Fortran 90 Handbook

Fortran 90 Handbook

Complete ANSI / ISO Reference

Jeanne C. Adams
Walter S. Brainerd
Jeanne T. Martin
Brian T. Smith
Jerrold L. Wagener

Intertext Publications
McGraw-Hill Book Company

New York St. Louis San Francisco Auckland Bogatá
Hamburg London Madrid Mexico Milan Montreal
New Delhi Panama Paris São Paolo
Singapore Sydney Tokyo Toronto

Library of Congress Catalog Card Number 91-77211

10 9 8 7 6 5 4 3 2 1

ISBN 0-07-000406-4

Intertext Publications/Multiscience Press, Inc.
One Lincoln Plaza
New York, NY 10023

McGraw-Hill Book Company
1221 Avenue of the Americas
New York, NY 10020

Composition by UNICOMP

F9⊙

Preface

The *Fortran 90 Handbook* is a definitive and comprehensive guide to Fortran 90 and its use. Fortran 90, the latest standard version of Fortran, has many excellent new features that will assist the programmer in writing efficient, portable, and maintainable programs. The *Fortran 90 Handbook* is an informal description of Fortran 90, developed to provide not only a readable explanation of features, but also some rationale for the inclusion of features and their use. In addition, "models" give the reader better insight as to why things are done as they are in the language.

This handbook is intended for anyone who wants a comprehensive survey of Fortran 90, including those familiar with programming language concepts but unfamiliar with Fortran. Experienced Fortran 77 programmers will be able to use this volume to assimilate quickly those features in Fortran 90 that are not in Fortran 77 (Fortran 90 is a superset of Fortran 77).

Chapter 0 provides a brief overview of several of the most important features that are new in Fortran 90. Chapters 1–14 correspond to Sections 1–14 in the standard. (The standard is the complete official description of the language, but it is written in a legally airtight, formal style without tutorial material and can be difficult to understand in places.) The handbook and the standard can be examined in parallel for insights into the Fortran language. This makes it feasible to use this handbook to "decipher" the standard, and this is an ideal use of this book.

Although the handbook is written for use in conjunction with the standard, it is also designed as a practical stand-alone description of Fortran 90. In the interest of readability, a few of the more obscure aspects of the standard may not be treated rigorously; any such cases should not impact the usefulness of this handbook in describing Fortran 90. On the other hand, in places where the standard is not completely clear, a reasonable interpretation is often given, together with ways to implement and program that will avoid potential problems due to misinterpretation of the standard. Of course, if information is being sought to understand

v

a fine point of compiler implementation, settle a bet, resolve a court case, or determine the answer to a Fortran trivia question, the standard itself should be considered the final authority.

The syntactic features of the language are described completely in the appendices, and these can serve as continual concise references for Fortran 90.

Other Sources of Information

Other parts of the book can be used to help find information.

- Each of the intrinsic functions is described in detail in Appendix A, although a general discussion of the intrinsic functions is included in Chapter 13.
- The complete syntax of Fortran 90 may be found in Appendix B. The syntax rules are numbered exactly as they are in the Fortran standard. There is a cross reference that lists, for each nonterminal syntactic term, the number of the rule in which it is defined, and all rules in which it is referenced.
- Appendix C contains a listing of the obsolescent features.
- The index is unusually comprehensive.
- There is an index of examples, giving the location of program examples that illustrate the use of many Fortran 90 features.

For an informal and tutorial approach to learning Fortran 90, the book, *Programmers Guide to Fortran 90*, by Brainerd, Goldberg, and Adams (McGraw-Hill, 1990) is more appropriate.

Style of the Programming Examples

In order to illustrate many features of the language and as many uses of these features as possible, no single particular style has been used when writing the examples. In many cases, the style illustrated is not necessarily one that the authors recommend.

Acknowledgments

Material in the appendices of this book was developed by the ANSI committee X3J3 and the ISO committee SC22/WG5 for inclusion in the Fortran 90 standard ISO/IEC 1539 : 1991. This material is reprinted with the permission of the International Standards Organization.

Comments provided by Charles Goldberg have increased the accuracy and readability of this book enormously.

Jeanne C. Adams	Walter S. Brainerd	Jeanne T. Martin
Brian T. Smith	Jerrold L. Wagener	
January 1992		

F9◐

Contents

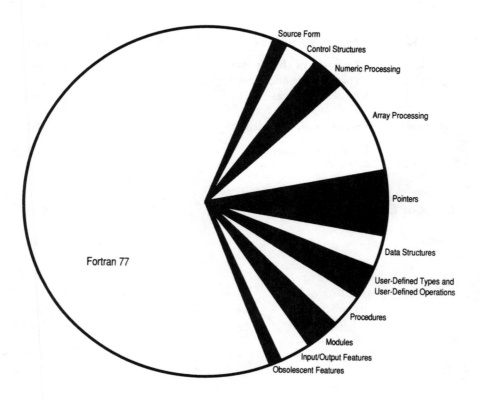

F90

O

Sneak Preview

This is Chapter 0. Fortran programmers, particularly old-timers, are accustomed to starting at 1. Prior to Fortran 77, a DO loop had to be executed at least once, and array subscripts started with one. Even though these restrictions were eliminated in Fortran 77, arrays had to have at least one element. In Fortran 90, the programmer can create strings of length zero and arrays of size zero. So this Chapter 0 will help Fortran 90 programmers get accustomed to other possibilities for the number 0. Seriously, though, the main reason for starting with Chapter 0 is that the remaining chapters of this book correspond with the fourteen chapters of the Fortran standard and are numbered 1–14 as they are in the standard. Chapter 0 provides the opportunity for a brief introduction to some of the exciting new features of Fortran 90.

The pie chart on the opposing page illustrates how Fortran 90 is made up of Fortran 77 plus several new features. The relative sizes of the slices are determined from the detailed syntax rules in Appendix B— each pie slice is roughly proportional to the number of syntax rules describing that part of Fortran 90. Thus the pie gives one measure of the relative complexity of the different parts of Fortran 90. It only indicates structural (syntactic) complexity, however, and should not be taken as an indication of conceptual (semantic) complexity; structural and conceptual complexity may or may not be related. It also should not be taken as an indication of implementation effort (which also may or may not be related). In fact, the cost pattern of implementation may be somewhat machine–architecture dependent or dependent upon the particular design strategy. Although this measure is crude, it shows clearly that the majority of statements in Fortran 90 are already familiar to Fortran 77 programmers.

Despite these caveats, the structure of a language is an important part of learning it and using it; therefore, the pie chart provides useful information about Fortran 90. The main purpose of this sneak preview is to provide a brief introduction to each new feature slice of the Fortran pie. Just a glance at the names of the new features should be enough to convince anyone that they will become very important to Fortran programmers.

Fortran always has been considered the premier language in scientific and engineering fields requiring numeric computations. The new features of Fortran 90 continue to enhance Fortran for these applications and also to extend the language in significant ways to other areas now very important in scientific and engineering programming. This chapter is a sneak preview of some of these features, illustrating briefly why it will be important to master and use these facilities.

 Fortran 77

One of the most important features of Fortran 90 is that it contains all of the features of Fortran 77. There are four relatively obscure things that are processor dependent in Fortran 77, but completely specified in Fortran 90; these are described in Section 1.5. If a program uses one of these features and it was done differently on a particular implementation than the way chosen for Fortran 90, this program could behave differently under Fortran 90. Otherwise, all standard-conforming Fortran 77 programs should run using a Fortran 90 compiler and produce equivalent results.

Source Form and Names

In Fortran 90 there is a new source form for which particular positions have no special meaning, names may have up to 31 characters and use the underscore character, blanks have significance in some circumstances, a semicolon may be used to separate multiple statements on one line, and comments may occur on any line following an exclamation (!). The old source form is still available and most of these new features are also available when using the old source form. SWAP_INTEGERS is a simple example of a subroutine written using the new source form.

```
SUBROUTINE SWAP_INTEGERS (ARG_A, ARG_B)
    INTEGER, INTENT (INOUT) :: ARG_A, ARG_B
    INTEGER :: TEMP   ! New form of declaration
    TEMP = ARG_A; ARG_A = ARG_B; ARG_B = TEMP
END
```

If the above code were written so that each line began in position 7 or beyond, it would also be acceptable as old source form.

Control Structures

Control structures have not been neglected; Fortran now has a complete suite of modern control structures. A CASE construct has been added. The DO construct has been improved significantly and now may utilize the CYCLE and EXIT statements. In addition, the DO construct can have a WHILE control clause, an iterative control clause, or no control clause. The DO, IF, and CASE constructs may have construct names to help identify the constructs, which is especially useful when constructs are nested. The following example illustrates a CASE construct and a DO construct that contains an IF construct and an EXIT statement.

```
SEARCH_LOOP: DO I = 1, TABLE_SIZE
    IF (ITEM == TABLE (I)) THEN
        LOCATION = I
        EXIT SEARCH_LOOP
    END IF
END DO SEARCH_LOOP

SELECT CASE (COLOR (LOCATION))
    CASE ("RED")
        STOP
    CASE ("YELLOW")
        PRINT *, "Look out!"
        CALL CAUTION
    CASE ("GREEN")
        CALL GO
END SELECT
```

Numeric Processing

One of the most difficult aspects of porting Fortran programs is the specification of numeric precision. Fortran 90 contains new features that allow the programmer to specify precision in a more portable manner and to inquire about properties of the precision used by a processor. It is possible to declare that real variables R1 and R2 have at least 10 decimal digits and a range extending to at least 10^{30} by using the declaration

```
REAL (SELECTED_REAL_KIND (10, 30)) :: R1, R2
```

The values of R1 and R2 may be represented using single precision on some machines and double precision on others.

The actual precision and range of any real variables can be determined using intrinsic functions provided for this purpose. Other intrinsic functions allow the programmer to manipulate the components of a real value in a portable manner. For example, the intrinsic function SPACING can be used to determine the convergence of an iterative process.

```
CONVERGED = ( ABS (XO - X) < 2 * SPACING (X) )
```

It is also possible to indicate a minimum required range of an integer value in a declaration, as illustrated by the following example.

```
INTEGER (SELECTED_INT_KIND (5)) :: I1, I2
```

In this case, the Fortran system must select an integer representation (if one is available) that allows the integer variables I1 and I2 to have all integer values between -10^5 and 10^5; if the programmer limits values assigned to I1 and I2 to this range, portability is guaranteed.

 ## Array Processing

Many Fortran programs process arrays of data. These programs usually are full of DO loops that process array elements one at a time. In fact, the more natural way to think of the process is that it performs some operation on the whole array. Allowing the programmer to manipulate arrays of data in this manner is perhaps the single most important enhancement in Fortran 90. This reflects not only the benefit of expressing array computations in a more natural manner, but also the development of computers having array processing hardware to achieve high processing speeds.

In Fortran 90 it is possible to treat a whole array as a single object. For example, suppose A, B, and C are 10 × 10 arrays of real values. For each element of B, the statement

```
A = 2 * B + C
```

doubles its value, adds it to the corresponding element of C, and places the result in the corresponding element of A.

Parts of an array may be referenced. For example,

```
PRINT *, A (3, :), B (:, 1:99:2)
```

prints the third row of the array A and the odd-numbered columns of B. A section of an array may be given another name with the use of a pointer, but that is another story.

There is a rich set of new intrinsic functions to process arrays. Users may define array-valued functions, and arrays may be allocated dynamically. This last feature alone will be a tremendous aid to programmers who have had to jump through hoops and often use nonstandard (and nonportable) features in an attempt to manage storage allocation. One use of dynamic allocation is illustrated by a simple example in which an array's size is determined as the program is executing.

```
REAL, ALLOCATABLE :: A (:,:)
   . . .
READ *, N
ALLOCATE (A (N,N))
```

There are many other new features designed to assist in array processing, such as the WHERE construct and the use of arrays with pointers.

 ## Pointers

The pointer features of Fortran 90 permit data to be accessed and processed dynamically.

```
REAL, POINTER :: A (:,:)
   . . .
READ *, N
ALLOCATE (A (N,N))
```

Note that, except for the replacement of the keyword "ALLOCATABLE" with the keyword "POINTER", this example is identical to the previous one in the section on arrays. Everything that can be done with allocatable arrays can also be done with pointers, but allocatable arrays can be used in simple situations where pointer concepts are not required. Any object may have the pointer attribute; it is not limited to arrays.

In addition, the effect of assignment can be achieved without the movement of data; and dynamic structures, such as linked lists and trees, can be created and processed.

In most cases, a pointer may be thought of as an *alias* to some data object. For example, a pointer may "point to" or "alias" a row of an array, a simple variable, a component of a structure, or an entire data structure.

```
REAL, TARGET :: A (100,100)
REAL, POINTER :: ITH_ROW (:), CORNERS (:,:), INNER (:,:)
   . . .
ITH_ROW => A (I, :)
CORNERS => A (1:100:99, 1:100:99)
INNER => A (2:99, 2:99)
```

In Fortran 90, pointers may point only to objects having the target attribute. This is to allow all optimization techniques in those cases that do not involve pointers.

Data Structures

In the past, scientific and engineering programs typically involved large amounts' of computation; if there were a large amount of data, it usually was organized in very simple ways. However, contemporary applications often process large and complex data structures, both numeric and nonnumeric. Fortran 90 provides the programmer with better tools to deal with such data by including data structures in the language. Unlike an array, the components of a Fortran 90 data structure do not have to be of the same data type. Data structures are introduced into a program with a type definition (see Section 0.7), such as the following:

```
TYPE EMPLOYEE
    ! An employee's name may have up to 20 characters.
    CHARACTER (LEN = 20)           :: NAME
    ! A social security number (SSN) has nine digits.
    INTEGER (SELECTED_INT_KIND (9))   :: SSN
    ! SALARY may be up to $1M and is kept to the penny.
    REAL (SELECTED_REAL_KIND (8, 6)) :: SALARY
END TYPE EMPLOYEE
```

Variables declared to be type EMPLOYEE have three components, NAME, SSN, and SALARY, each of a different data type. In the following example LARRY, MOE, and CURLY are structures of type EMPLOYEE.

```
TYPE (EMPLOYEE) :: LARRY, MOE, CURLY
```

An entire structure can be referenced by using its name, such as MOE. Individual components can be manipulated as follows:

```
MOE % SSN = 123456789
```

User-Defined Types and Operators

Programmers may extend the Fortran 90 built-in facilities in two ways. New data types may be built from the intrinsic types, and the programmer may extend the built-in operators, such as + and //, to other data types. In addition, new operators may be defined for any data types.

These facilities allow the programmer to define abstract data types and facilitate the utilization of the object-oriented programming paradigm in Fortran. For example, it is possible to define a new type called MATRIX and extend the operator * to mean matrix multiplication between two variables declared to be type MATRIX.

```
TYPE (MATRIX) :: M1, M2, M3
   . . .
M3 = M1 * M2
```

For this example, it is assumed that the type MATRIX has been defined as the type EMPLOYEE was defined in the example in Section 0.6. The form of each defined type must be a structure; in this case, it could be a structure with one component—a two-dimensional array of reals, for example, or it could be some sort of linked structure representing a sparse matrix. The operation (*) representing matrix multiplication is defined by a function with an operator interface, discussed in the next section.

 # Procedures

There are several new features in Fortran 90 that facilitate the use of procedures. Functions can extend existing operators and define new ones. Subroutines are used to redefine assignment for user-defined types, if desired. Procedure arguments may be made optional and keywords may be used when calling procedures, allowing them to be listed in any order. Default values may be specified for missing optional arguments.

```
SUBROUTINE CONCERT (LOCATION, TIME, BAND, BACKUP)
   INTEGER, OPTIONAL :: LOCATION, TIME, BAND, BACKUP
   . . .
```

With this declaration any of the following could be used to call the subroutine:

```
CALL CONCERT (1, 2, 3, 4)
CALL CONCERT (1, BACKUP=4)
CALL CONCERT (TIME=2, LOCATION=1)
```

A procedure interface block is used to describe the characteristics of an external procedure and its arguments, give a procedure a generic name, define a new operator or extend an old one, or define a new form of assignment.

Procedure interface blocks are necessary in some cases to allow the correct procedure call to be generated; their use also will permit the compiler to check that procedure calls are correct, particularly to check that argument types match. This provides the capability to guarantee the integrity of a procedure call and to guard against errors.

The programmer may define generic procedures in Fortran 90. Here are the subprograms and the interface blocks that create a generic function CUBE_ROOT that will find the cube root of either a real or double precision value.

```
INTERFACE  CUBE_ROOT

    FUNCTION  S_CUBE_ROOT(X)
       REAL ::  S_CUBE_ROOT
       REAL, INTENT(IN) ::  X
    END FUNCTION  S_CUBE_ROOT

    FUNCTION  D_CUBE_ROOT(X)
       DOUBLE PRECISION, INTENT(IN) ::  X
       DOUBLE PRECISION ::  D_CUBE_ROOT
    END FUNCTION  D_CUBE_ROOT

END INTERFACE


FUNCTION  S_CUBE_ROOT(X)
   REAL, INTENT(IN) ::  X
   REAL ::  S_CUBE_ROOT

   S_CUBE_ROOT = ...

END FUNCTION  S_CUBE_ROOT

FUNCTION  D_CUBE_ROOT(X)
   DOUBLE PRECISION, INTENT(IN) ::  X
   DOUBLE PRECISION ::  D_CUBE_ROOT

   D_CUBE_ROOT = ...

END FUNCTION  D_CUBE_ROOT
```

Fortran 90 also has recursion.

```
RECURSIVE SUBROUTINE QUICK_SORT (NUMBERS, START, END)
    . . .
    NEW_START = . . .
    NEW_END = . . .
    IF (START <= END - 10) THEN
        CALL QUICK_SORT (NUMBERS, NEW_START, NEW_END)
        . . .
    ELSE
        CALL SMALL_SORT (NUMBERS, NEW_START, NEW_END)
        . . .
    END IF
    . . .
```

 ## Modules

Modules can declare global data. This use of modules provides more power and is much less error-prone than the use of common blocks. Modules also may be used to collect related items, such as data, procedures, and procedure interfaces. A module can make a type definition widely accessible, an important functionality not provided by common blocks. To access the information in a module from another program unit, a USE statement is provided. The following simple example illustrates the use of a module to replace a common block.

```
MODULE T_FORD
    REAL, DIMENSION (100,100) :: A, B, C
    INTEGER :: I1, I2
END MODULE T_FORD
    . . .
SUBROUTINE SOUP
    USE T_FORD
    A = 0
    . . .
SUBROUTINE NUTS
    USE T_FORD
    B = 0
    . . .
```

Packaging with a module can be used to hide information. Objects can be kept inaccessible outside the module with a PRIVATE declaration. This provides some protection against inadvertent misuse or corruption, thereby improving program reliability. Packaging also can make the logical structure of a program more apparent by hiding complex details at lower levels. Programs are therefore easier to comprehend and less costly to maintain.

It is possible to place in a module the definitions needed to define the type MATRIX and its operations discussed in Section 0.7. The representation of the matrices—using arrays for dense matrices or linked lists for sparse matrices—can be hidden from the user so that the implementation can be modified without requiring changes in programs that use the module. Similarly, it is possible to hide the method used to implement operations such as matrix multiplication.

Input/Output Features

There are some additional input/output features, such as additional clauses for the OPEN and INQUIRE statements and namelist formatting. Perhaps the most significant input/output feature is nonadvancing or "stream" character-oriented input/output. For example, nonadvancing input/output makes it easier to write a program that counts the number of characters in a file.

```
PROGRAM CHAR_COUNT
    USE IO_PARAMETERS, ONLY : END_OF_RECORD, END_OF_FILE
    INTEGER :: IOS, COUNT = 0
    CHARACTER :: C
    DO
        READ (*, "(A)", ADVANCE = "NO", IOSTAT = IOS) C
        IF (IOS == END_OF_RECORD) CYCLE
        IF (IOS == END_OF_FILE) EXIT
        COUNT = COUNT + 1
    END DO
    PRINT *, "The file contains ", COUNT, " characters."
END PROGRAM CHAR_COUNT
```

Language Architecture

Everyone recognizes that there are features of Fortran (and other programming languages, too) that do not represent good programming practice. Modern features of the language may be used to achieve the same functionality more effectively. On the other hand, economics dictate that a language evolve slowly. There is a tremendous investment in Fortran programs; it must be possible to continue to run these programs, even as they are being revised and updated using more modern programming techniques. There is also a large investment in training programmers and perfecting their skill at Fortran programming. Ideally, it should be possible for a programmer to learn new features of Fortran 90 as they are needed and at a comfortable pace.

It is expected that most revisions of a programming language standard will include new features. One of the most significant, and perhaps controversial, concepts in Fortran 90 involves the attempt to identify features that are obsolescent and that should be phased out over time. The evolutionary scheme incorporated into Fortran 90 uses the concepts of **incremental** and **decremental** features. The decremental features are listed in Appendix C.

It is straightforward to recognize the incremental features. They are the new features added since the previous standard, Fortran 77. The handling of the decremental features is more complicated and controversial. In the Fortran 90 standard, there is an attempt to identify those features that should not be in the language, except for the fact that they were there in previous versions. Identifying these features in the standard gives notice to the programmer that they *might* be removed from the next version of the standard. Therefore, the programmer should avoid using these features when revising old programs or creating new ones. For each of the features indicated as decremental in Fortran 90, there was already a better equivalent facility in Fortran 77, although some of the features have even better replacements in Fortran 90.

If a feature is removed from the next standard, there is the possibility that it might get removed from some implementations; however, it is expected that obsolescent features will exist in most implementations for many generations in order to meet requirements for processing older programs that use them.

F 9◉

1

Introduction

For a programming language, Fortran has been around a long time. It was one of the first widely used "high-level" languages, as well as the first programming language to be standardized. It is still the premier language for scientific and engineering computing applications.

The purpose of this handbook is to describe the latest version of this language, Fortran 90. This chapter gives some history of the development and standardization of Fortran and describes the notation used to specify the syntax of Fortran 90.

1.1 History

1.1.1 Initial Development of Fortran

In 1954 a project was begun under the leadership of John Backus at IBM to develop an "automatic programming" system that would convert programs written in a mathematical notation to machine instructions for the IBM 704 computer. Many were skeptical that the project would be successful because, at the time, it was felt that computer memories were so small and expensive and execution time so valuable that it was necessary for the program produced by the compiler to be almost as efficient as that produced by a good assembly language programmer.

This project produced the first Fortran compiler, which was delivered to a customer in 1957. It was a great success by any reasonable criterion. The efficiency of the code generated by the compiler surprised even some of its authors. A more important achievement, but one that took longer to realize, was that programmers could express their computations in a much more natural way. This increased productivity and permitted the programmer to write a program that could be maintained and enhanced much more easily than an assembly language program.

About one year after the introduction of the first Fortran compiler, IBM introduced Fortran II. One of the most important changes in Fortran II was the addition of subroutines that could be compiled independently. Thus, Fortran changed substantially even during its first year; it has been changing continually ever since.

1.1.2 Standardization

By the early 1960s, many computer vendors had implemented a Fortran compiler. They all included special features not found in the original IBM compiler. These features usually were included to meet needs and requests of the users and thus provide an inducement for the customer to buy computer systems from the vendor providing the best compiler. Because the language was very young, a special added feature could be tested to see if it was a good long-term addition to the language. Unfortunately, the profusion of dialects of Fortran prevented programs written for one computer from being transported to a different computer system.

At about this time, the American Standards Association (ASA), later to become the American National Standards Institute (ANSI), began a project of standardizing many aspects of data processing. Someone had the daring idea of standardizing programming languages. A committee was formed to develop a standard for Fortran under the auspices of the Business Equipment Manufacturers Association (BEMA), later to become the Computer and Business Equipment Manufacturers Association (CBEMA). This standard was adopted in 1966; after the adoption of Fortran 77, it became known as Fortran 66 to distinguish the two versions.

The language continued to develop after 1966, along with general knowledge in the areas of programming, language design, and computer design. Work on a revision of Fortran 66 was completed in 1977 (hence the name Fortran 77) and officially published in 1978. The most significant features introduced in this version were the character data type, the

IF-THEN-ELSE construct, and many new input/output facilities, such as direct access files and the OPEN statement. Except for the character data type, most of these features had been implemented in many compilers or preprocessors. During this revision, Hollerith data was removed because the character data type is a far superior facility. Although this idea of removing features did not seem very controversial when Fortran 77 was introduced, it proved to be controversial later—so much so that no Fortran 77 features have been removed in Fortran 90.

As soon as the technical development of Fortran 77 was completed, ANSI X3J3 and (International Standards Organization (ISO) WG5, turned their attention to the next revision, which is now called Fortran 90 and is the subject of this book.

The work on Fortran 90 began so soon after the adoption of Fortran 77 because, contrary to the pronouncements of some that "Fortran is dead", the huge volume of public comments on the proposed standard indicated that there was a tremendous interest in the further development of the language. In fact, many of the public comments on Fortran 77 contained suggestions that have been adopted in Fortran 90.

Fortran is still the most widely used programming language for scientific and engineering applications, and the new standard version, Fortran 90, should continue this tradition.

1.2 Why a New Standard?

There are several reasons why Fortran or any other programming language needs to change over a period of years. Computing technology and programming methodology are evolving at a very rapid pace. Thus, the most obvious reason that programming languages must evolve is that, to be effective, a programmer must have a language that incorporates this new methodology. We now know how to incorporate certain features into a language better than we did ten, twenty, or thirty years ago. A good example is provided by control structures. In the 1970s a lot of effort was put into determining the best possible set of control structures that a language should have; this was done mainly from the point of view of providing facilities that encourage good program design and ease of program maintenance. In this area, Fortran's early lack of modern design was actually a benefit, because a very good set of control structures has been added to Fortran 90 without severely impacting the few older control mechanisms already in Fortran 77.

Another area in which both an awareness of the problem and the concomitant technology to cope with it have advanced is that of portability. As the cost of software maintenance increases and a wider variety of computing systems become available, it is increasingly important to be able to port Fortran programs from one system to another. The main purpose of a standard is to permit portability of programs; in spite of this, several features of each standard Fortran have been nonportable. Each time the standard is revised, features are added to enhance portability and replace features that do not port easily. Perhaps the most obvious example of this in Fortran 77 concerns numeric precision. The precision of real and double precision values varies greatly from one computer system to the next; when moving from a machine with many digits precision for reals to one with a smaller number of digits, it is often necessary to change many declarations from REAL to DOUBLE PRECISION. This problem was partially addressed in Fortran 77 by adding generic intrinsic functions so that function references in the program could remain unchanged; in Fortran 90 numeric quantities can be given a kind parameter that allows a programmer to specify numeric precision requirements in a portable way.

Another reason to change a programming language is that implementation techniques improve over time. Language features that required special implementation techniques, such as stack or heap storage management, were avoided because of their implementation cost and the possibility of reducing execution efficiency. Experience with these features in other languages over a long period of time has removed them from the category of features that are difficult to implement efficiently.

Advances in computer architecture also have an effect on language design. Increases in speed and decreases in the cost of hardware mitigate some concerns about efficiency. With decreases in computing costs have come increases in personnel costs. The economics of these trends indicate that there should be more features in a language that increase programmer productivity, even if they involve some decrease in machine efficiency.

Another important aspect of computer hardware that affects language design involves the changes in architecture that open up entirely new techniques for solving problems. Probably the most important recent development of this sort in the world of scientific and engineering computing is the use of synchronous parallel processing, or vector processing. Some of the fastest machines now available have this sort of architecture. For many algorithms to execute efficiently on these machines, the computations that can be vectorized or performed in parallel must be recognized either by the programmer or by software. There has been a lot of improvement in the ability of software to detect parallelism in old Fortran programs, but there are still many cases where it is necessary for the programmer to indicate these situations. Also, many algorithms involve parallel computations and these are expressed most naturally in a language like Fortran 90 that has special provisions, such as the new array processing facilities.

1.3　Why Not Use Another Language?

Many have suggested that we simply abandon Fortran and move on to a more modern language. They cite the peculiarities of the language present since its origins in the 1950s and the lack of features found in other programming languages. However, there are several reasons not to do this.

There is nothing that can be done about a few of the Fortran features. They always have been there and a change would cause an incompatibility with the previous standard and existing code. Some of the truly obsolescent features have been identified in the Fortran 90 standard and are candidates for removal from the next version of the standard. No new Fortran program need ever use these older peculiar features; Fortran 90 provides better ways of accomplishing the same thing.

Even if nothing were ever removed from standard Fortran, there are three compelling reasons not to switch to another programming language. The first and most important reason is that, although many programming languages have features superior to Fortran in various ways, it is by no means obvious that any language is sufficiently better than Fortran to justify making the switch. In fact, the ways many things are done in Fortran are now recognized as being superior to that of many other programming languages. One example involves the methods used to create and access global data. For a few years, the Algol/Pascal method involving block structure was considered superior, but now computer scientists think the Fortran model, particularly with the Fortran 90 module feature, is better.

The second reason is that there is a huge investment in Fortran programs. A switch to another programming language would mean rewriting many programs at great expense.

The third reason is a little more subtle: switching to another programming language would involve retraining a lot of programmers. This would have a particularly severe impact on those scientists and engineers who do not consider themselves primarily programmers, but just use Fortran to solve their problems. However, it is possible for a Fortran programmer to learn the new features of Fortran 90 gradually, picking features to master when the effort is justified by the improved problem-solving tools that are made available.

For these reasons, Fortran may well be the programming language of choice for scientists and engineers for many years.

1.4 Development of Fortran 90

During the period that the public reviewed the proposed Fortran 77 standard, many comments were received that contained good ideas. Some, like the IF construct, were adopted, but others would have required too much developmental work to enable them to be incorporated into the standard at that time. The quality and quantity of these proposed changes and the general interest in Fortran exhibited by the large number of comments indicated that there should be another revision of the standard.

Work on Fortran 90 began just as soon as the technical work on Fortran 77 was completed. Detailed proposals were put aside temporarily while the committee responsible for the standardization attempted to get a better idea of the overall requirements needed in a programming language used for scientific and engineering problem solving in the 1990s. To accomplish this, existing Fortran implementations were studied, features of other programming languages were examined carefully, and surveys were taken to determine the users' own perceptions of their needs in such a language.

During the years from 1978 to 1981, the committee heard many tutorials about general features thought desirable to be included in Fortran 90. These were presented by both members of the committee and outside experts. Between 1979 and 1985, most of the technical changes were presented as detailed proposals and were discussed and voted on by the committee.

Much of the technical work was in place by 1985. The last few years of the committee's work primarily involved polishing these proposals and creating a document that reflected the technical proposals developed and passed by the committee. The proposed standard was presented for public review and comment in the fall of 1987. Public comments were then reviewed and changes made as a result of these comments. The technical work was finished in 1990, and the language became known as "Fortran 90". It took until 1991 for it to become an official international standard (ISO/IEC 1539 : 1991) and it took until 1992 to become a U. S. national standard (ANSI X3.198-1992).

1.5 Fortran 77 Compatibility

Because of the large investment in existing software written in Fortran, the Fortran standards committee decided to include the entire previous standard (Fortran 77) in Fortran 90. Even though the standard describes a category called "deleted" features, there aren't any; as mentioned earlier, no Fortran 77 feature has been removed.

Fortran 90 restricts the behavior of some features that are processor dependent in Fortran 77. Therefore, a standard-conforming Fortran 77 program that uses any of these processor-dependent features may conform to the Fortran 90 standard and yet behave differently than with some Fortran 77 systems. In the following situations, the Fortran 90 interpretation may be different from that of Fortran 77.

1. Fortran 90 has more intrinsic functions than does Fortran 77 and has a few intrinsic subroutines. Therefore, a standard-conforming Fortran 77 program may have a different interpretation under this standard if it invokes an external procedure having the same name as one of the new standard intrinsic procedures, unless that procedure is specified in an EXTERNAL statement as recommended for nonintrinsic functions. Also, a program that used a nonstandard, vendor-supplied intrinsic function might behave differently if the function is one of the new intrinsic functions in Fortran 90. The chances of this happening are minimal, because most of the new intrinsic functions have names longer than six characters.

2. If a named variable that is not in a common block is initialized in a DATA statement, it has the SAVE attribute in Fortran 90. In Fortran 77, if the value of the variable is changed or becomes undefined, its value on re-entry into a procedure is processor dependent.

3. In Fortran 77, an input list must never require more characters than are present in a record during formatted input. In Fortran 90, this restriction has been removed when the PAD= specifier is YES; in this case, the input record is padded with as many blanks as necessary to satisfy the input item and the corresponding format.

4. Fortran 77 permits a processor to supply extra precision for a real constant when it is used to initialize a DOUBLE PRECISION data object in a DATA statement. Fortran 90 does not permit this.

1.6 Extensibility

New data types, new operators, and new meanings for the existing operators and assignment provide ways for the programmer to extend Fortran. These facilities allow the programmer to create abstract data types by defining new types and the operations to be performed on them. Modules have been introduced into Fortran as a convenient way to package these new data types and their operations. Modules can be used by the same user in different applications or may be distributed to a number of users on the same or different projects. This provides effective practical support for object-oriented programming, as well as enhancing both economy and efficiency.

1.7 Intrinsic and Standard Modules

An **intrinsic module** is one that is defined within the standard. There are no intrinsic modules in Fortran 90.

A **standard module** is one that might be standardized as a separate but related (collateral) standard in the revision cycle period between new standard releases, often a period of ten or more years. At this time, there are no standard modules, although a module for a varying length string data type has been proposed.

1.7.1 Syntax Forms

In this book, a simplified form is used to describe the syntax of Fortran 90 programs. The forms consist of program text in the same font used to display program examples (such as **END DO**) and syntactic terms that must be replaced with correct Fortran source for those terms, which are printed using a sans serif font (such as input-item-list). Optional items are enclosed in brackets; items enclosed in brackets followed by ellipses (...) may occur any number (including zero) of times. The ampersand (&) is used to continue a line, just as it is used to continue a line in a Fortran 90 program. Use of one of the syntactic forms always produces a syntactically correct part of a Fortran 90 program. These syntactic forms indicate how to construct most of the correct Fortran 90 statements, but may not be complete in that they do not describe all of the possible forms.

For example, the following syntax form occurs in Chapter 9. It describes one form that can be used to construct a direct-access formatted WRITE statement. The general syntax for the WRITE statement is quite complex and gives no hint as to which options are allowed for direct-access formatting. On the other hand, this rule is overly restrictive in that it indicates a particular order for the options, which is not required by the standard. Nevertheless, using this form always will produce a correct WRITE statement.

```
WRITE ( [ UNIT = ] unit-number  &
       , FMT = format  &
       , REC = record-number  &
       [ , IOSTAT = scalar-default-integer-variable ]  &
       [ , ERR = label ]  &
     ) [ output-item-list ]
```

Another property of the syntactic forms is that the terms used are descriptive and informal, and they are not necessarily defined precisely anywhere in the book. If you need to know the precise syntax allowed, refer to Appendix B, which contains all of the syntax rules of the Fortran 90 standard.

1.8 The Fortran 90 Language Standard

The Fortran 90 standard (ISO/IEC 1539 : 1991) describes the syntax and semantics of a programming language. However, the standard addresses certain aspects of the Fortran processing system, but does not address others. When specifications are not covered by the standard, the interpretation is processor dependent; that is, the processor defines the interpretation, but the interpretation for any two processors need not be the same. Programs that rely on processor-dependent interpretations typically are not portable.

The specifications that are included in the standard are:

1. the syntax of Fortran statements and forms for Fortran programs

2. the semantics of Fortran statements and the semantics of Fortran programs

3. specifications for correct input data

4. appearance of standard output data

The specifications that are not defined in the standard are:

1. the way in which Fortran compilers are written

2. operating system facilities defining the computing system

3. methods used to transfer data to and from peripheral storage devices and the nature of the peripheral devices

4. behavior of extensions implemented by vendors

5. the size and complexity of a Fortran program and its data

6. the hardware or firmware used to run the program

7. the way values are represented and the way numeric values are computed

8. the physical representation of data

9. the characteristics of tapes, disks, and various storage media

The Fortran standard is a technical and legal specification that describes the Fortran language. It is often used as the basis of procurement contracts; for example, Fortran compilers that are sold to government agencies often must pass a validation suite based on the Fortran standard.

1.8.1 Program Conformance

A program conforms to the standard if the statements are all syntactically correct, execution of the program causes no violations of the standard (such as dividing by zero), and the input data is all in the correct form. A program that uses a vendor extension is not standard conforming.

1.8.2 Processor Conformance

In the Fortran 90 standard, the term "processor" means the combination of a Fortran compiler and the computing system that executes the code. A processor conforms to the standard if it processes any standard-conforming program, provided the Fortran program is not too large or complex for the computer system in question. Except for certain restrictions in format specifications, the processor must be able to flag any nonstandard syntax used in the program. This includes the capability to flag any extensions available in the vendor software and used in the program. The standard now requires that certain other things be flagged, and that the reason they are flagged be given. These things are:

1.   obsolescent features

2.   kind values not supported

3.   violations of any syntax rules and their accompanying constraints

4.   characters not permitted by the processor

5.   illegal source form

6.   violations of the scope rules for names, labels, operators, and assignment symbols

These six conformance requirements were not present in previous Fortran standards.

Rules for the form of the output are less stringent than for other features of the language in the sense that the processor may have some options about the format of the output and the programmer may not have complete control over which of these options is used.

A processor may include extensions not in the standard; if it processes standard-conforming programs according to the standard, it is considered to be a standard-conforming processor.

1.8.3 Portability

One of the main purposes of a standard is to describe how to write portable programs. However, there are some things that are standard conforming, but not portable. An example is a program that computes a very large number like 10^{250}. Certain computing systems will not accommodate a number this large. Thus, such a number could be a part of a standard-conforming program, but may not run on all systems and thus may not be portable. Another example is a program that uses a deeper nesting of control constructs than is allowed by a particular compiler.

1.8.4 A Permissive Standard

The primary purpose of the Fortran standard is to describe a language with the property that, if a programmer uses the language, the difficulties of porting programs from one computer system to another will be minimized. But to handle the somewhat contradictory goal of permitting experimentation and development of the language, the standard is *permissive*; that is, a processor can conform to the standard even if it allows features that are not described in the standard. This has its good and bad aspects.

On the positive side, it allows implementors to experiment with features not in the standard; if they are successful and prove useful, they can become candidates for standardization during the next revision. Thus, a vendor of a compiler may choose to add some features not found in the standard and still conform to the standard by correctly processing all of the features that are described in the standard.

On the negative side, the burden is on the programmer to know about and avoid these extra features when the program is to be ported to a different computer system. The programmer is given some help with this problem in that a Fortran 90 processor is required to recognize and warn the programmer about syntactic constructs in a program that do not conform to the Fortran 90 standard. A good Fortran programmer's manual also will point out nonstandard features with some technique, such as shading on the page. But there is no real substitute for knowledge of the standard language itself. This handbook should help provide this knowledge.

1.9 References

1. American National Standards Institute, *American National Standard Programming Language FORTRAN, ANSI X3.9-1978*, New York, 1978.

2. Brainerd, Walter S., Fortran 77, *Communications of the ACM*, Vol. 21, No. 10, October 1978, pp. 806–820.

3. Brainerd, Walter S., Charles H. Goldberg, and Jeanne C. Adams, *Programmer's Guide to Fortran 90*, McGraw-Hill, New York, 1990.

4. Greenfield, Martin H., History of FORTRAN standardization, *Proceedings of the 1982 National Computer Conference*, AFIPS Press, Arlington, VA, 1982.

5. International Standards Organization, *ISO/IEC 1539 : 1991, Information technology—Programming languages—Fortran*, Geneva, 1991.

6. A programming language for information processing on automatic data processing systems, *Communications of the ACM*, Vol. 7, No. 10, October 1964, pp. 591–625.

F9⊘

2

Fortran Concepts and Terms

The features of Fortran 90 provide considerable power and expressiveness. In order to use these features effectively, it is necessary to become familiar with the basic concepts of the language. This is the first goal of this chapter.

Because terms are used in a precise way to describe a programming language, the second goal of this chapter is to introduce the fundamental terms needed to understand Fortran 90.

One of the major concepts involves the organization of a Fortran program. This topic is introduced in this chapter by presenting the high-level syntax rules for a Fortran program, including the principal constructs and statements that form a program. This chapter also describes the order in which constructs and statements must appear in a program and concludes with an example of a short, but complete, Fortran 90 program.

While there is some discussion of language features here to help explain various terms and concepts, Chapters 3–14 contain the complete description of all language features.

2.1 Scope and Association

In examining the basic concepts in Fortran, it helps to trace some of the important steps in its evolution. The results of the first few steps are familiar to Fortran programmers, but the later ones become relevant only when the new features of Fortran 90 are used.

The first version of Fortran produced in the late 1950s did not have user-defined subroutines or functions, but there were intrinsic functions, such as SINF and ABSF. Thus, while there were no tools to help organize a program, there were also no worries about such things as naming variables and sharing values between subprograms, except that a variable could not have the same name as an intrinsic function without the F (for example, a variable name could not be SIN or ABS) and there could not be an array ending with F with four or more characters in the name. Variables could not be typed explicitly, so the implicit typing rules for real and integer types applied to all variables. Then, as now, keywords such as IF and READ could be used as variable names, though this practice did not produce any more readable programs then than it does now.

To provide an example for this narrative, consider the problem of computing the sum $1 + 2 + \cdots + 100$. (Supposedly this is an arithmetic exercise given to Gauss as a young child; he solved it in a very few minutes, discovering the formula

$$\sum_{i=1}^{n} i = \frac{n(n+1)}{2}$$

for summing an arithmetic series in the process.) The following program to compute this sum the hard way would have run on the first Fortran compiler.

```
      M = 0
      DO 8 I = 1, 100
         M = M + I
    8 CONTINUE
      WRITE (6, 9) M
    9 FORMAT (I10)
      STOP
```

Early in the development of Fortran, it was recognized as a good idea to isolate definitive chunks of code into separate units. These were (and are) known as function and subroutine subprograms. This not only provided a mechanism for structuring a program, but permitted subprograms to be written once and then be called more than once by the same program or even be used by more than one program. Equally important, they could be compiled separately, saving hours of compilation time.

With this powerful tool come complications. For example, if both the main program and a subprogram use the variable named "X", what is the connection between them? The designers of the subprogram concept had the brilliance to answer that question by saying there is, in general, no connection between X in the main program and X in a subprogram. Of course, the same answer is obtained as a result of the fact that subprograms are separately compilable; an X in a different subprogram is not even known at compile time, so the simplest thing to do is have no connection between variables with the same name in different program units. Whatever the reason that led to this decision, it is a good one because if it is desirable to build a program by incorporating several subprograms, there is no need to worry about two or more subprograms using the same name. Thus, if two different programmers work on the different program units, neither needs to worry about names picked by the other. This idea is described by saying that the two Xs have different **scope**.

A subroutine could be written to do the summation and print the result of summing the first hundred integers, just in case someone else might want to take advantage of this mighty achievement. This one is written in Fortran 66, and would have been a legal Fortran II program.

```
      SUBROUTINE TOTAL
      M = 0
      DO 8 I = 1, 100
        M = M + I
    8 CONTINUE
      WRITE (6, 9) M
    9 FORMAT (I10)
      RETURN
      END
```

With this subroutine available, the main program can be:

```
      CALL TOTAL
      STOP
      END
```

Suppose now it is decided that the subroutine would be more generally useful if it just computed the sum, but did not print it.

```
      SUBROUTINE TOTAL
      M = 0
      DO 8 I = 1, 100
         M = M + I
    8 CONTINUE
      RETURN
      END
```

A first attempt to use this subroutine might produce the following erroneous program.

```
      CALL TOTAL
      WRITE (6, 9) M
    9 FORMAT (I10)
      STOP
      END
```

Of course, this does not work, because the variable M in the subroutine has nothing to do with the variable M in the main program. This is a case where there *should* be a connection between the two values. So, when subroutines and functions were introduced, two schemes were provided to communicate values between them and the main program. These are procedure arguments and common blocks. Here are two complete programs that do work and use a subroutine to compute the sum $1 + 2 + \cdots + 100$; one uses a subroutine argument and the other uses a common block to communicate values. Because the names in the different program units identify completely separate variables, yet their values are communicated from one to the other by using either arguments or common blocks, the name of the variable holding the sum in the subroutine has been changed. This example Fortran 77 program uses a subroutine argument.

```
      PROGRAM ARGSUM
      CALL TOTAL (M)
      WRITE (6, 9) M
    9 FORMAT (I10)
      END
```

```
      SUBROUTINE TOTAL (ITOTAL)
      ITOTAL = 0
      DO 8 I = 1, 100
         ITOTAL = ITOTAL + I
    8 CONTINUE
      END
```

A common block is used in the following Fortran 77 program COMSUM, which performs the same computation as the program ARGSUM.

```
      PROGRAM COMSUM
      COMMON / CB / M
      CALL TOTAL
      WRITE (6, 9) M
    9 FORMAT (I10)
      END

      SUBROUTINE TOTAL
      COMMON / CB / ITOTAL
      ITOTAL = 0
      DO 8 I = 1, 100
         ITOTAL = ITOTAL + I
    8 CONTINUE
      END
```

To describe even these simple cases and appreciate how they all work already requires the introduction of some terms and concepts. To precisely describe the phenomenon that the variable ITOTAL in the subroutine is not known outside the subroutine, the concept of **scope** is used. The scope of the variable ITOTAL is the subroutine and does not include the main program.

It is a common misconception that the scope of a variable in a common block is global; this is not the case. The scope of the variable ITOTAL is just the subroutine, whereas the scope of the variable M is just the main program. However, the scope of the common block name CB is global. It is **association** that is used to describe the connection between M in the main program and ITOTAL in the subroutine. In one case it is **argument association** and in the other it is **storage association**.

To summarize, very roughly, the scope of a variable is that part of the program in which it is known and can be used. Two variables may have the same name and nonoverlapping scopes; for example, there may be two completely different variables named X in two different subprograms. Association of variables means that there are two different names for the same object; this permits sharing values under certain conditions.

With arguments available, it is natural to generalize the computation somewhat to allow the upper limit of the sum (100 in the example) to vary. Also, a function is more natural than a subroutine, because the object of the computation is to return a single value. These changes produce the following Fortran 77 program.

```
      PROGRAM PTOTAL
      INTEGER TOTAL
      PRINT *, TOTAL (100)
      END

      FUNCTION TOTAL (N)
      INTEGER TOTAL
      TOTAL = 0
      DO 8 I = 1, N
         TOTAL = TOTAL + I
   8  CONTINUE
      END
```

In this example, the scope of N is the function TOTAL, but it gets the value 100 through argument association when the function TOTAL is called from the main program in the PRINT statement. The scope of the variable I is the function TOTAL. The scope of the function TOTAL is the whole program, but note that its type must be declared in the main program, because by the implicit typing rules, TOTAL is not of type integer. Another oddity is that there is a function named TOTAL, whose scope is global, and a variable named TOTAL that is local to the function. The variable TOTAL is used to compute and store the value that is returned as the value of the function TOTAL.

It is possible to rewrite the example using internal procedures introduced in Fortran 90. How the identifier TOTAL is used determines whether it is the local variable TOTAL or the global function name TOTAL. In the following example, when it is used with an argument list, it is the function name; when used inside the function subprogram defining the function TOTAL, it is the local variable.

```
      PROGRAM DO_TOTAL
         PRINT *, TOTAL (100)
```

```
CONTAINS

FUNCTION TOTAL (N)
   INTEGER TOTAL
   TOTAL = 0
   DO I = 1, N
      TOTAL = TOTAL + I
   END DO
END FUNCTION TOTAL

END PROGRAM DO_TOTAL
```

This looks almost like the previous example, except that the function is placed prior to the END statement of the main program and the CONTAINS statement is inserted to mark the beginning of any internal functions or subroutines. In this case, the function TOTAL is not global, but is local to the program DO_TOTAL. Also, the function statement for TOTAL and the specifications that follow it specify TOTAL as an internal function of type integer and with one integer argument N. Thus, the type of TOTAL must not be declared in the specification part of the program DO_TOTAL; to do so would create a duplicate declaration of TOTAL. The information about the type of the function and type of the argument is called the **interface** to the internal function.

To illustrate some different rules about scoping and association related to internal procedures, the example can be changed back to one that uses a subroutine, but one that is now internal.

```
PROGRAM DO_TOTAL
   INTEGER TOTAL
   CALL ADD_EM_UP (100)
   PRINT *, TOTAL

CONTAINS

SUBROUTINE ADD_EM_UP (N)
   TOTAL = 0
   DO I = 1, N
      TOTAL = TOTAL + I
   END DO
END SUBROUTINE ADD_EM_UP

END PROGRAM DO_TOTAL
```

The new twist here is that TOTAL in the internal subroutine and TOTAL in the main program are the same variable. It does not need to be declared type integer in the subroutine. This is the result of **host association**, wherein internal procedures **inherit** information about variables from their host, which is the main program in this case. Because the variable I is not mentioned in the main program, its scope is the internal subroutine.

Data declarations and procedures may be placed in a **module**, a new feature of Fortran 90. Then they may be used by other parts of the program. This scheme is illustrated using the simple example, with the summation done by a function again.

```
MODULE TOTAL_STUFF
CONTAINS
FUNCTION TOTAL (N)
   INTEGER TOTAL, N, I
   TOTAL = 0
   DO I = 1, N
      TOTAL = TOTAL + I
   END DO
END FUNCTION TOTAL
END MODULE TOTAL_STUFF

PROGRAM DO_TOTAL
   USE TOTAL_STUFF
   PRINT *, TOTAL (100)
END PROGRAM DO_TOTAL
```

The module and the program could be in completely different files and compiled at different times just like subroutines, but, unlike subroutines, the module must be available to the compiler when the program DO_TOTAL is compiled. The scope of the variables N and I is the function TOTAL; N gets its value 100 by argument association. The module name TOTAL_STUFF is global and any program can use the module, which causes the type and definition of the function TOTAL to become available within that program. This is called **use association**.

When more extensive examples are constructed using such features as internal procedures within a procedure in a module, there is a need to have a deeper understanding of the models underlying scope and association. These topics are introduced briefly below and discussed in more detail in Chapter 14.

2.1.1 Scoping Units

The scope of a program entity is the part of the program in which that entity is known, is available, and can be used. Some of the parts of a program that constitute the scope of entities have been classified specially as **scoping unit**s.

The scope of a label is a subprogram, which is one kind of scoping unit; however, some entities have scopes that are something other than a scoping unit. For example, the scope of a name, such as a variable name, can be any of the following:

1. a scoping unit

2. an executable program

3. a single statement

4. part of a statement

2.1.2 Association

Association is the concept that is used to describe how different entities in the same program unit or different program units can share values and other properties. It is also a mechanism by which the scope of an entity is made larger. For example, argument association allows values to be shared between a procedure and the program that calls it. Storage association, set up by the use of EQUIVALENCE and COMMON statements, for example, allows two or more variables to share storage, and hence values, under certain circumstances. Use association and host association allow entities described in one part of a program to be used in another part of the program. Use association makes entities defined in modules accessible, and host association makes entities in the containing environment available to an internal or module procedure. Examples of association are described earlier in this section, and the complete descriptions of all sorts of association are found in Chapter 14.

2.2 Program Organization

A collection of program units constitutes an executable program. Program units may contain other smaller units. Information may be hidden within part of a program or communicated to other parts of a program by various means. The programmer may control the parts of a program in which information is accessible.

2.2.1 Program Units

A Fortran 90 program unit is one of the following:

> main program
> external subprogram (subroutine or function)
> module
> block data

A Fortran program must contain one main program and may contain any number of the other kinds of program units. Program units contain Fortran constructs and statements that define the data environment and the steps necessary to perform calculations. Each program unit has an END statement to terminate the program unit. Each has a special initial statement as well, but the initial statement for a main program is optional. For example, a program might contain a main program, a subroutine, and a module:

```
PROGRAM MY_TASK
   . . .
END PROGRAM MY_TASK

SUBROUTINE MY_CALC (X)
   . . .
END SUBROUTINE MY_CALC

MODULE MY_DATA
   . . .
END MODULE MY_DATA
```

The main program is required and could be the only program unit in a program. If there are other program units, the main program acts as a controller; that is, it takes charge of the program tasks and controls the order in which they are executed.

An external subprogram (a function or a subroutine) may be used to perform a task or calculation on entities available to the external subprogram. These entities may be the arguments to the subprogram that are provided in the reference, entities defined in the subprogram, or entities made accessible by other means, such as common blocks. A CALL statement is used to invoke a subroutine. A function is invoked when its value is needed in an expression. The computational process that is specified by a function or subroutine subprogram is called a **procedure**. An external subprogram defines a procedure. It may be invoked from other program units of the Fortran program. Neither a module nor a block data program unit is executable, so they are not considered to be procedures.

A block data program unit contains data definitions only and is used to specify initial values for a restricted set of data objects.

The program units described so far (main program, external subprogram, and block data) are familiar to users of Fortran 77. There is a new kind of program unit in Fortran 90—the module—and Fortran 90 provides some new things that are similar to program units: module procedures, internal procedures, and procedure interface blocks.

A module contains definitions that can be made accessible to other program units. These definitions include data definitions, type definitions, definitions of procedures known as **module subprograms**, and specifications of procedure interfaces. Module subprograms may be either subroutine or function subprograms. A module subprogram may be invoked by another module subprogram in the module or by other program units that access the module.

Main programs, external subprograms, and module subprograms may contain internal subprograms, which may be either subroutines or functions. The procedures they define are called **internal procedures**. Internal subprograms must not themselves contain internal subprograms, however. The main program, external subprogram, or module subprogram that contains an internal subprogram is referred to as the internal subprogram's **host**. Internal subprograms may be invoked by their host or by other internal subprograms in the same host. A Fortran 90 internal procedure may contain any number of statements and constructs and thus is a generalization of the Fortran 77 statement function that specifies a procedure by a single statement. Of course the statement function is permitted in Fortran 90 programs as well. Figure 2-1 illustrates the organization of a sample Fortran program.

Fortran 77 has generic intrinsic procedures, such as SIN (the sine function) that can be referenced with a real, double precision, or complex argument. Fortran 90 has extended the concept of generic procedures and allows the programmer to specify a generic procedure so that user-defined procedures also can be referenced generically.

All program units, except block data, may contain procedure interface blocks. A procedure interface block is used to describe the interface of an external procedure; that is, the procedure name, the number of arguments, their types, attributes, names, and the type and attributes of a function. This information is necessary in some cases and, in others, allows the processor to check the validity of an invocation. An interface block with a generic interface may be used to ascribe generic properties.

Subprograms are described more fully in Chapters 11 and 12.

2.2.2 Packaging

Opportunities for applying packaging concepts are limited in Fortran 77. An external subprogram might be thought of as a package, but it can contain only procedures, not data declarations that can be made available to other parts of a program. An entire Fortran 77 program can be thought of as a package made up of program units consisting of a main program, subroutine and function program units, and block data program units. In contrast, Fortran 90, with internal procedures and modules, provides many more opportunities for packaging. This makes the packaging of a fair-sized program an important design consideration when a new Fortran application is planned.

The most important benefit of packaging is information hiding. Entities can be kept inaccessible except where they are actually needed. This provides some protection against inadvertent misuse or corruption, thereby improving program reliability. Packaging can make the logical structure of a program more apparent by hiding complex details at lower levels. Programs are therefore easier to comprehend and less costly to maintain. The Fortran 90 features that provide these benefits are internal procedures and modules.

Internal procedures may appear in main programs, subroutines, functions, and module subprograms. They are known only within their host. The name of an internal procedure must not be passed as an argument. The Fortran 90 standard further restricts internal procedures in that an internal procedure must not itself be the host of another internal procedure. However, a statement function may appear within an internal procedure. Thus, in some ways, internal procedures are like external procedures and in other ways they are like statement functions.

Modules provide the most comprehensive opportunities to apply packaging concepts, as illustrated in Figure 2-1. In addition to several levels of organization and hiding, the entities specified in a module (types, data objects, procedures, interfaces, etc.) may be kept private to the module or made available to other scoping units by use association. In Figure 2-1, the dashed lines with arrows represent subprogram references with the arrow pointing to the subprogram. The large solid arrows represent access by use association with the arrow pointing to the position of a USE statement.

2.3 Data Environment

Before a calculation can be performed, its data environment must be developed. The data environment consists of data objects that possess certain properties, attributes, and values. The steps in a computational process generally specify operations that are performed on operands (or

Program

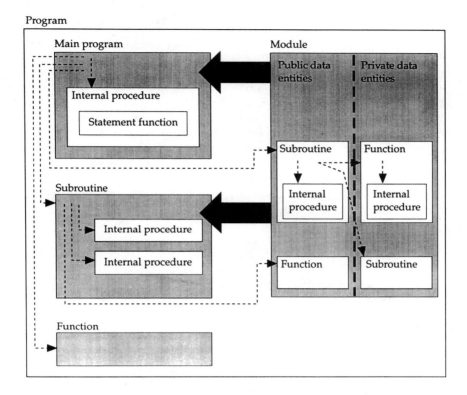

Figure 2-1 Example of program packaging. The large arrows represent use association with the USE statement at the arrow tip. The small arrows represent subprogram references with the "call" at the arrow base.

objects) to create desired results or values. Operands may be constants, variables, constructors, or function references; each has a data type and value, if defined. In some cases the type may be assumed by the processor; in other cases it may be declared. A data object has attributes other than type. Chapter 4 discusses data type in detail; Chapter 5 discusses the other attributes of program entities; and Chapters 6 and 7 describe how data objects may be used.

2.3.1 Data Type

The Fortran 90 language provides five intrinsic data types—real, integer, complex, logical, and character—and allows users to define additional types. Sometimes it is natural to organize data in combinations consisting of more than one type. For example, suppose a program is being written to monitor the patients in a hospital. For each patient, certain information must be maintained, such as the patient's name, room number, temperature, pulse rate, medication, and prognosis for recovery. Because all of this data describes one object (a particular patient), it would be convenient to have a means to refer to the aggregation of data by a single name. In Fortran 90, an aggregation of data values of different types is called a **structure**. To use a structure, a programmer must first define the type of the structure. Once the new type is defined, any number of structures of that type may be declared. This mechanism may seem slightly cumbersome if only one such structure is needed in a program, but usually several are needed; in addition, there are other advantages to defining a type for the structure. An example of a user-defined type with three components is:

```
TYPE PATIENT
   INTEGER              PULSE_RATE
   REAL                 TEMPERATURE
   CHARACTER (LEN = 300) PROGNOSIS
END TYPE PATIENT
```

Once the type PATIENT is defined, objects (structures) of the type may be declared. For example:

```
TYPE (PATIENT) JOHN_JONES, SALLY_SMITH
```

2.3.2 Kind

There may be more than one representation (or kind) of each of the intrinsic types. The Fortran 90 standard requires at least two different representations for the real and complex types that correspond to "single precision" and "double precision", and permits more. Fortran 90 provides portable mechanisms for specifying precision so that numerical algorithms that depend on at least a certain numeric precision can be programmed to produce reliable results regardless of the processor's characteristics. Fortran 90 permits more than one representation for the integer, logical, and character types. Alternative representations for the integer type permit different ranges of integers. Alternative representations for the logical type might include a "packed logical" type to conserve memory space and an "unpacked logical" type to increase speed of access. The large number of characters required for ideographic languages, such as those used in Asia with thousands of different graphical symbols, cannot be represented as concisely as alphabetic characters and require "more precision". Examples of such type declarations are:

```
COMPLEX (KIND = HIGH) X
INTEGER (KIND = SHORT) DAYS_OF_WEEK
CHARACTER (KIND = KANJI, LEN = 500) HAIKU
```

where HIGH, SHORT, and KANJI are named integer constants given appropriate processor-dependent values by the programmer.

Type is one attribute of a data object. There are 12 others, such as DIMENSION, POINTER, and ALLOCATABLE; they are discussed in Chapter 5. The DIMENSION attribute permits the creation of arrays. The POINTER and ALLOCATABLE attributes allow the declaration of dynamic objects.

2.3.3 Dimensionality

Single objects, whether intrinsic or user-defined, are scalar. Even though a structure has components, it is technically a scalar. A set of scalar objects, all of the same type, may be arranged in patterns involving columns, rows, planes, and higher-dimensioned configurations to form arrays. It is possible to have arrays of structures. An array may have up to seven dimensions. The number of dimensions is called the **rank** of the array. It is declared when the array is declared and cannot change. The size of the array is the total number of elements and is equal to the product of the extents in each dimension. The shape of an array is determined by its rank and its extents in each dimension. Two arrays that have the same shape are said to be **conformable**. Examples of array declarations are:

```
REAL COORDINATES (100, 100)
INTEGER DISTANCES (50)
TYPE (PATIENT) MATERNITY_WARD (20)
```

In Fortran 90, an array is treated as an object and is allowed to appear in an expression or be returned as a function result. Intrinsic operations involving arrays of the same shape are performed element-by-element to produce an array result of the same shape. There is no implied order in which the element-by-element operations are performed.

A portion of an array, such as an element or section, may be referenced as a data object. An array element is a single element of the array and is scalar. An array section is a subset of the elements of the array and is itself an array.

2.3.4 Dynamic Data

There are three sorts of dynamic data objects in Fortran 90: pointers, allocatable arrays, and automatic data objects.

Data objects in Fortran 90 may be declared to have the pointer attribute. Pointer objects must be associated with a target before they can be used in any calculation. This is accomplished by allocation of the space for the target or by assignment of the pointer to an existing target. The association of a pointer with a target may change dynamically as a program is executed. If the pointer object is an array, its size and shape may change dynamically, but its rank is fixed by its declaration. An example of pointer array declaration and allocation is:

```
REAL, POINTER :: LENGTHS (:)
ALLOCATE (LENGTHS (200))
```

An array may be declared to have the allocatable attribute. This functionality is exactly the same as provided by the simple use of pointers illustrated above. Space must be allocated for the array before it can be used in any calculation. The array may be deallocated and reallocated with a different size as the program executes. As with a pointer, the size and shape may change, but the rank is fixed by the declaration. An allocatable array cannot be made to point to an existing named target; the target array is always created by an ALLOCATE statement. An example of allocatable array declaration and allocation is:

```
REAL, ALLOCATABLE :: LENGTHS (:)
ALLOCATE (LENGTHS (200))
```

The similarities of these examples reflect the similarity of some of the uses of allocatable arrays and pointers, but pointers have more functionality. Pointers may be used to create dynamic data structures, such as linked lists and trees. The target of a pointer can be changed by reallocation or pointer assignment. The extents of an allocatable array can be changed only by deallocating and reallocating the array. If the values of the elements of an allocatable array are to be preserved, a new array must be allocated and the values moved to the new array before the old array is deallocated.

Automatic data objects, either arrays or character strings (or both), may be declared in a subprogram. These local data objects are created on entry to the subprogram and disappear when the execution of the subprogram completes. These are useful in subprograms for temporary arrays and characters strings whose sizes are different for each reference to the subprogram. An example of a subprogram unit with an automatic array TEMP is:

```
SUBROUTINE SWAP_ARRAYS (A, B)
   REAL, DIMENSION (:) :: A, B
   REAL, DIMENSION (SIZE (A)) :: TEMP

   TEMP = A
   A = B
   B = TEMP
END SUBROUTINE SWAP_ARRAYS
```

A and B are assumed-shape array arguments; that is, they take on the shape of the actual argument. TEMP is an automatic array that is created the same size as A on entry to subroutine SWAP. SIZE is an intrinsic function that is permitted in a declaration statement.

Even in Fortran 66, local variables with a fixed size could be allocated dynamically, but this was an implementation choice and many implementations allocated such variables statically. In Fortran 77 and Fortran 90, a programmer can force the effect of static allocation by giving the variable the SAVE attribute.

2.4 Program Execution

During program execution, constructs and statements are executed in a prescribed order. Variables become defined with values and may be redefined later in the execution sequence. Procedures are invoked, perhaps recursively. Space may be allocated and later deallocated. Pointers may change their targets.

2.4.1 Execution Sequence

Program execution begins with the first executable construct in the main program. An executable construct is an instruction to perform one or more of the computational actions that determine the behavior of the program or control the flow of the execution of the program. It may perform arithmetic, compare values, branch to another construct or statement in the program, invoke a procedure, or read from or write to a file or device. When a procedure is invoked, its execution begins with the first executable construct after the entry point in the procedure. On normal return from a procedure invocation, execution continues where it left off. Examples of executable statements are:

```
        READ (5, *) Z, Y
        X = (4.0 * Z) + BASE
        IF (X > Y) GO TO 100
        CALL CALCULATE (X)
100     Y = Y + 1
```

Unless a control construct is encountered, program statements are executed in the order in which they appear in a program unit until a STOP, RETURN, or END statement is executed. Control constructs include branch statements and IF, CASE, and DO constructs. Branch statements specify a change in the execution sequence and consist of the various forms of GO TO statements, a procedure reference with alternative return specifiers, and input/output statements with branch label specifiers, such as ERR=, END=, and EOR= specifiers. The control constructs (IF, CASE, and DO) can cause internal branching implicitly within the structure of the construct. Chapter 8 discusses in detail control flow within a program.

2.4.2 Definition and Undefinition

Most variables have no value when execution begins; they are considered to be **undefined**. Exceptions are variables that are initialized in DATA statements or type declaration statements; these are considered to be **defined**. A variable may acquire a value or change its current value, typically by the execution of an assignment statement or an input statement. Thus it may assume different values at different times, and under some circumstances it may become undefined. This is part of the dynamic behavior of program execution. **Defined** and **undefined** are the Fortran terms that are used to specify the definition status of a variable. The events that cause variables to become defined and undefined are described in Chapter 14.

A variable is considered to be defined only if all parts of it are defined. For example, all the elements of an array, all the components of a structure, or all characters of a character string must be defined; otherwise, the array, structure, or string is undefined. Fortran 90 permits zero-sized arrays and zero-length strings; these are always considered to be defined.

Pointers have both a definition status and an association status. When execution begins, the association status of all pointers is undefined. During execution a pointer may become nullified by the execution of a NULLIFY statement in which case its association status becomes **disassociated**, or it may become associated with a target by the execution of an ALLOCATE or pointer assignment statement, in which case its association status becomes **associated**. Even when the association status of a pointer is defined, the pointer is not considered to be defined unless the target with which it is associated is defined. Pointer targets become defined in the same way that any other variable becomes defined, typically by the execution of an assignment or input statement. When an allocatable array is allocated by the execution of an ALLOCATE statement, it is undefined until some other action occurs that causes it to become defined with values for all array elements.

2.4.3 Dynamic Behavior

There are new kinds of dynamic behavior that are introduced by Fortran 90:

1. recursion

2. allocation and deallocation

3. pointer assignment

Many algorithms can be expressed eloquently with the use of recursion, which occurs when a subroutine or function references itself, either directly or indirectly. The keyword RECURSIVE must be present in the SUBROUTINE or FUNCTION statement if the procedure is to be referenced recursively. Recursive subroutines and functions are described in Chapter 12.

Pointers and allocatable arrays can be declared in a program, but no space is set aside for them until the program is executed. The rank of array pointers and allocatable arrays is fixed by declaration, but the extents in each dimension (and thus the size of the arrays) is determined during execution by calculation or from input values.

The ALLOCATE and DEALLOCATE statements give Fortran programmers mechanisms to configure objects to the appropriate shape. Only pointers and allocatable arrays can be allocated. Only whole allocated objects can be deallocated. It is not possible to deallocate an object unless it was previously allocated, and it is not possible to deallocate a part of an object unless it is a named component of a structure. It is possible to inquire whether an object is currently allocated. Chapter 5 describes the declaration of pointers and allocatable arrays; Chapter 6 covers the ALLOCATE and DEALLOCATE statements; Chapter 13 and Appendix A discuss the ASSOCIATED intrinsic inquiry function for pointers and the ALLOCATED intrinsic inquiry function for allocatable arrays.

Pointers are more flexible than allocatable arrays, but they are more complicated as well. In the first place, a pointer need not be an array; it may be a scalar of any type. In the second place, a pointer need not be associated with allocated space; any object with the

TARGET attribute can become a pointer target. A pointer assignment statement is provided to associate a pointer with a target (declared or allocated). It makes use of the symbol pair => rather than the single character =; otherwise, it is executed in the same way that an ordinary assignment statement is executed, except that instead of assigning a value it associates a pointer with a target. For example,

```
REAL, TARGET :: VECTOR (100)
REAL, POINTER :: ODDS (:)
 . . .
ODDS => VECTOR (1:100:2)
```

The pointer assignment statement associates ODDS with the odd elements of VECTOR. The assignment statement

```
ODDS = 1.5
```

defines each odd element of VECTOR with the value 1.5. Later in the execution sequence, the pointer ODDS could become associated with a different target by pointer assignment or allocation, as long as the target is a one-dimensional, real array. Chapter 7 describes the pointer assignment statement.

2.5 Terms

Frequently used Fortran 90 terms are defined in this section. Some have a meaning slightly different from the same Fortran 77 term; for example, both an array and an array element are variables in Fortran 90, but not in Fortran 77. Definitions of less frequently used terms may be found by referencing the index of this handbook or Annex A of the Fortran 90 standard.

Entity	This is the general term used to refer to any Fortran 90 "thing", for example, a program unit, a common block, a variable, an expression value, a constant, a statement label, a construct, an operator, an interface block, a type, an input/output unit, a namelist group, etc.
Data object	A data object is a constant, a variable, or a part of a constant or variable.
Data entity	A data entity is a data object, the result of the evaluation of an expression, or the result of the

execution of a function reference (called the **function result**). A data entity always has a type.

Constant

A constant is a data object whose value cannot be changed. A named entity with the PARAMETER attribute is called a **named constant**. A constant without a name is called a **literal constant**.

Variable

A variable is a data object whose value can be defined and redefined. A variable may be a scalar or an array.

Subobject

Portions of a data object may be referenced and defined separately from other portions of the object. Portions of arrays are array elements and array sections. Portions of character strings are substrings. Portions of structures are structure components. Subobjects are referenced by designators and are considered to be data objects themselves.

Name

A name is used to identify many different entities of a program such as a program unit, a variable, a common block, a construct, a formal argument of a subprogram (dummy argument), or a user-defined type (derived type). A name may be associated with a specific constant (named constant). The rules for constructing names are given in Chapter 3.

Designator

Sometimes it is convenient to reference only part of an object, such as an element or section of an array, a substring of a character string, or a component of a structure. This requires the use of the name of the object followed by a selector that selects a part of the object. A name followed by a selector is called a **designator**.

Data type

A data type provides a means for categorizing data. Each intrinsic and user-defined data type has four characteristics—a name, a set of values, a set of operators, and a means to represent constant values of the type in a program.

Type parameter

There are two type parameters for intrinsic types: **kind** and **length**. The kind type parameter KIND indicates the decimal range for the integer type, the decimal precision and exponent range for the real and complex types, and the machine representation method for the character and logical types. The length type parameter LEN indicates the length of a character string.

Derived type

A derived type (or user-defined type) is a type that is not intrinsic; it requires a type definition to name the type and specify its components. The components may be of intrinsic or user-defined types. An object of derived type is called a **structure**. For each derived type, a structure constructor is available to specify values. Operations on objects of derived type must be defined by a function with an interface and the generic specifier OPERATOR. Assignment for derived type objects is defined intrinsically, but may be redefined by a subroutine with the ASSIGNMENT generic specifier. Data objects of derived type may be used as procedure arguments and function results, and may appear in input/output lists.

Scalar

A scalar is a single object of any intrinsic or derived type. A structure is scalar even if it has a component that is an array. The rank of a scalar is zero.

Array

An array is an object with the dimension attribute. It is a collected set of scalar data, all of the same type and type parameters. The rank of an array is at least one and at most seven. Arrays may be used as expression operands, procedure arguments, and function results, and may appear in input/output lists.

Declaration

A declaration is a nonexecutable statement that specifies the attributes of a program element. For example, it may be used to specify the type of a variable or function or the shape of an array.

Definition

This term is used in two ways. A data object is said to be defined when it has a valid or predictable value; otherwise it is undefined. It may be given a valid value by execution of statements such as assignment or input. Under certain circumstances described in Chapter 14, it may subsequently become undefined.

Procedures and derived types are said to be defined when their descriptions have been supplied by the programmer and are available in a program unit.

Statement keyword

A statement keyword is part of the syntax of a statement. Each statement, other than an assignment statement and a statement function definition, begins with a statement keyword. Examples of these keywords are IF, READ, and INTEGER. Statement keywords are not "reserved"; they may be used as names to identify program elements.

Argument keyword

An argument keyword is the name of a dummy (or formal) argument. These names are used in the subprogram definition and may also be used when the subprogram is invoked to associate dummy arguments with actual arguments that can appear in any order. Argument keywords for all of the intrinsic procedures are specified by the standard (see Appendix A). Argument keywords for user-supplied external procedures may be specified in a procedure interface block (described in Chapter 12).

Sequence

A sequence is a set ordered by a one-to-one correspondence with the numbers 1, 2, through n. The number of elements in the sequence is n. A sequence may be empty, in which case it contains no elements.

Operator

An operator indicates a computation involving one or two operands. Fortran defines a number of intrinsic operators; for example, +, -, *, /, ** with numeric operands, and .NOT., .AND., .OR. with logical operands. In addition, users may define operators for use with operands of intrinsic or derived types.

Expression

An expression is a sequence of operands, operators, and parentheses and represents some computation. The operands may be constants, variables, constructors, function references, or expressions enclosed in parentheses.

Construct

A construct is a sequence of statements starting with a CASE, DO, IF, or WHERE statement and ending with the corresponding terminal statement.

Executable construct

An executable construct is a statement (such as a GO TO statement) or a construct (such as a DO or CASE construct).

Control construct

A control construct is an action statement that can change the normal execution sequence (such as a GO TO, STOP, or RETURN statement) or a CASE, DO, or IF construct.

Procedure

A procedure is defined by a sequence of statements that expresses a computation that may be invoked as a subroutine or function during program execution. It may be an intrinsic procedure, an external procedure, an internal procedure, a module procedure, a dummy procedure, or a statement function. A subprogram may define more than one procedure if it contains an ENTRY statement.

Procedure interface

A procedure interface is a sequence of statements that specifies the name and characteristics of a procedure, the name and attributes of each dummy argument, and the generic specifier by which it may be referenced, if any.

Reference

A data object reference is the appearance of a name, designator, or associated pointer in an executable statement requiring the value of the object.

A procedure reference is the appearance of the procedure name, operator symbol, or assignment symbol in an executable program requiring execution of the procedure.

A module reference is the appearance of the module name in a USE statement.

Intrinsic

Anything that is defined by the language is intrinsic. There are intrinsic data types, procedures, and operators. These may be used freely in any scoping unit. The Fortran programmer may define types, procedures, and operators; these entities are not intrinsic.

Scoping unit

A scoping unit is a portion of a program in which a name has a fixed meaning. A program unit or subprogram generally defines a scoping unit. Type definitions and procedure interface blocks also constitute scoping units. Scoping units are nonoverlapping, though one scoping unit may contain another in the sense that it surrounds it. If a scoping unit contains another scoping unit, the outer scoping unit is referred to as the **host scoping unit** of the inner scoping unit.

Association

In general, association permits an entity to be referenced by different names in a scoping unit or by the same or different names in different scoping units. There are several kinds of association: the principal ones are pointer association, argument association, host association, use association, and storage association.

2.6 Summary of Forms

The forms of the most important components of a Fortran 90 program are given in this section. The notation used is the same as that used to show the syntax forms in all the remaining chapters. The complete Backus-Naur form (BNF) as given in the standard is part of Appendix B.

The form of a main program (R1101) is:

```
PROGRAM [ program-name ]
    [ specification-construct ] ...
    [ executable-construct ] ...
    [ CONTAINS
    [ internal-procedure ] ...
END [ PROGRAM [ program-name ] ]
```

The form of a subprogram (R203) is:

    procedure-heading
        [specification-construct] ...
        [executable-construct] ...
        [CONTAINS
        internal-procedure
        [internal-procedure] ...]
    procedure-ending

The form of a module (R1104) is:

    MODULE module-name
        [specification-construct] ...
        [CONTAINS
        subprogram
        [subprogram] ...]
    END [MODULE [module-name]]

The form of a block data program unit (R1110) is:

    BLOCK DATA [block-data-name]
        [specification-statement] ...
    END [BLOCK DATA [block-data-name]]

The form of an internal procedure (R211) is:

    procedure-heading
        [specification-construct] ...
        [executable-construct] ...
    procedure-ending

The forms of a procedure heading (R1216, R1220) are:

    [RECURSIVE] [type-spec] FUNCTION function-name   &
            ([dummy-argument-list]) [RESULT (result-name)]
    [RECURSIVE] SUBROUTINE subroutine-name   &
            [([dummy-argument-list])]

The forms of a procedure ending (R1218, R1222) are:

    END [FUNCTION [function-name]]
    END [SUBROUTINE [subroutine-name]]

The forms of a specification construct are:

    derived-type-definition
    interface-block
    specification-statement

The form of a derived-type definition (R422) is:

```
TYPE [ [ , access-spec ] :: ] type-name
   [ PRIVATE ]
   [ SEQUENCE ]
   [ type-spec [ [ , POINTER ] :: ] component-spec-list ] ...
END TYPE [ type-name ]
```

The form of an interface block (R1201) is:

```
INTERFACE [ generic-spec ]
   [ procedure-heading
       [ specification-construct ] ...
   procedure-ending ] ...
   [ MODULE PROCEDURE module-procedure-name-list ] ...
END INTERFACE
```

The forms of a specification statement are:

```
ALLOCATABLE [ :: ] allocatable-array-list
COMMON [ / [ common-block-name ] / ] common-block-object-list
DATA data-statement-object-list / data-statement-value-list /
DIMENSION array-dimension-list
EQUIVALENCE equivalence-set-list
EXTERNAL external-name-list
FORMAT ( [ format-item-list ] )
IMPLICIT implicit-spec
INTENT ( intent-spec ) [ :: ] dummy-argument-name-list
INTRINSIC intrinsic-procedure-name-list
NAMELIST / namelist-group-name / namelist-group-object-list
OPTIONAL [ :: ] optional-object-list
PARAMETER ( named-constant-definition-list )
POINTER [ :: ] pointer-name-list
PUBLIC [ [ :: ] module-entity-name-list ]
PRIVATE [ [ :: ] module-entity-name-list ]
SAVE [ [ :: ] saved-object-list ]
TARGET [ :: ] target-name-list
USE module-name [ , rename-list ]
USE module-name , ONLY : [ access-list ]
type-spec [ [ , attribute-spec ] ... :: ] object-declaration-list
```

The forms of a type specification (R502) are:

```
INTEGER [ ( [ KIND= ] kind-parameter ) ]
REAL [ ( [ KIND= ] kind-parameter ) ]
DOUBLE PRECISION
COMPLEX [ ( [ KIND= ] kind-parameter ) ]
```

```
CHARACTER [ ( [ KIND= ] kind-parameter ) ]
CHARACTER ( [ [ KIND= ] kind-parameter , ]   &
      [ LEN= ] length-parameter )
LOGICAL [ ( [ KIND= ] kind-parameter ) ]
TYPE ( type-name )
```

The forms of an attribute specification (R503) are:

```
ALLOCATABLE
DIMENSION ( array-spec )
EXTERNAL
INTENT ( intent-spec )
INTRINSIC
OPTIONAL
PARAMETER
POINTER
PRIVATE
PUBLIC
SAVE
TARGET
```

The forms of an executable construct (R215) are:

```
action-statement
case-construct
do-construct
if-construct
where-construct
```

The forms of an action statement (R216) are:

```
ALLOCATE ( allocation-list [ , STAT= scalar-integer-variable ] )
ASSIGN label TO scalar-integer-variable
BACKSPACE external-file-unit
BACKSPACE ( position-spec-list )
CALL subroutine-name [ ( [ actual-argument-spec-list ] ) ]
CLOSE ( close-spec-list )
CONTINUE
CYCLE [ do-construct-name ]
DEALLOCATE ( name-list [ , STAT= scalar-integer-variable ] )
ENDFILE external-file-unit
ENDFILE ( position-spec-list )
```

```
EXIT [ do-construct-name ]
GO TO label
GO TO ( label-list ) [ , ] scalar-integer-expression
GO TO scalar-integer-variable [ [ , ] ( label-list ) ]
IF ( scalar-logical-expression ) action-statement
IF ( scalar-numeric-expression ) label , label , label
INQUIRE ( inquire-spec-list ) [ output-item-list ]
NULLIFY ( pointer-object-list )
OPEN ( connect-spec-list )
PAUSE [ access-code ]
PRINT format [ , output-item-list ]
READ ( io-control-spec-list ) [ input-item-list ]
READ format [ , input-item-list ]
RETURN [ scalar-integer-expression ]
REWIND external-file-unit
REWIND ( position-spec-list )
STOP [ access-code ]
WHERE ( array-logical-expression ) array-assignment-statement
WRITE ( io-control-spec-list ) [ output-item-list ]
pointer-variable => target-expression
variable = expression
```

The form of a CASE construct (R808) is:

```
SELECT CASE ( case-variable )
   [ CASE case-selector
      [ executable-construct ] ... ] ...
   [ CASE DEFAULT
      [ executable-construct ] ... ]
END SELECT
```

The forms of a DO construct (R816) are:

```
DO [ label ]
   [ executable-construct ] ...
do-termination
```

```
DO [ label ] [ , ] loop-variable = initial-value , final-value &
      [ , increment ]
   [ executable-construct ] ...
do-termination
```

```
DO [ label ] [ , ] WHILE ( scalar-logical-expression )
    [ executable-construct ] ...
do-termination
```

The form of an IF construct (R802) is:

```
IF ( scalar-logical-expression ) THEN
    [ executable-construct ] ...
[ ELSE IF ( scalar-logical-expression ) THEN
    [ executable-construct ] ... ] ...
[ ELSE
    [ executable-construct ] ... ]
END IF
```

The form of a WHERE construct (R739) is:

```
WHERE ( array-logical-expression )
    array-assignment-block
ELSEWHERE
    array-assignment-block
END WHERE
```

Two miscellaneous forms (R1223) are:

```
ENTRY entry-name [ ( [ dummy-argument-list ] ) ]  &
        [ RESULT ( result-name ) ]

INCLUDE character-literal-constant
```

2.7 Ordering Requirements

Within program units and subprograms, there are ordering requirements for statements and constructs. The syntax rules above do not fully describe the ordering requirements. Therefore, they are illustrated in Tables 2-1 and 2-2. In general, data declarations and specifications must precede executable constructs and statements, although FORMAT, DATA, and ENTRY statements may appear among the executable statements. USE statements, if any, must appear first. Internal or module subprograms, if any, must appear last following a CONTAINS statement.

In Table 2-1, a vertical line separates statements and constructs that can be interspersed; a horizontal line separates statements that must not be interspersed.

There are restrictions on the places where some statements may appear. Table 2-2 summarizes these restrictions.

Table 2-1 Requirements on statement ordering

PROGRAM, FUNCTION, SUBROUTINE, MODULE, or BLOCK DATA statement		
USE statements		
FORMAT and ENTRY statements	IMPLICIT NONE	
	PARAMETER statements	IMPLICIT statements
	PARAMETER and DATA statements	Derived-type definitions, interface blocks, type declaration statements, statement function statements, and specification statements
	DATA statements	Executable constructs
CONTAINS statement		
Internal subprograms or module subprograms		
END statement		

Table 2-2 Restrictions on the appearance of statements

Kind of scoping unit:	Main program	Module	Block data	External subprog	Module subprog	Internal subprog	Interface body
USE statement	Yes	Yes	No	Yes	Yes	Yes	Yes
ENTRY statement	No	No	No	Yes	Yes	No	No
FORMAT statement	Yes	No	No	Yes	Yes	Yes	No
Misc. declarations (see note)	Yes	Yes	Yes	Yes	Yes	Yes	Yes
DATA statement	Yes	Yes	Yes	Yes	Yes	Yes	No
Derived-type definition	Yes	Yes	No	Yes	Yes	Yes	Yes
Interface block	Yes	Yes	No	Yes	Yes	Yes	Yes
Statement function	Yes	No	No	Yes	Yes	Yes	No
Executable statement	Yes	No	No	Yes	Yes	Yes	No
CONTAINS	Yes	Yes	No	Yes	Yes	No	No

Note: Misc. declarations are PARAMETER statements, IMPLICIT statements, DATA statements, type declaration statements, and specification statements.

2.8 Example Fortran 90 Program

Illustrated below is a very simple Fortran 90 program consisting of one program unit, the main program. Three data objects are declared: H, T, and U. These become the loop indices in a triply-nested loop structure (8.5) containing a logical IF statement (8.3.2) that conditionally executes an input/output statement (9.4).

```
PROGRAM SUM_OF_CUBES

! This program prints all 3-digit numbers that
! equal the sum of the cubes of their digits.

INTEGER H, T, U

DO H = 1, 9
   DO T = 0, 9
      DO U = 0, 9
         IF (100*H + 10*T + U == H**3 + T**3 + U**3) &
            PRINT "(3I1)", H, T, U
      END DO
   END DO
END DO

END PROGRAM SUM_OF_CUBES
```

This Fortran 90 program is standard conforming and should be compilable and executable on any standard Fortran 90 computing system, producing the following output:

```
153
370
371
407
```

2.9 Summary

Program Units

There are five kinds of program units:

> main program
> external subroutine
> external function
> module
> block data

The module is new to Fortran with Fortran 90. It may contain data definitions, type definitions, procedure definitions, and procedure interface
descriptions. Information in a module may be made available to other
program units or it may be kept private to the module. Type definitions
and procedure interface descriptions are also new to Fortran. Procedure
interface descriptions are used to describe the interfaces of external procedures and provide generic specifiers for external and module procedures.
For some new Fortran 90 features, procedure interfaces are required for
proper communication.

Scoping

The scope of an entity determines where it is accessible in the program.
A scope may be as large as an entire program or as small as a part of
one Fortran statement. The scope of an entity is often, but not always, a
scoping unit, which is one of the following:

1. a program unit or subprogram, excluding derived-type definitions,
    procedure interface bodies, and subprograms contained within it

2. a derived-type definition

3. a procedure interface body, excluding any derived-type definitions
    and procedure interface bodies contained within it

Association

Association allows more than one entity to share values and other properties. Storage association and argument association establish that different entities, possibly with different scopes, share values. Use and host
association extend the scope of entities into other procedures.

Packaging

Programs are made up of program units. Program units are made up of
Fortran constructs and statements and may contain other scoping units.
   Internal procedures may appear in the main program and in external and module procedures. They must not appear in internal procedures nor may the names of internal procedures be passed as arguments.
   Statement function statements may appear in the main program and
in external, internal, and module procedures.
   Interface blocks may appear in the main program, in modules, and
in external, internal, and module procedures. They must not appear in a
block data program unit.

Type definitions may appear in the main program, in modules, in block data subprograms, and in external, internal, and module procedures.

Packaging allows programs to be structured logically and information to be hidden unless it is needed. This permits more robust programs to be created.

Data Type

Fortran provides five intrinsic data types:

integer
real
complex
logical
character

A standard-conforming Fortran 90 processor must support at least two kinds (representations) of real and complex values; it may support more. It must support one kind of integer, logical, and character representations and may support more.

A Fortran 90 user may define new data types that are made up of components that are of intrinsic or user-defined type. An object of one of these new types is called a structure. It is considered to be a scalar.

Dimensionality

If a data object has the dimension attribute, it is an array; otherwise, it is a scalar. Arrays are treated as variables in Fortran 90; they may appear in expressions and be returned as function results. Either whole arrays or array sections may be referenced. A structure may have an array component, but it is still considered to be a scalar. Arrays of structures are permitted.

Dynamic Data

There are three dynamic data objects in Fortran 90:

pointers
allocatable arrays
automatic data objects

Dynamic data objects do not exist until a program is executed. They are declared, but no space is set aside by the compiler for these objects. During execution pointers may be allocated space, in which case new space is created for them; or they may be assigned to point to existing

space. Allocatable arrays must have space allocated for them during execution. Automatic data objects, which may be arrays or character
strings, can be declared only in subprograms. Space is created for them
when the subprogram is invoked, and they cease to exist when execution
of the subprogram completes.

Execution Sequence

Program execution begins with the first executable statement in the main
program. It continues with successive statements unless a statement or
construct is encountered that changes the flow of control. When a procedure is invoked, its execution begins with the first executable statement
after the entry point in the procedure. On normal return from a procedure, execution continues where it left off.

Definition and Undefinition

When program execution begins, most variables have no value. Their
definition status is considered to be **undefined**. If, however, the variable
was initialized by a DATA statement or a type declaration statement, its
definition status is **defined**. During the course of execution, a variable
may acquire a value or change its current value, which would cause its
definition status to be defined. On the other hand, some event could
occur that would cause its definition status to become undefined.

Pointers have both a definition status and an association status.
Initially, the association status of all pointers is undefined. When the
pointer becomes associated with a target, its status changes to associated.
Its definition status is defined only if it is associated with a target that is
defined.

In a like manner, allocatable arrays must be both allocated and
defined before their definition status is defined.

Dynamic Behavior

Fortran 90 introduces some new kinds of dynamic behavior:

1. recursion

2. allocation and deallocation

3. pointer assignment

The Fortran programmer can now write subprograms that invoke
themselves. The keyword RECURSIVE must appear in the SUBROU-
TINE or FUNCTION statement if this occurs.

The Fortran programmer can now control the utilization of space with ALLOCATE and DEALLOCATE statements.

Pointers can be allocated or they can be associated with existing space with a pointer assignment statement.

F90

3

Language Elements and Source Form

This chapter describes the language elements that a Fortran statement may contain. Language elements consist of lexical tokens, which include names, keywords, operators, and statement labels. Rules for forming lexical tokens from the characters in the Fortran character set are given.

The source form describes how to place these elements on a line in a Fortran program. There are two source forms in Fortran 90. One is oriented towards the Hollerith punched card common in the 1960s and is restricted to 80 positions. It is called **fixed source form**. The other is new in Fortran 90 and is oriented towards terminal input of source code. It is called **free source form**.

A processor must have a character set that includes the Fortran character set (described in the next section) but may permit other characters in certain contexts. These characters may include control characters (which may have no graphic representation, such as escape or newline) or may include characters with specified graphics. The characters with specified graphics are typically oriented towards other languages such as Greek, Arabic, Chinese, or Japanese. Such characters are not required to be part of the character set for the default character type, but would be part of some optional, nondefault character type, permitted by the standard and supplied by a particular implementation.

The INCLUDE line is a new feature in Fortran that permits the inclusion of source code from a specified file. It is a convenient way to place the same text in several places in a program.

3.1 The Processor Character Set

The **processor character set** contains:

- the Fortran character set with specified graphics except for the currency symbol ($). The Fortran 90 character set includes the Fortran 77 character set plus the characters >, <, ;, !, ?, %, _, ", and &.

- as an option, a processor-dependent set of control characters that have no graphic representation, such as "newline" or "escape"

- as an option, a set of characters with graphics (such as Greek letters, Japanese ideographs, or characters in the shape of a heart or a diamond)

It is recommended that the programmer consult the implementor's documentation describing the processor-dependent features of each particular Fortran 90 implementation.

3.1.1 The Fortran Character Set

Characters in the **Fortran character set** are shown in Table 3-1.

Rules and restrictions:

1. Lowercase letters are permitted, but a processor is not required to recognize them. If a processor does recognize them, they are considered the same as uppercase letters except within a character constant or a quote, apostrophe, or H edit descriptor, where uppercase and lowercase letters are different data values. Thus, for a processor that accepts lowercase letters, the following two statements are equivalent:

```
PRINT *, N
Print *, n
```

Whether uppercase and lowercase letters are distinguished in the FILE= or NAME= specifier in an OPEN or an INQUIRE statement is processor dependent.

Table 3-1 The Fortran character set

Alphanumeric characters

Letters   A B C D E F G H I J K L M N O P Q R S T U V W X Y Z
Digits   0 1 2 3 4 5 6 7 8 9
Underscore ___

Special characters

Graphic	Name of character	Graphic	Name of character
	Blank	:	Colon
=	Equals	!	Exclamation point
+	Plus	"	Quotation mark or quote
—	Minus	%	Percent
*	Asterisk	&	Ampersand
/	Slash	;	Semicolon
(	Left parenthesis	<	Less than
)	Right parenthesis	>	Greater than
,	Comma	?	Question mark
.	Decimal point or period	$	Currency symbol
'	Apostrophe		

2. The digits are assumed to be decimal numbers when used to describe a numeric value, except in binary, octal, and hexadecimal (BOZ) literal constants or input/output records corresponding to B, O, or Z edit descriptors. For example, consider the following DATA statement:

```
DATA  X, I, J / 4.89, B'1011', Z'BAC91' /
```

The digits of the first constant are decimal digits, those of the second constant are binary digits, and those of the third are hexadecimal digits.

3. The underscore is used to make names more readable. For example, in the identifier NUMBER_OF_CARS, each underscore is used to separate the obvious English words. It is a significant character in any name. It cannot be used as the first character of a name; however, it may be the last character. An underscore is also used to separate the kind value from the actual value of a literal constant (for example, 123_2).

4. Except for the currency symbol ($), the graphic for each character must be the same as in Table 3-1; however, any style, font, or printing convention may be used.

There are twenty-one special characters used for operators like multiply and add, and as separators or delimiters in Fortran statements. Separators and delimiters make the form of a statement unambiguous. The special characters, $ and ?, are not required for any Fortran statement.

Fortran's treatment of uppercase and lowercase letters may lead to portability problems when calling subprograms written in other languages. The problem occurs because the standard does not specify the case of letters used for external names. To illustrate the problem, consider the program fragment:

```
EXTERNAL   FOO
   . . .
CALL   FOO
   . . .
END
```

One Fortran processor may use FOO as the external name whereas another Fortran system may use foo. If FOO were to be written in a programming language such as C, which is case sensitive, the external name used in C would then be different for different programming systems.

Undoubtedly, most implementations will use the case that makes the Fortran 90 compiled code compatible with previous Fortran implementations on the same system. For example, Unix implementations of Fortran generally use lowercase letters for external names in Fortran implementations, and thus can be expected to continue to use lowercase letters for all externals. Consult your vendor's documentation for the specific details.

3.1.2 Other Characters

In addition to the Fortran character set, other characters may be included in the processor character set. These are either control characters with no graphics or additional characters with graphics. The selection of the other characters and where they may be used is processor dependent. However, wherever they are permitted, the other characters are restricted in use to character constants, quote, apostrophe, and H edit descriptors, comment lines, and input/output records. All characters of the Fortran character set may be used in character constants, quote, apostrophe, and H edit descriptors, comment lines, and input/output records.

A processor is required to support the Fortran character set as part of a character set referred to as the **default character set**. A processor is allowed to support more than one character set, each set using a different kind value of the intrinsic character type (4.3.5). The choice of characters in such sets is processor dependent except that each such set must contain a character that can be used as a blank. This specially designated character is used where blank padding is required.

The choice of the representable characters beyond the Fortran character set is expected to be dependent on the particular implementation. It is recommended that the implementor's documentation be consulted for specific details.

3.2 Lexical Tokens

A statement is constructed from low-level syntax. The low-level syntax describes the basic language elements, called **lexical tokens**, in a Fortran statement. A lexical token is the smallest meaningful unit of a Fortran statement and may consist of one or more characters. Tokens are names, keywords, literal constants (except for complex literal constants), labels, operator symbols, comma, =, = >, :, ::, ;, %, and delimiters. A complex literal (4.3.3.4) consists of several tokens. Examples of operator symbols are + and //.

Delimiters in Fortran are pairs of symbols that enclose parts of a Fortran statement. The delimiters are slashes (in pairs), left and right parentheses, and the symbol pair (/ and /).

```
/ ... /
( ... )
(/ ... /)
```

In the statements:

```
DATA  X, Y/ 1.0, -10.2/
CALL PRINT_LIST (LIST, SIZE)
VECTOR = (/ 10, 20, 30, 40 /)
```

the slashes distinguish the value list from the object list in a DATA statement, the parentheses are delimiters marking the beginning and end of the argument list in the CALL statement, and the pairs (/ and /) mark the beginning and end of the elements of an array constructor.

3.2.1 Statement Keywords

Statement keywords appear in uppercase letters in the syntax rules. Some statement keywords also identify the statement, such as in the DO statement:

```
DO I = 1, 10
```

where DO is a statement keyword identifying the DO statement. Other keywords delimit parts of a statement such as ONLY in a USE statement, or WHILE in one of the forms of a DO construct, as, for example:

```
DO WHILE( .NOT. FOUND )
```

Others specify options in the statement such as IN, OUT, or INOUT in the INTENT statement.

There are three statements in Fortran that have no statement keyword. They are the assignment statement, the pointer assignment statement, and the statement function.

A dummy argument keyword, a different sort of keyword, is discussed in Section 12.5.4.

3.2.2 Names

Variables, named constants, program units, common blocks, procedures, arguments, constructs, derived types (types for structures), namelist groups, structure components, dummy arguments, and function results are among the elements in a program that have a name.

Rules and restrictions:

1. A name must begin with a letter and consist of letters, digits, and underscores. Note that an underscore must not be the first character of a name—see the syntax rule for *name* in 3.6.

2. Fortran 90 permits up to 31 characters in names.

Examples of names:

```
A
CAR_STOCK_NUMBER
A__BUTTERFLY
Z_28
TEMP_
```

3.2.3 Constants

A **constant** is a syntactic notation for a value. The value may be of any intrinsic type, that is, a numeric (integer, real, or complex) value, a character value, or a logical value.

A value that does not have a name is a **literal constant**. Examples of literal constants are:

```
1.23
400
( 0.0, 1.0 )
"ABC"
B'0110110'
.TRUE.
```

No literal constant can be array-valued or of derived type. The forms of literal constants are given in more detail in Section 4.3.

A value that has a name is called a **named constant** and may be of any type, including a derived type. A named constant may also be array-valued. Examples of named constants are:

```
X_AXIS
MY_SPOUSE
```

where these names have been specified in a declaration statement as follows:

```
REAL, DIMENSION(2), PARAMETER :: X_AXIS = (/ 0.0, 1.0 /)
TYPE(PERSON), PARAMETER :: MY_SPOUSE = PERSON( 39, 'PAT' )
```

Note, however, that the entity on the right of the equal sign is not itself a constant but a constant expression (7.2.9.1). The forms for defining named constants are described in more detail in Section 5.5.2.

3.2.4 Operators

Operators are used with operands in expressions to produce other values. Examples of language-supplied operators are:

*	representing multiplication of numeric values
//	representing concatenation of character values
==	representing comparison for equality (same as .EQ.)
.OR.	representing logical disjunction
.NOT.	representing logical negation

The complete set of the intrinsic operators built into Fortran 90 is given by the class *intrinsic-operator* (R310) in Appendix B.2.

Users may define operators (12.6.4) in addition to the intrinsic operators. User-defined operators begin with a period (.), followed by a sequence of up to 31 letters, and end with a period (.), except that the letter sequence must not be the same as any intrinsic operator or the logical constants .FALSE. or .TRUE.

3.2.5 Statement Labels

A label may be used to identify a statement. A **label** consists of one to five decimal digits, one of which must be nonzero. If a Fortran statement has a label, it is uniquely identified and the label can be used in DO constructs, CALL statements, branching statements, and input/output statements. In most cases, two statements in the same program unit must not have the same label (there are exceptions because a program unit may contain more than one scoping unit, for example, several internal procedures). Leading zeros in a label are not significant so that the labels 020 and 20 are the same label. The cases in which duplicate labels can be used in the same program unit are explained in Chapter 14 as part of the general treatment of the scope of entities. Examples of statements with labels are:

```
100 CONTINUE
 21 X = X + 1.2
101 FORMAT (1X, 2F10.2)
```

The Fortran 90 syntax does not permit a statement with no content, sometimes referred to as a blank statement. Such a statement is always treated as a comment; therefore, if such a statement is created, it must not be labeled. For example, each of the following lines is nonstandard Fortran 90:

```
10
        X=0;101;
```

3.3 Source Form

A Fortran program consists of Fortran statements, comments, and INCLUDE lines; this collection of statements, comments, and lines is called **source text**. A Fortran statement consists of one or more complete or partial lines of source text and is constructed from low-level syntax (3.6). A complete or partial line is a sequence of characters. The following examples illustrate how statements can be formed from partial or complete lines:

```
! This example is written for one of the source forms,
! called free source form (3.3.1).  It uses the & on the
! continued line to indicate continuation, and ! to
! indicate the beginning of a comment.
```

```
10 FORMAT( 2X, I5 )          ! A statement on a complete line
13 FORMAT( 2X, &             ! A statement on two complete
          I5 )               !   lines

X = 5; 10 FORMAT( 2X, I5)    ! Two statements, each as part
                             !   of a line

X = 5 + &                    ! A statement consisting of a
    Y; 10 FORMAT( 2X, I5 )   !   complete line and a partial
                             !   line

X = 5 + &                    ! A statement made up of two
    Y; 10 FORMAT( 2X, &      !   partial lines
          I5);   READ &
       (5, 10)  A, B, C
```

The lines within a program unit (except comment lines) and the order of the lines are in general significant (see Table 2-1), except that the order of the subprograms following a CONTAINS statement and before the END statement for the containing program unit is insignificant. Because all program units terminate with their own END statement, lines following such an END statement are never part of the preceding program unit; they are part of the program unit that follows.

There are two source forms for writing source text: free source form, which is new, and fixed source form, which is the traditional Fortran form. Programmers must use either fixed or free source form throughout a program unit, although different program units within the program may use different source forms. Each Fortran processing system must provide a way to indicate which source form is being used; for example, this might be indicated with a compiler option or compiler directive, or the processor might assume one of the forms by default. Section 3.4 describes a way to write Fortran statements so that the source text is acceptable to both free and fixed source forms.

Characters that form the value of a character literal constant or a character string edit descriptor (quote, apostrophe, or H edit descriptor) are said to be in a **character context**. Note that the characters in character context do not include the delimiters used to indicate the beginning and end of the character constant or string. Also, the ampersands in free source form, used to indicate that a character string is being continued and used to indicate the beginning of the character string on the continued line, are never part of the character string value and thus are not in character context—see Section 3.3.1.1.

The rules that apply to characters in a character context are different from the rules that apply to characters in other contexts. For example, blanks are always significant in a character context, but are never significant in other parts of a program written using fixed source form.

```
CHAR = CHAR1 // "Mary K. Williams"
! The blanks within the character string
! (within the double quotes) are significant.

! The next two statements are equivalent
! in fixed source form.
DO2I=1,N
DO 2 I = 1, N
```

Comments may contain any graphic character that is in the processor character set. For fixed source form, comments may contain, in addition, certain control characters as allowed by the processor—see the implementor's manual for the specific control characters allowed.

3.3.1 Free Source Form

In free source form, there are no restrictions limiting statements to specific positions on a Fortran line. The blank character is significant and may be required to separate lexical tokens.

Rules and restrictions:

1. Blank characters are significant everywhere except that a sequence of blank characters outside a character context is treated as a single blank character. They may be used freely between tokens and delimiters to improve the readability of the source text. For example, the two statements

    ```
    SUM=SUM+A(I)
    SUM = SUM + A (I)
    ```

    are the same.

2. Each line may contain from 0 to 132 characters, provided that are they are of default character kind. If any character is of a nondefault character kind, the processor may limit the number of characters to fewer than 132 characters. For example, a line such as

    ```
    TEXT = GREEK_'This line has 132 characters and contains α'
    ```

may use exactly 132 graphic characters, but the implementation may require more space to represent this source line than 132 Fortran characters. The processor may thus limit how many graphic characters may be used on a line if any of them are of nondefault character kind.

3. The exclamation mark (!), not in character context, is used to indicate the beginning of a comment that ends with the end of the line. A line may contain nothing but a comment. Comments, including the !, are ignored and do not alter the interpretation of Fortran statements in any way. There is no language limit on the number of comments in a program unit, although the processor may impose such a limit. A line whose first nonblank character is an exclamation mark is called a **comment line**. An example of a Fortran statement with a trailing comment is:

```
ITER = ITER + 1    ! Begin the next iteration.
```

An example of a comment line is:

```
! Begin the next iteration.
```

4. An ampersand, not in character context, is a continuation symbol and can only be followed by zero or more blanks or a comment and the end of the line. The line following that is not a comment line is called a **continuation line**. An example of a continued line and a continuation line is:

```
FORCE = G * MASS1 *  & ! This is a continued line.
        MASS2 / R**2   ! This is a continuation line.
```

No more than 39 continuation lines are allowed in a Fortran statement. No line may contain an ampersand as the only nonblank character before an exclamation mark. Comment lines cannot be continued; that is, the ampersand as the last character in a comment is part of the comment and does not indicate continuation. The next section gives more details on the use of the ampersand in free source form as a continuation symbol.

5. A line with only blank characters or with no characters is treated as a comment line.

6. More than one statement or partial statements may appear on a line. The statement separator is the semicolon (;), provided it is

not in a character context; multiple successive semicolons on a line with or without blanks intervening are considered as a single separator. The end of a line is also a statement separator, but a semicolon at the end of a line that is not part of a comment is considered as a single separator. For example:

```
! The semicolon is a statement separator.
X = 1.0;   Y = 2.0

! However, the semicolon below at the end of a line is
! not treated as a separator and is ignored.
Z = 3.0;

! Also, consecutive semicolons are treated as one
! semicolon, even if blanks intervene.
Z = 3.0; ; W = 4.0
```

The effect of these rules is as if a null statement were a legal Fortran statement.

7. A label may appear before a statement, provided it is not part of another statement, but it must be separated from the statement by at least one blank. For example:

```
10 FORMAT(10x,2I5)        ! 10 is a label
   IF (X == 0.0) 200 Y = SQRT(X)  ! Label 200 is
                          ! not allowed.
```

8. Any graphic character in the processor character set may be used in character literal constants (4.3.5.4) and character string edit descriptors (10.2.3). Note that this excludes control characters; it is recommended that the implementor's manual be consulted for the specific details.

3.3.1.1 The Ampersand as a Continuation Symbol. The ampersand (&) is used as the continuation symbol in free source form. If it is the last nonblank character after any comments are deleted and it is not in a character context, the statement is continued on the next line that does not begin with a comment. If the first nonblank character on the continuing line is an ampersand, the statement continues after the ampersand; otherwise, the statement continues with the first position of the line. The ampersand or ampersands used as the continuation symbols are not considered part of the statement. For example, the following statement takes two lines (one continuation line) because it is too long to fit on one line:

```
STOKES_LAW_VELOCITY = 2 * GRAVITY * RADIUS ** 2 * &
        (DENSITY_1 - DENSITY_2) / (9 * COEFF_OF_VISCOSITY)
```

The leading blanks on the continued line are included in the statement and are allowed in this case because they are between lexical tokens.

The double-ampersand convention must be used to continue a name, a character constant, or a lexical token consisting of more than one character split across lines. The following statement is the same statement as in the previous example:

```
STOKES_LAW_VELOCITY = 2 * GRAVITY * RADIUS * 2 * (DEN&
        &SITY_1 - DENSITY_2) / (9 * COEFF_OF_VISCOSITY)
```

However, splitting names across lines makes the code difficult to read and is not recommended.

Ampersands may be included in a character constant. Only the last ampersand on the line is the continuation symbol, as illustrated in the following example:

```
LAWYERS = "Jones & Clay & &
Davis"
```

The value of this constant is "Jones & Clay & Davis" (provided the lines begin in position 1). The first two ampersands are in character context; they are part of the value of the character string.

To continue a character constant so that the continued line is indented, an ampersand must be used as the first character of the continued line, as in:

```
NAME = "Mary K. W&
        &illiams"
```

In this case, the first nonblank character on the next line (that is not a comment) must be an ampersand because Williams is split between lines; otherwise the blanks at the beginning of the second line will be included as part of the character constant. The statement continues with the character following the ampersand. The value in NAME is "Mary K. Williams". This allows character strings (that could be quite long) to be continued.

3.3.1.2 Blanks as Separators. Blanks in free source form may not appear within tokens, such as names or symbols consisting of more than one character, except that blanks may be freely used in format specifications. For instance, blanks may not appear between the characters of multicharacter operators such as ** and .NE. Format specifications are an exception because blanks may appear within edit descriptors such as BN, SS, or TR in format specifications. On the other hand, a blank must be used to separate a statement keyword, name, constant, or label from an adjacent name, constant, or label. For example, the blanks in the following statements are required.

```
INTEGER SIZE
PRINT 10,N
DO I=1,N
```

Table 3-2 Where blanks are optional and required separating statement keywords

Blanks optional	Blank mandatory
BLOCK DATA	CASE DEFAULT
DOUBLE PRECISION	DO WHILE
ELSE IF	IMPLICIT type-spec
END BLOCK DATA	IMPLICIT NONE
END DO	INTERFACE ASSIGNMENT
END FILE	INTERFACE OPERATOR
END FUNCTION	MODULE PROCEDURE
END IF	RECURSIVE FUNCTION
END INTERFACE	RECURSIVE SUBROUTINE
END MODULE	RECURSIVE type-spec
END PROGRAM	type-spec FUNCTION
END SELECT	type-spec RECURSIVE
END SUBROUTINE	
END TYPE	
END WHERE	
GO TO	
IN OUT	
SELECT CASE	

Adjacent keywords require a blank separator in some cases (for example, CASE DEFAULT) whereas in other cases two adjacent keywords may be written either with or without intervening blanks (for example, BLOCK DATA); Table 3-2 gives the situations where blank separators are optional or mandatory. Despite these rules, blank separators between statement keywords make the source text more readable and clarify the statements. In general, if common rules of English text are followed, everything will be correct. For example, blank separators in the following statement make them quite readable, even though the blank between the keywords RECURSIVE and FUNCTION in the first statement is the only one that is required.

```
RECURSIVE FUNCTION F(X)
DOUBLE PRECISION X
END FUNCTION F
```

3.3.1.3 Sample Program, Free Source Form. A sample program in free source form is:

```
123456789.......
------------------------------------------------------
|PROGRAM LEFT_RIGHT
| REAL  X(5), Y(5)
|        ! Print arrays X and Y
|        PRINT 100, X, Y
|        100 FORMAT (F10.1, F10.2, F10.3, F10.4,  &
|                       F10.5)
|  . . .
|END
```

3.3.2 Fixed Source Form

Fixed source form is position oriented on a line using the conventions for position that were used historically for Fortran written on punched cards. Currently, most programmers use Fortran systems that permit a less stilted style of source form; this is the free source form described in the previous sections.

Rules and restrictions:

1. Fortran statements or parts of Fortran statements must be written between positions 7 and 72. Character positions 1 through 6 are reserved for special purposes.

2. Blanks are not significant in fixed source form except in a character context. For example, the two statements

```
D O  10  I = 1, L O O P E N D
DO 10 I = 1, LOOPEND
```

are the same.

3. A C or * in position 1 identifies a comment. In this case, the entire line is a comment and is called a **comment line**. A ! in any position except position 6 and not in character context indicates that a comment follows to the end of the line. Comments are not significant, and there is no language limit on the number of comment lines. However, a processor may impose a limit.

4. A line with only blank characters or with no characters is treated as a comment line.

5. Multiple statements on a line are separated by one or more semicolons, and semicolons may occur at the end of a line, which are ignored.

6. Any character (including ! and ;) other than blank or zero in position 6 indicates that the line is a continuation of the previous line. Such a line is called a **continuation line**. The text on the continuation line begins in position 7. There must be no more than 19 continuation lines for one statement in fixed source form. The first line of a continued statement is called the **initial line**.

7. Statement labels may appear only in positions 1 through 5. Labels may appear only on the first line of a continued statement. Thus, positions 1 through 5 of continuation lines must contain blanks.

8. An END statement must not be continued. END also must not be an initial line of a statement other than an END statement. For example, an assignment statement for the variable ENDLESS may not be written as

        END
        +LESS = 3.0

    because the initial line of this statement is identical to an END statement.

9. Any character from the processor character set (including graphic and control characters) may be used in a character literal constant and character edit descriptors, except that the processor is permitted to limit the use of some of the control characters in such character contexts. Consult the implementor's documentation for such limitations.

3.3.3 Sample Program, Fixed Source Form

A sample program in fixed source form is:

```
123456789.....
-----------------------------------------------
|        PROGRAM LEFT_RIGHT
|        REAL  X(5), Y(5)
|C       Print arrays X and Y
|        PRINT 100, X, Y
|   100 FORMAT (F10.1, F10.2, F10.3, F10.4,
|     1         F10.5)
|         . . .
|        END
```

3.4 Rules for Fixed/Free Source Form

For many purposes, such as an included file (3.5), it is desirable to use a form of the source code that is valid and equivalent for either free source form or fixed source form. Such a fixed/free source form can be written by obeying the following rules and restrictions:

1. Limit labels to positions 1 through 5, and statements to positions 7 through 72. These are the limits required in fixed source form.

2. Treat blanks as significant. Because blanks are ignored in fixed source form, using the rules of free source form will not impact the requirements of fixed source form.

3. Use the exclamation mark (!) for a comment, but don't place it in position 6, which indicates continuation in fixed source form. Do not use the C or * forms for a comment.

4. To continue statements, use the ampersand in both position 73 of the line to be continued, and in position 6 of the continuation. Positions 74 to 80 must remain blank or have only a comment there. Positions 1 through 5 must be blank. The first ampersand continues the line after position 72 in free source form and is ignored in fixed source form. The second ampersand indicates continuation in fixed source form and in free source form indicates that the text for the continuation of the previous line begins after the ampersand.

3.4.1 Sample Program, Use with Either Source Form

A sample program that is acceptable for either source form is:

```
    123456789.....                                       73
    ---------------------------------------.....----
    |      PROGRAM LEFT_RIGHT
    |      REAL  X(5), Y(5)
    |!     Print arrays X and Y
    |      PRINT 100, X, Y
    |  100 FORMAT (F10.1, F10.2, F10.3, F10.4,          &
    |      &         F10.5)
    |         . . .
    |      END
```

3.5 The INCLUDE Line

Source text may be imported from another file and included within a program file during processing. An **INCLUDE line** consists of the keyword INCLUDE followed by a character literal constant. For example,

```
    INCLUDE  'MY_COMMON_BLOCKS'
```

The specified text is substituted for the INCLUDE line before compilation and is treated as if it were part of the original program source text. The location of the included text is specified by the value of the character constant in some processor-dependent manner. A frequent convention is that the character literal constant is the name of a file containing the text to be included. Use of the INCLUDE line provides a convenient way to include source text that is the same in several program units. For example, the specification of interface blocks or objects in common blocks may constitute a file that is referenced in the INCLUDE line.

The form for an INCLUDE line is:

```
    INCLUDE   character-literal-constant
```

Rules and restrictions:

1. The character literal constant used must not have a kind parameter that is a named constant.

2. The INCLUDE line is a directive to the compiler; it is not a Fortran statement.

3. The INCLUDE line is placed where the included text is to appear in the program.

4. The INCLUDE line must appear on one line with no other text except possibly a trailing comment. There must be no statement label.

5. INCLUDE lines may be nested. That is, a second INCLUDE line may appear within the text to be included. The permitted level of nesting is not specified and is processor dependent. However, the text inclusion must not be recursive at any level; for example, included text A must not include text B, which includes text A.

6. A file intended to be referenced in an INCLUDE line must not begin or end with an incomplete Fortran statement.

An example of a program unit with an INCLUDE line follows:

```
PROGRAM MATH
REAL, DIMENSION (10,5,79) :: X, ZT
!  Some arithmetic
INCLUDE 'FOURIER'
!  More arithmetic
   . . .
END
```

The Fortran source text in the file FOURIER in effect replaces the INCLUDE line. The INCLUDE line behaves like a compiler directive.

3.6 Low-Level Syntax

The basic lexical elements of the language consist of the classes *character* (R301), *name* (R304), *constant* (R305), *intrinsic-operator* (R310), *defined-operator* (R311), and *label* (R313), which are defined in Appendix B.2. These items are defined in terms of the classes *letter*, *digit*, *underscore*, and *special-character* which are defined in Section 3.1.1.

3.7 Summary

The Fortran and Processor Character Sets

The Fortran character set consists of the 26 uppercase letters of the English alphabetic, the 10 decimal digits, and 21 special characters. The processor character set consists of the Fortran character set plus, as an option, a set of control characters with no graphics plus, as an option, a set of additional characters with graphics. The characters of the default character type must include the Fortran character set and may include other characters.

The processor may support other character sets, one for each non-default character type. Each of these additional character sets is a subset of the processor character set and must contain a character designated as a blank character.

The characters of the processor character set may be used in character context, in comments, and in input/output records. (Recall that characters in a character literal constant or in a character string edit descriptor are in character context.) The processor may also represent and recognize lowercase letters. However, each lowercase letter is considered the same as its corresponding uppercase letter in all contexts except character context and input/output records.

Low-Level Syntax and Lexical Tokens

A Fortran statement is constructed from low-level syntax. The lexical tokens are the basic language elements. They are described by low-level syntax rules in terms of the characters of the Fortran character set. The lexical tokens consist of names, keywords, literal constants, labels, delimiters, operators, and various other basic symbols such as =, = >, :, ::, ;, and %.

Source Forms

Fortran has two source forms: fixed source form and free source form.

Fixed Source Form

Fixed source form is oriented towards a fixed-size record of 80 characters with positional restrictions. Labels must be in positions 1 through 5, the Fortran statements must be in positions 7 through 72, and positions 73 through 80 are unused. If needed, a character in position 6 indicates the line is continuing the previous line. Any line with the letter C or an asterisk in position 1 is a comment. An exclamation (!) in any position except 6 and not in character context indicates that the characters to the end of the line represent a comment. More than one statement may be written on one line with a semicolon separating the statements. Blanks are insignificant except in a character context; that is, they may be inserted anywhere within a statement. Of course, they may be used to make the Fortran source text readable.

Free Source Form

Free source form is oriented towards variable-length records with no position restrictions. Source records with up to 132 characters must be accepted by the processor. Blanks are significant and must not be used within tokens, particularly identifiers, keywords, literal constants, and multicharacter operators. More than one statement may be written on one line with a semicolon separating the statements. Comments begin with an exclamation (!) and may appear on a separate line or at the end of any line. Lines are continued by using an ampersand as the last non-blank character not in a comment on the line to be continued and, optionally, using an ampersand as the first character of the continued line. An ampersand may be used as the first nonblank character on the continuation line to indicate that the continuation line begins after the ampersand. If a character string is to be continued between lines, ampersands can be used on both the end of the line to be continued and at the beginning of the continued line so that no blanks are inserted between the end of the continued line and the beginning of the continuation line.

Source Form That Is Both Fixed and Free

Fortran statements can be written so that their form is acceptable for both fixed and free source form. Briefly, the form of such statements must be that labels appear in positions 1 through 5, statements in positions 7 through 72, blanks are significant, the exclamation mark (!) is used to begin a comment in any position except 6, and statements are continued by placing an ampersand in position 73 of the continued line and in position 6 of the continuation line.

Within a given program unit, the source forms must not be mixed; that is, one source form must be used throughout a program unit.

The INCLUDE Mechanism

An INCLUDE line specifies the location of text to be included in the source in place of the INCLUDE line. The location is specified by a character string which normally is the name of a file. The line before the INCLUDE line and the final line of the included text must not be continued. The first line of the included text and the line after the INCLUDE line must not be continuation lines. The included text may contain INCLUDE lines, provided that the included text does not recurse directly or indirectly.

F9○

4

Data Types

Fortran was designed to give scientists and engineers an easy way to solve problems using computers. Statements could be presented that looked like formulas or English sentences. For example:

```
X = B + A * C
```

might be performing typical numeric calculations.

```
CX = SQRT (CY)
```

might be performing a calculation in the complex domain.

```
I = I + 1
```

could be counting the number of times some calculation is performed.

```
IF (LIMIT_RESULTS .AND. X .GT. XMAX) X = XMAX
```

could specify that a certain action is to be taken based on a logical decision.

```
PRINT *, "CONVERGENCE REACHED"
```

could be used to communicate the results of a calculation to a scientist or engineer in a meaningful way.

Each of these statements performs a task that makes use of a different type of data.

Task	Type of data
Calculating typical numeric results	Real data
Calculating in the complex domain	Complex data
Counting	Integer data
Making decisions	Logical data
Explaining	Character data

These are the five commonly needed data types, and the Fortran language provides them. Anything provided by the language is said to be **intrinsic** to the language. Other types, not intrinsic to the language, may be specified by a programmer; this is a facility that is new in Fortran 90. The new types are built of (or derived from) the intrinsic types and thus are called **derived types**. The Fortran 90 data types are categorized in Figure 4-1.

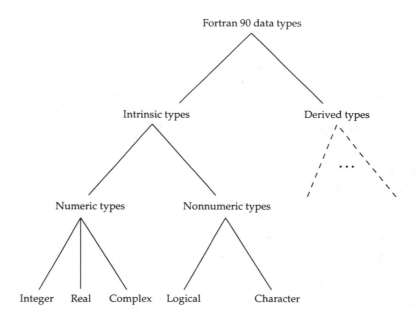

Figure 4-1 Fortran 90 data types

The type of the data determines the operations that can be performed on it. For example:

Type of data	Operations
Real, complex, integer	Addition, subtraction, multiplication, division, exponentiation, negation, comparison
Logical	Negation, conjunction, disjunction, and equivalence
Character	Concatenation, comparison
User defined	User defined

That is, the intrinsic types have the appropriate built-in (intrinsic) operations. On the other hand, operations performed on data of user-defined type must themselves be defined by the user.

This chapter discusses the data environment (the collection of necessary data objects) for a problem solution. It explains what is meant by a data type in Fortran 90. It then describes each of the intrinsic types. It ends with a discussion of derived types and the facilities provided by the language that allow users to define types and declare and manipulate objects of these types in ways that are analogous to the ways in which objects of the intrinsic types can be manipulated.

4.1 Building the Data Environment for a Problem Solution

When envisioning a computer solution to a problem, a scientist or engineer usually focuses initially on the operations that must be performed and the order in which they must be performed. It is a good idea, however, to consider the variables that will be needed before determining all the computational steps that are required. The variables that are chosen, together with their types and attributes, sometimes determine the course of computation, particularly when variables of user-defined type are involved.

Choosing the Type and Other Attributes of a Variable. There are a number of decisions to make about a variable in a program. Usually, if the variable is of an intrinsic type, the intended use of the variable will readily determine its type, so this is an easy decision. While type is the most important attribute of a variable, there are other attributes. Certainly it will be necessary to decide very early whether the variable is to be a single data object (a scalar) or an array. Fortran 90 provides many new facilities for manipulating arrays as objects, making it possible to specify computations as straightforward array operations that, in Fortran 77, require program loops. The fact that these facilities exist may have some influence on the choice.

Because Fortran 90 provides allocatable arrays and pointers, it is no longer necessary to decide at the outset how big an array must be. In fact, determining sizes may be postponed until the finished program is executed, when sizes may be read in as input or calculated. Setting aside space for an array may thus be deferred until the appropriate size needed for a particular calculation is known. Before these dynamic facilities were added to the language, it was necessary for array declarations to specify the maximum size that would ever be needed in any execution of the program. This frequently caused programs to consume a great deal more memory than was actually required for a particular calculation or, if the size estimate was insufficient, prevented the execution of a particular calculation, at least until the program was recompiled. Now, instead of making a decision about the size of an array, a programmer may decide to make the array a dynamic object.

Another decision that can be made about a variable is its accessibility. Control of accessibility is a new feature available in modules. If the variable is needed only within the module, then it can be kept private or hidden from other program units which prevents it from being corrupted inadvertently. This new feature can be used to make Fortran 90 programs safer and more reliable.

In addition to type, dimensionality, dynamic determination, and accessibility, there are other attributes that can be applied to data objects. The attributes that are permitted depend on where and how the object is to be used; for example, there are a number of attributes that can be applied only to subprogram arguments. All of the attributes of data objects are described in Chapter 5.

Choosing the Kind of a Variable of Intrinsic Type. Once the type of a variable is decided, it may be necessary for the programmer to consider which "kind" of the type to use. "Kind" is a technical term that is new with Fortran 90. Each of the intrinsic types may be specified with a **kind parameter** that selects a processor-dependent representation of objects of that type and kind. If no kind parameter is specified, the default kind is assumed. Fortran 77 does not have kind parameters but it does provide two kinds for the real type: REAL and DOUBLE PRECISION. It treats double precision real as a separate type, but it is really a different kind of real. Fortran 90, while remaining compatible with Fortran 77, treats it as a separate kind of real. That is, there are two ways to declare real variables with higher precision in Fortran 90: one is with a REAL statement specifying a nondefault kind, and the other is with a DOUBLE PRECISION statement. Fortran 77 provides only one kind for the other four types (integer, complex, logical, and character). Fortran 90 requires a processor to support at least two kinds for the real and complex types and at least one kind for the other three intrinsic types. An implementation may include any number of additional kinds of any intrinsic type.

The Fortran 90 addition of kind parameters for each of the intrinsic types addresses several problems that exist with Fortran 77.

1. **Real.** Programs with REAL and DOUBLE PRECISION declarations are not numerically portable across machine architectures with different word sizes. Each compiler vendor chooses a representation for the real type that is efficient on the host machine. For example, a representation that will fit into 32 bits is chosen on a 32-bit-word machine while a representation that fits into 64 bits is chosen for a 64-bit-word machine. If 64 bits is required for the numerical stability of the algorithm, DOUBLE PRECISION declarations must be used on the 32-bit machine. When the program is moved to a 64-bit machine, the DOUBLE PRECISION declarations must be changed to REAL declarations because a 128-bit representation is not needed and would degrade the performance of the program. With Fortran 90, a programmer can use kind parameters in REAL declarations to specify a required minimum precision. When the program is run on a 32-bit machine, it will use two words for each real object. When the same program (without any changes) is run on a 64-bit machine, one word will be used. Some processors may provide more than two representations for the real type. These could reflect different sizes or different methods of representation such as the standard IEEE method and the native method. Kind parameters give the Fortran 90 user access to and control over the use of these different machine representations.

2. **Complex.** The Fortran 77 standard does not require a double precision complex type. This is an inconsistency that is corrected by the kind parameters specified in the Fortran 90 standard. Fortran 90 does not need a DOUBLE PRECISION COMPLEX declarative because it uses a COMPLEX declarative with a nondefault kind parameter to specify double precision complex. As with the real type, more than two representations for complex may be available on a given processor, but at least two are required.

3. **Character.** The character data type usually has an underlying machine representation of a single byte (8 bits). This is adequate to represent 2^8 or 256 different characters, which is more than enough for alphabetic languages. However, ideographic languages, such as

Japanese and Chinese, have several thousand graphic symbols that require at least a two-byte representation (16 bits). Japanese and Chinese scientists and engineers need readable explanatory information in their printouts just as American and European scientists and engineers do. To accommodate this spectrum of users, Fortran 90 makes provision for (although it does not require implementation of) different kinds of character data. Because these additional kinds of character data are not required for standard-conforming Fortran 90 processors, many processors intended for English-speaking Fortran users may not support ideographic languages. Nevertheless, the character kind mechanism allows an implementation to support an alphabetic language or an ideographic language or both simultaneously.

4. **Logical.** Because the logical data type has only two values (true and false), it could be represented in a single bit. Fortran 77 requires that logical data and real data be represented in the same size machine unit. This is especially wasteful on 64-bit word machines. In Fortran 90, the default logical type retains this requirement, but Fortran 90 permits alternative representations of logical data; that is, a nondefault logical kind might be represented in a byte on byte-addressable machines and in a bit on machines that have large word sizes or small memories.

5. **Integer.** One motivation for alternative representations of integer data is the same, to a lesser degree, as that for logical data: memory conservation. An alternative representation might also provide an integer kind with a very large range. As with the logical data type, only one representation is required in a standard-conforming Fortran 90 processor, but more are permitted.

Choosing to Define a Type for a Variable. Sometimes it is easier to think about an essential element of a problem as several pieces of related data, not necessarily all of the same type. Arrays can be used to collect homogeneous data (all of the same type) into a single variable. In Fortran 90, a **structure** is a collection of nonhomogeneous data in a single variable. To declare a structure, it is first necessary to define a type that has components of the desired types. The structure is then declared as an object of this user-defined (or derived) type. An example of objects declared to be of user-defined type was given in Section 2.3.1. It is repeated here. First a type, named PATIENT, is defined; then two structures JOHN_JONES and SALLY_SMITH are declared.

```
TYPE PATIENT
    INTEGER          PULSE_RATE
    REAL             TEMPERATURE
    CHARACTER *300   PROGNOSIS
END TYPE PATIENT

TYPE (PATIENT)      JOHN_JONES, SALLY_SMITH
```

Type PATIENT has three components, each of a different intrinsic type (integer, real, and character). In practice, a type of this nature probably would have even more components, such as the patient's name and address, insurance company, room number in the hospital, etc. For purposes of illustration, three components are sufficient. JOHN_JONES and SALLY_SMITH are structures (or variables) of type PATIENT. A type definition indicates names, types, and attributes for its components; it does not declare any variables that have these components. Just as with the intrinsic types, a type declaration is needed to declare variables of this type. But because there is a type definition, any number of structures can be created that have the components specified in the type definition for PATIENT; subprogram arguments and function results can be of type PATIENT; there can be arrays of type PATIENT; and operations can be defined that manipulate objects of type PATIENT. Thus the derived-type definition can be used merely as a way to specify a pattern for a particular collection of related but nonhomogeneous data; but, because the pattern is specified by a type definition, a number of other capabilities are available.

4.2 What Is Meant by "Type" in Fortran?

Knowing exactly what is meant by type in Fortran becomes more important now that a user can define types in addition to the intrinsic types. A data type provides a means to categorize data and thus determine which operations may be applied to the data to get desired results. For each data type there is:

1. a name

2. a set of values

3. a set of operations

4. a form for constants of the type

4.2.1 Data Type Names

Each of the intrinsic types has a name supplied by the standard. The names of derived types must be supplied in type definitions. The name of the type is used to declare entities of the type unless the programmer chooses to let the processor determine the type of an entity implicitly by the first character of its name. Chapter 5 describes declarations and implicit typing.

4.2.2 Data Type Values

Each type has a set of valid values. The logical type has only two values: true and false. The integer type has a processor-dependent set of integral numeric values that may be positive, negative, or zero. For complex or derived types, the set of valid values is the set of all combinations of the values of the individual components.

The kind of an intrinsic type determines the set of valid values for that type and kind. For example, if there are two integer data types, the default type and a "short" integer type, the short integer type will have a set of values that is (probably) a subset of the default integer values. There must be two kinds of the real data type to correspond to real and double precision in Fortran 77. In most implementations, the higher-precision real kind permits a superset of the values permitted for the lesser-precision real kind. The kind of a type is referred to as a "kind parameter" or "kind type parameter" of the type. The character data type has a length parameter as well as a kind parameter. The length parameter specifies the number of characters in an object, and this determines the valid values for a particular character object. Derived types do not have parameters, even though their components may.

4.2.3 Data Type Operations

For each of the intrinsic data types, a set of operations with corresponding operators is provided by the language. These are described in Chapter 7.

A user may specify new operators and define operations for the new operators. The form of a new operator is an alphabetic name of the user's choice delimited by periods. These new operators are analogous to intrinsic operators such as .GT., .AND., and .NEQV. For example, a user might specify and define the operations .PLUS., .REMAINDER., and .REVERSE. In defining the operation, the types of allowable operands must be specified. Such new operations may apply to objects of intrinsic type and in these cases extend the set of operations for the type. Perhaps more often a user would define operations for objects of derived type. It is not possible to redefine an intrinsic operation, but it is possible to define meanings for intrinsic operator symbols when at least one operand is not of an intrinsic type or for intrinsic operands for which the intrinsic operation does not apply. For example, consider the expression A + B. If both A and B are of numeric type, the operation is intrinsically defined. However, if either A or B is of derived type or nonnumeric type, then the plus operation between A and B is not intrinsically defined, and the user may provide a meaning for the operation. New operations are defined by functions with the OPERATOR interface. These are described in Chapter 12.

Assignment is defined intrinsically for each intrinsic and derived type. Structure assignment is component-by-component intrinsic or pointer assignment, though this may be replaced by a defined assignment. No other intrinsically defined assignment, including array assignment, can be redefined. Beyond this, any assignment between objects of different type may be defined with the ASSIGNMENT interface as described in Chapter 12.

4.2.4 Forms for Constants

The language specifies the syntactic forms for literal constants of each of the intrinsic types. Syntactic mechanisms (called derived-type constructors) specify derived-type values and named constants. The form indicates both the type and a particular member of the set of valid values for the type (see Table 4-1). Array constructors are used to specify arrays of any type.

Table 4-1 The form of a constant indicates both a type and a valid value of the type

Syntax	Type	Value
1	integer	1
103.1 or 1.031E2	real	103.1
(1.0, 1.0)	complex	$1 + i$
.TRUE.	logical	true
"Hello"	character	Hello
PATIENT (70, 99.7, "Recovering")	patient	70 / 99.7 / Recovering

If a constant is not of default kind, some indication of its kind must be included in its syntactic form. This form is the default literal constant separated from the kind value by an underscore. Kind specifications follow integer, real, and logical values and precede character values. Kinds are known to the processor as integer values, but if a program is to be portable, the actual numbers should not be used because the kind values are processor dependent. Instead, a kind value should be assigned to a named constant, and this name should always be used. For example,

real	1.31415926535897932384626433383_QUAD
complex	(1.75963_HIGH, -2.0)
integer	7_SHORT
logical	.FALSE._BYTE
character	SPANISH_"Olé, Señor"

where QUAD, HIGH, SHORT, BYTE, and SPANISH are named constants for processor dependent kind values. The kind of a complex constant is determined by the kind of its parts (see 4.3.3.4).

4.3 Intrinsic Data Types

The Fortran 77 data types are based on a storage model in which a real, integer, and logical object each are represented in a numeric storage unit, and a complex and double precision object each are represented in two numeric storage units. A character in Fortran 77 is represented in a character storage unit, which is different from a numeric storage unit. Fortran 90, while remaining compatible with Fortran 77, extends this underlying model. The default kinds for Fortran 90 intrinsic types conform to the Fortran 77 model. That is, the storage units for default real kind, default integer kind, and default logical kind must all be the same. Default complex (which is really two default reals) requires two of these storage units, and double precision real requires two of these storage units. Because Fortran 90 requires at least two representations of the real type, one of these must require two storage units to conform with the specifications for the Fortran 77 double precision type.

Beyond these requirements, Fortran 90 standard conforming processors may provide additional representations for real, complex, integer, logical, and character data that bear no relationship to an underlying storage model. Variables of these other kinds may be declared. Literal constants of these other kinds must be specified with an explicit indication of their kind.

Fortran 77 depends on COMMON statements to permit objects to be accessible from more than one subprogram. COMMON statements depend on an underlying storage model. Although Fortran 90 allows nondefault kinds of objects in COMMON statements, restrictions must be placed on their appearance. Global access to any kind of object without such restrictions is provided in Fortran 90 with modules.

Each of the intrinsic types is described below. The descriptions include a simple statement form to show how objects of these types may be declared. These simple forms do not give the complete story. If they are used to construct statements, the statements will be correct, but other variations are permitted. A complete form may be found in Section 5.1. The kind parameter that appears in the forms is limited to a scalar integer initialization expression, which is described in Section 7.2.9.2.

4.3.1 Integer Type

4.3.1.1 Name. The name of the integer type is INTEGER. A form that shows how integer objects may be declared is:

```
INTEGER  [ ( [ KIND = ] kind-parameter ) ]  &
    [ , attribute-list  :: ]  entity-list
```

Examples are:

```
INTEGER X
INTEGER COUNT, K, TEMPORARY_COUNT
INTEGER (SHORT) PARTS
INTEGER, DIMENSION (0:9) :: SELECTORS, IX
```

4.3.1.2 Values. The integer data type has values that represent a subset of the mathematical integers. The set of values varies from one processor to another. The intrinsic inquiry function RANGE provides the decimal exponent range for integers of the kind of its argument. Only one kind of integer is required by the standard, but a processor may provide more. The intrinsic function KIND can be used to determine the kind parameter of its integer argument.

There is an intrinsic function, SELECTED_INT_KIND, that returns the integer kind parameter required to represent as many decimal digits as are specified by the function argument. If there is no such integer type available from the processor, –1 is returned. For example:

```
INTEGER (SELECTED_INT_KIND (5)) I, J
```

declares I and J to be integer objects with a representation method that permits at least five decimal digits; that is, it includes all integers between -10^5 and 10^5.

4.3.1.3 Operators. There are both binary and unary intrinsic operators for the integer type. Binary operators have two operands and unary operators have only one. The binary arithmetic operations for the integer type are: +, –, *, /, and **. The unary arithmetic operations are + and –. The relational operations (all binary) are: .LT., <, .LE., < =, .EQ., = =, .NE., /=, .GE., > =, .GT., and >. The result of an intrinsic arithmetic operation on integer operands is an integer entity; the result of an intrinsic relational operation is a logical entity of default logical kind.

4.3.1.4 Form for Constant Values. An integer constant is a string of decimal digits, optionally preceded by a sign and optionally followed by an underscore and a kind parameter.

The form of a signed integer literal constant (R403) is:

[sign] digit-string [_ kind-parameter]

where a sign is either + or – and the kind parameter is one of:

digit-string
scalar-integer-constant-name

Examples are:

42
999999999999999999999999_LONG
+64
10000000
–258_SHORT

where LONG and SHORT are named constants with values that are valid integer kind parameters for the processor.

Integer constants are interpreted as decimal values. However, in a DATA statement, it is possible to initialize an object with a value that is presented as if it had a nondecimal base. The allowed forms are unsigned binary, octal, and hexadecimal constants.

A binary constant (R408) has one of the forms:

B ' digit [digit] ... '
B " digit [digit] ... "

where a digit is restricted to 0 or 1.

An octal constant (R409) has one of the forms:

O ' digit [digit] ... '
O " digit [digit] ... "

where a digit is restricted to the values 0 through 7.

A hexadecimal constant (R410) has one of the forms:

Z ' digit [digit] ... '
Z " digit [digit] ... "

where a digit is 0 through 9 or one of the letters A through F (representing the decimal values 10 through 15). If a processor supports lowercase letters, the hexadecimal digits A through F may be represented by their lowercase equivalents, a through f.

In these constants, the binary, octal, and hexadecimal digits are interpreted according to their respective number systems. Examples (all of which have a value equal to the decimal value 10 on a machine with a traditional representation) are:

B"1010"
O'12'
Z"A"

The standard does not specify what these bit patterns actually represent.

4.3.2 Real Type

4.3.2.1 Name. The name of the real data type is REAL. The name DOUBLE PRECISION is used for another kind of the real type. Forms that show how objects of real type may be declared are:

REAL [([KIND =] kind-parameter)] &
     [, attribute-list ::] entity-list
DOUBLE PRECISION [, attribute-list ::] entity-list

Examples are:

REAL X, Y
REAL (KIND = HIGH), SAVE :: XY(10, 10)
REAL, POINTER :: A, B, C
DOUBLE PRECISION DD, DXY, D

4.3.2.2 Values. The values of the real data type approximate the mathematical real numbers. The set of values varies from processor to processor. A processor must provide at least two approximation methods for the real type. Each method has its kind type parameter. One of the required approximation methods is for the default real type and the other is for the double precision real type, which must have more precision than the default real type.

Intrinsic functions are available to inquire about the representation methods provided on a processor. The intrinsic function KIND can be used to determine the kind parameter of its real argument. The intrinsic functions PRECISION and RANGE return the decimal precision and exponent range of the approximation method used for the kind of the argument. The intrinsic function SELECTED_REAL_KIND returns the kind value required to represent as many digits of precision as specified by the first argument and the decimal range specified by the optional second argument. For example:

```
REAL (SELECTED_REAL_KIND (5)) X
```

declares X to have at least five decimal digits of precision and no specified minimum range.

```
REAL (SELECTED_REAL_KIND (8, 70)) Y
```

declares Y to have at least eight decimal digits of precision and a range that includes values between 10^{-70} and 10^{+70} in magnitude.

4.3.2.3 Operators. The intrinsic binary arithmetic operators for the real type are: +, –, *, /, and **. The intrinsic unary arithmetic operators are: + and –. The relational operators are: .LT., <, .LE., < =, .EQ., = =, .NE., /=, .GE., > =, .GT., and >. The result of an intrinsic arithmetic operation on real operands is a real entity. If one of the operands of an arithmetic operation is an integer entity, the result is still a real entity. The result of an intrinsic relational operation is a logical entity of default logical kind.

4.3.2.4 Forms for Constants. A real constant is distinguished from an integer constant by containing either a decimal point, an exponent, or both. Forms for a signed real literal constant (R412) are:

```
[ sign ] digit-string &
        exponent-letter exponent [ _ kind-parameter ]
[ sign ] whole-part . [ fraction-part ] &
        [ exponent-letter exponent ] [ _ kind-parameter ]
[ sign ] . fraction-part &
        [ exponent-letter exponent ] [ _ kind-parameter ]
```

where the exponent letter is E or D, the whole part and fraction part are digit strings (R401), and an exponent (R416) is a signed digit string. If both a kind parameter and an exponent letter are present, the exponent letter must be E. If a kind parameter is present, the real constant is of that kind; if a D exponent letter is present, the constant is of type double precision real; otherwise the constant is of type default real. A real constant may have more decimal digits than will be used to approximate the real number. Examples of signed real literal constants are:

```
-14.78
+1.6E3
2.1
-16.E4_HIGH
0.45_LOW
.123
3E4
2.718281828459045D0
```

The parameters HIGH and LOW must have been defined and their values must be kind parameters for the real data type permitted by the processor. If a real literal constant has a kind parameter, it takes precedence over an exponent letter, for example:

```
1.6E4_HIGH
```

will be represented by the method specified for HIGH, even though

```
1.6E4
```

would be represented by a different method.

4.3.3 Complex Type

4.3.3.1 Name. The name of the complex type is COMPLEX. A form for declaring objects of this type is:

```
COMPLEX [ ( [ KIND = ] kind-parameter ) ]  &
         [ , attribute-list :: ] entity-list
```

Examples are:

```
COMPLEX CC, DD
COMPLEX (KIND = QUAD), POINTER :: CTEMP (:)
```

4.3.3.2 Values. The complex data type has values that approximate the mathematical complex numbers. A complex value is a pair of real values; the first is called the **real part** and the second is called the **imaginary part**. Each approximation method used to represent data entities of type real is available for entities of type complex with the same kind parameter values. Therefore, there are at least two approximation methods for complex, one of which corresponds to default real and one of which corresponds to double precision real. When a complex entity is declared with a kind specification, this kind is used for both parts of the complex entity. There is no special double precision complex declaration, as such. If no kind parameter is specified, the entity is of type default complex which corresponds to default real. The SELECTED_REAL_KIND intrinsic function may be used in a declaration of a complex object. For example:

```
COMPLEX (SELECTED_REAL_KIND (8, 70)) CX
```

CX must be represented by an approximation method with at least 8 decimal digits of precision and at least a decimal exponent range between 10^{-70} and 10^{+70} in magnitude for the real and imaginary parts.

4.3.3.3 Operators. The intrinsic binary arithmetic operators for the complex type are: +, −, *, /, and **. The intrinsic unary arithmetic operators are: + and −. The intrinsic relational operators are: .EQ., ==, .NE., and /=. The arithmetic operators specify complex arithmetic; the relationals compare operands to produce default logical results. The result of an intrinsic arithmetic operation on complex operands is a complex entity. If one of the operands is an integer or real entity, the result is still a complex entity.

4.3.3.4 Form for Constants. A complex literal constant is written as two literal constants that are real or integer, separated by a comma, and enclosed in parentheses. The form for a complex literal constant (R417) is:

(real-part , imaginary-part)

where the real part and imaginary part may be either a signed integer literal constant (R403) or a signed real literal constant (R412).

Examples are:

```
(3.0, -3.0)
(6, -7.6E9)
(3.0_HIGH, 1.6E9_LOW)
```

A real kind parameter may be specified for either one of the two real values. If a different real kind parameter is given for each of the two real values, the complex value will have the kind parameter that specifies the greater precision, unless the kind parameters specify the same precision. In this case one part is converted to the kind of the other part, and the choice of which part is converted is processor dependent. If both parts are integer, each part is converted to default real. If one part is of integer type and the other is of real type, the integer value is converted to the kind and type of the real value.

4.3.4 Logical Type

4.3.4.1 Name. The name of the logical type is LOGICAL. A form for declaring objects to be of this type is:

```
LOGICAL [ ( [ KIND = ] kind-parameter ) ]  &
        [ , attribute-list :: ] entity-list
```

Examples are:

```
LOGICAL IR, XT
LOGICAL (KIND = BIT), SAVE :: XMASK (3000)
```

4.3.4.2 Values. The logical data type has two values that represent true and false. A processor is required to provide one logical kind, but may provide other kinds to allow the packing of logical values; for example, one value per bit or one per byte. (An object of default logical type must occupy the same unit of storage as an object of default real type.) The KIND intrinsic function may be used to determine the kind number of its argument. There is no SELECTED_LOGICAL_KIND intrinsic function analogous to the functions SELECTED_INT_KIND and SELECTED_REAL_KIND.

4.3.4.3 Operators. The intrinsic binary operators for the logical type are: conjunction (.AND.), inclusive disjunction (.OR.), logical equivalence (.EQV.), and logical nonequivalence (or exclusive disjunction) (.NEQV.). The intrinsic unary operation is negation (.NOT.).

4.3.4.4 Form for Constants. There are only two logical literal constants. Optionally, they may be followed by an underscore and a kind parameter. The forms for logical literal constants (R421) are:

```
.TRUE. [ _ kind-parameter ]
.FALSE. [ _ kind-parameter ]
```

The kind parameter specified must be available on the processor. If a kind is not specified, the type of the constant is default logical.

Examples are:

```
.FALSE.
.TRUE._BIT
```

4.3.5 Character Type

4.3.5.1 Name. The name of the character type is CHARACTER. Declarations for objects of this type may take several different forms. One of these is:

```
CHARACTER [ ( [ LEN = ] length-parameter   &
         [ , [ KIND = ] kind-parameter ] ) ]   &
         [ , attribute-list :: ] entity-list
```

The length parameter length-parameter may be an asterisk or a specification expression, which is described in Section 7.2.9.3. The various forms of the CHARACTER statement are described in Section 5.1.6, but the following examples use the form given above:

```
CHARACTER (80) LINE
CHARACTER (*, HANZI) GREETING
CHARACTER (LEN = 30, KIND = CYRILLIC), DIMENSION (10) :: C1
```

4.3.5.2 Values. The character data type has a set of values composed of character strings. A character string is a sequence of characters, numbered from left to right 1, 2, ..., n, where n is the length of (number of characters in) the string. Both length and kind are type parameters for the character type. If no length parameter is specified, the length is 1. A character string may have length 0. The maximum length permitted for character strings is processor-dependent.

A standard-conforming processor must support one character kind and may support more. Each kind must contain a character designated as a blank that can be used as a padding character in character operations and input/output data transfer. The characters in all processor-supported character sets are considered to be representable characters. The default character kind must include the characters that make up the Fortran character set as described in Section 3.1.1.

A partial collating sequence is required so that operations that compare character objects containing only characters from the Fortran character set will be portable across different processors. The blank must precede both the alphabetic and numeric characters in the collating sequence. The alphabetic characters, whether uppercase or lowercase (if lowercase is supported by the processor), must be in the normal alphabetic sequence. The numeric characters must be in the normal numeric sequence, 0, 1, ..., 9. Numeric characters and alphabetic characters must not be interspersed. Other than blank, there are no constraints on the position of the special characters and the underscore, nor is there any specified relationship between the uppercase and lowercase alphabetic letters. Thus, the standard does not require that a processor provide the ASCII encoding, but does require intrinsic functions (ACHAR and IACHAR) that convert between the processor's encoding and the ASCII encoding. Intrinsic functions (LGT, LGE, LLE, and LLT) provide comparisons between strings based on the ASCII collating sequence.

4.3.5.3 Operators. The binary operation concatenation (//) is the only intrinsic operation on character entities that has a character entity as a result. A number of intrinsic functions are provided that perform character operations. These are described in Chapter 13 and Appendix A. The intrinsic relational operators on objects of type character are .LT., <, .LE., <=, .EQ., ==, .NE., /=, .GE., >=, .GT., and >. The relational operations may be used to compare character entities, but, because of possible processor-dependent collating sequences, care must be taken if the results are intended to be portable.

4.3.5.4 Form for Constants. A character literal constant is written as a sequence of characters, enclosed either by apostrophes or quotation marks. Forms for character literal constants (R420) are:

    [kind-parameter _] ' [representable-character] ... '
    [kind-parameter _] " [representable-character] ... "

where a representable character is any character in that character set kind that the processor can represent. The use of control characters in character literal constants may be restricted by the processor. Note that, unlike the other intrinsic types, the kind parameter for the character literal constant precedes the constant. The kind parameter specified must be available on the processor. If a kind is not specified, the type of the constant is default character. If the string delimiter character (either an apostrophe or quotation mark) is required as part of the constant, two consecutive such characters with no intervening blanks serve to represent a single such character in the string.

Examples are:

```
GREEK_"πβφ"
GERMAN_"gemütlichkeit"
"DON'T"
'DON''T'
```

The last two both have the value DON'T. A zero-length character constant may be written as " " or ''.

4.4 Derived Types

Unlike the intrinsic types that are defined by the language, derived types must be defined by the programmer. It is intended that these types have the same utility as the intrinsic types. That is, for example, variables of these types may be declared, passed as procedure arguments, and returned as function results.

A derived-type definition specifies a name for the type; this name is used to declare objects of the type. A derived-type definition also specifies components of the type, of which there must be at least one. A component may be of intrinsic or derived type; if it is of derived type, it can be resolved into components, called the **ultimate components**. These ultimate components are of intrinsic type and may be pointers. If the complex type were not provided by the language and had to be derived, it could be defined as a derived type with two real components.

A type definition may contain the keywords PUBLIC and PRIVATE if the type definition appears in a module. In general, entities specified in a module may be kept private to the module and will not be available outside the module. This is true of data objects, module subprograms, and type definitions. By default, entities specified in a module are available to any program unit that accesses the module. That is, they have PUBLIC accessibility by default. This default can be changed by inserting a PRIVATE statement ahead of the specifications and definitions in the module. Individual entities can be specified to have either the PUBLIC or PRIVATE attribute regardless of the default. For a type definition, one way this may be accomplished is by an optional PUBLIC or PRIVATE specifier in the TYPE statement of the type definition. Actually, the keyword PRIVATE may be used in two ways in type definitions in a module. One makes the entire type private to the module; the other allows the type name to be known outside the module, but not the names or attributes of its components. A separate PRIVATE statement that mentions the type name or a PRIVATE specifier in the TYPE statement of the type definition provides the first of these. An optional PRIVATE statement inside the type definition provides the second. There are examples of a private type and a public type with private components in Section 4.4.1

A type definition may contain a SEQUENCE statement. In general, no storage sequence is implied by the order of components in a type definition. However, if a SEQUENCE statement appears inside the type definition, the type is considered to be a **sequence type**. In this case, the order of the components specifies a storage sequence for objects of the type so that such objects may appear in COMMON and EQUIVALENCE statements. There is an example of a sequence type in Section 4.4.1.

A derived type has a set of values that is every combination of the permitted values for the components of the type. The language provides a syntax for constants of complex type; it provides a somewhat similar mechanism, called a **structure constructor**, to specify values of derived types. These constructors can be used in PARAMETER statements and type declaration statements to define derived-type named constants; they can be used in DATA statements to specify initial values; and they can be used as structure-valued operands in expressions.

Special functions and subroutines are used to define operations on entities of derived type. Thus, the four properties of the intrinsic types (possession of a name, a set of values, a set of operations, and a syntactic mechanism to specify constants) are also provided for derived types.

4.4.1 Derived-Type Definition

A type definition gives a new type a name and specifies the types and attributes of its components. A type definition begins with a derived-type statement of the general form:

    TYPE type-name

ends with an END TYPE statement, and has component declarations in between. An example is the definition of type PATIENT given earlier in this chapter:

```
TYPE PATIENT
    INTEGER         PULSE_RATE
    REAL            TEMPERATURE
    CHARACTER *300  PROGNOSIS
END TYPE PATIENT
```

More precisely, the form of a type definition (R422) is:

    TYPE [[, access-spec] ::] type-name
       [private-sequence-statement] ...
       component-definition-statement
       [component-definition-statement] ...
    END TYPE [type-name]

where an access specifier is either PRIVATE or PUBLIC and a private-sequence statement is PRIVATE or SEQUENCE. A type containing a SEQUENCE statement is called a **sequence type**.

A component definition statement (R426) contains a type specification (R502). A component definition has the form:

type-spec [[, component-attribute-list] ::] &
    component-declaration-list

where component attributes (R427) are limited to POINTER and DIMEN-SION. A component array (R428) must be a deferred-shape array if the POINTER attribute is present; otherwise, it must be an explicit-shape array. A component declaration (R429) has the form:

component-name [(component-array-spec)] &
    [* character-length]

Rules and restrictions:

1. The name of the derived type must not be the same as any locally accessible name; it has the scope of local names declared in the scoping unit, which means that it may be accessible by use or host association in other scoping units. A component name has the scope of the type definition only; another type definition in the same scoping unit may specify the same component name (14.2.1.2, item 5).

2. If the END TYPE statement is followed by a name, it must be the name specified in the derived-type statement.

3. A type may be defined at most once within a scoping unit.

4. A PRIVATE statement must not appear more than once in a given type definition.

5. A SEQUENCE statement must not appear more than once in a given type definition

6. The keywords PUBLIC and PRIVATE may appear only if the definition is in the specification part of a module.

7. If SEQUENCE is present, all derived types specified as components must also be sequence types.

8. There must be at least one component definition statement in a type definition.

9. No component attribute may appear more than once in a given component definition statement.

10. A component may be declared to have the same type as the type being defined only if it has the POINTER attribute.

11. An array component without the POINTER attribute must be specified with an explicit-shape specification where the bounds are integer constant expressions.

12. If a component is of type character with a specified length, the length must be an integer constant specification expression.

An example of a derived-type definition with four components (three integer and one character) is:

```
TYPE COLOR
    INTEGER HUE, SHADE, INTENSITY
    CHARACTER (LEN = 30) NAME
END TYPE COLOR
```

A form for declaring variables of derived type is:

TYPE (type-name) [, attribute-list ::] entity-list

For example, variables of type COLOR may be declared as follows:

```
TYPE (COLOR) MY_FAVORITE
TYPE (COLOR) RAINBOW (7)
TYPE (COLOR), DIMENSION (100) :: CURRENT_SELECTIONS
```

The object MY_FAVORITE is a structure. The objects RAINBOW and CURRENT_SELECTIONS are arrays of structures.

Note that the initial statement of a type definition and the statement used to declare objects of derived type both begin with the keyword TYPE. The initial statement of a type definition is called a **derived-type statement**, and the statement used to declare objects of derived type is called a **TYPE statement**. The type name in a derived-type statement is not enclosed in parentheses, whereas the type name in a TYPE statement is.

A component of a structure is referenced using a percent sign, as in the following template:

parent-structure % component-name

For example:

```
MY_FAVORITE % HUE
RAINBOW (3) % NAME
```

Following are several examples of definitions of derived types. Each example illustrates a different aspect of a type definition:

1. a derived type with a component of a different derived type

2. a derived type with a pointer component

3. a derived type with a pointer component of the type being defined

4. a private type definition

5. a public type definition with private components

There is an example of a sequence type on page 110.

Example 1. A derived type may have a component that is of a different derived type. The type WEATHER in the following example has a component of type TEMPERATURES.

```
TYPE TEMPERATURES
    INTEGER HIGH, LOW
END TYPE TEMPERATURES

TYPE WEATHER
    CHARACTER (LEN = 32) CITY
    TYPE (TEMPERATURES) RANGE (1950:2050)
END TYPE WEATHER

TYPE (WEATHER) WORLDWIDE (200)
```

WORLDWIDE is an array of type WEATHER. Components of an element of the array are referenced as shown below.

```
WORLDWIDE (I) % CITY = "Nome"
WORLDWIDE (I) % RANGE (1990) % LOW = -83
```

Example 2. A derived type may have a component that is a pointer.

```
TYPE ABSTRACT
    CHARACTER (LEN = 50) TITLE
    INTEGER NO_OF_PAGES
    CHARACTER, POINTER :: TEXT(:)
END TYPE ABSTRACT
```

Any object of type ABSTRACT will have three components: TITLE, NO_OF_PAGES, and TEXT. TEXT is a pointer to an array of character strings, each of which is of length one. The size of the array is determined during program execution. The space for the target of TEXT may be allocated (6.5.1), or TEXT may be pointer-assigned (7.5.3) to existing space.

Example 3. A derived type may have a pointer component that is of the type being defined. This is useful in creating linked lists and trees. For example:

```
TYPE LINK
   REAL VALUE
   TYPE (LINK), POINTER :: PREVIOUS
   TYPE (LINK), POINTER :: NEXT
END TYPE LINK
```

Example 4. A type definition in a module may be kept private to the module.

```
TYPE, PRIVATE :: FILE
   INTEGER DRAWER_NO
   CHARACTER (LEN = 20) FOLDER_NAME
   CHARACTER (LEN = 5) ACCESS_LEVEL
END TYPE FILE
```

When a module containing this type definition is accessed by another scoping unit, the type FILE is not available.

Example 5. A type definition may be public while its components are kept private.

```
MODULE COORDINATES
   TYPE POINT
      PRIVATE
      REAL X, Y
   END TYPE POINT
      ...
END MODULE COORDINATES
```

In a program unit that uses module COORDINATES, variables of type POINT may be declared; values of type POINT may be passed as arguments; and if the program unit is a function, a value of type POINT may be returned as the result. However, the internal structure of the type (its components) is not available. If, at some future time, the type POINT is changed to (for example):

```
TYPE POINT
   PRIVATE
   REAL RHO, THETA
END TYPE POINT
```

no other program unit that uses COORDINATES will have to be changed.

If a subprogram argument is of derived type, the corresponding actual argument must be of the same type. There are two ways in which objects in different scoping units may be declared to be of the same type. Two data entities have the same type if they are declared with reference to the same type definition. The definition may appear in a module that is accessed or, in the case of an internal or module procedure, in the host scoping unit. For example:

```
MODULE SHOP
   TYPE COMPONENT
      CHARACTER (LEN = 20) NAME
      INTEGER CATALOG_NO
      REAL WEIGHT
   END TYPE COMPONENT
   TYPE (COMPONENT) PARTS(100)
CONTAINS
   SUBROUTINE GET_PART (PART, NAME)
      TYPE (COMPONENT) PART
      CHARACTER (LEN = *) NAME
      DO I = 1, 100
         IF (NAME .EQ. PARTS(I) % NAME) THEN
            PART = PARTS(I)
            RETURN
         END IF
      END DO
      PRINT *, "Part not available"
      PART % NAME = "none"
      PART % CATALOG_NO = 0
      PART % WEIGHT = 0.0
   END SUBROUTINE GET_PART
      . . .
END MODULE SHOP
```

```
PROGRAM BUILD_MACHINE
   USE SHOP
   TYPE (COMPONENT) MOTOR(20)
   TOTAL_WEIGHT = 0.0
   CALL GET_PART (MOTOR(1), "VALVE")
   TOTAL_WEIGHT = TOTAL_WEIGHT + MOTOR(1) % WEIGHT
   . . .
END PROGRAM BUILD_MACHINE
```

Module procedure GET_PART has access to the type COMPONENT because the type definition appears in its host. Program BUILD_MACHINE has access to the type because it uses module SHOP. This allows a variable of the type, such as MOTOR(1), to be passed as an actual argument.

   The other way to declare data entities in different scoping units to be of the same type is provided for programmers who, for some reason, choose not to use a module. Instead of a single type definition in the module, a sequence type may be defined in each of the scoping units that need access to the type. Each of the type definitions must specify the same name; the SEQUENCE property; have no PRIVATE components; and have components that agree in order, name, and attributes. If this is the case, data entities declared in any of these scoping units to be of the named type are considered to be of the same type. The example for program BUILD_MACHINE above is restated to illustrate the differences between the two ways:

```
PROGRAM BUILD_MACHINE
   TYPE COMPONENT
      SEQUENCE
      CHARACTER (LEN = 20) NAME
      INTEGER CATALOG_NO
      REAL WEIGHT
   END TYPE COMPONENT
   TYPE (COMPONENT) PARTS, MOTOR(20)
   COMMON /WAREHOUSE/ PARTS(100)
   TOTAL_WEIGHT = 0.0
   CALL GET_PART (MOTOR(1), "VALVE")
   TOTAL_WEIGHT = TOTAL_WEIGHT + MOTOR(1) % WEIGHT
   . . .
END PROGRAM BUILD_MACHINE
```

```
SUBROUTINE GET_PART (PART, NAME)
   TYPE COMPONENT
      SEQUENCE
      CHARACTER (LEN = 20) NAME
      INTEGER CATALOG_NO
      REAL WEIGHT
   END TYPE COMPONENT
   TYPE (COMPONENT) PART, PARTS
   CHARACTER (LEN = *) NAME
   COMMON /WAREHOUSE/ PARTS(100)
   DO I = 1, 100
      IF (NAME .EQ. PARTS(I) % NAME) THEN
         PART = PARTS(I)
         RETURN
      END IF
   END DO
   PART % NAME = "none"
   PART % CATALOG_NO = 0
   PART % WEIGHT = 0.0
   PRINT *, "Part not available"
END SUBROUTINE GET_PART
   . . .
```

In this example, type COMPONENT in program BUILD_MACHINE and type COMPONENT in subroutine GET_PART are the same because they are sequence types with the same name; have no private components; and have components that agree in order, name, and attributes. This allows variables of the type to appear in COMMON and be passed as arguments. Note that this example is less concise, particularly if there are more procedures that need access to the type definition, and therefore may be more error prone than the previous example.

   Type COMPONENT is a sequence type because its definition contains a SEQUENCE statement. If all of the ultimate components of a sequence type are of type default integer, default real, double precision real, default complex, or default logical, and are not pointers, the type is a **numeric sequence type**. An object of numeric sequence type may appear in a common block that contains only objects that occupy numeric storage units and be equivalenced to default numeric objects without the restrictions that otherwise apply to objects of user-defined type in COMMON and EQUIVALENCE statements. If all of the ultimate components of a sequence type are of type default character and are not pointers, the type is a **character sequence type.** An object of character sequence type may appear in a common block that contains only objects that occupy character storage units and be equivalenced to default character objects without the restrictions that otherwise apply to objects of user-defined type in COMMON and EQUIVALENCE statements.

4.4.2 Derived-Type Values

The set of values of a derived type consists of all combinations of the possibilities for component values that are consistent with the components specified in the type definition.

4.4.3 Derived-Type Operations

Any operation on derived-type entities must be defined explicitly by a function with an OPERATOR interface. Assignment, other than the intrinsic assignment provided for entities of the same derived type, must be defined by a subroutine with an ASSIGNMENT interface. These are described in Chapter 12.

A simple example is provided. Suppose it is desirable to determine the number of words and lines in a section of text. The information is available for each paragraph. A type named PARAGRAPH is defined as follows:

```
TYPE PARAGRAPH
    INTEGER NO_OF_WORDS, NO_OF_LINES
    CHARACTER (LEN = 30) SUBJECT
END TYPE PARAGRAPH
```

It is now desirable to define an operator for adding the paragraphs. An OPERATOR interface is required for the function that defines the addition operation for objects of type PARAGRAPH.

```
INTERFACE OPERATOR (+)
    MODULE PROCEDURE ADDP
END INTERFACE
```

This definition of addition for objects of type PARAGRAPH adds the words and lines, but does nothing with the component SUBJECT because that would have no useful meaning.

```
TYPE (PARAGRAPH) FUNCTION ADDP (P1, P2)
   TYPE (PARAGRAPH) P1, P2
   ADDP % NO_OF_WORDS = P1 % NO_OF_WORDS + P2 % NO_OF_WORDS
   ADDP % NO_OF_LINES = P1 % NO_OF_LINES + P2 % NO_OF_LINES
END FUNCTION ADDP
```

If the following variables were declared:

```
TYPE (PARAGRAPH) BIRDS, BEES
```

the expression BIRDS + BEES would be defined and could be evaluated in the module subprograms as well as any program unit accessing the module.

4.4.4 Syntax for Specifying Derived-Type Constant Expressions

When a derived type is defined, a structure constructor for that type is defined automatically. The structure constructor is used to specify values of the type. It specifies a sequence of values, one for each of the components of the type. A structure constructor whose values are all constant expressions is a derived-type constant expression. A named constant of user-defined type may be given such a value. Structure constructors are described in Section 4.5.

A component of a derived type may be an array (6.4). In this case a mechanism called an array constructor is used to specify that component of a scalar value of the type. An array constructor whose values are all constant expressions is an array-valued constant expression. Such an expression may be specified for an array component of a named constant. Array constructors have utility beyond specifying the value of a component of a structure, however. They may be used to specify array values for objects of any type including objects of derived type. Array constructors are described in Section 4.6.

4.5 Structure Constructors

A **structure constructor** is a mechanism that is used to specify a scalar value of a derived type by specifying a sequence of values for the components of the type. If a component is of derived type, an embedded structure constructor is required to specify the value of that component. A structure constructor is the name of the type followed by a sequence of component values in parentheses. For example, a value of type COLOR (defined in 4.4.1) may be constructed with the following structure constructor:

```
COLOR (I, J, K, "MAGENTA")
```

The form for a structure constructor (R430) is:

type-name (expression-list)

Rules and restrictions:

1. There must be a value in the expression list for each component.

2. The expressions must agree in number, order, and rank with the components of the derived type. Values may be converted to agree in type, kind, and length with the components.

3. If a component is specified as an explicit shape array, the values for it in the expression list must agree in shape with the component.

4. If a component is a pointer, the value for it in the expression list must evaluate to an allowable target for the pointer. A constant is not an allowable target.

5. A structure constructor must not appear before that type is defined.

6. The structure constructor for a private type or a public type with private components is not available outside the module in which the type is defined.

If all of the values in a structure constructor are constants, the structure constructor may be used to specify a named constant, for example:

```
PARAMETER ( TEAL = COLOR (14, 7, 3, "TEAL") )
PARAMETER ( NO_PART = COMPONENT ("none", 0, 0.0) )
```

Following are several examples of structure constructors for types with somewhat different components:

1. a type with a component that is of derived type

2. a type with an array component

3. a type with a pointer component

Example 1. A structure constructor for a type that has a derived type as a component must provide a value for each of the components. A component may be of derived type, in which case a structure constructor is required for the component. In the example below, type RING has a component of type STONE.

```
TYPE STONE
      REAL           CARETS
      INTEGER        SHAPE
      CHARACTER (30) NAME
END TYPE STONE

TYPE RING
      REAL           EST_VALUE
      CHARACTER (30) INSURER
      TYPE (STONE)   JEWEL
END TYPE RING
```

If OVAL is a named integer constant, a structure constructor for a value of type RING is:

```
RING (5000.00, "Lloyds", STONE (2.5, OVAL, "emerald") )
```

Example 2. If a type is specified with an array component, the value that corresponds to the array component in the expression list of the structure constructor must conform with the specified shape. For example, type ORCHARD has an array component:

```
TYPE ORCHARD
      INTEGER              AGE, NO_OF_TREES
      CHARACTER (LEN = 20) VARIETIES (10)
END TYPE
```

Given the declarations:

```
CHARACTER (LEN = 20) CATALOG (16, 12)
PARAMETER (LEMON = 3)
```

a structure constructor for a value of type ORCHARD is:

```
ORCHARD (5, ROWS * NO_PER_ROW, CATALOG (LEMON, 1:10) )
```

Example 3. When a component of the type is a pointer, the corresponding structure constructor expression must evaluate to an object that would be an allowable target for such a pointer in a pointer assignment statement (7.5.3). If the variable SYNOPSIS is declared:

```
CHARACTER, TARGET :: SYNOPSIS (4000)
```

a value of the type ABSTRACT (defined in 4.4.1) may be constructed:

    ABSTRACT ("War and Peace", 1025, SYNOPSIS)

A constant expression cannot be constructed for a type with a pointer component because a constant is not an allowable target in a pointer assignment statement.

4.6 Array Constructors

An array constructor is used to specify the value of an array. More precisely, an **array constructor** is a mechanism that is used to specify a sequence of scalar values that is interpreted as a rank-one array. Syntactically, it is a sequence of scalar values and implied-do specifications enclosed in parentheses and slashes. For example:

    REAL VECTOR_X(3), VECTOR_Y(2), RESULT(100)
        . . .
    RESULT (1: 8) = (/ 1.3, 5.6, VECTOR_X, 2.35, VECTOR_Y /)

The value of the first eight elements of RESULT is constructed from the values of VECTOR_X and VECTOR_Y and three real constants in the specified order. If a rank-two or greater array appears in the value list, the values of its elements are taken in array element order. If it is necessary to construct an array of rank greater than one, the RESHAPE intrinsic function may be applied to an array constructor.

The form for an array constructor (R431) is:

    (/ ac-value-list /)

where an ac-value is either an expression (R723) or an ac-implied-do.
The form for an ac-implied-do (R433) is:

    (ac-value-list , ac-do-variable = scalar-integer-expression , &
        scalar-integer-expression [, scalar-integer-expression]

Rules and restrictions:

1. Each ac-value expression in the array constructor must have the same type and type parameters.

2. The type and type parameters of an array constructor are those of its ac-value expressions.

3. If there are no ac-value expressions or the ac-implied-do yields no values, the array is a rank-one, zero-sized array.

4. An ac-do-variable must be a scalar integer named variable. This variable has the scope of this ac-implied-do.

5. If an ac-implied-do is contained within another ac-implied-do, they must not have the same ac-do-variable.

There are three possibilities for an ac-value:

1. It may be a scalar expression as is each ac-value in:

   (/ 1.2, 3.5, 1.1 /)

2. It may be an array expression as is each ac-value in:

   (/ A (I, 1:3), A (I+1, 6:8) /)

3. It may be an implied-do specification as in:

   (/ (SQRT (REAL (I)), I = 1, 9) /)

Of course, the possibilities may be mixed in a single array constructor as in:

   (/ 1.2, B (2:6,:), (REAL (I), I = 1, N), 3.5 /)

If an ac-value is an array expression, the values of the elements of the expression in array element order (6.4.7) become the values of the array constructor. For example, the values that result from the example in possibility 2 above are:

   (/ A(I,1), A(I,2), A(I,3), A(I+1,6), A(I+1,7), A(I+1,8) /)

If an ac-value is an implied-do specification, it is expanded to form a sequence of values under control of the ac-do-variable as in the DO construct (8.5). For example, the values that result from the example in possibility 3 above are:

   (/1.0, 1.414, 1.732, 2.0, 2.236, 2.449, 2.645, 2.828, 3.0/)

If every expression in an array constructor is a constant expression, the array constructor is a constant expression as in the example above. Such an array constructor may be used to give a value to a named constant, for example:

```
REAL X(3), EXTENDED_X(4)
PARAMETER (X = (/ 2.0, 4.0, 6.0 /) )
PARAMETER (EXTENDED_X = (/ 0.0, X /) )
```

Following are several examples of array constructors. Examples 1 and 2 demonstrate the construction of arrays; examples 3 and 4 demonstrate the construction of values of derived type when the type has an array component:

1. a constructor for a rank-two array

2. a constructor for an array of derived type

3. a constructor for a value of derived type with an array component

4. a constructor for a value of derived type with a rank-two array component

Example 1. To create a value for an array of rank greater than one, the RESHAPE intrinsic function (A.88) must be used. With this function, a one-dimensional array may be reshaped into any allowable array shape.

```
Y = RESHAPE (SOURCE = (/ 2.0, (/ 4.5, 4.0 /), Z /),  &
       SHAPE = (/ 3, 2 /))
```

If Z has the value given in possibility 1 above, then Y is a 3×2 array with the elements:

```
2.0    1.2
4.5    3.5
4.0    1.1
```

Example 2. It may be necessary to construct an array value of derived type.

```
TYPE PERSON
    INTEGER AGE
    CHARACTER (LEN = 40) NAME
END TYPE PERSON

TYPE (PERSON) CAR_POOL (3)

CAR_POOL = (/ PERSON (35, "SCHMITT"),  &
       PERSON (57, "LOPEZ"), PERSON (26, "YUNG") /)
```

Example 3. When one of the components of a derived type is an array, then an array constructor must be used in the structure constructor for a scalar value of the derived type. Suppose that the definition for type COLOR differed slightly from that given above:

```
TYPE COLOR
    INTEGER PROPERTIES (3)
    CHARACTER (LEN = 30) NAME
END TYPE COLOR
```

A value of the revised type COLOR can be constructed:

```
COLOR ((/ 5, 20, 8 /), "MAGENTA")
```

Example 4. A derived type might contain an array of rank two or greater.

```
TYPE LINE
    REAL      COORD (2, 2)
    REAL      WIDTH
    INTEGER   PATTERN
END TYPE LINE
```

where the values of COORD are the coordinates x_1, y_1 and x_2, y_2 representing the end points of a line; WIDTH is the line width in centimeters; and PATTERN is 1 for a solid line, 2 for a dashed line, and 3 for a dotted line. An object of type line is declared and given a value as follows:

```
TYPE (LINE) SLOPE
    . . .
SLOPE = LINE (RESHAPE ((/ 0.0, 1.0, 0.0, 2.0 /),   &
        (/ 2, 2 /)), 0.1, 1)
```

The RESHAPE intrinsic function is used to construct a value that represents a solid line from $(0, 0)$ to $(1, 2)$ of width 0.1 centimeters.

4.7 Summary

The following are intrinsic data types in both Fortran 77 and Fortran 90:

integer
real
complex
logical
character

Type is the most important attribute of a data entity, but there are others such as dimensionality. The other attributes are described in Chapter 5.

Fortran 90 introduces two new ideas to the Fortran 77 data capabilities: kind parameters for the intrinsic types and nonintrinsic, derived (or user-defined) types.

The Fortran 90 standard requires a processor to provide two different kinds of each of the real and complex types and allows a processor to provide other kinds of real and complex types. A standard-conforming processor must provide one kind for each of the integer, logical, and character types, and may provide more. Examples of type declarations are:

```
REAL PRESSURE(500)
INTEGER (SHORT) AGE
COMPLEX (QUAD) SOLUTION
```

PRESSURE is a real array variable of rank one. AGE is an integer variable of kind SHORT where SHORT is a named constant whose value is a processor-dependent kind number for the integer type. SOLUTION is a complex variable of kind QUAD where QUAD is a named constant whose value is a processor-dependent kind number for the real data type.

A data type in Fortran has a name, a set of values, a set of operations, and a means to represent constants of the type. This is the case for the intrinsic types as well as for the new derived types.

The five intrinsic types and their various kinds may be used as components to derive other types. A type definition specifies the name of the new type as well as the names and attributes of its components. A component may be of derived type and may be a pointer or an array. An example of a simple type is:

```
TYPE EMPLOYEE
    CHARACTER (LEN = 30) NAME
    INTEGER SSN
    INTEGER (SHORT) EMP_NO
END TYPE EMPLOYEE
```

An object of user-defined type is called a structure. The name of the user-defined type is used to declare structures of the type. For example:

```
TYPE (EMPLOYEE) J_JONES, W_WILLIAMS, JANITOR
```

Operations for the intrinsic types are provided by the language, whereas operations for derived types must be defined in terms of functions provided by the user. A means, called a structure constructor, is provided to specify a value of derived type. For example:

```
J_JONES = EMPLOYEE ("Jones, John", 123456789, 35)
```

Structure constructors may be used to create nonconstant values of derived type as well.

Array constructors are also provided to create array-valued objects. These may be array components in structures or arrays of any intrinsic or derived type. If all the values specified are constant, the result is an array-valued constant expression. For example:

```
PRESSURE(1:5) = (/ 80., 45.1, 100., 23.5, 60. /)
```

F9⊘

5

Declarations

Declarations are used to specify the type and other attributes of program entities. The attributes that an entity possesses determine how the entity may be used in a program. Every variable and function has a type, which is the most important of the attributes; type is discussed in Chapter 4. However, type is only one of a number of attributes that an entity may possess. Some entities, such as subroutines and namelist groups, do not have a type but may possess other attributes. In addition, there are relationships among objects that can be specified by EQUIVALENCE, COMMON, and NAMELIST statements. Declarations are used to specify these attributes and relationships.

In general, Fortran keywords are used to declare the attributes for an entity. The following list summarizes these keywords:

Type	INTEGER
	REAL (and DOUBLE PRECISION)
	COMPLEX
	LOGICAL
	CHARACTER
	TYPE (user-defined name)

Array properties	DIMENSION
	ALLOCATABLE
Pointer properties	POINTER
	TARGET
Setting values	DATA
	PARAMETER
Object accessibility and use	PUBLIC
	PRIVATE
	INTENT
	OPTIONAL
	SAVE
Procedure properties	EXTERNAL
	INTRINSIC

The attributes are described and illustrated in turn using each of the two forms that attribute specifications may take: entity-oriented and attribute-oriented.

In Fortran 77, it is necessary to use a different statement for each attribute given to a variable or a collection of variables, for example:

```
INTEGER A, B, C
SAVE    A, B, C
```

In Fortran 90, for objects that have a type, the other attributes may be included in the type declaration statement. For example:

```
INTEGER, SAVE :: A, B, C
```

Collecting the attributes into a single statement is sometimes more convenient for readers of programs. It eliminates searching through many declaration statements to locate all the attributes of a particular object. Emphasis can be placed on an object and its attributes (entity-oriented declaration) or on an attribute and the objects that possess the attribute (attribute-oriented declaration), whichever is preferred by a programmer. In both forms, dimensionality may be specified as an attribute or as an attachment to the object name. For example:

• entity-oriented declarations

```
REAL, DIMENSION(20), SAVE :: X
```

or

```
REAL, SAVE :: X(20)
```

- attribute-oriented declarations

```
REAL X
DIMENSION X(20)
SAVE X
```

or

```
REAL X (20)
SAVE X
```

In the following description of each attribute, the entity-oriented method of specification is described first, followed by the attribute-oriented. In most cases these are equivalent, but not always.

If no attributes are declared for a data object, defaults apply. In general, if an attribute is not specified for an object, it is assumed that the object does not possess the attribute. However, every data object has a type, and if this is not explicitly specified, it is assumed from the first letter of its name. The IMPLICIT statement may be used to specify any intrinsic or user-defined type for an initial letter or a range of initial letters. The IMPLICIT NONE statement, on the other hand, removes implicit typing and thus requires explicit type declarations for every named data object in the scoping unit.

Fortran 90 provides new dynamic data objects that can be sized at the time a program is executed. These include allocatable arrays and objects with the POINTER attribute. They also include automatic data objects (arrays of any type and character strings) that are created on entry into a procedure. Only objects whose size may vary are called automatic.

Other declarations (NAMELIST, EQUIVALENCE, and COMMON) establish relationships among data objects. The NAMELIST statement is used to name a collection of objects so that they can be referenced by a single name in an input/output statement. In Fortran 77, storage (the location of an object in a computer's memory) is an important concept. EQUIVALENCE is used to reference storage by more than one name. COMMON is used to share storage among the different units of a program. Fortran 90 provides new features that deemphasize the concept of storage. Objects may be referenced by name, and modules (11.6) provide shared access to named objects. In new programs, there is no need for COMMON and EQUIVALENCE statements; they are provided in Fortran 90 for compatibility with existing Fortran 77 programs.

5.1 Type Declaration Statements

A type statement begins with the name of the type, optionally lists other attributes, then ends with a list of variables that possess these attributes. In addition, a type declaration statement may include an initial value for a variable. It must include the value of a named constant. The form of a type declaration statement (R501) is:

type-spec [[, attribute-spec] ... ::] entity-declaration-list

where a type specification (R502) is one of:

INTEGER [kind-selector]
REAL [kind-selector]
DOUBLE PRECISION
COMPLEX [kind-selector]
CHARACTER [character-selector]
LOGICAL [kind-selector]
TYPE (type-name)

with a kind selector (R505) taking the form:

([KIND =] scalar-integer-initialization-expression)

and where an attribute specification (R503) is one of:

PARAMETER
access-spec
ALLOCATABLE
DIMENSION (array-spec)
EXTERNAL
INTENT (intent-spec)
INTRINSIC
OPTIONAL
POINTER
SAVE
TARGET

with an access specification being either PUBLIC or PRIVATE. An entity declaration (R504) has one of the forms:

object-name [(array-spec)] [* character-length]   &
    [= initialization-expression]
function-name [(array-spec)] [* character-length]

Rules and restrictions:

1. The type specification may override or confirm the implicit type indicated by the first letter of the entity name according to the implicit typing rules in effect.

2. The same attribute must not appear more than once in a given type declaration statement.

3. An entity must not be given any attribute more than once in a scoping unit.

4. The value specified in a kind selector must be a kind type parameter allowed for that type by the implementation.

5. The character length option may appear only when the type specification is CHARACTER.

6. If an initialization expression appears, a double colon separator must be used.

7. An initialization expression must be included if the PARAMETER attribute is specified.

8. A function name must be the name of an external function, an intrinsic function, a function dummy procedure, or a statement function.

9. An array function name must be specified as an explicit-shape array (5.3.1.1) unless it has the POINTER attribute, in which case it must be specified as a deferred-shape array (5.3.1.3).

There are other rules and restrictions that pertain to particular attributes; these are covered in the sections describing that attribute. The attributes that may be used with the attribute being described are also listed. The simple forms that appear in the following sections to illustrate attribute specification in a type declaration statement seem to imply that the attribute being described must appear first in the attribute list, but this is not the case; attributes may appear in any order. If these simple forms are used to construct statements, the statements will be correct, but other variations are permitted. The complete form appears earlier in this section.

Some example type declaration statements are:

```
REAL A(10)
LOGICAL, DIMENSION(5, 5) :: MASK_1, MASK_2
COMPLEX :: CUBE_ROOT = (-0.5, 0.867)
INTEGER, PARAMETER :: SHORT = SELECTED_INT_KIND(4)
INTEGER(SHORT) K          ! Range of -9999 to 9999
REAL, ALLOCATABLE :: A1(:, :), A2(:, :, :)
TYPE(PERSON) CHAIRMAN
TYPE(NODE), POINTER :: HEAD_OF_CHAIN, END_OF_CHAIN
REAL, INTENT(IN) :: ARG1
REAL, INTRINSIC :: SIN
```

5.1.1 Integer

An INTEGER statement declares the named variables and functions to be of type integer (4.3.1). If a kind selector is present, it specifies the representation method. A simple form for declaring objects of this type is:

```
INTEGER [ ( [ KIND = ] kind-value ) ] [ , attribute-list :: ]   &
   entity-list
```

For example:

- entity-oriented

```
INTEGER, DIMENSION(:), POINTER :: MILES, HOURS
INTEGER (SHORT), POINTER :: RATE, INDEX
```

- attribute-oriented

```
INTEGER MILES, HOURS
INTEGER (SHORT) RATE, INDEX
DIMENSION MILES (:), HOURS (:)
POINTER MILES, HOURS, RATE, INDEX
```

5.1.2 Real

A REAL statement declares the named variables and functions to be of type real (4.3.2). If a kind selector is present, it specifies the representation method. A simple form for declaring objects of this type is:

```
REAL [ ( [ KIND = ] kind-value ) ] [ , attribute-list :: ] entity-list
```

For example:

- entity-oriented

```
REAL (KIND = HIGH), OPTIONAL :: VARIANCE
REAL, SAVE :: A1(10, 10), A2(100, 10, 10)
```

- attribute-oriented

```
REAL (KIND = HIGH) VARIANCE
REAL A1(10, 10), A2(100, 10, 10)
OPTIONAL VARIANCE
SAVE A1, A2
```

5.1.3 Double Precision

A DOUBLE PRECISION statement declares the named variables and functions to be of type real with a representation method that represents more precision than the default real representation (4.3.2). DOUBLE PRECISION is not needed in Fortran 90, as REAL with the appropriate kind parameter value is equivalent. A kind selector is not permitted in the DOUBLE PRECISION statement. A simple form for declaring objects of this type is:

```
DOUBLE PRECISION [ , attribute-list :: ] entity-list
```

For example:

- entity-oriented

```
DOUBLE PRECISION, DIMENSION(N,N) :: MATRIX_A, MATRIX_B
DOUBLE PRECISION, POINTER :: C, D, E, F(:, :)
```

- attribute-oriented

```
DOUBLE PRECISION MATRIX_A, MATRIX_B, C, D, E, F
DIMENSION MATRIX_A (N, N), MATRIX_B (N, N), F(:, :)
POINTER C, D, E, F
```

If DOUBLE is a named integer constant that has the value of the kind parameter of the double precision real type, the entity-oriented declarations above could be written as:

```
REAL (DOUBLE), DIMENSION (N,N) :: MATRIX_A, MATRIX_B
REAL (DOUBLE), POINTER :: C, D, E, F(:,:)
```

5.1.4 Complex

A COMPLEX statement declares the named variables and functions to be
of type complex (4.3.3). If a kind selector is present, it specifies the representation method. A simple form for declaring objects of this type is:

```
COMPLEX [ ( [ KIND = ] kind-value ) ] [ , attribute-list :: ]   &
    entity-list
```

For example:

- entity-oriented

```
COMPLEX (KIND = LOW), POINTER :: ROOTS(:)
COMPLEX, POINTER :: DISCRIMINANT, COEFFICIENTS (:)
```

- attribute-oriented

```
COMPLEX (KIND = LOW) ROOTS(:)
COMPLEX DISCRIMINANT, COEFFICIENTS (:)
POINTER ROOTS, DISCRIMINANT, COEFFICIENTS
```

5.1.5 Logical

A LOGICAL statement declares the named variables and functions to be
of type logical (4.3.4). If a kind selector is present, it specifies the representation method. A simple form for declaring objects of this type is:

```
LOGICAL [ ( [ KIND = ] kind-value ) ] [ , attribute-list :: ] entity-list
```

For example:

- entity-oriented

```
LOGICAL, ALLOCATABLE :: MASK_1(:), MASK_2(:)
LOGICAL (KIND = BYTE), SAVE :: INDICATOR, STATUS
```

- attribute-oriented

```
LOGICAL MASK_1(:), MASK_2(:)
LOGICAL (KIND = BYTE) INDICATOR, STATUS
ALLOCATABLE MASK_1, MASK_2
SAVE INDICATOR, STATUS
```

5.1.6 Character

A CHARACTER statement declares the named variables and functions to be of type character (4.3.5). A simple form for declaring objects of this type is:

CHARACTER [character-selector] [, attribute-list ::] entity-list

The length of a character entity may be specified in a character selector (R506). It has one of the forms:

length-selector
(LEN = type-param-value , &
   KIND = scalar-integer-initialization-expression)
(type-param-value , &
   [KIND =] scalar-integer-initialization-expression)
(KIND = scalar-integer-initialization-expression &
   [, LEN = type-param-value])

where a length selector (R507) has one of the forms:

([LEN =] type-param-value)
* character-length [,]

and a character length (R508) has one of the forms:

(type-param-value)
scalar-integer-literal-constant

where a type parameter value (R509) is one of:

specification-expression
*

Rules and restrictions:

1. The optional comma in a length selector is permitted only if no double colon separator appears in the type declaration statement.

2. A character type declaration that appears in a procedure or a procedure interface may specify a character length that is a nonconstant expression. The length is determined on entry into the procedure and is not affected by any changes in the values of variables in the expression during the execution of the procedure. A character object declared this way that is not a dummy argument is called an **automatic data object**.

3. The length of a named character entity or a character component in a type definition is specified by the character selector in the type specification unless there is a character length in an entity or component declaration; if so, the character length specifies an individual length and overrides the length in the character selector. If a length is not specified in either a character selector or a character length, the length is 1.

4. If the length parameter has a negative value, the length of the character entity is 0.

5. The scalar integer literal constant that specifies a character length must not include a kind parameter. (This could produce an ambiguity when fixed source form is used.)

6. A length parameter value of * may be used only in the following ways:

    a. It may be used to declare a dummy argument of a procedure, in which case the dummy argument assumes the length of the associated actual argument when the procedure is invoked.

    b. It may be used to declare a named constant, in which case the length is that of the constant value.

    c. It may be used to declare the result variable for an external function. Any scoping unit that invokes the function must declare the function with a length other than *, or it must access such a declaration by host or use association. When the function is invoked, the length of the result is the value specified in the declaration in the program unit referencing the function.

    Note that an implication of this rule is that a length of * must not appear in an IMPLICIT statement.

7. A function name must not be declared with a length of * if the function is an internal or module function, or if it is array-valued, pointer-valued, or recursive.

8. The length of a character-valued statement function or statement function dummy argument of type character must be an integer constant expression.

Examples of character type declaration statements are:

- entity-oriented

```
CHARACTER (LEN = 10, KIND = KANJI), SAVE :: GREETING
CHARACTER (10) :: PROMPT = "PASSWORD?"
CHARACTER (*), INTENT(IN) :: HOME_TEAM, VISITORS
CHARACTER *3, SAVE :: NORMAL_1, LONGER *20, NORMAL_2
CHARACTER :: GRADE = "A"
```

- attribute-oriented

```
CHARACTER (LEN = 10, KIND = KANJI) GREETING
CHARACTER (10) PROMPT
CHARACTER (*) HOME_TEAM, VISITORS
CHARACTER *3 NORMAL_1, LONGER *20, NORMAL_2
CHARACTER GRADE
SAVE GREETING, NORMAL_1, LONGER, NORMAL_2
INTENT (IN) HOME_TEAM, VISITORS
DATA PROMPT / "PASSWORD?" /  GRADE / "A" /
```

5.1.7 Derived Type

A TYPE declaration statement declares the named variables and functions to be of the specified user-defined type (4.4). The type name appears in parentheses following the keyword TYPE. A form for declaring objects of user-defined type is:

TYPE (type-name) [, attribute-list ::] entity-list

For example, using types defined in Chapter 4:

- entity-oriented

```
TYPE (COLOR), DIMENSION (:), ALLOCATABLE :: HUES_OF_RED
TYPE (PERSON), SAVE :: CAR_POOL (3)
TYPE (PARAGRAPH), SAVE :: OVERVIEW, SUBSTANCE, SUMMARY
```

- attribute-oriented

```
TYPE (COLOR) HUES_OF_RED
TYPE (PERSON) CAR_POOL(3)
```

```
TYPE (PARAGRAPH) OVERVIEW, SUBSTANCE, SUMMARY
DIMENSION HUES_OF_RED (:)
ALLOCATABLE HUES_OF_RED
SAVE CAR_POOL, OVERVIEW, SUBSTANCE, SUMMARY
```

Rules and restrictions:

1. An object of derived type must not have the PUBLIC attribute if its type is private.

2. A structure constructor (4.4.5) must be used to initialize an object of derived type. Each component of the structure must be an initialization expression.

5.2 Implicit Typing

Each variable, named constant, and function has a type and a name. If the type is not declared explicitly, it is assumed from the first letter of the name. This method of determining type is called **implicit typing**. In each scoping unit, there is in effect a mapping of each of the letters A, B, ..., Z to one of the accessible types or to no type. IMPLICIT statements in a scoping unit may be used to specify a mapping different from the default mapping; this makes it easier to transform an external procedure into an internal or module procedure. If a new mapping for a letter is not specified in an IMPLICIT statement, the default mapping continues to apply for that letter. An IMPLICIT NONE statement specifies that there is no mapping for any letter and thus all variables, named constants, and functions must be declared in type declaration statements. If the host of a scoping unit contains the IMPLICIT NONE statement and the scoping unit contains IMPLICIT statements for some letters, the other letters retain the null mapping. This is the only situation in which some initial letters specify an implied type and other initial letters require explicit declarations. A program unit is treated as if it had a host with the mapping shown in Figure 5-1. That is, each undeclared variable or function whose name begins with any of the letters I, J, K, L, M, or N is of type integer and all others are of type real.

The IMPLICIT statement (R540) has two forms:

IMPLICIT type-spec (letter-spec-list)
IMPLICIT NONE

where a letter specification (R542) is:

letter [– letter]

$$\underbrace{\text{Real}}\quad\underbrace{\text{Integer}}\quad\underbrace{\text{Real}}$$

A B C D E F G H I J K L M N O P Q R S T U V W X Y Z

Figure 5-1 Default implicit mapping for a program unit

Rules and restrictions:

1. If IMPLICIT NONE appears, it must precede any PARAMETER statements and there must be no other IMPLICIT statements in the scoping unit.

2. If the – letter option appears in a letter specification, the second letter must follow the first alphabetically.

3. The same letter must not appear as a single letter or be included in a range of letters more than once in all of the IMPLICIT statements in a scoping unit.

4. An IMPLICIT statement may be used to specify implicit mappings for user-defined types as well as for intrinsic types.

The IMPLICIT statement specifies that all variables, named constants, and functions beginning with the indicated letters are implicitly given the indicated data type (and type parameters). For example, the statement

```
IMPLICIT COMPLEX (A-C, Z)
```

indicates that all undeclared variables, named constants, and functions beginning with the letters A, B, C, and Z are of type default complex. If this is the only IMPLICIT statement, undeclared variables, named constants, and functions beginning with I–N will still be of type integer; undeclared variables, named constants, and functions beginning with D–H and O–Y will be of type real.

The statement

```
IMPLICIT NONE
```

indicates that there is no implicit typing in the scoping unit and that each variable, named constant, and function used in the scoping unit must be declared explicitly in a type statement. This statement is useful for detecting inadvertent misspellings in a program because misspelled names become undeclared rather than implicitly declared.

An IMPLICIT statement may specify a user-defined type. Some examples of IMPLICIT statements are:

```
IMPLICIT INTEGER (A-G), LOGICAL (KIND = BIT) (M)
IMPLICIT CHARACTER *10 (P, Q)
IMPLICIT TYPE (COLOR) (X-Z)
```

The additional complexity that implicit typing causes in determining the scope of an undeclared variable in a nested scope is explained in Section 11.4.

5.3 Array Properties

An array object has the dimension attribute. An array specification determines the array's rank, or number of dimensions. The extents of the dimensions may be declared or left unspecified. If they are left unspecified, the array must also have the ALLOCATABLE or POINTER attribute, or it must be a dummy argument.

5.3.1 Array Specifications

There are four forms that an array specification (R512) may take:

> explicit-shape-spec-list
> assumed-shape-spec-list
> deferred-shape-spec-list
> assumed-size-spec-list

Rules and restrictions:

1. The maximum rank of an array is 7. A scalar is considered to have rank 0.

2. An array with a deferred-shape specification list must have the POINTER or ALLOCATABLE attribute.

3. An array with an assumed-shape specification list or an assumed-size specification list must be a dummy argument.

5.3.1.1 Explicit-Shape Arrays. An explicit-shape array has bounds specified in each dimension. Each dimension is specified by an explicit-shape specification (R513), which has the form:

> [lower-bound :] upper-bound

where the lower bound, if present, and the upper bound are specification expressions (7.2.9.3).

Rules and restrictions:

1. The number of sets of bounds specified is the number of dimensions (rank) of the array.

2. If the lower bound is omitted, the default value is 1.

3. The value of a lower bound or an upper bound may be positive, negative, or 0.

4. The subscript range of the array in a given dimension is the set of integer values between and including the lower and upper bounds, provided the upper bound is not less than the lower bound. If the upper bound is less than the lower bound, the range is empty, the extent in that dimension is 0, and the size of the array is 0.

5. The expression for a bound may involve variables that cause the expression to have different values each time the procedure in which it is declared is executed. If so, the array must be a dummy argument, a function result, or an automatic array, in which case the actual bounds are determined when the procedure is entered. The bounds of such an array are unaffected by any redefinition or undefinition of the specification variables during the execution of the procedure.

For example:

- entity-oriented

```
REAL Q (-10:10, -10:10, 2)
```

or in a subroutine

```
SUBROUTINE EX1 (Z, I, J)
   REAL, DIMENSION (2:I + 1, J) :: Z
      . . .
```

- attribute-oriented

```
REAL Q (-10:10, -10:10, 2)
```

or in a subroutine

```
SUBROUTINE EX1 (Z, I, J)
   REAL Z
   DIMENSION Z (2:I + 1, J)
      . . .
```

5.3.1.2 Assumed-Shape Arrays. An assumed-shape array is a dummy argument that takes the shape of the actual argument passed to it. An assumed-shape specification (R516) has the form:

[lower-bound] :

Rules and restrictions:

1. The rank is equal to the number of colons in the assumed-shape specification.

2. The lower bound of the assumed-shape array is the specified lower bound, if present, and is 1 otherwise.

3. The upper bound is the extent of the corresponding dimension of the associated array plus the lower bound minus 1.

4. An assumed-shape array must not have the POINTER or ALLO-CATABLE attribute.

For example:

*   entity-oriented

```
REAL, DIMENSION (2:, :) :: X
   . . .
```

*   attribute-oriented

```
SUBROUTINE EX2 (A, B, X)
   REAL A (:), B (0:), X
   DIMENSION X (2:, :)
   INTENT (IN) A, B
   . . .
```

Suppose EX2 is called by the statement

```
CALL EX2 ( U, V, W (4:9, 2:6))
```

For the duration of the execution of subroutine EX2, the dummy argument X is an array with bounds (2:7, 1:5). The lower bound of the first dimension is 2 because X is declared to have a lower bound of 2. The upper bound is 7 because the dummy argument takes its shape from the actual argument W.

5.3.1.3 Deferred-Shape Arrays. A deferred-shape array is either an array pointer or an allocatable array. An array pointer is an array that has the POINTER attribute. Its extent in each dimension is determined when the pointer is allocated or when a pointer assignment statement for the pointer is executed. An allocatable array is an array that has the ALLOCATABLE attribute. Its bounds, and thus its shape, are determined when the array is allocated. In both cases the declared bounds are specified by just a colon; that is, the form of a deferred-shape specification (R517) is:

:

Rules and restrictions:

1. The rank is equal to the number of colons in the deferred-shape specification.

2. The bounds of an allocatable array are specified in an ALLOCATE statement when the array is allocated.

3. The lower bound of each dimension of an array pointer is the result of the LBOUND intrinsic function applied to the corresponding dimension of the target. The upper bound of each dimension is the result of the UBOUND intrinsic function applied to the corresponding dimension of the target. This means, in effect, that if the bounds are determined by allocation of the pointer, they may be specified by the user; if the bounds are determined by pointer assignment, there are two cases:

    a. If the pointer target is a named whole array, the bounds are those declared in the array declaration or those specified when the array was allocated.

    b. If the pointer target is an array section, the lower bound is 1 and the upper bound is the extent in that dimension.

4. The bounds, and thus the shape, of an array pointer or allocatable array are unaffected by any subsequent redefinition or undefinition of variables involved in determination of the bounds.

For example:

- entity-oriented

```
REAL, POINTER :: D (:, :), P (:) ! array pointers
REAL, ALLOCATABLE :: E (:)       ! allocatable array
```

- attribute-oriented

      REAL D (:, :), P (:), E (:)
      POINTER D, P
      ALLOCATABLE E

5.3.1.4 Assumed-Size Arrays. An assumed-size array is a dummy argument array whose size is assumed from that of the associated actual argument. Only the size is assumed—the rank, extents, and bounds (except for the upper bound and extent in the last dimension) are determined by the declaration of the dummy array. There are four rules for argument association between an actual argument and an assumed-size array.

- They have the same initial array element.

- Successive array elements are storage associated (5.10).

- Declarations for the dummy argument determine the rank. They also determine lower bounds for all dimensions and the extents and upper bounds for all dimensions except the last.

- The size of the actual argument determines the size of the dummy argument as explained in rule 2 below.

The upper bound of the last dimension of an assumed-size array is an asterisk (*). The form of an assumed-size specification (R518) is:

      [explicit-shape-spec-list ,] [lower-bound :] *

Rules and restrictions:

1. The rank of an assumed-size array is the number of explicit-shape specifications plus one.

2. The size of an assumed-size array is determined as follows:

    a. If the actual argument associated with the assumed-size dummy argument is an array of any type other than default character, the size is that of the actual array.

    b. If the actual argument associated with the assumed-size dummy array is an array element of any type other than default character with a subscript order value (6.4.7) of v in an array of size x, the size of the dummy argument is $x - v + 1$.

    c. If the actual argument is a default character array, default character array element, or a default character array element substring (6.2), and if it begins at character storage unit t of an array with c character storage units, the size of the dummy array is

$$\text{MAX (INT } ((c - t + 1)/e), 0)$$

where e is the length of an element in the dummy character array.

3. If r is the rank of the array, the bounds of the first $r - 1$ dimensions are those specified by the explicit-shape specification list, if present. The lower bound of the last dimension is the specified lower bound, if present, and 1 otherwise.

4. The expression for a bound may involve variables that cause the expression to have different values each time the procedure in which it is declared is executed. If so, the bounds are unaffected by any subsequent redefinition or undefinition of such variables involved in the determination of the bounds.

5. A function result must not be an assumed-size array.

6. An assumed-size array must not appear in a context where the shape of the array is required, such as a whole array reference.

For example:

*   entity-oriented

```
SUBROUTINE EX3 (N, S, Y)
   REAL, DIMENSION (N, *) :: S
   REAL Y (10, 5, *)
   . . .
```

*   attribute-oriented

```
SUBROUTINE EX3 (N, S, Y)
   REAL S, Y (10, 5, *)
   DIMENSION S (N, *)
   . . .
```

5.3.2 DIMENSION Attribute and Statement

The dimensions of an array may be specified by the appearance of a DIMENSION attribute or by the appearance of an array specification following the name of the array in a type declaration statement. In fact, both a DIMENSION attribute and an array specification following the name may appear in a type declaration statement. In this case, the array specification following the name overrides the array specification following the DIMENSION attribute. A form for a type declaration statement with a DIMENSION attribute is:

> type , **DIMENSION** (array-spec) [, attribute-list] **::** entity-list

See the examples below. Other attributes that are allowed with the DIMENSION attribute are:

> initialization
> ALLOCATABLE
> INTENT
> OPTIONAL
> POINTER
> PARAMETER
> PRIVATE
> PUBLIC
> SAVE
> TARGET

In addition, an array specification can appear following a name in several different kinds of statements to declare an array. They are DIMENSION, type specification, ALLOCATABLE, POINTER, TARGET, and COMMON statements.

The DIMENSION statement (R525) is the statement form of the DIMENSION attribute.

> **DIMENSION** [**::**] array-name (array-spec) **&**
> [, array-name (array-spec)] ...

For example:

- entity-oriented

```
INTEGER, DIMENSION (10), TARGET, SAVE :: INDICES
INTEGER, ALLOCATABLE, TARGET :: LG (:, :, :)
```

- attribute-oriented

```
INTEGER INDICES, LG (:, :, :)
DIMENSION INDICES (10)
TARGET INDICES, LG
ALLOCATABLE LG
SAVE INDICES
```

- with the array specification in other statements

```
INTEGER INDICES, LG
TARGET INDICES (10), LG
ALLOCATABLE LG (:, :, :)
SAVE INDICES
```

- an additional example with the array specification in a COMMON statement

```
COMMON / UNIVERSAL / TIME (80), SPACE (20, 20, 20, 20)
```

5.3.3 ALLOCATABLE Attribute and Statement

Arrays are the only objects that can have the ALLOCATABLE attribute. An allocatable array is one for which the bounds are determined when an ALLOCATE statement is executed for the array. Such arrays must be deferred-shape arrays. A form for a type declaration statement with an ALLOCATABLE attribute is:

type , **ALLOCATABLE** [, attribute-list] :: entity-list

Other attributes that may be used with the ALLOCATABLE attri-bute are:

DIMENSION (with deferred shape)
PRIVATE
PUBLIC
SAVE
TARGET

The form of the ALLOCATABLE statement (R526) is:

ALLOCATABLE [::] array-name [(deferred-shape-spec-list)] &
    [, array-name [(deferred-shape-spec-list)]] ...

Rules and restrictions:

1. The array must not be a dummy argument or function result.

2. If the array is given the DIMENSION attribute elsewhere, the bounds must be specified as colons (deferred shape).

For example:

- entity-oriented

    ```
    REAL, ALLOCATABLE :: A (:, :)
    LOGICAL, ALLOCATABLE, DIMENSION (:) :: MASK1
    ```

- attribute-oriented

    ```
    REAL A (:, :)
    LOGICAL MASK1
    DIMENSION MASK1 (:)
    ALLOCATABLE A, MASK1
    ```

5.4 Pointer Properties

Most attributes, when applied to an ordinary object, add characteristics that the object would not have otherwise. The POINTER attribute, in some sense, takes away a characteristic that an ordinary object has. An ordinary object has storage space set aside for it. If the object has the POINTER attribute, it has no space initially and must not be referenced until space is associated with it. An ALLOCATE statement creates new space for a pointer object. A pointer assignment statement permits the pointer to borrow the space from another object. The space that becomes associated with a pointer is called the pointer's **target**. The target may change during the execution of a program. A pointer target is either an object or part of an object declared to have the TARGET attribute; or it is an object or part of an object that was created by the allocation of a pointer. A pointer may be assigned the target (or part of the target) of another pointer. An array with the ALLOCATABLE attribute may be a pointer target only if it also has the TARGET attribute.

Another way of thinking about a pointer is as a **descriptor** that contains information about the type, type parameters, rank, extents, and location of the pointer's target. Thus, a pointer to a scalar object of type real would be quite different from a pointer to an array of user-defined type. In fact, each of these pointers is considered to occupy a different unspecified storage unit. When an object with the POINTER attribute is declared to be in a common block, it is likely to be the descriptor that occupies the storage. This is why every declaration of a common block that contains a pointer must specify the same sequence of storage units.

5.4.1 POINTER Attribute and Statement

A form for a type declaration statement with a POINTER attribute is:

type , **POINTER** [, attribute-list] **::** entity-list

Other attributes that may be used with the POINTER attribute are:

DIMENSION (with deferred shape)
OPTIONAL
PRIVATE
PUBLIC
SAVE

The POINTER statement (R527) also provides a means for declaring pointers. Its form is:

POINTER [**::**] object-name [(deferred-shape-spec-list)] &
    [, object-name [(deferred-shape-spec-list)]] ...

Rules and restrictions:

1. The target of a pointer may be a scalar or an array.

2. A pointer that is an array must be declared as a deferred-shape array.

3. A pointer must not be referenced or defined unless it is associated with a target that may be referenced or defined. (A pointer on the right-hand side of a pointer assignment is not considered to be a pointer reference.)

For example:

*   entity-oriented

        TYPE (NODE), POINTER :: CURRENT
        REAL, POINTER :: X (:, :), Y (:)

*   attribute-oriented

        TYPE (NODE) CURRENT
        REAL X (:, :), Y (:)
        POINTER CURRENT, X, Y

5.4.2 TARGET Attribute and Statement

An object with the TARGET attribute may become the target of a pointer during execution of a program. The sole purpose of the

TARGET attribute is to provide aid to a compiler in the production of efficient code. If an object does not have the target attribute or has not been allocated, no part of it can be accessed via a pointer. A form for a type declaration statement with a TARGET attribute is:

    type , TARGET [, attribute-list] :: entity-list

Other attributes that may be used with the TARGET attribute are:

    data initialization
    ALLOCATABLE
    DIMENSION
    INTENT
    OPTIONAL
    PRIVATE
    PUBLIC
    SAVE

The TARGET statement (R528) also provides a means for specifying pointer targets. It has the form:

    TARGET [::] object-name [(array-spec)] &
       [, object-name [(array-spec)]] ...

For example:

- entity-oriented

```
TYPE (NODE), TARGET :: HEAD_OF_LIST
REAL, TARGET, DIMENSION (100, 100) :: V, W (100)
```

- attribute-oriented

```
TYPE (NODE) HEAD_OF_LIST
REAL V, W (100)
DIMENSION V (100, 100)
TARGET HEAD_OF_LIST, V, W
```

5.5 Value Attributes

Variables may be given values before execution of the program begins; named constant values must be specified prior to execution. The general provisions for these two cases are:

1. A variable may be given an initial value by an entity-oriented type declaration statement that contains an entity declaration of the form:

object-name = initialization-expression

or by a DATA statement. The value may be redefined later in the program. This gives the programmer a convenient and efficient way to establish initial values.

2. A named constant is declared and defined with a value by an entity-oriented declaration statement that contains the PARAME-TER attribute and an entity declaration of the form:

object-name = initialization-expression

or by a PARAMETER statement. The value associated with the name cannot be changed during the execution of the program. For example, PI or E may be associated with the familiar mathematical constants to provide more convenient access to these values. Named constants are also used to give names to values (such as a sales tax rate) that may change at some later time. When a change is necessary, it can be made at one place in the program and not every place where the value is used. The program can be recompiled to effect the change.

5.5.1 Data Initialization and the DATA Statement

The DATA statement is the only attribute specification statement for which there is no corresponding attribute that may appear in a type declaration statement. It is, however, possible to initialize a variable in an entity-oriented type declaration statement. When an initialization expression appears in a declaration for an object that does not have the PARAMETER attribute, the object (which is a variable) is given the specified initial value. The same rules apply to the assignment of the initial value as apply when an assignment statement is executed. For example, if the variable is of type real but the value is an integer value, the variable will be assigned the real equivalent of the integer value. If the kind of the variable is different from the kind of the value, the value will be "converted" to the kind of the variable. Array constructors may be used to initialize arrays, and structure constructors may be used to initialize variables of user-defined type. The form of a type declaration statement that provides an initial value for a variable is:

type [, attribute-list] :: object-name [(array-spec)] &
    [* character-length] = initialization-expression

Other attributes that may be used with variable initialization are:

DIMENSION
PRIVATE

PUBLIC
SAVE
TARGET

The PARAMETER attribute may appear, but in this case the object is a named constant.

Initialization of a variable in a type declaration statement or any part of a variable in a DATA statement implies that the variable has the SAVE attribute unless the variable is in a named common block. The automatically acquired SAVE attribute may be reaffirmed by the appearance of SAVE as an attribute in its type declaration statement or by inclusion of the variable name in a separate SAVE statement.

The DATA statement (R529) is somewhat complicated. It has the form:

DATA data-object-list / data-value-list /   &
    [[**,**] data-object-list / data-value-list] ...

where a data object (R531) is one of:

variable
data-implied-do

and a data value (R532) is:

[repeat-factor *] data-constant

where a repeat factor (R534) is a scalar integer constant and a data constant (R533) is one of:

scalar-constant
signed-integer-literal-constant
signed-real-literal-constant
structure-constructor
boz-literal-constant

The form of a data-implied do (R535) is:

(data-implied-do-object-list **,** scalar-integer-variable =   &
    scalar-integer-expression **,** scalar-integer-expression   &
    [**,** scalar-integer-expression])

where a data-implied-do object (R536) is one of:

array-element
structure-component
data-implied-do

Rules and restrictions:

1. If an object is of type character or logical, the constant used for initialization must be of the same type. If an object is of type real or complex, the corresponding constant must be of type integer, real, or complex. If the object is of type integer, the corresponding constant must be of type integer, real, or complex; or, if the initialization is specified in a DATA statement, the corresponding constant may be a binary, octal, or hexadecimal literal constant. If an object is of derived type, the corresponding constant must be of the same type.

2. The value of the constant must be such that it could be assigned to the variable using an intrinsic assignment statement. The variable becomes initially defined with the value of the constant.

3. A variable, or the same part of a variable, must not be initialized more than once in an executable program.

4. None of the following may be initialized:

    a dummy argument
    an object made accessible by use or host association
    a function result
    an automatic object
    a pointer
    an allocatable array
    an object in a named common block, unless the data initialization
        is in a block data program unit
    an object in a blank common block
    an external or intrinsic procedure

5. For an object being initialized, any subscript, section subscript, substring starting point, or substring ending point must be an initialization expression.

6. Each component of a structure constructor used for initialization must be an initialization expression.

7. A variable that appears in a DATA statement and is thereby declared and typed implicitly may appear in a subsequent type declaration statement only if that declaration confirms the implicit declaration. An array name, array section, or array element appearing in a DATA statement must have had its array properties established previously.

8. An array element or structure component that appears in a DATA statement must not have a constant parent.

9. The DATA statement repeat factor must be positive or zero and if it is a named constant, the value must be specified in a prior statement in the same scoping unit when the DATA statement is encountered.

10. A subscript in an array element of an implied-do list must contain as operands only constants or DO variables of the containing implied-dos.

11. A scalar integer expression in an implied-do must contain as operands only constants or DO variables and each operation must be an intrinsic operation.

12. The data object list is expanded to form a sequence of scalar variables. An array or array section is equivalent to the sequence of its array elements in array element order. A data-implied-do is expanded to form a sequence of array elements and structure components, under the control of the implied-do variable, as in the DO construct. A zero-sized array or an implied-do with an iteration count of zero contributes no variables to the expanded list, but a character variable declared to have zero length does contribute a variable to the list.

13. The data value list is expanded to form a sequence of scalar constant values. Each value must be a constant that is known to the processor when the DATA statement is encountered. A DATA statement repeat factor indicates the number of times the following constant is to be included in the sequence. If the repeat factor is zero, the following constant is not included in the sequence.

14. Scalar variables and constant values of the expanded sequence must be in one-to-one correspondence. Each constant specifies the initial value for the corresponding variable. The lengths of the two expanded sequences must be the same.

For example:

• entity-oriented

```
CHARACTER (LEN = 10) :: NAME = "JOHN DOE"
INTEGER, DIMENSION (0:9) :: METERS = (/ (0, I = 1, 10) /)
TYPE (PERSON) :: ME = PERSON (21, "JOHN SMITH"), &
    YOU = PERSON (35, "FRED BROWN")
```

```
REAL :: SKEW(100,100) = RESHAPE ( (/ (1.0, K = 1,J-1), &
        ( 0.0, K = J,100 ), J = 1,100 /), (/ 100, 100 /) )
```

- attribute-oriented

```
CHARACTER (LEN = 10) NAME
INTEGER METERS
DIMENSION METERS (0:9)
DATA NAME / "JOHN DOE" /, METERS / 10*0 /
TYPE (PERSON) ME, YOU
DATA ME / PERSON (21, "JOHN SMITH") /
DATA YOU % AGE, YOU % NAME / 35, "FRED BROWN" /

REAL SKEW (100, 100)
DATA ((SKEW (K, J), K = 1, J-1), J = 1, 100) / 4950 * 1.0 /
DATA ((SKEW (K, J), K = J, 100), J = 1, 100) / 5050 * 0.0 /
```

In both forms, the character variable NAME is initialized with the value JOHN DOE with padding on the right because the length of the constant is less than the length of the variable. All ten elements of the integer array METERS are initialized to 0; an array constructor is used in the entity-oriented form; a repeat factor is used for the attribute-oriented form. ME and YOU are structures declared using the user-defined type PERSON defined in Section 4.6. In both forms ME is initialized using a structure constructor. In the attribute-oriented form YOU is initialized by supplying a separate value for each component.

In both forms, the two-dimensional array SKEW is initialized so that the lower triangle is 0 and the strict upper triangle is 1. The RESHAPE intrinsic function is required in the entity-oriented form because SKEW is of rank 2. Repeat factors are used in the attribute-oriented form.

5.5.2 PARAMETER Attribute and Statement

Constants may be given a name in a type declaration statement with the PARAMETER attribute or in a separate PARAMETER statement. A form for a type declaration statement with a PARAMETER attribute is:

type , PARAMETER [, attribute-list] :: name = initialization-expression

More than one named constant can be specified in a single type declaration statement; see the examples below. Other attributes that are allowed with the PARAMETER attribute are:

initialization (must be present)
DIMENSION

PRIVATE
PUBLIC
SAVE

The named constant becomes defined with the value determined from the initialization expression in accordance with the rules for intrinsic assignment. Any named constant that appears in the initialization expression must have been either: 1) defined previously in this type declaration statement or in a previous type declaration statement, or 2) otherwise made known to the processor (through host or use association).

The PARAMETER statement (R538) also provides a means of defining a named constant. It takes the form:

```
PARAMETER ( named-constant = initialization-expression   &
   [ , named-constant = initialization-expression ] ... )
```

Rules and restrictions:

1. The PARAMETER attribute must not be specified for dummy arguments, functions, or objects in a common block.

2. A named constant that appears in a PARAMETER statement and is thereby declared and typed implicitly may appear in a subsequent type declaration statement only if that declaration confirms the implicit declaration.

3. A named array constant appearing in a PARAMETER statement must have had its array properties established previously.

4. A named constant must not appear in a format specification because of a possible ambiguity.

For example:

- entity-oriented

```
INTEGER, PARAMETER :: STATES = 50
INTEGER, PARAMETER :: M = MOD (28, 3),  &
      NUMBER_OF_SENATORS = 2 * STATES
```

- attribute-oriented

```
INTEGER STATES, M, NUMBER_OF_SENATORS
PARAMETER (STATES = 50)
PARAMETER (M = MOD (28, 3),  &
      NUMBER_OF_SENATORS = 2 * STATES)
```

5.6 Object Accessibility and Use

Several attributes indicate where an object may be accessed and how it may be used. Some of these attributes apply only to objects in a module and others only to dummy arguments or other variables declared in a subprogram.

Entities specified in a module are generally available (PUBLIC attribute) to a program unit that contains a USE statement for the module, or they are restricted (PRIVATE attribute) to use in the module. The INTENT attribute determines the use of a dummy argument within a subprogram. The OPTIONAL attribute allows a subprogram argument to be omitted in a particular reference to the subprogram. The SAVE attribute preserves the values of variables between subprogram references.

5.6.1 PUBLIC and PRIVATE Accessibility

The PUBLIC and PRIVATE attributes control access to type definitions, variables, nonintrinsic functions, and named constants in a module. The PUBLIC attribute declares that entities in a module are available outside the module by use association; the PRIVATE attribute prevents access outside the module by use association. The default accessibility is PUBLIC, but it can be changed to PRIVATE.

Forms for type declaration statements with PUBLIC and PRIVATE attributes are:

```
type , PUBLIC [ , attribute-list ] :: entity-list
type , PRIVATE [ , attribute-list ] :: entity-list
```

PUBLIC and PRIVATE specifications may also appear in the derived-type statement of a derived-type definition to specify the accessibility of the type definition (4.4.1).

```
type , PUBLIC :: type-name
type , PRIVATE :: type-name
```

Further, if a PRIVATE statement without an access-id list appears inside a type definition, it specifies that, although the type may be accessible outside the module, its components are private.

Other attributes that are allowed with the PUBLIC and PRIVATE attributes in type declaration statements are:

initialization
ALLOCATABLE
DIMENSION
EXTERNAL
INTRINSIC

> PARAMETER
> POINTER
> TARGET
> SAVE

PUBLIC and PRIVATE statements provide another means for controlling the accessibility of variables, functions, type definitions, and named constants. In addition, PUBLIC and PRIVATE statements can control the accessibility of some entities that do not have a type and thus cannot appear in type declaration statements; these are nonintrinsic subroutines, generic specifiers, and namelist groups. Forms for PUBLIC and PRIVATE statements (R521) are:

> PUBLIC [[::] access-id-list]
> PRIVATE [[::] access-id-list]

where an access-id (R522) is one of:

> use-name
> generic-spec

A generic specification (R1206) is one of:

> generic-name
> OPERATOR (defined-operator)
> ASSIGNMENT (=)

Generic specifications are explained in Section 12.6. Examples of PUBLIC and PRIVATE statements that might be used with generic specifications are:

```
PUBLIC HYPERBOLIC_COS, HYPERBOLIC_SIN      ! generic names
PRIVATE HY_COS_RAT, HY_SIN_RAT             ! specific names
PRIVATE HY_COS_INF_PREC, HY_SIN_INF_PREC   ! specific names
PUBLIC :: OPERATOR ( .MYOP. ), OPERATOR (+), ASSIGNMENT (=)
```

Rules and restrictions:

1. PUBLIC and PRIVATE may appear only in a module.

2. A use name may be a variable, procedure, derived type, named constant, or namelist group.

3. Only one PUBLIC or PRIVATE statement with an omitted access-id list is permitted in the scoping unit of a module. It determines the default accessibility of the module.

4. A PRIVATE statement (but not a PUBLIC statement) may appear within a derived-type definition to indicate that the components of a structure of the type are not accessible outside the module.

5. A procedure that has a generic identifier that is public is accessible through the generic identifier even if its specific name is private.

6. A module procedure that has a private argument or function result must be private and must not have a generic identifier that is public.

The default accessibility of entities defined in a module is PUBLIC. A PUBLIC statement without an access-id list may appear in the module to confirm the default accessibility. A PRIVATE statement without an access-id list may appear in the module to change the default accessibility.

For example:

*   entity-oriented

```
REAL, PUBLIC :: GLOBAL_X
TYPE, PRIVATE :: LOCAL_DATA
   LOGICAL :: FLAG
   REAL, DIMENSION (100) :: DENSITY
END TYPE LOCAL_DATA
```

*   attribute-oriented

```
REAL GLOBAL_X
PUBLIC GLOBAL_X
TYPE LOCAL_DATA
   LOGICAL FLAG
   REAL DENSITY
   DIMENSION DENSITY (100)
END TYPE LOCAL_DATA
PRIVATE LOCAL_DATA
```

*   a public type with private components

```
TYPE LIST_ELEMENT
   PRIVATE
   REAL VALUE
   TYPE (LIST_ELEMENT), POINTER :: NEXT, FORMER
END TYPE LIST_ELEMENT
```

- changing the default accessibility

```
MODULE M
  PRIVATE
  REAL R, K, TEMP (100)   ! R, K, and TEMP are private
  REAL, PUBLIC :: A(100), B(100) ! A and B are public
  . . .
END MODULE M
```

5.6.2 INTENT Attribute and Statement

The INTENT attribute specifies the intended use of a dummy argument. If specified, it can help detect errors, provide information for readers of the program, and give the compiler information that can be used to make the code more efficient. It is particularly valuable in creating software libraries.

Some dummy arguments are referenced but not redefined within the subprogram; some are defined before being referenced within the subprogram; others may be referenced before being redefined. INTENT has three forms: IN, OUT, and INOUT which correspond respectively to the above three situations.

If the intent of an argument is IN, the subprogram must not change the value of the argument nor must the argument become undefined during the course of the subprogram. If the intent is OUT, the subprogram must not use the argument before it is defined, and it must be definable. If the intent is INOUT, the argument may be used to communicate information to the subprogram and return information; it must be defined on entry into the subprogram and must be definable. If no intent is specified, the use of the argument is subject to the limitations of the associated actual argument; for example, the actual argument may be a constant (for example, 2) or a more complicated expression (for example, $N+2$), and in these cases the dummy argument can only be referenced but not defined.

A form for a type declaration statement with an INTENT attribute is:

type , **INTENT** (intent-spec) [, attribute-list] **::** &
    dummy-argument-list

where an intent specification is IN, OUT, or INOUT.

Other attributes that are allowed with the INTENT attribute are:

DIMENSION
OPTIONAL
TARGET

The INTENT statement (R519) also provides a means of specifying an intent for an argument. It has the form:

INTENT (intent-spec) [**::**] dummy-argument-list

where an intent specification is one of:

IN
OUT
INOUT

Rules and restrictions:

1. The INTENT attribute may be specified only for dummy arguments.

2. An INTENT statement may appear only in the specification part of a subprogram or interface body.

3. An intent must not be specified for a dummy argument that is a dummy procedure because it is not possible to change the definition of a procedure. It would not be clear whether an intent specified for a dummy pointer applied to the pointer or to its target, so intent for a dummy pointer must not be specified either.

For example:

- entity-oriented

```
SUBROUTINE MOVE (FROM, TO)
   USE PERSON_MODULE
   TYPE (PERSON), INTENT (IN) :: FROM
   TYPE (PERSON), INTENT (OUT) :: TO
    . . .
SUBROUTINE SUB (X, Y)
   INTEGER, INTENT (INOUT) :: X, Y
    . . .
```

- attribute-oriented

```
SUBROUTINE MOVE (FROM, TO)
   USE PERSON_MODULE
   TYPE (PERSON) FROM, TO
   INTENT (IN) FROM
   INTENT (OUT) TO
    . . .
```

```
SUBROUTINE SUB (X, Y)
   INTEGER X, Y
   INTENT (INOUT) X, Y

   . . .
```

5.6.3 OPTIONAL Attribute and Statement

Sometimes there are procedures that are used most frequently to perform a special case of a more general calculation, but on occasion are called upon to perform the fully general calculation. In the more frequent special case, there are arguments that do not change from one invocation to the next, but in the general case, all the arguments are different. It is inconvenient to supply the same arguments for 90 percent of the invocations just to accommodate the 10 percent where the arguments are different. The OPTIONAL attribute allows a procedure reference to omit arguments with this attribute. Default values can then be used instead of the omitted arguments. The PRESENT intrinsic function can be used to test the presence of an optional argument in a particular invocation and this test can be used to control the subsequent processing in the procedure. If the argument is not present, a default value may be used or the subprogram may use an algorithm that is not based on the presence of the argument.

A form for a type declaration statement with an OPTIONAL attribute is:

type , OPTIONAL [, attribute-list] :: dummy-argument-list

Other attributes that are allowed with the OPTIONAL attribute are:

DIMENSION
EXTERNAL
INTENT
POINTER
TARGET

The OPTIONAL statement (R520) also provides a means for specifying an argument that may be omitted. It has the form:

OPTIONAL [::] dummy-argument-name-list

Rules and restrictions:

1. The OPTIONAL attribute may be specified only for dummy arguments.

2. An OPTIONAL statement may appear only in the scoping unit of a subprogram or interface body.

For example:

- entity-oriented declarations (in a program fragment)

```
CALL SORT_X (X = VECTOR_A)
   . . .

SUBROUTINE SORT_X (X, SIZEX, FAST)
   REAL, INTENT (INOUT) :: X (:)
   INTEGER, INTENT (IN), OPTIONAL :: SIZEX
   LOGICAL, INTENT (IN), OPTIONAL :: FAST
      . . .
   INTEGER TSIZE
      . . .
   IF (PRESENT (SIZEX)) THEN
      TSIZE = SIZEX
   ELSE
      TSIZE = SIZE (X)
   END IF
   IF (.NOT. PRESENT (FAST) .AND. TSIZE > 1000) THEN
      CALL QUICK_SORT (X)
   ELSE
      CALL BUBBLE_SORT (X)
   END IF
      . . .
```

- attribute-oriented declarations (to be inserted in the same program fragment)

```
SUBROUTINE SORT_X (X, SIZEX, FAST)
   REAL X (:)
   INTENT (INOUT) X
   INTEGER SIZEX
   LOGICAL FAST
   INTENT (IN) SIZEX, FAST
   OPTIONAL SIZEX, FAST
      . . .
   INTEGER TSIZE
      . . .
```

5.6.4 SAVE Attribute and Statement

Variables with the SAVE attribute retain their value and their definition, association, and allocation status after the subprogram in which they are declared completes execution. Variables without the SAVE attribute cannot be depended on to retain their value and status, although in some Fortran implementations all local variables and common blocks are treated as if they had the SAVE attribute. With virtual memory, multi-processors, and modern operating systems, this is becoming less common. The SAVE attribute should always be specified for an object or the object's common block, if it is necessary for the object to retain its value and status.

Objects declared in a module may be given the SAVE attribute, in which case they always retain their value and status when a procedure that uses the module completes execution.

Objects declared in recursive subprograms may be given the SAVE attribute. Such objects are shared by all instances of the subprogram.

Any object that is data initialized (in a DATA statement or a type declaration statement) has the SAVE attribute by default.

A form for a type declaration statement with a SAVE attribute is:

type **,** **SAVE** [**,** attribute-list] **::** entity-list

Other attributes that are allowed with the SAVE attribute are:

initialization
ALLOCATABLE
DIMENSION
PARAMETER
POINTER
PRIVATE
PUBLIC
TARGET

An object with the PARAMETER attribute (named constant) is always available, so there is no need to specify the SAVE attribute for it; however, it is not prohibited.

The SAVE statement (R523) provides a means for specifying the SAVE attribute for objects and also for common blocks. It has the form:

SAVE [[**::**] saved-entity-list]

where a saved entity (R524) is either of:

object-name
/ common-block-name **/**

Rules and restrictions:

1. A SAVE statement without a saved entity list is treated as though it contained the names of all items that could be saved in the scoping unit. No other SAVE statements or attributes may appear in the scoping unit.

2. If SAVE appears in a main program as an attribute or a statement, it has no effect.

3. The following objects must not be saved:

   > a procedure
   > a function result
   > a dummy argument
   > an automatic data object
   > an object in a common block
   > a namelist group

4. Variables in a common block cannot be saved individually; the entire common block must be saved if any variables in it are to be saved.

5. If a common block is saved in one scoping unit of a program, it must be saved in every scoping unit of the program in which it is defined (other than the main program).

6. If a named common block is specified in a main program, it is available to any scoping unit of the program that specifies the named common block; it does not need to be saved.

For example:

- entity-oriented

      CHARACTER (LEN = 12), SAVE :: NAME

- attribute-oriented

      CHARACTER (LEN = 12) NAME
      SAVE NAME

- saving objects and common blocks

      SAVE A, B, / BLOCKA /, C, / BLOCKB /

5.7 Procedure Properties

If an external or dummy procedure is to be an actual argument to a sub-program, the procedure name must be declared to be EXTERNAL. (A dummy procedure is a dummy argument that is a procedure.) If an external procedure has the same name as an intrinsic procedure, again the name must be declared to be EXTERNAL. When this occurs, the intrinsic procedure of that name is no longer accessible to that program unit. If an intrinsic procedure is to be an actual argument, the name of the procedure must be declared to be INTRINSIC. Sections 12.4.4 and 12.4.5 discuss further the usage of these attributes.

Because only functions, not subroutines, are declared to have a type (the type of the result), only function names can appear in type declaration statements. The EXTERNAL and INTRINSIC attributes in type declaration statements therefore apply only to functions. The EXTERNAL and INTRINSIC statements can be used to specify properties of subroutines (12.4.4, 12.4.5), and the EXTERNAL statement can specify block data program units (11.7).

Module procedures can have an accessibility attribute. They may be accessible outside the module (PUBLIC) or their accessibility may be restricted to the module in which they are defined (PRIVATE). See Section 5.6.1.

5.7.1 EXTERNAL Attribute and Statement

The EXTERNAL attribute is used to indicate that a name is the name of an external function or a dummy function and permits the name to be used as an actual argument.

A form for a type declaration statement with an EXTERNAL attribute is:

type , **EXTERNAL** [, attribute-list] :: function-name-list

Other attributes that are allowed with the EXTERNAL attribute are:

OPTIONAL
PRIVATE
PUBLIC

If a function returns an array or a pointer, the interface of the function must be explicit. Interface blocks are used to describe the interfaces of external functions. A function described by an interface block thus has the external attribute by default; it need not be declared explicitly.

The EXTERNAL statement (R1207) provides a means for declaring subroutines and block data program units, as well as functions, to be external. It has the form:

> **EXTERNAL** external-name-list

Rules and restrictions:

1. Each external name must be the name of an external procedure, a dummy argument, or a block data program unit.

2. If a dummy argument is specified to be EXTERNAL, the dummy argument is a dummy procedure.

3. An interface block specifies the external attribute (12.6.2) for all procedures in the interface block, with the exception of module procedures specified in MODULE PROCEDURE statements within the block. The attribute given by an interface block may be specified redundantly in an EXTERNAL statement.

For example:

- entity-oriented

```
SUBROUTINE SUB (FOCUS)
    INTEGER, EXTERNAL :: FOCUS
    LOGICAL, EXTERNAL :: SIN
```

- attribute-oriented

```
SUBROUTINE SUB (FOCUS)
    INTEGER FOCUS
    LOGICAL SIN
    EXTERNAL FOCUS, SIN
```

FOCUS is declared to be a dummy procedure. SIN is declared to be an external procedure. Both are functions. To declare an external subroutine, the EXTERNAL statement or an interface block must be used because a subroutine does not have a type, and thus its attributes cannot be specified in a type declaration statement. The specific name SIN of the intrinsic function SIN is no longer available to subroutine SUB.

5.7.2 INTRINSIC Attribute and Statement

The INTRINSIC attribute is used to indicate that a name is the name of an intrinsic function and permits the name to be used as an actual argument.

A form for a type declaration statement with an INTRINSIC attribute is:

> type , INTRINSIC [, attribute-list] :: intrinsic-function-name-list

Other attributes that are allowed with the INTRINSIC attribute are:

PRIVATE
PUBLIC

The INTRINSIC statement (R1208) provides a means for declaring intrinsic subroutines, as well as functions. Its form is:

INTRINSIC intrinsic-procedure-name-list

Rules and restrictions:

1. Each intrinsic procedure name must be the name of an intrinsic procedure.

2. Within a scoping unit, a name may be declared INTRINSIC only once.

3. A name must not be declared to be both EXTERNAL and INTRINSIC in a scoping unit.

4. A type may be specified for an intrinsic function even though it has a type as specified in Appendix A. If a type is specified for the generic name of an intrinsic function, it does not remove the generic properties of the function name.

5. The documentation provided with a compiler may specify intrinsic procedures in addition to the ones required by the standard. These procedures have the status of intrinsic procedures, but programs that use them may not be portable to other computer systems.

For example:

- entity-oriented

      ```
      REAL, INTRINSIC :: SIN, COS
      ```

- attribute-oriented

      ```
      REAL SIN, COS
      INTRINSIC SIN, COS
      ```

Because the interfaces of intrinsic procedures are explicit (known), it is not necessary to specify a type for them, but it is not incorrect to do so.

5.8 Automatic Data Objects

Automatic data objects are especially useful as working storage in a procedure. These objects may be declared only in procedures or procedure interfaces; they are created when the procedure is entered and disappear when the procedure completes execution. They can be created the same size as an argument to the procedure, so they can be tailored to each invocation.

There are two kinds of automatic data objects: automatic arrays of any type and objects of type character. Note that in Fortran 90 the term "automatic object" does not include noncharacter scalar local variables. For an array, the extents in each dimension are determined when the procedure is entered. For a character object, the length is determined when the procedure is entered. Apart from dummy arguments, this is the only character object whose length may vary. For arrays, extents may vary for allocatable arrays and array pointers as well as dummy arguments. An automatic object is not a dummy argument, but it is declared with a specification expression that is not a constant expression. The specification expression may be the length of the character object or the bounds of the array. Automatic objects cannot be saved or initialized. For example:

```
SUBROUTINE SWAP_ARRAYS (A, B, A_NAME, B_NAME)
   REAL, DIMENSION (:), INTENT (INOUT) :: A, B
   CHARACTER (LEN = *), INTENT(IN)     :: A_NAME, B_NAME

   REAL C (SIZE (A))
   CHARACTER (LEN = LEN (A_NAME) + LEN (B_NAME) + 17) &
      MESSAGE
   C = A
   A = B
   B = C
   MESSAGE = A_NAME // " and " // B_NAME // " are swapped"
   PRINT *, MESSAGE
END SUBROUTINE SWAP_ARRAYS
```

In the example, C is an automatic array and MESSAGE is an automatic character object.

5.9 NAMELIST Statement

A NAMELIST statement establishes the name for a collection of objects that can then be referenced by the group name in certain input/output statements. The form of the NAMELIST statement (R543) is:

```
NAMELIST / namelist-group-name / variable-name-list  &
    [ [ , ] / namelist-group-name / variable-name-list ] ...
```

Rules and restrictions:

1. A variable in the variable name list must not be an array dummy argument with nonconstant bounds, a variable with assumed character length, an automatic object, a pointer, an object of a type that has a pointer component at any level, an allocatable array, or a subobject of any of the preceding objects.

2. If a namelist group name has the PUBLIC attribute, no item in the namelist group object list may have the PRIVATE attribute.

3. The order in which the data objects (variables) are specified in the NAMELIST statement determines the order in which the values appear on output.

4. A namelist group name may occur in more than one NAMELIST statement in a scoping unit. The variable list following each successive appearance of the same namelist group name in a scoping unit is treated as a continuation of the list for that namelist group name.

5. A variable may be a member of more than one namelist group.

6. A variable either must have its type, type parameters, and shape specified previously in the same scoping unit, or must be determined by implicit typing rules. If a variable is typed by the implicit typing rules, its appearance in any subsequent type declaration statement must confirm this implicit type.

Examples of NAMELIST statements are:

```
NAMELIST / N_LIST / A, B, C
NAMELIST / S_LIST / A, V, W, X, Y, Z
```

5.10 Storage Association

In general, the physical storage units or storage order for data objects cannot be specified. However, the COMMON, EQUIVALENCE, and

SEQUENCE statements provide sufficient control over the order and layout of storage units to permit data to share storage units.

In Fortran 77, the COMMON statement provides the primary means of sharing data between program units. The EQUIVALENCE statement provides a means whereby two or more objects can share the same storage units. These two statements are powerful tools that can accomplish tasks for which no other mechanisms exist in Fortran 77, but they also permit the construction of programs that are difficult to understand and maintain.

In Fortran 90, modules, pointers, allocatable arrays, and automatic data objects provide more effective tools for sharing data and managing storage. The SEQUENCE statement has been introduced in Fortran 90 to define a storage order for structures. This permits structures to appear in common blocks and be equivalenced. The SEQUENCE statement can appear only in derived-type definitions to define sequence types. The components of a sequence type have an order in storage sequences that is the order of their appearance in the type definition.

The concept of storage association involves storage units and storage sequence. These concepts are used to explain how the COMMON and EQUIVALENCE mechanisms work. This description does not imply that any particular memory allocation scheme is required by a Fortran system, but the system must function as though storage were actually managed according to these descriptions.

5.10.1 Storage Units

In Fortran 77, there are only two kinds of storage units: numeric and character. Fortran 90 introduces new types (the nondefault types), user-defined types, and pointers. Objects of these types and pointers cannot be accommodated by the two storage units allowed in Fortran 77, and, in fact, it is not desirable to specify storage units for the space these objects occupy. Fortran 90 uses the term "unspecified storage unit" for these objects. A new Fortran 90 object (a pointer, an object of nondefault type, or a structure containing components that are of nondefault types or are pointers) is said to occupy an unspecified storage unit, but this unit is different for each different sort of object. If a processor provides a quadruple precision real type and a small-size logical type, they each occupy an unspecified storage unit, but the quadruple precision object will probably take more storage than the small-size logical object. A pointer occupies a single unspecified storage unit that is different from that of any nonpointer object and is different for each combination of type, type parameters, and rank.

There are two kinds of structures, sequence structures and nonsequence structures, depending on whether the type definition contains a SEQUENCE statement or not. A nonsequence structure occupies a single unspecified storage unit that is different for each type. There are three kinds of sequence structures:

1. numeric sequence structures (containing only numeric and logical entities of default kind)

2. character sequence structures (containing only character entities of default kind)

3. sequence structures (containing a mixture of components including objects that occupy numeric, character, and unspecified storage units)

Table 5-1 lists objects of various types and attributes and the storage units they occupy.

5.10.2 Storage Sequence

A storage sequence is an ordered sequence of storage units. The storage units may be elements in an array, characters in a character variable, components in a sequence structure, or variables in a common block. A sequence of storage sequences forms a composite storage sequence. The order of the storage units in such a composite sequence is the order of the units in each constituent taken in succession, ignoring any zero-sized sequences.

Storage is associated when the storage sequences of two different objects have some storage in common. This permits two or more variables to share the same storage. Two objects are **totally associated** if they have the same storage sequence; two objects are **partially associated** if they share some storage but are not totally associated.

5.10.3 EQUIVALENCE Statement

To indicate that two or more variables are to share storage, they may be placed in an equivalence set in an EQUIVALENCE statement. If the objects in an equivalence set have different types or type parameters, no conversion or mathematical relationship is implied. If a scalar and an array are equivalenced, the scalar does not have array properties and the array does not have the properties of a scalar. The form of the EQUIVALENCE statement (R545) is:

```
EQUIVALENCE ( equivalence-object , equivalence-object-list )   &
   [ , ( equivalence-object , equivalence-object-list ) ] ...
```

Table 5-1 Types and attributes and the storage units they occupy

Type and attributes of object	Storage units
Default integer	1 numeric
Default real	1 numeric
Default logical	1 numeric
Double precision	2 numeric
Default complex	2 numeric
Default character of length 1	1 character
Default character of length s	s character
Nondefault integer	1 unspecified
Real other than default real or double precision	1 unspecified
Nondefault logical	1 unspecified
Nondefault complex	1 unspecified
Nondefault character of length 1	1 unspecified
Nondefault character of length s	s unspecified
Nonsequence structure	1 unspecified
Numeric sequence structure	n numeric, where n is the number of numeric storage units the structure occupies
character sequence structure	n character, where n is the number of character storage units the structure occupies
Sequence structure	1 unspecified
Any type with the pointer attribute	1 unspecified
Any intrinsic or sequence type with the dimension attribute	The size of the array times the number of storage units for the type (will appear in array element order)
Any nonintrinsic, nonsequence type with the dimension attribute	Unspecified number of unspecified storage units
Any type with the pointer attribute and the dimension attribute	1 unspecified

where an equivalence object (R547) is one of:

variable-name
array-element
substring

Rules and restrictions:

1. An equivalence object must not be:

    a dummy argument
    a pointer
    an allocatable array

a nonsequence structure
a structure containing a pointer at any level
an automatic object
a function name, result name, or entry name
a named constant
a subobject of any of the above

2.   An equivalence set list must contain at least two items.

3.   Any subscripts and subscript ranges must be integer initialization expressions.

4.   If an equivalence object is of type default integer, default real, double precision real, default complex, default logical, or numeric sequence type, all of the objects in the set must be of these types.

5.   If an equivalence object is of type default character or character sequence type, all of the objects in the set must be of these types. The lengths do not need to be the same.

6.   If an equivalence object is of sequence type other than numeric or character sequence type, all of the objects in the set must be of the same type.

7.   If an equivalence object is of intrinsic type other than default integer, default real, double precision real, default complex, default logical, or default character, all of the objects in the set must be of the same type with the same kind type parameter value.

8.   The use of an array name unqualified by a subscript list in an equivalence set specifies the first element of the array; that is, A means the first element of A.

9.   An EQUIVALENCE statement must not specify that the same storage unit is to occur more than once in a storage sequence. For example, the following is illegal because it would indicate that storage for X(2) and X(3) is shared.

    ```
    EQUIVALENCE (A, X (2)), (A, X (3))
    ```

10. An EQUIVALENCE statement must not specify the sharing of storage units between objects declared in different scoping units.

An EQUIVALENCE statement specifies that the storage sequences of the data objects in an equivalence set are storage associated. All of the nonzero-sized sequences in the set, if any, have the same first storage unit, and all of the zero-sized sequences, if any, are storage associated with one another and with the first storage unit of any nonzero-sized sequences. This causes storage association of the objects in the set and may cause storage association of other data objects.

For example:

```
CHARACTER (LEN = 4) :: A, B
CHARACTER (LEN = 3) :: C (2)
EQUIVALENCE (A, C (1)), (B, C (2))
```

causes the alignment illustrated below:

A(1:1)	A(2:2)	A(3:3)	A(4:4)				
			B(1:1)	B(2:2)	B(3:3)	B(4:4)	
C(1)(1:1)	C(1)(2:2)	C(1)(3:3)	C(2)(1:1)	C(2)(2:2)	C(2)(3:3)		

As a result, the fourth character of A, the first character of B, and the first character of C(2) all share the same character storage unit.

```
REAL, DIMENSION (6) :: X, Y
EQUIVALENCE (X (5), Y(3))
```

causes the alignment illustrated below:

X(1)	X(2)	X(3)	X(4)	X(5)	X(6)		
		Y(1)	Y(2)	Y(3)	Y(4)	Y(5)	Y(6)

5.10.4 COMMON Statement

The COMMON statement establishes blocks of storage called **common blocks** and specifies objects that are contained in the blocks. Two or more program units may share this space and thus share the values of variables stored in the space. Thus, the COMMON statement provides a global data facility based on storage association. Common blocks may be named, in which case they are called **named common blocks**, or may be unnamed, in which case they are called **blank common**.

Fortran 77 restricts a common block to contain only numeric storage units or to contain only character storage units. Fortran 90 relaxes this restriction. Common blocks may contain mixtures of storage units and may contain unspecified storage units; however, if a common block contains a mixture of storage units, every declaration of the common block in the program must contain the same sequence of storage units, thereby matching types, kind type parameters, and attributes (dimension and pointer). The form of the COMMON statement (R548) is:

COMMON [/ [common-block-name] /] common-block-object-list &
   [[,] / [common-block-name] / common-block-object-list] ...

where a common block object (R549) is:

   variable-name [(explicit-shape-spec-list)]

Rules and restrictions:

1. A common block object must not be:

        a dummy argument
        an allocatable array
        a nonsequence structure
        an automatic object
        a function name, result name, or entry name

2. The appearance of two slashes with no common block name between them declares the objects in the following object list to be in blank common.

3. A common block name or an indication of blank common may appear more than once in one or more COMMON statements in the same scoping unit. The object list following each successive block name or blank common indication is treated as a continuation of the previous object list.

4. A variable may appear in only one common block within a scoping unit.

5. If a variable appears with an explicit-shape specification list, it is an array, and each bound must be a constant specification expression.

6. If a variable appears with a deferred-shape specification list, it is a pointer array and must be given the POINTER attribute in the scoping unit. It must not be an allocatable array.

7. A nonpointer object of type default integer, default real, double precision real, default complex, default logical, or numeric sequence type must become associated only with nonpointer objects of these types.

8. A nonpointer object of type default character or character sequence must become associated only with nonpointer objects of these types.

9. If an object of numeric sequence or character sequence type appears in a common block, it is as if the individual components were enumerated in order directly in the common block object list.

10. A nonpointer object of sequence type other than numeric or character sequence type must become associated only with nonpointer objects of the same type.

11. A nonpointer object of intrinsic type other than default integer, default real, double precision real, default complex, default logical, or default character must become associated only with nonpointer objects of the same type with the same kind type parameter value.

12. A pointer must become associated only with pointers of the same type, type parameters, and rank.

13. Only a named common block may be saved, not individual variables in the common block.

For each common block, a common block storage sequence is formed. It consists of the sequence of storage units of all the variables listed for the common block in the order of their appearance in the common block list. The storage sequence may be extended (on the end) to include the storage units of any variable equivalenced to a variable in the common block. Data objects storage associated with a variable in a common block are considered to be in that common block. The size of a common block is the size of its storage sequence including any extensions of the sequence resulting from equivalence association.

Within an executable program, the common block storage sequences of all nonzero-sized common blocks with the same name have the same first storage unit and must have the same size. Zero-sized common blocks are permitted. Frequently a program is written with array extents and character lengths specified by named constants. When there is a need for a different-sized data configuration, the values of the named constants can be changed and the program recompiled. Allowing extents and lengths to be specified to have the value zero, and thus possibly specifying zero-length common blocks, permits the maximum generality. All zero-sized common blocks with the same name are storage associated with one another. The same is true of all blank common blocks except that because they may be of different sizes, it is possible for a zero-sized blank common block in one scoping unit to be associated with the first storage unit of a nonzero-sized blank common block in another scoping unit. In this way, many subprograms may use the same storage. They may specify common blocks to communicate global values or to reuse and thus conserve storage.

A blank common block has the same properties as a named common block except for the following:

1. Variables in blank common must not be initially defined.

2. Blank common is always saved; a named common block is not saved unless it is mentioned in a SAVE statement.

3. Named common blocks of the same name must be the same size in all scoping units of a program. Blank common blocks may be of different sizes.

For example:

```
SUBROUTINE FIRST

    INTEGER, PARAMETER :: SHORT = 2
    REAL B(2)
    COMPLEX C
    LOGICAL FLAG
    TYPE COORDINATES
       SEQUENCE
       REAL X, Y
       LOGICAL Z_0        ! zero origin?
    END TYPE COORDINATES
    TYPE (COORDINATES) P
    COMMON / REUSE / B, C, FLAG, P

    REAL MY_VALUES (100)
    CHARACTER (LEN = 20) EXPLANATION
    COMMON / SHARE / MY_VALUES, EXPLANATION
    SAVE / SHARE /

    REAL, POINTER :: W (:, :)
    REAL, TARGET, DIMENSION (100, 100) :: EITHER, OR
    INTEGER (SHORT) :: M (2000)
    COMMON / MIXED / W, EITHER, OR, M
        . . .
```

```
SUBROUTINE SECOND

    INTEGER, PARAMETER :: SHORT = 2
    INTEGER I(8)
    COMMON / REUSE / I

    REAL MY_VALUES (100)
    CHARACTER (LEN = 20) EXPLANATION
    COMMON / SHARE / MY_VALUES, EXPLANATION
    SAVE / SHARE /

    REAL, POINTER :: V (:)
    REAL, TARGET, DIMENSION (10000) :: ONE, ANOTHER
    INTEGER (SHORT) :: M (2000)
    COMMON / MIXED / V, ONE, ANOTHER, M    ! ILLEGAL
        . . .
```

Common block REUSE has a storage sequence of 8 numeric storage units. It is being used to conserve storage. The storage referenced in subroutine FIRST is associated with the storage referenced in subroutine SECOND as shown below:

B(1)	B(2)	C		FLAG	X	Y	Z_O
I(1)	I(2)	I(3)	I(4)	I(5)	I(6)	I(7)	I(8)

There is no guarantee that the storage is actually retained and reused because, in the absence of a SAVE attribute for REUSE, some processors may release the storage when either of the subroutines completes execution.

Common block SHARE contains both numeric and character storage units and is being used to share data between subroutines FIRST and SECOND.

The declaration of common block MIXED in subroutine SECOND is illegal because it does not have the same sequence of storage units as the declaration of MIXED in subroutine FIRST. The array pointer in FIRST has two dimensions; the array pointer in SECOND has only one. With common blocks, it is the sequence of storage units that must match, not the names of variables.

5.10.5 Restrictions on Common and Equivalence

An EQUIVALENCE statement must not cause two different common blocks to become associated and must not cause a common block to be extended by adding storage units preceding the first storage unit of the common block.

For example:

```
COMMON A (5)
REAL B (5)
EQUIVALENCE (A (2), B (1))
```

is legal and results in the following alignment:

A(1)	A(2)	A(3)	A(4)	A(5)	
	B(1)	B(2)	B(3)	B(4)	B(5)

On the other hand, the following is not legal:

```
EQUIVALENCE (A (1), B (2))
```

because it would place B (1) ahead of A (1) as in the following alignment:

	A(1)	A(2)	A(3)	A(4)	A(5)
B(1)	B(2)	B(3)	B(4)	B(5)	

and a common block must not be extended from the beginning of the block.

COMMON and EQUIVALENCE statements may appear in a module. If a common block is declared in a module, it must not also be declared in a scoping unit that accesses the module. The name of a PUBLIC data object from a module must not appear in a COMMON or EQUIVALENCE statement in any scoping unit that has access to the data object.

5.11 Summary

Declarations are used to specify the attributes and relationships of the entities in a program. Variables, functions, and named constants have a type which is the most important of the attributes.

Type

Fortran 90 has five intrinsic types and permits users to define additional types. The types are:

    integer
    real
    complex
    logical
    character
    user-defined

The following are type declaration statements:

```
REAL (KIND = HIGH) ROOT, ANSWER
INTEGER INDEX, SELECTOR, COUNTER
TYPE (VEHICLE) CAR, BIKE, TRAIN
CHARACTER (LEN = STRING_LEN) WORK_STRING
```

The only character objects that may have a length that is specified as a variable are dummy arguments and automatic character variables in a procedure. The length is determined each time the procedure is invoked.

If there is no type declaration for a variable, named constant, or function, its type is determined implicitly by the first letter of its name. Unless there is an IMPLICIT NONE statement in the scoping unit, there is a default mapping for each letter to one of the permissible types. IMPLICIT statements may be used to change the default mapping rules. In the absence of any other mapping, it is as if the following IMPLICIT statements defined the mapping:

```
IMPLICIT REAL (A-H, O-Z)
IMPLICIT INTEGER (I-M)
```

Entities such as subroutines, common blocks, and namelist groups do not have a type but may possess other attributes.

Other Attributes

There are 12 other attributes, as well as initialization, for variables. In general, attributes may be specified in type declaration statements (entity-oriented form) or in separate attribute declaration statements (attribute-oriented form). For example:

- entity-oriented

```
INTEGER, TARGET, SAVE :: SCORES (50)
INTEGER, POINTER :: TEAM (:)
```

- attribute-oriented

```
INTEGER SCORES (50), TEAM (:)
TARGET SCORES
SAVE SCORES
POINTER TEAM
```

Initialization and the DATA Statement. A variable is given an initial value (that may change during program execution) in a type declaration statement or in a separate DATA statement. For example:

- entity-oriented

```
REAL :: DELTA = .01
LOGICAL, SAVE :: STATES(3) = (/.TRUE.,.FALSE.,.FALSE./)
```

- attribute-oriented

```
REAL DELTA
LOGICAL STATES(3)
SAVE STATES
DATA DELTA /.01/, STATES / (/.TRUE.,.FALSE.,.FALSE./) /
```

ALLOCATABLE. An array may have the ALLOCATABLE attribute. No space is set aside for such an array until an ALLOCATE statement, specifying the extent of each dimension, is executed. A DEALLOCATE statement may be executed to release the space. Such an array may be declared as:

- entity-oriented

```
REAL, ALLOCATABLE :: MATRIX_X (:, :), MATRIX_Y (:, :)
```

- attribute-oriented

```
REAL MATRIX_X (:, :), MATRIX_Y (:, :)
ALLOCATABLE MATRIX_X, MATRIX_Y
```

DIMENSION. An array has the DIMENSION attribute. There are four ways to declare arrays:

- with explicit shape

- with assumed shape

- with deferred shape

- with assumed size

An explicit-shape array is declared with all upper bounds specified. The only arrays that may have a dimension specified by a variable are dummy arguments and automatic arrays in a procedure. In these cases, the extents are determined each time the procedure is invoked.

An assumed-shape array is a dummy argument that takes its shape from the actual argument. The interface of the procedure in which the dummy argument appears must be explicit in the scope of the procedure reference.

A deferred-shape array must have the POINTER or ALLOCATABLE attribute. If an array argument or array function result has the POINTER attribute, the interface of the procedure must be explicit in the scope of the procedure reference.

An assumed-size array is a dummy argument with an asterisk (*) as its last dimension and explicit upper bounds for all other dimensions. The interface of the procedure in which the dummy argument appears need not be explicit in the scope of the procedure reference.

There are some limitations on appearances in a program of arrays declared in each of these four ways. Table 5-2 gives a partial summary of the allowable appearances.

There are several ways to specify an array. It may be specified by a DIMENSION attribute in a type declaration statement or in a separate DIMENSION statement; or it may be specified by attaching the dimension specification to the array name in a type declaration, ALLOCATABLE, COMMON, POINTER, or TARGET statement. For example:

- entity-oriented

```
REAL, DIMENSION(:,:), ALLOCATABLE :: MX_X, MX_Y
COMPLEX (HIGH), SAVE :: HYPER_SPACE (20,20,20,20)
LOGICAL, INTENT(IN) :: MASK1(SIZE(ARG1))
```

Table 5-2 Partial summary of allowable appearances of arrays declared in each of the four ways

	An array declared with			
May appear as a	Explicit shape	Assumed shape	Deferred shape	Assumed size
Primary in an expression	Yes	Yes	Yes	No
Vector subscript	Yes	Yes	Yes	No
Dummy argument	Yes	Yes	Yes[1]	Yes
Actual argument	Yes	Yes	Yes	Yes
Equivalence object	Yes	No	No	No
Common object	Yes	No	Yes[1]	No
Namelist object	Yes[2]	No	No	No
Saved object	Yes[2]	No	Yes	No
Data initialized object	Yes[2]	No	No	No
I/O list item	Yes	Yes	Yes	No
Format	Yes	Yes	Yes	Yes
Internal file	Yes	Yes	Yes	No
Allocate object	No	No	Yes	No
Pointer object in pointer assignment statement	No	No	Yes[1]	No
Target object in pointer assignment statement	Yes	Yes	Yes	No

[1] Must have the POINTER attribute

[2] Must have constant bounds

- attribute-oriented

```
REAL MX_X, MX_Y
COMPLEX (HIGH) HYPER_SPACE (20,20,20,20)
LOGICAL MASK1 (SIZE(ARG1))
DIMENSION MX_X (:, :), MX_Y (:, :)
ALLOCATABLE MX_X, MX_Y
SAVE HYPER_SPACE
INTENT (IN) MASK
```

EXTERNAL and INTRINSIC. These attributes permit the names of external or intrinsic procedures to be actual arguments in subroutine calls and function references. If the procedure is a subroutine, then the attribute must be specified in an EXTERNAL or INTRINSIC statement because subroutines must not appear in type declaration statements. The type of an intrinsic function is known to the processor, but it may be specified in a type declaration statement as well. For example:

- entity-oriented

```
REAL, EXTERNAL :: INVERT
EXTERNAL MY_SUB
COMPLEX, INTRINSIC :: CSIN, CCOS
```

- attribute-oriented

```
REAL INVERT
EXTERNAL INVERT, MY_SUB
INTRINSIC CSIN, CCOS
```

INTENT. The INTENT attribute specifies the intended use of a dummy argument. There are three possible intents: IN, OUT, and INOUT. For example:

- entity-oriented

```
INTEGER, INTENT (IN) :: SIGNAL (N)
REAL, INTENT (OUT) :: SOLUTION
COMPLEX, INTENT (INOUT) :: CX_VAL
```

- attribute-oriented

```
INTEGER SIGNAL (N)
REAL SOLUTION
COMPLEX CX_VAL
INTENT (IN) SIGNAL
INTENT (OUT) SOLUTION
INTENT (INOUT) CX_VAL
```

OPTIONAL. If a dummy argument has the OPTIONAL attribute, the corresponding actual argument may be omitted from a reference to the procedure. The PRESENT intrinsic function may be used within the procedure to inquire about the presence of the actual argument. Thus, it is possible to establish defaults within a procedure that may be reset when an optional argument is actually present. Example declarations are:

- entity-oriented

```
REAL, INTENT (IN), OPTIONAL :: ORIGIN (2)
CHARACTER (*), OPTIONAL :: REPLY
```

- attribute-oriented

  ```
  REAL ORIGIN (2)
  CHARACTER (*) REPLY
  INTENT (IN) ORIGIN
  OPTIONAL ORIGIN, REPLY
  ```

PARAMETER. If an object has the PARAMETER attribute, it is a named constant. As with any constant, its value does not change during execution. The value of a named constant may be specified in a type declaration statement or in a separate PARAMETER statement.

- entity-oriented

  ```
  REAL, PARAMETER :: PI = 3.14159
  TYPE (COLOR), PARAMETER :: &
        MAUVE = COLOR (12, 22, 3, "mauve")
  ```

- attribute-oriented

  ```
  REAL PI
  TYPE (COLOR) MAUVE
  PARAMETER ( PI = 3.14159,  &
        MAUVE = COLOR (12, 22, 3, "mauve") )
  ```

POINTER. An object with the POINTER attribute has no space set aside for it until an ALLOCATE statement is executed for the pointer or the pointer is assigned to point to existing space. An object that is accessed by a pointer is called the target of the pointer. The pointer's target may change during program execution. Examples of pointer declarations are:

- entity-oriented

  ```
  REAL, POINTER :: BUFFER (10000)
  TYPE (LINK), POINTER :: HEAD_OF_CHAIN
  ```

- attribute-oriented

  ```
  REAL BUFFER (10000)
  TYPE (LINK) HEAD_OF_CHAIN
  POINTER BUFFER, HEAD_OF_CHAIN
  ```

PUBLIC and PRIVATE. A programmer can control the accessibility of entities specified in a module. The default accessibility of module entities is PUBLIC, but it can be changed to PRIVATE by the insertion of a PRIVATE statement after the MODULE statement. Accessibility of the following entities can be controlled:

> variables
> functions
> named constants
> type definitions
> subroutines
> generic procedures
> namelist groups

There are two ways to specify accessibility individually for variables, functions, and named constants: with PUBLIC and PRIVATE attributes in type declaration statements or with PUBLIC and PRIVATE statements. There are two ways to specify accessibility for a type definition: with a PUBLIC or PRIVATE attribute in the derived-type statement of the definition or with a PUBLIC or PRIVATE statement containing the type name. Further, the type name may be public, but the components kept private by the insertion of a PRIVATE statement following the derived-type statement in the type definition. There is only one way to specify accessibility for subroutines, generic procedures, and namelist groups: with a PUBLIC or PRIVATE statement containing their names. Examples of declarations of accessibility for two objects and for a type are:

- entity-oriented

```
CHARACTER (10), PUBLIC, SAVE :: ACCESS_NAME = "ALPHA"
CHARACTER (10), PRIVATE :: PASSWORD = "rosebud"
TYPE, PRIVATE :: VEHICLE
    INTEGER         NO_WHEELS
    CHARACTER (10)  FUEL
    REAL            WEIGHT
END TYPE VEHICLE
```

- attribute-oriented

```
CHARACTER (10) ACCESS_NAME, PASSWORD
DATA ACCESS_NAME /"ALPHA"/, PASSWORD /"rosebud"/
```

```
TYPE :: VEHICLE
    INTEGER        NO_WHEELS
    CHARACTER (10) FUEL
    REAL           WEIGHT
END TYPE VEHICLE
PRIVATE PASSWORD, VEHICLE
PUBLIC ACCESS_NAME
SAVE ACCESS_NAME
```

SAVE. Local variables and data in named common blocks are not necessarily saved when a subprogram completes execution. To guarantee that they are, the variables and common blocks must have the SAVE attribute. Because common blocks have no type, the SAVE statement must be used to give the attribute to them. Examples of such declarations are:

- entity-oriented

```
INTEGER, SAVE :: NO_OF_WEIGHTS, NO_OF_MEASURES
```

- attribute-oriented

```
INTEGER NO_OF_WEIGHTS, NO_OF_MEASURES
SAVE NO_OF_WEIGHTS, NO_OF_MEASURES
SAVE /BLOCK1/, /BLOCK2/
```

TARGET. If an object has the TARGET attribute, it may become a pointer target. If it does not have the TARGET attribute (and is not a pointer), it can never be referenced by a pointer. This knowledge gives the processor much more leeway in the optimization of code. An allocatable array may have the TARGET attribute. Example TARGET declarations are:

- entity-oriented

```
LOGICAL, ALLOCATABLE, TARGET :: MASK (:, :)
REAL, TARGET :: COEFFICIENTS
```

- attribute-oriented

```
LOGICAL MASK (:, :)
REAL COEFFICIENTS
ALLOCATABLE MASK
TARGET MASK, COEFFICIENTS
```

Attribute Compatibility. No single entity can possess all of the attributes because some attributes are incompatible with others. For example, OPTIONAL is an attribute that can be applied only to dummy arguments, and dummy arguments must not have the SAVE attribute. Table 5-3 shows which attributes may be used together to specify an entity.

Table 5-3 Attribute compatibility. If two attributes can appear in the same type declaration statement, a check mark appears at their intersection in the chart. A cross indicates incompatibility.

Attribute compatibility	Initialization	ALLOCATABLE	DIMENSION	EXTERNAL	INTENT	INTRINSIC	OPTIONAL	PARAMETER	POINTER	PRIVATE	PUBLIC	SAVE	TARGET
Initialization		✕	✓	✕	✕	✕	✕	✓	✕	✓	✓	✓	✓
ALLOCATABLE	✕		✓	✕	✕	✕	✕	✕	✕	✓	✓	✓	✓
DIMENSION	✓	✓		✕	✓	✕	✓	✓	✓	✓	✓	✓	✓
EXTERNAL	✕	✕	✕		✕	✕	✓	✕	✕	✓	✓	✕	✕
INTENT	✕	✕	✓	✕		✕	✓	✕	✕	✕	✕	✕	✓
INTRINSIC	✕	✕	✕	✕	✕		✕	✕	✕	✓	✓	✕	✕
OPTIONAL	✕	✕	✓	✓	✓	✕		✕	✓	✕	✕	✕	✓
PARAMETER	✓	✕	✓	✕	✕	✕	✕		✕	✓	✓	✓	✕
POINTER	✕	✕	✓	✕	✕	✕	✓	✕		✓	✓	✓	✕
PRIVATE	✓	✓	✓	✓	✕	✓	✕	✓	✓		✕	✓	✓
PUBLIC	✓	✓	✓	✓	✕	✓	✕	✓	✓	✕		✓	✓
SAVE	✓	✓	✓	✕	✕	✕	✕	✓	✓	✓	✓		✓
TARGET	✓	✓	✓	✕	✓	✕	✓	✕	✕	✓	✓	✓	

Relationships

Other statements are used to declare relationships among objects.

NAMELIST

A NAMELIST statement specifies a name for a list of objects so that the entire list of objects can be referenced simply by the name in certain input/output statements. For example:

```
NAMELIST /MY_GROUP/ FRIENDS, ROMANS, COUNTRYMEN
```

EQUIVALENCE

The EQUIVALENCE statement is used to indicate that a group of variables share storage. For example:

```
EQUIVALENCE (FIRST_A, A(1,1,1)), (LAST_A, A(100,100,100))
```

COMMON

The COMMON statement is used to specify a name for a block of storage and to declare objects that are contained in the block. Two or more program units may declare the same named common block, and thus they can share the values of variables contained in the block. Fortran 90 permits objects of numeric type and objects of character type to appear in the same common block. Fortran 90 also permits pointers, sequence structures, and objects of nondefault type to appear in common blocks, as long as each specification of the common block contains the same sequence of storage units. For example:

```
TYPE LINK
   REAL VALUE
   TYPE (LINK) NEXT
END TYPE LINK
CHARACTER (20) NAME_OF_SPARSE_ARRAY
LOGICAL (KIND = BIT) MASK (1000, 1000)
TYPE (LINK) HEAD_OF_CHAIN, END_OF_CHAIN
     . . .
COMMON /SPARSE_ARRAY/ NAME_OF_SPARSE_ARRAY, MASK, &
      HEAD_OF_CHAIN, END_OF_CHAIN
```

F9◑

6

Using Data

Chapter 5 explained how data objects are created and how their attributes are specified. Chapter 6 goes further and explains how these objects can be used. To use a data object, its name or designator must appear in a Fortran statement. The appearance of the name or designator where its value is required is a **reference** to the object. When an object is referenced, it must be **defined**; that is, it must have a value. The reference makes use of the value. For example:

```
A = 1.0
B = A + 4.0
```

In the first statement, the constant value 1.0 is assigned to the variable A. It does not matter whether A was previously defined with a value or not; it now has a value and can be referenced in an executable statement. In the second statement, A is referenced; its value is obtained and added to the constant 4.0 to obtain a value that is then assigned to the variable B. The appearances of A in the first statement and B in the second statement are not considered to be references because their values are not required. The appearance of A in the second statement is a reference.

A data object may be a constant or a variable. If it is a constant, either a literal or a named constant, its value will not change. If it is a variable, it may take on different values as program execution proceeds. Variables and constants may be scalar objects (with a single value) or arrays (with any number of values, all of the same type).

Variables generally have storage space set aside for them by the compiler and are always found in the same place. If, however, the variable is a pointer or an allocatable array, the compiler does not set aside any space. The programmer must allocate space or, in the case of a pointer, the programmer might assign existing space.

Arrays are said to be dynamic if their size as well as their position may change. Automatic arrays were discussed in Section 5.8; they are created on entry to a procedure and their size and location are determined at that time. Allocatable arrays or pointer arrays may change size as well as location. The declared rank cannot change, but the extents of the dimensions may change with each reallocation or pointer assignment.

If a variable or constant is a portion of another object, it is called a **subobject**. A subobject is one of:

an array element
an array section
a structure component
a substring

A variable is referenced by its name, whereas a subobject is referenced by a designator. A **designator** indicates the portion of an object that is being referenced. Each subobject is considered to have a **parent** and is a portion of the parent. Each of the subobjects is described in this chapter; first, substrings and structure components, and then array subobjects (array elements and array sections) along with the use of subscripts, subscript triplets, and vector subscripts. A number of additional aspects of arrays are covered: array terminology, use of whole arrays, and array element order.

A reference to a variable or subobject is called a **data reference**. There are guidelines for determining whether a particular data reference is classified as a character string, character substring, structure component, array, array element, or array section. These classifications are perhaps of more interest to compiler writers than to users of the language, but knowing how a data reference is classified makes it clearer which rules and restrictions apply to the reference and easier to understand some of the explanations for the formation of expressions. Briefly, character strings and substrings must be of type character. Arrays have the dimension attribute. Some data references may be classified as both structure components and arrays sections. In general, if a data reference contains a percent, it is a structure component, but its actual classification may be determined by other factors such as a section subscript or the rightmost element of the reference. If a substring range appears in a data reference, it must appear at the right end of the reference, and the reference is considered to be a substring unless some component of the reference is an array section, in which case the data reference is considered to be an array section that just happens to have elements that are substrings. For a component reference to be classified as an array element, every component must have rank zero and a subscript list must appear at the right end of the reference. Sections 6.1 through 6.4.5 contain many examples that demonstrate how these guidelines for classification apply.

Finally, Chapter 6 explains how pointers and allocatable arrays can be created and released by using ALLOCATE and DEALLOCATE statements. In addition, pointers can be disassociated from any target object by using the NULLIFY statement.

6.1 Constants and Variables

A constant has a value that cannot change; it may be a literal constant or a named constant (parameter). As explained in Chapter 4, each of the intrinsic types has a form that specifies the type, type parameters, and value of a literal constant of the type. For user-defined types, there is a structure constructor to specify values of the type. If all of the components of a value are constants, the resulting derived-type value is a constant expression. Array constructors are used to form array values of any intrinsic or user-defined type. If all array elements are constant values, the resulting array is a constant array expression. A reference to a constant is always permitted, but a constant cannot be redefined.

A variable has a name such as A or a designator such as B(I), and may or may not have a value. If it does not have a value, it must not be referenced. A variable (R601) may be one of the following:

    scalar-variable-name
    array-variable-name
    subobject

where a subobject (R602) is one of:

    array-element
    array-section
    structure-component
    substring

Rules and restrictions:

1. Variables may be of any type. There are contexts in which a variable must be of a certain type. In some of these cases, terms, such as logical-variable, character-variable, or default-character-variable, provide precise limitations.

2. A subobject with a constant parent is not a variable.

A single object of any of the intrinsic or user-defined types is a scalar. A set of scalar objects, all of the same type and type parameters, may be arranged in a pattern involving columns, rows, planes, and higher-dimensioned configurations to form arrays. An array has a rank between one and seven; a Fortran processor is not required to support the processing of arrays of rank greater than seven. A scalar has rank zero. In simple terms, an array is an object with the DIMENSION attribute; a scalar is not an array.

For example, given the declarations:

```
TYPE PERSON
   INTEGER AGE
   CHARACTER (LEN = 40) NAME
END TYPE PERSON

TYPE(PERSON) FIRECHIEF, FIREMEN(50)
CHARACTER (20) DISTRICT, STATIONS(10)
```

the following data references are classified as indicated by the comments on each line.

```
DISTRICT            ! character string
DISTRICT(1:6)       ! substring
FIRECHIEF % AGE     ! structure component
FIREMEN % AGE       ! array of integers
STATIONS            ! array of character strings
STATIONS(1)         ! array element (character string)
STATIONS(1:4)       ! array section of character strings
```

A subobject may have a constant parent, for example:

```
CHARACTER (*), PARAMETER :: MY_DISTRICT = "DISTRICT 13"
CHARACTER (2) DISTRICT_NUMBER
DISTRICT_NUMBER = MY_DISTRICT (10:11)
```

DISTRICT_NUMBER has the value 13, a character string of length 2.

6.2 Substrings

A **character string** consists of zero or more characters. Even though it is made up of individual characters, a character string is considered to be scalar. As with any data type, it is possible to declare an array of character strings, all of the same length.

A **substring** is a contiguous portion of a character string that has a starting point and an ending point within the character string. It is possible to reference a substring of a character scalar variable or constant. The form of a substring (R609) is:

parent-string (substring-range)

where a parent string (R610) is one of:

scalar-variable-name
array-element
scalar-structure-component
scalar-constant

and a substring range (R611) is:

[starting-position] : [ending-position]

The starting position and ending position must be scalar integer expressions.

Rules and restrictions:

1. The parent string of a substring must be of type character. The substring is of type character.

2. A substring is the contiguous sequence of characters within the string beginning with the character at the starting position and ending at the ending position. If the starting position is omitted, the default is 1; if the ending position is omitted, the default is the length of the character string.

3. The length of a character string or substring may be 0, but not negative. Zero-length strings result when the starting position is greater than the ending position. The formula for calculating the length of a string is:

MAX (ending-position – starting-position + 1, 0)

4. The first character of a parent string is at position 1 and the last character is at position n where n is the length of the string. The starting position of a substring must be greater than or equal to 1 and the ending position must be less than or equal to the length n,

unless the length of the substring is 0. If the parent string is of length 0, the substring must be of length 0.

In the following example,

```
CHARACTER (14) NAME
NAME = "John Q. Public"
NAME(1:4) = "Jane"
PRINT *, NAME (9:14)
```

NAME is a scalar character variable, a string of 14 characters, that is assigned the value "John Q. Public" by the first assignment statement. NAME(1:4) is a substring of four characters that is reassigned the value "Jane" by the second assignment statement, leaving the remainder of the string NAME unchanged; the string name then becomes "Jane Q. Public". The PRINT statement prints the characters in positions 9 through 14, in this case, the surname, "Public".

Given the definition and declarations:

```
TYPE PERSON
    INTEGER AGE
    CHARACTER (LEN = 40) NAME
END TYPE PERSON

TYPE(PERSON) FIRECHIEF, FIREMEN(50)
CHARACTER (20) DISTRICT, STATIONS(10)
```

the following are all substrings:

```
STATIONS (1) (1:5)      ! array element as parent string
FIRECHIEF % NAME (4:9)  ! structure component as parent string
DISTRICT (7:14)         ! scalar variable as parent string
'0123456789' (N:N+1)    ! character constant as parent string
```

The reference STATIONS (:) (1:5) is permitted. It is an array whose elements are substrings, but it is not considered to be a substring reference. Even though the entire array is indicated, this reference is considered to be an array section reference, and the description can be found in Section 6.4.5. STATIONS (1:5) (1:5) is also permitted. It is an array section whose elements are substrings. Whenever an array is constructed of character strings and any part of it (other than the whole object) is referenced, an array section subscript must appear before the substring range specification, if any. Otherwise, the substring range specification will be treated as an array section specification because the two have the same form. STATIONS (1:5) is an array section reference that references the entire character strings of the first five elements of STATIONS. The last example is a substring where the parent is a constant and the starting and ending positions are variable. This substring is considered to be neither a constant nor a variable. It is in a category all by itself.

6.3 Structure Components

A structure is an aggregate of components of intrinsic or derived types. It is itself an object of derived type. The types and attributes of the components are specified in the type definition; they may be scalars or arrays. Each structure has at least one component. There may be arrays of structures. In the example given above, FIRECHIEF is a structure; FIREMEN is an array of structures of type PERSON.

A component of a structure may be referenced by placing the name of the component after the name of the parent structure, separated by a percent sign (%). For example, FIRECHIEF % NAME references the character string component of the variable FIRECHIEF of type PERSON.

A structure component (R614) is a data reference (R612) that has the form:

part-reference   [% part-reference] ...

where a part reference (R613) has the form

part-name   [(section-subscript-list)]

and a section subscript (R618) is one of:

subscript
subscript-triplet
vector-subscript

Rules and restrictions:

1. For a data reference to be considered a structure component reference, there must be more than one part reference.

2. For a data reference to be classified as a structure component reference, the rightmost part reference must be a part name. If the rightmost component is of the form

    part-name (section-subscript-list)

    the reference is considered to be an array section or array element (the simplest form of a section subscript list is a subscript list).

3. In a data reference, each part name except the rightmost must be of derived type.

4. In a data reference, each part name except the leftmost must be the name of a component of the derived-type definition of the type of the preceding part name.

5. In a part reference containing a section subscript list, the number of section subscripts must equal the rank of the part name.

6. It is possible to create a structure with more than one array part, but in a data reference to the structure, there must not be more than one part reference with nonzero rank. This is a somewhat arbitrary restriction imposed for the sake of simplicity.

7. In a data reference, a part name to the right of a part reference with nonzero rank must not have the POINTER attribute. It is possible to declare an array of structures that have a pointer as a component, but it is not possible to reference such an object as an array.

The rank of a part reference consisting of just a part name is the rank of the part name. The rank of a part reference of the form

    part-name (section-subscript-list)

is the number of subscript triplets and vector subscripts in the list. The rank is less than the rank of the part name if any of the section subscripts are subscripts other than subscript triplets or vector subscripts. The shape of a data reference is the shape of the part reference with nonzero rank, if any; otherwise, the data reference is a scalar and has rank zero.

The **parent structure** in a data reference is the data object specified by the leftmost part name. If the parent object has the INTENT, TARGET, or PARAMETER attribute, the structure component has the attribute. The type and type parameters of a structure component are those of the rightmost part name. A structure component is a pointer only if the rightmost part name has the POINTER attribute.

Given the type definition and structure declarations:

```
TYPE PERSON
   INTEGER AGE
   CHARACTER (LEN = 40) NAME
END TYPE PERSON

TYPE(PERSON) FIRECHIEF, FIREMEN(50)
```

examples of structure components are:

```
FIRECHIEF % AGE     ! scalar component of scalar parent
FIREMEN(J) % NAME   ! component of array element parent
FIREMEN(1:N) % AGE  ! component of array section parent
```

If a derived-type definition contains a component that is of derived type, then a reference to an ultimate component can contain more than two part references as do the references in the first two PRINT statements in the following example.

```
TYPE REPAIR_BILL
    REAL PARTS
    REAL LABOR
END TYPE REPAIR_BILL

TYPE VEHICLE
    CHARACTER (LEN = 40) OWNER
    INTEGER MILEAGE
    TYPE(REPAIR_BILL) COST
END TYPE VEHICLE

TYPE (VEHICLE) BLACK_FORD, RED_FERRARI

PRINT *, BLACK_FORD % COST % PARTS
PRINT *, RED_FERRARI % COST % LABOR
PRINT *, RED_FERRARI % OWNER
```

6.4 Arrays

An **array** is a collection of scalar elements of any intrinsic or derived type. All of the elements of an array must have the same type and kind parameter. There may be arrays of structures. An object of any type that is specified to have the DIMENSION attribute is an array. The value returned by a function may be an array. The appearance of an array name or designator has no implications for the order in which the individual elements are referenced unless array element ordering is specifically required.

6.4.1 Array Terminology

An array consists of elements that extend in one or more dimensions to represent columns, rows, planes, etc. There may be up to seven dimensions in an array declaration in a standard-conforming program. The number of dimensions in an array is called the **rank** of the array. The number of elements in a dimension is called the **extent** of the array in that dimension. Limits on the size of extents are not specified in the Fortran standard. The **shape** of an array is determined from the rank and the extents; to be precise, the shape is a vector where each element of the vector is the extent in the corresponding dimension. The **size** of an array is the product of the extents; that is, it is the total number of elements in the array.

For example, given the declaration

```
REAL X (0:9, 2)
```

the rank of X is 2; X has two dimensions. The extent of the first dimension is 10; the extent of the second dimension is 2. The shape of X is 10 by 2, that is, a vector of two values, (10, 2). The size is 20, the product of the extents.

An object is given the DIMENSION attribute in a type declaration or in one of several declaration statements. The following are some ways of declaring that A has rank 3 and shape (10, 15, 3):

```
DIMENSION A(10, 15, 3)
REAL, DIMENSION(10, 15, 3) :: A
REAL A(10, 15, 3)
COMMON A(10, 15, 3)
ALLOCATABLE A(10, 15, 3)
TARGET A(10, 15, 3)
```

Arrays of nonzero size have a lower and upper bound along each dimension. The **lower bound** is the smallest subscript value along a dimension; the **upper bound** is the largest subscript value along that dimension. The default lower bound is 1 if the lower bound is omitted in the declaration. Array bounds may be positive, zero, or negative. In the example:

```
REAL Z(-3:10, 12)
```

the first dimension of Z ranges from –3 to 10, that is, –3, –2, –2, 0, 1, 2, ..., 9, 10. The lower bound is –3; the upper bound is 10. In the second dimension, the lower bound is 1; the upper bound is 12. The bounds for array expressions are described in Section 7.2.8.4.

6.4.2 Whole Arrays

Some arrays are named. The name is either an array variable name or the name of a constant. If the array name appears without a subscript list or section subscript list, all of the elements of the array are referenced and the reference is considered to be a **whole array** reference. References to a single element of an array or a section of an array are permitted. If the array has the INTENT, TARGET, or PARAMETER attribute, an element or section of the array also has the attribute. An element or section of an array never has the POINTER attribute.

6.4.3 Array Elements

An **array element** is one of the scalar elements that make up an array. A subscript list is used to indicate which element is referenced. If A is declared to be a one-dimensional array:

```
REAL, DIMENSION (10) :: A
```

then A(1) refers to the first element, A(2) to the second, and so on. The number in the parentheses is the subscript that indicates which scalar element is referenced. If B is declared to be a seven-dimensional array:

```
REAL B (5, 5, 5, 5, 4, 7, 5)
```

then B (2, 3, 5, 1, 3, 7, 2) refers to one scalar element of B, indexed by a subscript in each dimension. The set of numbers that indicate the position along each dimension in turn (in this case, 2, 3, 5, 1, 3, 7, 2) is called a **subscript list**.

6.4.4 Array Sections

Sometimes only a portion of an array is needed for a calculation. It is possible to refer to a selected portion of an array as an array; this portion is called an **array section**. A **parent array** is the whole array from which the portion that forms the array section is selected.

An array section is specified by an array variable name and a section subscript list that consists of subscripts, triplet subscripts, or vector subscripts. At least one subscript must be a triplet or vector subscript; otherwise, the reference indicates an array element, not an array. The following example uses a section subscript to create an array section:

```
REAL A (10)
   . . .
A (2:5) = 1.0
```

The parent array A has 10 elements. The array section consists of the elements A (2), A (3), A (4), and A (5) of the parent array. The section A (2:5) is an array itself and the value 1.0 is assigned to all four of its elements.

6.4.5 Form of Array Elements and Array Sections

The form of an array element is a data reference (R612) and the form of an array section (R616) is a data reference followed by an optional substring range enclosed in parentheses; the form of a substring range is found in Section 6.2.

A part name in a data reference may be followed by an optional section subscript list. A section subscript (R618) can be any of:

subscript
subscript-triplet
vector-subscript

where a subscript triplet (R619) is:

[subscript] : [subscript] [: stride]

Subscripts and strides must be scalar integer expressions and a vector subscript (R621) must be an integer array expression of rank one.

Rules and restrictions:

1. For a data reference to be classified as an array element, every part reference must have rank zero and the last part reference must contain a subscript list.

2. For a data reference to be classified as an array section, exactly one part reference must have nonzero rank, and either the final part reference must have a section subscript list with nonzero rank or another part reference must have nonzero rank.

3. In an array section that is a data reference followed by a substring range, the rightmost part name must be of type character.

4. In an array section of an assumed-size array, the second subscript must not be omitted from a subscript triplet in the last dimension.

5. A section subscript must be present for each dimension of an array. If any section subscript is simply a subscript, the section will have a lesser rank than its parent.

Examples of array elements and array sections are:

```
ARRAY_A (1,2)            ! array element
ARRAY_A (1:N:2,M)        ! rank-one array section
ARRAY_B (:,:,:) (2:3)    ! array whose elements are
                         ! substrings of length 2
SCALAR_A % ARRAY_C(L)                    ! array element
SCALAR_A % ARRAY_C(1:L)                  ! array section
SCALAR_B % ARRAY_D(1:N) % SCALAR_C       ! array section
ARRAY_E(1:N:2) % ARRAY_F(I,J) % STRING(K)(:) ! array section
```

If any part of a reference is an array section, the reference is considered to be an array section reference. In a data reference, there may be at most one part with rank greater than zero. As mentioned earlier, this is a somewhat arbitrary restriction imposed for the sake of simplicity.

Only the last component of a data reference may be of type character. In the last example above, each component of the type definition is an array and the object ARRAY_E is an array. The reference is valid because each component in the reference is scalar. The substring range is not needed because it specifies the entire string; however, it serves as a reminder that the last component is of type character.

The following examples demonstrate the allowable combinations of scalar and array parents with scalar and array components.

```
TYPE REPAIR_BILL
    REAL PARTS (20)
    REAL LABOR
END TYPE REPAIR_BILL

TYPE (REPAIR_BILL) FIRST
TYPE (REPAIR_BILL) FOR_1990 (6)
```

Scalar parent

```
1. FIRST % LABOR            ! structure component
2. FIRST % PARTS (I)        ! array element
3. FIRST % PARTS            ! component (array-valued)
4. FIRST % PARTS (I:J)      ! array section

5. FOR_1990 (K) % LABOR          ! structure component
6. FOR_1990 (K) % PARTS (I)      ! array element
7. FOR_1990 (K) % PARTS          ! component (array-valued)
8. FOR_1990 (K) % PARTS (I:J)    ! array section
```

Array parent

```
 9.  FOR_1990 % LABOR              ! component and array section
10.  FOR_1990 % PARTS (I)          ! array section
11.  FOR_1990 % PARTS              ! ILLEGAL
12.  FOR_1990 % PARTS (I:J)        ! ILLEGAL

13.  FOR_1990 (K:L) % LABOR        ! component and array section
14.  FOR_1990 (K:L) % PARTS (I)    ! array section
15.  FOR_1990 (K:L) % PARTS        ! ILLEGAL
16.  FOR_1990 (K:L) % PARTS (I:J)  ! ILLEGAL
```

References 11, 12, 15, and 16 are illegal because only one component may be of rank greater than zero. References 3 and 7 are compact (contiguous) array objects and are classified as array-valued structure components. References 9, 10, 13, and 14 are noncontiguous array objects and are classified as sections. These distinctions are important when such objects are actual arguments in procedure references.

6.4.5.1 Subscripts. In an array element reference, each subscript must be within the bounds for that dimension. A subscript may appear in an array section reference. Whenever this occurs, it decreases the rank of the section by one less than the rank of the parent array. A subscript used in this way must be within the bounds for the dimension.

6.4.5.2 Subscript Triplets. The first subscript in a subscript triplet is the lower bound; the second is the upper bound. If the lower bound is omitted, the declared lower bound is used. If the upper bound is omitted, the declared upper bound is used. The stride is the increment between successive subscripts in the sequence. If it is omitted, it is assumed to be 1. If the subscripts and stride are omitted and only the colon (:) appears, the entire declared range for the dimension is used.

When the stride is positive, an increasing sequence of integer values is specified from the first subscript in increments of the stride, up to the last value that is not greater than the second subscript. The sequence is empty if the first subscript is greater than the second. If any subscript sequence is empty, the array section is a zero-sized array, because the size of the array is the product of its extents. For example, given the array declared A(5, 4, 3) and the section A(3:5, 2, 1:2), the array section is of rank 2 with shape (3, 2) and size 6. The elements are:

```
A (3, 2, 1)    A (3, 2, 2)
A (4, 2, 1)    A (4, 2, 2)
A (5, 2, 1)    A (5, 2, 2)
```

The stride must not be 0.

When the stride is negative, a decreasing sequence of integer values is specified from the first subscript, in increments of the stride, down to the last value that is not less than the second subscript. The sequence is empty if the second subscript is greater than the first, and the array section is a zero-sized array. For example, given the array declared B(10) and the section B (9:4:–2), the array section is of rank 1 with shape (3) and size 3. The elements are:

B (9)
B (7)
B (5)

However, the array section B (9:4) is a zero-sized array.

A subscript in a subscript triplet is not required to be within the declared bounds for the dimension as long as all subscript values selected by the triplet are within the declared bounds. For example, the section B (3:11:7) is permitted. It has rank 1 with shape (2) and size 2. The elements are:

B (3)
B (10)

6.4.5.3 Vector Subscripts. While subscript triplets specify values in increasing or decreasing order with a specified stride to form a regular pattern, vector subscripts specify values in arbitrary order. The values must be within the declared bounds for the dimension. A vector subscript is a rank-one array of integer values used as a section subscript to select elements from a parent array. For example:

```
INTEGER J (3)
REAL A (30)
   . . .
J = (/ 8, 4, 7 /)
A(J) = 1.0
```

The last assignment statement assigns the value 1.0 to A(4), A(7), and A(8). The section A(J) is a rank-one array with shape (3) and size 3.

If J were assigned (/ 4, 7, 4 /) instead, the element A(4) would be accessed in two ways: as A(J(1)) and as A(J(3)). Such an array section is called a many-one array section. A many-one section must not appear on the left of the equal sign in an assignment statement or as an input item in a READ statement. The reason is that the result will depend on the order of evaluation of the subscripts, which is not specified by the language. The results would not be predictable and the program containing such a statement would not be portable.

There are places where array sections with vector subscripts must not appear:

1. as internal files

2. as pointer targets

3. as actual arguments for INTENT (OUT) or INTENT (INOUT) dummy arguments

6.4.6 Using Array Elements and Array Sections

Subscripts, subscript triplets, and vector subscripts may be mixed in a single section subscript list used to specify an array section. A triplet section may specify an empty sequence (for example 1:0), in which case the resulting section is a zero-sized array.

If B were declared:

REAL B (10, 10, 5)

then the section:

B (1:4:3, 6:8:2, 3)

consists of four elements:

B (1, 6, 3)	B (1, 8, 3)
B (4, 6, 3)	B (4, 8, 3)

The stride along the first dimension is 3, resulting in a subscript-value list of 1 and 4. The stride along the second subscript is 2 resulting in a subscript-value list of 6 and 8. In the third position there is a subscript that reduces the rank of the section by 1. The section has shape (2, 2) and size 4.

Assume IV is declared:

INTEGER, DIMENSION (3) :: IV = (/ 4, 5, 4 /)

then the section:

B (8:9, 5, IV)

is a 2 × 3 array consisting of the six elements:

B (8, 5, 4)	B (8, 5, 5)	B (8, 5, 4)
B (9, 5, 4)	B (9, 5, 5)	B (9, 5, 4)

B (8:9, 5:4, IV) is a zero-sized array of rank 3.

6.4.7 Array Element Order

When whole arrays are used as operands in an executable statement, the indicated operation is performed element-by-element, but no order is implied for these elemental operations. They may be executed in any order or simultaneously. Although there is no order of evaluation when whole array operations are performed, there is an ordering of the elements in an array itself. An ordering is required for the input and output of arrays and for certain intrinsic functions such as MAXLOC. The elements of an array form a sequence whose ordering is called **array element order**. This is the sequence that occurs when the subscripts along the first dimension vary most rapidly, and the subscripts along the last dimension vary most slowly. Thus, for an array declared as:

```
REAL A (3, 2)
```

the elements in array element order are: $A(1,1)$, $A(2,1)$, $A(3,1)$, $A(1,2)$, $A(2,2)$, $A(3,2)$.

The position of an array element in this sequence is its **subscript order value**. Element $A(1,1)$ has a subscript order value of 1. Element $A(1,2)$ has a subscript order value of 4. Table 6-1 shows how to compute the subscript order value for any element in arrays of rank 1 through 7.

The subscript order of the elements of an array section is that of the array object that the section represents. That is, given the array A(10) and the section A(2:9:2) consisting of the elements A(2), A(4), A(6), and A(8), the subscript order value of A(2) in the array section A(2:9:2) is 1; the subscript order value of A(4) in the section is 2 and A(8) is 4.

6.5 Pointers and Allocatable Arrays

Fortran 90 provides several dynamic data objects. Automatic objects (arrays and character strings) were discussed in Section 5.8. In addition, there are two data attributes that can be used to specify dynamic data objects: ALLOCATABLE and POINTER. Arrays of any type may have the ALLOCATABLE attribute; scalars or arrays of any type may have the POINTER attribute. Chapter 5 described how such objects are declared. This section describes how space is created for these objects with the ALLOCATE statement, how it may be released with the DEALLOCATE statement, and how pointers can be disassociated from any

Table 6-1 Computation of subscript order value

Rank	Explicit shape specifier	Subscript list	Subscript order value
1	$j_1{:}k_1$	s_1	$1 + (s_1 - j_1)$
2	$j_1{:}k_1, j_2{:}k_2$	s_1, s_2	$1 + (s_1 - j_1)$ $\quad + (s_2 - j_2) \times d_1$
3	$j_1{:}k_1, j_2{:}k_2, j_3{:}k_3$	s_1, s_2, s_3	$1 + (s_1 - j_1)$ $\quad + (s_2 - j_2) \times d_1$ $\quad + (s_3 - j_3) \times d_2 \times d_1$
.	.	.	.
.	.	.	.
.	.	.	.
7	$j_1{:}k_1, \ldots, j_7{:}k_7$	$s_1, \ldots, s_7$	$1 + (s_1 - j_1)$ $\quad + (s_2 - j_2) \times d_1$ $\quad + (s_3 - j_3) \times d_2 \times d_1$ $\quad + \cdots$ $\quad + (s_7 - j_7) \times d_6$ $\quad\quad \times d_5 \times \cdots \times d_1$

Notes for Table 6-1:
1. $d_i = \max (k_i - j_i + 1, 0)$ is the size of the ith dimension.
2. If the size of the array is nonzero, $j_i \le s_i \le k_i$ for all $i = 1, 2, \ldots, 7$.

target with the NULLIFY statement. The association status of a pointer may be defined or undefined; initially (when a pointer is declared), it is undefined. If it is defined, the pointer may be associated with a target or disassociated from any target. The target is referenced by the name of the pointer and is like any other variable in that it is defined when it acquires a value. Figure 6-1 shows the various states that a pointer may assume.

Section 7.5.3 describes how pointers can be associated with existing space and how dynamic objects can acquire values.

6.5.1 ALLOCATE Statement

The ALLOCATE statement creates space for:

1. arrays with the ALLOCATABLE attribute

2. variables with the POINTER attribute

The pointer becomes associated with the newly created space.

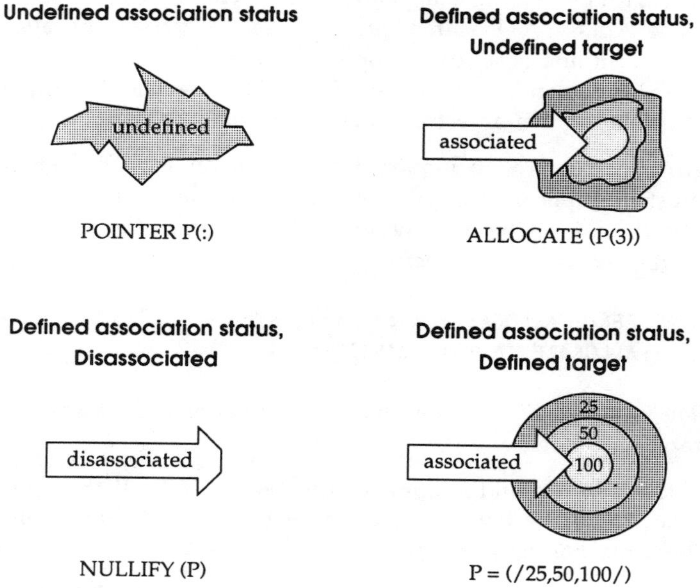

Undefined association status

undefined

POINTER P(:)

**Defined association status,
Undefined target**

associated

ALLOCATE (P(3))

**Defined association status,
Disassociated**

disassociated

NULLIFY (P)

**Defined association status,
Defined target**

associated   25 50 100

P = (/25,50,100/)

Figure 6-1 States in the lifetime of a pointer

The form of the ALLOCATE statement (R622) is:

ALLOCATE (allocation-list [**,** **STAT =** stat-variable] **)**

where an allocation (R624) is:

allocate-object [**(** allocate-shape-spec-list **)**]

An allocate object (R625) is one of:

variable-name
structure-component

and an allocate shape specification (R626) is:

[allocate-lower-bound **:**] allocate-upper-bound

Rules and restrictions:

1. The STAT= variable, allocate lower bound, and allocate upper bound must be scalar integer expressions.

2. Each allocate object must be a pointer or an allocatable array.

3. Attempts to allocate space for allocatable arrays that are currently allocated result in an error condition.

4. If a STAT= variable appears, it must not also be allocated in the same ALLOCATE statement. It is set to zero if the allocation is successful and is set to a processor-dependent positive value if there is an error condition. If there is no STAT= variable, the program terminates when an error condition occurs.

5. An argument to an inquiry function in an ALLOCATE statement must not appear as an allocate object in that statement. For example, the use of the intrinsic inquiry function SIZE (A.99) in the following example is not permitted.

```
REAL, ALLOCATABLE :: A(:), B(:)
ALLOCATE (A(10), B(SIZE(A)))
```

6. The number of allocate shape specifications must agree with the rank of the array.

7. If the lower bound is omitted, the default is 1. If the upper bound is less than the lower bound, the extent in that dimension is 0 and the array has zero size.

8. An allocate object may be of type character and it may have a length of 0, in which case no memory is allocated.

9. The values of the bounds expressions at the time an array is allocated determine the shape of the array. If an entity in a bounds expression is subsequently redefined, the shape of the allocated array is not changed.

6.5.1.1 Allocation of Allocatable Arrays. The rank of an allocatable array is declared. The bounds, extents, shape, and size are determined when the array is allocated. After allocation the array may be defined and redefined. The array is said to be **currently allocated**. It is an error to allocate a currently allocated allocatable array. The intrinsic function ALLOCATED (A.9) may be used to query the allocation status of an allocatable array if the allocation status is defined. For example:

```
REAL, ALLOCATABLE :: X(:, :, :)
    . . .
IF (.NOT. ALLOCATED (X) ) ALLOCATE (X (-6:2, 10, 3))
```

X is not available for use in the program until it has been allocated space by an ALLOCATE statement. X must be declared with a deferred-shape array specification and the ALLOCATABLE attribute.

6.5.1.2 Allocation of Pointers. When an object with the POINTER attribute is allocated, space is created, and the pointer is associated with that space, which becomes the pointer target. A reference to the pointer name can be used to define or access its target. The target may be an array or a scalar. Additional pointers may become associated with the same target by pointer assignment (described in Section 7.5.3). A pointer target may be an array with the ALLOCATABLE attribute if the array also has the TARGET attribute. Allocation of a pointer creates an object that implicitly has the TARGET attribute. It is not an error to allocate a pointer that is currently associated with a target. In this case, a new pointer target is created and the previous association of the pointer is lost. If there was no other way to access the previous target, it becomes inaccessible. The ASSOCIATED intrinsic function may be used to query the association status of a pointer if the association status of the pointer is defined. The ASSOCIATED function (A.13) also may be used to inquire whether a pointer is associated with a target or whether two pointers are associated with the same target.

Pointers can be used in many ways; an important usage is the creation of linked lists. For example,

```
TYPE NODE
    INTEGER :: VALUE
    TYPE (NODE), POINTER :: NEXT
END TYPE NODE

TYPE(NODE), POINTER :: LIST
    . . .

ALLOCATE (LIST)
LIST % VALUE = 17
ALLOCATE (LIST % NEXT)
```

The first two executable statements create a node pointed to by LIST and put the value 17 in the VALUE component of the node. The third statement creates a second node pointed to by the NEXT component of the first node.

6.5.2 NULLIFY Statement

The NULLIFY statement causes a pointer to be disassociated from any target. Pointers have an initial association status that is undefined. To initialize a pointer to point to no target, it is necessary to execute a NULLIFY statement for the pointer.

The form of the NULLIFY statement (R629) is:

NULLIFY (pointer-object-list)

where a pointer object (R630) is one of:

variable-name
structure-component

Rules and restrictions:

1.   Each pointer object must have the POINTER attribute.

6.5.3 DEALLOCATE Statement

The DEALLOCATE statement releases the space allocated for an allocatable array or a pointer target and nullifies the pointer. After an allocatable array or pointer has been deallocated, it cannot be accessed or defined until it is allocated again or, in the case of a pointer, assigned to an existing target.

In some cases the execution of a RETURN statement in a subprogram may cause the allocation status of an allocatable array or the association status of a pointer to become undefined. This can be avoided if the array or pointer is given the SAVE attribute or if it is declared in a subprogram that remains active. The main program is always active. Variables declared in modules accessed by the main program and named common blocks specified in the main program do not need to be given the SAVE attribute; these entities have the attribute automatically. If the main program calls subroutine A and subroutine A calls function B, then the main program, subroutine A, and function B are active until a return from function B is executed, at which time only the main program and subroutine A are active. If a recursive subprogram becomes active, it remains active until the return from its first invocation is executed.

The form of the DEALLOCATE statement (R631) is:

DEALLOCATE (allocate-object-list [, STAT = stat-variable])

where an allocate object is (R625) one of:

variable-name
structure-component

Rules and restrictions:

1.   The STAT= variable must ·be a scalar integer variable.

2.   Each allocate object must be a pointer or an allocatable array.

3.   If there is a STAT= variable and it is a pointer, it must not be deallocated in the same DEALLOCATE statement. The STAT=

variable is set to zero if the deallocation is successful and is set to a processor-dependent positive value if there is an error condition. If there is no STAT= variable, the program terminates when an error condition occurs.

6.5.3.1 Deallocation of Allocatable Arrays. To be deallocated, an allocatable array must be currently allocated; otherwise, an error condition will occur. The inquiry function ALLOCATED (A.9) may be used to determine if an array is currently allocated.

An allocatable array may have the TARGET attribute. If such an array is deallocated, the association status of any pointer associated with the array will become undefined. Such an array must be deallocated by the appearance of its name in a DEALLOCATE statement. It must not be deallocated by the appearance of the pointer name in a DEALLOCATE statement.

When a RETURN or END statement is executed in a subprogram, allocatable arrays become undefined and their allocation status becomes undefined unless:

1. the array has the SAVE attribute

2. the array is specified in a module that is accessed by an active subprogram

3. the array is accessed by host association

Any other allocatable arrays should be deallocated before leaving the subprogram because if an allocatable array acquires an undefined allocation status, it can no longer be referenced, defined, allocated, or deallocated.

An example of the allocation and deallocation of an allocatable array is:

```
REAL, ALLOCATABLE :: X (:, :)
   . . .
ALLOCATE (X (10, 2), STAT = IERR)
IF (IERR) .GT. 0) CALL HANDLER
X = 0.0
   . . .
DEALLOCATE (X)
   . . .
ALLOCATE (X (-10:10), 5), STAT = JERR)
```

X is declared to be a deferred-shape, two-dimensional, real array with the ALLOCATABLE attribute. Space is allocated for it and it is given bounds, extents, shape, and size and then initialized to have zero values in all elements. Later X is deallocated, and still later, it is again allocated with different bounds, extents, shape, and size, but its rank remains as declared.

6.5.3.2 Deallocation of Pointers. Only a pointer with defined association status may be deallocated. Deallocating a pointer with an undefined association status or a pointer associated with a target that was not created by allocation causes an error condition in the DEALLOCATE statement. A pointer associated with an allocatable array must not be deallocated. (Of course, the array itself may be deallocated.)

It is possible (by pointer assignment) to associate a pointer with a portion of an object such as an array section, an array element, or a substring. A pointer associated with only a portion of an object cannot be deallocated. If more than one pointer is associated with an object, deallocating one of the pointers causes the association status of the others to become undefined. Such pointers must not be arguments to the ASSOCIATED inquiry function.

When a RETURN or END statement is executed in a procedure, the association status of a pointer declared or accessed in the procedure becomes undefined unless:

1. the pointer has the SAVE attribute

2. the pointer is specified in a module that is accessed by an active subprogram

3. the pointer is accessed by host association

4. the pointer is in blank common

5. the pointer is in a named common block that is specified in an active subprogram or has the SAVE attribute

6. the pointer is the return value of a function declared to have the POINTER attribute

If the association status of a pointer becomes undefined, the pointer can no longer be referenced, defined, or deallocated. It may be allocated, nullified, or pointer assigned to a new target.

An example of the allocation and deallocation of a pointer is:

```
REAL, POINTER :: X (:, :)
    . . .
ALLOCATE (X (10, 2), STAT = IERR)
IF (IERR .GT. 0) CALL HANDLER
X = 0.0
```

```
    . . .
DEALLOCATE (X)
    . . .
ALLOCATE (X (-10:10), 5), STAT = JERR)
```

X is declared to be a deferred-shape, two-dimensional, real array with the POINTER attribute. Space is allocated for it and it is given bounds, extents, shape, and size and then initialized to have zero values in all elements. Later X is deallocated, and still later, it is again allocated with different bounds, extents, shape, and size. This example is quite similar to the previous example for allocatable arrays, except that, in the case of pointers, it is not necessary to deallocate X before allocating it again. If a compiler has the ability to collect and reuse released space, explicit deallocation may lead to more space efficient programs.

6.6 Summary

A data object may be categorized in several ways. It may be a variable or a constant; it may be a scalar or an array; it may be a whole object or part of an object; and finally, it may be dynamic.

Variables and Constants

Variables must become defined with a value before they can be used (referenced) in a program. They may have several values during program execution. Constants may be referenced any time. They have a specified value and cannot be redefined. There are two kinds of constants: literal and named.

Scalars and Arrays

A data object can be categorized by its rank. A scalar has a rank of zero and can have only a single value from the set of values permitted for its type. An array is a set of scalar data, all with the same type and type parameters, that is arranged in a regular pattern. The pattern will have columns, rows, planes, etc., depending on the rank of the array. An array may have a rank between one and seven, inclusively. The rank is the number of dimensions in the array declaration. The number of elements in a dimension is called the extent in that dimension. The shape of an array is determined by the rank and the extents, and the size of the array is the product of the extents. A constant, as well as a variable, may be a scalar or an array.

Whole Objects and Parts of Objects

Fortran 90 permits several objects that are aggregations of data. Some
are scalar objects. A character string, even though it may consist of several characters, is a scalar. It is possible to reference a substring of a
character object; even a substring of a character constant. For example:

```
CHARACTER (3)      HIGH_THREE, ANY_THREE
CHARACTER (10) :: NUMBERS = "0123456789"
    . . .
HIGH_THREE = NUMBERS ( 8:10 )
ANY_THREE = "7302694815" (N : N + 2)
```

A structure, even though it may contain a component that is an
array, is a scalar. It is possible to reference a single component of a
structure. For example, if the type ADDRESS_BOOK is defined and the
variable CLIENTS is declared to be of this type:

```
TYPE ADDRESS_BOOK
    INTEGER NO_ADDRESSES (26)
    TYPE (DATE) FIRST_ENTRY, LAST_ENTRY
END TYPE ADDRESS_BOOK
    . . .
TYPE (ADDRESS_BOOK) CLIENTS
```

then CLIENTS % NO_ADDRESSES refers to a rank-one integer array
even though CLIENTS refers to a scalar of type ADDRESS_BOOK.

It is possible to reference a scalar element of an array. For example, if X is declared:

```
REAL X (40, 20, 30)
```

then X (3, 5, 21) refers to a scalar element. It is also possible to reference a section of an array, for example X(1:10, 3:4, 15:30). A section is
itself an array.

A whole object is referenced by its name if it is a variable or a
named constant. A part of an object is referenced by a designator which
is a whole object reference followed by a substring selector, a component
selector, an array element selector, or an array section selector.

An array section selector is a list of section subscripts, one for each
dimension of the array. There are three possibilities for section subscripts: a single subscript, a subscript triplet, or a vector subscript.

If a single subscript appears in a section selector, it will reduce by one the rank of the resulting array section. For example, X(1:10, 3, 15:30) is a rank-two array.

A subscript triplet selects a regularly formed section. For example, X (2:40:2, 1, 1) is a rank-one array that consists of the even-numbered elements in the first dimension of X. A subscript triplet may be reduced to a single colon (:). In this case, the entire range of the dimension is selected. X (:, 1, 1) references the entire first column of X.

A vector subscript may select an irregularly formed section. If II = (/ 3, 7, 19, 2 /), then X (II, 1, 1) is a rank-one array consisting of the elements X (3, 1, 1), X (7, 1, 1), X (19, 1, 1), and X (2, 1, 1).

When operations on arrays are performed, no order of evaluation is required; however, there is an order for array elements that is reflected in input and output sequences and in certain intrinsic functions. This order is "column-wise"; that is, the subscripts along the first dimension vary most rapidly.

Dynamic Data Objects

Fortran 90 introduces three new categories of data objects with dynamic properties: automatic objects, allocatable arrays, and pointers. Automatic objects are character objects and arrays of any type that may be declared only in procedures or procedure interfaces. These are described in Section 5.8. The declaration of allocatable arrays and pointers is described in Sections 5.3.3 and 5.4.1. These objects can not be referenced, however, until space is created for them. For allocatable arrays, this can be accomplished with an ALLOCATE statement. For pointers, it may be accomplished with an ALLOCATE statement or the pointer may be assigned to already existing space by a pointer assignment statement (7.5.3). A pointer may be declared as a scalar or an array. Neither pointers nor allocatable arrays can be named constants. Allocatable arrays and pointers are allocated as whole objects, but an element or section of an allocatable array can be referenced. A pointer target may be any part of an existing object including substrings, components, array elements, and array sections. A pointer target may be the whole or part of an allocatable array if the array has the TARGET attribute.

The ALLOCATE statement has an optional STAT= specifier that may be used to determine whether the requested allocation was successful. For example:

```
REAL, ALLOCATABLE :: A ( :. : ), B ( :, : )
        . . .
ALLOCATE ( A (100, 100), STAT = DID_IT)
IF (DID_IT .GT. 0) GO TO ALLOC_ERR
```

It is an error to allocate an already allocated allocatable array. An intrinsic function ALLOCATED is provided to test the status of an allocatable array. For example:

```
IF (.NOT. ALLOCATED (B) ) ALLOCATE ( B ( -10:10, 3) )
```

It is not an error to allocate an already allocated pointer.

The ALLOCATED intrinsic function is not available for pointers; instead, there is an ASSOCIATED intrinsic function to test the status of a pointer. Initially, a pointer has an undefined association status. A NULLIFY statement may be used to set its status to disassociated. For example:

```
TYPE (LINK), POINTER :: NEXT
NULLIFY (NEXT)
     . . .
IF (.NOT. ASSOCIATED (NEXT) ) ALLOCATE (NEXT)
```

The DEALLOCATE statement releases space that was previously allocated. If a pointer is deallocated, the DEALLOCATE statement nullifies the pointer. Only whole objects may be deallocated. The DEALLOCATE statement also has an optional status specifier STAT that may be used to determine whether the requested deallocation was successful. For example:

```
DEALLOCATE ( A, B, NEXT, STAT = ALL_GONE )
```

F9⦿

7

Expressions and Assignment

In Fortran, calculations are specified by writing **expressions**. Expressions look much like algebraic formulas in mathematics, particularly when the expressions involve calculations on numerical values. In fact, the attempt to give the programmer a programming language that reflects, as much as possible, ordinary mathematical notation is what inspired the name Fortran (**Formula tran**slation).

Expressions often involve nonnumeric values, such as character strings, logical values, or structures; these also can be considered to be formulas—ones that involve nonnumeric quantities rather than numeric ones.

This chapter describes how valid expressions can be formed, how they are interpreted, and how they are evaluated. One of the major uses of expressions is in assignment statements where the value of an expression is assigned to a variable. The assignment statement appears in four forms: intrinsic assignment, defined assignment, masked array assignment, and pointer assignment. In the first three forms, a value is computed by performing the computation specified in an expression and the value is assigned to a variable. In the fourth form, a pointer, the object on the left side, is made to point to the object or target on the right side.

The four forms of the assignment statement are also described in detail in this chapter.

7.1 Introduction to Fortran 90 Expressions

Fortran 90 extensions allow the programmer to define new data types, operators for these types, and new operators for intrinsic types. These additional capabilities are provided within the general Fortran 77 framework for expressions which consists of three parts:

- the rules for forming a valid expression (7.2)

- the rules for interpreting the expression (giving it a meaning) (7.3)

- the rules for evaluating the expression (how the computation may be carried out) (7.4)

An expression is formed from operators and operands. There is no change from Fortran 77 in the rules for forming expressions, except that a new class of operators has been defined. These are user-defined operators, which are either unary or binary operators. They have the form of a sequence of letters surrounded by periods; .INVERSE. and .PLUS. are examples of possible user-defined operators.

The formal (BNF) rules for forming expressions imply an order for combining operands with operators. These rules specify that expressions enclosed in parentheses are combined first and that, for example, the multiply operator * is combined with its operands before the addition operator + is combined with its operands. This order for operators in the absence of specific parentheses is called the **operator precedence** and is summarized in Section 7.2.5. Operator precedence for Fortran 77 operators is unchanged in Fortran 90. There are also some new operators, such as = = and > =, that are equivalent, including precedence, to their corresponding Fortran 77 operators; for example, = = and > = have the same precedence and meaning as .EQ. and .GE., respectively.

The formation rules for expressions imply that the defined unary operators have highest precedence of all operators, and defined binary operators have the lowest precedence of all operators. When they appear in a context where two or more of these operators of the same precedence are adjacent, the operands are combined with their operators in a left-to-right manner, as is the case for the familiar + and – operators, or in a right-to-left manner for the exponentiation operator (**).

Intrinsic operators (3.6) are generic in the sense that they can operate on operands of different types. For example, the plus operator + operates on operands of type integer as well as real and complex. Intrinsic operators can be extended further by the programmer to operate on operands of types for which there are no intrinsic operations. Similarly, defined unary and defined binary operators can be extended by the programmer to operate on operands of types for which there are no previous definitions. Section 12.6.4 describes how any operator can be made generic by the programmer using a generic specifier on an interface block.

The rules for interpretation of an expression are provided by the interpretation of each operator in the expression. When the operator is an intrinsic operator such as $+$, $*$, or .NOT., and the operands are of intrinsic types allowed for the intrinsic operator, the interpretation is provided by the usual mathematical or symbolic meaning of the operation. Thus, $+$ with two numeric operands means that the two operands are added together. For the user-defined operators, the interpretation is provided by a user-supplied function subprogram with a designation that this subprogram is to be used to define the operation. This aspect is new to Fortran 90. In addition, Fortran 90 allows the intrinsic operator symbols to be extended to cases in which the operands are not of the usual intrinsic types defined by the standard. For example, the $+$ operator can be defined for operands of type RATIONAL (a user-defined type) or for operands of type logical with the interpretation provided by a user-supplied function subprogram. The rules for construction of expressions (the syntax rules) are the same for user-defined operators as for intrinsic operators.

The general rule for evaluation of a Fortran expression remains unchanged in Fortran 90. In essence, the rule states that any method that is mathematically equivalent to that provided by the construction and interpretation rules for the expression is permitted, provided the order of evaluation indicated by explicit parentheses in the expression is followed. Thus, a compiler has a great deal of freedom to rearrange or optimize the computation, provided the rearranged expression has the same mathematical meaning. Because the definitions of user-defined operations are provided by subprograms, the opportunities for determining mathematical equivalent forms for expressions involving user-defined operations are more limited than for expressions involving only intrinsic operations.

New to Fortran 90 are arrays and pointers as objects that can appear in expressions and assignment statements. This chapter describes the use of arrays and pointers in the following contexts:

- as operands of intrinsic and user-defined operations

- as the variables being assigned in intrinsic assignment statements

- as the variables in pointer assignment statements and masked array assignment statements, new in Fortran 90

7.1.1 Assignment

The result obtained from the evaluation of an expression can be used in many ways. For example, it can be printed or passed to a subprogram. In many cases, however, the value is **assigned** to a variable and that value may be used later in the program by referencing the variable.

Execution of the assignment statement causes the expression to be evaluated (by performing the computation indicated), and then the value of the expression is assigned to the variable on the left of the equal sign. The form of assignment and the process of assignment is illustrated in Figure 7-1.

$$\overleftarrow{\text{Variable} \quad = \quad \text{Computation}}$$

Figure 7-1   The assignment operation

An example of an assignment statement is:

```
REAL_AGE = REPORTED_AGE + 3.0
```

REPORTED_AGE + 3.0 is the expression that indicates how to compute a value, which is assigned to the variable REAL_AGE.

Use of the equal sign for assignment is a little misleading because assignment is not equality in the algebraic sense. It indicates a replacement of the value of the variable named on the left-hand side of the equal sign with the value of the expression on the right. Assigning a value to the variable on the left-hand side is performed after all expressions in the statement have been evaluated. Additional examples of assignment statements are:

```
X = C + 1.0
PI = 3.1416
Z = 3.1 * (PI + X)
```

In the first statement, the value of C is added to 1.0 in order to compute the value of the expression C + 1.0; the resulting value is given to X, replacing any value X already has with the new value. In the second statement, PI is assigned the constant value 3.1416. In the third statement, the value of Z is determined from a more complicated expression; first the values of X and PI are added and then the result is multiplied by 3.1; the final value is assigned to Z.

An example involving subscripts is:

```
A (I+3) = PI + A (I-3)
```

The value of the subscript expression I-3 is determined and the value of the I-3 element of A is added to the value of PI to produce a sum. Before the result of this expression is assigned, the value of the subscript expression I+3 is determined, and the value of the sum is assigned to the element I+3 of A. Whether I+3 is evaluated before or after PI + A (I-3) is computed is not specified and therefore is processor dependent.

The above examples are arithmetic; Fortran has expressions of other types, such as logical, character, and derived type. Values of expressions of these other types can be assigned to variables of these other types. As with operators, the programmer can extend the meaning of assignment to types not defined intrinsically and can redefine assignment for two objects of the same derived type—such assignments are called **defined assignments** (7.5.2, 12.6.5). New to Fortran 90 are arrays and pointers of any type. Arrays and the targets associated with the pointers can be assigned values in intrinsic assignment statements. In addition, arrays and pointers each have a special form of assignment statement called **masked array assignment** (7.5.4) and **pointer assignment** (7.5.3), respectively.

7.1.2 Expressions

An assignment statement is only one of the Fortran statements where expressions may occur. Expressions also may appear in subscripts, actual arguments, IF statements, PRINT statements, WHERE statements, declaration statements, and many other statements.

An expression represents a computation that results in a value and may be as simple as a constant or variable. The value of an expression has a type and may have zero, one, or two type parameter values. In addition, the value is a scalar (including a structure) or an array. If the value is of a derived type, it has no type parameter. If it is of an intrinsic type, it has a kind type parameter, and if, in addition, it is of the type character, it has a length type parameter. Complicated expressions can be formed from simpler expressions, for example:

```
A ** (-B) + 3.0 / C - C * (A + B)
```

A complex value or a structure value is a scalar, even though it may consist of more than one value (for example, a complex value consists of two real values).

Arrays and pointers may be used as operands of intrinsic and defined operators. For intrinsic operators, when an array is an operand, the operation is performed elementwise on the elements of the array. For intrinsic operators, when a pointer is an operand, the value of the target pointed to by (associated with) the pointer is used as the operand. For defined operators, the array or pointer is used in a manner determined by the procedure defining the operation.

As indicated in the introduction to this chapter, the presentation of expressions is described in terms of the following three basic parts:

- The rules for forming expressions (syntax)

- The rules for interpreting expressions (semantics)

- The rules for evaluating expressions (optimization)

The syntax rules indicate which forms of expressions are valid. The semantics indicate how each expression is to be interpreted. Once an expression has been given an interpretation, a compiler may evaluate another completely different expression, provided the expression evaluated is mathematically equivalent to the one written.

To see how this works, consider the expression 2 * A + 2 * B in the following PRINT statement:

```
PRINT *, 2 * A + 2 * B
```

The syntax rules described later in this chapter indicate that the expression is valid and suggest an order of evaluation. The semantic rules specify the operations to be performed which, in this case, are the multiplication of the values of A and B by 2 and the addition of the two results. That is, the semantic rules indicate that the expression is to be interpreted as if it were

```
((2 * A) + (2 * B))
```

and not, for example

```
(((2 * A) + 2) * B)
```

Once the correct interpretation has been determined, the Fortran rules of evaluation permit a different expression to be used to evaluate the expression, provided the different expression is mathematically equivalent to the one written. For example, the computer may first add A and B and then multiply the result by 2, because the expression

```
2 * (A + B)
```

is mathematically equivalent to the one written.

When reading the rules about allowed alternative evaluations, three properties should be noted:

- Parentheses must not be violated. For example, the expression

    (2 * A) + (2 * B)

  must not be evaluated as

    2 * (A + B)

  This gives the programmer some control over the method of evaluation.

- Integer division is not mathematically equivalent to real division. The value of 3/2 is 1 and so cannot be evaluated as 3 * 0.5, which is 1.5.

- Mathematically equivalent expressions may produce computationally different results, due to the implementation of arithmetic and rounding on computer systems. For example, the expression X/2.0 may be evaluated as 0.5*X, even though the results may be slightly different. Also, for example, the expression 2 * A + 2 * B may be evaluated as 2*(A+B); when A and B are of type real, the two mathematically equivalent expressions may yield different values because of different rounding errors and different arithmetic exceptions in the two expressions.

7.2 Formation of Expressions

An expression is formed from operands, operators, and parentheses. The simplest form of an expression is a constant or a variable. Some examples are:

3.1416	A real constant
.TRUE.	A logical constant
X	A scalar variable
Y	An array variable
Y (K)	A variable that is an array element of Y
Y (2:10:2)	A variable that is an array section of Y
M % N	A variable that is a component of a structure M
Y (K) (I:I+3)	A variable that is a substring of array element Y (K)

The values of these simple expressions are the constant value 3.1416, the constant value .TRUE., the value of the variable X, the value of the array Y, the value of the array element Y (K), the value of the array section Y (2:10:2), the value of the component N of structure M, and the value of a substring of an array element Y (K), respectively.

7.2.1 Operands

An **operand** in an expression may be one of the following:

* a constant or subobject of a constant

* a variable (for example, a scalar, an array, a substring, or a pointer—see Section 6.1)

* an array constructor

* a structure constructor

* a function reference (returning, for example, a scalar, an array, a substring, or a pointer—see Section 12.3.3)

* another expression in parentheses

Examples of operands are:

```
A                ! a scalar or an array
B(1)             ! an array element or function
C(3:5)           ! an array section or a substring
(A + COS(X))     ! an expression in parentheses
(/ 1.2, 2.41 /)  ! an array constructor
RATIONAL(1,2)    ! a structure constructor or function
I_PTR            ! a pointer to an integer target
```

7.2.2 Binary and Unary Operations

There are two forms that operations may take in an expression. One is an operation involving two operands such as multiplying two numbers together. The other is an operation on one operand such as making a number negative. These forms are called **binary** and **unary** operations, respectively.

Table 7-1 lists the intrinsic operators. A programmer may define additional operators using function subprograms. User-defined operators are either binary or unary operators.

A binary operator combines two operands as in:

x_1 operator x_2

Examples are:

```
A + B
2 * C
```

The examples show an addition between two operands A and B, and a multiplication of two operands, the constant 2 and the operand C.

A unary operation acts on one operand as in:

operator x_1

Examples are:

```
- C
+ J
.NOT. L
```

The first example results in the value minus C. The second example yields the value J; a unary plus operator is, in effect, the identity operator. The third example produces a value that is the logical complement of L; the operator .NOT. is the only intrinsic operator that is a unary operator and is never a binary operator.

Note that the operators + and – may be used as operators with one operand as well as two. With two operands, the value of the expression is the sum or difference of the operands and, with one operand, the value of the expression is the operand itself or the negation of the operand.

7.2.3 Intrinsic and Defined Operations

Intrinsic operations are those whose definitions are known to the compiler. They are built into Fortran and are always available for use in expressions. Table 7-1 lists the operators built into Fortran as specified by the standard. There may, of course, be other operations that are intrinsic to the compiler.

The relational operator symbols $==$, $/=$, $>$, $>=$, $<$, and $<=$ are new to Fortran and are synonyms for the operators .EQ., .NE., .GT., .GE., .LT., and .LE., respectively.

In addition to the Fortran operators that are intrinsic (built in), there may be user-defined operators in expressions.

Defined operations are those that the user defines in the Fortran program and makes available to each program unit that uses them. The computation performed by a defined operation is described explicitly in a function that must appear as a subprogram in the Fortran program where

Table 7-1 Intrinsic operators and the allowed types of their operands

Operator category	Intrinsic operator	Operand types
Arithmetic	**, *, /, +, -, unary +, unary -	Numeric of any combination of numeric types and kind type parameters
Character	//	Character of any length with the same kind type parameter
Relational	.EQ., .NE., ==, /=	Both of any numeric type and any kind type parameter, or both of type character with any length type parameter and with the same kind type parameter
Relational	.GT., .GE., .LT., .LE., >, >=, <, <=	Both of any numeric type except complex and any kind type parameter, or both of type character with any length type parameter and with the same kind type parameter
Logical	.NOT., .AND., .OR., .EQV., .NEQV.	Both of type logical with any combination of kind type parameters

it is used. The operator used in a defined operation is called a **defined operator**. In this way, users extend the repertoire of operations so that computations can be expressed in a natural way using operator notation. Function subprograms that define operators are explained in detail in Section 12.6.4.

A defined operator uses a symbol that is either the symbol for an intrinsic operator or is a new operator symbol. The synonyms described above for the relational operators remain synonyms in all contexts, even when there are defined operators. For example, if the operator < is defined for a new type, say STRING, the same definition applies to the operator .LT. for the type STRING; if the operator .LT. is specified as private, the operator < is also private.

A distinction is made between a defined (or new) operator and an extended intrinsic operator. An extended intrinsic operator is one that uses the same symbol as an intrinsically defined Fortran operator, like plus + or multiply *. It also causes the operations to be combined in the same order as is specified for the intrinsic operator. A **new operator** is one where the operator symbol is not the same as an intrinsic operator but is new, such as .INVERSE. New operators, however, have a fixed precedence; new unary operators have the highest precedence of all operators and new binary operators have the lowest precedence of all operators. The precedences of all operators are described in more detail in Section 7.2.5.

7.2.4 Rules for Forming Expressions

Expressions are formed by combining operands. Operands may be constants, variables (scalars, array elements, arrays, array sections, structures, structure components, and pointers), array constructors, structure constructors, functions, and parenthesized expressions with intrinsic and defined operators. Examples of expressions satisfying the expression formation rules are:

```
A
A + B
A + B / C
A * (B + C) / D - F ** 10 .EQ. G
```

The method used to specify these formation rules is a collection of syntax rules that determine the forms of expressions. The order of evaluation of the operations in an expression is determined by the usual semantics for the operations, and the syntax rules are designed to be consistent with these semantics. In fact, the order of evaluation defines a precedence order for operators that is summarized in Table 7-2 on page 233.

The set of syntax rules defines at the highest level an expression in terms of operators and operands which are themselves expressions. As a result, the formal set of rules is recursive. The basic or lowest level of an expression is a primary, which, for example, can be a variable, a constant, or a function, or recursively an expression enclosed in parentheses. The rules for forming expressions are described from the lowest or most primitive level to the highest or most complex level; that is, the rules are stated from a primary up to an expression.

Primary. A primary has one of the following forms (R701):

> constant
> constant-subobject
> variable
> array-constructor
> structure-constructor
> function-reference
> (expression)

Rules and restrictions:

1. A constant subobject is a subobject whose parent is a constant.

2. A variable that is a primary must not be an assumed-size array (5.3.1.4) or a section of an assumed-size array name, unless the last

subscript position of the array is specified with a scalar subscript or a section subscript in which the upper bound is specified.

Examples of primaries are:

3.2	A real constant
ONE	A named constant
'ABCS' (I:I)	A constant subobject
A	A variable (scalar, array, structure, or pointer)
B (:,1:N)	An assumed-size array with an upper bound in the last dimension
C (I)	An array element
CH (I:J)	A substring
(/ 1, J, 7 /)	An array constructor
RATIONAL (I, J)	A structure constructor
FCN (A)	A function reference
(A * B)	A parenthesized expression

In the above examples, ONE is a named constant if it has the PARAMETER attribute or appears in a PARAMETER statement. 'ABCS'(I:I) is a constant subobject even though I may be a variable because its parent is a constant; it is a constant subobject because it cannot be defined like a variable can be defined. RATIONAL is a derived type and FCN is a user-defined function.

When an array variable is a primary, the whole array is used, except in a masked assignment statement (7.5.4). In a masked assignment statement, only that part of the array specified by the mask is used. When a pointer is a primary, the target associated with (pointed to by) the pointer is used, except possibly when the pointer is an actual argument of a procedure, or is an operand of a defined operation or a defined assignment. Whether the pointer or the target is used in these exceptional cases is determined by the procedure invoked by the reference.

Recall that an assumed-size array (5.3.1.4) is a dummy argument whose shape is not completely specified in the subprogram in that the extent in the last dimension is determined by its corresponding actual argument. The implementation model is that the extent in the last dimension is never known to the subprogram but is specified by the use of a subscript, section subscript, or vector subscript expression which defines an upper bound in the last dimension. Unless the extent is specified in this way, such an object must not be used as a primary in an expression. On the other hand, if a subscript, section subscript with an extent for the upper bound, or a vector subscript is specified for the last dimension, the array value has a well-defined shape and hence can be used as a primary in any expression. For example, if A is declared as

```
REAL  A(3,*)
```

A(:,3) has a well-defined shape and can be used as a primary in an expression.

Expressions are used as actual arguments in procedure references (function references or subroutine calls). Because actual arguments can be expressions involving operations, actual arguments must not contain assumed-size arrays, unless their shape is well-defined, as described above. An actual argument, however, can be just a variable, which then allows the actual argument to be the name of an assumed-size array. This implies that such actual arguments can be assumed-size arrays, unless the procedure requires the shape of the argument to be specified by the actual argument. Most of the intrinsic procedures that allow array arguments require the shape to be specified for the actual array arguments, and therefore assumed-size arrays cannot be used as actual arguments for most intrinsic functions. The exceptions are all references to the intrinsic function LBOUND, and certain references to the intrinsic functions UBOUND and SIZE—see their descriptions in Appendix A.

Defined-Unary Expression. A defined-unary expression is a defined operator followed by a primary. Its form (R703) is:

> [defined-operator] primary

where defined operator has the form (R704)

> . letter [letter] ... .

Rules and restrictions:

1. A defined operator must not contain more than 31 letters.

2. A defined operator must not be the same name as the name of any intrinsic operator (.NOT., .AND., .OR., .EQV., .NEQV., .EQ., .NE., .GT., .GE., .LT., or .LE.) or any logical literal constant (.FALSE. or .TRUE.).

Examples of defined-unary expressions are:

.INVERSE. B   A defined-unary expression

A   A primary is also a defined-unary expression

where .INVERSE. is a defined operator.

Exponentiation Expression. An exponentiation expression is an expression in which the operator is the exponentiation operator **. Its form (R705) is:

defined-unary-expression [** exponentiation-expression]

Note that the definition is right recursive (that is, the defined term appears to the right of the operator **) which indicates that the precedence of the ** operator in contexts of equal precedence is right-to-left. Thus, the interpretation of the expression A ** B ** C is A ** (B ** C). Examples of exponentiation expressions are:

A ** B	An exponentiation expression
A ** B ** C	An exponentiation expression with right-to-left precedence
.INVERSE. B	A defined-unary expression is also an exponentiation expression
A	A primary is also an exponentiation expression

Multiplication Expression. A multiplication expression is an expression in which the operator is either * or /. Its forms (R706) are:

[multiplication-expression *] exponentiation-expression
multiplication-expression / exponentiation-expression

Note that the definition is left recursive (that is, the defined term appears to the left of the operator * or /) which indicates that the precedence of the * and / operators in contexts of equal precedence is left-to-right. Thus, the interpretation of the expression A * B * C is (A * B) * C, or A / B * C is (A / B) * C. This left-to-right precedence rule applies to the remaining binary operators except the relational operators. Examples of multiplication expressions are:

A * B	A multiplication expression
A * B * C	A multiplication expression with left-to-right precedence
A / B	A multiplication expression
A / B / C	A multiplication expression with left-to-right precedence
A * B / C	A multiplication expression with left-to-right precedence
A ** B	An exponentiation expression is also a multiplication expression
.INVERSE. B	A defined-unary expression is also a multiplication expression
A	A primary is also a multiplication expression

Summation Expression. A summation expression is an expression in which the operator is either + or −. Its forms (R707) are:

[summation-expression +] multiplication-expression
summation-expression − multiplication-expression
+ multiplication-expression
− multiplication-expression

Examples of summation expressions are:

A + B	A summation expression
A + B − C	A summation expression with left-to-right precedence
− A − B − C	A summation expression with left-to-right precedence
+ A	A summation expression using unary +
− A	A summation expression using unary −
A * B	A multiplication expression is also a summation expression
A ** B	An exponentiation expression is also a summation expression
.INVERSE. B	A defined-unary expression is also a summation expression
A	A primary is also a summation expression

Concatenation Expression. A concatenation expression is an expression in which the operator is //. Its form (R711) is:

[concatenation-expression //] summation-expression

Examples of concatenation expressions are:

A // B	A concatenation expression
A // B // C	A concatenation expression with left-to-right precedence
A − B	A summation expression is also a concatenation expression
− A	A summation expression is also a concatenation expression
A * B	A multiplication expression is also a concatenation expression
A ** B	An exponentiation expression is also a concatenation expression
.INVERSE. B	A defined-unary expression is also a concatenation expression
A	A primary is also a concatenation expression

Comparison Expression. A comparison expression is an expression in which the operator is a relational operator. Its form (R713) is:

[concatenation-expression relational-operator]   **&**
            concatenation-expression

where a relational operator (R714) is one of the operators .EQ., ==, .NE., /=, .LT., <, .LE., <=, .GT., >, .GE., and >=. The opera-tors ==, /=, <, <=, >, and >= are synonyms in all contexts for the operators .EQ., .NE., .LT., .LE., .GT., and .GE., respectively.

Note that the definition of a comparison expression is not recursive, and therefore comparison expressions cannot contain relational operators in contexts of equal precedence. Examples of comparison expressions are:

A .EQ. B	A comparison expression
A < B	A comparison expression
A // B	A concatenation expression is also a comparison expression
A – B	A summation expression is also a comparison expression
– A	A summation expression is also a comparison expression
A * B	A multiplication expression is also a comparison expression
A ** B	An exponentiation expression is also a comparison expression
.INVERSE. B	A defined-unary expression is also a comparison expression
A	A primary is also a comparison expression

Not Expression. A not expression is an expression in which the operator is .NOT. Its form (R715) is:

[**.NOT.**] comparison-expression

Note that the definition of a not expression is not recursive, and there-fore not expressions cannot contain adjacent .NOT. operators. Exam-ples of not expressions are:

.NOT. A	A not expression
A .EQ. B	A comparison expression is also a not expression
A // B	A concatenation expression is also a not expression
A – B	A summation expression is also a not expression
– A	A summation expression is also a not expression
A * B	A multiplication expression is also a not expression
A ** B	An exponentiation expression is also a not expression
.INVERSE. B	A defined-unary expression is also a not expression
A	A primary is also a not expression

Conjunct Expression. A conjunct expression is an expression in which the operator is .AND. Its form (R716) is:

  [conjunct-expression **.AND.**] not-expression

Note that the definition of a conjunct expression is left recursive, and therefore the precedence of the .AND. operator in contexts of equal precedence is left-to-right. Thus, the interpretation of the expression A .AND. B .AND. C is (A .AND. B) .AND. C. Examples of conjunct expressions are:

A .AND. B	A conjunct expression
A .AND. B .AND. C	A conjunct expression with left-to-right precedence
.NOT. A	A not expression is also a conjunct expression
A .EQ. B	A comparison expression is also a conjunct expression
A // B	A concatenation expression is also a conjunct expression
A – B	A summation expression is also a conjunct expression
– A	A summation expression is also a conjunct expression
A * B	A multiplication expression is also a conjunct expression
A ** B	An exponentiation expression is also a conjunct expression
.INVERSE. B	A defined-unary expression is also a conjunct expression
A	A primary is also a conjunct expression

Disjunct Expression. A disjunct expression is an expression in which the operator is .OR. Its form (R717) is:

  [disjunct-expression **.OR.**] conjunct-expression

Note that the definition of a disjunct expression is left recursive, and therefore the precedence of the .OR. operator in contexts of equal precedence is left-to-right. Thus, the interpretation of the expression A .OR. B .OR. C is (A .OR. B) .OR. C. Examples of disjunct expressions are:

A .OR. B	A disjunct expression
A .OR. B .OR. C	A disjunct expression with left-to-right precedence
A .AND. B	A conjunct expression is also a disjunct expression

.NOT. A	A not expression is also a disjunct expression
A .EQ. B	A comparison expression is also a disjunct expression
A // B	A concatenation expression is also a disjunct expression
A – B	A summation expression is also a disjunct expression
– A	A summation expression is also a disjunct expression
A * B	A multiplication expression is also a disjunct expression
A ** B	An exponentiation expression is also a disjunct expression
.INVERSE. B	A defined-unary expression is also a disjunct expression
A	A primary is also a disjunct expression

Equivalence Expression. An equivalence expression is an expression in which the operator is either .EQV. or .NEQV. Its forms (R718) are:

    [equivalence-expression **.EQV.**] disjunct-expression
    equivalence-expression **.NEQV.** disjunct-expression

Note that the definition of an equivalence expression is left recursive, and therefore the precedence of the .EQV. or .NEQV. operators in contexts of equal precedence is left-to-right. Thus, the interpretation of the expression A .EQV. B .NEQV. C is (A .EQV. B) .NEQV. C. Examples of equivalence expressions are:

A .EQV. B	An equivalence expression
A .NEQV. B	An equivalence expression
A .NEQV. B .EQV. C	An equivalence expression with left-to-right precedence
A .OR. B	A disjunct expression is also an equivalence expression
A .AND. B	A conjunct expression is also an equivalence expression
.NOT. A	A not expression is also an equivalence expression
A .EQ. B	A comparison expression is also an equivalence expression
A // B	A concatenation expression is also an equivalence expression

A – B   A summation expression is also
                       an equivalence expression
– A   A summation expression is also
                       an equivalence expression
A * B   A multiplication expression is also
                       an equivalence expression
A ** B   An exponentiation expression is also
                       an equivalence expression
.INVERSE. B   A defined-unary expression is also
                       an equivalence expression
A   A primary is also an equivalence expression

Expression. The most general form of an expression (R723) is:

[expression defined-operator] equivalence-expression

Note that the definition of an expression is left recursive, and therefore the precedence of the binary defined operator in contexts of equal precedence is left-to-right. The interpretation of the expression A .PLUS. B .MINUS. C is thus (A .PLUS. B) .MINUS. C. Examples of expressions are:

A .PLUS. B   An expression
A .CROSS. B .CROSS. C   An expression with left-to-right precedence
A .EQV. B   An equivalence expression is also an expression
A .OR. B   A disjunct expression is also an expression
A .AND. B   A conjunct expression is also an expression
.NOT. A   A not expression is also an expression
A .EQ. B   A comparison expression is also an expression
A // B   A concatenation expression is also an expression
A – B   A summation expression is also an expression
– A   A summation expression is also an expression
A * B   A multiplication expression is also an expression
A ** B   An exponentiation expression is also an expression
.INVERSE. B   A defined-unary expression is also an expression
A   A primary is also an expression

where .PLUS., .MINUS., and .CROSS. are defined operators.

Summary of the Forms and Hierarchy for Expressions. The previous sections have described in detail the sorts of expressions that can be formed. These expressions form a hierarchy that can best be illustrated by two figures. Figure 7-2 describes the hierarchy by placing the simplest form of an expression, namely, a variable, at the center of a set of nested rectangles. The more general forms of an expression are the enclosing rectangles, from a primary to an exponential expression, to a summation expression, and finally to a general expression using a defined binary operator .CROSS. Thus, Figure 7-2 demonstrates that an expression is indeed all of these special case forms, including the simplest form, a primary.

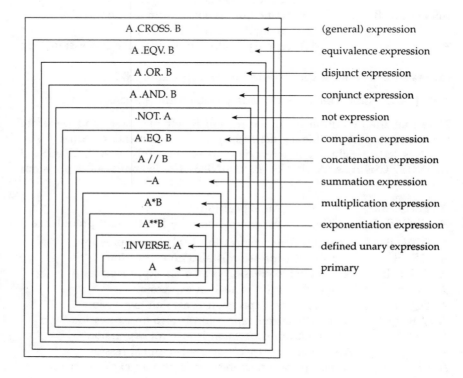

Figure 7-2 The hierarchy of expressions by examples

Figure 7-3 illustrates the relationship between the different sorts of expressions by summarizing the definitional forms in one table. The simplest form of an expression is at the bottom and is the primary as in Figure 7-2. The next, more general, form is second from the bottom and is the defined unary expression; it uses the primary in its definition. At the top of the figure is the most general form of an expression.

The following are examples of more complicated expressions:

A + B .CROSS. C – D   An expression mixing new operators
                             and old ones

(A + B) .CROSS. (C – D)   An expression which has
                            the same interpretation
                            as the previous expression

A + (B .CROSS. C) – D   An expression which has
                            a different interpretation from
                            the previous two expressions

A .CROSS. (B .CROSS. C)   An expression which in general is not
                            the same as the expression
                            A .CROSS. B .CROSS. C

Term	Definition
expression	[expression defined-operator] equivalence-expression
equivalence-expression	[equivalence-expression .EQV.] disjunct-expression
	equivalence-expression .NEQV. disjunct-expression
disjunct-expression	[disjunct-expression .OR.] conjunct-expression
conjunct-expression	[conjunct-expression .AND.] not-expression
not-expression	[.NOT.] comparison-expression
comparison-expression	[concatenation-expression relational-operator] &
	concatenation-expression
concatenation-expression	[concatenation-expression //] summation-expression
summation-expression	[summation-expression +] multiplication-expression
	summation-expression – multiplication-expression
	+ multiplication-expression
	– multiplication-expression
multiplication-expression	[multiplication-expression *] exponentiation-expression
	multiplication-expression / exponentiation-expression
exponentiation-expression	defined-unary-expression [** exponentiation-expression]
defined-unary-expression	[defined-operator] primary
primary	constant
	constant-subobject
	variable
	array-constructor
	structure-constructor
	function-reference
	(expression)

Figure 7-3 The hierarchy of expressions via forms

7.2.5 Precedence of Operators

The above formation rules suggest a precedence among the operators—
that is, the order in which operands are combined with operators to form
values of subexpressions. Table 7-2 summarizes the relative precedence
of operators, including the precedence when operators of equal

precedence are adjacent. An entry "N/A" in the column titled "In context of equal precedence" indicates that the operator cannot appear in such contexts. The column titled "Category of operator" classifies the operators as extension, numeric, character, relational, and logical operators. Note that these operators are not intrinsic operators unless the types of the operands are those specified in Table 7-3.

Table 7-2 Categories of operations and relative precedences

Category of operator	Operator	Precedence	In context of equal precedence
Extension	Unary defined-operator	Highest	N/A
Numeric	**	.	Right-to-left
Numeric	* or /	.	Left-to-right
Numeric	Unary + or –	.	N/A
Numeric	Binary + or –	.	Left-to-right
Character	//	.	Left-to-right
Relational	.EQ., .NE., .LT., .LE., .GT., .GE. == , /=, <, <=, >, >=	.	N/A
Logical	.NOT.	.	N/A
Logical	.AND.	.	Left-to-right
Logical	.OR.	.	Left-to-right
Logical	.EQV. or .NEQV.	.	Left-to-right
Extension	Binary defined-operator	Lowest	Left-to-right

For example, in the expression

```
A .AND. B .AND. C .OR. D
```

Table 7-2 indicates that the .AND. operator is of higher precedence than the .OR. operator, and the .AND. operators are combined left-to-right when in contexts of equal precedence; thus, A and B are combined by the .AND. operator, the result A .AND. B is combined with C using the .AND. operator, and that result is combined with D using the .OR. operator. This expression is thus interpreted the same way as the following fully parenthesized expression

```
(((A .AND. B) .AND. C) .OR. D)
```

Notice that the defined (or new) operators have fixed precedences; new unary operators have the highest precedence of all operators and are all of equal precedence; new binary operators have the lowest precedence, are all of equal precedence, and are combined left-to-right when in contexts of equal precedence. Both kinds of new operators may have multiple definitions in the program unit and therefore may be generic just as intrinsic operators and intrinsic procedures are generic.

As a consequence of the expression formation rules, unary operators cannot appear in a context of equal precedence; the precedence must be specified by parentheses. There is thus no left-to-right or right-to-left rule for any unary operators. Similarly, the relational operators cannot appear in a context of equal precedence; consequently, there is no left-to-right or right-to-left rule for the relational operators.

7.2.6 Intrinsic Operations

Intrinsic operations are those known to the processor. For an operation to be intrinsic, an intrinsic operator symbol must be used, and the operands must be of the intrinsic types specified in Table 7-3.

Table 7-3 Type of operands and result for intrinsic operations

Intrinsic operator	Type of x_1	Type of x_2	Type of result
Unary +, −		I, R, Z	I, R, Z
Binary +, −, *, /, **	I	I, R, Z	I, R, Z
	R	I, R, Z	R, R, Z
	Z	I, R, Z	Z, Z, Z
//	C	C	C
.EQ., .NE.	I	I, R, Z	L, L, L
==, /=	R	I, R, Z	L, L, L
	Z	I, R, Z	L, L, L
	C	C	L
.GT., .GE., .LT., .LE.	I	I, R	L, L
>, >=, <, <=	R	I, R	L, L
	C	C	L
.NOT.		L	L
.AND., .OR., .EQV., .NEQV.	L	L	L

Note: The symbols I, R, Z, C, and L stand for the types integer, real, complex, character, and logical, respectively. Where more than one type for x_2 is given, the type of the result of the operation is given in the same relative position in the next column. For the intrinsic operators requiring operands of type character, the kind type parameters of the operands must be the same.

The intrinsic operations are either binary or unary. The binary operations use the binary intrinsic operator symbols +, −, *, /, **, //,

.EQ., .NE., .LT., .GT., .LE., .GE. (and their synonyms ==, /=, <, >, <=, and >=), .AND., .OR., .EQV., and .NEQV. The unary operations use the unary intrinsic operator symbols +, -, and .NOT.

The intrinsic operations are divided into four classes with different rules and restrictions for the types of the operands. The four classes are numeric intrinsic, character intrinsic, logical intrinsic, and numeric relational intrinsic operations.

The numeric intrinsic operations use the intrinsic operators +, -, *, /, and **. The operands may be of any numeric type and with any kind type parameters. The result of the operation is of a type specified by Table 7-3 and has type parameters as specified in Section 7.2.8.2.

For example, the expressions

```
I + R
I * I
I - D
I / Z
```

where I, R, D, and Z are declared to be of types integer, real, double precision real, and complex have the types and type parameters of the variables R, I, D, and Z, respectively.

7.2.7 Defined Operations

A **defined operation** is any nonintrinsic operation that is interpreted and evaluated by a function subprogram specified by an interface block with a generic specifier of the form OPERATOR (defined-operator). A defined operation uses either a defined operator or an intrinsic operator symbol, and is either unary or binary. Its forms (R703, R723) are:

intrinsic-unary-operator x_2
defined-operator x_2
x_1 intrinsic-binary-operator x_2
x_1 defined-operator x_2

where x_1 and x_2 are operands. When either an intrinsic unary or binary operator symbol is used, the type of x_2 and types of x_1 and x_2 must not be the same as the types of the operands specified in Table 7-3 for the particular intrinsic operator symbol. Thus, intrinsic operations on intrinsic types cannot be redefined by the user. Examples of each of the previous forms are:

```
- A
.PLUS. A
A * B
A .HIGHER. B
```

When a defined operation uses an intrinsic operator symbol, the generic properties of that operator are extended to the new types specified by the interface block. When a defined operation uses a defined operator, the defined operation is called an **extension operation**, and the operator is called an **extension operator**. An extension operator may have generic properties by specifying more than one interface block with the same generic specifier of the form OPERATOR (defined-operator) or by specifying more than one function subprogram in an interface block.

7.2.8 Data Type, Type Parameters, and Shape of an Expression

The data type, type parameters, and shape of a complete expression are determined by the data type, type parameters, and shape of each constant, variable, constructor, and function reference appearing in the expression. The determination is inside-out in the sense that the properties are determined first for the primaries. These properties are then determined repeatedly for the operations in precedence order, resulting eventually in the properties for the expression.

For example, consider the expression A + B * C, where A, B, and C are of numeric type. First, the data types, type parameter values, and shapes of the three variables A, B, and C are determined. Because * has a higher precedence than +, the operation B * C is performed first. The type, type parameters, and shape of the expression B * C are determined next, and then these properties for the entire expression are determined from those of A and B * C.

7.2.8.1 Data Type and Type Parameters of a Primary.
The type, type parameters, and shape of a primary that is a nonpointer variable or constant is straightforward because these properties are determined by specification statements for the variable or named constant, or by the form of the constant (4.2.4). For example, if A is a variable, its declaration in a specification statement such as

```
REAL  A (10, 10)
```

determines it as an explicit-shaped array of type real with a default kind parameter. For a constant such as

(1.3, 2.9)

the form of the constant indicates that it is a scalar constant of type complex and of default kind.

For a pointer variable, the type, type parameters, and rank are determined by the declaration of the pointer variable. However, if the pointer is of deferred shape, the shape (in particular, the extents in each dimension) is determined by the target of the pointer, Consider the declarations

```
REAL, POINTER :: A (:, :)
REAL, TARGET  :: B (10, 20)
```

and suppose that the pointer A is associated with the target B. Then the shape of A is (10, 20).

The type, type parameters, and shape of an array constructor are determined by the form of the constructor. Its shape is of rank one and of size equal to the number of elements. Its type and type parameters are those of any element of the constructor because they must all be of the same type and type parameters. Therefore, the type and type parameters of the array constructor

```
(/ 1_1, 123_1, -10_1 /)
```

are integer and kind value 1.

The type of a structure constructor is the derived type used as the name of the constructor. A structure constructor is always a scalar. A structure has no type parameters. So, the type of the structure constructor

```
PERSON( 56, 'Father' )
```

is the derived type PERSON. (See Section 4.6 for the type definition PERSON.)

The type, type parameters, and shape of a function are determined either by:

- an implicit type declaration for the function within the program unit referencing the function,

- an explicit type declaration for the function within the program unit referencing the function (just like a variable), or

- an explicit interface to the function (12.6.1). (When the interface is not explicit, the function is either an external function or a statement function.)

In case the interface is explicit, these properties are determined by:

- the type and other specification statements for the function in an interface block within the program unit referencing the function

- the type and other specification statements for the internal or module procedure specifying the function

- the description of the particular intrinsic function being referenced (see Appendix A)

Note, however, that because intrinsic functions and functions with interface blocks may be generic, these properties are determined by the type, type parameters, and shapes of the actual arguments of the particular function reference.

For example, consider the statements

```
REAL FUNCTION FCN (X)
DIMENSION FCN (10, 15)
```

as part of the program unit specifying an internal function FCN. A reference to FCN (3.3) is of type default real with shape (10, 15). As a second example, consider

```
REAL ( SINGLE ) X (10, 10, 10)
   . . .
   . . . SIN (X) . . .
```

The interface to SIN is specified by the definition of the sine function in Appendix A. In this case, the function reference SIN (X) is of type real with kind parameter value SINGLE and of shape (10, 10, 10).

As mentioned above, the interface is implicit if the function is external (and no interface block is provided) or is a statement function. In these cases, the shape is always that of a scalar, and the type and type parameters are determined by the implicit type declaration rules in effect, or by an explicit type declaration for the function name. For example, given the code fragment:

```
IMPLICIT INTEGER ( SHORT ) (A-F)
   . . .
   . . . FCN (X) . . .
```

FCN (X) is a scalar of type integer with kind type parameter value SHORT.

The one case for variables and functions that is not straightforward is the determination of the shape of a variable when it is of deferred shape or of assumed shape. For deferred-shape arrays, the rank is known from the declaration but the sizes in each dimension are determined as the result of executing an ALLOCATE statement or a pointer assignment statement. For assumed-shape arrays, the rank is also known from the declaration but the sizes are determined by information passed into the subprogram through a descriptor in the argument sequence. In the case of pointers, the shape of the object is that of the target associated with (pointed to by) the pointer. The shape of deferred-shape and assumed-shape arrays thus cannot be determined in general until execution time.

7.2.8.2 Type and Type Parameters of the Result of an Operation. The type of the result of an intrinsic operation is determined by the type of the operands and the intrinsic operation and is specified by Table 7-3.

For nonnumeric operations, the type parameters of the result of an operation are determined as follows. For the relational intrinsic operations, the kind type parameter is that for the default logical type. For the logical intrinsic operations, the kind type parameter is that of the operands if the operands have the same kind type parameter, and otherwise is processor dependent. For the character intrinsic operation (note—there is only one, namely //), the operands must have the same kind type parameter and the result has that kind type parameter. The length type parameter value for the result is the sum of the length type parameters of the operands.

For example, consider the operation C1 // C2 where C1 and C2 are of type character with kind type parameters 2 and lengths 7 and 18. The result is of type character with kind type parameter value 2 and length type parameter value 25.

For numeric intrinsic operations, the kind type parameter value of the result is determined as follows:

- For unary operations, it is that of the operand.

- For binary operations, if the operands are of different types (for example, I+R), it is the kind type parameter of the operand with the same type as the result (as specified by Table 7-3).

- For binary operations, if the operands are of the same type and kind type parameters, it is the kind type parameter of the operands.

- For binary operations, if the operands are both of type integer but with different kind type parameters, it is the kind type parameter of the operand with the larger decimal exponent range. If the decimal exponent ranges of the two kinds are the same, it is processor dependent.

- For binary operations, if the operands are both of type real or complex but with different kind type parameters, it is the kind type parameter of the operand with the larger decimal precision. If the decimal precisions are the same, the kind type parameter is processor dependent.

For numeric intrinsic operations, an easy way to remember the result type and type parameter rules is to consider that the three numeric types—integer, real, and complex—are ordered by the increasing generality of numbers: integers are contained in the set of real numbers and real numbers are contained in the set of complex numbers. Within the integer type, the kinds are ordered by increasing decimal exponent ranges. Within the real and complex types, the kinds for each type are ordered by increasing decimal precision. If there is more than one kind of integer with the same decimal exponent range, the ordering is processor dependent; a similar processor-dependent ordering is selected for the real and complex types, if there is more than one kind with the same decimal precision.

Using this model, the result type of a numeric intrinsic operation is the same type as the operand of the greater generality. For the result type parameter, the rule is complicated: if one or both of the operands is of type real or complex, the type parameter is that of the set of numbers of the more general type described above and with a precision at least as large as the precision of the operands; if both are of type integer, the result type parameter is of a set of numbers that has a range at least as large as the range of the operands.

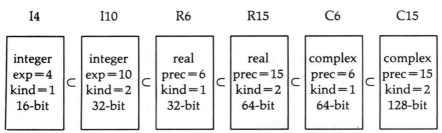

Figure 7-4 Example ordering of numeric types

To illustrate this ordering, consider an implementation that has two kinds of integers (kind=1 is a 16-bit format; kind=2 is a 32-bit format) with decimal exponent ranges 4 and 10, two kinds of reals (kind=1 is a 32-bit format; kind=2 is a 64-bit format) with decimal precisions 6 and

15, and two kinds of complex numbers (kind=1 is a 64-bit format; kind=2 is a 128-bit format) with decimal precisions 6 and 15. Figure 7-4 gives the ordering of the integer, real, and complex types that are likely for the common 32- and 64-bit representations used by most workstations. Let variables of the 6 numeric types be I4, I10, R6, R15, C6, and C15, where the letter designates the type and the digits designate the decimal exponent range or decimal precision. Using this ordering, Table 7-4 gives the type and type parameters of some simple expressions.

Table 7-4 Type and type parameters of some simple expressions

Expressions	Type and type parameters are the same as the variable
I4 + R6	R6
I10 * C15	C15
C6 / C15	C15
I4 - I10	I10
I4 ** C6	C6
R15 + C6	C15
C6 ** I4	C6
I10 - R6	R6

The type and type parameter values of a defined operation are determined by the interface block (or blocks) for the referenced operation and are the type and type parameters of the name of the function specified by the interface block. Note that the operator may be generic and therefore the type and type parameters may be determined by the operands. For example, consider the interface:

```
INTERFACE OPERATOR (.PLUS.)

   TYPE (SET) FCN_SET_PLUS (X, Y)
      TYPE (SET)  X, Y
   END FUNCTION FCN_SET_PLUS

   TYPE (RATIONAL) FCN_RAT_PLUS (X, Y)
      TYPE (RATIONAL)  X, Y
   END FUNCTION FCN_RAT_PLUS

END INTERFACE  OPERATOR (.PLUS.)
```

The operation A .PLUS. B where A and B are of type RATIONAL is an expression of type RATIONAL with no type parameters. The operation

C .PLUS. D where C and D are of type SET is an expression of type SET with no type parameters.

7.2.8.3 Shape of an Expression. The shape of an expression is determined by the shape of each operand in the expression in the same recursive manner as for the type and type parameters for an expression. That is, the shape of an expression is the shape of the result of the last operation determined by the interpretation of the expression.

However, the shape rules are simplified considerably by the requirement that the operands of binary intrinsic operations must be in shape conformance; that is, two operands are in **shape conformance** if both are arrays of the same shape, or one or both operands are scalars. The operands of a defined operation have no such requirement but must match the shape of the corresponding dummy arguments of the defining function.

For primaries that are constants, variables, constructors, or functions, the shape is that of the constant, variable, constructor, or function name. Recall that structure constructors are always scalar, and array constructors are always rank-one arrays of size equal to the number of elements in the constructor. For unary intrinsic operations, the shape of the result is that of the operand. For binary intrinsic operations, the shape is that of the array operand if there is one and is scalar otherwise. For defined operations, the shape is that of the function name specifying the operation.

For example, consider the intrinsic operation A + B where A and B are of type default integer and default real respectively; assume A is a scalar and B is an array of shape (3, 5). Then, the result is of type default real with shape (3, 5).

As a second example, consider the expression A // B as a defined operation where A is a scalar of type character with kind type parameter value 1 and of length 25, and B is an array of type character with kind type parameter value 2, of length 30, and of shape (10). Suppose further there is the following interface for the // operator:

```
INTERFACE OPERATOR (//)

    FUNCTION FCN_CONCAT (X, Y)
        CHARACTER (*, 1) X
        CHARACTER (*, 2) Y (:)
        CHARACTER (LEN (X) + LEN (Y), 2) FCN_CONCAT (SIZE (Y))
    END FUNCTION FCN_CONCAT

END INTERFACE
```

The type declaration for FCN_CONCAT determines that the result of the expression A // B is of type character with kind type parameter 2. In addition, the same type declaration specifies that the length of the result is the sum of the lengths of the operands A and B, that is, of length 55. The shape is specified to be of rank one and of size equal to the size of the actual argument B corresponding to the dummy argument Y, that is, of shape (10).

7.2.8.4 The Extents of an Expression. For most contexts, the extents (lower and upper bounds) of an array expression are not needed; only the sizes of each dimension are needed to satisfy array conformance requirements for expressions. The extents of an array expression when it is the ARRAY argument (first positional argument) of the LBOUND and UBOUND intrinsic functions are needed, however.

The functions LBOUND and UBOUND have two keyword arguments ARRAY and DIM; ARRAY is an array expression and DIM, which is optional, is an integer. If the DIM argument is present, LBOUND and UBOUND return the lower and upper bounds, respectively, of the dimension specified by the DIM argument. If DIM is absent, they return a rank-one array of the lower and upper bounds, respectively, of all dimensions of the ARRAY argument. As described below, these functions distinguish the special cases when the array argument is a name or structure component with no section subscript list from the general case when the array argument is a more general expression. Note that if A is a structure with an array component B, A % B is treated as if it were an array name and not an expression.

When the ARRAY argument is an array expression that is not a name or a structure component, the function LBOUND returns 1 if the DIM argument is specified and returns a rank-one array of 1s if the DIM argument is absent. For the same conditions, the function UBOUND returns as the upper bound the size of the requested dimension or the size of all dimensions in a rank-one array.

When the ARRAY argument is an array name or a structure component with no section subscript list, there are four cases to distinguish depending on the array specifier for the name.

Explicit-Shape Specifier. LBOUND and UBOUND functions return the declared lower and upper bounds of the array name or the structure component with no section subscript list.

Examples:

```
INTEGER A (2:10, 11:12)
```

```
TYPE PASSENGER_INFO
   INTEGER NUMBER
   INTEGER TICKET_IDS (2:500)
END TYPE PASSENGER_INFO

TYPE (PASSENGER_INFO) PAL, MANY (3:10)
```

LBOUND (A) has the value (2, 11), and UBOUND (A, 1) has the value 10. LBOUND (PAL % TICKET_IDS) has the value (2) and UBOUND (MANY % TICKET_IDS(2), 1) has the value 10.

Assumed-Shape Specifier. The name is a dummy argument whose extents are determined by the corresponding actual argument. The dummy argument may have its lower bound in a particular dimension specified but if not, the lower bound is defined to be 1. The LBOUND function returns these lower bounds. The upper bound for a particular dimension is the extent of the actual argument in that dimension, if no lower bound is specified for the dummy argument, and is the extent minus 1 plus the lower bound if a lower bound is specified. The UBOUND function returns these upper bounds.

Example:

```
REAL   C (2:10, 11:12)
   . . .
CALL  S (C (4:8, 7:9) )
CONTAINS
   SUBROUTINE  S (A)
     REAL  A (:, 2:)
      . . .
     ! Reference to LBOUND (A)  and  UBOUND (A)
      . . .
```

Inside the body of subroutine S, LBOUND (A) has the value (1, 2), because the array starts at subscript position 1 by default in the first dimension and starts at subscript position 2 by declaration in the second dimension. UBOUND (A) has the value (5, 4), because there are 5 subscript positions (4 to 8) in the first dimension of the actual argument corresponding to A, and 3 subscript positions (7 to 9) in the second dimension of the same actual argument and the subscripts are specified to start at 2 by the declaration of the dummy argument A.

Assumed-Size Specifier. The name is a dummy argument whose upper and lower bounds in all but the last dimension are declared for the dummy argument. The lower bound for the last dimension may be specified in the assumed-shape specifier but, if absent, the lower bound is 1. The LBOUND function returns these lower bounds. The upper bound for all dimensions except the last one is known to the subprogram but the upper bound in the last dimension is not known. The UBOUND function, therefore, must not be referenced with the first argument being the name of an assumed-size array and no second argument, or the first argument being the name of an assumed-size array and the second argument specifying the last dimension of the array. Otherwise, the UBOUND function returns the upper bounds as declared for all but the last dimension.

Example:

```
REAL  C (2:10, 11:12)
   . . .
CALL  S (C (4:8, 7:9) )
CONTAINS
  SUBROUTINE  S (A)
    REAL  A (-2:2, *)
      . . .
    ! Reference to LBOUND (A, 1)  and  UBOUND (A (:, 2))
    ! A reference to UBOUND (A) would be illegal.
    ! A reference to UBOUND (A, 2) would be illegal.
      . . .
```

Inside the body of subroutine S, LBOUND (A, 1) has the value -2, and UBOUND (A (:, 2)) has the value (5) because A(:,2) is an expression, which is an array section, not an array name.

Deferred-Shape Specifier. The name is the name of an allocatable array, an array pointer, or a structure component with one of its part references being an allocatable or pointer array. As such, if the array or a part reference has not been allocated or associated with a target, the LBOUND and UBOUND functions must not be invoked with the ARRAY argument equal to such an array name. If it is allocated, the functions LBOUND and UBOUND return the lower and upper bounds specified in the ALLOCATE statement that allocated the array. If no lower bound is specified, it is taken as 1. If it is an array pointer, either its target has been allocated by an ALLOCATE statement or its target has become associated with the pointer using a pointer assignment statement. In the former case, the LBOUND and UBOUND functions return the lower and upper bounds specified in the ALLOCATE statement. In the latter case, the LBOUND and UBOUND functions return values as if the ARRAY argument were equal to the target used in the pointer assignment statement that created the last association for the pointer.

Example:

```
REAL, ALLOCATABLE ::  A (:, :)
   . . .
ALLOCATE  ( A (5, 7:9) )
   . . .
! Reference to LBOUND (A)  and  UBOUND (A)
   . . .
```

After the ALLOCATE statement above is executed, LBOUND (A) has the value (1, 7), and UBOUND (A) has the value (5, 9).

7.2.9 Special Expressions

Expressions may appear in statements other than assignment statements, in particular in specification statements. In many cases, such expressions are restricted in some way; for example, the operands in expressions in a PARAMETER statement are restricted to essentially constants. Throughout the standard, there are terms used for the various categories of expressions allowed in specific syntactic contexts. For example, the expressions that can be used in PARAMETER statements are called **initialization expressions** and can be evaluated at the time the program is compiled. Initialization expressions are restricted forms of constant expressions.

The expressions that can be used as array bounds and character lengths in specification statements are called **specification expressions** and are those that are scalar and of type integer that can be evaluated on entry to the program unit at the time of execution. The remainder of this subsection describes and defines such limited expressions and summarizes where they can be used.

7.2.9.1 Constant Expressions.

A constant expression is an extended constant or is an expression consisting of intrinsic operators whose operands are extended constants. An extended constant in this context is defined as any one of the following:

1. a literal or named constant, or a subobject of a constant where each subscript, section subscript, or starting and ending point of a substring range is a constant expression

2. an array constructor where every subexpression has primaries that are constant expressions or are implied-DO variables of the array constructor

3. a structure constructor where each component is a constant expression

4. an intrinsic function reference that can be evaluated at compile-time

5. a constant expression enclosed in parentheses.

The restriction in item (4) above to intrinsic functions that can be evaluated at compile-time eliminates the use of the intrinsic functions PRESENT, ALLOCATED, and ASSOCIATED, and requires that each argument of the intrinsic function reference be a constant expression or a variable whose type parameters or bounds are known at compile-time. This restriction excludes, for example, named variables that are assumed-shape arrays, assumed-size arrays for inquiries requiring the size of the last dimension, and variables that are pointer arrays or allocatable arrays. For example, if an array X has explicit bounds in all dimensions, an inquiry such as SIZE (X) can be computed at compile-time, and SIZE (X) + 10 is considered a constant expression.

Constant expressions may be used in any executable statement where general expressions (that is, unrestricted expressions) are permitted.

Examples of constant expressions are:

2	An integer literal constant
3.0E+01	A real literal constant
–7.5_QUAD	A real literal constant where QUAD is a named integer constant
7_LONG	An integer literal constant where LONG is a named integer constant
(/ 7, (I, I = 1, 10) /)	An array constructor
RATIONAL (1, 2+J)	A structure constructor where RATIONAL is a derived type and J is a named integer constant
LBOUND (A,1)+3	A reference to an inquiry intrinsic function where A is an explicit-shape array
INT (N, 2)	An intrinsic function where N is a named constant
KIND (X)	An intrinsic function where X is a real variable with known type parameter
REAL (10+I)	An intrinsic function where I is a named integer constant
COUNT (A)	An intrinsic function where A is a named logical constant
LOG (2.0)	An intrinsic function

I/3.3 + J**3.3   A numeric expression where I and J are
          named integer constants

SUM (A)   A reference to a transformational intrinsic function
          where A is a named integer array constant

7.2.9.2 Initialization Expressions. An **initialization expression** is a constant expression restricted as follows:

1. The exponentiation operator (**) is allowed only when the power (second operand) is of type integer; that is, X ** Y is allowed only if Y is of type integer.

2. Subscripts, section subscripts, starting and ending points of substring ranges, components of structure constructors, and arguments of intrinsic functions must be initialization expressions.

3. The elements of array constructors must be initialization expressions or implied-DOs for which the array constructor values and implied-DO parameters are expressions whose primaries are initialization expressions or implied-DO variables.

4. An elemental intrinsic function in an initialization expression must have arguments of type integer or character, and must return a result of type integer or character.

5. A transformational intrinsic function in an initialization expression must be one of the transformational intrinsic functions REPEAT, RESHAPE, SELECTED_INT_KIND, SELECTED_REAL_KIND, TRANSFER, and TRIM, and must have initialization expressions as arguments; this excludes the use of the transformational functions ALL, ANY, COUNT, CSHIFT, DOT_PRODUCT, EOSHIFT, MATMUL, MAXLOC, MAXVAL, MINLOC, MINVAL, PACK, PRODUCT, SPREAD, SUM, TRANSPOSE, and UNPACK.

6. An inquiry intrinsic function is allowed, except that the arguments must either be initialization expressions or variables whose type parameters or bounds inquired about are not assumed, not defined by an ALLOCATE statement, or not defined by pointer assignment.

7. Any subexpression enclosed in parentheses must be an initialization expression.

All but the last five examples in Section 7.2.9.1 are initialization expressions. The last five are not because initialization expressions cannot contain functions that return results of type real (REAL, LOG), must not reference certain transformational functions (COUNT, SUM), or use the exponentiation operator when the second operand is of type real.

Further examples of initialization expressions are:

SIZE (A, 1) * 4	An integer expression where A is an array with an explicit shape
KIND (0.0D0)	An inquiry function with a constant argument
SELECTED_REAL_KIND (6, 30)	An inquiry function with constant arguments
SELECTED_INT_KIND (2 * R)	An inquiry function with an argument that is an initialization expression, where R is a previously declared named constant of type integer

Initialization expressions must be used in the following contexts:

1. as initial values following the equal signs in PARAMETER statements and in type declaration statements with the PARAMETER attribute

2. as initial values following the equal signs for entities in type declaration statements

3. as expressions in structure constructors in the DATA statement value list

4. as kind type parameter values in type declaration statements; in this case, they also must be scalar and of type integer

5. as actual arguments for the KIND dummy argument of the conversion intrinsic functions AINT, ANINT, CHAR, INT, LOGICAL, NINT, REAL, CMPLX; in this case, they also must be scalar and of type integer

6. as case values in the CASE statement; in this situation, they must be scalar and of type integer, logical, or character

7. as subscript or substring range expressions of equivalence objects in an EQUIVALENCE statement; in this case, they must be scalar and of type integer

Thus, initialization expressions must be used for situations where the value of the expression is needed at compile time. Note that the initialization expressions do not include intrinsic functions that return values of type real, logical, or complex, or have arguments of type real, logical, or complex.

7.2.9.3 Specification Expressions. Specification expressions are forms of restricted expressions (defined below), limited in type and rank. Briefly, a restricted expression is limited to constants and certain variables accessible to the scoping unit whose values can be determined on entry to the programming unit before any executable statement is executed. For example, variables that are dummy arguments, are in a common block, are in a host program unit, or are in a module made accessible to the program unit can be evaluated on entry to a program unit. Array constructors, structure constructors, intrinsic function references, and parenthesized expressions made up of these primaries must depend only on restricted expressions as building blocks for operands in a restricted expression. To be specific, a restricted expression is an expression in which each operation is intrinsic and each primary is limited to one of the following:

1. a constant or constant subobject

2. a variable that is a dummy argument

3. a variable that is in a common block

4. a variable made accessible from a module

5. a variable from the host program unit

6. an array constructor where every expression has primaries that are restricted expressions or are implied-DO variables of the array constructor

7. a structure constructor where each component is a restricted expression

8. an elemental intrinsic function whose result is of type integer or character and whose arguments are all of type integer or character

9. one of the transformational intrinsic functions REPEAT, RESHAPE, SELECTED_INT_KIND, SELECTED_REAL_KIND, TRANSFER, and TRIM, where each argument is a restricted expression of type integer or character (this excludes the use of the transformational functions ALL, ANY, COUNT, CSHIFT, DOT_PRODUCT, EOSHIFT, MATMUL, MAXLOC, MAXVAL, MINLOC, MINVAL, PACK, PRODUCT, SPREAD, SUM, TRANSPOSE, and UNPACK).

10. an inquiry intrinsic function except PRESENT, ALLOCATED, and ASSOCIATED where each argument is either:

a.   a restricted expression, or

b.   a variable whose bounds or type parameters inquired about are not assumed, not defined by an ALLOCATE statement, and not defined by a pointer assignment statement

where any subscript, section subscript, and starting or ending point of a substring range is a restricted expression.

A **specification expression** is a restricted expression that has a scalar value and is of type integer. Specification expressions are used as bounds for arrays and length parameter values for character entities in type declarations, attribute specifications, dimension declarations, and other specification statements (see Table 7-5).

7.2.9.4 Initialization   and   Specification   Expressions   in Declarations. The following rules and restrictions apply to the use of initialization and specification expressions in specification statements.

Rules and restrictions:

1. The type and type parameters of a variable or named constant in one of these expressions must be specified in a prior specification in the same scoping unit, in a host scoping unit, in a module scoping unit made accessible to the current scoping unit, or by the implicit typing rules in effect. If the variable or named constant is explicitly given these attributes in a subsequent type declaration statement, it must confirm the implicit type and type parameters.

2. If an element of an array is referenced in one of these expressions, the array bounds must be specified in a prior specification.

3. If a specification expression includes a variable that provides a value within the expression, the expression must appear within the specification part of a subprogram. For example, the variable N in the program segment:

```
INTEGER  N
COMMON   N
REAL   A (N)
```

is providing a value that determines the size of the array A. This program segment must not appear in a main program but may appear in the specification part of a subprogram.

A prior specification in the above cases may be in the same specification statement, but to the left of the reference. For example, the following declarations are valid:

```
INTEGER, DIMENSION (4), PARAMETER :: A = (/ 4, 3, 2, 1 /)
REAL, DIMENSION (A (2)) :: B, C (SIZE (B))
```

B and C are of size 3 (the second element of the constant array A). But the following declaration is invalid because SIZE (E) precedes E:

```
REAL, DIMENSION (2) :: D (SIZE (E)), E
```

7.2.9.5 Uses of the Various Kinds of Expressions. The various kinds of expressions are somewhat confusing and it is difficult to remember where they can be used. To summarize the differences, Section 7.2.4 specifies the most general kind of expression; the other kinds of expressions are restrictions of the most general kind. The classification of expressions forms two orderings, each from most general to least general, as follows:

- expression, restricted expression, and specification expression
- expression, constant expression, and initialization expression

The relationship between the various kinds of expression can be seen in the diagram in Figure 7-5.

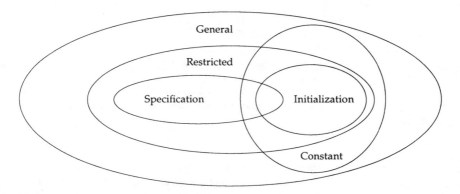

Figure 7-5 Diagram describing relationships between the kinds of expressions

Note that initialization expressions are not a subset of specification expressions because the result of an initialization expression can be of any type, whereas the result of a specification expression must be of type integer and scalar. Also, specification expressions are not a subset of initialization expressions because specification expressions allow certain variables (such as dummy arguments and variables in common blocks) to be primaries, whereas initialization expressions do not allow such variables.

Table 7-5 Differences and similarities between initialization and specification expressions

Property	Kind of expression Initialization	Specification
Character result	Yes	No[1]
Integer result	Yes	Yes
Scalar result	Yes	Yes
Array result	Yes	No
Variables as primaries (limited to dummy arguments, common objects, host objects, module objects)	No	Yes
Elemental intrinsic functions of type integer and character as primaries	Yes	Yes
Elemental intrinsic functions of type real, complex, logical, and derived type as primaries	No	No
Only constants as primaries	Yes	No
Only constant subscripts, strides, character lengths	Yes	No
One of the transformational intrinsic functions REPEAT, RESHAPE, SELECTED_INT_KIND, SELECTED_REAL_KIND, TRANSFER, or TRIM as primaries	Yes	Yes
Inquiry intrinsic functions (not including ALLOCATED, ASSOCIATED, or PRESENT) as primaries	Yes	Yes

Note 1: Expression results of type character are allowed if they are arguments of an intrinsic function.

Table 7-5 describes in detail the differences between the various kinds of expressions. Table 7-6 summarizes where each of these kinds of expressions are used in other Fortran statements and gives the restrictions as to their type and rank when used in the various contexts. For example, Table 7-5 indicates that initialization and specification expressions are different in that initialization expressions can be array valued, whereas specification expressions are scalar. A consequence of this difference, as indicated in Table 7-6, is that an initialization expression is used in a type declaration statement or a PARAMETER statement to specify the value of a named constant array, whereas a specification expression is used to specify the bounds of an array in a declaration statement.

Table 7-6 Kinds of expressions and their uses

Context	Arb. expr.	Init. expr.	Spec. expr.	Type[1]	Rank[2]
Bounds in declaration statement[3]	No	No	Yes	I	Scalar
Lengths in declaration statement[4]	No	No	Yes	I	Scalar
Subscripts and substring ranges in EQUIVALENCE statement	No	Yes	No	I	Scalar
Values in CASE statement	No	Yes	No	I,L,C	Scalar
Kind parameters in declaration statement[5]	No	Yes	No	I	Scalar
Kind arguments in intrinsics	No	Yes	No	I	Scalar
Initial value in PARAMETER and type declaration statement	No	Yes	No	Any	Any
Data-implied-DO parameters	No	Restr.[3]	No	I	Scalar
Assignment	Yes	Yes	Yes	Any	Any
Subscripts in executable statement	Yes	Yes	Yes	I	≤ 1
Strides in executable statement	Yes	Yes	Yes	I	Scalar
Substring ranges in executable statement	Yes	Yes	Yes	I	Scalar
Expression in SELECT CASE	Yes	Yes	Yes	I,L,C	Scalar
IF-THEN statement	Yes	Yes	Yes	L	Scalar
ELSE-IF statement	Yes	Yes	Yes	L	Scalar
IF statement	Yes	Yes	Yes	L	Scalar
Arithmetic IF statement	Yes	Yes	Yes	I,R	Scalar
DO statement	Yes	Yes	Yes	I,R	Scalar
Mask in WHERE statement	Yes	Yes	Yes	L	Array
Mask in WHERE construct	Yes	Yes	Yes	L	Array
Output item list	Yes	Yes	Yes	Any	Any
I/O specifier values except FMT= specifier	Yes	Yes	Yes	I,C	Scalar
I/O FMT= specifier value	Yes	Yes	Yes	C(def)	Any
RETURN statement	Yes	Yes	Yes	I	Scalar
Computed GO TO statement	Yes	Yes	Yes	I	Scalar
Array-constructor-implied-DO parameters	Yes	Yes	Yes	I	Scalar
I/O-implied-DO parameters	Yes	Yes	Yes	I,R	Scalar
Actual arguments	Yes	Yes	Yes	Any	Any
Expressions in statement function definitions	Yes	Yes	Yes	Any	Scalar

Note 1: "Any" in this column means any intrinsic or derived type.

Note 2: "Any" in this column means that the result may be a scalar or an array of any rank (less than 8).

Note 3: The relevant declaration statements are type declaration, component definition, DIMENSION, TARGET, and COMMON statements.

Note 4: The relevant declaration statements are type declaration, component definition, IMPLICIT, and FUNCTION statements.

Note 5: The allowed expressions are limited even further to have as primaries only constants and variables of any containing implied-do. Also, only intrinsic functions are allowed.

Also in Table 7-6 are the kinds of expressions that can be used as data-implied-do parameters and subscripts of DATA statement objects in a DATA statement; such expressions must be scalar integer expressions in which each primary is either a constant or a variable of a containing implied-do, and each operation must be an intrinsic operation. (These expressions are anomalous in terms of the above categorization of expressions mainly because of the limited scope of the DO variables in data-implied-do lists and because the DATA statement is treated by many implementations as a compile-time assignment statement.) For example,

```
DATA ((A (I*3), I = 1+2*J, 5*J/3), J = 1, 10)/ ... /
```

the expressions I*3, 1+2*J, 5*J/3, 1, and 10 are all expressions allowed in subscripts and DO parameter expressions in an implied-do list in a DATA statement. However, expressions such as:

```
RADIX(I)
N  ! where N is not a named constant nor an
   !    implied-do variable in a containing implied-do list
```

are not allowed expressions for data-implied-do parameters or subscripts of DATA statement objects.

Thus, such special expressions are restricted forms of initialization expressions in the sense that the primaries must not include references to any intrinsic function. On the other hand, they are extended forms of initialization expressions in the sense that they permit the use of implied-do variables that have the scope of the implied-do list—namely, are implied-do variables of the implied-do or a containing implied-do in the DATA statement.

7.3 Interpretation of Expressions

The interpretation of an expression specifies the value of the expression when it is evaluated. As with the rules for forming an expression, the rules for interpreting an expression are described from the bottom up, from the interpretation of constants, variables, constructors, and functions to the interpretation of each subexpression to the interpretation of the entire expression.

When an expression is interpreted, the value of each constant and variable is determined. Once these are determined, the operations for which they are operands are interpreted in precedence order, and a value for the operation is determined by the interpretation rules for each operator. This repeats recursively until the entire expression is interpreted and a value is determined.

The interpretation rules for operations are of two sorts: rules for the intrinsic operations (intrinsic operators with operands of the intrinsic types specified by Table 7-3) and rules for the defined operations (provided by the programmer using function subprograms). Except for integer division, the intrinsic operations are interpreted in the usual mathematical way, subject to representation limitations imposed by a computer (for example, a finite range of integers, or finite precision of real numbers). The defined operations are interpreted by a function program that is specified in an interface block with a generic specifier of the form OPERATOR (defined-operator).

The interpretation rules for an intrinsic or a defined operation are independent of the context in which the expression occurs. That is, the type, type parameters, and interpretation of any expression do not depend on any part of a larger expression in which it occurs. This statement is often misunderstood. It does not mean that in all cases the results of individual operations with the same operands must be the same in all contexts. The reason is that the actual results of the intrinsic operations (except for logical, character, and possibly integer operations) are not specified precisely. For example, the expression A + B in the assignment statement X = A + B where A and B are of type real may not yield the same results as the same expression A + B in the expression A+B .EQ. X. The result of A + B is required to be only an approximation of the mathematical result of adding A to B, and different numerical approximations are allowed in different contexts. In terms of understanding the behavior of a program, this behavior is not desirable and rarely happens in practice. On the other hand, it allows an implementation the freedom to optimize the evaluation of certain expressions to speed up the program.

7.3.1 Interpretation of the Intrinsic Operations

When the arguments of the intrinsic operators satisfy the requirements of Table 7-3, the operations are intrinsic and are interpreted in the usual mathematical way as described in Table 7-7, except for integer division. For example, the binary operator * is interpreted as the mathematical operation multiplication and the unary operator – is interpreted as negation.

Table 7-7 Interpretation of the intrinsic operations

Use of operator			Interpretation
x_1	**	x_2	Raise x_1 to the power x_2
x_1	/	x_2	Divide x_1 by x_2
x_1	*	x_2	Multiply x_1 by x_2
x_1	−	x_2	Subtract x_2 from x_1
	−	x_2	Negate x_2
x_1	+	x_2	Add x_1 and x_2
	+	x_2	Same as x_2
x_1	//	x_2	Concatenate x_1 with x_2
x_1	.LT.	x_2	x_1 less than x_2
x_1	<	x_2	x_1 less than x_2
x_1	.LE.	x_2	x_1 less than or equal to x_2
x_1	<=	x_2	x_1 less than or equal to x_2
x_1	.GT.	x_2	x_1 greater than x_2
x_1	>	x_2	x_1 greater than x_2
x_1	.GE.	x_2	x_1 greater than or equal to x_2
x_1	>=	x_2	x_1 greater than or equal to x_2
x_1	.EQ.	x_2	x_1 equal to x_2
x_1	==	x_2	x_1 equal to x_2
x_1	.NE.	x_2	x_1 not equal to x_2
x_1	/=	x_2	x_1 not equal to x_2
	.NOT.	x_2	True if x_2 is false
x_1	.AND.	x_2	True if x_1 and x_2 are both true
x_1	.OR.	x_2	True if x_1 and/or x_2 is true
x_1	.NEQV.	x_2	True if either x_1 or x_2 is true, but not both
x_1	.EQV.	x_2	True if both x_1 and x_2 are true or both are false

7.3.1.1 Interpretation of Numeric Intrinsic Operations. Except for exponentiation to an integer power, when an operand for a numeric intrinsic operation does not have the same type or type parameters as the result of the operation, the operand is converted to the type, type parameter, and shape of the result and the operation is then performed. For exponentiation to an integer power, the operation may be performed without the conversion of the integer power, say, by developing binary powers of the first operand and multiplying them together to obtain an efficient computation of the result.

For integer division, when both operands are of type integer, the result must be of type integer, but the mathematical quotient is, in general, not an integer. In this case, the result is specified to be the integer value closest to the quotient and between zero and the quotient inclusively.

For exponentiation, there are three cases that need to be further described. When both operands are of type integer, the result must be of type integer; when x_2 is negative, the operation x_1 ** x_2 is interpreted as the quotient $1/(x_1$ ** $(-x_2))$. Note that it is subject to the rules for integer division. For example, 4 ** (–2) is 0.

The second case occurs when the first operand is negative and the second operand is of type real. In this case, the result is, in general, a complex number but the returned type is real. A program is invalid if it causes a reference to the exponentiation operator with such values. For example, a program that contains the expression (–1.0) ** 0.5 and causes the expression to be evaluated is an invalid program.

The third case occurs when both operands are of type complex. In this case, the result returned is the principal value of the mathematical power function $x_1{}^{x_2}$.

7.3.1.2 Interpretation of Nonnumeric Intrinsic Operations. The intrinsic character operation performs the usual concatenation operation. For this operation, the operands must be of type character with the same kind type parameters. The length parameter values may be different. The result is of type character with the kind type parameter of its operands and a length type parameter value equal to the sum of the lengths of the operands. The result consists of the characters of the first operand in order followed by those of the second operand in order. For example, 'Fortran$b$' // 'b90' yields the result 'Fortranbb90'.

The intrinsic relational operations perform the usual comparison operations for character and most numeric operands. For these operations, the operands must both be of numeric type or both be of character type. The kind type parameter values of the operands of the numeric types may be different but must be the same for operands of type character. However, the lengths of the character operands may be different. Complex operands must only be compared for equality and inequality; the reason is that complex numbers are not totally ordered. The result in all cases is of type default logical.

When the operands of an intrinsic relational operation are both numeric, but of different types or type parameters, each operand is converted to the type and type parameters of the sum of the two operands. Then, the operands are compared according to the usual mathematical interpretation of the particular relational operator.

When the operands are both of type character, the shorter one is padded on the right with blank padding characters until the operands are of equal length. Then, the operands are compared one character at a time in order, starting from the leftmost character of each operand until the corresponding characters differ. The first operand is less than, equal to, or greater than the second operand according to whether the characters in the first position where they differ are less than, equal to, or greater than in the processor collating sequence. The operands are equal if both are of zero length or all corresponding characters are equal, including the padding characters. Note that the padding character is the Fortran blank (3.1.1) when the operands are of default character type and is a processor specified character for nondefault character types. Also, all comparisons, except equality (.EQ. or ==) and inequality (.NE. or /=), are processor dependent as they depend on the processor-dependent collating sequence.

There is no ordering defined for logical values. However, logical values may be compared for equality and inequality by using the logical equivalence and not equivalence operators .EQV. and .NEQV. That is, L1 .EQV. L2 is true when L1 and L2 are equal and is false otherwise; L1 .NEQV. L2 is true if L1 and L2 are not equal and is false otherwise.

The intrinsic logical operations perform many of the common operations for logical computation. For these operations, the operands must both be of logical type but may have different kind type parameters. When the kind type parameters are the same, the kind parameter value of the result is that value; if different, the kind parameter value of the result is processor dependent. The values of the result in all cases are specified in Table 7-8.

Table 7-8 The values of operations involving logical intrinsic operators

x_1	x_2	.NOT. x_2	x_1 .AND. x_2	x_1 .OR. x_2	x_1 .EQV. x_2	x_1 .NEQV. x_2
true	true	false	true	true	true	false
true	false	true	false	true	false	true
false	true	false	false	true	false	true
false	false	true	false	false	true	false

7.3.1.3 Interpretation of Intrinsic Operations with Array Operands. Each of the intrinsic operations may have array operands; however, for the binary intrinsic operations, the operands must both be of the same shape, if both are arrays. When one operand is an array and the other is a scalar, the operation behaves as if the scalar operand were broadcast to an array of the result shape and the operation performed. Broadcasting a scalar to an array means creating an array of elements all equal to the scalar. This broadcast need not actually occur if the operation can be performed without it.

For both the unary and binary intrinsic operators, the operation is interpreted element-by-element; that is, the scalar operation is performed on each element of the operand or operands. For example, if A and B are arrays of the same shape, the expression A * B is interpreted by taking each element of A and the corresponding element of B and multiplying them together using the scalar intrinsic operation * to determine the corresponding element of the result. Note that this is not the same as matrix multiplication. As a second example, the expression –A is interpreted by taking each element of A and negating it to determine the corresponding element of the result.

For intrinsic operations that appear in masked assignment statements (7.5.4) (in WHERE blocks, ELSEWHERE blocks, or in a WHERE statement), the scalar operation is performed only for those elements selected by the logical mask expression.

Note that there is no order specified for the interpretation of the scalar operations. Indeed, a processor is allowed to perform them in any order, including all at once (possible for vector and array processors). For masked operations in masked assignment statements, the scalar operations on the unselected elements may still be performed, provided they have no side effects; that is, the computation on the unselected elements must not change any value in the expression or statement, or cause any execution-time error.

7.3.1.4 Interpretation of Intrinsic Operations with Pointer Operands. The intrinsic operations may have pointers for their operands. In such cases, each pointer must be associated with a target that is defined, and the value of the target is used as the operand. The target may be scalar or array-valued; the rules for interpretation of the operation are those appropriate for the operand being a scalar or an array, respectively.

Recall that an operand may be a structure component that is the component of a structure variable that is itself a pointer. In this case, the value used for the operand is the named component of the target structure associated with the structure variable. For example, consider the declarations:

```
TYPE( RATIONAL )
   N, D :: INTEGER
END TYPE

TYPE( RATIONAL ), POINTER :: PTR
TYPE( RATIONAL ), TARGET  :: T
```

and suppose the pointer PTR is associated with T. If PTR % N appears as an operand, its value is the component N of the target T, namely T % N.

7.3.2 Interpretation of Defined Operations

The interpretation of a defined operation is provided by a function sub-program with an OPERATOR interface (see Section 12.6.4). When there is more than one function with the same OPERATOR interface, the function giving the interpretation of the operation is the one whose dummy arguments match the operands in order, types, kind type parameters, and ranks (if the operands are arrays). For example, for the operation A .PLUS. B, where A and B are structures of the derived type RATIONAL, the interface

```
INTERFACE OPERATOR (.PLUS.)

    FUNCTION RATIONAL_PLUS (L, R)
        USE RATIONAL_MODULE
        TYPE (RATIONAL), INTENT (IN) :: L, R
        TYPE (RATIONAL)              :: RATIONAL_PLUS
    END FUNCTION RATIONAL_PLUS

    FUNCTION LOGICAL_PLUS (L, R)
        LOGICAL, INTENT (IN) :: L, R
        LOGICAL              :: LOGICAL_PLUS
    END FUNCTION LOGICAL_PLUS

    END INTERFACE
```

specifies that the function RATIONAL_PLUS provides the interpretation of this operation.

Rules and restrictions:

1. A defined operation is declared using a function with one or two dummy arguments. (Note that the function may be an entry in an external or module function.)

2. The dummy arguments to the function represent the operands of the operation; if there is only one, the operation is a unary operation, and otherwise it is a binary operation. For a binary operation, the first argument is the left operand and the second is the right operand.

3. There must be an interface block for the function with the generic specifier of the form OPERATOR (defined-operator).

4. The types and kind type parameters of the operands in the expression must be the same as those of the dummy arguments of the function.

5. The rank of the operands in the expression must match the ranks of the corresponding dummy arguments of the function.

6. Either one of the dummy arguments must be of a derived type, or both are of intrinsic type but do not match the types and kind type parameters for intrinsic operations as specified in Table 7-3.

The requirement that the shapes of the dummy arguments and operands match implies that the defined operators are never elemental; that is, if a defined operation is specified for a scalar operator, it does not apply to array operands of the same shape as is the case for intrinsic operations. Thus, user-defined elemental procedures (functions or subroutines) are not allowed. Note also that the operands of a defined operation need not be in shape conformance as is required for the intrinsic operations.

As with the intrinsic operations, the type, type parameters, and interpretation of a defined operation are independent of the context of the larger expression in which the defined operation appears. The interpretation of the same defined operation in different contexts is the same; however, the results may be different because the results of the procedure being invoked may depend on values that are not operands and that are different for each invocation.

The relational operators $==$, $/=$, $>$, $>=$, $<$, and $<=$ are synonyms for the operators .EQ., .NE., .GT., .GE., .LT., and .LE., even when they are defined operators. It is invalid, therefore, to have an interface block for both $==$ and .EQ., for example, for which the order, types, type parameters, and rank of the dummy arguments of two functions are the same.

Defined operations are either unary or binary. An existing unary operator (that is, one that has the same name as an intrinsic operator) cannot be defined as a binary operator unless it is also a binary operator. Similarly, an existing binary operator cannot be defined as a unary operator unless it is also a unary operator. However, a defined operator, .PLUS. say, (that is, one that does not have a name that is the same as an intrinsic operator) can be defined as both a unary and binary operator.

7.4 Evaluation of Expressions

The form of the expression and the meaning of the operations establish the interpretation; once established, the compiler evaluates the expression in any way that provides the same interpretation with one exception; parentheses specify an order of evaluation that cannot be modified. This applies to both intrinsic operations and defined operations. For defined operations, it is more difficult to determine whether an alternative evaluation scheme provides the same interpretation.

There are essentially two sorts of alternative evaluations that are permitted. They are:

- the rearrangement of an expression that yields an equivalent expression; for example, A + B + C can be evaluated equivalently as A + (B + C) and would improve the efficiency of the compiled program if B + C were a subexpression whose value had already been computed.

- the partial evaluation of an expression because the value of the unevaluated part can be proven not to affect the value of the entire expression. For example, once one operand of a disjunction (.OR. operator) is known to be true, the other operand need not be evaluated to determine the result of the operation. To be specific, the operand A * B < C need not be evaluated in the expression A < B .OR. A * B < C if A < B is true.

This freedom for the compiler to use alternative equivalent evaluations permits the compiler to produce code that is more optimal in some sense (for example, fewer operations, array operations rather than scalar operations, or a reduction in the use of registers or work space), and thereby produce more efficient executable code.

7.4.1 Possible Alternative Evaluations

Before describing in more detail the possible evaluation orders, four basic issues need to be addressed, namely, definition of operands, well-defined operations, functions (and defined operations) with side effects, and equivalent interpretations.

Definition status is described in detail in Section 14.4. For the purpose of evaluation of expressions, it is required that each operand is defined, including all of its parts, if the operand is an aggregate (an array, a structure, or a string). If the operand is a subobject (part of an array, structure, or string), only the selected part is required to be defined. If the operand is a pointer, it must be associated with a target that is defined. An integer operand must be defined with an integer value rather than a statement label.

For the numeric intrinsic operations, the operands must have values for which the operation is well-defined. For example, the divisor for the division operation must be nonzero, and the result of any of the numeric operations must be within the exponent range for the result data type; otherwise, the program is not standard conforming. Other cases include limitations on the operands of the power operation **: for example, a zero-valued first operand must not be raised to a nonpositive second operand; and a negative-valued first operand of type real cannot be raised to a real power.

The third issue is functions with side effects. In Fortran, functions are allowed to have side effects; that is, they are allowed to modify the state of the program so that the state is different after the function is invoked than before it is invoked. This possibility potentially affects the equivalence of two schemes for evaluating an expression (see below), particularly if the function modifies objects appearing in other parts of the expression. However, Fortran outlaws the formation of statements with these kinds of side effects. That is, a function (or defined operation) within a statement is not permitted to change any entity in the same statement. Exceptions are those statements that have statements within them, for example, an IF statement or a WHERE statement. In these cases, the evaluation of functions in the logical expressions in parentheses after the IF keyword or WHERE keyword are allowed to affect objects in the statement following the closing right parenthesis. For example, if F and G below are functions that change their actual argument I, the statements

```
IF (F (I))  A = I
WHERE (G (I))  B = I
```

are valid, even though I is changed when the functions are evaluated. Examples of invalid statements are:

```
A (I) = F (I)
Y = G (I) + I
```

because F and G change I, which is used elsewhere in the same statement.

In case the reader is wondering, it is also illegal for there to be two function references in a statement, if each causes a side effect and the order in which the functions are invoked yields a different final status, even though nothing in the statement is changed.

The fourth issue is equivalent interpretation. For the numeric intrinsic operations, the definition of equivalent interpretation is defined as being mathematical equivalence of the expression, not computational equivalence. Mathematical equivalence assumes exact arithmetic (no rounding errors and infinite exponent range) and thus assumes the rules of commutativity, associativity, and distributivity as well as other rules that can be used to determine equivalence (except that the order of operations specified by parentheses must be honored). Under these assumptions, two evaluations are mathematically equivalent if they yield the same values for all possible values of the operands. A + B + C and A + (B + C) are thus mathematically equivalent but are not necessarily numerically equivalent because of possible different rounding errors. On the other hand, I / 2 and 0.5 * I (where I is an integer) is a mathematical difference because of the special Fortran definition of integer division.

For example, Table 7-9 gives examples of equivalent evaluations of expressions where A, B, and C are operands of type real or complex, and X, Y, and Z are of any numeric type. All of the variables are assumed to be defined and have values that make all of the operations in this table well-defined.

Table 7-9 Equivalence evaluations for numeric intrinsic operations

Expression	Equivalent evaluations
X + Y	Y + X
X * Y	Y * X
– X + Y	Y – X
X + Y + Z	X + (Y + Z)
X – Y + Z	X – (Y – Z)
X * A / Z	X * (A / Z)
X * Y – X * Z	X * (Y – Z)
A / B / C	A / (B * C)
A / 5.0	0.2 * A

Table 7-10 provides examples of invalid alternative evaluations that are not mathematically equivalent to the original expression. In addition to the operands of the same names used in Table 7-9, Table 7-10 uses I and J as operands of type integer. Recall that when both operands of the division operator are of type integer, a Fortran integer division truncates the result toward zero to obtain the nearest integer quotient.

Table 7-10 Nonequivalent evaluations of numeric expressions

Expression	Prohibited evaluations
I / 2	0.5 * I
X * I / J	X * (I / J)
I / J / A	I / (J * A)
(X + Y) + Z	X + (Y + Z)
(X * Y) – (X * Z)	X * (Y – Z)
X * (Y – Z)	X * Y – X * Z

7.4.2 Partial Evaluations

For character, relational, and logical intrinsic operations, the definition of the equivalence of two evaluations is that, given the same values for their operands, each evaluation produces the same result. The definition for equivalence of two evaluations of the same defined operation also requires the results to be the same; note that this definition is more restrictive than for the numeric intrinsic operations, because only mathematical equivalence need be preserved for numeric operations. As described for numeric intrinsic operations, the compiler may choose any evaluation scheme equivalent to that provided by the interpretation. Table 7-11 gives some equivalent schemes for evaluating a few example expressions. For these examples, I and J are of type integer; L1, L2, and L3 are of type logical; and C1, C2, and C3 are of type character of the same length. All of the variables are assumed to be defined.

Table 7-11 Equivalent evaluations of other expressions

Expression	Equivalent evaluations
I .GT. J	(J−I) .GT. 0
L1 .OR. L2 .OR. L3	L1 .OR. (L2 .OR. L3)
L1 .AND. L1	L1
C3 = C1 // C2	C3 = C1 (C1, C2, C3 all of the same length)

These rules for equivalent evaluation schemes allow the compiler to not evaluate any part of an expression that has no effect on the resulting value of the expression. Consider the expression $X * F(Y)$, where F is a function and X has the value 0. The result will be the same regardless of the value of F(Y); therefore, it need not be evaluated. This shortened evaluation is allowed in all cases, even if F(Y) has side effects. In this case every data object that F could affect is considered to be undefined after the expression is evaluated—that is, it does not have a predictable value.

The execution of an array element, an array section, or a character substring reference requires, in most cases, the evaluation of the expressions that are the subscripts, strides, or substring ranges. The type or type parameters of an expression are not affected by the evaluation of such expressions. It is not necessary for these expressions to be evaluated, if the array section can be shown to be zero-sized or the substring can be shown to be of a zero-length by other means. For example, in the expression $A (1:0) + B (expr_1:expr_2)$, $expr_1$ and $expr_2$ need not be evaluated as the conformance rules for intrinsic operations require that the section of B be zero-sized.

In contrast, and in apparent contradiction to the rule above, the standard states that the appearance of an array constructor requires the evaluation of all elements of the constructor. This rule also requires the evaluation of any implied-DO parameters. It is the authors' opinion that the general rule above overrides this special treatment of array constructors.

The type and type parameters, if any, of the constructor are not affected by the evaluation of any of the expressions within the constructor.

Parentheses within the expression must be honored. This is particularly important for computations involving numeric values where rounding errors or range errors may occur or for computations involving functions with side effects. Of course, if there is no computational difference between two evaluation schemes where parentheses are provided, the compiler can violate the parentheses integrity because no one can tell the difference. For example, the expression (1.0/3.0)*3.0 must be evaluated by performing the division first because of the explicit parentheses. Evaluating the expression as 1.0 would be valid if the value obtained by performing the division first and then the multiplication produced a result that is equal to 1.0 despite rounding errors. Although this sort of rearrangement might be possible in theory, it is not a practical option in general, unless all of the operands are constants as in the above example.

7.5 Assignment

The most common use of the result of an expression is to give a value to a variable. This is done with an assignment statement. For example,

```
RUG = BROWN + 2.34 / TINT
```

An assignment statement has three parts:

- the variable being assigned a value
- the assignment symbol (= or =>)
- the computation (an expression)

Assignment establishes a value for the variable on the left of the assignment symbol in an assignment statement. Execution of the assignment statement causes the expression to be evaluated (by performing the computation indicated), and then the value of the expression is assigned to the variable. If the variable has subscripts, section subscripts, or a substring range, the execution of the assignment statement must behave as if they were evaluated before any part of the value is assigned.

There are four forms of the assignment statement: intrinsic assignment, defined assignment, pointer assignment, and masked array assignment. All but the first are new in Fortran 90 and apply specifically to new entities in Fortran. In addition, intrinsic assignment has been extended to arrays, pointers, and structure objects.

The form of intrinsic assignment, defined assignment, and masked array assignment (R735) is the same, namely:

variable = expression

An assignment statement is a defined assignment if:

1. there is a subroutine subprogram with an assignment interface of the form ASSIGNMENT (=)

2. the types, kind type parameters, and ranks (if arrays) of the variable and expression match in order the dummy arguments of the subroutine with the assignment interface

An assignment statement is a masked array assignment if it appears in a WHERE construct or WHERE statement. Otherwise, it is an intrinsic or defined assignment.

The form of the pointer assignment statement is similar to the assignment statement except that the assignment operator is => instead of =.

The rules and restrictions for each of these forms of assignment are different and are described in the subsections below for each form of assignment.

Examples of the four forms of assignment are:

X = X + 1	Intrinsic assignment for reals
CHAR (1:4) = "A123"	Intrinsic assignment for characters
STUDENT = B_JONES	Intrinsic assignment for structures
STRING = "Brown"	Defined assignment for varying string structure
WHERE (Z /= 0.0)	
A = B / Z	Masked array assignment
END WHERE	
PTR => X	Pointer assignment

7.5.1 Intrinsic Assignment

Intrinsic assignment may be used to assign a value to a nonpointer variable of any type or to the target associated with a pointer variable. The assignment statement defines or redefines the value of the variable or the target, as appropriate. The value is determined by the evaluation of the expression on the right-hand side of the equal sign.

Rules and restrictions:

1. The types and kind parameters of the variable and expression in an intrinsic assignment statement must be of the types given in Table 7-12.

    Table 7-12 Types of the variable and expression in an intrinsic assignment

Type of the variable	Type of the expression
Integer	Integer, real, complex
Real	Integer, real, complex
Complex	Integer, real, complex
Character	Character with the same kind
	Type parameter as the variable
Logical	Logical
Derived type	Same derived type as the variable

2. If the variable is an array, the expression must either be a scalar or an array of the same shape as the variable. If the variable is a scalar, the expression must a scalar. The shape of the variable may be specified in specification statements if it is an explicit-shape array; it may be determined by the section subscripts in the variable, by an actual argument if it is a assumed-shape array, or by an ALLO-CATE statement or a pointer assignment statement if it is a deferred-shape array. It must not be an assumed-size array unless there is a vector subscript, a scalar subscript, or a section subscript containing an upper bound in the last dimension of the array. The shape of the expression is determined by the shape of the operands, the operators in the expression, and the functions referenced in the expression. A complete description of the shape of an expression appears in Section 7.2.8.3.

3. If the variable is a pointer, it must be associated with a target; the assignment statement assigns the value of the expression to the target of the pointer. The pointer may be associated with a target that is an array; the pointer determines the rank of the array, but the extents in each dimension are that of the target.

4. The evaluation of the expression on the right-hand side of the equal sign, including subscript and section subscript expressions that are part of the expression and part of the variable, must be performed before any portion of the assignment is performed. Before the assignment begins, any necessary type conversions are completed if the variable has a different numeric type or type parameter from

the expression. The conversion is the same as that performed by the conversion intrinsic functions INT, REAL, CMPLX, and LOGICAL, as specified in Table 7-13.

Table 7-13 Conversion performed on an expression before assignment

Type of the variable	Value assigned
Integer	INT (expression, KIND (variable))
Real	REAL (expression, KIND (variable))
Complex	CMPLX (expression, KIND (variable))
Logical	LOGICAL (expression, KIND (variable))

5. An expression may use parts of the variable that appear on the left side of an assignment statement. (Note that this is not allowed in Fortran 77.) For example, in evaluating a character string expression on the right-hand side of an assignment, the values in the variable on the left-hand side may be used, as in

    ```
    DATE (2:5) = DATE (1:4)
    ```

6. If the variable and expression are of character type, they must have the same kind type parameter value.

7. If the variable and expression are of character type with different lengths, the assignment occurs as follows: if the length of the variable is less than that of the expression, the value of the expression is truncated from the right; if the length of the variable is greater than the expression, the value of the expression is filled with blanks on the right. The character used as the blank character for default character type is the blank character specified in Section 3.1.1 and otherwise is a blank padding character specified by the processor for nondefault character types.

8. The evaluation of expressions in the variable on the left-hand side, such as subscript expressions, has no affect on, nor is affected by, the evaluation of the expression on the right-hand side, which is evaluated completely first.

9. When a scalar is assigned to an array, the assignment behaves as if the scalar is broadcast to an array of the shape of the variable; it is then in shape conformance with the variable. In the example:

```
REAL A (10)
A = 1.0
```

all ten elements of the array A are assigned the value 1.0.

10.   Array assignment is element-by-element but the order is not speci-
       fied. If A and B are real arrays of size 10, and the whole array
       assignment were:

```
A = B
```

the first element of B would be assigned to the first element of A,
the second element of B would be assigned to the second element of
A, and this would continue element-by-element for 10 elements.
The assignment of elements, however, may be performed in any
order, as long as the effect is as if all elements were assigned simultaneously.

11.   For derived-type intrinsic assignment, the derived types of the vari-
       able and the expression must be the same. Derived-type intrinsic
       assignment is performed component-by-component following the
       above rules, except when a component is a pointer. For pointer
       components, pointer assignment between corresponding compo-
       nents is used.

7.5.2 Defined Assignment

Defined assignment is an assignment operation provided by a subroutine
with an assignment interface ASSIGNMENT (=)—see Section 12.6.5.
When the variable and expression in the assignment statement are of
intrinsic types and do not satisfy the type matching rules in Table 7-12 or
are of derived type, a defined assignment operation will be used, provided the assignment interface and subroutine are accessible. For example, a defined assignment may apply when character objects of different
kinds are to be assigned, provided a subroutine with a generic assignment interface is accessible. Assignment thus may be extended to types
other than the intrinsic types or may replace the usual assignment operation for derived types, if the programmer defines the rules for this assignment in a subroutine.

Rules and restrictions:

1.   An assignment operation is declared using a subroutine with two
      dummy arguments. (Note that the subroutine may be an entry in
      an external or module subroutine.)

2.   The dummy arguments to the subroutine represent the variable and the expression, in that order.

3.   There must be an interface block for the subroutine with the generic specifier of the form ASSIGNMENT (=).

4.   The types and kind type parameters of the variable and expression in the assignment statement must be the same as those of the dummy arguments.

5.   The rank of the variable and the expression in the assignment must match the ranks of the corresponding dummy arguments.

6.   Either one of the dummy arguments must be of a derived type, or both are of intrinsic type but do not match the types and kind type parameters for intrinsic assignment as specified in Table 7-12.

Example:

```
INTERFACE  ASSIGNMENT (=)

    SUBROUTINE  RATIONAL_TO_REAL (L, R)
       USE  RATIONAL_MODULE
       TYPE (RATIONAL), INTENT (IN) :: R
       REAL, INTENT(OUT)            :: L
    END SUBROUTINE  RATIONAL_TO_REAL

    SUBROUTINE  REAL_TO_RATIONAL (L, R)
       USE  RATIONAL_MODULE
       REAL, INTENT(IN)             :: R
       TYPE (RATIONAL), INTENT (OUT) :: L
    END SUBROUTINE  REAL_TO_RATIONAL

END INTERFACE
```

The above interface block specifies two defined assignments for two assignment operations in terms of two external subroutines, one for assignment of objects of type RATIONAL to objects of type real and other for assignment of objects of type real to objects of type RATIONAL. With this interface block, the following assignment statements are defined:

```
REAL   R_VALUE
TYPE (RATIONAL)   RAT_VALUE

R_VALUE = RATIONAL (1, 2)
RAT_VALUE = 3.7
```

The effect of the defined assignment on variables in the program is determined by the referenced subroutine. The variable being assigned may be a pointer, or the expression on the right may yield a pointer. How such pointers are used is determined by the declarations and uses of the corresponding dummy arguments of the subroutine.

7.5.3 Pointer Assignment

Recall that a pointer is a variable that points to another object. The term (**pointer**) **association** is used for the concept of "pointing to" and the term **target** is used for the object associated with a pointer.

A pointer assignment associates a pointer with a target, unless the target is disassociated or undefined. If the target is disassociated or undefined, the pointer becomes disassociated or undefined according to the status of the target. Once a pointer assignment has been executed, the association status of the pointer remains unchanged, until another pointer assignment or ALLOCATE, DEALLOCATE, or NULLIFY statement is executed redefining the pointer.

The form of a pointer assignment statement (R736) is:

pointer-object => target

where a pointer object (R630) has one of the forms:

variable-name
structure-component

and a target (R737) is of one of the forms:

variable
expression

The form of the expression permitted as a target is limited severely—see item 12 of the rules and restrictions below.

Rules and restrictions:

1. If the pointer object is a variable name, the name must have the POINTER attribute. If the pointer object is a structure component, the component must have the POINTER attribute.

2. If the target is a variable, then

    a. it must have the TARGET attribute

    b. it must be the component of a structure, the element of an array variable, or the substring of a character variable that has the TARGET attribute, or

    c. it must have the POINTER attribute

3. The type, type parameters (kind and length, if character), and rank of the target must be the same as the pointer object.

4. If the variable on the right of $=>$ has the TARGET attribute, the pointer object on the left of $=>$ becomes associated with this target.

5. If the variable on the right of $=>$ has the POINTER attribute and is associated, the pointer object on the left of $=>$ points to the same data that the target points to after the pointer assignment statement is executed.

6. If the variable on the right of $=>$ has the POINTER attribute and is disassociated, the pointer object on the left of $=>$ becomes disassociated.

7. If the variable on the right of $=>$ has the POINTER attribute and has an undefined association status, the association status of the pointer object on the left of $=>$ becomes undefined.

8. A pointer assignment statement terminates any previous association for that pointer and creates a new association.

9. If the pointer object is a deferred-shape array, the pointer assignment statement establishes the extents for each dimension of the array, unless the target is a disassociated or undefined pointer. Except for the case of a disassociated or undefined pointer, the extents are those of the target. For example, if the following statements have been processed:

```
INTEGER, TARGET :: T (11:20)
INTEGER, POINTER :: P1 (:), P2 (:)
P1 => T
P2 => T (:)
```

the extents of P1 are those of T, namely 11 and 20, but those of P2 are 1 and 10, because T (:) has a section subscript list (7.2.8.4).

10. The target must not be a variable that is an assumed-size array. If it is an array section of an assumed-size array, the upper bound for the last dimension must be specified.

11. If the target is an array section, it must not have a vector subscript.

12. If the target is an expression, it must deliver a pointer result. This implies that the expression must be a user-defined function reference or defined operation that returns a pointer (there are no intrinsic operations or functions that return results with the POINTER attribute).

13. If the target of a pointer may not be referenced or defined, the pointer must not be referenced or defined.

14. If a structure has a component with the POINTER attribute and the structure is assigned a value using an intrinsic derived-type assignment, pointer assignment is used for each component with the POINTER attribute. Also, defined assignment may cause pointer assignment between some components of a structure.

Note that, when a pointer appears on the right side of $=>$ in a pointer assignment, the pointer on the left side of $=>$ is defined or redefined to be associated with the target on the right side of the $=>$; neither the pointer on the right nor its target are changed in any way.

Examples:

```
MONTH => DAYS (1:30)
PTR => X (:, 5)
NUMBER => JONES % SOCSEC
```

An example where a target is another pointer is:

```
REAL, POINTER :: PTR, P
REAL, TARGET :: A
REAL  B
A = 1.0
P => A
PTR => P
B = PTR + 2.0
```

The previous program segment defines A with the value 1.0, associates P with A; then PTR is associated with A as well (through P). The value assigned to B in the regular assignment statement is 3.0, because the reference to PTR in the expression yields the value of the target A which is the value 1.0. An example in which the target is an expression is:

```
INTERFACE
    FUNCTION POINTER_FCN (X)
        REAL  X
        REAL, POINTER :: POINTER_FCN
    END FUNCTION
END INTERFACE

REAL, POINTER :: P
REAL  A

P => POINTER_FCN (A)
```

In this example, the function POINTER_FCN takes a real argument and returns a pointer to a real target. After execution of the pointer assignment statement, the pointer P points to this real target.

Pointers may become associated using the ALLOCATE statement instead of a pointer assignment statement. Pointers may become disassociated using the DEALLOCATE or NULLIFY statements, as well as with the pointer assignment statement.

A pointer may be used in an expression (see Section 7.3.1.4 for the details). Briefly, any reference to a pointer in an expression, other than in a pointer assignment statement, or in certain procedure references, yields the value of the target associated with the pointer. When a pointer appears as an actual argument corresponding to a dummy argument that has the pointer attribute, the reference is to the pointer and not the value. Note that a procedure must have an explicit interface (12.6.1), if it has a dummy argument with a pointer attribute.

7.5.4 Masked Array Assignment

Sometimes, it is desirable to assign only certain elements of one array to another array. To invert the elements of an array element-by-element, for example, one has to avoid elements that are 0. The masked array assignment is ideal for such selective assignment, as the following example using a WHERE construct illustrates:

```
REAL  A(10,10)
   ...

WHERE( A /= 0.0 )
    RECIP_A = 1.0 / A     ! Assign only where the
                          !    elements are nonzero
ELSEWHERE
    RECIP_A = 1.0         ! Use the value 1.0 for
                          !    the zero elements.
END WHERE
```

The first array assignment statement is executed for only those elements where the mask A /= 0.0 is true. Next, the second assignment statement (after the ELSEWHERE statement) is executed for only those elements where the same mask is false. If the values of RECIP_A where A is 0 are never used, this example can be simply written using the WHERE statement rather than the WHERE construct as follows:

```
WHERE( A /= 0.0 ) RECIP_A = 1.0 / A
```

A **masked array assignment** is an intrinsic assignment statement in a WHERE block, an ELSEWHERE block, or a WHERE statement for which the variable being assigned is an array. The WHERE statement and WHERE construct appear to have the characteristics of a control statement or construct such as the IF statement and IF construct. But there is a major difference; every assignment statement in a WHERE construct is executed, whereas at most one block in the IF construct is executed. Similarly, the assignment statement following a WHERE statement is always executed. For this reason, WHERE statements and constructs are discussed here under assignment rather than under control constructs.

In a masked array assignment, the assignment is made to certain elements of an array based on the value of a logical array expression serving as a mask for picking out the array elements. The logical array expression acts as an array-valued condition on the elemental intrinsic operations, functions, and assignment for each array assignment statement in the WHERE statement or WHERE construct.

As in an intrinsic array assignment, a pointer to an array may be used as the variable, and a pointer to a scalar or an array may be used as a primary in the expression. In case the target of the pointer is an array, the target array is masked in the same manner as a nonpointer array used in a masked array assignment.

7.5.4.1 WHERE Statement. The form of the WHERE statement (R738) is:

WHERE (logical-expression) array-intrinsic-assignment-statement

The logical expression is evaluated resulting in a logical array, which is treated as a mask. The mask array must conform with the variable on the right side in the array intrinsic assignment statement. Each element of the array on the left side of the array assignment statement is assigned a value from the expression on the right, if the corresponding element in the mask is true. Where the mask is false, the array elements are not assigned a value. Any elemental intrinsic operations or functions within the expression are evaluated only for the selected elements.

The expression in the array assignment statement may contain nonelemental function references. Nonelemental function references are references to any function or operation defined by a subprogram, or any intrinsic function that is a transformational or an inquiry function. If it does, all elements of the arguments of such functions and returned results (if arrays) are evaluated in full. If the result of the nonelemental function is an array and is an operand of an elemental operation or function, then only the selected elements are used in evaluating the remainder of the expression.

Example:

```
WHERE( TEMPERATURES > 90.0 )   HOT_TEMPS = TEMPERATURES
WHERE( TEMPERATURES < 32.0 )   COLD_TEMPS = TEMPERATURES
```

7.5.4.2 WHERE Construct. The form of the WHERE construct (R739) is:

```
WHERE ( logical-expression )
     [ array-intrinsic-assignment-statement ] ...
[ ELSEWHERE
     [ array-intrinsic-assignment-statement ] ... ]
END WHERE
```

The **WHERE block** is the set of assignments between the WHERE construct statement and the ELSEWHERE statement (or END WHERE statement, if the ELSEWHERE statement is not present). The **ELSEWHERE block** is the set of assignment statements between the ELSEWHERE and the END WHERE statements.

Rules and restrictions:

1. The logical expression is evaluated resulting in a logical array, which is treated as a mask. The mask array must conform with the

variables on the right side in all of the array assignment statements in the construct.

2. Each assignment in the WHERE block assigns a value to each element of the array that corresponds with an element of the mask array that is true.

3. Each assignment in the ELSEWHERE block assigns a value to each element of the array that corresponds with an element of the mask array that is false.

4. The ELSEWHERE block is optional; when it is not present, no assignment is made to elements corresponding to mask array elements that are false.

5. All of the assignment statements are executed in sequence as they appear in the construct (in both the WHERE and ELSEWHERE blocks).

6. Any elemental intrinsic operation or function within the expression is evaluated only for the selected elements. For example:

```
REAL  A (10, 20)
   ...
WHERE( A > 0.0 )
   SQRT_A = SQRT (A)
END WHERE
```

the square roots are taken only of the elements of A that are positive.

7. Nonelemental function references in the array assignment statements are completely evaluated, even though all elements of the resulting array may not be used. For example:

```
REAL  A (2, 3), B (3, 10), C (2, 10), D (2, 10)
INTRINSIC  MATMUL
   ...
WHERE( D < 0.0 )
   C = MATMUL(A, B)
END WHERE
```

the matrix product $A \times B$ is performed, yielding all elements of the product, and only for those elements of D that are negative are the assignments to the corresponding elements of C made.

8. An elemental function reference is evaluated independently for each element, and only those elements needed in the array assignment are referenced. Elemental function references are only those intrinsic functions classified as elemental functions, such as ABS, INT, and COS.

9. In a WHERE construct, only the WHERE statement may be labeled as a branch target statement.

Example:

```
WHERE( VALUES > 0.0 )
    A = VALUES
ELSEWHERE
    A = 0.0
END WHERE
```

7.5.4.3 Differences between the WHERE Construct and Control Constructs. One major difference between the WHERE construct and control constructs has been described in Section 7.5.4. Another difference is that no transfers out of WHERE or ELSEWHERE blocks are possible (except by a function reference) because only intrinsic assignment statements are permitted within these blocks. Note that the execution of statements in the WHERE block can affect variables referenced in the ELSEWHERE block (because the statements in both blocks are executed).

7.6 Summary

Expression

An expression is formed using operands, operators, and parentheses. When evaluated, an expression produces a value. An expression has a type, type parameters when of intrinsic type, and a shape. Operands may be scalars, arrays, pointers, or structures of derived type. When a pointer is used in an expression, the value of the target is used.

Scalar Expression

The result of a scalar expression is a scalar value.

```
X + 1.
```

Array Expression

The result of an array expression is an array value.

```
A (1:10) = B (1:10) + C (2:11)
```

Constant Expression

A constant expression is constructed from values that can be determined at compile time. These include constants, references to intrinsic functions with constant arguments, and references to certain other intrinsic functions whose values can be evaluated at compile time.

```
10 / 2 + 7
SIZE (X) + K
```

Specification Expression

A specification expression is a scalar expression of type integer that can be evaluated on entry to a program before any executable statement in the program unit is executed. Specification expressions are used to specify array bounds and character length parameter values in specification statements.

Initialization Expressions

Initialization expressions are restricted forms of constant expressions. The restrictions are essentially that the exponentiation operator is limited to integer powers, and no intrinsic functions that use or return values of type real, logical, or complex are allowed. This excludes many of the transformational intrinsic functions such as SUM, ALL, and SPREAD, and many of the floating point and logical elemental intrinsic functions such as CONJG, COS, DBLE, SQRT, LGE, LOGICAL, EXPONENT, and SCALE.

Expressions are limited to initialization expressions in only a few contexts. In brief, these contexts include the initialization of named constants and variables in declaration statements, kind type parameter values in all contexts, and subscript and subrange expressions in EQUIVALENCE statements.

Expressions Resulting in Scalar and Array Values

Constants, variables, structures, and functions may be used as operands in expressions. Each of these forms may be a scalar or an array. If all operands are scalars, the operations are performed on scalar values. If both operands are arrays, the operations are performed on all the elements of the arrays named as operands. If one operand is a scalar and the other is an array in a binary operation, the scalar is broadcast to an array of the appropriate shape, that is, the scalar is repeated as many times as there are elements in the array.

Example:

X + 1.	Scalar expression
Y + 1.0	Array expression
W + Z	Array expression

where X is a scalar variable, Y is a one-dimensional array of size 100, and W and Z are two 10 × 100 arrays.

In the first example, the single value of X is added to 1.0. In the second example, each of the 100 elements of Y is added to 1.0. The scalar 1.0 is broadcast 100 times, once for each element of Y. In the third example, the arrays are "conformable" (both have 1000 elements) and the operation is performed element-by-element for all elements W and Z.

Assignment

The outcome of an assignment replaces a value for a variable on the left of an equal sign (the assignment symbol) with the result of evaluating the expression on the right-hand side of the equal sign. The variable may be a scalar, an array, a pointer, or a structure.

```
X = Y * Z / (2.3 - U)
```

X is assigned a value obtained by evaluating the expression Y * Z / (2.3 - U).

Intrinsic Assignment

Intrinsic assignment is an assignment operation (using the equal sign) that is understood by the Fortran processor; it is built in. Intrinsic assignment applies to all intrinsic and derived types, provided the types of the variable and expression in the assignment satisfy the requirements for intrinsic assignment specified in Table 7-12.

```
X = X + 1.0
L = CHAR (3:4) == C1 (1:2)
```

Defined Assignment

A defined assignment statement is not built into Fortran. The program must define the assignment in a subroutine subprogram for which an interface block with an assignment generic specifier is provided.

Masked Array Assignment

The variable on the left of the equal sign and the elemental operations on the right are controlled by a mask. Elements of an array are assigned values based on an array of logical values, serving as the mask. The array assignment statements must be controlled by a WHERE statement or a WHERE construct.

```
WHERE (I == J)
    X = 1.0
ELSEWHERE
    X = 0.0
END WHERE
WHERE (I >= 0)  X = 3.0
```

Pointer Assignment

A pointer assignment statement associates a pointer with a target. The target is either a variable or a function that returns a pointer. The pointer may be a scalar or an array. If it is an array, it must be of deferred shape and the pointer assignment statement establishes the extents of the array. In the example

```
REAL, POINTER :: PTR, ARRAY_PTR (:, :)
REAL, TARGET :: A (10, 100)

PTR => A (7, 6)
ARRAY_PTR => A
```

after the pointer assignment statements are executed, the pointer PTR points to the element A (7, 6), and the pointer ARRAY_PTR points to the entire array and has the shape (10, 100).

F9🌀

8

Controlling Execution

A program performs its computation by executing the statements in sequence from beginning to end. Control constructs and statements modify this normal sequential execution of a program. The modification may select blocks of statements and constructs for execution or repetition, or may transfer control to another statement in the program. Repetition occurs until some condition is met and a branch to some other statement in the program occurs.

As outlined in Chapter 2, the statements and constructs making up a program are of two sorts—nonexecutable and executable. The **nonexecutable statements** "set the stage" or establish the environment under which the program runs. In particular, they determine the properties and attributes for data and consist mostly of those statements described in Chapters 4 and 5. The **executable statements** and **executable constructs**, referred to sometimes as **action statements**, perform computations, assign values, perform input/output operations, or control the sequence in which the other executable statements and constructs are executed. This chapter describes the latter group of executable statements—the control statements and control constructs.

Control constructs and control statements alter the usual sequential execution order of statements and constructs in a program. This execution order is called the **normal execution sequence**. The control constructs are block constructs and consist of the IF construct, the DO construct, and the CASE construct. Individual statements that alter the normal execution sequence include the CYCLE and EXIT statements which are special statements for DO constructs, branch statements such as arithmetic IF statements, various forms of GO TO statements, and the statements that cause execution to cease such as the STOP and PAUSE statements.

With any of the block constructs, construct names may be used to identify the constructs and also to identify which DO constructs, particularly in a nest of DO constructs, are being terminated or cycled when using the EXIT or CYCLE statements. Construct names are described in the introductory material for blocks (8.2) and also with each construct and statement that uses them.

8.1 The Execution Sequence

There is an established execution sequence for action statements in a Fortran program. Normally, a program or subprogram begins with the first executable statement in that program or subprogram and continues with the next executable statement in the order in which these statements appear. However, there are executable constructs and statements that cause statements to be executed in an order that is different from the order in which they appear in the program. These are either control constructs or branching statements.

There are two basic ways to affect the execution sequence. One is to use an executable construct that selects a block of statements and constructs for execution. The second is to execute a statement that branches to a specific statement in the program. In almost all cases, the use of constructs will result in programs that are more readable and maintainable, so constructs are discussed first, followed by branching statements.

8.2 Blocks and Executable Constructs

A **control construct** consists of one or more blocks of Fortran statements and constructs and the control logic that explicitly or implicitly encloses these blocks. Based on a control condition, a block of statements and constructs is selected for execution. A block (R801) is a sequence of zero or more statements and constructs, and has the form:

[execution-part-construct] ...

A block of statements and constructs is treated as a whole. Either the block as a whole is executed or it is not executed. Whether or not the block is executed is determined by expressions in the control logic of the construct. Note that not every statement or construct in the block need be executed; for example, a branch statement early in the block may prevent subsequent statements in the block from being executed. This is still considered a complete execution of the block.

An executable construct consists of one or more blocks of statements surrounded by control statements. The construct usually contains an initial statement before a block and a terminal statement after the block. There are constructs that contain more than one block. The construct includes conditions that determine which block in the construct is executed. Some of the constructs contain additional statements between blocks that may determine which block is chosen. The DO construct determines how many times a block will be executed. An example of an executable construct controlling a block of statements is:

```
IF (I <= 1) THEN   ! Initial statement of the IF construct
   X = 1.2 * I     ! First statement of the block
   Y = COS (X)     ! Final statement of the block
END IF             ! Terminal statement of the IF construct
```

There are three executable constructs that contain blocks:

1. IF construct

2. CASE construct

3. DO construct

There is also a construct called the WHERE construct that controls array assignment for individual elements (masked array assignment) as opposed to controlling flow of the program statements. Even though it looks like a control construct, it really is a construct for unconditional but masked array assignment. Every statement in the construct is executed independent of the control conditions; the condition is used to determine how much of each array assignment in the blocks is executed. This construct is discussed in detail in Section 7.5.4.

Naming a construct is a new option in Fortran 90; the name, if used, must appear on the same line as the initial statement of the construct and a matching name must appear on the terminal statement of the construct.

The IF construct is in Fortran 77. The CASE construct is new in Fortran 90. Extensions have been made to the Fortran 77 DO loop, which permit more flexible control of blocks.

Some of the general rules and restrictions that apply to blocks and control of blocks follow.

Rules and restrictions:

1. The first statement or construct of a block is executed first. The statements of the block are executed in order unless there is a control construct or statement within the block that changes the sequential order.

2. A block, as an integral unit, must be completely contained within a construct. A block may be empty; that is, it may contain no statements or constructs at all.

3. A branching or control construct within a block that transfers to a statement or construct within a block is permitted.

4. Exiting from a block may be done from anywhere within the block.

5. Branching to a statement or construct within a block from outside the block is prohibited. (Even branching to the first executable statement within a block from outside the block is prohibited.)

6. References to procedures are permitted within a block.

7. Constructs may have construct names.

8.3 IF Construct and IF Statement

An IF construct selects at most one block of statements and constructs within the construct for execution. It was introduced in Fortran 77. The IF statement controls the execution of only one statement; formerly it was called the logical IF statement and was present in Fortran 66. The arithmetic IF statement, the only IF statement in the original Fortran, is not the same as the IF statement; it is a branching statement that is designated as obsolescent and is discussed in Section 8.7.2.

8.3.1 The IF Construct

The IF construct contains one or more executable blocks; at most one block is executed, and it is possible for no block to be executed when there is no ELSE statement. The logical expression determining whether a particular block is executed appears prior to the block except the block following the ELSE statement. These expressions are evaluated in turn until one of them is true. The block immediately following the control statement containing the first true logical expression is executed. If none of the expressions is true, the block following the ELSE statement, if present, is executed. If there is no ELSE statement, the IF construct terminates. At most one block is chosen for execution, after which the IF construct is completed and it terminates. If more than one logical expression is true, only the block following the first one is executed.

8.3.1.1 Form of the IF Construct. The form of the IF construct (R802) is:

```
[ if-construct-name : ] IF ( scalar-logical-expression ) THEN
          block
[ ELSE IF ( scalar-logical-expression ) THEN [ if-construct-name ]
          block ] ...
[ ELSE  [ if-construct-name ]
          block ]
END IF [ if-construct-name ]
```

Rules and restrictions:

1. At most one of the blocks in the construct is executed. It is possible that no block is executed.

2. ELSE IF statements cannot follow an ELSE statement.

3. Branching to an ELSE IF or an ELSE statement is prohibited.

4. Branching to an END IF is allowed from any block within the IF construct. Branching to an END IF from outside the IF construct is allowed but is designated as an obsolescent feature.

5. If a construct name appears on the IF-THEN statement, the same name must appear on the corresponding END IF statement.

6. The construct names on the ELSE IF and ELSE statements are optional, but if present must be the same name as the one on the IF-THEN statement. If one such ELSE IF or ELSE statement has a construct name, the others are not required to have a construct name.

7. The same construct name must not be used for different named constructs in the same scoping unit; thus, two IF blocks must not be both named INNER in the same executable part, for example.

8.3.1.2 Execution of the IF Construct. The logical expressions are evaluated in order until one is found to be true. The block following the first true condition is executed, and the execution of the IF construct terminates. Subsequent true conditions in the construct have no effect. There may be no logical expressions found to be true in the construct. In this case, the block following the ELSE statement is executed if there is one; otherwise, no block in the construct is executed.

Figure 8-1 indicates the execution flow for an IF construct.

Example:

```
IF (I < J) THEN
   X = Y + 5.0
ELSE IF (I > 100) THEN
   X = 0.0
   Y = -1.0
ELSE
   X = -1.0
   Y = 0.0
END IF
```

If I is less than J, the statement $X = Y + 5.0$ is executed and execution proceeds following the END IF statement. If I is not less than J and if I is greater than 100, the two statements following the ELSE IF statement are executed and execution proceeds following the END IF statement. If neither of these conditions is true, the block after the ELSE statement is executed.

8.3.2 The IF Statement

The IF statement is the logical IF statement of Fortran 77.

8.3.2.1 Form of the IF Statement. The form of the IF statement (R807) is:

IF (scalar-logical-expression) action-statement

Example:

```
IF (S < T) S = 0.0
```

8.3.2.2 Execution of the IF Statement. The scalar logical expression is evaluated. If true, the action statement is executed. If false, the action statement is not executed, and control passes to the next statement in the program.

Rules and restrictions:

1. The action statement must not be an IF statement or an END statement for a program, function, or subroutine.

2. If the logical expression contains a function reference, its evaluation may have side effects that modify the action statement. This is permitted.

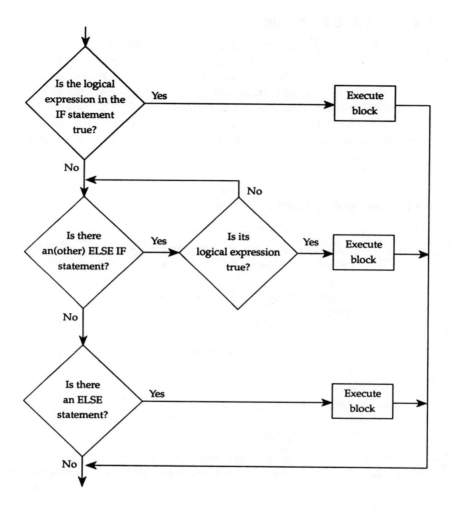

Figure 8-1 Execution flow for an IF construct

A complete list of the action statements can be found in Section 2.6. Fundamentally, action statements change the definition state of variables or the condition of the input/output system, or are control statements. Examples of action statements are the assignment, WRITE, and GO TO statements. Specification statements such as type declaration statements, FORMAT statements, and ENTRY statements are not action statements. Note that constructs are not action statements.

8.4 The CASE Construct

The CASE construct is a new feature in Fortran 90. It, like the IF construct, consists of a number of blocks, of which at most one is selected for execution. The selection is based on the value of the scalar expression in the SELECT CASE statement at the beginning of the construct; the value of this expression is called the **case index**. The case selected is the one for which the case index matches a case selector value in a CASE statement. Case selector values must not overlap. There is an optional default case that, in effect, matches all values not matched by any CASE statement in the construct.

8.4.1 Form of the CASE Construct

The form of the CASE construct (R808) is:

```
[ case-construct-name : ] SELECT CASE ( case-expression )
[ CASE ( case-value-range-list ) [ case-construct-name ]
       block ] ...
[ CASE DEFAULT [ case-construct-name ]
       block ]
END SELECT [ case-construct-name ]
```

where case expression is a scalar expression. The forms of a case value range (R814) are:

```
case-value
case-value :
: case-value
case-value : case-value
```

where each case value is a scalar initialization expression of the same type as the case expression. Recall that an initialization expression is an expression that can be evaluated at compile time; that is, a constant expression, essentially. The types of the case expression and case values are limited to the "discrete" intrinsic types, namely integer, character, and logical.

The statement containing the keywords SELECT CASE is called the **SELECT CASE statement**. The statement beginning with the keyword CASE is called the **CASE statement**. The statement beginning with the keywords END SELECT is called the **END SELECT statement**. A case value range list enclosed in parenthesis or the DEFAULT keyword is called a **case selector**.

Rules and restrictions:

1. If a construct name is present on a SELECT CASE statement, it must also appear on the END SELECT statement.

2. Any of the case selector statements may or may not have a construct name. If one does, it must be the same name as the construct name on the SELECT CASE statement.

3. A CASE statement with the case selector DEFAULT is optional; however, the general form (R808) of the CASE construct does not require that such a CASE statement be the last CASE statement.

4. Within a particular CASE construct, the case expression and all case values must be of the same type. If the character type is used, different character lengths are allowed. But, the kind type parameter values must be the same for all of these expressions.

5. The colon forms of the case values expressing a range may be used for expressions in the construct of type integer and character (but not logical). For example, a CASE statement of the form

    ```
    CASE ('BOOK':'DOG')
    ```

    would select all character strings that collate between BOOK and DOG inclusive, using the processor-dependent collating sequence for the default character type.

6. After expression evaluation, there must be no more than one case selector that matches the case index. In other words, overlapping case values and case ranges are prohibited.

An example of the CASE construct is:

```
FIND_AREA: &  ! Compute the area with a formula
              ! appropriate for the shape of the object
   SELECT CASE (OBJECT)
     CASE (CIRCLE)  FIND_AREA
        AREA = PI * RADIUS ** 2
     CASE (SQUARE)  FIND_AREA
        AREA = SIDE * SIDE
     CASE (RECTANGLE)  FIND_AREA
        AREA = LENGTH * WIDTH
     CASE DEFAULT  FIND_AREA
   END SELECT  FIND_AREA
```

8.4.2 Execution of the CASE Construct

The case index (the scalar expression) in the SELECT CASE statement is evaluated in anticipation of matching one of the case values preceding the blocks. The case index must match at most one of the selector values. The block following the case matched is executed, the CASE construct terminates, and control passes to the next executable statement or construct following the END SELECT statement of the construct. If no match occurs and the CASE DEFAULT statement is present, the block after the CASE DEFAULT statement is selected. If there is no CASE DEFAULT statement, the CASE construct terminates, and the next executable statement or construct following the END SELECT statement of the construct is executed. If the case value is a single value, a match occurs if the index is equal to the case value (determined by the rules used in evaluating the equality or equivalence operator [see Sections 7.3.1.2]). If the case value is a range of values, there are three possibilities to determine a match depending on the form of the range:

Case value range	Condition for a match
case-value$_1$: case-value$_2$	case-value$_1 \leq$ case-index $\leq$ case-value$_2$
case-value :	case-value $\leq$ case-index
: case-value	case-value $\geq$ case-index

Rules and restrictions:

1. Overlapping case ranges are not allowed.

2. The execution of the construct concludes with the execution of the block selected, if there is one. At most one block is executed. There must not be a case value that would select more than one block.

3. If there is no match and no default case. the CASE construct terminates. None of the blocks within the construct is executed.

4. Branching to the END SELECT statement is allowed only from within the construct.

5. Branching to a CASE statement is prohibited; branching to the SELECT CASE statement is allowed, however.

Figure 8-2 illustrates the execution of a CASE construct.

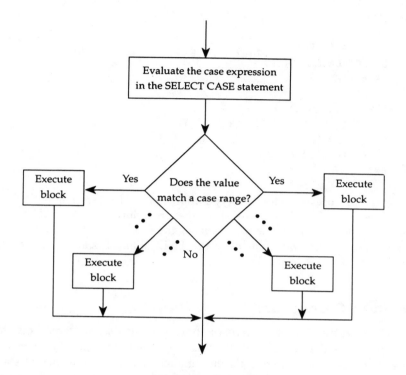

Figure 8-2 Execution flow for a CASE construct

Example:

```
INDEX = 2
SELECT CASE (INDEX)
CASE (1)
   X = 1.0
CASE (2)
   X = 2.0
CASE DEFAULT
   X = 99.0
END SELECT
```

The case expression INDEX has the value 2. The block following the case value of 2 is executed; that is, the statement $X = 2.0$ is executed, and execution of the CASE construct terminates.

Example:

```
COLOR = 'GREEN'
SELECT CASE (COLOR)
CASE ('RED')
   STOP
CASE ('YELLOW')
   CALL  STOP_IF_YOU_CAN_SAFELY
CASE ('GREEN')
   CALL  GO_AHEAD
END SELECT
```

This example uses selectors of type character. The expression COLOR has the value GREEN, and therefore the procedure GO_AHEAD is executed. When it returns, the execution of the CASE statement terminates, and the executable statement after the END SELECT statement executes next.

8.5 The DO Construct

The DO construct contains zero or more statements and constructs that are repeated under control of other parts of the construct. More specifically, the DO construct controls the number of times a sequence of statements and constructs within the range of a loop is executed. There are three steps in the execution of a DO construct:

1. First, if execution of the DO construct is controlled by a DO variable, the expressions representing the parameters that determine the number of times the range is to be executed are evaluated (step 1 of Figure 8-3).

2. Next, a decision is made as to whether the range of the loop is to be executed (step 2 of Figure 8-3).

3. Finally, if appropriate, the range of the loop is executed (step 3a of Figure 8-3); the DO variable, if present, is updated (step 3b of Figure 8-3); and step 2 is repeated.

In Fortran 77, execution of a DO loop is controlled by a DO variable that is incremented a certain number of times as prescribed in the initial DO statement. In Fortran 90, this option remains available, but there are two additional ways of controlling the loop; one is the DO WHILE and the other is the simple DO, sometimes called "DO forever". The execution of the simple DO construct must be terminated by

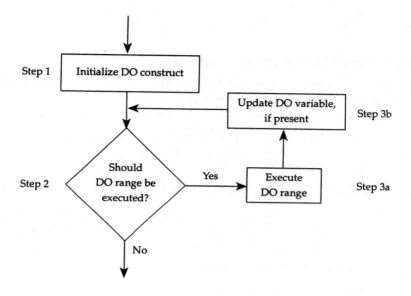

Figure 8-3 Execution flow for a DO construct

executing a statement, such as an EXIT statement, that transfers control out of the DO range.

There are two basic forms of the DO construct—the block DO and the nonblock DO. Modern programming practice favors the block DO form and therefore the block DO form is the recommended construct. The nonblock DO form is there for compatibility with Fortran 77. The block DO contains all of the functionality of the nonblock DO and vice versa. Indeed, both forms of DO construct permit the DO WHILE and DO forever forms of loops. The feature distinguishing the two forms is that the block DO construct is always terminated by an END DO or CONTINUE statement whereas the nonblock DO construct either terminates with an action statement or construct or shares a termination statement with another DO construct.

An example of a block DO construct is:

```
DO I = 1, N
  SUM = SUM + A (I)
END DO
```

An example of a nonblock DO construct to perform the same computation is:

```
    DO 10 I = 1, N
10 SUM = SUM + A (I)
```

8.5.1 Form of the Block DO Construct

The block DO construct is a DO construct that terminates with an END
DO statement or a CONTINUE statement that is not shared with another
DO construct. The form of a block DO construct (R817) is:

> [do-construct-name :] DO [label] [loop-control]
>   [execution-part-construct] ...
> [label] end-do

where the forms of the loop control (R821) are:

> [,] scalar-variable-name = scalar-numeric-expression , &
>   scalar-numeric-expression [, scalar-numeric-expression]
> [,] WHILE (scalar-logical-expression)

and the forms of the end-do (R824) are:

> END DO [do-construct-name]
> CONTINUE

The statement beginning with the keyword DO after the optional construct name is called a **DO statement**. The statement beginning with the
keywords END DO is called an **END DO statement**. The statement
beginning with the keyword CONTINUE is called a **CONTINUE statement**.

Rules and restrictions:

1. The DO variable must be a scalar named variable of type integer,
    default real, or double precision real. (This excludes scalar vari-
    ables that are array elements, arrays, and components of struc-
    tures.) The use of a real or double precision DO variable is obso-
    lescent.

2. Each scalar numeric expression in the loop control must be of type
    integer, default real, or double precision real. The use of numeric
    expressions of type real or double precision real for the DO loop
    parameters is obsolescent.

3. If the DO statement of a block DO construct has a construct name,
    the corresponding end-do must be an END DO statement that has
    the same construct name. If the DO statement of a block DO con-
    struct does not have a construct name, the corresponding end-do
    must not have a construct name.

4. If the DO statement does not contain a label, the corresponding end-do must be an END DO statement. If the DO statement does contain a label, the corresponding end-do must be identified with the same label. Note that a block DO construct can never share its terminal statement with another DO construct, even if it is a labeled statement. If a DO construct does share its terminal statement with another DO construct, it is a nonblock DO construct.

Examples:

```
SUM = 0.0
DO I = 1, N
  SUM = SUM + X (I) ** 2
END DO

FOUND = .FALSE.
I = 0
DO WHILE (.NOT. FOUND .AND. I < LIMIT )
  IF (KEY == X (I))   THEN
    FOUND = .TRUE.
  ELSE
    I = I + 1
  END IF
END DO

NO_ITERS = 0
DO
  ! F and F_PRIME are functions
  X1 = X0 - F (X0) / F_PRIME (X0)
  IF (ABS(X1-X0) < SPACING (X0) .OR. &
      NO_ITERS > MAX_ITERS )  EXIT
  X0 = X1
  NO_ITERS = NO_ITERS + 1
END DO

    INNER_PROD = 0.0
    DO 10 I = 1, 10
      INNER_PROD = INNER_PROD + X (I) * Y (I)
10 CONTINUE

LOOP: DO I = 1, N
        Y (I) = A * X (I) + Y (I)
      END DO LOOP
```

Although a DO construct can have both a label and a construct name, use of both is not in the spirit of modern programming practice where the use of labels is minimized.

8.5.2 Form of the Nonblock DO Construct

The nonblock DO construct is a DO construct that either shares a terminal statement with another DO construct, or the terminal statement is a construct or an action statement. The nonblock DO construct always uses a label to specify the terminal statement of the construct. The two forms for a nonblock DO construct (R826) are:

    action-terminated-do-construct
    outer-shared-do-construct

where the form of an action terminated DO construct (R827) is:

    [do-construct-name :] DO label [loop-control]
        [execution-part-construct] ...
    label action-statement

and the form of an outer shared DO construct (R830) is:

    [do-construct-name :] DO label [loop-control]
        [execution-part-construct] ...
    label shared-termination-do-construct

where the forms of a shared termination DO construct (R831) are:

    outer-shared-do-construct
    inner-shared-do-construct

An inner shared DO construct (R832) is:

    [do-construct-name :] DO label [loop-control]
        [execution-part-construct] ...
    label action-statement

The action statement terminating an action terminated DO construct is called a **DO terminated action statement**. The action statement terminating an inner shared DO construct is called a **DO terminated shared statement**. The DO terminated action statement, DO terminated shared statement, or shared terminated DO construct at the end of a nonblock DO construct is called the **DO termination** or the **terminal statement** of that construct.

Rules and restrictions:

1. A DO terminated action statement must not be a CONTINUE statement, a GO TO statement, a RETURN statement, a STOP

statement, an EXIT statement, a CYCLE statement, an END statement for a program or subprogram, an arithmetic IF statement, or
an assigned GO TO statement.

2. The DO terminated action statement must be identified with a label
   and the corresponding DO statement must refer to the same label.

3. A DO terminated shared statement must not be a GO TO statement, a RETURN statement, a STOP statement, an EXIT statement,
   a CYCLE statement, an END statement for a program or subprogram, an arithmetic IF statement, or an assigned GO TO statement.

4. The DO terminated shared statement must be identified with a label
   and all DO statements of the shared terminated DO construct must
   refer to the same label.

Examples:

```
      PROD = 1.0
      DO 10 I = 1, N
10    PROD = PROD * P (I)


      DO 10 I = 1, N
        DO 10 J = 1, N
10      HILBERT (I, J) = 1.0 / REAL (I + J)


      FOUND = .FALSE.
      I = 0
      DO 10 WHILE (.NOT. FOUND .AND. I < LIMIT)
        I = I + 1
10    FOUND = KEY == X (I)


      DO 20 I = 1, N
        DO 20 J = I+1, N
          T = A (I, J); A (I, J) = A (J, I); A (J, I) = T
20 CONTINUE
```

8.5.3 Range of a DO Construct

The range of a DO construct consists of all statements and constructs following the DO statement, bounded by and including the terminal statement. The DO range may contain constructs, such as an IF construct, a
CASE construct, or another DO construct, but the inner construct or
constructs must be entirely enclosed within the nearest outer construct.
If the range of a DO construct contains another DO construct, the DO
constructs are said to be **nested**.

Although a nest of DO constructs sharing a terminal statement is obsolescent and is earmarked for removal in the next revision of the standard, it is still permitted. A branch to a statement within a DO construct range from outside the DO construct is prohibited.

8.5.4 Active and Inactive DO Constructs

A DO construct is either active or inactive. A DO construct becomes **active** when the DO statement is executed. A DO construct becomes **inactive** when any one of the following situations occurs:

1. the iteration count is zero at the time it is tested

2. the WHILE condition is false at the time it is tested

3. an EXIT statement is executed that causes an exit from the DO construct or any DO construct containing the DO construct

4. a CYCLE statement is executed that causes cycling of any DO construct containing the DO construct

5. there is a transfer of control out of the DO construct

6. a RETURN statement in the DO construct is executed

7. the program terminates for any reason

8.5.5 Execution of DO Constructs

There are essentially three forms of DO constructs, each with their own rules for execution. These forms are: a DO construct with an iteration count, a DO WHILE construct, and a simple DO construct. Each form of the DO construct may contain executable statements that alter the sequential execution of the DO range (8.5.6); in addition, some render the DO construct inactive as described in Section 8.5.4.

8.5.5.1 DO Construct with an Iteration Count. In this case, an iteration count controls the number of times the range of the loop is executed.
    The form of a DO statement (R818) using an iteration count is:

```
DO [ label ] [ , ]   &
    do-variable = expression₁ , expression₂ [ , expression₃ ]
```

The DO variable and the expressions may be of any arithmetic type, except complex, but the use of any type except integer is considered obsolescent. Examples of the DO statement are:

```
DO 10 I = 1, N
DO, J = -N, N
DO K = N, 1, -1
```

The Iteration Count. An iteration count is established for counting the number of times the program executes the range of the DO construct. This is done by evaluating the expressions expression$_1$, expression$_2$, and expression$_3$, and converting these values to the type of the DO variable. Let m_1, m_2, and m_3 be the values obtained. The value of m_3 must not be zero. If expression$_3$ is not present, m_3 is given the value 1. Thus:

> m_1 is the initial value of the DO variable
> m_2 is the terminal value the DO variable may assume
> m_3 is an optional parameter, specifying the DO variable increment

The iteration count is calculated from the formula:

$$\text{MAX (INT} ((m_2 - m_1 + m_3) / m_3), 0)$$

Note that the iteration count is 0 if:

> $m_1 > m_2$ and $m_3 > 0$
> or
> $m_1 < m_2$ and $m_3 < 0$

Controlling Execution of the Range of the DO Construct. The steps that control the execution of the range of the DO construct are:

1. The DO variable is set to m_1, the initial parameter (step 1 of Figure 8-3).

2. The iteration count is tested (step 2 of Figure 8-3). If it is 0, the DO construct terminates.

3. If the iteration count is not 0, the range of the DO construct is executed (step 3a of Figure 8-3). The iteration count is decremented by 1, and the DO variable is incremented by m_3 (step 3b of Figure 8-3). Steps 2 and 3 are repeated until the iteration count is 0.

After termination, the DO variable retains its last value, the one that it had when the iteration count was tested and found to be 0.

The DO variable must not be redefined or become undefined during the execution of the range of the DO construct. Note that changing the variables used in the expressions for the loop parameters during the execution of the DO construct does not change the iteration count; it is fixed each time the DO construct is entered.

Example:

```
N = 10
SUM = 0.0
DO 2 I = 1, N
    SUM = SUM + X (I)
    N = N + 1
2 CONTINUE
```

The loop is executed 10 times; after execution $I = 11$ and $N = 20$.

Example:

```
X = 20.
DO 41 I = 1, 2
    DO 40 J = 1, 5
        X = X + 1.0
40      CONTINUE
41 CONTINUE
```

The inner loop is executed 10 times. After completion of the outer DO construct, $J = 6$, $I = 3$, $X = 30$.

If the second DO statement had been

```
DO 40 J = 5, 1
```

the inner DO construct would not have executed at all; X would remain equal to 20; J would equal 5, its initial value; and I would be equal to 3. Note that labels in DO constructs can be used in both free and fixed source forms.

8.5.5.2 The DO WHILE Construct. The DO WHILE form of the DO construct provides the ability to repeat the DO range while a specified condition remains true.

The form of the DO WHILE statement is:

DO [label] [,] **WHILE** (scalar-logical-expression)

Examples of the DO WHILE statement are:

```
DO WHILE( K >= 4 )
DO 20 WHILE( .NOT. FOUND )
DO, WHILE( A(I) /= 0 )
```

The DO range is executed repeatedly as follows. Prior to each execution of the DO range, the logical expression is evaluated. If it is true, the range is executed; if it is false, the DO WHILE construct terminates.

```
SUM = 0.0
I = 0
DO WHILE (I < 5)
    I = I + 1
    SUM = SUM + I
END DO
```

The loop would execute 5 times, after which SUM = 15.0 and I = 5.

8.5.5.3 The Simple DO Construct. A DO construct without any loop control provides the ability to repeat statements in the DO range until the DO construct is terminated explicitly by some statement within the range. When the end of the DO range is reached, the first executable statement of the DO range is executed next.

The form of the simple DO statement is:

```
DO [ label ]
```

Example:

```
DO
    READ *, DATA
    IF (DATA < 0) STOP
    CALL PROCESS (DATA)
END DO
```

The DO range executes repeatedly until a negative value of DATA is read, at which time the DO construct (and the program, in this case) terminates. The previous example, rewritten using a label, is:

```
    DO 100
        READ *, DATA
        IF (DATA < 0) STOP
        CALL PROCESS (DATA)
100 CONTINUE
```

8.5.6 Altering the Execution Sequence within the Range of a DO Construct

There are two special statements that may appear in the range of any DO construct that alter the execution sequence in a special way. One is the EXIT statement; the other is the CYCLE statement. Other statements, such as branch statements, RETURN statements, and STOP statements also alter the execution sequence but are not restricted to DO constructs as are the EXIT and CYCLE statements.

8.5.6.1 EXIT Statement. The EXIT statement immediately causes termination of the DO construct. No further action statements within the range of the DO construct are executed. It may appear in either the block or nonblock form of the DO construct, except that it must not be the DO termination action statement or DO termination shared statement of the nonblock form.

The form of the EXIT statement (R835) is:

    EXIT [do-construct-name]

Rules and restrictions:

1. The EXIT statement must be within a DO construct.

2. If the EXIT statement has a construct name, it must be within the DO construct with the same name; when it is executed, the named DO construct is terminated as well as any DO constructs containing the EXIT statement and contained within the named DO construct.

3. If the EXIT statement does not have a construct name, the innermost DO construct in which the EXIT statement appears is terminated.

Example:

```
LOOP_8 : DO
   . . .
   IF (TEMP == INDEX) EXIT LOOP_8
   . . .
END DO LOOP_8
```

The DO construct has a construct name, LOOP_8; the DO range is executed repeatedly until the condition in the IF statement is met, when the DO construct terminates.

8.5.6.2 CYCLE Statement. In contrast to the EXIT statement, which terminates execution of the DO construct entirely, the CYCLE statement interrupts the execution of the DO range and begins a new cycle of the DO construct, with appropriate adjustments made to the iteration count and DO variable, if present. It may appear in either the block or nonblock form of the DO construct, except it must not be the DO termination action statement or DO termination shared statement of the nonblock form. When the CYCLE statement is in the nonblock form, the DO termination action statement or DO termination shared statement is not executed.

The form of the CYCLE statement (R834) is:

CYCLE [do-construct-name]

Rules and restrictions:

1. The CYCLE statement must be within a DO construct.

2. If the CYCLE statement has a construct name, it must be within the DO construct with the same name; when it is executed, the execution of the named DO construct is interrupted, and any DO construct containing the CYCLE statement and contained within the named DO construct is terminated.

3. If the CYCLE statement does not have a construct name, the innermost DO construct in which the CYCLE statement appears is interrupted. The CYCLE statement may be used with any form of the DO statement and causes the next iteration of the DO range to begin, if permitted by the condition controlling the loop.

4. Upon interruption of the DO construct, if there is a DO variable, it is updated and the iteration count is decremented by 1. Then, in all cases, the processing of the next iteration begins.

Example:

```
DO
    . . .
    INDEX = . . .
    . . .
    IF (INDEX < 0) EXIT
    IF (INDEX == 0) CYCLE
    . . .
END DO
```

In the above example, the loop is executed as long as INDEX is nonnegative. If INDEX is negative, the loop is terminated. If INDEX is 0, the latter part of the loop is skipped.

8.6 Branching

Branching is a transfer of control from the current statement to another statement or construct in the program unit. A branch alters the execution sequence. This means that the statement or construct immediately following the branch is usually not executed. Instead, some other statement or construct is executed, and the execution sequence proceeds from that point. The terms **branch statement** and **branch target statement** are used to distinguish between the transfer statement and the statement to which the transfer is made.

An example of branching is provided by the GO TO statement. It is used to transfer to a statement in the execution sequence that is usually not the next statement in the program, although this is not prohibited.

The statements that may be branch target statements are those classified as action statements plus the IF-THEN statement, SELECT CASE statement, a DO statement, a WHERE statement, and a few additional statements in limited situations. However, it is not permitted to branch to a statement within a block from outside the block. The additional statements that may be branch targets in limited contexts are:

1. an END SELECT statement, provided the branch is taken from within the CASE construct

2. an END DO statement provided the branch is taken from within the DO construct

3. an END IF statement provided the branch is taken from within the IF construct; also from outside the IF construct, but this use is designated as obsolescent

4. an END DO statement, a DO termination action statement, or a DO termination shared statement, provided the branch is taken from within the DO construct, but this use is also designated as obsolescent

8.6.1 Use of Labels in Branching

A statement label is a means of identifying the branch target statement. Any statement in a Fortran program may have a label. However, if a branch statement refers to a statement label, some statement in the program unit must have that label, and the statement label must be on an allowed branch target statement (8.6).

As described in Section 3.2.5, a label is a string of from one to five decimal digits; leading zeros are not significant. Note that labels can be used in both free and fixed source forms.

8.6.2 The GO TO Statement

The GO TO statement is an unconditional branching statement altering the execution sequence.

8.6.2.1 Form of the GO TO Statement. The form of the GO TO statement (R836) is:

```
GO TO   label
```

Rules and restrictions:

1. The label must be a branch target statement in the same scoping unit as the GO TO statement (that is, in the same program unit, excluding labels on statements in internal procedures, derived-type definitions, and interface blocks).

8.6.2.2 Execution of the GO TO Statement. When the GO TO statement is executed, the next statement that is executed is the branch target statement identified with the label specified. Execution proceeds from that point. For example:

```
GO TO 200    ! This is an unconditional branch and
             ! always goes to 200.

X = 1.0      ! Because this statement is not labeled
             ! and follows a GO TO statement, it is
             ! not reachable.

GO TO 10
GO TO 010    ! 10 and 010 are the same label.
```

8.6.3 The Computed GO TO Statement

The computed GO TO statement transfers to one of a set of the branch target statements based on the value of an integer expression, selecting the branch target from a list of labels. The CASE construct provides a similar functionality in a more structured form.

8.6.3.1 Form of the Computed GO TO Statement. The form of the computed GO TO statement (R837) is:

> GO TO (label-list) [,] scalar-integer-expression

Examples:

```
GO TO ( 10, 20 ), SWITCH
GO TO ( 100, 200, 3, 33 ),  2*I-J
```

Rules and restrictions:

1. If there are n labels in the list and the expression has one of the values from 1 to n, the value identifies a statement label in the list: the first, second, ..., or nth label. A branch to the statement with that label is executed.

2. If the value of the expression is less than 1 or greater than n, no branching occurs and execution continues with the next executable statement or construct following the computed GO TO statement.

3. Each label in the list must be the label of a branch target statement in the same scoping unit as the computed GO TO statement.

4. A label may appear more than once in the list of target labels.

Example:

```
      SWITCH = . . .
      GO TO (10, 11, 10) SWITCH
      Y = Z
   10 X = Y + 2.
      . . .
   11 X = Y
```

If SWITCH has the value 1 or 3, the assignment statement labeled 10 is executed; if it has the value 2, the assignment statement labeled 11 is executed. If it has a value less than 1 or greater than 3, the assignment statement Y = Z is executed, because it is the next statement after the computed GO TO statement, and the statement with label 10 is executed next.

8.6.4 The CONTINUE Statement

The form of the CONTINUE statement (R841) is:

```
CONTINUE
```

Normally, the statement has a label and is used for DO termination; however, it may serve as some other place holder in the program or as a branch target statement. It may appear without a label. The statement by itself does nothing and has no effect on the execution sequence or on program results. Examples are:

```
100 CONTINUE
CONTINUE
```

8.6.5 The STOP Statement

This statement terminates the program whenever and wherever it is executed.

The forms of the STOP statement (R842) are:

```
STOP [ scalar-character-constant ]
STOP digit [ digit [ digit [ digit [ digit ] ] ] ]
```

Rules and restrictions:

1. The character constant or list of digits identifying the STOP statement is optional and is called a **stop code**.

2. The character constant must be of default character type.

3. When the STOP code is a string of digits, leading zeros are not significant; 10 and 010 are the same STOP code.

The stop code is accessible following program termination. This might mean that the processor prints this code to identify where the program stopped if there are multiple STOP statements. Using a stop code is dependent on the local termination procedures used by the processor. Examples are:

```
STOP
STOP 'Error #823'
STOP 20
```

8.7 Obsolescent Control Statements

Three Fortran 77 control facilities have been declared obsolescent and may be removed from the next revision of the standard. These are, however, part of the current standard, but their use is discouraged because of their potential removal after the next revision of the standard. These statements are the ASSIGN and the assigned GO TO statements, the arithmetic IF statement, and the PAUSE statement.

8.7.1 The ASSIGN and Assigned GO TO Statements

The ASSIGN statement gives an integer variable a statement label. During program execution, the variable may be assigned labels of branch target statements, providing a dynamic branching capability in a program. The unsatisfactory property of these statements is that the integer variable name may be used to hold both a label and an ordinary integer value, leading to errors that are hard to discover and programs that are difficult to read.

A frequent use of the ASSIGN statement and assigned GO TO statement is to simulate internal procedures, using the ASSIGN statement to record the return point after a reusable block of code has completed. The new internal procedure mechanism of Fortran 90 provides this capability. A second use of these constructs is to simulate dynamic format specifications by assigning labels corresponding to different format statements to an integer variable and using this variable in input/output statements as a format specifier. This use can be accomplished in a clearer way by using character strings as format specifications. Thus, it is no longer necessary to use the ASSIGN statement and assigned GO TO statement.

Execution of an ASSIGN statement assigns a label to an integer variable. Subsequently, this value may be used by an assigned GO TO statement or by an input/output statement to reference a FORMAT statement.

Execution of the assigned GO TO statement causes a transfer of control to the branch target statement with the label that had previously been assigned to the integer variable.

8.7.1.1 Form of the ASSIGN and Assigned GO TO Statements. The form of the ASSIGN statement (R838) is:

ASSIGN label TO scalar-integer-variable

Rules and restrictions:

1. The variable must be a named variable of default integer type. That is, it must not be an array element, an integer component of a structure, or an object of nondefault integer type.

2. The label must be the label of a branch target statement or the label of a FORMAT statement in the same scoping unit as the ASSIGN statement.

3. When defined with an integer value, the integer variable may not be used as a label.

4. When assigned a label, the integer variable must not be used as anything other than a label.

5. When the integer variable is used in an assigned GO TO statement, it must be assigned a label.

6. The variable may be redefined during program execution with either another label or an integer value.

Example:

```
ASSIGN 100 TO K
```

The form of the assigned GO TO statement (R839) is:

```
GO TO  scalar-integer-variable [ [ , ] ( label-list ) ]
```

Rules and restrictions:

1. The variable must be a named variable of default integer type. That is, it must not be an array element, an integer component of a structure, or an object of nondefault integer type.

2. The variable must be assigned the label of a branch target statement in the same scoping unit as the assigned GO TO statement.

3. If the label list appears, the variable must have been assigned a label value that is in the list.

Example:

```
GO TO K
GO TO K (10, 20, 100)
```

8.7.2 Arithmetic IF Statement

The arithmetic IF statement is a three-way branching statement based on an arithmetic expression.

The form of the arithmetic IF statement (R840) is:

```
IF ( scalar-numeric-expression ) label , label , label
```

Rules and restrictions:

1. The same label may appear more than once in the same arithmetic IF statement.

2. The numeric expression must not be of type complex.

3. Each statement label must be the label of a branch target statement in the same scoping unit as the arithmetic IF statement itself.

The execution begins with the evaluation of the expression. If the expression is negative, the branch is to the first label; if zero, to the second label; and if positive, to the third label.

8.7.3 PAUSE Statement

The execution of the PAUSE statement suspends the execution of a program until the operator or system starts the execution again. This is now redundant, because a WRITE statement may be used to send a message to any device (such as the operator console or terminal) and a READ statement may be used to wait for and receive a message from the same device.

The forms of the PAUSE statement (R844) are:

PAUSE [scalar-character-constant]
PAUSE digit [digit [digit [digit [digit]]]]

The character constant or list of digits identifying the PAUSE statement is called the **pause code** and follows the same rules as those for the stop code (8.6.5). The pause code, as with the stop code, is accessible following program suspension and may be printed as a code to identify where the program has been suspended. Using a pause code is dependent on the local termination procedures used by the processor. Examples are:

PAUSE
PAUSE 'Wait #823'
PAUSE 100

8.8 Summary

IF Construct

If the logical expression in the IF-THEN statement is true, the block following that statement is executed and the construct completes. If the logical expression is not true, the block is not executed. If there is an ELSE IF statement, its logical expression is evaluated and, if it is true, the block following it is executed, and the construct terminates. There may be several ELSE IF statements with a block following each one of them. At most one block in the construct is executed. An ELSE statement is optional, and the optional block following it is executed if none of the logical expressions in the IF-THEN or ELSE IF statements is true. The construct may be named with a construct name. Recall that the blocks may be empty; that is, they may contain no executable statements or constructs.

```
SUM = S
SUMXY : IF (X > Y) THEN
    SUM = SUM + X
ELSE
    SUM = SUM + Y
END IF SUMXY
```

IF Statement

An action statement is executed if the logical expression in the IF statement is true. If it is not true, the next statement in the execution sequence is executed and the action statement is not executed.

```
IF (I == J) X = X + 1.0
```

CASE Construct

The case index is evaluated and compared with all case selectors. If there is a match, the block following the matched case is executed. There may be a default case that is executed when no match occurs. The construct may be named. At most one block in the construct is executed. The construct may be named with a construct name. The case index is limited to an expression of type integer, character, or logical.

```
I = 2
    . . .
SELECT CASE (I)
CASE (0)
    Z = 4.5
    A = A + 1.0
CASE (2)      .
    A = A + 2.0
CASE DEFAULT
    A = 999.0
END SELECT
```

DO Construct

The DO construct is used to repeat zero or more times a sequence of statements and constructs that constitute its range. The DO construct includes the Fortran 77 DO loop as well as the new iterated DO construct, the DO WHILE, and the simple DO loop. The repetition of the DO construct range may be controlled by an iteration count or a logical condition. A DO construct may contain EXIT and CYCLE statements. The construct may be named with a construct name.

Simple DO Loop

The range of the loop is repeated until it is terminated explicitly by a statement within the range.

```
DO
    S (K) =  . . .
    K = . . .
    IF (K < LIMIT) THEN
        K = 0
        EXIT
    END IF
    . . .
END DO
```

DO Loop with Iteration Count

The range of the DO construct is executed as many times as the iteration count. The iteration count is determined initially from the expressions in the DO statement and decremented until the count is zero. The DO construct may contain EXIT and CYCLE statements.

```
DO I = 1, 100
    X (I) =  2 * I
    Y (I) = COS (R * X(I))
END DO
```

DO WHILE Loop

The range of the DO WHILE construct is executed while the value of a logical expression in the DO statement is true.

```
DO WHILE (J < K)
   X (J) = COS (Y (J) * J)
   J = J + 2
END DO
```

GO TO Statement

The statement branches unconditionally to the statement with the label referenced.

```
GO TO 100
```

Computed GO TO Statement

A transfer to a branch target statement takes place based on the value of a scalar integer expression.

```
GO TO (1, 2, 99) SWITCH
```

If the scalar integer expression has the value i, there is a transfer to the branch target statement with the ith label in the list.

STOP Statement

A program terminates unconditionally when a STOP statement is executed. A stop code is optional.

```
STOP
```

ASSIGN and Assigned GO TO Statements

An integer variable may be given a label by execution of an ASSIGN statement. Subsequently, the variable may be used in an assigned GO TO statement to designate a branch target. The label of a FORMAT statement also may be assigned and used in an input/output statement to designate the format to be used.

```
        ASSIGN 100 TO FORMAT_SPEC
        WRITE (6, FORMAT_SPEC) X
           . . .
        ASSIGN 98 TO ERROR_HANDLER
        GO TO ERROR_HANDLER
100 FORMAT(3A5)
```

Arithmetic IF Statement

The arithmetic IF statement provides a three-way branch based on whether the value of an expression is negative, zero, or positive.

```
IF (IOSTAT_RESULT) 10, 20, 30
```

The branch is to the first label if it is negative, the second label if it is zero, and the third label if it is positive.

F9(

9

Input and Output Processing

Many programs need data to begin a calculation. After the calculation is completed, often the results need to be printed, displayed graphically, or saved for later use. During execution of a program, sometimes there is a large amount of data produced by one part of the program that needs to be saved for use by another part of the program, and the amount of data is too large to store in variables, such as arrays. Also, the editing capabilities of the data transfer statements for internal files are so powerful that they can be used for processing character strings. Each of these tasks is accomplished using Fortran input/output statements described in this chapter.

The input/output statements are:

READ
PRINT
WRITE
OPEN
CLOSE
INQUIRE
BACKSPACE
ENDFILE
REWIND

The READ statement is a **data transfer input statement** and provides a means for transferring data from an external media to internal storage or from an internal file to internal storage through a process called **reading**. The WRITE and PRINT statements are both **data transfer output statements** and provide a means for transferring data from internal storage to an external media or from internal storage to an internal file. This process is called **writing**. The OPEN and CLOSE statements are both **file connection statements**. The INQUIRE statement is a **file inquiry statement**. The BACKSPACE, ENDFILE, and REWIND statements are both **file positioning statements**.

The first part of this chapter discusses terms and concepts needed to gain a thorough understanding of all of the input/output facilities. These include internal and external files, formatted and unformatted records, sequential and direct access methods for files, advancing and nonadvancing input/output for the sequential formatted access method, file and record positions, units, and file connection properties. Following the concepts are descriptions of the READ, WRITE, and PRINT data transfer statements and the effect of these statements when they are executed. A model for the execution of data transfer statements and a description of the possible error and other conditions created during the execution of data transfer statements are provided next. Following the model are the descriptions of the OPEN, CLOSE, and INQUIRE statements that establish respectively the connection properties between units and files, that disconnect units and files, and that permit inquiry about the state of the connection between a unit and file. Lastly, file position statements are specified, which include the BACKSPACE and REWIND statements, followed by the description of the ENDFILE statement that creates end-of-file records.

The reader should keep in mind that the processor is not required to perform any input/output operation that cannot be supported by the processor. This and other restrictions are described in Section 9.9. For example, the processor is not required to skip a page when the output unit is connected to a nonprinting device, because skipping a page has no meaning for a file connected to a card punch. This statement is the "way out" for implementations in the input/output area and is sometimes referred to as the "cop-out clause".

The chapter concludes with a summary of the terms, concepts, and statements used for input and output processing and some examples.

9.1 Records, Files, Access Methods, and Units

Collections of data are stored in files. The data in a file is organized into records. Fortran treats a record, for example, as a line on a computer terminal, a line on a printout, or a logical record on a magnetic tape or disk file. However, the general properties of files and records do not depend on how the properties are acquired or how the files and records are stored. This chapter discusses the properties of records and files, and the various kinds of data transfer.

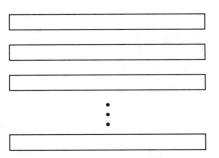

Figure 9-1   Schematic representations of records in a file

A **file** is a sequence of records that can be represented schematically with each box representing a record as shown in Figure 9-1. Before dis-⁀cussing further the general properties of files, we will discuss the properties of records.

9.1.1 Records

There are two kinds of records: data and end-of-file. A **data record** is a sequence of values; thus, it can be represented schematically as a collection of small boxes, each containing a value, as shown in Figure 9-2.

Figure 9-2   Schematic representations of the values in a record

The values in a data record may be represented in one of two ways: formatted or unformatted. **Formatted** data consists of characters that are representable by the processor and are viewable on some medium. For example, a record may contain the four character values "6", ",", "1", and "1" that are intended to represent the two numbers, 6 and 11. In this case, the record might be represented schematically as shown in Figure 9-3. **Unformatted** data consists of values represented usually just as they are stored in computer memory. For example, if integers are stored using a binary representation, an unformatted record, consisting of two integer values, 6 and 11, might look like Figure 9-4.

Figure 9-3 A formatted record with four character values

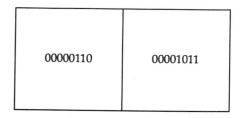

Figure 9-4 An unformatted record with two integer values

The values in a data record are either all formatted or all unformatted. A **formatted record** is one that contains only formatted data. It may be created by a person typing at a terminal or by a Fortran program that converts values stored internally into character strings that form readable representations of those values. When formatted data is read into the computer, the characters must be converted to the computer's internal representation of values, which is often a binary representation. Even character values may be converted from one character representation in the record to another internal representation. The length of a formatted record is the number of characters in it; the length may be zero.

An **unformatted record** is one that contains only unformatted data. Unformatted records usually are created by running a Fortran program, although with the knowledge of how to form the bit patterns correctly, they could be created by other means. Unformatted data often requires less space on an external device. Also, it is usually faster to read and write because no conversion is required. However, it is not as suitable for reading by humans and usually it is not suitable for transferring data from one computer to another because the internal representation of values is machine dependent. The length of an unformatted data record depends on the number of values in it, but is measured in some processor-dependent units; it may be zero. The length of an unformatted record that will be produced by a particular output list may be determined by the INQUIRE statement (9.7.1).

In general, a formatted record is read and written by a formatted data transfer input/output statement, and an unformatted record is read and written by an unformatted data transfer input/output statement.

The other kind of record is the **end-of-file record**; it has no value and has no length. There can be at most one end-of-file record in a file and it must be the last record of a file. It is used to mark the end of a file. It may be written explicitly for files connected for sequential access by using the ENDFILE statement; it may be written implicitly with a file positioning statement (REWIND or BACKSPACE statement) or by closing the file (CLOSE statement).

9.1.2 Kinds of Files

The records of a file must be either all formatted or all unformatted, except that the file may contain an end-of-file record as the last record. A file may have a name, but the length of a file name and the characters that may be used in a file name depend on the processor.

A distinction is made between files that are located on an external device like a disk, and files in memory accessible to the program. The two kinds of files are:

1. external files

2. internal files

The use of these files is illustrated schematically in Figure 9-5.

9.1.2.1 External Files.
External files are located on external devices such as tapes, disks, or computer terminals. For each external file, there is a set of allowed access methods, a set of allowed forms, a set of allowed actions, and a set of allowed record lengths. How these characteristics are established is not described by the standard, but usually is determined by a combination of requests by the user of the file and by actions of the operating system. Each of these characteristics will be discussed later in this chapter. An external file connected to a unit has the position property; that is, the file is positioned at the current record (at the beginning or end), and in some cases, is positioned within the current record.

9.1.2.2 Internal Files.
The contents of internal files are stored as values of variables of type default character. The character values may be created using all the usual means of assigning character values, or they may be created with an output statement specifying the variable as an internal

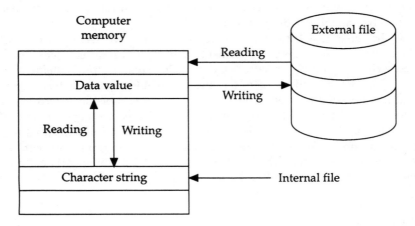

Figure 9-5 Internal and external files

file. Data transfer to and from internal files is described in detail in Section 9.2.9.

File connection, file positioning, and file inquiry must not be used with internal files. If the variable representing the internal file is a scalar, the file has just one record; if the variable is an array, the file has one record for each element of the array. The order of the records is the order of the elements in the array. The length of each record is the length of one array element.

9.1.2.3 Existence of Files.

Certain files are made known to the processor for any executing program, and these files are said to **exist** at the time the program begins executing. On the other hand, a file may not exist because it is not anywhere on the disks accessible to a system. A file may not exist for a particular program because the user of the program is not authorized to access the file. For example, Fortran programs usually are not permitted to access special system files, such as the operating system or the compiler, in order to protect them from user modification.

In addition to files that are made available to programs by the processor for input, output, and other special purposes, programs may create files needed during and after program execution. When the program creates a file, it is said to exist, even if no data has been written into it. A file no longer exists after it has been deleted. Any of the input/output statements may refer to files that exist for the program at that point during execution. Some of the input/output statements (INQUIRE, OPEN, CLOSE, WRITE, PRINT, REWIND, and ENDFILE) may refer to files that do not exist. A WRITE or PRINT statement may create a file that does not exist and put data into that file, unless an error condition occurs.

An internal file always exists.

9.1.3 File Position

Each file being processed by a program has a **position**. During the course of program execution, records are read or written, causing the file position to change. Also, there are other Fortran statements that cause the file position to change; an example is the BACKSPACE statement. The action produced by the input/output statements is described in terms of the file position, so it is important that file position be discussed in detail.

The **initial point** is the point just before the first record. The **terminal point** is the point just after the last record. If the file is empty, the initial point and the terminal point are the same. Initial and terminal points of a file are illustrated in Figure 9-6. A file position may become indeterminate, in particular, when an error condition occurs. When the file position becomes indeterminate, the programmer cannot rely on the file being in any particular position.

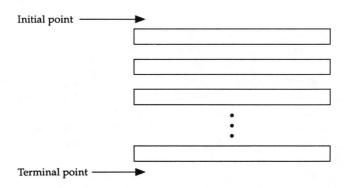

Figure 9-6 Initial and terminal points of a file

A file may be positioned between records. In the example pictured in Figure 9-7, the file is positioned between records 2 and 3. In this case, record 2 is the **preceding record** and record 3 is the **next record**. Of course, if a file is positioned at its initial point, there is no preceding record, and there is no next record if it is positioned at its terminal point.

There may be a current record during execution of an input/output statement or after completion of a nonadvancing input/output statement as shown in Figure 9-8, where record 2 is the current record. If the file is

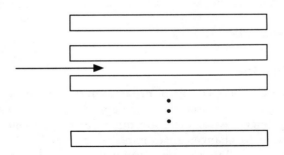

Figure 9-7 A file positioned between records

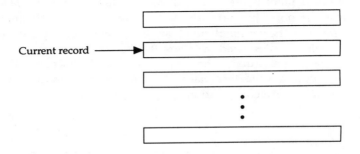

Figure 9-8 A file positioned with a current record

positioned within a current record, the preceding record is the record immediately previous to the current record, unless the current record is also the initial record, in which case there is no preceding record. Similarly, the next record is the record immediately following the current record, unless the current record is also the final record in which case there is no next record.

When there is a current record, the file is positioned at the initial point of the record, between values in a record, or at the terminal point of the record as illustrated in Figure 9-9.

An internal file is always positioned at the beginning of a record just prior to data transfer.

Advancing input/output is record oriented; completion of such an operation always positions a file at the end of a record or between records, unless an error condition occurs. In contrast, nonadvancing input/output is character oriented; after reading and writing, the file may be positioned between characters within the current record.

The position of a nonadvancing file is never changed following a data transfer, unless an error, end-of-file, or end-of-record condition

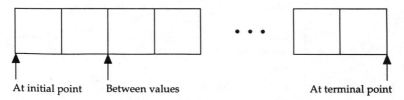

At initial point   Between values   At terminal point

Figure 9-9 Positions within a record of a file

occurs while reading the file. The file position is indeterminate following an error condition when reading a file.

9.1.4 File Access Methods

There are two access methods:

1. sequential access

2. direct access

Some files may be accessed by both methods; other files may be restricted to one access method or the other. For example, a magnetic tape may be accessed only sequentially. While each file is connected, it has a set of permissible access methods, which usually means that it may be accessed either sequentially or directly. However, a file must not be connected for both direct and sequential access simultaneously; that is, if a file is connected for direct access, it must be disconnected with a CLOSE statement and/or reconnected with an OPEN statement specifying sequential access before it can be referenced in a sequential access data transfer statement, and vice versa.

The actual file access method used to read or write the file is *not* a property of the file itself, but is indicated when the file is connected to a unit or when the file is created, if the file is preconnected. The same file may be accessed sequentially by a program, then disconnected, and then later accessed directly by the same program, if both types of access are permitted for the file.

9.1.4.1 Sequential Access. Sequential access to the records in the file begins with the first record of the file and proceeds sequentially to the second record, and then to the next record, record-by-record. The records are accessed serially as they appear in the file. It is not possible to begin at some particular record within the file without reading down to that record in sequential order, as illustrated in Figure 9-10.

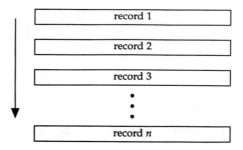

Figure 9-10 Sequential access

When a file is being accessed sequentially, the records are read and written sequentially. For example, if the records are written in any arbitrary order using direct access (see below) and then read using sequential access, the records are read beginning with record number 1 of the file, regardless of when it was written.

9.1.4.2 Direct Access. When a file is accessed directly, the records are selected by record number. Using this identification, the records may be read or written in any order. Therefore, it is possible to write record number 47 first, then number 13. In a new file, this produces a file represented by Figure 9-11. Reading or writing such records is accomplished by direct access data transfer input/output statements.

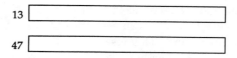

Figure 9-11 A file written using direct access

Either record may be written without first accessing the other.

A file can be accessed using both the direct and sequential access methods (but not both at the same time). However, direct access reads are restricted to records that have been written, and direct access writes are restricted to files connected for direct access (9.2.6). If a file contains an end-of-file record and is connected for direct access, the end-of-file record is not considered part of the file. If the sequential access method is not an allowed access method between the unit and the file, the file must not contain an end-of-file record.

9.1.5 Units

Input/output statements refer to a particular file by providing an **input/output unit**. An input/output unit is either an external unit or an internal unit. An external unit is either a nonnegative integer or an asterisk (*). When an external file is a nonnegative integer, it is called an **external file unit**.

An internal unit is a default character variable. The name of an internal file also is called a unit. A unit number identifies one and only one external unit in all program units in a Fortran program.

File positioning, file connection, and inquiry statements must use an external unit.

9.1.5.1 Unit Existence. The collection of unit numbers that can be used in a program for external files is determined by the processor and the operating system. The unit numbers that may be used are said to **exist**. Some unit numbers on some processors are always used for data input (for example, unit 5), others are always used for output (for example, unit 6). There may be certain unit numbers that are never allowed for user files because they are restricted by the operating system. Input/output statements must refer to units that exist, except for those that close a file or inquire about a unit.

9.1.5.2 Establishing a Connection to a Unit. In order to transfer data to or from an external file, the file must be connected to a unit. An internal file is always connected to the unit that is the name of the character variable. There are two ways to establish a connection between a unit and an external file:

1. execution of an OPEN statement in the executing program

2. preconnection by the operating system

Only one file may be connected to a unit at any given time and vice versa. If the unit is disconnected after its first use on a file, it may be reconnected later to another file or to the same file. A file that is not connected to a unit must not be used in any statement, except the OPEN, CLOSE, or INQUIRE statements.

Some units may be **preconnected** to files for each Fortran program by the operating system without any action necessary by the program. For example, on most systems, units 5 and 6 are always preconnected to the default input and default output files, respectively. Preconnection of units also may be done by the operating system when requested by the user in the operating system command language. In either of these cases, the user program does not require an OPEN statement to connect the file; it is preconnected.

Once a file has been disconnected, the only way to reference it is by its name using an OPEN or INQUIRE statement. There is no means of referencing an unnamed file once it is disconnected.

9.2 Data Transfer Statements

When a unit is connected, either by preconnection or execution of an OPEN statement, data may be transferred by reading and writing to the file associated with the unit. The transfer may occur to or from internal or external files.

The **data transfer statements** are the READ, WRITE, and PRINT statements. The general form of the data transfer statements is presented first, and then they are followed by the forms that specify the major uses of data transfer statements.

9.2.1 General Form for Data Transfer Statements

There are three general forms for data transfer statements:

- the READ statement (R909) in two forms

    READ (io-control-spec-list) [input-item-list]
    READ format [, input-item-list]

- the WRITE statement (R910)

    WRITE (io-control-spec-list) [output-item-list]

- the PRINT statement (R911)

    PRINT format [, output-item-list]

The forms of input and output items are given in Section 9.2.2.1. The form of the item format is described as part of the FMT= specifier in Section 9.2.2. The format item is called a **format specifier**.

9.2.1.1 The Input/Output Control Specifiers. The forms of the input/output control specifier (R912) are:

    [**UNIT** =] io-unit
    [**FMT** =] format
    [**NML** =] namelist-group-name
    ADVANCE = scalar-default-character-expression
    END = label
    EOR = label
    ERR = label

```
IOSTAT = scalar-default-integer-variable
REC = scalar-integer-expression
SIZE = scalar-default-integer-variable
```

The UNIT= specifier, with or without the keyword UNIT, is called a **unit specifier**; the FMT= specifier, with or without the keyword FMT, is called a **format specifier**; and the NML= specifier, with or without the keyword NML, is called a **namelist specifier**;

The data transfer statement is called a **formatted input/output statement** if a format or namelist group name specifier is present; it is called an **unformatted input/output statement** if neither is present. If a namelist group name specifier is present, it is also called a **namelist input/output statement**. It is called a **direct access input/output statement** if a REC= specifier is present; otherwise, it is called a **sequential access input/output statement**.

Rules and restrictions:

1. The input/output control specification list must contain a unit specifier and may contain any of the other input/output control specifiers (but none can appear more than once). A FMT= and NML= specifier may not both appear in the list.

There are many additional rules describing the valid combinations of the input/output control specifiers. These rules are covered in the descriptions of each specifier in Section 9.2.2, where appropriate, and in terms of straightforward forms specifying the various kinds of data transfer statements (see Sections 9.2.3 to 9.2.9).

9.2.2 Specifiers for Data Transfer Statements

This section describes the form and effect of the control information specifiers that are used in the data transfer statements. The NML=, ADVANCE=, END=, EOR=, REC=, and SIZE= specifiers are each unique to one of the forms of the data transfer statements, whereas the other specifiers are used in more than more form. In particular, NML= is used in the namelist data transfer statement; the ADVANCE=, EOR=, and SIZE= specifiers are used in input data transfer statements to specify nonadvancing formatted sequential data transfer; and the REC= specifier is used for direct access data transfer.

[UNIT=] input/output unit (R901)

    scalar integer expression   indicates an external unit (R902)

    *   indicates a processor-dependent external unit. It is the same unit number that the

processor would define if a READ or PRINT statement appeared without the unit number

default character variable   indicates an internal unit (R903)

Rules:

1. If a scalar integer expression is used as an input/output unit, it must be nonnegative.

2. A unit specifier is required.

3. A unit number identifies one and only one external unit in all program units in a Fortran program.

4. If the UNIT keyword is omitted, the input/output unit must be first. In this case, the keyword FMT or NML may be omitted from the format or namelist specifier and either item must be second in the list.

5. The unit specified by an asterisk may be used only for formatted sequential access.

[FMT =] format

default character expression

provides the format specification (10.1.1) in the form of a character string, indicating formatted input/output

*   indicates list-directed formatting

label   provides the statement label of a FORMAT statement containing the format specification (10.1.1), indicating formatted input/output.

scalar default integer variable

provides an integer variable that has been assigned the label of a FORMAT statement, using an ASSIGN statement (8.7.1), and indicates formatted input/output

Rules:

1. The keyword FMT= may be omitted if the format specifier is the second specifier in the control information list; otherwise, it is required.

2. If a format specifier is present, a namelist specifier (NML=) must not be present.

3. A format specifier may appear in a PRINT statement and the short form of the READ statement.

4. The scalar default character expression must be a valid format specification (10.1.1). If the expression is an array, it is treated as if all elements of the array were concatenated together in array element order and must be a valid format specification.

5. If a label or a variable with a label value is used, the label must be the label of a FORMAT statement in the same scoping unit as the data transfer statement.

6. The use of a scalar default integer variable is considered obsolescent.

[NML=] namelist group name

name   is the name of a namelist group declared in a NAMELIST statement

Rules:

1. The namelist group name identifies the list of data objects to be transferred by the READ or WRITE statement with the NML= specifier.

2. If a namelist specifier is present, a format specifier must not be present.

ADVANCE= scalar default character expression

NO   indicates   nonadvancing   formatted sequential data transfer

YES   indicates advancing formatted sequential data transfer

Rules:

1. The default value is YES.

2. Trailing blanks in the scalar default character expression are ignored. The value of the specifier is without regard to case (upper or lower); that is, the value no is the same as NO.

3. If an ADVANCE= specifier appears in the control information list, the data transfer must be a formatted sequential data

transfer statement connected to an external unit. List-directed or namelist input/output is not allowed and neither is data transfer to or from an internal unit.

4. If the EOR= or SIZE= specifier appears in the control information list, an ADVANCE= specifier must also appear with the value NO.

END= label

label   is the label of a branch target statement taken when an end-of-file condition occurs

Rules:

1. The END= specifier may appear only in a sequential access READ statement; note that the END= specifier must not appear in a WRITE statement.

2. If an IOSTAT= specifier is present, an end-of-file condition occurs, and no error condition occurs, the IOSTAT variable specified becomes defined with a processor-dependent negative value.

3. If the file is an external file, it is positioned after the end-of-file record.

4. If an end-of-file condition occurs and no error condition occurs during the execution of the READ statement, the program branches to the label in the END= specifier. The label must be a branch target in the same scoping unit as the READ statement.

EOR= label

label   is the label of a branch target statement taken when an end-of-record condition occurs

Rules:

1. The program branches to the labeled statement specified by the EOR= specifier if an end of record is encountered for a nonadvancing READ statement. The label must be a branch target in the same scoping unit as the statement containing the EOR= specifier.

2. The EOR= specifier may appear only in a READ statement with an ADVANCE= specifier with a value of NO, that is, a nonadvancing READ statement.

3. If an end-of-record condition occurs and no error condition occurs during the execution of the READ statement:

   a. The file is positioned after the current record.

   b. The variable given in the IOSTAT= specifier, if present, becomes defined with a processor-dependent negative value.

   c. If the connection has been made with the PAD= specifier of YES, the record is padded with blanks to satisfy the input item list and the corresponding data edit descriptor that requires more characters than are provided in the record.

   d. The variable given in the SIZE= specifier, if present, becomes defined with an integer value (9.2.2) equal to the number of characters read from the input record; however, blank padding characters inserted because the PAD= specifier is YES are not counted.

   e. Execution of the READ statement terminates, and the program branches to the label in the EOR= specifier.

ERR= label

   label   is the label of a branch target statement taken when an error condition occurs

Rules:

1. If an error condition occurs, the position of the file becomes indeterminate.

2. The program branches to the label in the ERR= specifier if an error occurs in a data transfer statement. The label must be a branch target in the same scoping unit as the data transfer statement.

3. If an IOSTAT= specifier is also present and an error condition occurs, the IOSTAT variable specified becomes defined with a processor-dependent positive value.

4. If the data transfer statement is a READ statement, contains a SIZE= specifier, and an error condition occurs, then the variable specified by the SIZE= specifier becomes defined with an integer value equal to the number of characters read from the input record; however, blank padding characters inserted because the PAD= specifier is YES are not counted.

IOSTAT= scalar default integer variable

positive integer	indicates an error condition occurred
negative integer	indicates an end-of-file or end-of-record condition occurred
0	indicates that no error, end-of-file, or end-of-record condition occurred

Rules:

1. The negative value indicating the end-of-file condition must not be the same as the negative value indicating the end-of-record condition.

2. The IOSTAT= specifier applies to the execution of the data transfer statement itself.

3. The variable specified in the IOSTAT= specifier must not be the same as or associated with any entity in the input/output item list or in the namelist group or with the variable specified in the SIZE= specifier, if present.

4. If the variable specified in the IOSTAT= specifier is an array element, its subscript values must not be affected by the data transfer, by any implied-do item or processing, or with the definition or evaluation of any other specifier in the control specifier list.

REC= scalar integer expression

integer	indicates the record number to be read or written

Rules:

1. The REC= specifier may appear only in a data transfer statement with a unit that is connected for direct access.

2. If the REC= specifier is present in a control information list, the data transfer is for a unit connected for direct access, and an END=, namelist, or format specifier with an asterisk (for

list-directed data transfer) must not be specified in the same control information list.

SIZE= scalar default integer variable

nonnegative integer   indicates the number of characters read before an end-of-record condition occurred

Rules:

1. The SIZE= specifier applies to the execution of the READ statement itself and can appear only in a READ statement with an ADVANCE= specifier with the value NO.

2. Blanks inserted as padding characters when the PAD= specifier is YES for the connection (see Section 9.5.5) are not counted.

3. The variable specified in the SIZE= specifier must not be the same as or associated with any entity in the input/output item list or in the namelist group or with the variable specified in the IOSTAT= specifier, if present.

4. If the variable specified in the SIZE= specifier is an array element, its subscript values must not be affected by the data transfer, by any implied-do item or processing, or with the definition or evaluation of any other specifier in the control specifier list.

9.2.2.1 The Input/Output Item List. The input/output item list consists basically of lists of variables in a READ statement and lists of expressions in a WRITE or PRINT statement. In addition, in any of these statements, the input/output item list may contain an input/output implied-do list, containing a list of variables or expressions indexed by the DO variables.

The forms of an input item (R914) are:

variable
io-implied-do

and the forms of an output item (R915) are:

expression
io-implied-do

where the form of an input/output implied-do (R916) is:

(io-implied-do-object-list , io-implied-do-control)

and the forms of an input/output implied-do object (R917) are:

input-item
output-item

and the form of an input/output DO control (R918) is:

do-variable = scalar-numeric-expression , &
    scalar-numeric-expression [, scalar-numeric-expression]

Rules and restrictions:

1. The DO variable must be a scalar integer or real variable. If it is real, it must be default real or double precision real; the use of real DO variables is considered obsolescent.

2. Each scalar numeric expression must be of type integer or real. If it is of type real, each must be of type default real or default double precision; the use of such real expressions is considered obsolescent. They need not be all of the same type nor of the type of the DO variable.

3. The DO variable must not be one of the input items in the implied-do; it must not be associated with an input item either.

4. Two nested implied-do must not have the same (or associated) DO variables.

5. An implied-do object, when it is part of an input item, must itself be an input item; that is, it must be a variable or an implied-do object whose objects are ultimately variables. Similarly, an implied-do object, when it is part of an output item, must itself be an output item; that is, it must be an expression or an implied-do object whose objects are ultimately expressions.

6. For an input/output implied-do, the loop is initialized, executed, and terminated in the same manner as for the DO construct (8.5.5). Its iteration count is established at the beginning of processing of the items that constitute the input/output implied-do.

7. An array appearing without subscripts in an input/output list is treated the same as if all elements of the array appeared in array-element order. For example, if UP is an array of shape (2,3),

        READ *, UP

    is the same as

```
READ *, UP(1,1), UP(2,1), UP(1,2),  &
        UP(2,2), UP(1,3), UP(2,3)
```

8. When a subscripted array is an input item, it is possible that when a value is transferred from the file to the variable, it might affect another part of the input item. This is not permitted. Consider the following READ statements, for example:

    ```
    INTEGER  A(100), V(10)

    ! Suppose V's elements are defined with values in the
    ! range 1 to 100.

    READ *, A(A)
    READ *, A(A(1):A(9))
    READ *, A(V)
    ```

    All three READ statements are invalid because the data values read affect other parts of the array A.

9. Assumed-size arrays may not appear in input/output lists, unless a subscript, a section subscript specifying an upper bound, or a vector subscript appears in the last dimension.

10. In formatted input/output, a structure is treated as if, in place of the structure, all components were listed in the order of the components in the derived-type definition. For example, if FIRECHIEF is a structure of type PERSON defined in Section 4.6,

    ```
    READ *, FIRECHIEF
    ```

    is the same as

    ```
    READ *, FIRECHIEF % AGE, FIRECHIEF % NAME
    ```

11. In unformatted input/output, a structure is treated as a single object and its components are arranged in some processor-dependent order; it is not necessarily processed as if all components appeared in the order given in the derived-type definition, even if it is of a sequence type.

12. All components of a structure in an input/output list must be accessible in that scoping unit.

13. A pointer may be an input/output list item but it must be associated with a target at the time the data transfer statement is executed. For an input item, the data in the file is transferred to the associated target. For an output item, the target associated with the pointer must be defined, and the value of the target is transferred to the file.

14. No structure with an ultimate component that is a pointer may appear in an input/output list.

15. An input or output list item must not be of nondefault character type if the data transfer statement specifies an internal file.

16. A constant or an expression with operators, parentheses, or function references may not appear as an input list item, but may appear as an output list item. A function reference in an output list must not cause execution of another input/output statement.

17. An input list item, or an entity associated with it, must not contain any portion of an established format specification.

18. On output, every entity whose value is to be written must be defined.

9.2.3 Explicitly Formatted Advancing Sequential Access Data Transfer

For formatted input and output, the file consists of characters. These characters are converted into representations suitable for storing in the computer memory during input and converted from an internal representation to characters on output. When a file is accessed sequentially, records are processed in the order in which they appear in the file.

Explicitly formatted advancing sequential access data transfer statements have the forms:

```
READ ( [ UNIT = ] io-unit  &
      , [ FMT = ] format  &
      [ , IOSTAT = scalar-default-integer-variable ]  &
      [ , ERR = label ]  &
      [ , END = label ]  &
      [ , ADVANCE = 'YES' ]  &
      ) [ input-item-list ]
```

```
READ format [ , input-item-list ]
```

```
WRITE ( [ UNIT = ] io-unit  &
      , [ FMT = ] format  &
      [ , IOSTAT = scalar-default-integer-variable ]  &
      [ , ERR = label ]  &
      [ , ADVANCE = 'YES' ]  &
      ) [ output-item-list ]
```

PRINT format [, output-item-list]

Rules and restrictions:

1. The input/output unit is either a scalar integer expression with a nonnegative value indicating a formatted sequential access external unit or an asterisk (*) indicating a formatted sequential access external unit.

2. The format must not be an asterisk (*).

3. When an advancing input/output statement is executed, reading or writing of data begins with the next character in the file. If a previous input/output statement was a nonadvancing statement, the next character transferred may be in the middle of a record, even if the statement being executed is an advancing statement. The essential difference between advancing and nonadvancing sequential data transfer is that an advancing input/output statement always leaves the file positioned at the end of the record.

4. During the data transfer, data are transferred with editing between the file and the entities specified by the input/output list. Format control is initiated and editing is performed as described in Chapter 10. The current record and possibly additional records are read or written.

5. For the data transfer, values may be transmitted to or from objects of intrinsic or derived types. In the latter case, the transmission is in the form of values of intrinsic types to or from the components of intrinsic types, which ultimately comprise these structured objects.

6. For input data transfer, the file must be positioned so that the record read is a formatted record or an end-of-file record.

7. For input data transfer, the input record is logically padded with blanks to satisfy an input list and format specification that requires more characters than the record contains, unless the PAD= specifier is specified as NO in the OPEN statement. If the PAD=

specifier is NO, the input list and format specification must not require more characters from the record than the record contains. The action of the processor at this point is processor dependent; it may report this erroneous condition by setting the variable of the IOSTAT= specifier, if it is present, or it may terminate execution of the program.

8. For output data transfer, the output list and format specification must not specify more characters for a record than the record size; recall that the record size for an external file is specified by a RECL= specifier in the OPEN statement.

9. If the file is connected for formatted input/output, unformatted data transfer is prohibited.

10. Execution of an advancing sequential access data transfer statement terminates when:

    a. format processing encounters a data or colon edit descriptor, and there are no remaining elements in the input item list or output item list

    b. on input, an end-of-file condition is encountered

    c. an error condition is encountered

Examples of formatted reading are:

```
! Assume that FMT_5 is a character string
! whose value is a valid format specification.
READ (5, 100, ERR = 99, END = 100)  &
              A, B, (C (I), I = 1, 40)
READ (9, IOSTAT = IEND, FMT = FMT_5) X, Y
READ (FMT = "(5E20.0)", UNIT = 5,  &
      ADVANCE = "YES") (Y (I), I = 1, KK)
READ 100, X, Y
```

Examples of formatted writing are:

```
! Assume FMT_103 is a character string with a valid
! format specification.

WRITE (9, FMT_103, IOSTAT = IS, ERR = 99)  A, B, C, S
WRITE (FMT = 105, ERR = 9, UNIT = 7)  X
WRITE (*, "(F10.5)")  X
PRINT "(A, E14.6)", " Y = ", Y
```

In free source form, blank characters are required in some contexts and are not allowed in others. A blank is not required to separate the name of the specifier and its value from the equal sign. For example, the following statement uses blanks in various places adjacent to the equal sign and is a correct WRITE statement:

```
WRITE (FMT=105, IOSTAT =IST,ERR= 9 , UNIT=7)
```

9.2.4 Unformatted Sequential Access

For unformatted sequential input and output, the file consists of values stored using a representation that is close to or the same as that used in program memory. This means that little or no conversion is required during input and output. Sequential access processes records in the order in which the records appear in the file.

Unformatted sequential access data transfer statements are the READ and WRITE statements with no format specifier or namelist group name specifier. The forms are:

```
READ ( [ UNIT = ] scalar-integer-expression  &
       [ , IOSTAT = scalar-default-integer-variable ]  &
       [ , ERR = label ]  &
       [ , END = label ]  &
     ) [ input-item-list ]
WRITE ( [ UNIT = ] scalar-integer-expression  &
       [ , IOSTAT = scalar-default-integer-variable ]  &
       [ , ERR = label ]  &
     ) [ output-item-list ]
```

Rules and restrictions:

1. Data are transferred without editing between the current record and the entities specified by the input/output list. Exactly one record is read or written.

2. Objects of intrinsic or derived types may be transferred through an unformatted data transfer statement.

3. For input data transfer, the file must be positioned so that the record read is an unformatted record or an end-of-file record.

4. For input data transfer, the number of values required by the input list must be less than or equal to the number of values in the record. Each value in the record must be of the same type as the corresponding entity in the input list, except that one complex value

may correspond to two real list entities or two real values may correspond to one complex list entity. The type parameters of the corresponding entities must be the same. Note that if an entity in the input list is of type character, the character entity must have the same length and the same kind type parameter as the character value. Also note that if two real values correspond to one complex entity or one complex value corresponds to two real entities, all three must have the same kind type parameter values.

5. On output, if the file is connected for unformatted sequential access data transfer, the record is created with a length sufficient to hold the values from the output list. This length must be one of the set of allowed record lengths for the file and must not exceed the value specified in the RECL= specifier, if any, of the OPEN statement that established the connection.

6. Execution of an unformatted sequential access data transfer statement terminates when:

    a.   the input item list or output item list is exhausted

    b.   on input, an end-of-file condition is encountered

    c.   an error condition is encountered

7. If the file is connected for unformatted input/output, formatted data transfer is prohibited.

Examples of unformatted sequential access reading are:

```
READ (5, ERR = 99, END = 100)  A, B, (C (I), I = 1, 40)
READ (IOSTAT = IEND, UNIT = 9) X, Y
READ (5) Y
```

Examples of unformatted sequential access writing are:

```
WRITE (9, IOSTAT = IS, ERR = 99) A, B, C, S
WRITE (ERR = 99, UNIT = 7) X
WRITE (9) X
```

If the access is sequential, the file is positioned at the beginning of the next record prior to data transfer and positioned at the end of the record when the input/output is finished, because nonadvancing unformatted input/output is not permitted.

9.2.5 Nonadvancing Formatted Sequential Data Transfer

Nonadvancing formatted sequential input/output provides the capability of reading or writing part of a record. It leaves the file positioned after the last character read or written, rather than skipping to the end of the record. Processing of nonadvancing input continues within a current record, until an end-of-record condition occurs. Nonadvancing input statements can read varying-length records and determine their lengths. Nonadvancing input/output is sometimes called **partial record** or **stream input/output**. It may be used only with explicitly formatted, external files connected for sequential access.

The forms of the nonadvancing input/output statements are:

```
READ ( [ UNIT = ] io-unit  &
     , [ FMT = ] format  &
     , ADVANCE = 'NO'  &
     [ , SIZE = scalar-default-integer-variable ]  &
     [ , EOR = label ]  &
     [ , IOSTAT = scalar-default-integer-variable ]  &
     [ , ERR = label ]  &
     [ , END = label ]  &
     ) [ input-item-list ]

WRITE ( [ UNIT = ] io-unit  &
      , [ FMT = ] format  &
      , ADVANCE = 'NO'  &
      [ , IOSTAT = scalar-default-integer-variable ]  &
      [ , ERR = label ]  &
      ) [ output-item-list ]
```

Rules and restrictions:

1. The input/output unit is either a scalar integer expression with a nonnegative value, indicating a formatted sequential access external unit, or an asterisk (*), indicating a formatted sequential access external unit.

2. The format must not be an asterisk (*).

3. During the data transfer, data are transferred with editing between the file and the entities specified by the input/output list. Format control is initiated and editing is performed as described in Chapter 10. The current record and possibly additional records are read or written.

4. For the data transfer, values may be transmitted to or from objects of intrinsic or derived types. In the latter case, the transmission is in the form of values of intrinsic types to or from the components of intrinsic types, which ultimately comprise these structured objects.

5. For input data transfer, the file must be positioned at the beginning of, end of, or within a formatted record or at the beginning of an end-of-file record.

6. For input data transfer, the input record is logically padded with blanks to satisfy an input list and format specification that requires more characters than the record contains, unless the PAD= specifier is specified as NO in the OPEN statement. If the PAD= specifier is NO, the input list and format specification must not require more characters from the record than the record contains, except in the presence of an ADVANCE= specifier with the value NO and either the EOR= or IOSTAT= specifier. In the exceptional cases during nonadvancing input, the actions and execution sequence are described in Section 9.4.

7. For output data transfer, the output list and format specification must not specify more characters for a record than the record size; recall that the record size for an external file is specified by a RECL= specifier in the OPEN statement.

8. The variable in the SIZE= specifier is assigned the number of characters read on input. Blanks inserted as padding characters when the PAD= specifier is YES are not counted.

9. The program branches to the label given by the EOR= specifier, if an end-of-record condition is encountered during input. The label must be the label of a branch target statement in the same scoping unit as the data transfer statement.

10. Execution of a nonadvancing formatted sequential access data transfer statement terminates when:

   a. format processing encounters a data or colon edit descriptor, and there are no remaining elements in the input item list or output item list

   b. on input, an end-of-file or end-of-record condition is encountered

   c. an error condition is encountered

11.   Unformatted data transfer is prohibited.

Examples: If N has the value 7, the statements

```
WRITE (*, '(A)', ADVANCE = "NO") "The answer is "
PRINT '(I1)', N
```

produce the single output record:

```
The answer is 7
```

If SSN is a rank-one array of size 9 with values (1, 2, 3, 0, 0, 9, 8, 8, 6), the following statements

```
DO I = 1, 3
  WRITE (*, '(I1)', ADVANCE = "NO") SSN(I)
ENDDO
WRITE (*, '("-")', ADVANCE = "NO")
DO I = 4, 5
  WRITE (*, '(I1)', ADVANCE = "NO") SSN(I)
ENDDO
WRITE (*, '(A1)', ADVANCE = "NO")   '-'
DO I = 6, 9
  WRITE (*, '(I1)', ADVANCE = "NO") SSN(I)
ENDDO
```

produce the record:

```
123-00-9886
```

9.2.6 Direct Access Data Transfer

In direct access data transfer, the records are selected by record number. The record number is a scalar integer expression whose value represents the record number to be read or written. The records may be written in any order, but all records must be of the length specified by the RECL= specifier in an OPEN statement.

If a file is connected using the direct access method, then nonadvancing, list-directed, and namelist input/output is prohibited. Also, an internal file must not be accessed using the direct access method.

It is not possible to delete a record using direct access. However, records may be rewritten so that a record can be erased by writing blanks into it.

9.2.6.1 Formatted Direct Access Data Transfer. For formatted input and output, the file consists of characters. These characters are converted into representations suitable for storing in computer memory during input and converted from an internal representation to characters on output. When a file is accessed directly, the record to be processed is given by reference to the record number.

Formatted direct access data transfer statements are READ and WRITE statements with a REC= specifier and a format specifier. The forms for formatted direct access data transfer statements are:

```
READ ( [ UNIT = ] scalar-integer-expression   &
     , [ FMT = ] format   &
     , REC = scalar-integer-expression   &
     [ , IOSTAT = scalar-default-integer-variable ]   &
     [ , ERR = label ]   &
     ) [ input-item-list ]
WRITE ( [ UNIT = ] scalar-integer-expression   &
      , [ FMT = ] format   &
      , REC = scalar-integer-expression   &
      [ , IOSTAT = scalar-default-integer-variable ]   &
      [ , ERR = label ]   &
      ) [ output-item-list ]
```

Rules and restrictions:

1. The format must not be an asterisk (*).

2. On input, an attempt to read a record of a file connected for direct access that has not previously been written causes all entities specified by the input list to become undefined.

3. During the data transfer, data are transferred with editing between the file and the entities specified by the input/output list. Format control is initiated and editing is performed as described in Chapter 10. The current record and possibly additional records are read or written.

4. For the data transfer, values may be transmitted to or from objects of intrinsic or derived types. In the latter case, the transmission is in the form of values of intrinsic types to or from the components of intrinsic types, which ultimately comprise these structured objects.

5. For input data transfer, the file must be positioned so that the record read is a formatted record or an end-of-file record.

6. For input data transfer, the input record is logically padded with blanks to satisfy an input list and format specification that requires more characters than the record contains, unless the PAD= specifier was specified as NO in the OPEN statement. If the PAD= specifier is NO, the input list and format specification must not require more characters from the record than the record contains. The action of the processor at this point is processor dependent; it may report this erroneous condition by setting the variable of the IOSTAT= specifier, if it is present, or it may terminate execution of the program.

7. For output data transfer, the output list and format specification must not specify more characters for a record than the record size; recall that the record size for an external file is specified by a RECL= specifier in the OPEN statement.

8. If the format specification specifies another record (say, by the use of the slash edit descriptor), the record number is increased by one as each succeeding record is read or written by that input/output statement.

9. For output data transfer, if the number of characters specified by the output list and format do not fill a record, blank characters are added to fill the record.

10. Execution of a formatted direct access data transfer statement terminates when:

    a. format processing encounters a data or colon edit descriptor, and there are no remaining elements in the input item list or output item list

    b. an error condition is encountered

11. If the file is connected for formatted input/output, unformatted data transfer is prohibited.

12. Note the above forms are intentionally structured so that the unit cannot be an internal file, and the END=, ADVANCE=, and namelist specifiers cannot appear.

Examples of formatted direct access input/output statements are:

```
READ (7, FMT_X, REC = 32, ERR = 99) A
READ (IOSTAT = IO_ERR, REC = 34, &
      FMT = 185, UNIT = 10, ERR = 99)  A, B, D
WRITE (8, "(2F15.5)", REC = N + 2) X, Y
```

9.2.6.2 Unformatted Direct Access Data Transfer. For unformatted input and output, the file consists of values stored using a representation that is close to or the same as that used in program memory. This means that little or no conversion is required during input and output. When a file is accessed directly, the record to be processed is given by reference to the record number.

Unformatted direct access data transfer statements are READ and WRITE statements with a REC= specifier and no format specifier. The forms for unformatted direct access data transfer statements are:

```
READ ( [ UNIT = ] scalar-integer-expression   &
     , REC = scalar-integer-expression   &
     [ , IOSTAT = scalar-default-integer-variable ]   &
     [ , ERR = label ]   &
     ) [ input-item-list ]
WRITE ( [ UNIT = ] scalar-integer-expression   &
     , REC = scalar-integer-expression   &
     [ , IOSTAT = scalar-default-integer-variable ]   &
     [ , ERR = label ]   &
     ) [ output-item-list ]
```

Rules and restrictions:

1. On input, an attempt to read a record of a file connected for direct access that has not previously been written causes all entities specified by the input list to become undefined.

2. The number of items in the input list must be less than or equal to the number of values in the input record.

3. Data are transferred without editing between the current record and the entities specified by the input/output list. Exactly one record is read or written.

4. Objects of intrinsic or derived types may be transferred.

5. For input data transfer, the file must be positioned so that the record read is an unformatted record or an end-of-file record.

6. For input data transfer, the number of values required by the input list must be less than or equal to the number of values in the record. Each value in the record must be of the same type as the corresponding entity in the input list, except that one complex value may correspond to two real list entities or two real values may correspond to one complex list entity. The type parameters of the corresponding entities must be the same. Note that if an entity in the input list is of type character, the character entity must have the

same length and the same kind type parameter as the character value. Also note that if two real values correspond to one complex entity or one complex value corresponds to two real entities, all three must have the same kind type parameter values.

7. The output list must not specify more values than can fit into the record. If the file is connected for direct access and the values specified by the output list do not fill the record, the remainder of the record is undefined.

8. Execution of an unformatted direct access data transfer statement terminates when:

    a. the input item list or output item list is exhausted

    b. an error condition is encountered

9. If the file is connected for unformatted direct access input/output, formatted data transfer is prohibited.

10. Note the above forms are intentionally structured so that the unit cannot be an internal file, and the FMT =, END =, ADVANCE =, and namelist specifiers cannot appear.

Examples of unformatted direct access input/output statements are:

```
READ (7, REC = 32, ERR = 99) A
READ (IOSTAT = MIS, REC = 34, UNIT = 10, ERR = 99) A, B, D
WRITE (8, REC = N + 2) X, Y
```

9.2.7 List-Directed Data Transfer

List-directed formatting may occur only with files connected for sequential access; however, the file may be an internal file. The input/output data transfer must be advancing. The records read and written are formatted.

List-directed data transfer statements are any data transfer statement, for which the format specifier is an asterisk (*). The forms of the list-directed data transfer statements are:

```
READ ( [ UNIT = ] io-unit  &
     , [ FMT = ] *  &
     [ , IOSTAT = scalar-default-integer-variable ]  &
     [ , END = label ]  &
     [ , ERR = label ]  &
     ) [ input-item-list ]

READ * [ , input-item-list ]
```

```
WRITE ( [ UNIT = ] io-unit  &
      , [ FMT = ] *  &
      [ , IOSTAT = scalar-default-integer-variable ]  &
      [ , ERR = label ]  &
      ) [ output-item-list ]

PRINT * [ , output-item-list ]
```

Rules and restrictions:

1. During the data transfer, data are transferred with editing between the file and the entities specified by the input/output list. The rules for formatting the data transferred are discussed in Section 10.10. The current record and possibly additional records are read or written.

2. For the data transfer, values may be transmitted to or from objects of intrinsic or derived types. In the latter case, the transmission is in the form of values of intrinsic types to or from the components of intrinsic types, which ultimately comprise these structured objects.

3. For input data transfer, the file must be positioned so that the record read is a formatted record or an end-of-file record.

4. For output data transfer, the output list and list-directed formatting must not specify more characters for a record than the record size; recall that the record size for an external file is specified by a RECL= specifier in the OPEN statement.

5. If the file is connected for list-directed data transfer, unformatted data transfer is prohibited.

6. Execution of a list-directed data transfer statement terminates when:

    a. the input item list or the output item list is exhausted

    b. on input, an end-of-file is encountered, or a slash (/) is encountered as a value separator

    c. an error condition is encountered

7. Note the above forms are intentionally structured so that the ADVANCE= and namelist specifiers cannot appear.

Examples of list-directed input and output statements are:

```
READ (5, *, ERR = 99, END = 100)  &
               A, B, (C (I), I = 1, 40)
READ (FMT = *, UNIT = 5) (Y (I), I = 1, KK)
READ *, X, Y
WRITE (*, *) X
PRINT *, " Y = ", Y
```

9.2.8 Namelist Data Transfer

Namelist input/output uses a group name for a list of variables that are transferred. Before the group name can be used in the transfer, the list of variables must be declared in a NAMELIST statement, a specification statement. Using the namelist group name eliminates the need to specify the list of variables in the sequence for a namelist data transfer. Namelist input/output is convenient for initializing the same variables with different values in successive runs. It is also convenient for changing the values of a few variables among a large list of variables that are given default initial values. The formatting of the input or output record is not specified in the program; it is determined by the contents of the record itself or the items in the namelist group. Conversion to and from characters is implicit for each variable in the list.

9.2.8.1 Form of a Namelist Group Declaration. All namelist input/output data transfer statements use a namelist group name, which must be declared. As described in Section 5.9, the form of a namelist group name declaration (R543) is:

```
NAMELIST / namelist-group-name / &
       variable-name [ , variable-name ] ... &
    [ [ , ] / namelist-group-name / &
       variable-name [ , variable-name ] ...
```

Examples are:

```
NAMELIST / GOAL / G, K, R
NAMELIST / XLIST / A, B / YLIST / Y, YY, YU
```

9.2.8.2 Forms of Namelist Input and Output Statements. Namelist input and output data transfer statements are READ and WRITE statements with a namelist specifier. The forms for namelist data transfer statements are:

```
READ ( [ UNIT = ] io-unit  &
        , [ NML = ] namelist-group-name  &
        [ , IOSTAT = scalar-default-integer-variable ]  &
        [ , END = label ]  &
        [ , ERR = label ]
      )
WRITE ( [ UNIT = ] io-unit  &
         , [ NML = ] namelist-group-name  &
         [ , IOSTAT = scalar-default-integer-variable ]  &
         [ , ERR = label ]  &
       )
```

Rules and restrictions:

1. The input/output unit is either a scalar integer expression with a nonnegative value indicating a formatted sequential access external unit or an asterisk (*) indicating a formatted sequential access external unit.

2. During namelist data transfer, data are transferred with editing between the file and the entities specified by the namelist group name. Format control is initiated and editing is performed as described in Section 10.11. The current record and possibly additional records are read or written.

3. For the data transfer, values may be transmitted to or from objects of intrinsic or derived types. In the latter case, the transmission is in the form of values of intrinsic types to or from the components of intrinsic types, which ultimately comprise these structured objects.

4. For namelist input data transfer, the file must be positioned so that the record read is a formatted record or an end-of-file record.

5. For namelist output data transfer, the output list and namelist formatting must not specify more characters for a record than the record size; recall that the record size for an external file is specified by a RECL= specifier in the OPEN statement.

6. If an entity appears more than once within the input record for a namelist input data transfer, the last value is the one that is used.

7. For namelist input data transfer, all values following a *name=* part within the input record are transmitted before processing any subsequent entity within the namelist input record.

8. Execution of a namelist data transfer statement terminates when:

a.   on input, an end-of-file is encountered, or a slash (/) is encountered as a value separator

b.   on input, the end of the namelist input record is reached and a name-value subsequence has been processed for every item in the namelist group object list

c.   on output, the namelist group object list is exhausted

d.   an error condition is encountered

9.   If the file is connected for namelist data transfer, unformatted data transfer is prohibited.

10.   Note the above forms are intentionally structured so that the unit cannot be an internal file. Also, the REC=, FMT=, and ADVANCE= specifiers cannot appear, and there must be no input or output item list.

Examples of namelist data transfer statements are:

```
READ (NML = NAME_LIST_23, IOSTAT = KN,   UNIT = 5)
WRITE (6, NAME_LIST_23, ERR = 99)
```

9.2.9 Data Transfer on Internal Files

Transferring data from machine representation to characters or from characters back to machine representation can be done between two variables in an executing program. A formatted sequential access input or output statement, including list-directed formatting, is used. The format is used to interpret the characters. The internal file and the internal unit are the same character variable.

With this feature, it is possible to read in a string of characters without knowing its exact format, examine the string, and then interpret it according to its contents.

Formatted sequential access data transfer statements on an internal file have the forms:

```
READ ( [ UNIT = ] default-character-variable   &
      , [ FMT = ] format   &
      [ , IOSTAT = scalar-default-integer-variable ]   &
      [ , ERR = label ]   &
      [ , END = label ]   &
      ) [ input-item-list ]
WRITE ( [ UNIT = ] default-character-variable   &
      , [ FMT = ] format   &
      [ , IOSTAT = scalar-default-integer-variable ]   &
```

```
            [ , ERR = label ]   &
          ) [ output-item-list ]
```

Examples of data transfer on internal files are:

```
READ (CHAR_124, 100, IOSTAT = ERR)   MARY, X, J, NAME
WRITE (FMT = *, UNIT = CHAR_VAR) X
```

Rules and restrictions:

1. The unit must be a default character variable that is not an array section with a vector subscript.

2. Each record of an internal file is a scalar character variable of default character kind.

3. If the character variable is an array or an array section, each element of the array or section is a scalar character variable and thus a record. The order of the records is array element order. The length, which must be the same for each record, is the length of one array element.

4. If the character variable is an array or part (component, element, section, or substring) of an array that has the allocatable attribute, the variable must be allocated before its use as an internal file. It must be defined if it is used as an internal file in a READ statement.

5. If the character variable is a pointer, it must be associated with a target. The target must be defined if it is used as an internal file in a READ statement.

6. During data transfer, data are transferred with editing between the file and the entities specified by the input/output list. Format control is initiated and editing is performed as described in Chapter 10. The current record and possibly additional records are read or written.

7. For the data transfer, values may be transmitted to or from objects of intrinsic or derived types. In the latter case, the transmission is in the form of values of intrinsic types to or from the components of intrinsic types, which ultimately comprise these structured objects.

8. For output data transfer, the output list and format specification must not specify more characters for a record than the record size; recall that the record size for an internal file is the length of the character variable representing the internal file. The format

specification must not be part of the internal file or associated with the internal file or part of it.

9. If the number of characters written is less than the length of the record, the remaining characters are set to blank.

10. The records in an internal file are defined when the record is written. An input/output list item must not be in the internal file or associated with the internal file. An internal file also may be defined by a character assignment statement, or some other means, or may be used in expressions in other statements. For example, an array element may be given a value with a WRITE statement and then used in an expression on the right-hand side of an assignment statement.

11. In order to read a record in an internal file, the scalar character object must be defined.

12. Before a data transfer occurs, an internal file is positioned at the beginning of the first record (that is, before the first character, if a scalar, and before the first character of the first element, if an array). This record becomes the current record.

13. Only formatted sequential access, including list-directed formatting, is permitted on internal files. Namelist formatting is prohibited.

14. On input, an end-of-file condition occurs when there is an attempt to read beyond the last record of the internal file.

15. During input processing, all nonleading blanks in numeric fields are treated as if they were removed, right justifying all characters in the field (as if a BN edit descriptor were in effect [10.8.6]). In addition, records are blank padded when an end of record is encountered before all of the input items are read (as if PAD=YES were in effect [9.5.5]).

16. For list-directed output, character values are not delimited (10.10.2).

17. File connection, positioning, and inquiry must not be used with internal files.

18. Execution of a data transfer statement on an internal file terminates when:

    a. format processing encounters a data or colon edit descriptor, and there are no remaining elements in the input item list or output item list

b.   if list-directed processing is specified, the input item list or the output item list is exhausted; or on input, a slash (/) is encountered as a value separator

c.   on input, an end-of-file condition is encountered

d.   an error condition is encountered

9.2.10 Printing of Formatted Records

Sometimes output records are sent to a device that interprets the first character of the record as a control character. This is usually the case with line printers. If a formatted record is transferred to such a device, the first character of the record is not printed, but instead is used to control vertical spacing. The remaining characters of the record, if any, are printed on one line beginning at the left margin. This transfer of information is called **printing**.

The first character of such a record must be of default character type and determines vertical spacing as specified in Table 9-1.

Table 9-1 Interpretation of the first character for printing control

Character	Vertical spacing before printing
Blank	One line (single spacing)
0	Two lines (double spacing)
1	To first line of next page (begin new page)
+	No advance (no spacing—print on top of previous line)

If there are no characters in the record, a blank line is printed. If the first character is not a blank, 0, 1, or +, the interpretation is processor dependent; usually the character is treated as a blank.

The PRINT statement does not imply that printing will occur actually on a printer, and the WRITE statement does not imply that printing will not occur. Whether printing occurs depends on the device connected to the unit number.

9.3 Execution Model for Data Transfer Statements

When a data transfer statement is executed, these steps are followed in the order given:

1.   Determine the direction of data transfer. A READ statement indicates that data is to be transferred from a file to program variables.

A WRITE or PRINT statement indicates that data is to be transferred from program variables to a file.

2. Identify the unit. The unit identified by a data transfer input/output statement must be connected to a file when execution of the statement begins. Note that the file may be preconnected.

3. Establish the format, if one is specified. If specified, the format specifier is given in the data transfer statement and implies list-directed, namelist, or formatted data transfer.

4. Position the file prior to transferring the data. The position depends on the method of access (sequential or direct) and is described in Section 9.3.2.

5. Transfer data between the file and the entities specified by the input/output item list (if any). The list items are processed in the order of the input/output list for all data transfer input/output statements, except namelist input data transfer statements which are processed in the order of the entities specified within the input records. For namelist output data transfer, the output items are specified by the namelist when a namelist group name is used.

6. Determine if an error, end-of-record, or end-of-file condition exists. If one of these conditions occurs, the status of the file and the input/output items is specified in Section 9.4.

7. Position the file after transferring the data (9.3.3). The file position depends on whether one of the conditions in step 6 above occurred or if the data transfer was advancing or nonadvancing.

8. Cause the variables specified in the IOSTAT= and SIZE= specifiers, if present, to become defined. See the description of these specifiers in the READ and WRITE data transfer statements in Section 9.2.2.

9. If ERR=, END=, or EOR= specifiers appear in the statement, transfer to the branch target corresponding to the condition that occurs. If an IOSTAT= specifier appears in the statement and the label specifier corresponding to the condition that occurs does not appear in the statement, the next statement in the execution sequence is executed. Otherwise, the execution of the program terminates. See the descriptions of these label specifiers in Section 9.2.2.

9.3.1 Data Transfer

Data are transferred between records in the file and entities in the input/output list or namelist. The list items are processed in the order of the input/output list for all data transfer input/output statements except namelist data transfer statements. The list items for a namelist formatted data transfer input statement are processed in the order of the entities specified within the input records. The list items for a namelist data transfer output statement are processed in the order in which the data objects (variables) are specified in the namelist group object list.

The next item to be processed in the input or output item list is the **next effective item**, which is used to determine the interaction between the input/output item list and the format specification (see Section 10.3).

Zero-sized arrays and implied-do lists with zero iteration counts are ignored in determining the next effective item.

Before beginning the input/output processing of a particular list item, all values needed to determine which entities are specified by the list item are evaluated first. For example, the subscripts of a variable in an input/output list are evaluated before any data is transferred.

The value of an item that appears early in an input/output list may affect the processing of an item that appears later in the list. In the example,

```
READ (N) N, X (N)
```

the old value of N identifies the unit, but the new value of N is the subscript of X.

9.3.2 File Position Prior to Data Transfer

The file position prior to data transfer depends on the method of access: sequential or direct.

For sequential access on input, if there is a current record, the file position is not changed; this will be the case if the previous data transfer was nonadvancing. Otherwise, the file is positioned at the beginning of the next record and this record becomes the current record. Input must not occur if there is no next record (there must be an end-of-file record at least) or if there is a current record and the last data transfer statement accessing the file performed output.

If the file contains an end-of-file record, the file must not be positioned after the end-of-file record prior to data transfer. However, a REWIND or BACKSPACE statement may be used to reposition the file.

For sequential access on output, if there is a current record, the file position is not changed; this will be the case if the previous data transfer was nonadvancing. Otherwise, a new record is created as the next record of the file; this new record becomes the last and current record of the file and the file is positioned at the beginning of this record.

For direct access, the file is positioned at the beginning of the record specified. This record becomes the current record.

9.3.3 File Position After Data Transfer

If an error condition exists, the file position is indeterminate. If no error condition exists, but an end-of-file condition exists as a result of reading an end-of-file record, the file is positioned after the end-of-file record.

If no error condition or end-of-file condition exists, but an end-of-record condition exists, the file is positioned after the record just read. If no error condition, end-of-file condition, or end-of-record condition exists, and the data transfer was a nonadvancing input or output statement, the file position is not changed. In all other cases, the file is positioned after the record just read or written, and that record becomes the preceding record.

9.4 Error and Other Conditions in Input/Output Statements

In step 6 of the execution model in Section 9.3, the data transfer statements admit the occurrence of error and other conditions during the execution of the statement. The same is true for the OPEN, CLOSE, INQUIRE, and file positioning statements.

The set of error conditions is processor dependent. Whenever an error condition is detected, the variable of the IOSTAT= specifier is assigned a positive value, if it is present. Also, if the ERR= specifier is present, the program transfers to the branch target specified by the ERR= specifier upon completion of the input/output statement. Note, then, that the set of conditions that set the variable of the IOSTAT= specifier or cause a transfer to the branch target specified by the ERR= specifier is processor dependent.

In addition, two other conditions described below must be detected by the processor: end-of-file and end-of-record. For each of these conditions, error branches may be provided using the END= and EOR= specifiers in a READ statement to which the program branches upon completion of the READ statement. Also, the variable of the IOSTAT= specifier, if present, is set to a unique negative integer value, indicating which condition occurred.

An **end-of-file** condition occurs when either an end-of-file record is encountered during a sequential READ statement, or an attempt is made to read beyond the end of an internal file. An end-of-file condition may occur at the beginning of the execution of an input statement or during the execution of a formatted READ statement when more than one record is required by the interaction of the format specification and the input item list.

An **end-of-record** condition occurs when a nonadvancing input statement (9.2.5) attempts to transfer data from beyond the end of the record.

Two or more conditions may occur during a single execution of an input/output statement. If one or more of the conditions is an error condition, one of the error conditions takes precedence, in the sense that the IOSTAT= specifier is given a positive value designating the particular error condition and the action taken by the input/output statement is as if only that error condition occurred. If no error condition occurs, but both an end-of-file and end-of-record condition occur, the end-of-file condition takes precedence in the same sense as above.

In summary, an error condition may be generated by any of the input/output statements, and an end-of-file or end-of-record condition may be generated by a READ statement. The IOSTAT=, END=, EOR=, and ERR= specifiers allow the program to recover from such conditions rather than terminate execution of the program. In particular, when any one of these conditions occurs, the following actions are taken:

1. If an end-of-record condition occurs and if the connection has been made with the PAD= specifier of YES, the record is padded, as necessary, with blanks to satisfy the input item list and the corresponding data edit descriptor.

2. Execution of the input/output statement terminates.

3. If an error condition occurs, the position of the file becomes indeterminate; if an end-of-file condition occurs, the file is positioned after the end-of-file record; if an end-of-record condition occurs, the file is positioned after the current record.

4. If the statement also contains an IOSTAT= specifier, the variable specified becomes defined with a processor-dependent nonzero integer value; the value is positive if an error condition occurs and is negative if either an end-of-file or end-of-record condition occurs.

5. If an error or end-of-record condition occurs, the statement is a READ statement, and contains a SIZE= specifier, then the variable specified by the SIZE= specifier becomes defined with an integer value equal to the number of characters read from the input record;

blank padding characters inserted because the PAD= specifier is YES are not counted.

6. Any implied-do variables in the input/output statement become undefined; if an error or end-of-file condition occurs during execution of a READ statement, all list items become undefined; if an error condition occurs during the execution of an INQUIRE statement, all specifier variables except the IOSTAT= variable become undefined.

7. If an END= specifier is present and an end-of-file condition occurs, execution continues with the statement specified by the label in the END= specifier; if an EOR= specifier is present and an end-of-record condition occurs, execution continues with the statement specified by the label in the EOR= specifier; if an ERR= specifier is present and an error condition occurs, execution continues with the statement specified by the label in the ERR= specifier; if none of the above cases applies, but the input/output statement contains an IOSTAT= specifier, the normal execution sequence is resumed; if there is no IOSTAT=, END=, EOR=, or ERR= specifier, the program terminates execution.

The following program segment illustrates how to handle end-of-file and error conditions.

```
READ (FMT = "(E8.3)", UNIT=3, IOSTAT = IOSS) X

IF (IOSS < 0) THEN

    ! PERFORM END-OF-FILE PROCESSING ON THE
    ! FILE CONNECTED TO UNIT 3.
    CALL END_PROCESSING

ELSE IF (IOSS > 0) THEN

    ! PERFORM ERROR PROCESSING
    CALL ERROR_PROCESSING

END IF
```

The procedure END_PROCESSING is used to handle the case where an end-of-file condition occurs and the procedure ERROR_PROCESSING is used to handle all other error conditions, because an end-of-record condition cannot occur.

9.5 The OPEN Statement

The OPEN statement establishes a connection between a unit and an external file and determines the connection properties. In order to perform data transfers (reading and writing), the file must be connected with an OPEN statement or preconnected by the processor. It may also be used to change certain properties of the connection between the file and the unit, to create a file that is preconnected, or create a file and connect it.

The OPEN statement may appear anywhere in a program, and once executed, the connection of the unit to the file is valid in the main program or any subprogram for the remainder of that execution, unless a CLOSE statement affecting the connection is executed.

If a file is already connected to one unit, it must not be connected to a different unit.

9.5.1 Connecting a File to a Unit

In what is probably the most common situation, the OPEN statement connects an external file to a unit. If the file does not exist, it is created. If a unit is already connected to a file that exists, an OPEN statement referring to that unit may be executed. If the FILE= specifier is not included, the unit remains connected to the file. If the FILE= specifier names the same file, the OPEN statement may change the connection properties as described in Section 9.5.3. If it specifies a different file by name, the effect is as if a CLOSE statement without a STATUS= specifier is executed on that unit and the OPEN statement is then executed. (The default value of the STATUS= specifier is KEEP, unless the prior status of the file was SCRATCH, in which case the default value is DELETE.)

9.5.2 Creating a File on a Preconnected Unit

If a unit is preconnected to a file that does not exist, the OPEN statement creates the file and establishes properties of the connection.

9.5.3 Changing the Connection Properties

Execution of an OPEN statement may change the properties of a connection that is already established. The properties that may be changed are those indicated by BLANK=, DELIM=, PAD=, ERR=, and IOSTAT= specifiers. If new values for DELIM=, PAD=, and BLANK= specifiers are specified, these will be used in subsequent data transfer statements; otherwise, the old ones will be used. However, the values in ERR= and IOSTAT= specifiers, if present, apply only to the

OPEN statement being executed; after that, the values of these specifiers have no effect. If no ERR= or IOSTAT= specifier appears in the new OPEN statement, error conditions will terminate the execution of the program.

9.5.4 Form of the OPEN Statement

The form of the OPEN statement (R904) is:

    OPEN (connection-spec-list)

where the forms of a connection specifier (R905) are:

    [UNIT =] scalar-integer-expression
    ACCESS = scalar-default-character-expression
    ACTION = scalar-default-character-expression
    BLANK = scalar-default-character-expression
    DELIM = scalar-default-character-expression
    ERR = label
    FILE = file-name-expression
    FORM = scalar-default-character-expression
    IOSTAT = scalar-default-integer-variable
    PAD = scalar-default-character-expression
    POSITION = scalar-default-character-expression
    RECL = scalar-integer-expression
    STATUS = scalar-default-character-expression

Rules and restrictions:

1. A unit specifier is required. If the keyword UNIT is omitted, the scalar integer expression must be the first item in the list.

2. A specifier must not appear more than once in an OPEN statement.

3. The character expression established for many of the specifiers must contain one of the permitted values from the list of alternative values for each specifier described in Section 9.5.5. For example, OLD, NEW, REPLACE, UNKNOWN, or SCRATCH are permitted for the STATUS= specifier; any other combination of letters is not permitted. Trailing blanks in any specifier are ignored. If a processor is capable of representing both uppercase and lowercase letters, the value specified is without regard to case.

4. Note that the form * for the unit specifier is not permitted in the OPEN statement. However, in cases where the default external unit specified by an asterisk also corresponds to a nonnegative unit specifier (such as unit numbers 5 and 6 on many systems), inquiries about these default units and connection properties are possible.

Examples are:

```
OPEN (STATUS = "SCRATCH", UNIT = 9)
OPEN (8, FILE = "PLOT_DATA", ERR = 99, ACCESS = "DIRECT")
```

9.5.5 The Connection Specifiers

The OPEN statement specifies the connection properties between the file and the unit, using keyword specifiers, which are described in this section. Table 9-2 indicates the possible values for the specifiers in an OPEN statement and their default values when the specifier is omitted.

Table 9-2 Values for keyword specifier variables in an OPEN statement

Specifier	Possible values	Default value
ACCESS=	DIRECT, SEQUENTIAL	SEQUENTIAL
ACTION=	READ, WRITE, READWRITE	Processor dependent
BLANK=	NULL, ZERO	NULL
DELIM=	APOSTROPHE, QUOTE, NONE	NONE
ERR=	Label	No default
FILE=	Character expression	Processor determined
FORM=	FORMATTED	FORMATTED for sequential access
	UNFORMATTED	UNFORMATTED for direct access
IOSTAT=	Scalar default integer variable	No default
PAD=	YES, NO	YES
POSITION=	ASIS, REWIND, APPEND	ASIS
RECL=	Positive scalar integer expression	Processor dependent
STATUS=	OLD, NEW, UNKNOWN, REPLACE, SEARCH	UNKNOWN
UNIT=	Scalar integer expression	No default

[UNIT=] scalar integer expression

Rules:

1. The value of the scalar integer expression must be nonnegative.

2. A unit specifier with an external file unit is required. If the keyword UNIT is omitted, the unit specifier must be the first item in the list.

3. A unit number identifies one and only one external unit in all program units in a Fortran program.

ACCESS = scalar default character expression

DIRECT	specifies the direct access method for data transfer
SEQUENTIAL	specifies the sequential access method for data transfer

Rules:

1. The default value is SEQUENTIAL.

2. If the file exists, the method specified must be an allowed access method for the file.

3. If the file is new, the allowed access methods given for the file must include the one indicated.

ACTION = scalar default character expression

READ	indicates that WRITE and ENDFILE statements are prohibited
WRITE	indicates that READ statements are prohibited
READWRITE	indicates that any input/output statement is permitted

Rules:

1. The default value is processor dependent.

2. If READWRITE is an allowed ACTION= specifier, READ and WRITE must also be allowed ACTION= specifiers.

3. For an existing file, the specified action must be an allowed action for the file.

4. For a new file, the value of the ACTION= specifier must be one of the allowed actions for the file.

BLANK = scalar default character expression

NULL	ignore all blanks in numeric fields
ZERO	interpret all blanks except leading blanks as zeros

Rules:

1. The default value is NULL.

2. A field of all blanks evaluates to zero in both cases.

3. The BLANK= specifier may be specified for files connected only for formatted input/output.

DELIM= scalar default character variable

APOSTROPHE	use the apostrophe as the delimiting character for character constants written by a list-directed or namelist formatted data transfer statement
QUOTE	use the quotation mark as the delimiting character for character constants written by a list-directed or namelist-formatted data transfer statement
NONE	use no delimiter to delimit character constants written by a list-directed or namelist-formatted data transfer statement

Rules:

1. The default value is NONE.

2. If the DELIM= specifier is APOSTROPHE, any occurrence of an apostrophe within a character constant will be doubled; if the DELIM= specifier is QUOTE, any occurrence of a quote within a character constant will be doubled.

3. The specifier is permitted only for a file connected for formatted input/output; it is ignored for formatted input.

ERR= label

label	is the label of a branch target statement taken when an error condition occurs

Rules:

1. If an error condition occurs, the position of the file becomes indeterminate.

2. If an IOSTAT= specifier is present and an error condition occurs, the IOSTAT variable specified becomes defined with a processor-dependent positive value.

3. The program branches to the label in the ERR= specifier if an error occurs in the OPEN statement. The label must be a branch target in the same scoping unit as the OPEN statement.

FILE= scalar default character expression

expression   indicates the name of the file to be connected. It is called the **file name expression**

Rules:

1. If the name is omitted, the connection can be made to a processor-determined file.

2. Trailing blanks in the name are ignored.

3. The name must be a file name allowed by the processor.

4. If the processor allows uppercase and lowercase letters in file names, the interpretation of the case of the letters is processor dependent; for example, the processor may distinguish file names by case or it may interpret the name all in uppercase or lowercase letters.

5. The FILE= specifier must appear if the STATUS= specifier is OLD, NEW, or REPLACE; the FILE= specifier must not appear if the STATUS= specifier is SCRATCH.

6. If the FILE= specifier is omitted and the unit is not already connected to a file, the STATUS= specifier (see below) must have the value SCRATCH; in case the unit is not already connected, the unit becomes connected to a processor-dependent file.

FORM= scalar default character expression

FORMATTED   indicates that all records are formatted

UNFORMATTED   indicates that all records are unformatted

Rules:

1. The default value is UNFORMATTED, if the file is connected for direct access and the FORM= specifier is absent.

2. The default value is FORMATTED, if the file is connected for sequential access and the FORM= specifier is absent.

3. If the file is new, the allowed forms given for the file must include the one indicated.

4. If the file exists, the form specified by the FORM= specifier must be one of the allowed forms for the file.

IOSTAT= scalar default integer variable

positive integer	indicates an error condition occurred
0	indicates that no error condition occurred

Rules:

1. The IOSTAT= specifier applies to the execution of the OPEN statement itself. Note that the value cannot be negative.

PAD= scalar default character expression

YES	use blank padding when the input item list and format specification require more data than the record contains
NO	requires that the input record contains the data indicated by the input list and format specification

Rules:

1. The default value is YES.

2. The specifier is permitted only for a file connected for formatted input/output; it is ignored for formatted output.

3. The blank padding character used for nondefault character types is processor dependent.

4. If this specifier has the value YES and an end-of-record condition occurs, the data transfer behaves as if the record were padded with sufficient blanks to satisfy the input item and the corresponding data edit descriptor.

POSITION= scalar default character expression

ASIS	indicates the file position is to remain unchanged for a connected file and is unspecified for a file that is not connected
REWIND	indicates the file is to be positioned at its initial point

APPEND   indicates the file is to be positioned at
                            the terminal point or just before an
                            end-of-file record, if there is one

Rules:

1. The default value is ASIS, permitting an OPEN statement to
    change other connection properties of a file that is already
    connected without changing its position.

2. The file must be connected for sequential access.

3. If the file is new, it is positioned at its initial point, regardless
    of the value of the POSITION= specifier.

RECL= scalar integer expression

positive value   specifies the length of each record if the
                           access method is direct, or the maximum
                           length of a record if the access method is
                           sequential

Rules:

1. The default value is processor dependent, if the RECL= speci-
    fier is absent for a file connected for sequential access.

2. The RECL= specifier must be present for a file connected for
    direct access.

3. If the file is connected for formatted input/output, the length
    is the number of characters.

4. If the file is connected for unformatted input/output, the
    length is measured in processor-dependent units. In this case,
    the length may be the number of computer words, for exam-
    ple.

5. If the file exists, the length of the record specified must be an
    allowed record length.

6. If the file does not exist, the file is created with the specified
    length as an allowed length.

STATUS= scalar default character expression

OLD   requires that the file exist

NEW   requires that the file not exist

UNKNOWN   indicates that the file has a processor-
                           dependent status

REPLACE   requires that, if the file does not exist, the file is created and given a status of OLD; if the file does exist, the file is deleted, a new file is created with the same name, and the file is given a status of OLD

SCRATCH   indicates that an unnamed file is to be created and connected to the specified unit; it is to exist either until the program terminates or a CLOSE statement is executed on that unit.

Rules:

1. The default value is UNKNOWN.

2. Scratch files must be unnamed; that is, the STATUS= specifier must not be SCRATCH when a FILE= specifier is present. The term **scratch file** refers to this temporary file.

3. Note that, if the STATUS= specifier is REPLACE, the specifier in this statement is not changed to OLD; only the file status is considered to be OLD when the file is used in subsequently executed input/output statements, such as a CLOSE statement.

9.6 The CLOSE Statement

Execution of a CLOSE statement terminates the connection of a file to a unit. Any connections not closed explicitly by a CLOSE statement are closed by the operating system when the program terminates, unless an error condition has terminated the program. The form of the CLOSE statement (R907) is:

CLOSE (close-spec-list)

where the forms of a close specifier (R908) are:

[UNIT =] scalar-integer-expression
IOSTAT = scalar-default-integer-variable
ERR = label
STATUS = scalar-default-character-expression

Rules and restrictions:

1. A unit specifier is required. If the keyword UNIT is omitted, the scalar integer expression must be the first item in the list.

2.   A specifier must not appear more than once in a CLOSE statement.

3.   A CLOSE statement may appear in any program unit in an executing program.

4.   A CLOSE statement may refer to a unit that is not connected or does not exist, but it has no effect.

5.   When an executing program terminates, all files are closed, unless the program has been terminated by an error condition.

6.   After a unit has been disconnected by a CLOSE statement, it may be connected again to the same or a different file. Similarly, after a file has been disconnected by a CLOSE statement, it may also be connected to the same or a different unit, provided the file still exists.

Examples are:

```
CLOSE (ERR = 99, UNIT = 9)
CLOSE (8, IOSTAT = IR, STATUS = "KEEP")
```

9.6.1 The CLOSE Specifiers

This section describes the form and effect of the specifiers that may appear in a CLOSE statement.

[UNIT =] scalar integer expression

Rules:

1.   The value of the scalar integer expression must be nonnegative.

2.   A unit specifier is required. If the keyword UNIT is omitted, a scalar integer expression unit must be the first item in the list.

3.   A unit number identifies one and only one external unit in all program units in a Fortran program.

ERR= label

label   is the label of a branch target statement taken when an error condition occurs

Rules:

1.   If an error condition occurs, the position of the file becomes indeterminate.

2. If an IOSTAT= specifier is present and an error condition occurs, the IOSTAT variable specified becomes defined with a processor-dependent positive value.

3. The program branches to the label in the ERR= specifier if an error occurs in the CLOSE statement. The label must be a branch target in the same scoping unit as the CLOSE state-ment.

IOSTAT= scalar default integer variable

positive integer	indicates an error condition occurred
0	indicates that no error condition occurred

Rules:

1. The IOSTAT= specifier applies to the execution of the CLOSE statement itself. Note that the value cannot be nega-tive.

STATUS= scalar default character expression

KEEP	indicates that the file is to continue to exist after closing the file
DELETE	indicates that the file will not exist after closing the file

Rules:

1. The default value is DELETE, if the unit has been opened with a STATUS= specifier of SCRATCH.

2. The default value is KEEP, if the unit has been opened with any other value of the STATUS= specifier.

3. KEEP must not be specified for a file whose file status is SCRATCH.

4. If KEEP is specified for a file that does not exist, the file does not exist after the CLOSE statement is executed.

9.7 Inquiring about Files

An inquiry may be made about a file's existence, connection, access method, or other properties. For each property inquired about, a scalar variable of default kind is supplied; that variable is given a value that answers the inquiry. The variable may be tested and optional execution paths may be selected based on the answer returned. The inquiry specifiers are determined by keywords in the INQUIRE statement. The only exception is the unit specifier, which, if no keyword is specified, must be the first specifier. A file inquiry may be made by unit number, file name, or an output item list. When inquiring by an output item list, an output item list that might be used in an unformatted direct access output statement must be present.

9.7.1 The INQUIRE Statement

There are three kinds of INQUIRE statements (R923): inquiry by unit, by name, and by an output item list. The first two kinds use the first form of the INQUIRE statement below, whereas the third kind uses the second form below. Inquiry by unit uses a unit specifier, whereas inquiry by file uses a file specifier with the keyword FILE=. The form of an inquiry by unit or file is:

```
INQUIRE ( inquiry-spec-list )
```

The form of an inquiry by an output item list is:

```
INQUIRE ( IOLENGTH = scalar-default-integer-variable )   &
         output-item-list
```

where the forms of an inquiry specifier (R924) are:

```
[ UNIT = ] scalar-integer-expression
ACCESS = scalar-default-character-variable
ACTION = scalar-default-character-variable
BLANK = scalar-default-character-variable
DELIM = scalar-default-character-variable
DIRECT = scalar-default-character-variable
ERR = label
EXIST = scalar-default-logical-variable
FILE = scalar-default-character-expression
FORM = scalar-default-character-variable
FORMATTED = scalar-default-character-variable
IOSTAT = scalar-default-integer-variable
NAME = scalar-default-character-variable
NAMED = scalar-default-logical-variable
NEXTREC = scalar-default-integer-variable
NUMBER = scalar-default-integer-variable
OPENED = scalar-default-logical-variable
PAD = scalar-default-character-variable
POSITION = scalar-default-character-variable
READ = scalar-default-character-variable
```

    READWRITE = scalar-default-character-variable
    RECL = scalar-default-integer-variable
    SEQUENTIAL = scalar-default-character-variable
    UNFORMATTED = scalar-default-character-variable
    WRITE = scalar-default-character-variable

Rules and restrictions:

1. An INQUIRE statement with an inquiry specifier list must have a unit specifier or a FILE= specifier, but not both. If the keyword UNIT is omitted, a scalar integer expression must be the first item in the list and must have a nonnegative value.

2. No specifier may appear more than once in a given inquiry specifier list.

3. For an inquiry by an output item list, the output item list must be a valid output list. The length value returned in the scalar default integer variable must be a value that is acceptable when used as the value of the RECL= specifier in an OPEN statement. This value may be used in a RECL= specifier to connect a file whose records will hold the data indicated by the output list of the INQUIRE statement.

4. The value taken by a variable given in an inquiry specifier is the value that would be obtained if the specified value were assigned to the variable using an intrinsic assignment statement.

5. An INQUIRE statement may be executed before or after a file is connected to a unit. The specifier values returned by the INQUIRE statement are those current at the time at which the INQUIRE statement is executed.

6. A variable appearing in a keyword specifier or any entity associated with it must not appear in another specifier in the same INQUIRE statement if that variable can become defined or undefined as a result of executing the INQUIRE statement. That is, do not try to assign two inquiry results to the same variable!

7. Except for the NAME= specifier, the processor must return character values in uppercase, even if it can process both uppercase and lowercase. For the NAME= specifier, the allowed characters used in the value returned are processor determined. For the same reason, the allowed characters for the value for the FILE= specifier are processor dependent.

8. If an error condition occurs during the execution of an INQUIRE statement, all the inquiry specifier variables become undefined except the IOSTAT= specifier.

Examples of the INQUIRE statement are:

```
INQUIRE (9, EXIST = EX)
INQUIRE (FILE = "T123", OPENED = OP, ACCESS = AC)
INQUIRE (IOLENGTH = IOLEN)  X, Y, CAT
```

9.7.2 Specifiers for Inquiry by Unit or File Name

This section describes the form and effect of the inquiry specifiers that may appear in the inquiry by unit and file forms of the INQUIRE statement.

[UNIT=] scalar integer expression

    expression   indicates an external unit (R902)

    Rules:

1. The value of the scalar integer expression must be nonnegative.

2. A unit specifier is required. If the keyword UNIT is omitted, a scalar integer expression must be the first item in the list.

3. A unit number identifies one and only one external unit in all program units in a Fortran program.

4. The file is the file connected to the unit, if one is connected; otherwise, the file does not exist.

ACCESS= scalar default character variable

SEQUENTIAL	indicates the file is connected for sequential access
DIRECT	indicates the file is connected for direct access
UNDEFINED	indicates the file is not connected

ACTION= scalar default character variable

READ	indicates the file is connected with access limited to input only
WRITE	indicates the file is connected with access limited to output only
READWRITE	indicates the file is connected for both input and output
UNDEFINED	indicates the file is not connected

BLANK= scalar default character variable

NULL	indicates null blank control is in effect
ZERO	indicates zero blank control is in effect
UNDEFINED	indicates the file is not connected for formatted input/output or the file is not connected at all

Rules:

1. See the BLANK= specifier for the OPEN statement in Section 9.5.5 for the meaning of null and zero blank control.

DELIM= scalar default character variable

APOSTROPHE	indicates an apostrophe is used as the delimiter in list-directed and namelist-formatted output
QUOTE	indicates the quotation mark is used as the delimiter in list-directed and namelist-formatted output
NONE	indicates there is no delimiting character in list-directed and namelist-formatted output
UNDEFINED	indicates the file is not connected or the file is not connected for formatted input/output

DIRECT= scalar default character variable

YES	indicates direct access is an allowed access method
NO	indicates direct access is not an allowed access method
UNKNOWN	indicates the processor does not know if direct access is allowed

ERR= label

label	is the label of a branch target statement taken when an error condition occurs

Rules:

1.   If an error condition occurs, the position of the file becomes indeterminate.

2.   If an IOSTAT= specifier is present and an error condition occurs, the IOSTAT variable specified becomes defined with a processor-dependent positive value. All other inquiry specifier variables become undefined.

3.   The program branches to the label in the ERR= specifier if there is an error in the execution of the INQUIRE statement itself. The label must be a branch target in the same scoping unit as the INQUIRE statement.

EXIST= scalar default logical variable

true	indicates the file or unit exists
false	indicates the file or unit does not exist

FILE= scalar default character expression

expression	indicates the name of the file

Rules:

1.   The value of the scalar default character expression must be a file name acceptable to the processor. Trailing blanks are ignored. If the processor can represent both uppercase and lowercase letters, the interpretation is processor dependent.

2.   The file name may refer to a file not connected or to one that does not exist.

FORM= scalar default character variable

FORMATTED	indicates the file is connected for formatted input/output
UNFORMATTED	indicates the file is connected for unformatted input/output
UNDEFINED	indicates the file is not connected

FORMATTED= scalar default character variable

YES	indicates formatted input/output is an allowed form for the file
NO	indicates formatted input/output is not an allowed form for the file

UNKNOWN
indicates the processor cannot determine if formatted input/output is an allowed form for the file

IOSTAT= scalar default integer variable

positive integer
indicates an error condition occurred

0
indicates no error condition occurred

Rules:

1. The IOSTAT= specifier applies to the execution of the INQUIRE statement itself. Note that the value cannot be negative.

NAME= scalar default character variable

file name
indicates the name of the file connected to the unit, if the file has a name

undefined value
indicates the file does not have a name or no file is connected to the unit

Rules:

1. The processor may return a name different from the one specified in the FILE= specifier by the program, because a user identifier or some other processor requirement for file names may be added.

2. Whatever the name returned, it must be acceptable for use as a FILE= specifier in an OPEN statement.

3. The interpretation of the case (upper or lower) of letters used and allowed in a file name is determined by the processor.

NAMED= scalar default logical variable

true
indicates the file has a name

false
indicates the file does not have a name

NEXTREC= scalar default integer variable

last record number + 1
indicates the next record number to be read or written in a file connected for direct access. The value is one more than the last record number read or written.

1	indicates no records have been processed
undefined value	indicates the file is not connected for direct access or the file position is indeterminate because of a previous error condition

Rules:

1.   This inquiry is used for files connected for direct access.

NUMBER= scalar default integer variable

unit number	indicates the number of the unit connected to the file
–1	indicates there is no unit connected to the file

OPENED= scalar default logical variable

true	indicates the file or unit is connected (that is, opened)
false	indicates the file or unit is not connected (that is, not opened)

PAD= scalar default character variable

NO	indicates the file or unit is connected with the PAD= specifier set to NO
YES	indicates the file or unit is connected with the PAD= specifier other than NO, or the file or unit is not connected

POSITION= scalar default character variable

REWIND	indicates the file is connected with its position at the initial point
APPEND	indicates the file is connected with its position at the terminal point
ASIS	indicates the file is connected without changing its position
UNDEFINED	indicates the file is not connected or is connected for direct access

Rules:

1. If any repositioning has occurred since the file was connected, the value returned is processor dependent, but it is not equal to REWIND unless positioned at the initial point, and it is not equal to APPEND unless positioned at the terminal point.

READ= scalar default character variable

YES	indicates READ is one of the allowed actions for the file
NO	indicates READ is not one of the allowed actions for the file
UNKNOWN	indicates the processor is unable to determine whether READ is one of the allowed actions for the file

READWRITE= scalar default character variable

YES	indicates READWRITE is an allowed action for the file
NO	indicates READWRITE is not an allowed action for the file
UNKNOWN	indicates the processor is unable to determine whether READWRITE is an allowed action for the file

RECL= scalar default integer variable

maximum record length	indicates an integer value which is the maximum record length of the file
undefined value	indicates the file does not exist

Rules:

1. For a formatted file that contains only default characters, the length is the number of characters for all records.

2. For a formatted file containing nondefault characters or for an unformatted file, the length is in processor-dependent units.

SEQUENTIAL= scalar default character variable

YES	indicates sequential access is an allowed access method

NO   indicates sequential access is not an allowed access method

UNKNOWN   indicates the processor does not know whether sequential access is allowed

UNFORMATTED = scalar default character variable

YES   indicates unformatted input/output is an allowed form for the file

NO   indicates unformatted input/output is not an allowed form for the file

UNKNOWN   indicates the processor cannot determine whether unformatted input/output is an allowed form for the file

WRITE = scalar default character variable

YES   indicates WRITE is an allowed action for the file

NO   indicates WRITE is not an allowed action for the file

UNKNOWN   indicates the processor is unable to determine whether WRITE is an allowed action for the file

9.7.3 Table of Values Assigned by the INQUIRE Statement

Table 9-3 summarizes the values assigned to the various variables by the execution of an INQUIRE statement.

9.8 File Positioning Statements

Execution of a data transfer statement usually changes the file position. In addition, there are three statements whose main purpose is to change the file position. Changing the position backwards by one record is called **backspacing** and is performed by the BACKSPACE statement. Changing the position to the beginning of the file is called **rewinding** and is performed by the REWIND statement. The ENDFILE statement writes an end-of-file record and positions the file after the end-of-file record.

The forms of the BACKSPACE statement (R919) are:

BACKSPACE scalar-integer-expression
BACKSPACE (position-spec-list)

Table 9-3 Values for keyword specifier variables in an INQUIRE statement

	INQUIRE by file		INQUIRE by unit	
Specifier	Unconnected	Connected	Connected	Unconnected
ACCESS=	UNDEFINED	SEQUENTIAL or DIRECT		UNDEFINED
ACTION=	UNDEFINED	READ, WRITE, or READWRITE		UNDEFINED
BLANK=	UNDEFINED	NULL, ZERO, or UNDEFINED		UNDEFINED
DELIM=	UNDEFINED	APOSTROPHE, QUOTE, NONE, or UNDEFINED		UNDEFINED
DIRECT=	UNKNOWN	YES, NO, or UNKNOWN		UNKNOWN
EXIST=	.TRUE. if file exists, .FALSE. otherwise		.TRUE. if unit exists, .FALSE. otherwise	
FORM=	UNDEFINED	FORMATTED or UNFORMATTED		UNDEFINED
FORMATTED=	UNKNOWN	YES, NO, or UNKNOWN		UNKNOWN
IOSTAT=	0 for no error, a positive integer for an error			
NAME=	Filename (may not be same as FILE= value)	Filename if named, else undefined		Undefined
NAMED=	.TRUE.		.TRUE. if file named, .FALSE. otherwise	.FALSE.
NEXTREC=	Undefined	If direct access, next record #; else undefined		Undefined
NUMBER=	-1	Unit number		-1
OPENED=	.FALSE.	.TRUE.		.FALSE.
PAD=	YES	YES or NO		YES
POSITION=	UNDEFINED	REWIND, APPEND, ASIS, or UNDEFINED		UNDEFINED
READ=	UNKNOWN	YES, NO, or UNKNOWN		UNKNOWN
READWRITE=	UNKNOWN	YES, NO, or UNKNOWN		UNKNOWN
RECL=	Undefined	If direct access, record length; else maximum record length		Undefined
SEQUENTIAL=	UNKNOWN	YES, NO, or UNKNOWN		UNKNOWN
UNFORMATTED=	UNKNOWN	YES, NO, or UNKNOWN		UNKNOWN
WRITE=	UNKNOWN	YES, NO, or UNKNOWN		UNKNOWN
IOLENGTH=	RECL= value for output-item-list			

The forms of the REWIND statement (R920) are:

REWIND scalar-integer-expression
REWIND (position-spec-list)

The forms of the ENDFILE statement (R921) are:

ENDFILE scalar-integer-expression
ENDFILE (position-spec-list)

The forms of a position specifier (R922) are (none may be repeated in a position specifier list):

[**UNIT** =] scalar-integer-expression
ERR = label
IOSTAT = scalar-default-integer-variable

Rules and restrictions:

1. The scalar integer expression in the first form of each file positioning statement is a unit specifier and must have a nonnegative value. A unit specifier in the second form of each file positioning statement is required, and its scalar integer expression must have a nonnegative value. Thus, the BACKSPACE, REWIND, and ENDFILE statements are used only to position external files.

2. The files must be connected for sequential access.

Example file positioning statements are:

```
BACKSPACE 9
BACKSPACE (UNIT = 10)
BACKSPACE (ERR = 99, UNIT = 8, IOSTAT = STATUS)
REWIND (ERR = 102, UNIT = 10)
ENDFILE (10, IOSTAT = IERR)
ENDFILE (11)
```

9.8.1 Specifiers for File Position Statements

This section describes the form and effect of the position specifiers that may appear in the file positioning statements.

[UNIT=] scalar integer expression

expression   indicates an external unit (R902)

Rules:

1. The value of the scalar integer expression must be nonnegative.

2. A unit specifier is required.

3. There must be a file connected to the unit, and the unit must be connected for sequential access.

4. If the keyword UNIT is omitted, the scalar integer expression must be the first item in the position specifier list.

5. A unit number identifies one and only one external unit in all program units in a Fortran program.

ERR= label

label   is the label of a branch target statement taken when an error condition occurs

Rules:

1. If an error condition occurs, the position of the file becomes indeterminate.

2. If an IOSTAT= specifier is present and an error condition occurs, the IOSTAT variable specified becomes defined with a processor-dependent positive value.

3. The program branches to the label in the ERR= specifier if there is an error in the execution of the particular file positioning statement itself. The label must be a branch target label in the same scoping unit as the file positioning statement.

IOSTAT= scalar default integer variable

positive integer   indicates an error condition occurred

0   indicates no error condition occurred

Rules:

1. The IOSTAT= specifier applies to the execution of the file positioning statement itself. Note that the value cannot be negative.

9.8.2 The BACKSPACE Statement

Execution of a BACKSPACE statement causes the file to be positioned before the current record if there is a current record, or before the preceding record if there is no current record. If there is no current record and no preceding record, the file position is not changed. If the preceding record is an end-of-file record, the file becomes positioned before the end-of-file record. If a BACKSPACE statement causes the implicit writing of an end-of-file record and if there is a preceding record, the file becomes positioned before the record that precedes the end-of-file record.

If the file is already at its initial point, a BACKSPACE statement has no effect. If the file is connected, but does not exist, backspacing is prohibited. Backspacing over records written using list-directed or namelist formatting is prohibited.

Examples of BACKSPACE statements are:

```
BACKSPACE  ERROR_UNIT      ! ERROR_UNIT is an
                          !    integer variable.
BACKSPACE (10, &          ! STAT is an integer variable
          IOSTAT = STAT)  !    of default type.
```

9.8.3 The REWIND Statement

A REWIND statement positions the file at its initial point. Rewinding has no effect on the file position when the file is already positioned at its initial point. If a file does not exist, but it is connected, rewinding the file is permitted, but has no effect. Examples of REWIND statements are:

```
REWIND  INPUT_UNIT      ! INPUT_UNIT is an integer variable.
REWIND (10, ERR = 200)  ! 200 is a label of branch target
                        !    in this scoping unit.
```

9.8.4 The ENDFILE Statement

The ENDFILE writes an end-of-file record as the next record and positions the file after the end-of-file record written. Writing records past the end-of-file record is prohibited. After executing an ENDFILE statement, it is necessary to execute a BACKSPACE or REWIND statement to position the file ahead of the end-of-file record before reading or writing the file. If the file is connected but does not exist, writing an end-of-file record creates the file. Examples of ENDFILE statements are:

```
ENDFILE  OUTPUT_UNIT    ! OUTPUT_UNIT is an integer variable.
ENDFILE (10, &          ! 200 is a label of a branch target
         ERR = 200, &   !    in this scoping unit.  ST is a
         IOSTAT = ST)   !    default scalar integer variable.
```

A file may be connected for sequential and direct access, but not for both simultaneously. If a file is connected for sequential access and an ENDFILE statement is executed on the file, only those records written before the ENDFILE statement is executed are considered to have been written. Consequently, when the file is subsequently connected for direct access, only those records before the end-of-file record may be read.

9.9 Restrictions on Input/Output Specifiers, List Items, and Statements

Any function reference appearing in a keyword specifier value or in an input/output list must not cause the execution of another input/output statement. Note that such function references also must not have side effects that change any object in the same statement (7.4.1). For example:

```
WRITE (10, FMT = "(10I5)", REC = FCN(I) )  X(FCN(J)), I, J
```

The function FCN must not contain an input/output statement and must not change its argument, because I and J are also output list items.

A unit or file may not have all of the properties (for example, all access methods or all forms) required for it by execution of certain input/output statements. If this is the case, such input/output statements must not refer to files or units limited in this way. For example, if unit 5 cannot support unformatted sequential files, the following OPEN statement must not appear in a program:

```
OPEN (UNIT = 5, IOSTAT = IERR,  &
      ACCESS = "SEQUENTIAL", FORM = "UNFORMATTED")
```

9.10 Summary

Fortran Files

A Fortran file consists of records. Files may be internal or external.

Record

Data records are sequences of data values. End-of-file records are processor determined.

Formatted and Unformatted Data

Records of formatted data may not be mixed with unformatted data. Formatted data is converted to characters according to the editing in a format statement, or by namelist or list-directed editing. Unformatted data is not converted.

File Positioning

The file position determines the data record to be processed. The file may be at the initial point, the terminal point, between data records, within a record, or be undetermined.

Backspacing

The BACKSPACE statement positions the file ahead of the previous record.

```
BACKSPACE 9
```

Rewinding

The REWIND statement positions the file at the initial point.

```
REWIND (10, ERR = 99)
```

Ending a File

The ENDFILE statement writes an end-of-file record and the file is positioned after the end-of-file record. Reading or writing beyond an end-of-file record is prohibited.

```
ENDFILE 8
```

Unit

A unit number is a nonnegative integer that identifies a file. The valid unit numbers are processor dependent. On any system, the files that exist for connection to a unit are processor determined.

```
REWIND (UNIT = 9)
```

A unit may also be a character variable in the program. In this case, an internal file is being specified, and the internal file is the character variable.

```
CHARACTER (100) INTERNAL_FILE
READ (UNIT = INTERNAL_FILE, FMT = '(2I5)') I, J
```

File Connection

File connection, preconnection, and disconnection apply to external files and a unit number. Internal files are always connected.

Opening Files

The OPEN statement connects a file to a unit and determines file connection characteristics.

```
OPEN (UNIT = 10, IOSTAT = IERR,  &
      ACCESS = "DIRECT", RECL = 100)
```

Closing Files

The CLOSE statement disconnects a file from a unit.

```
CLOSE (10, ERR = 99, STATUS = "KEEP")
```

Unformatted Sequential Access Input/Output

Data is transferred without any format conversion. The transfer proceeds sequentially from the current file position to the next data record.

```
READ (9, IOSTAT = IER) X, Y
WRITE (10) A
```

Formatted Sequential Access Input/Output

Data is transferred with format conversion. The transfer proceeds sequentially from the current file position to the next data record.

```
READ (9, 100, IOSTAT = IER) X, Y
WRITE (10, 101) A
```

Namelist Input/Output

Variables are established in a list with a group name. Conversion takes place implicitly without a format specification. The data transfer uses the group name rather than the list of variables.

```
NAMELIST / GROUP_NAME / A, B, C
   . . .
READ (9, NML = GROUP_NAME, ERR = 99)
   . . .
WRITE (19, NML = GROUP_NAME)
```

List-Directed Input/Output

Data is converted without a format specification. The data consists of sequences of values edited implicitly. Sequential access is required. An asterisk as the format specification indicates list-directed data transfer.

```
READ (9, *, ERR = 99) X
WRITE (UNIT = 8, FMT = *, IOSTAT = IERR) Y
```

Nonadvancing Input/Output

Nonadvancing reading and writing is character oriented. Positioning is after the last character read or written. Nonadvancing data transfer is indicated by an ADVANCE= specifier with the value NO.

```
READ (9, 100, ADVANCE = "NO", &
      SIZE = NCOUNT, EOR = 200) CHAR
WRITE (FMT = 12, ADVANCE = "NO", UNIT = 8, IOSTAT = K)   NAME
```

Data Transfer on Internal Files

The transfer is memory to memory using a format specification for conversion to or from characters. Only formatted sequential access is allowed. The unit is a character variable.

```
READ (CHAR, FMT = 103) X, Y, KK
WRITE (UNIT = CH, FMT = 104, ERR = 99)   A, I, J
```

Unformatted Direct Access Input/Output

Access is by record number. The records in the file are all unformatted. Direct access data transfer is indicated by a REC= specifier in the data transfer statement.

```
READ (9, IOSTAT = IERR, REC = 64) X, Y
WRITE (UNIT = 8, ERR = 99, REC = 30) Z
```

Formatted Direct Access Input/Output

Access is by record number. The records in the file are all formatted.

```
READ (9, 100, IOSTAT = IERR, REC = 64) X, Y
WRITE (UNIT = 8, FMT = 105, ERR = 99, REC = 30) Z
```

F9 🌀

10

Input and Output Editing

Data usually are stored in memory as the values of variables in some binary form. For example, the integer 6 may be stored as 0000000000000110, where the 0s and 1s represent binary digits. On the other hand, formatted data records in a file consist of characters. Thus, when data is read from a formatted record, it must be converted from characters to the internal representation. When data is written to a formatted record, it must be converted from the internal representation into a string of characters.

A **format specification** provides the information necessary to determine how these conversions are to be performed. The format specification is basically a list of **edit descriptors**, of which there are three general types: data edit descriptors, control edit descriptors, and string edit descriptors. There is a data edit descriptor for each data value in the input/output list of the data transfer statement. Control edit descriptors specify the spacing and position within a record, new records, interpretation of blanks, and plus sign suppression. String edit descriptors transfer strings of characters represented in format specifications to output records.

The format reference that indicates where to find the format may be a statement label that identifies a FORMAT statement, or it may be a character expression giving the format directly. Using either method is called **explicit formatting**.

There are two other cases where formatting of a different sort applies. These are list-directed and namelist formatting. Formatting (that is, conversion) occurs without specifically providing the editing information usually contained in a format specification. In these cases, the editing or formatting is implicit; that is, the details about the width of fields, forms of output values, and location of output fields within the records is determined by the processor.

This chapter describes the two methods of specifying explicit formatting, namely, using a FORMAT statement and using a character expression representing a format specification. It then lists and subsequently describes in detail the three kinds of edit descriptors that determine the conversion, location, and transfer of data values to and from input and output records. An algorithm is given that describes the correspondence of the data edit descriptors and items in the data item list of the data transfer statement. Next, the two methods of implicit formatting—list-directed and namelist formatting—are described. Finally, the chapter concludes with a brief summary of the formatting methods available in Fortran 90.

Tables 10-1, 10-2, and 10-3 list all of the edit descriptors—control, data, and string edit descriptors—and provide a brief description of each.

Table 10-1 Summary of control edit descriptors

Descriptor	Description
BN	Ignore nonleading blanks in numeric input fields
BZ	Treat nonleading blanks in numeric input fields as zeros
S	Printing of optional plus sign is processor dependent
SP	Print optional plus sign
SS	Do not print optional plus sign
T	Tab to specified position
TL	Tab left the specified number of positions
TR	Tab right the specified number of positions
X	Tab right the specified number of positions
/	End current record and move to beginning of next record
:	Stop format processing when no further input/output list items
P	Interpret certain real numbers with a specified scale factor

Table 10-2 Summary of data edit descriptors

Descriptor	Description
A	Convert data of type character
B	Convert data of type integer to/from a binary base
D	Convert data of type real—same as E edit descriptor
E	Convert data of type real with an exponent
EN	Convert data of type real to engineering notation
ES	Convert data of type real to scientific notation
F	Convert data of type real with no exponent on output
G	Convert data of all intrinsic types
I	Convert data of type integer
L	Convert data of type logical
O	Convert data of type integer to/from an octal base
Z	Convert data of type integer to/from a hexadecimal base

Table 10-3 Summary of string edit descriptors

Descriptor	Description
H	Transfer of text to output record
'text'	Transfer of a character literal constant to output record
"text"	Transfer of a character literal constant to output record

10.1 Explicit Formatting

As indicated above, explicit formatting information may be:

1. contained in a FORMAT statement

```
        WRITE (6, 100) LIGHT, AND, HEAVY
    100 FORMAT (F10.2, I5, E16.8)
```

2. given as the value of a character expression

```
    WRITE (6, '(F10.2, I5, E16.8)' ) LIGHT, AND, HEAVY
```

10.1.1 The FORMAT Statement

The form of the FORMAT statement (R1001) is:

    FORMAT ([format-item-list])

A **format specification** (R1002) consists of the parentheses and the format item list (10.2).

The FORMAT statement must be labeled. The label is used in the input/output statement to reference a particular FORMAT statement.

There may be many FORMAT statements in a program—as many as one for each input/output statement; or, FORMAT statements may be used repeatedly in different input/output statements.

10.1.2 Character Expression Format Specifications

A character expression may be used in the input/output statement as a format specification. The leading part of the character expression must be a valid format specification including the parentheses; that is, the value of the expression must be such that the first nonblank character is a left parenthesis, followed by a list of valid format items, followed by a right parenthesis.

Rules and restrictions:

1. All variables in the character expression must be defined when the input/output statement is executed.

2. Characters may appear following the last right parenthesis in the character expression; they have no effect.

3. If the expression is a character array, the format is scanned in array element order. For example, the following format specification is valid (where A is a character array of length at least 6 and size at least 2):

```
A (1) = '(1X,I3,'
A (2) = ' I7, I9)'
PRINT  A, MUTT, AND, JEFF
```

4. If the expression is an array element, the format must be entirely contained within that element.

5. If the expression is a character variable, it or any part of it must not be redefined or become undefined during the execution of the input/output statement.

6. If the expression is a character constant delimited by apostrophes, two apostrophes must be written to represent each apostrophe in the format specification. If a format specification contains, in turn, a character constant delimited by apostrophes, there must be two apostrophes for each of the apostrophe delimiters, and each apostrophe within the character constant must be represented by four apostrophes (see the example below). If quotes are used for the string delimiters and quotes are used within the string, a similar doubling of the quote marks is required. One way to avoid problems is to use delimiters different from the characters within the

format specification, if possible. The best way to avoid the problem is to put the character expression in the input/output list instead of the format specification as shown in the second line of the following example.

```
PRINT '(''I can''''t hear you'')'
PRINT "(A16)", "I can't hear you"
```

where A16 is a character edit descriptor specifying a field width of 16 positions.

The last example can be written without a field width (character count) as in:

```
PRINT "(A)", "I can't hear you"
```

When a character expression is used as a format specification, the processor is not required to detect at compile-time any syntax or constraint violations in the format specification. The reason for relaxing the requirements for detection of such errors is that the format specification may not be complete or known until the data transfer statement is executed and therefore cannot be checked for validity until execution time. The same relaxation on the requirements for error detection also applies to the use of deleted, obsolescent, and extended features used in format specifications.

10.2 Format Specifications

Each item in the format item list of a format specification is an **edit descriptor**, which may be a data edit descriptor, control edit descriptor, or character string edit descriptor. Each data list item must have a corresponding data edit descriptor; other descriptors specify spacing, tabulation, scale factors for real data, and printing of optional signs.

Blanks may be used freely in format specifications without affecting the interpretation of the edit descriptors, both in the free and fixed source forms. Named constants are not allowed in format specifications because they would create ambiguities in the interpretation of the format specifications. For example, if N12 were a named integer constant with value 15, the engineering format edit descriptor E N12.4 could be interpreted as the edit descriptor EN12.4 or E15.4.

The forms of a format item (R1003) are:

[r] data-edit-descriptor
control-edit-descriptor

character-string-edit-descriptor
[r] (format-item-list)

where r is a default integer literal constant and is called a **repeat factor.**
If a repeat factor is optional and is not present, it is as if it were present
with the value of 1.

Rules and restrictions:

1.   r must not have a kind value specified for it.

2.   The comma between edit descriptors may be omitted in the follow-
     ing cases:

     a.   between the scale factor (P) and the numeric edit descriptors
          F, E, EN, ES, D, or G

     b.   before a new record indicated by a slash when there is no
          repeat factor present

     c.   after the slash for a new record

     d.   before or after the colon edit descriptor

3.   Blanks may be used as follows:

     a.   before the first left parenthesis

     b.   anywhere in the format specification except within a character
          string; the blanks have no effect on the formatting. It is rec-
          ommended that blanks be used to enhance the readability of
          the format specification

4.   r must be a positive integer.

5.   Edit descriptors may be nested within parentheses and may be pre-
     ceded by a repeat factor indicating that the edit descriptor is
     repeated; a parenthesized list of edit descriptors may also be pre-
     ceded by a repeat factor, indicating that the entire list is to be
     repeated.

     The following examples illustrate many of the edit descriptors that
are described in detail in the next sections.

```
100 FORMAT (2(5E10.1, I10) / (1X, SP, I7, ES15.2))
110 FORMAT (I10, F14.1, EN10.2)
120 FORMAT (TR4, L4, 15X, A20)
130 FORMAT (9HMORE SNOW)
140 FORMAT (9X, 3A5, 7/ 10X, 3L4)
```

10.2.1 Data Edit Descriptor Form

Data edit descriptors specify the conversion of values to and from the internal representation to the character representation in the formatted record of a file. The forms of the data edit descriptors (R1005) are:

```
I w [ . m ]
B w [ . m ]
O w [ . m ]
Z w [ . m ]
F w . d
E w . d [ E e ]
EN w . d [ E e ]
ES w . d [ E e ]
G w . d [ E e ]
L w
A [ w ]
D w . d
```

where w, m, d, and e are default integer literal constants, and

        w   is the width of the field
        m   is the least number of digits in the field
        d   is the number of decimal digits in the field
        e   is the number of digits in the exponent

Rules and restrictions:

1.   w, m, d, and e must not have a kind value specified for them.

2.   w and e must be positive.

3.   The values of m, d, and e must not exceed the value of w.

4.   The I, B, O, Z, F, E, EN, ES, G, L, A, and D edit descriptors indicate the manner of editing.

The detailed meanings of the data edit descriptors are described in Sections 10.5 through 10.7.

10.2.2 Control Edit Descriptor Form

Control edit descriptors determine the position, form, layout, and interpretation of characters transferred to and from formatted records in a file. The forms of a control edit descriptor (R1010) are:

```
T n
TL n
TR n
```

n X
[r] /
:
S
SP
SS
k P
BN
BZ

where n and r are default integer literal constants, k is a signed default integer literal constant, and

k   is a scale factor
n   is a position in the record to tab for descriptor T
n   is the number of spaces to tab for descriptors X, TR, and TL
r   is a repeat factor

The control edit descriptors T, TL, TR, and X are called **position edit descriptors** (R1012). The control edit descriptors S, SP, and SS are called **sign edit descriptors** (R1014). The control edit descriptors BN and BZ are called **blank interpretation edit descriptors** (R1015).

Rules and restrictions:

1.   n must be positive.

2.   n, k, and r must not have a kind value specified for them.

In kP, k is called the **scale factor**. T, TL, TR, X, slash, colon, S, SP, SS, P, BN, and BZ indicate the manner of editing and are described in detail in Section 10.8.

10.3 Character String Edit Descriptor Form

Character string edit descriptors specify character strings to be transmitted to the formatted output record of a file. The forms of the character string edit descriptor (R1016) are:

character-literal-constant
n H representable-character [representable-character] ...

where n is a default integer literal constant and is a character count.

Rules and restrictions:

1.   n must not have a kind value specified for it.

2.   n must be positive.

3.   If the edit descriptor is a character literal constant, it must not have a kind value specified for it.

The character string edit descriptors are described in detail in Section 10.9.

10.4 Formatted Data Transfer

The format specification indicates how data are transferred by READ, WRITE, and PRINT statements. The data transfer typically involves a conversion of a data value. The particular conversion depends on the next data input or output item, along with the current edit descriptor in the format specification.

Examples:

READ (*, '(A7, I10, E16.8)') X, Y, Z
WRITE (*, 100) X, Y, Z 100 FORMAT (A7, I10, E16.3)
An empty format specification ( ) is restricted to input/output statements with no items in the input/output data item list or a list of items all of which have zero size. On the other hand, a scalar zero-length character string requires an A edit descriptor.
The effect on input and output of an empty format specification depends on whether the data transfer is advancing or nonadvancing, and on whether there is a current record. The effect is described by the following eight cases:

1.   The data transfer is advancing:

   a.   if there is no current record, then:

      i.   on input, skip the next record

      ii.   on output, write an empty record

   b.   if there is a current record, then:

      i.   on input, skip to the end of the current record

      ii.   on output, terminate the current record

2.   The data transfer is nonadvancing:

   a.   if there is no current record, then:

      i.   on input, move to the initial point of the next record

    ii.   on output, create an empty record and move to its initial point

  b.   if there is a current record, then:

    i.   on input, there is no effect

    ii.   on output, there is no effect

Example:

```
DO I = 1, N
   READ (5, '(A1)', ADVANCE='NO')  (CHARS(I)(J:J), J = 1, M)
ENDDO
READ (5, '()', ADVANCE = 'YES')
```

The above program segment reads N character strings, each of length M, from a single record and then advances to the beginning of the next record.

    The data and the edit descriptors are converted in a left-to-right fashion, except for repeated items, which are repeated until either the data items are exhausted or the repeat number is reached. A complex data item requires two data edit descriptors for data items of type real; that is, two of the edit descriptors E, F, D, ES, EN, or G (they may be different).

    Control edit descriptors and character edit descriptors do not require a corresponding data item in the list. The effect is directly on the record transferred. When the data items are completed, no further change is made to record on output, and no change is made to the position in the file on input.

10.4.1 Parentheses Usage

The effect of parentheses in a format specification depends on the nesting level of the parentheses.

Rules and restrictions:

1.   When the rightmost right parenthesis of a complete format specification is encountered and there are no more data items, the input/output data transfer terminates. Remember that the format specification may be given by a character string expression. In such a case, the right parenthesis matching the leftmost left parenthesis may be followed by any characters, including parentheses. None of these trailing characters are relevant to the rules and restrictions in this section. For example, the following character string

'(I5,E16.8,A5)   (This part is ignored)'

may be used as a format specification in a character string, and the part after the first right parenthesis is ignored.

2. When the rightmost right parenthesis is encountered and there are more data items, format control continues beginning at the left parenthesis corresponding to the last preceding right parenthesis in the specification, if there is one, with an implied slash (/) to cause a new record to begin. If there is no preceding right parenthesis, the reversion is to the beginning of the format.

3. If there is a repeat factor encountered when reverting, the repeat before the parenthesis is reused.

4. Reversion does not affect the scale factors, the sign control edit descriptor, or blank interpretation. These remain in effect for the duration of the format action.

Example:

```
CHR_FMT = '(I5, 4(3F10.2, 10X), E20.4)'
```

If the above character string were used in a formatted output data transfer statement, the first output data item must be an integer. The remaining items must be of type real (or complex): 13 real values are printed on the first line after the integer, and then the next real values are printed on each new line, 13 at a time, until the data items are exhausted. All but the last line will have 13 real values printed, 3 real values using the F10.2 edit descriptor, 10 blanks, followed by 3 more real values and 10 blanks repeated 4 times in total, followed by a real value using the E20.4 edit descriptor. This behavior is described in more detail in the next section.

10.4.2 Correspondence between a Data-Edit Descriptor and a List Item

The best way to describe how this correspondence is determined is to think of two markers, one beginning at the first item of input/output data item list and the other beginning at the first left parenthesis of the format specification. Before describing how each marker proceeds through each list, the input/output data item list is considered to be expanded by writing out each element of an array, each component of a structure, each part (real and imaginary) of each item of type complex, and each iteration of each implied-do list. The expanded item list is called the **effective data item list**, and each item in the list is called an **effective item**. Note that zero-sized arrays yield no effective items, but zero-length character objects yield effective items. Also, the format specification is considered expanded for each repeat factor preceding any (data or slash) edit descriptor but *not* a parenthesized format item list. If the data item list is nonempty, there must be at least one data edit descriptor in the format specification. Given the effective data item list and expanded format specification, the markers proceed as follows:

1. The marker proceeds through the format specification until the first data edit descriptor or right parenthesis is encountered. Any control edit descriptor or string edit descriptor encountered before the first data edit descriptor is encountered is interpreted according to its definition, each possibly changing the position within the record or the position within the file, or changing the interpretation of data in the record or conversion of data to the record.

2. If a data edit descriptor is encountered first, the effective data item pointed to by the marker in the data item list is transferred and converted according to the data edit descriptor, and the marker in the data item list proceeds to the next effective data item.

3. If a right parenthesis is encountered and the right parenthesis is not the outermost one of the format specification, the repeat factor in front of the matching left parenthesis is reduced by one. If the reduced factor is nonzero, the marker scans right from this left parenthesis, looking for a data edit descriptor as above. If the repeat factor becomes zero, the format specification marker then proceeds right from the right parenthesis, again looking for a data edit descriptor. If the right parenthesis is the outermost right parenthesis, the marker reverts to the left parenthesis corresponding to the last preceding right parenthesis, if there is one; if there is no preceding right parenthesis, it reverts to the first left parenthesis of the format specification. Upon reversion, a slash edit descriptor is interpreted implicitly, and the format marker proceeds right from this left parenthesis, honoring any repeat factor in front of it.

4. If no effective data item remains when a data edit descriptor is encountered or when a colon edit descriptor is encountered, the input/output operation terminates.

To illustrate how this works, consider the following example:

```
INTEGER  A(3)
COMPLEX  C
TYPE RATIONAL
   INTEGER  N, D
END TYPE
TYPE (RATIONAL)  R
   . . .
WRITE (*, &
     "('A and C appear on line 1, R appears on line 2' &
     / (1X, 3I5, 2F5.2) )" )  A, C, R
```

The data item list is first expanded as described above. The expanded data item list becomes:

```
A(1), A(2), A(3), REAL(C), AIMAG(C), R % N, R % D
```

The format specification is also expanded and becomes:

```
('A and C appear on line 1, R appears on line 2'  &
   / (1X, I5, I5, I5, F5.2, F5.2) )
```

A marker is established in the data item list, which initially points at the item A(1). A marker is also established in the format specification and initially points to the first left parenthesis. The marker in the format specification proceeds right to the first edit descriptor, which is the first I5. In so doing, it sees the string edit descriptor which is transferred to the output record, the slash edit descriptor which causes the previous record to terminate and to begin a new record, and the position edit descriptor which positions the record at the second character, blank filling the record. The item A(1) is then converted according to the I5 specification and the converted value is transferred to the output record. The marker in the data item list is moved to A(2). The format specification marker is moved left to the second I5 edit descriptor, and A(2) is converted and transferred to the output record. Similarly, A(3), the real part of C, and the imaginary part of C are converted and transferred to the output record. At this point, the data item list marker is pointing at R % N, and the format specification marker begins scanning after the second F5.2 edit descriptor looking for the next edit descriptor. The first right parenthesis is encountered and the scan reverts back to the corresponding left parenthesis. The repeat factor in front of this parenthesis is 1 by default and is reduced by 1 to 0. The marker in the format specification proceeds right from the first right parenthesis, encountering the outermost right parenthesis and then reverts to the left parenthesis before the edit descriptor 1X. As a result, an implicit slash edit descriptor is interpreted, causing the previous output record to be completed and a new record to be started. The format specification marker scans right looking for a data edit descriptor, which is the first I5. In the process of the scan right, the position edit descriptor is interpreted, which positions the file at the second character of the next record (and blank fills the skipped characters). Finally, the N and D components of R are converted and transferred to the output record, using the first two I5 edit descriptors. The data item list marker finds no further items, and the output operation terminates.

An example of writing a zero-sized array and zero-length character string using formatted output data transfer is:

```
REAL  A(10)
CHARACTER(4)  CHR
  . . .
WRITE( 6, '()' )  A(1:0)
WRITE( 6, '(A4)' )  CHR(4:3)
```

An empty format specification is allowed for the first WRITE statement, because the array to be printed is a zero-sized array section. The format specification in the second WRITE statement is required to have at least one A edit descriptor, because the effective data item is a zero-length character string, not a zero-sized array. In the first case, an empty record is written, and, in the second case, a record consisting of four blank characters is written (see Section 10.7).

10.5 File Positioning by Format Control

There is a current record being processed. After each data edit descriptor is used, the file position within that record is following the last character read or written by the particular edit descriptor. On output, after a string edit descriptor is used, the file is positioned within that record following the last character written. (See the description of the control edit descriptors T, TL, TR, and X for any special positioning within the current record; see the description of the slash edit descriptor for special positioning within the file.) The remaining control edit descriptors do not affect the position within a record or within the file; they affect only the interpretation of the input characters or the form of the output character string or how subsequent edit descriptors are interpreted. The interpretation of the edit descriptors is not affected by whether the operation is an advancing or nonadvancing input/output operation.

10.6 Numeric Editing

There are seven edit descriptors that cover numeric editing: I, F, E, EN, ES, D, and G. The following rules apply to all of them.

Rules and restrictions:

On input:

1. Leading blanks are never significant.

2. Plus signs may be omitted in the input data.

3. A blank field is considered to be zero, regardless of the BN edit descriptor or the BLANK= specifier in effect.

4. Within a field, blanks are interpreted in a manner that depends on the BLANK= specifier default for preconnected files, the BLANK= specifier provided in an OPEN statement for the unit, and any BN or BZ blank edit descriptor in effect.

5. In numeric fields that have a decimal point and correspond to F, E, EN, ES, D, or G edit descriptors, the decimal point in the input field overrides the placement of the decimal point specified by the edit descriptor specification.

6. Data input is permitted to have more digits of significance than the processor can use to represent a number.

7. If the processor is capable of representing both uppercase and lowercase letters in input records, the lowercase exponent letters e and d are equivalent to the corresponding uppercase exponent letters.

8. The constants in the input records may have kind parameters specified for them, but the kind parameters are restricted to integer literal constants; named constants are prohibited.

On output:

1. A positive or zero value may have a plus sign, depending on the sign edit descriptors used.

2. Negative values must have a negative sign, unless the printed value would be zero (because of the conversion rules). Negative zero must never be produced. For example, suppose the variable SMALL has the value -0.000314. On output, the characters transferred to output unit 6 by the statements

```
        WRITE(6,10)  SMALL
    10  FORMAT(F5.2)
```

must not contain a negative sign, and may be either

b0.00   or bb.00

Because a negative zero must not be printed.

3. The number is right justified in the field. Leading blanks may be inserted.

4. If the number or the exponent is too large for the field width specified in the edit descriptor, the entire output field is filled with asterisks.

5. The processor must not produce asterisks when the optional characters can be omitted and the output character string fits in the output field.

10.6.1 Integer Editing

The input/output list item corresponding to an integer edit descriptor must be of type integer, except for the G edit descriptor.

The integer edit descriptors are:

```
I w [ . m ]
B w [ . m ]
O w [ . m ]
Z w [ . m ]
G w . d [ E e ]
```

where:

w   is the field width
m   is the minimum number of digits in the constant

Rules and restrictions:

On both input and output:

1. The value of m must not exceed the value of w.

2. For an integer input/output list item, the edit descriptor Gw.d[Ee] is the same as the Iw for the given value of w.

On input:

1. m has no effect on an input field.

2. For the I edit descriptor, the character string in the file must be an optionally signed integer constant.

3. For the B, O, or Z edit descriptors, the character string must be a string of blanks and digits of binary, octal, or hexadecimal base, respectively. For example, the character string corresponding to a B edit descriptor must not contain digits 2 through 9. The character string corresponding to an O edit descriptor must not contain the digits 8 or 9. The character string corresponding to a Z edit descriptor may consist only of the blank character, the digits 0 through 9, and the letters A through F (or equivalently the letters a through f if the processor supports lowercase letters).

Example:

```
     READ (5, 100)  K, J
100 FORMAT (I5, G8.0)
```

If the input field is

bb–24bbbbb117

K is read using the integer I5 edit descriptor, while J is read with a G8 edit descriptor. The resulting values of K and J are –24 and 117, respectively.

On output:

1. If m is not present, each edit descriptor behaves as if it were present with the value 1.

2. For the Iw.m edit descriptor with m positive, the field is w characters wide and consists of zero or more leading blanks, followed by an optional sign, followed by an unsigned integer consisting of at least m digits. Leading zeros pad an integer field until there are m digits.

3. If m is not present and the value of the output list item is nonzero, the first digit must be nonzero; otherwise, the field consists of only one 0 digit with no sign character. Negative zero must never be produced.

4. For the Iw.0 edit descriptor, if the output list item has the value 0, the field consists entirely of blanks.

5. For the B, O, or Z edit descriptors, the rules for forming the output field for the values w and m are the same as for the I edit descriptor

except that no sign is allowed and the unsigned integer must consist of digits from the binary, octal, or hexadecimal base, respectively. A negative value must be indicated in the encoding of the digits written; for example, –1 might be printed as 80000001 using a hexadecimal edit descriptor, encoding the negative sign as a leading 1 bit.

The interpretation of the digits under B, O, and Z edit descriptors is not specified in the standard particularly for negative values. Encodings other than those illustrated above are permitted, and so the interpretation of the binary, octal, or hexadecimal digits is processor dependent. For example, the constant 80000001 may be interpreted as –1 if the first bit is the sign bit, or $2^{31} + 1$ if the sign bit is further to the left in the representation. Therefore, the B, O, and Z edit descriptors are basically nonportable. Most implementations will choose the machine representation for these patterns.

10.6.2 Real Editing

The F, E, EN, ES, and D edit descriptors specify editing for real and complex input/output list items. The G edit descriptor may also be used for real and complex items. Two such edit descriptors are required for each complex data item.

The forms of the edit descriptors for real values are:

```
F w . d
E w . d [ E e ]
EN w . d [ E e ]
ES w . d [ E e ]
D w . d
G w . d [ E e]
```

10.6.2.1 F Editing. Fw.d editing converts to or from a string occupying w positions.

Rules and restrictions:

On both input and output:

1. d must not exceed w.

2. The value in the input field or the value transferred to the output field may be signed.

On input:

1. d specifies the number of decimal places in the input value if a decimal point is not present in the input field.

2. The input field may be:

   a. a signed integer or real literal constant but without an underscore and kind parameter value

   b. a signed digit string followed by a sign followed by an unsigned digit string treated as an exponent

   c. a signed digit string containing a decimal point followed by a sign followed by an unsigned digit string treated as an exponent

   except that blanks may be freely inserted anywhere in the input field.

3. If the input field contains a decimal point, the value of d has no effect.

4. If there is no decimal point, a decimal point is inserted in front of the rightmost d digits of the nonexponent part, treating blanks as 0 digits or as if they were not present, according to the BLANK= specifier or the BZ or BN edit descriptor currently in effect.

   Example: consider the format specification F5.1. The input data item

   1bb99

   is treated as the real number 19.9, if the BLANK= specifier is NULL or the BN edit descriptor is in effect, and is treated as the real number 1009.9 if the BLANK= specifier is ZERO or the BZ edit descriptor is in effect.

5. There may be more digits in the number than the processor can use.

6. The number may contain an E or D indicating an exponent value; a field with a D exponent letter is processed identically to the same field with an E exponent letter. If there is no exponent field on input, the assumption is that the character string is followed by an exponent with the value $-k$ where k is the scalar factor established by a previous kP edit descriptor.

On output:

1. d specifies the number of digits after the decimal point.

2. The form of the output field consists of w positions comprised of leading blanks, if necessary, and an optionally signed real constant

with a decimal point, rounded to d digits after the decimal point but with no exponent, underscore, or kind parameter value. The rounding algorithm is not specified by the standard; most systems round up when the d+1-*st* digit is 5 or greater.

3. Leading 0s are not permitted unless the number is less than 1, in which case the processor may place a 0 in front of the decimal point.

4. At least one zero must be output if no other digits would appear.

5. The scale factor has no effect on F editing on output.

6. Negative zero must never be produced (see Section 10.5).

Example:

```
      READ (5, 100) X, Y
100 FORMAT (F10.2, F10.3)
```

If the input field is

*bbbb*6.42181234567890

the values assigned to X and Y are 6.4218 and 1234567.89, respectively. The value of d is ignored for X because the input field contains a decimal point.

The rounding algorithm for either input or output is not specified by the standard; recent articles (SIGPLAN '90 Conference, *SIGPLAN Notices*, Vol. 25, No. 6, June 1990, pp. 92–101, pp. 112–123) describe reasonable rounding algorithms with many desirable properties.

10.6.2.2 E and D Editing. The Ew.d[Ee] and Dw.d edit descriptors convert to and from a string occupying w positions. For the edit descriptors Ew.d[Ee] and Dw.d, the field representing the floating point number contains w characters, including an exponent.

Rules and restrictions:

On both input and output:

1. w is the field width, d is the number of places after the decimal, and e is the exponent width.

2. d and e must not exceed w.

On input:

1. The form Ew.d[Ee] is the same as for Fw.d editing, where either E or D in the input data record may indicate an exponent. e has no effect on input.

On output:

1. The form of the output field for a scale factor of zero is:

    $[\pm][0].x_1x_2\cdots x_d\, exp$

    where:

    a. $\pm$ signifies a plus or a minus.

    b. $x_1x_2\cdots x_d$ are the d most significant digits of the datum value after rounding.

    c. *exp* is a decimal exponent having one of the forms specified in Table 10-4, where each z_i is a decimal digit.

    Table 10-4 Forms for the exponent *exp* in E and D editing

Edit descriptor	Absolute value of exponent	Form of exponent
Ew.d	$\|exp\| \le 99$ $99 < \|exp\| \le 999$	$E\pm z_1z_2$ or $\pm 0z_1z_2$ $\pm z_1z_2z_3$
Ew.dEe	$\|exp\| \le 10^e - 1$	$E\pm z_1z_2\cdots z_e$
Dw.d	$\|exp\| \le 99$ $99 < \|exp\| \le 999$	$D\pm z_1z_2$ or $E\pm z_1z_2$ or $\pm 0z_1z_2$ $\pm z_1z_2z_3$

2. The sign in the exponent is required.

3. Plus is used for zero exponents.

4. If the exponent exceeds 999 in magnitude, the forms Ew.dEe must be used with a sufficiently large value of e to represent the exponent *exp*.

5. A scale factor kP may be used to specify the number of digits to the left of the decimal point, with the exponent adjusted accordingly; that is, the scale factor k controls the decimal normalization. If $-d < k \le 0$, the output field contains the decimal point, exactly $|k|$ leading zeros, and $d - |k|$ significant digits. If

$0 < k < d + 2$, the output field contains exactly k significant digits to the left of the decimal point and $d - k + 1$ significant digits to the right of the decimal point. Other values of k are not permitted; that is, those values of k that will produce no digits to the left of the decimal point or specify fewer than zero digits to the right of the decimal point.

6. The precise form of zero on output is not specified, except that it must contain a decimal point, d zero digits, and an exponent of at least 4 characters whose digits are not specified. However, a reasonable, sensible, and likely value of the exponent is zero.

Example:

```
    WRITE (6, 105)  Y, Z
105 FORMAT (E15.3,4PD15.3)
```

If the values of Y and Z are -2.12×10^1 and 2.65421232×10^4 respectively, the output record produced is:

bbbbb−0.212E+02*bbb*2654.212E+01

10.6.2.3 Engineering Edit Descriptor EN. The EN edit descriptor converts to or from a string using engineering notation for a value occupying w positions.

Rules and restrictions:

On input:

1. The form ENw.d[Ee] is the same as for Fw.d editing (10.5.2.1).

On output:

1. The output of the number is in the form of engineering notation, where the exponent is divisible by 3 and the absolute value of the significand is $1000 > |\text{significand}| \geq 1$. This is the same form as the E edit descriptor, except for the restriction on the exponent and significand.

Example:

```
    WRITE (6, 110)  B
110 FORMAT (EN13.3)
```

If the value of B is 0.212, the output record produced is:

*bb*212.000E-03

2. The precise form of zero is not specified, except for the same restrictions as noted for the E edit descriptor with the additional restriction that there must be exactly one zero digit before the decimal point.

3. The form of the output field is:

$$[\ \pm\ ]\ yyy.x_1x_2 \cdots x_d\ exp$$

where:

a. $\pm$ signifies a plus or a minus.

b. yyy are the 1 to 3 decimal digits representing the most significant digits of the value of the datum after rounding (yyy is an integer such that $1 \leq yyy < 1000$ or, if the output value is zero, $yyy = 0$).

c. $x_1x_2 \cdots x_d$ are the d next most significant digits of the value of the datum after rounding. If the output value is zero, the x_i are all 0.

d. exp is a decimal integer, divisible by 3, representing the exponent and of one of the forms, given in Table 10-5, where each z_i is a decimal digit.

Table 10-5 Forms for the exponent exp in EN editing

Edit descriptor	Absolute value of exponent	Form of exponent
ENw.d	$\|exp\| \leq 99$ $99 < \|exp\| \leq 999$	$E\pm z_1z_2$ or $\pm 0z_1z_2$ $\pm z_1z_2z_3$
ENw.dEe	$\|exp\| \leq 10^e - 1$	$E\pm z_1z_2 \cdots z_e$

4. The sign in the exponent is produced. A plus sign is produced if the exponent value is zero. The form ENw.dEe must be used with a sufficiently large value of e if $|exp| > 999$.

Examples:

Internal value	Output field using SS, EN12.3
6.421	6.421E+00
-.5	-500.000E-03
.00217	2.170E-03
4721.3	4.721E+03

10.6.2.4 Scientific Edit Descriptor ES. The scientific edit descriptor ES converts to or from a string using scientific notation for a value occupying w positions.

Rules and restrictions:

On input:

1. The form ESw.d[Ee] is the same as for Fw.d editing (10.5.2.1) .

On output:

1. The output of the number is in the form of scientific notation, where the absolute value of the significand is $10 > |significand| \geq 1$. This is the same form as the E edit descriptor, except for the restriction on the significand.

Example:

```
    WRITE (6, 110)  B
110 FORMAT (ES12.3)
```

If the value of B is 0.12345678, the output record produced is:

*bbb*1.235E-01

2. The precise form of zero is not specified, except for the same restrictions as noted for the EN edit descriptor.

3. The form of the output field is:

$$[\pm]\, y.x_1 x_2 \cdots x_d\, exp$$

where:

a. $\pm$ signifies a plus or a minus.

b. y is a decimal digit representing the most significant digit of the value of the datum after rounding (y is an integer such that $1 \le y < 10$ or, if the output value is zero, $y = 0$).

c. $x_1 x_2 \cdots x_d$ are the d next most significant decimal digits of the value of the datum after rounding. If the output value is zero, the x_i are all 0.

d. exp is a decimal exponent of one of the forms, given in Table 10-6, where each z_i is a decimal digit.

Table 10-6 Forms for the exponent exp in ES editing

Edit descriptor	Absolute value of exponent	Form of exponent
ESw.d	$\|exp\| \le 99$ $99 < \|exp\| \le 999$	$E \pm z_1 z_2$ or $\pm 0 z_1 z_2$ $\pm z_1 z_2 z_3$
ESw.dEe	$\|exp\| \le 10^e - 1$	$E \pm z_1 z_2 \cdots z_e$

4. The sign in the exponent is produced.

5. A plus sign is produced if the exponent value is zero.

6. The form ESw.dEe must be used with a sufficiently large value of e if $|exp| > 999$.

Examples:

Internal value	Output field using SS, ES12.3
6.421	6.421E+00
-.5	-5.000E-01
.00217	2.170E-03
4721.3	4.721E+03

10.6.2.5 Complex Editing. Complex editing follows the rules for numeric editing. Editing of complex numbers requires two real edit descriptors, the first one for the real part and the second one for the imaginary part. Different edit descriptors may be used for the two parts. Control and character string edit descriptors may be inserted between the edit descriptors for the real and imaginary parts.

Example:

```
COMPLEX CM (2)
READ (5, "(4E7.2)") (CM (I), I = 1, 2)
```

If the input record is:

bb55511bbb2146bbbb100bbbb621

the values assigned to CM (1) and CM (2) are $555.11 + 21.46\iota$ and $1 + 6.21\iota$, respectively.

10.6.2.6 Generalized Editing of Real Data. Gw.d[Ee] converts to or from a string using generalized editing. The form for generalized editing is determined by the magnitude of the value of the number.

Rules and restrictions:

On input:

1. The Gw.d[Ee] edit descriptor is the same as the Fw.d edit descriptor (10.5.2.1).

On output:

1. Let N be the magnitude of a number to be printed using a G edit descriptor. If $N = 0$ or is approximately between 0.1 and 10^d, Table 10-7 specifies the form of the output, where n is 4 for Gw.d and n is $e + 2$ for Gw.dEe. A kP scale factor has no effect.

2. If N is outside this range, output editing with the edit descriptor kPGw.d[Ee] is the same as that with kPEw.d[Ee].

Examples:

```
PRINT "(G10.1)", 8.76E1
```

produces the output

bbb0.9E+02

because the magnitude of N is such that rule 2 applies, yielding the format E10.1.

```
PRINT "(G10.3)" , 8.76E1
```

produces the output:

Table 10-7 The form of the output using a G edit descriptor for a number of magnitude N

Magnitude of datum	s	t	Equivalent conversion
$N = 0$	$w - n$	$d - 1$	$Fs.t, nX$
$0.1 - 0.5 \times 10^{-d-1} \leq N < 1 - 0.5 \times 10^{-d}$	$w - n$	d	$Fs.t, nX$
$1 - 0.5 \times 10^{-d} \leq N < 10 - 0.5 \times 10^{-d+1}$	$w - n$	$d - 1$	$Fs.t, nX$
$10 - 0.5 \times 10^{-d+1} \leq N < 100 - 0.5 \times 10^{-d+2}$	$w - n$	$d - 2$	$Fs.t, nX$
$\vdots$	$\vdots$	$\vdots$	
$10^d - 2 - 0.5 \times 10^{-2} \leq N < 10^d - 1 - 0.5 \times 10^{-1}$	$w - n$	1	$Fs.t, nX$
$10^d - 1 - 0.5 \times 10^{-1} \leq N < 10^d - 0.5$	$w - n$	0	$Fs.t, nX$

    bb87.6bbbb

because n is 4, and the format reduces to F6.1,4X (the fourth line in Table 10-7) because of the range of the magnitude of the number.

Example:

    PRINT "(G10.3E1)" , 8.76E1

produces the output:

    bbb87.6bbb

because n is 3 ($=1+2$) and the format reduces to F7.1,3X.

10.7 Logical Editing

The logical edit descriptors convert to or from a string representing a logical value that is true or false. The edit descriptors used for logical editing are:

    L w
    G w . d [E e]

Rules and restrictions:

On both input and output:

1. w is the field width.

2. Generalized logical editing Gw.d[Ee] follows the rules for Lw editing.

On input:

1. The input field for a logical value consists of any number of blanks, followed by an optional period, followed by T or F, for a true and false value respectively, followed by any representable characters.

Example: Using the READ statement:

```
READ (5, "(2L8)")  L1, L2
```

to read the input record:

```
.TRUE.bb .FALSE.b
```

will cause L1 and L2 to have the values true and false, respectively. The result would be the same if the input record were:

```
TUESDAYb FRIDAYbb
```

On output:

1. The output field consists of $w-1$ leading blanks, followed by T or F, for a true and false value, respectively, of the output item.

Example:

```
WRITE (6, "(2L7)")  L1, L2
```

If L1 and L2 are true and false, respectively, the output record will be:

```
bbbbbb Tbbbbbb F
```

10.8 Character Editing

Character editing converts to or from a string of characters. The edit descriptors for character editing are:

```
A [ w ]
G w . d [ E e ]
```

Rules and restrictions:

On both input and output:

1. w is the field width measured in characters.

2. A Gw.d[Ee] general edit descriptor is the same as an Aw edit descriptor for character data.

3. All characters transferred under the control of a particular A or G edit descriptor must be of the same kind.

4. If w is omitted, the length of the character data object being transferred is used as the field width.

On input:

1. If w is greater than or equal to the length *len* of the character datum read, *len* rightmost characters of the input field are read.

2. If w is less than the length *len* of the character data read, the w characters of the character datum will be read from the input field and placed left justified in the character list item followed by *len* −w trailing blanks.

On output:

1. If w exceeds the length *len* of the character datum written, w−*len* blank padding characters are written followed by *len* characters of the character datum.

2. If w is less than or equal to the length *len* of the character data written, the w leftmost characters of the character datum will appear in the output field.

3. If the character datum is of the nondefault kind, the character used for "blank padding" is processor dependent.

Example:

```
CHARACTER (LEN = 14), PARAMETER :: &
      SLOGAN = "SAVE THE RIVER"
WRITE (*, "(A)")  SLOGAN
```

produces the output record:

```
SAVE THE RIVER
```

10.9 Control Edit Descriptors

No data is transferred or converted with the control edit descriptors. Control edit descriptors affect skipping, tabbing, scale factors, and printing of optional signs. These edit descriptors may affect how the data is input or output using the subsequent data edit descriptors in the format specification.

10.9.1 Position Editing

Position edit descriptors control relative tabbing left or right in the record before the next list item is processed. The edit descriptors for tabbing are:

T n	tab to position n
TL n	tab left n positions
TR n	tab right n positions
n X	tab right n positions

The tabbing operations to the left are limited by a position called the **left tabbing limit**. This position is normally the first position of the current record but, if the previous operation on the file was a nonadvancing formatted data transfer, the left tabbing limit is the current position within the record before the data transfer begins. If the file is positioned to another record during the data transfer, the left tabbing limit changes to the first position of the new record.

The Tn edit descriptor positions the record just before the character in position n relative to the left tabbing limit. TRn and nX move right n characters from the current position. TLn moves left n characters from the current position, but is limited by the left tabbing limit.

Rules and restrictions:

On both input and output:

1. n must be a positive integer constant with no kind parameter value specified for it.

2. Left tabbing is always limited so that even if left tabbing specifies a position to the left of the left tabbing limit, the record position is set to the left tabbing limit in the record.

3. The left tabbing limit in the record is determined by the position in the record before any data transfer begins for a particular data transfer statement.

4. If a file is positioned to another record during a particular data transfer statement, the left tabbing limit is the first position of the record.

On input:

1. The resulting position in the record after tabbing over nondefault characters in the output record is processor dependent.

2. The T descriptor may move the position within a record either left or right from the current position.

3. Moving to a position left of the current position allows input to be processed twice, provided the same input statement is performing the processing for advancing input, or provided nonadvancing input is in effect.

4. The X descriptor always moves the position to the right and skips characters.

On output:

1. The positioning does not transmit characters, and does not by itself cause the record to be shorter or longer.

2. Positions that are skipped and have not been filled previously behave as if they are blank filled.

3. Positions previously filled may be replaced with new characters, but are not blank filled when they are skipped using any of the position edit descriptors.

Example: If DISTANCE and VELOCITY have the values 12.66 and −8654.123,

```
      PRINT 100, DISTANCE, VELOCITY
100 FORMAT (F9.2, 6X, F9.3)
```

produces the record:

*bbbb*12.66*bbbbbb*−8654.123

and

```
      PRINT 100, DISTANCE, VELOCITY
100 FORMAT (F9.2, T7, F9.3)
```

produces the record:

*bbbb*12−8654.123

because T7 specifies the first position for VELOCITY as the seventh character in the record.

10.9.2 Slash Editing

The slash edit descriptor consists of the single slash character (/). The current record is ended when a slash is encountered in a format specification.

Rules and restrictions:

On input:

1. If the file is connected for sequential access, the file is positioned at the beginning of the next record. The effect is to skip the remainder of the current record.

2. For direct access, the record number is increased by one, and the file is positioned at the beginning of the record with this increased record number, if it exists; it becomes the current record.

3. A record may be skipped entirely on input.

On output:

1. If the file is connected for sequential access, a new empty record is created after the current record, and the file is positioned at the beginning of a new record. In completing the previous record, no characters may be written to the file (for example, for systems that support variable length records).

2. For direct access, the current record is blank filled, the record number is increased by one, and this record becomes the current record.

3. For an internal file, the current record is blank filled, and the file is positioned at the beginning of the next array element.

Example: If ALTER, POSITION, and CHANGE have the values 1.1, 2.2, and 3.3, respectively,

```
PRINT "(F5.1, /, 2F6.1)", ALTER, POSITION, CHANGE
```

produces two records:

```
bb1.1
bbb2.2bbb3.3
```

10.9.3 Colon Editing

The colon edit descriptor consists of the character colon (:). If the list of items in a formatted READ or WRITE statement is exhausted, a colon stops format processing at that point. If the list is not exhausted, the colon edit descriptor has no effect.

Example: If ALTER, POSITION, and CHANGE have the values 1.1, 2.2, and 3.3, respectively,

```
WRITE (6, 100) ALTER, POSITION, CHANGE
100 FORMAT (3F5.2, :, "STOP")
```

produces:

   *bb*1.1*bb*2.2*bb*3.3

The characters STOP are not printed because the output list is exhausted when the colon edit descriptor is processed. If the colon edit descriptor were not present in the above format, the string "STOP" would be printed.

10.9.4 Sign Editing

Sign editing applies to the output data transfer of positive integer and real values only. It controls the writing of the optional plus sign when the edit descriptor I, F, E, EN, ES, D, or G is used. The sign edit descriptors are:

S	the optional plus may or may not be printed; the choice is processor dependent
SP	the optional plus must be printed
SS	the optional plus must not be printed

Rules and restrictions:

1. The descriptors have effect until another sign edit descriptor is encountered in the format specification.

2. The descriptors have no effect during formatted input data transfers.

Example: If SPEED(1) and SPEED(2) are 1.46 and 2.3412 respectively,

```
WRITE (6, 110) (SPEED (K), K = 1, 2)
110 FORMAT (SP, 2F10.2)
```

produces the record:

  bbbbb+1.46*bbb*+234.12

10.9.5 Scale Factors

The kP edit descriptor indicates scaling, where the scale factor k is a signed integer literal constant.

  The scale factor is zero at the beginning of a formatted input/output statement. When a kP descriptor occurs, the scale factor becomes k, and all succeeding numeric fields processed with an F, E, EN, ES, D, or G edit descriptor may be affected by this scale factor until another kP edit descriptor occurs.

Rules and restrictions:

On input:

1. If the input field has no exponent, the external number equals the internal number multiplied by a scale factor 10^k.

2. The scale factor has no effect if the input field has an exponent.

Example: If the input record contains 10.12:

```
      READ (5,100) MASS
 100 FORMAT (3PF15.3)
```

gives MASS the value 10120.0.

On output:

1. For the F edit descriptor, the scale factor has no effect.

2. For the E and D edit descriptors, the nonexponent part (significand) of the number appearing in the output is multiplied by 10^k and the exponent is reduced by k.

3. The G edit descriptor is not affected by the scale factor if the number will print correctly with the appropriate F edit descriptor as described in Table 10-7. Otherwise, the scale factor for the G edit descriptor has the same effect as for the E edit descriptor.

4. EN and ES edit descriptors are not affected by a scale factor.

Example: If TREE has the value 12.96:

```
    WRITE (6,200) TREE
200 FORMAT (2PG10.1)
```

produces:

```
b1296.E-02
```

10.9.6 Blanks in Numeric Fields

Blanks other than leading blanks may be ignored or interpreted as zero characters in numeric input fields as determined by the blank edit descriptors:

BN treat nonleading blanks in numeric input fields as nonexistent
BZ treat nonleading blanks in numeric input fields as zeros

The interpretation is for input fields only when the field is processed using an I, B, O, Z, F, E, EN, ES, D, or G edit descriptor; output fields are not affected. The BLANK= specifier in the OPEN statement affects the interpretation of blanks if no BN or BZ descriptor is used.

Rules and restrictions:

On input:

1. The BLANK= specifier for an internal file is NULL.

2. If the BLANK= specifier is NULL, or a BN edit descriptor is in effect, the nonleading blanks are ignored and treated as if they were not in the input field.

3. If the BLANK= specifier is ZERO, or a BZ edit descriptor is in effect, the nonleading blanks are interpreted as zeros in succeeding numeric fields.

4. The BN and BZ edit descriptors override the effect of the BLANK= specifier during the execution of a particular input data transfer statement.

Example:

```
    READ (5, 100) N1, N2
100 FORMAT (I5, BZ, I5)
```

If the input record is:

   *b*9*b*9*b*9*b*9*b*9

and unit 5 has been opened with a BLANK= specifier equal to NULL, the values assigned to N1 and N2 are 99 and 90909, respectively.

10.9.7 Character String Edit Descriptors

Character string edit descriptors are used to transfer characters to an output record. The character string edit descriptors must not be used on input. The character string edit descriptors are apostrophe, quote, and Hollerith and are respectively:

   ' characters '
   " characters "
   n H characters

Rules and restrictions:

On output:

1. The apostrophe and quote edit descriptors have the form of literal character constants with no kind parameter values and cause those constants to be placed in the output.

2. The Hollerith descriptor nH . . . may be used to print the n characters following the H. n must be a positive integer and must not have a kind value specified for it.

3. To print a quote in the output field when a quote is the delimiting character, use two consecutive quotes; to print an apostrophe in the output field when an apostrophe is the delimiting character, use two consecutive apostrophes.

4. The field width is the length of the character constant, but does not include doubled apostrophes or quotes.

Example: If TEMP has the value 32.120001,

```
    WRITE (6, 120)  TEMP
120 FORMAT (' TEMPERATURE = ', F13.6)
```

produces the record:

   *b*TEMPERATURE*b*=*bbbbb*32.120001

10.10 List-Directed Formatting

List-directed formatting is one of the implicit formatting methods in Fortran. Conversion to and from characters in READ and WRITE statements does not use an explicit format specification. The editing occurs based on the type of the list item. Data is separated by commas or blanks. The input/output statement uses an asterisk (*) instead of an explicit format specification.

Example:

```
READ (5, *)  HOT, COLD, WARM
```

Rules and restrictions:

On both input and output:

1. A list-directed record consists of values and value separators.

2. **Values.** The values allowed in a list-directed input record are:

null	a null value, specified for example by two consecutive commas (,,)
c	a noncharacter literal constant with no embedded blanks, a character literal constant, or a nondelimited character string with no embedded blanks (see Section 10.10.1.1 for the detailed requirements for nondelimited character constants)
$r*c$	r repetitions of the constant c
$r*$	r repetitions of the null value

    Embedded blanks are not allowed within values except in a delimited character constant.

3. **Value Separators.** The value separators allowed in a list-directed input record are:

    *   a comma, optionally preceded or followed by contiguous blanks

    *   a slash, optionally preceded or followed by contiguous blanks

    *   one or more contiguous blanks between two nonblank values or following the last nonblank value, where a nonblank value is a constant, an $r*c$ form, or an $r*$ form

4. List-directed formatting must not be specified for direct-access or nonadvancing sequential data transfer.

5.   If there are no list items and there is no current record, an input record is skipped or an output record that is empty is written. If there are no list items and there is a current record, the current record is skipped (the file is positioned at the end of the current record) or the current record is terminated at the current position. (Recall that a current record exists only if the previous input/output data transfer to the unit was nonadvancing.) An empty record is either a blank-filled record or a record with no characters in it, depending on the processor.

6.   The end of a record has the same effect as a blank, unless it occurs within a delimited character literal constant. Similarly, a sequence of two or more consecutive blanks is treated as a single blank.

10.10.1 List-Directed Input

Input values are generally accepted as list-directed input if they are the same as those required for explicit formatting with an edit descriptor. There are some exceptions. They are:

1.   When the data list item is of type integer, the constant must be of a form suitable for the I edit descriptor. Binary, octal, or hexadecimal based values must not appear in a list-directed input record.

2.   When the data list item is of type real, the constant must be of a form suitable for the F edit descriptor. If no decimal point appears in the constant, the constant has no fractional digits specified for it.

3.   Blanks are never zeros.

4.   Embedded blanks are not allowed, except within a delimited character constant. Values of type complex include the parentheses for a complex constant, and blanks may occur before or after the comma, and before or after the parentheses.

Examples are:

```
"NICE DAY"
(1.2, 5.666 )
TODAY
```

5.   Logical items must not use value separators as the optional characters following the T or F. TUESDAY is allowed; T,TOO is not.

6.   An end of record may not occur within a constant, except a complex constant or a delimited character constant: for a complex

constant, the end of record may occur between the real part and the comma, or between the comma and the imaginary part; for a character constant, the end of record may occur anywhere in the constant except between any consecutive (doubled) quotes or apostrophes in the constant. The end of record does not cause a blank or any other character to become part of the character value. A complex or character constant may be continued on as many records as needed.

7.   Value separators may appear in any delimited default character constant. They are, however, not interpreted as value separators, but are characters in the delimited character constant.

8.   If *len* is the length of the corresponding input list item, and w is the number of effective characters in the character value, and if:

> $len \leq w$ the leftmost *len* characters of the constant are used
>
> $len > w$ the w characters of the constant are left justified in the input list item and the list item is blank filled on the right

For example, consider the code:

```
CHARACTER (2) NAME
       . . .
READ (5,*)  NAME
```

where the input record is:

```
JONES
```

After the READ statement, the value in NAME is JO, because *len* ($=2$) is less than w ($=5$).

10.10.1.1 Requirements for Nondelimited Character Strings as Values.

In certain cases, the delimiters are not required for character values on input. However, nondelimited character strings impose certain requirements which are:

1.   The corresponding data list item must be of type character.

2.   The character string must not contain any value separator.

3.   The character string must not be continued across a record boundary.

4. The first nonblank character is neither an apostrophe (') nor a quote (").

5. The leading characters are not a string of digits followed immediately by an asterisk.

In any of these cases, the character constant represented by the character string is terminated by the first value separator or end of record, and apostrophes (') and quotes (") are not doubled.

10.10.1.2 Null Values. Null values are used to specify no change of the items in the input item list. Null values have the forms:

1. no value between separators, such as ,,

2. a nonblank value separator as the first entity in the record; for example, a record beginning with slash as the first nonblank character represents a null value, as in /4.56

3. $r*$ followed by a value separator as in:

```
7*,'TODAY'
```

Rules and restrictions:

1. An end of record does not signify a null value.

2. The null value does not affect the definition status or value of the corresponding list item.

3. For a complex constant, the entire constant may be null, but not one of the parts.

4. If a slash terminates input, the remaining characters in the record are ignored, and the remaining list items are treated as though null values had been read. This applies to any remaining items in an implied-DO or to any remaining elements of an array.

Example:

```
REAL AVERAGE (2)
READ (5, *)  NUMBER, AVERAGE
```

If the input record is:

```
b6,,2.418
```

the result is that NUMBER = 6, AVERAGE (1) is unchanged, and AVERAGE (2) = 2.418.

10.10.2 List-Directed Output

List-directed output uses similar conventions to those used for list-directed input. The rules and restrictions that are the same are:

Rules and restrictions:

1. A blank or a comma optionally preceded or followed by a blank is used as a separator except for nondelimited character values.

2. The processor begins new records, as needed, at any point in the list of output items. A new record does not begin in the middle of a value, except as noted below for complex and character values. Each new record begins with a blank for carriage control, except for delimited character constants.

3. Slashes and null values are not output.

4. The processor has the option of using the repeat factor $r*c$ for two or more consecutive values that are identical.

There are a few exceptions that are noted below for each of the intrinsic types.

Integer. The effect is as though an Iw edit descriptor were used, using a suitable processor-dependent value for w.

Real. The effect is as though an 0PFw.d or an 1PEw.dEe edit descriptor were used, using suitable processor-dependent values for w, d, and e. Which edit descriptor is chosen by the compiler depends on the magnitude of the number written.

Complex. The real and imaginary parts are enclosed in parentheses and separated by a comma (with optional blanks surrounding the comma). If the length of the complex number is longer than an entire record, the processor may separate the real and imaginary parts on two consecutive records with the real part in the first record.

Logical. List-directed output prints T or F depending on the value of the logical data item.

Character. The form of the output for character values depends on the value of the DELIM= specifier in the OPEN statement for that unit.

1. If there is no DELIM= specifier, if the value of the DELIM= specifier is NONE, or if the file is an internal file:

    a.   Character values are not delimited.

    b.   Character values are not surrounded by value separators.

    c.   Only one quote or apostrophe is needed for each quote or apostrophe in the string transferred.

    d.   A blank is inserted at the beginning of new records for a continued character value.

2.   If the DELIM= specifier is QUOTE or APOSTROPHE:

    a.   Character values are delimited with the specified delimiter quote or apostrophe.

    b.   All values are surrounded by value separators.

    c.   A character that is the same as the specified delimiter is doubled when written to the output record.

    d.   An underscore followed by a kind parameter is allowed, if applicable.

    e.   No blank is inserted at the beginning of a continued record for carriage control in the case of a character value continued between records.

Example:

```
REAL                 :: TEMPERATURE = -7.6
INTEGER              :: COUNT = 3
CHARACTER(*), PARAMETER :: PHRASE = "This isn't so"

OPEN( 10, DELIM = 'NONE' )
WRITE( 10, * )  TEMPERATURE, COUNT, PHRASE
```

The output record on unit 10 would be:

```
-7.6    3.0   This isn't so
```

10.11 Namelist Formatting

In some programs, it is convenient to create a list of variables that can be read or written by referencing the name of the list. The term **namelist** denotes this kind of data transfer. Before input or output can begin using this facility, the NAMELIST specification statement (5.9) is used to define the list and give it a **group name**. In the following example, the

NAMELIST statement defines the group name MEETING made up of the data objects JAKE, JOE, and JANE.

```
NAMELIST /MEETING/ JOE, JAKE, JANE
```

The namelist input and output records consist of an ampersand (&) followed by a namelist group name followed by a sequence of name-value pairs followed by a slash (/). A **name-value pair** is a name or a subobject designator, an equal sign, and one or more values separated by value separators; that is, *name = value* or *name = value, value, ...* The name in a name-value pair must appear in the NAMELIST statement specifying the namelist group name. The name-value pairs provide a convenient form of documentation.

For example, the following input data transfer statement

```
READ (*, NML = MEETING)
```

sets the variables JAKE and JOE when the input record is:

```
&MEETING  JAKE = 3505,  JOE = 1 /
```

and does not change the value of the variable JANE.

Namelist output is convenient for debugging or writing values in a form that can later be read by a READ statement referencing the same namelist group name. All variables in the namelist group name appear in the output record but must be defined when the output statement is executed. For example, the WRITE statement

```
WRITE (*, NML = MEETING)
```

creates the output record (assuming JANE is defined with the value 0)

```
&MEETING  JAKE = 3505, JOE = 1, JANE = 0 /
```

In namelist input/output records, blanks may be before or after the ampersand, after the namelist group name, before or after the equal sign in the name-value pairs, or before the slash terminating the namelist input statement.

The rules and restrictions for a blank and an end of record in a character constant are the same as for delimited character constants in list-directed formatting. Nondelimited character strings are not permitted in namelist records.

10.11.1 Namelist Input

Namelist input consists of an ampersand (&), followed by the group name, followed by one or more blanks, followed by a sequence of zero or more name-value pairs whose names (10.11.1.1) are in the namelist group and whose values are described in Section 10.11.1.2, are separated by value separators, and followed by a slash which terminates the namelist input.

Name-Value Pairs. The name-value pairs are separated by value separators that are of the form:

- a comma, optionally preceded or followed by contiguous blanks

- a slash, optionally preceded or followed by contiguous blanks

- one or more contiguous blanks between two name-value pairs

Rules and restrictions:

1. Blanks may precede the ampersand or the slash.

2. When the name in the name-value pair is a subobject designator, it must not be a zero-sized array, zero-sized array section, or a zero-length character string.

3. If the processor supports uppercase and lowercase characters, a lowercase letter is the same as an uppercase letter and vice versa when used in the group name.

   An example of namelist input is:

   ```
   READ (*, NML = MEETING)
   ```

The input record might be:

```
&MEETING JAKE = 3500, JOE = 100, JANE = 0/
```

10.11.1.1 Names in Name-Value Pairs. There are rules and restrictions for the names used in the name-value pairs in the namelist records.

Rules and restrictions:

1. The name-value pairs may appear in any order in the input records.

2. The name-value pairs are evaluated serially, in left-to-right order.

3. A name in the namelist group may be omitted.

4. Each name must correspond with a name in the designated namelist group; a component name, if any, must also be the name of a component of the structure named in the namelist group.

5. Optionally-signed integer literal constants with no kind parameter values must be used in all expressions that appear in subscripts, section designators, or substring designators.

6. The name of a structure or a subobject designator may be the name in a name-value pair.

7. A name in an input record must not contain embedded blanks. A name in the name-value pair may be preceded or followed by one or more blanks.

8. If the processor supports uppercase and lowercase characters, a lowercase letter is the same as an uppercase letter and vice versa when used in the name of a name-value pair.

9. A namelist group object name or subobject designator may appear in more than one name-value pair in a sequence.

10. Recall that each name must not be the name of an array dummy argument with nonconstant bounds, an automatic object, a character variable with nonconstant length, a pointer, or a structure variable of a type with a component that is a pointer, or an allocatable array.

10.11.1.2 Values in Name-Value Pairs. The value in a name-value pair must be in a form acceptable for a format specification for the type of the name, except for restrictions noted below.

Null values have the forms:

1. no value between value separators

2. no value between the equal sign and the first value separator

3. the $r*$ form, followed by one or more blanks.

Null values do not change the value of the named item or its definition status. An entire complex constant may be null; neither of the parts can be. The end of a record following a value separator does not specify a null value.

Each value is a null value or one of these forms:

    c indicates a literal constant

$r*c$ indicates r successive literal constants c where r is a repeat factor and is a nonzero, unsigned integer literal constant

$r*$ indicates r successive null values

Rules and restrictions:

1. The form of a value must be acceptable to a format specification for an entity of the type of the corresponding list item, except as noted below; for example, the value c corresponding to a list item of type real can be of the forms:

    ```
    1
    1.0_2
    1.0E0
    ```

    but cannot be of the forms:

    ```
    (1.0,0.0)
    A0
    1.0EN-3
    2.2_QUAD
    ```

2. Blanks are never zero, and embedded blanks may not appear in numeric or logical constants. The exception is that a blank may appear as a character in a character constant, or preceding or following the real or imaginary parts of a complex constant.

3. The number of values following the equal sign must not be larger than the number of elements of the array when the name in the name-value pair is an array, or must not be larger than the ultimate number of components when the name in the name-value pair is that of a structure. Any array or component that is an array is filled in array element order.

    For the example:

    ```
    TYPE PERSON
          INTEGER LEN
          CHARACTER (10) NAME
    END TYPE PERSON
    TYPE (PERSON) PRESIDENT, VICE_PRES
    NAMELIST/PERSON_LIST/PRESIDENT, VICE_PRES
    READ (5, NML = PERSON_LIST)
    ```

the input record might be:

```
&PERSON_LIST PRESIDENT%LEN=4, PRESIDENT%NAME="BUSH",
             VICE_PRES%LEN=6, VICE_PRES%NAME="QUAYLE"/
```

4. If there are fewer values in the expanded sequence than array elements or structure components, null values are supplied for the missing values.

5. If a slash occurs in the input, it is as if null values were supplied for the remaining list items, and the namelist input data transfer is terminated. The remaining values after the slash within the current record are ignored.

6. An integer value is interpreted as if the data edit descriptor were Iw for a suitable value of w; for example, the integer value must not be a hexadecimal based digit string.

7. A complex value consists of a pair of parentheses surrounding the real and imaginary parts, separated by a comma. Blanks may appear before and after these values.

8. A logical value must not contain slashes, commas, or blanks as part of the optional characters after the .T, .F, T, or F.

9. A character literal constant may contain slashes, commas, or blanks as part of the constant. The character constant must have the same kind parameter value as the name in the name-value pair. On namelist input, the DELIM= specifier is ignored.

10.11.1.3 Blanks. Blanks are part of the value separator except for the use of blanks:

1. in a character constant

2. before or after the parts of a complex constant

3. before or after an equal sign, unless after the equal sign the blanks are followed immediately by a comma or slash

4. before the ampersand indicating the namelist group name and after the namelist group name

10.11.1.4 Use of Namelist Input. Namelist input requires the namelist group name, preceded by an ampersand, to be on the first nonblank record read by the namelist READ statement.

Example of namelist input:

```
REAL A (3), B (3)
CHARACTER (LEN = 3) CHAR
COMPLEX X
LOGICAL LL
NAMELIST / TOKEN / I, A, CHAR, X, LL, B
READ (*, NML = TOKEN)
```

If the input record is:

```
&TOKEN A(1:2) = 2*1.0   CHAR = "NOP" B = ,3.13,
       X = (2.4,0.0)   LL = T /
```

results of the READ statement are:

Name	Value
I	Unchanged
A (1)	1.0
A (2)	1.0
A (3)	Unchanged
B (1)	Unchanged
B (2)	3.13
B (3)	Unchanged
CHAR	"NOP"
X	(2.4, 0.0)
LL	True

10.11.2 Namelist Output

On namelist output, the processor may produce uppercase and lowercase letters if it supports them. Value separators may be blanks, commas, or a combination of blanks and commas. A new record may begin anywhere, except within a name or value, unless the value is a character constant or a complex constant; a record may begin anywhere within a character constant, or may begin before or after the comma, or left or right parenthesis of a complex constant. A blank may occur anywhere, except in a name or a noncharacter value. The only blanks that may occur in a character value are those that are in the character string; no additional blanks may be added.

10.11.2.1 Use of Namelist Output. A number of rules, similar to those for list-directed formatting, apply for namelist output.

Rules and restrictions:

1. Namelist output consists of a series of records. The first nonblank record begins with an ampersand, followed by the namelist group name, followed by a sequence of name-value pairs, one pair for each variable name in the namelist group object list of the NAMELIST statement and ends with a slash.

2. A logical value is either T or F.

3. An integer value is one that would be produced by an Iw edit descriptor using a suitable value of w.

4. For real output, the rules for list-directed output are followed using reasonable values for the w, e, and d that appear in real data edit descriptors and are appropriate for the output value.

5. Parentheses enclose the value of a complex constant, and the parts are separated by a comma. An end of record may occur after the comma only if the value is longer than the entire record. Blanks may be embedded after the comma and before the end of the record.

6. Character constants follow the rules for list-directed output.

7. Repeat factors of the form $r*c$ are allowed on output for successive identical values.

8. Null values are not output.

9. Each record begins with a blank for carriage control.

10. No values are written for zero-sized arrays or array sections.

11. For zero-length character strings, the name is written, followed by an equal sign, followed by a zero-length character string, and followed by a value separator or slash.

Example:

```
NAMELIST / CALC / DEPTH, PRESSURE
DIMENSION DEPTH (3), PRESSURE (3)
WRITE (6, NML = CALC)

&CALC DEPTH (1) = 1.2, DEPTH (2) = 2.2, DEPTH (3) = 3.2,
    PRESSURE = 3.0, 3.1, 3.2 /
```

10.11.2.2 DELIM= Specifier for Character Constants. The form of the output for character values depends on the value of the DELIM= specifier in the OPEN statement for that unit.

1. If there is no DELIM= specifier or the value of the DELIM= specifier is NONE:

    a. Character values are not delimited.

    b. Character values are not surrounded by value separators.

    c. Only one quote or apostrophe is needed for each quote or apostrophe in the string transferred.

    d. A blank is inserted in new records for a continued character value to allow for carriage control.

2. If the DELIM= specifier is QUOTE or APOSTROPHE:

    a. Character values are delimited with the specified delimiter, either quote or apostrophe.

    b. A character that is the same as the specified delimiter is doubled when written to the output record.

    c. A kind parameter followed by an underscore all preceding a delimited character value is allowed if applicable.

Example: for LEFT and RIGHT with values "SOUTH" and "NORTH", the program with the DELIM= specifier of QUOTE for unit 10:

```
CHARACTER (5) LEFT, RIGHT
NAMELIST / TURN / LEFT, RIGHT
WRITE (10, NML = TURN)
```

produces the output record:

```
&TURN  LEFT = "SOUTH",  RIGHT = "NORTH" /
```

Note that if the DELIM= specifier is NONE in an OPEN statement, namelist output may not be usable as namelist input when character values are transferred, because namelist input of character values requires delimited character values.

10.12 Summary

Explicit Formatting

Explicit formatting uses edit descriptors that are contained in a FORMAT statement or contained in a character expression used as a format specification.

```
      READ (5,200) DIFFICULTY
200 FORMAT (F5.1)
```

or

```
READ (5, "(F5.1)") DIFFICULTY
```

Format Specifications

Format specifications are lists of edit descriptors enclosed in parentheses. There are data edit descriptors, control edit descriptors, and character string edit descriptors. The format specification, including the parentheses and the edit descriptors, are placed in the input/output statement itself.

```
READ (5, "(2F10.1)") LATITUDE, LONGITUDE
```

The format specification also may appear in a FORMAT statement, for example, as in:

```
    WRITE (6, 500) A(1:2), B, TITLE
500 FORMAT (1H0, 2F10.3, E15.1, TR1, A10, 7HIN BOOK)
```

The FORMAT Statement

This statement contains edit descriptors corresponding to an input or output list. The statement labeled 100 in the example is the FORMAT statement. The list of data items is in the WRITE statement.

```
      WRITE (6, 100)  LATITUDE, LONGITUDE
100 FORMAT (1H0, F10.1, 7HDEGREES, F10.1, &
            7HDEGREES)
```

Data Edit Descriptors

There must be at least one data edit descriptor for each effective item in the expanded input/output item list. Edit descriptors can be reused as a result of reversion back to the previous parenthetical group. The descriptor must be appropriate for the type of the item in the list. The data edit descriptors are listed in Section 10.2.1.

```
      WRITE (6, 100)  (SEASONS (I), I = 1,4)
100 FORMAT (1H0, 4A20)
```

Control Edit Descriptors

Control edit descriptors do not correspond to items in the input/output list. They control the position, as well as the scale factor for real values, transferred to the output file (10.2.2). Examples are the tabbing facility (Tn, TLn, TRn, or nX edit descriptors), the sign interpretation (BN and BZ edit descriptors), and blank interpretation (SS and SP edit descriptors).

In the example:

```
100 FORMAT (TR4, F6.1, SS, 5F10.2)
```

TR4 and SS are control edit descriptors.

Character String Edit Descriptors

A string of characters may be transferred to an output device or file by using apostrophes or quotes to delimit the string or preceding the string by nH where n is the number of characters in the string. See Section 10.9.

```
100 FORMAT (1H , "KEEP", 'SAVE', 6HDELETE)
```

Implicit Formatting

List-directed and namelist data transfer in Fortran 90 are implicit input/output conversion and transfer operations. They do not require a format specification. Instead they behave as though appropriate edit descriptors were supplied.

List-Directed Formatting

Editing occurs based on the type of the list item. An asterisk as a format specifier signifies list-directed data transfer in an input/output statement.

```
READ (5, *)  TEMP, I, CHAR
```

Namelist Formatting

Editing occurs based on the type of the list item included in the namelist group. The namelist group name appears in the input/output statement after the NML= specifier in the input/output statement.

```
NAMELIST / BOOK_ONE / X, Y, Z
NAMELIST / TURN / TED, MARY, JOAN, BOB
WRITE (*, NML = BOOK_ONE)
READ (*, NML = TURN)
```

The input might be:

```
&TURN TED = 98, MARY = 80, JOAN = 99,
      BOB = 100  /
```

The output for the namelist group BOOK_ONE might be:

```
&BOOK_ONE  X = 2.4,  Y = 0.64E-07, Z = 6/
```

F9○

11

Program Units

There are several kinds of executable and nonexecutable program units in Fortran. Each of these program units provides unique functionality. The executable program units are the main program and procedure subprograms; the nonexecutable program units are block data units, which are now effectively obsolescent, and modules, which provide definitions used by other program units. This chapter describes each of these as well as the closely related concepts of host association and use association. Only one of these program units—the module—is new in Fortran 90, although internal procedures, which are procedure subprograms, represent a significant addition to the executable program units. A section on the major uses of modules is included.

A complete Fortran program might be compared to a complete meal. There are a number of parts to a meal—the main course, salad, dessert, etc. Each course has a specific part in the meal, just like each program unit (main program, subroutine, etc.) plays a specific part in a complete program. The parts work together, and in a well-planned program, as with a well-designed meal, the net result is something analogous to the whole being greater than the sum of its parts.

11.1 Overview

A Fortran program is a collection of program units. One and only one of these units must be a main program. In all but the simplest programs, the individual tasks are typically organized into a collection of function and subroutine subprograms and module program units. The program may be organized so that the main program drives (or manages) the collection of program units making up the executable program, but other program organizations can work as well.

Each program unit is an ordered set of constructs and statements. The heading statement identifies the kind of program unit it is, such as a subroutine or a module; it is optional in a main program. An ending statement marks the end of the unit. The five principal kinds of program units are:

> main program
> external function subprogram
> external subroutine subprogram
> module program unit
> block data program unit

As already noted, the module program unit is new in Fortran 90 and is intended to help the programmer organize elements of the program. A module itself is not executable but contains data declarations, derived-type definitions, procedure interface information, and subprogram definitions used by other program units. Block data program units are also nonexecutable and are used only to specify initial values for variables in named common blocks. With the addition of modules to Fortran, block data program units are no longer needed for new programs because modules can provide global data initializations.

Program execution begins with the first executable statement in the main program. Chapter 2 explains the high-level syntax of Fortran and how to put a Fortran program together. It is a good place to review the ways statements can be combined to form a program unit.

The Fortran program in Figure 11-1 is an example of a program that contains four program units: a main program, a module, and two subroutines.

Module STOCK_ROOM contains data and procedure information used by subroutines MECHANIC and PARTS. The main program DRIVER invokes the task represented by subroutine MECHANIC, but DRIVER does not itself need the information in STOCK_ROOM.

```
┌─────────────────────────────────────┐
│  PROGRAM DRIVER                      │
│                                      │
│     ...                              │
│                                      │
│     CALL MECHANIC (TUNEUP)           │
│                                      │
│     ...                              │
│                                      │
│  END PROGRAM DRIVER                  │
└─────────────────────────────────────┘
```

```
┌─────────────────────────────────────┐
│  MODULE STOCK_ROOM                   │
│                                      │
│     ...                              │
│                                      │
│  END MODULE STOCK_ROOM               │
└─────────────────────────────────────┘
```

```
┌─────────────────────────────────────┐
│  SUBROUTINE PARTS &                  │
│         (PART, MODEL, YEAR)          │
│  USE STOCK_ROOM                      │
│                                      │
│     ...                              │
│                                      │
│  END SUBROUTINE PARTS                │
└─────────────────────────────────────┘
```

```
┌─────────────────────────────────────┐
│  SUBROUTINE MECHANIC (SERVICE)       │
│  USE STOCK_ROOM                      │
│                                      │
│     ...                              │
│                                      │
│  CALL PARTS (PLUGS, "CRX", 1992)     │
│                                      │
│     ...                              │
│                                      │
│  END SUBROUTINE MECHANIC             │
└─────────────────────────────────────┘
```

Figure 11-1 Four program units

11.2 Main Program

The main program specifies the overall logic of a Fortran program and is where execution of the program begins. A main program is similar to the other program units (particularly external subprograms), and has three principal parts:

specification-part   defines the data environment of the program

execution-part   where execution begins, and program logic
                            is detailed

internal-procedure-part if the main program contains internal procedures

The principal ways of stopping the execution are:

1. executing a STOP statement anywhere in the program—that is, in any program unit making up the program

2. reaching the end of the main program

11.2.1 Main Program Organization

The form of a main program (R1101) is:

```
[ PROGRAM program-name ]
    [ specification-part ]
    [ execution-part ]
    [ internal-subprogram-part ]
END [ PROGRAM [ program-name ] ]
```

The simplest of all programs is:

```
END
```

Of course, this is not a very interesting program! A more interesting simple program is:

```
PROGRAM  SIMPLE
    PRINT*,  'Hello, world.'
END
```

The main program organization is essentially an extension of that for Fortran 77, with the optional internal subprogram part as the principal new feature.

Rules and restrictions:

1. The PROGRAM statement is optional in main programs (but a program heading is required for all other program units).

2. The program name on the END statement, if present, must be the same as the name on the PROGRAM statement and must be preceded by the keyword PROGRAM.

3. Main programs have no provisions for dummy arguments.

4. Main programs must not be referenced anywhere—that is, main programs must not be recursive (either directly or indirectly).

5. Main programs must not contain RETURN or ENTRY statements (but internal procedures in a main program can have RETURN statements).

11.2.2 The Specification Part

The principal purpose of the specification part is to describe the nature of the data environment of the program—the arrays, types and attributes of variables, initial values, etc. The complete list of specification part statements is given in Chapter 2. A summary of these statements that are valid in a main program is (R204):

ALLOCATABLE	PARAMETER
COMMON	POINTER
DATA	SAVE
DIMENSION	TARGET
EQUIVALENCE	USE
EXTERNAL	derived-type definition
FORMAT	interface block
IMPLICIT	statement function
INTRINSIC	type declaration statement
NAMELIST	

The statements in this list that are new in Fortran 90 are:

1. USE statements to provide access to entities packaged in modules

2. derived-type definitions and declarations

3. procedure interface blocks, which make procedure interfaces explicit

4. "entity-oriented" style of declarations, where all attributes of an entity may be declared in the same statement

5. NAMELIST statement, for namelist data transfer

6. ALLOCATABLE attribute and statement, for dynamic arrays

7. POINTER attribute and statement, to specify dynamic objects

8. TARGET attribute and statement, to specify a target for a pointer

Rules and restrictions:

1. OPTIONAL and INTENT attributes or statements do not appear in the specification part of a main program; they are applicable only to dummy arguments.

2. The accessibility specifications, PUBLIC and PRIVATE, do not appear in a main program; they are applicable only within modules.

3. Automatic objects (5.8) have no meaning in main programs.

4. The SAVE attribute or statement may appear, but it has no effect in a main program.

11.2.3 The Execution Part

The complete list of execution part statements (R208) is given in Chapter 2. A summary of these statements that are valid in a main program is:

ALLOCATE	IF construct
ASSIGN	INQUIRE
BACKSPACE	NULLIFY
CALL	OPEN
CASE construct	PAUSE
CLOSE	PRINT
CONTINUE	READ
CYCLE	REWIND
DATA	STOP
DEALLOCATE	WHERE
DO construct	WHERE construct
ENDFILE	WRITE
END	arithmetic IF
ENTRY	assigned GO TO
EXIT	assignment statement
FORMAT	computed GO TO
GO TO	pointer assignment statement
IF	

The statements that are new in Fortran 90 are:

1. the DO construct, including the EXIT and CYCLE statements

2. the SELECT CASE control construct, including the CASE statement

3. the WHERE statement and construct

4. the ALLOCATE and DEALLOCATE statements for dynamically allocatable objects

5. pointer statements, including pointer assignment and the NULLIFY statement

11.2.4 The Internal Subprogram Part

A set of internal procedures comprises the internal subprogram part. Internal procedures are described in the following section.

11.3 Internal Procedures

Internal procedures are very much like Fortran 77 external procedures, except that they are packaged inside main programs or other procedure subprograms. This makes their names local, rather than global like Fortran 77 external procedures, and an internal procedure can be referenced only within the program unit that contains its definition. Internal procedures may be recursive, must not contain ENTRY statements, and must not be passed as actual arguments. There are three principal reasons for providing internal procedures in Fortran 90:

1. to provide a procedure facility that has convenient access to the host environment (the host is the program unit containing the internal procedure)

2. to provide a multistatement form of the statement function functionality

3. to facilitate modular design and better software engineering

The use of internal procedures can increase programmer productivity and program reliability by making modular design easier. Safety and reliability are enhanced because interfaces are known explicitly. Internal procedures can be expanded easily inline and therefore can increase efficiency.

The form of the internal procedure part (R210) of the host is:

```
CONTAINS
    internal-subprogram
    [ internal-subprogram ] ...
```

where each internal procedure is either a function (R1215) or subroutine (R1219):

```
function-statement
    [ specification-part ]
    [ execution-part ]
END FUNCTION [ function-name ]

subroutine-statement
    [ specification-part ]
    [ execution-part ]
END SUBROUTINE [ subroutine-name ]
```

An example of an internal procedure is:

```
PROGRAM WEATHER
   . . .
CONTAINS
   FUNCTION STORM (CLOUD)
      . . .
   END FUNCTION STORM
END
```

Rules and restrictions:

1. Internal procedures must not themselves contain internal procedures—that is, internal procedures must not be "nested".

2. Internal procedures must not contain ENTRY statements.

3. Internal procedures must not contain PUBLIC or PRIVATE attributes or statements.

4. Internal procedures must not be passed as actual arguments.

5. The specification part of an internal procedure may contain the same statements as the specification part of a main program (11.2.2), plus the INTENT statement and the OPTIONAL statement.

6. The execution part of an internal procedure may contain the same statements as the execution part of a main program (11.2.3), plus the RETURN statement.

7. There must be at least one internal subprogram after the CONTAINS statement.

An internal procedure can be referenced in the execution part of its host (for example, the main program that contains it), and in the execution part of any internal procedure contained in the same host. This includes itself—that is, internal procedures may be referenced recursively, either directly or indirectly.

An internal procedure name is a local name in the host and therefore is subject to the rules governing such names. An internal procedure name:

- gives the internal procedure precedence over any external procedure or intrinsic procedure with the same name

- must be different from the names of other internal procedures in that host and different from the imported names of any module procedures either imported into the host or into the internal procedure itself

- must be different from any other local name in the host or itself, and from names made accessible by a USE statement

The rules governing other names that appear in the host and/or the internal procedure are described under the topic of "host association" (11.4). Because the host association rules apply to a module procedure and its host module, as well as to an internal procedure and its host (such as a main program), they are described separately in the following section.

11.4 Host Association

The program unit containing an internal procedure is called the **host** of the internal procedure. The program unit (which must be a module) containing a module procedure is called the **host** of the module procedure. An important property of internal and module procedures is that the data environment of the host is available to the procedure (see Figure 11-2). When data in the host are available within the contained procedure, they are said to be accessible by **host association**. Because the internal (or module) procedure also has a local data environment, rules are needed to determine whether a given reference inside that procedure identifies a host entity or one local to the procedure.

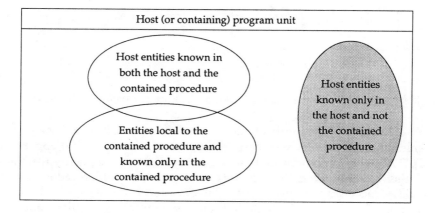

Figure 11-2 Host association

In a language in which the attributes of all entities must be declared explicitly, this is not a problem. In such languages, local declarations typically override host declarations, and any host declarations not over-ridden are available in the contained procedure. Fundamentally these are the rules used in Fortran 90, and this clean situation can be simulated by using IMPLICIT NONE in both the host and the contained procedure; IMPLICIT NONE forces explicit declaration of all entities.

However, Fortran allows implicit declarations—use of an entity name in the execution part without an explicit declaration of that name in the specification part—and that complicates the situation. For example, suppose the variable TOTAL is referenced in an internal procedure, and neither the internal procedure nor its host explicitly declares TOTAL. Is TOTAL a host or local entity? Or worse, suppose that TOTAL is used in two internal procedures in the same host, without declaration anywhere. Are they (it) the same TOTAL? The possibilities are shown in Figure 11-3.

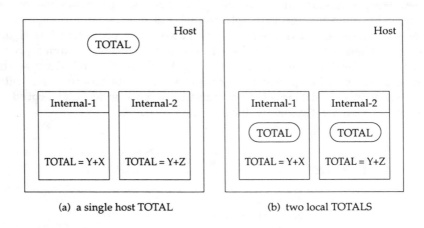

(a) a single host TOTAL   (b) two local TOTALS

Figure 11-3 Is there one TOTAL in the host or two local TOTALs?

The answer to both of these questions is case (b) in Figure 11-3, unless TOTAL is also referenced in the host, in which case (a) applies. If TOTAL is referenced in the host, it becomes declared implicitly there and is therefore a host entity. In this case, any internal procedure use of TOTAL accesses the host entity. The situation is the same (TOTAL is a host entity) if it is declared but not referenced in the host and not declared in the internal procedure. Of course, if TOTAL is declared in the internal procedure, then case (b) applies (TOTAL is local) regardless of whether TOTAL is declared or referenced in the host.

Implicit declarations are governed by the implicit typing rules and the use of the IMPLICIT statement. The detailed rules governing implicit typing in hosts and contained procedures are given in Section 5.2, and the detailed rules governing host association are given in Section 14.3.1.3. These rules are combined and summarized below.

Rules and restrictions:

1. A name (of a variable or other identifiable object) is local if it is declared explicitly in the contained procedure, regardless of any declarations in the host. A dummy argument in a contained procedure is an explicit local declaration, even though the name may be implicitly typed. (A dummy argument, if not explicitly typed, is typed according to the implicit typing rules of the contained procedure.)

2. An entity not declared explicitly in a contained procedure is nevertheless local (via implicit declaration) if and only if it is neither explicitly nor implicitly declared in the host.

3. If it is not local based on rules 1 and 2 above, the entity is host associated.

4. The default implicit rules (the implicit typing rules in the absence of IMPLICIT statements) in a contained procedure are the implicit typing rules of the host, as established by the default implicit rules in the host and modified by any IMPLICIT statements in the host.

5. IMPLICIT statements in the contained procedure, if any, modify the implicit typing rules inherited from the host. Note that these modified rules apply to implicitly typed dummy arguments of the contained procedure.

A summary of the implicit typing rules is:

$$\text{host implicit typing rules} \ = \ \text{host default implicit rules} \\ + \ \text{host IMPLICIT statements}$$

$$\text{contained procedure typing rules} \ = \ \text{host implicit typing rules} \\ + \ \text{contained procedure} \\ \text{IMPLICIT statements}$$

In the expression $X = A+B+P+Q+Y$ in the following example, the operands in the expression are from different places as determined from the above rules (see Figure 11-4).

```
PROGRAM HOST
   USE GLOBAL_DATA      ! accesses integer X and real Y
   IMPLICIT LOGICAL (E-J)
   ! implicit typing: A-D real
   !                  E-J logical
   !                  K-N integer
   !                  O-Z real
   REAL  A, B
     . . .
        READ *,  P       ! this reference declares P
                         ! implicitly in host
     . . .
   CALL CALC(Z)          ! This reference implicitly
     . . .               ! declares Z
CONTAINS
     . . .
   ! X declared explicitly in internal procedure CALC
   SUBROUTINE CALC (X)
      IMPLICIT REAL (G-I)
      ! implicit typing: A-D real
      !                  E-F logical
      !                  G-I real
      !                    J logical
      !                  K-N integer
      !                  O-Z real
      REAL  B
         . . .
         . . .
      X = A + B + P + Q + Y
      ! in subroutine CALC (all are type real):
      !    X is local (dummy argument)
      !    A is host associated
      !    B is local (explicitly declared)
      !    P is host associated
      !    Q is local (implicitly declared)
      !    Y is use associated (from the module)
         . . .
   END SUBROUTINE CALC
     . . .
END PROGRAM HOST
```

A particularly interesting case of the host associated implicit rules is when the host has IMPLICIT NONE. With IMPLICIT NONE, no other

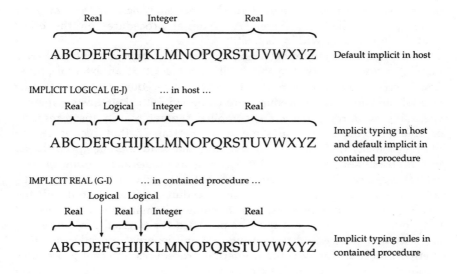

Figure 11-4 How the mapping of implicit typing progresses from host to contained procedure

implicit statements are allowed in that scoping unit, and explicit typing is required for all data objects in the host. IMPLICIT NONE is therefore the default in the contained procedure, although this may be modified by IMPLICIT statements in the contained procedure. This can result in some of the letters having implicit types in the contained procedure and some not. For example, suppose that the host has IMPLICIT NONE and the contained procedure has the following IMPLICIT statements:

```
IMPLICIT COMPLEX ( C,Z )
IMPLICIT LOGICAL ( J-L )
```

Then data objects in the contained procedure with names starting with C or Z may be declared implicitly of type complex; data objects with names starting with J, K, or L may be declared implicitly of type logical. IMPLICIT NONE continues to apply to letters A–B, D–I, and M–Y, and data object names beginning with these letters must be explicitly declared.

11.5 External Subprograms

External subprograms are global to the Fortran program; they may be referenced or called anywhere. An internal procedure, on the other hand, is known only within its host.

The major difference between external procedures and internal (and module) procedures is not syntactic; it is the fact that an external procedure interface is not known at the point of procedure reference. Also, internal (and module) procedures are compiled with their hosts, whereas external procedures usually are compiled separately. In these respects external procedures are the same as in Fortran 77 (but see procedure interface blocks in Chapter 12). For internal (and module) procedures, on the other hand, interface information is available at the point of procedure reference. This is a very significant difference and a major practical advantage of internal and module procedures; Section 12.6 details the benefits of explicit interfaces, which come automatically with internal and module procedures, but must be provided for external procedures.

Another difference between internal and external procedures is that external procedures may contain internal procedures; internal procedures cannot. There is no compelling reason for this difference, and a common implementation extension is likely to allow nesting of internal procedures.

The organization of external subprograms is very much like that of main programs. External subprograms (R203) come in two flavors, functions (R1215) and subroutines (R1219):

```
function-statement
    [ specification-part ]
    [ execution-part ]
    [ internal-subprogram-part ]
END [ FUNCTION [ function-name ] ]

subroutine-statement
    [ specification-part ]
    [ execution-part ]
    [ internal-subprogram-part ]
END [ FUNCTION [ function-name ] ]
```

Examples of external procedures are:

```
FUNCTION FOOTBALL (GAME)
   INTEGER FOOTBALL
   FOOTBALL = N_PLAYERS
      . . .
END FUNCTION FOOTBALL

SUBROUTINE SATURDAY (SEVEN)
   X = . . .
END
```

Rules and restrictions:

1. Unlike the main program, the program unit heading (FUNCTION or SUBROUTINE statement) is required in an external subprogram.

2. The procedure name on the END statement, if present, must be the same as that in the heading statement.

3. OPTIONAL and INTENT attributes and statements for dummy arguments are allowed in the specification part of an external subprogram, but only for dummy arguments specified in the heading statement.

4. The specification and execution parts of an external subprogram may contain ENTRY statements and the execution part may contain RETURN statements.

5. External subprograms must not contain PUBLIC or PRIVATE attributes or statements.

6. External procedures may be directly or indirectly recursive, in which case the RECURSIVE keyword is required on the heading statement.

7. An external subprogram is the host to any internal procedures defined within it.

8. An external procedure name may be used as an actual argument in a procedure reference, corresponding to a dummy procedure argument in the procedure referenced.

Procedures, including internal, external, and module procedures, are described in detail in Chapter 12.

11.6 Modules

The module program unit is a new feature in Fortran 90; it offers a wealth of versatility in packaging data specifications and procedures in one place for use in any computational task in the program.

This functionality was sorely needed in Fortran 77, primarily for making information available to more than one program unit. The standard did not provide it, however, and to prevent errors in the course of duplicating common block code, most implementations were extended with an INCLUDE facility. Because this was such a common extension, the INCLUDE line was added to Fortran 90 (see Section 3.5). It operates as if the included lines of text were copied into a program unit, which then become part of the local program unit; included material is treated as if it had been part of the program unit in the first place.

There is an even greater need in Fortran 90 for a way to locate data "centrally", available to all program units. The module program unit provides this capability. As such, it provides all of the data configuration and declaration functionality of the INCLUDE line and a lot more, using syntax that is clean and simple.

Module program units solve the following specific problems for Fortran:

1. The reliability problems associated with the use of common blocks for global data are legion, and therefore a "name association" rather than "storage association" form of global data is needed.

2. For similar reliability reasons, there must be a way of defining derived types in a central location.

3. Certain situations in Fortran 90 require explicit procedure interfaces (see Section 12.6); thus a way to centrally provide such definitions is needed.

4. "Information hiding" is important for improving program reliability and therefore Fortran 90 needs better packaging and information hiding capabilities than Fortran 77.

The major uses of modules are summarized in Section 11.6.5.

Anything required by more than one program unit may be packaged in modules and made available where needed. A module is not itself executable, though the procedures it contains can be individually referenced in the execution part of other program units. The number of modules is not restricted, and a module may use any number of other modules as long as the access path does not lead back to itself. Modules, therefore, are powerful tools for managing program organization and simplifying program design.

11.6.1 Module Organization

The form of a module (R1104) is:

```
MODULE module-name
    [ specification-part ]
    [ module-subprogram-part ]
END [ MODULE [ module-name ] ]
```

The module name on the END statement, if present, must be the same as on the MODULE statement.

11.6.2 The Specification Part

The form of the specification part (R204) of a module is similar to that for other program units. The statements it may contain are:

ALLOCATABLE	POINTER
COMMON	PRIVATE
DATA	PUBLIC
DIMENSION	SAVE
EQUIVALENCE	TARGET
EXTERNAL	USE
IMPLICIT	derived-type definition
INTRINSIC	interface block
NAMELIST	type declaration statement
PARAMETER	

The following rules and restrictions apply to the specification part of a module; the specification parts of the module procedures, however, have the same rules as those for external procedures.

Rules and restrictions:

1. OPTIONAL or INTENT attributes or statements are not allowed.

2. ENTRY statements are not allowed.

3. FORMAT statements are not allowed.

4. Automatic objects are not allowed.

5. Statement function statements are not allowed.

6. PUBLIC and PRIVATE attributes and statements are allowed.

The SAVE attribute and statement may be used in the specification part of a module to ensure that module data object values remain intact. Without SAVE, module data objects remain defined as long as any program unit using the module has initiated, but not yet completed, execution. However, when all such program units become inactive, any data objects in the module not having the SAVE attribute become undefined. SAVE can be used to specify that module objects continue to be defined under these conditions.

The following is an example of a simple module for providing global data:

```
MODULE T_DATA
   INTEGER  ::  A, KA
   REAL     ::  X = 7.14
   REAL     ::  Y (10,10), Z (20,20)
END MODULE T_DATA


! This module declares three scalar variables (A, KA, and X)
! and two arrays (Y and Z). X is given an initial value.
! These five variables can be considered to be "global"
! variables that can selectively be made available to
! other program units.

! The USE statement makes A, KA, X, Y, and Z
! available to subroutine TASK_2

SUBROUTINE TASK_2
   USE T_DATA
   . . .
END SUBROUTINE TASK_2
```

11.6.3 The Module Subprogram Part

The module subprogram part is similar to the internal procedure part of main programs and external subprograms. It is a collection of procedures local to the module and sharing its data environment via host association. The two principal differences between module subprograms and internal subprograms are that:

1. The organization, rules, and restrictions of module procedures are those of external procedures rather than internal procedures. For example, module procedures may contain internal procedures.

2. Module procedures are not strictly local to the host module, nor are they global to the program. Only program units using the module can access the module's procedures not specified to be PRIVATE.

The form of the module subprogram part (R212) is:

```
CONTAINS
    module-subprogram
    [ module-subprogram ] ...
```

where each module subprogram is a function (R1215) or subroutine (R1219):

```
function-statement
    [ specification-part ]
    [ execution-part ]
    [ internal-subprogram-part ]
END FUNCTION [function-name ]

subroutine-statement
    [ specification-part ]
    [ execution-part ]
    [ internal-subprogram-part ]
END SUBROUTINE [subroutine-name ]
```

An example of a module procedure is:

```
MODULE INTERNAL
    . . .
CONTAINS
    FUNCTION SET_INTERNAL (KEY)
        . . .
    END FUNCTION
END
```

The rules for host association and implicit typing in a module procedure are the same as described for internal procedures in Section 11.4. A module procedure acquires access to entities in its host module via host association, but not to entities in a program unit that uses the module. There must be at least one internal subprogram after the CONTAINS statement.

11.6.4 Using Modules

A program unit may use the specifications and definitions in a module by referencing (using) the module. This is accomplished with a USE statement in the program unit requiring access to the specifications and definitions of that module. Such access causes an association between named objects in the module and the using program unit and is called **use association**. USE statements immediately follow the program unit heading and there is no restriction on their number.

Each entity in a module has the PUBLIC or PRIVATE attribute, which determines the accessibility of that entity in a program unit using the module. A PRIVATE entity is not accessible (that is, is hidden) from program units using the module. A PUBLIC entity is accessible, although its accessibility may be further limited by the USE statement itself. Figure 11-5 depicts these phenomena.

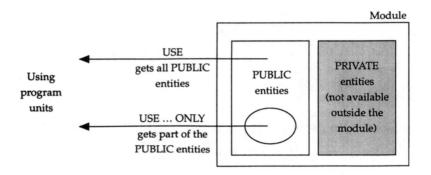

Figure 11-5 Public and private entities in a module

11.6.4.1 Accessing All Public Entities in a Module. The simplest form of the USE statement (R1107) gives the program unit access to all public entities in the module.

    USE module-name

The USE statement with the rename option

    USE module-name , rename-list

allows any of the public entities in the module to be renamed to avoid name conflicts or to blend with the readability flavor in the using program unit. Each item in the rename list (R1108) has the form:

    local-name => module-entity-name

Examples:

```
USE FOURIER
USE S_LIB,  PRESSURE => X_PRES
```

With both USE statements in this example, all public entities in the respective modules are made accessible. In the case of FOURIER, the names are those specified in the module. In the case of S_LIB, the entity named X_PRES is renamed PRESSURE in the program unit using the module. The other entities accessed from S_LIB have the same name in the using program unit as in the module. Note the similarity between the rename syntax and pointer assignment (the only difference is that a rename is part of a statement, not a complete statement itself); this is because the local name is conceptually similar to a local pointer to the module entity.

11.6.4.2 Accessing Only Part of the Public Entities. Restricting the entities accessed from a module is accomplished with the ONLY form of the USE statement (R1107), which is:

    USE module-name   , ONLY :   access-list

In this case the using program unit has access only to those entities explicitly identified in the ONLY clause of the USE statement. All items in this list must identify public entities in the module. As with the unrestricted form of the USE statement, accessed entities may be renamed for local purposes. The form of each item in the access list (R1109) is:

    [local-name   =>] module-entity-name

The local name, if present, specifies the name of the module entity in the using program unit.

Examples:

    USE MTD, ONLY : X, Y
    USE MONTHS, &
         ONLY : JANUARY => JAN, MAY, JUNE => JUN

In the case of MTD, only X and Y are accessed from the module, with no renaming. In the case of MONTHS, only JAN, MAY, and JUN are accessed from the module. JAN is renamed JANUARY and JUN is renamed JUNE.

11.6.4.3 Entities Accessible from a Module. The following may be defined, declared, or specified in a module, and may be public. They are accessed via the USE statement by other program units, and any public entity may be renamed in the using program unit.

1. declared variables

2. named constants

3. derived-type definitions

4. procedure interfaces

5. module procedures

6. generic identifiers

7. namelist groups

Note that this list does not contain the implicit type rules of the module; these are not accessible via a USE statement.

Common blocks may be placed in modules, and their names are always global. Therefore, there is no need to access common block names via a USE statement. However, the variables in the common blocks may be renamed using the ONLY option in a USE statement.

The default accessibility for all entities in a module is PUBLIC unless this default has been changed by a PRIVATE statement with an empty entity list. An entity may be specified to be PRIVATE in a PRIVATE statement or in a type declaration statement that contains the PRIVATE attribute. If the default has been turned to PRIVATE, the entity may be made PUBLIC by its appearance in a PUBLIC statement or in a type declaration that contains the PUBLIC attribute.

In any event, each named entity in a module is classified as either public or private. Regardless of this classification, all module entities may be used freely within the module, including within module procedures in the module; within a module procedure a module entity is governed only by the rules of host association. Outside the module, however, only the public entities are accessible (via the USE statement). Figure 11-6 illustrates these rules.

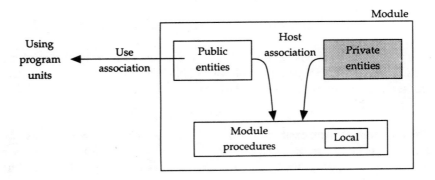

Figure 11-6 Use of public and private module entities

A module limits access to just those entities of the module designed for use outside the module. Entities needed only within the module may be PRIVATE and thus hidden. This is a valuable form of information hiding.

PUBLIC and PRIVATE attributes are prescribed by the module writer, and the module user has no say in these decisions. However, both the ONLY option on the USE statement and the renaming provisions give the module user additional forms of information hiding and environment tailoring. Between PUBLIC and PRIVATE accessibility and the USE...ONLY feature, the module facilities provide considerable flexibility for program design that effectively employs information hiding.

11.6.4.4 Name Conflicts When Using Modules.
There are two ways in which name conflicts can occur when using modules:

1. A public entity in a module may have the same name as a local entity in the using program.

2. Two modules being used may each have a public entity with the same name.

Such a name conflict is allowed if and only if that name is never referenced in the using program. If a name is to be referenced in the using program, potential conflicts involving that name must be prevented via the rename or ONLY facilities of the USE statement. This is the case even if the using program is another module.

For example:

```
MODULE BLUE
    INTEGER  A, B, C
END MODULE BLUE

MODULE GREEN
    USE BLUE, ONLY : AX => A
    REAL  B, C
END MODULE GREEN

                          ! in program RED:
                          ! integer A is accessed as AX or A
                          ! integer B is accessed as B
                          !    real B is accessed as BX
                          ! neither C is accessible, because
                          !    there is a name conflict
PROGRAM RED
    USE BLUE              ! accesses A, B, and C
    USE GREEN, BX => B    ! accesses A as AX, B as BX, and C
      . . .
END
```

11.6.4.5 Use Association. The USE statement gives a program unit access to other entities not defined or specified locally within the using program. As mentioned earlier, the association between a module entity and a local entity in the using program unit is termed **use association**. Host association is analogous, but host association applies only to a module and its module procedures and to internal procedures and their hosts. There are many similarities between use association and host association. Their rules, however, are different in the following two ways.

First, it is not desirable that a module's implicit typing rules form the default implicit rules for a using program unit, especially because a program unit may use any number of modules. Therefore, implicit rules do not "flow into" a using program unit from a module like they do in host association. Second, respecification of a name accessed from a module is disallowed. This is motivated by the fact that the USE...ONLY provision, which is not feasible with host association, is a safer approach to excluding entities from the local environment than by use of an overriding respecification. Thus, in summary, the two ways that use association differs from host association are:

1. The implicit typing rules of a module have no effect on a using program unit's environment.

2. Entities accessed via a USE statement must not be respecified locally.

The only exception to the second rule is that if the using program unit is another module, then the using module may specify an entity from the used module to be PRIVATE in the using module, rather than maintaining public accessibility. This is perhaps best illustrated with an example: program units using module M2, defined as follows, may access X but not Y, even though Y is a public entity of M1.

```
MODULE M2
   USE M1, ONLY:  X, Y
   PRIVATE  Y
      . . .
END MODULE M2
```

The prohibition on respecifying entities accessed via use association includes the use of module data objects in locally specified COMMON and EQUIVALENCE specifications.

While a name accessed from a module must not be respecified locally, the same name can be imported from another module under either of the following conditions:

1. both accesses are to the same entity (for example, if a program unit uses both M1 and M2 in the above example, both give access to the same X; this is allowed)

2. the accesses are to different entities, but the using program unit makes no reference to that name

11.6.5 Typical Applications of Modules

A number of different Fortran applications are easier to write and understand using modules. Modules provide a way of packaging:

1. global data, including data structures and common blocks

2. user-defined operators

3. software libraries

4. data abstraction

These uses for modules are summarized in the following sections.

11.6.5.1 Global Data. A module provides an easy way of making type definitions and data declarations global in a program. Notice that COMMON is not used in the example below, although it could have been. Data in a module does not have an implied storage association or an assumption of any form of sequence or any order of appearance, unless it is a sequence structure or in a common block. Global data in a module may be of any type or combination of types.

Example:

```
MODULE MODELS
    COMPLEX           :: GTX (100, 6)
    REAL              :: X (100)
    REAL, ALLOCATABLE :: Y (:), Z (:, :)
    INTEGER           CRX, GT, MR2
END MODULE
```

There are alternative ways to "use" this module. For example,

```
USE MODELS
```

makes all the data (and their attributes) of the module available using it.

```
USE MODELS, ONLY : X, Y
```

makes only the data named X and Y and their attributes available to the program using the module.

```
USE MODELS, T => Z
```

makes the data object named Z available, but it is renamed to T for that particular application. In addition, it makes the other public entities of the module MODELS available with the same names they have in the module.

11.6.5.2 COMMON Blocks in a Module. One way of packaging common blocks is by putting them in a module. This makes migration of Fortran 77 programs that use common blocks easier.

For example:

```
MODULE LATITUDE
   COMMON . . .
   COMMON . . .
   COMMON / BLOCK1 / . . .
END MODULE
   . . .
PROGRAM NAVIGATE
USE LATITUDE
   . . .
END
```

The USE statement in this example makes all of the variables in the common blocks in the module available to the program NAVIGATE. These common blocks may be made available to other program units in the same way. This technique minimizes errors in transcription and omission when the module LATITUDE is used in many routines in the program.

11.6.5.3 Global User-Defined Types. A derived type defined in a module is a user-defined type that can be made accessible to other program units. The same type definition can be referenced via a USE statement by more than one program unit.

Example:

```
MODULE NEW_TYPE
   TYPE TAX_PAYER
      INTEGER SSN
      CHARACTER(20) NAME
   END TYPE TAX_PAYER
END MODULE NEW_TYPE
```

The module NEW_TYPE contains the definition of a new type called TAX_PAYER. Procedures using the module NEW_TYPE may declare objects of type TAX_PAYER.

11.6.5.4 Operator Extensions. An interface block may declare new operators or give additional meanings to the intrinsic ones, such as +, .EQ., .OR., and //. The assignment symbol = also may be given additional meanings and may be redefined for derived-type intrinsic assignment. (Derived-type assignment is the only instance of intrinsic operators or assignment that can be redefined.) These extensions require that the OPERATOR or ASSIGNMENT options be on the interface block, the details of which appear in Section 12.6. A simple example of an OPERATOR interface for matrix inversion requires a function and an interface block defining the new operator. In the following example, which normally (but not necessarily) would be in a module, the function INVERSE defines the desired operation, and the operator .INVERSE. may be used in an expression to reference the function.

```
INTERFACE OPERATOR (.INVERSE.)
   FUNCTION INVERSE (MATRIX_1)

      TYPE (MATRIX), INTENT (IN) :: MATRIX_1
      TYPE (MATRIX) :: INVERSE

   END FUNCTION INVERSE
END INTERFACE
```

An example of its use might be (assuming + also has been extended to add a real value and a MATRIX):

```
1.0 + (.INVERSE. A)
```

11.6.5.5 Data Abstraction. Data type definitions and operations may be packaged together in a module. Program units using this module will have the convenience of a new data type specific to a particular application. A simple example might be:

```
MODULE POLAR_COORDINATES

    TYPE POLAR
       PRIVATE
       REAL RHO, THETA
    END TYPE POLAR

    INTERFACE OPERATOR (*)
       MODULE PROCEDURE POLAR_MULT
    END INTERFACE

CONTAINS
    FUNCTION POLAR_MULT (P1, P2)
       TYPE (POLAR) P1, P2, POLAR_MULT
       POLAR_MULT = &
               POLAR (P1 % RHO   * P2 % RHO,  &
                      P1 % THETA + P2 % THETA)
    END FUNCTION POLAR_MULT
       . . .
END MODULE POLAR_COORDINATES
```

In the function POLAR_MULT, the structure constructor POLAR computes a value that represents the result of multiplication of two arguments in polar coordinates. Any program unit using the module POLAR_COORDINATES has access to both the type POLAR and the extended intrinsic operator * for polar multiplication.

11.6.5.6 Procedure Libraries. A module may contain a collection of interface blocks for related procedures. Argument keywords, as well as optional arguments, may be used to differentiate various applications using these procedures.

```
MODULE ENG_LIBRARY
    INTERFACE
       FUNCTION FOURIER (X, Y)
            . . .
       END
```

```
      SUBROUTINE INPUT (A, B, C, L)
         OPTIONAL C
         . . .
      END SUBROUTINE INPUT
   END INTERFACE
END MODULE ENG_LIBRARY
```

An input routine may be called using optional or keyword arguments.

```
CALL INPUT (AXX, L = LXX, B = BXX)
```

A collection of related procedures that need to access the same type definitions and data declarations may be placed in a module.

```
MODULE BOOKKEEPING
   TYPE, PRIVATE :: ID_DATA
      INTEGER ID_NUMBER
      CHARACTER (20) NAME, ADDRESS (3)
      REAL BALANCE_OR_SALARY
   END TYPE ID_DATA
   REAL, PRIVATE :: GROSS_INCOME, EXPENSES, &
                    PROFIT, LOSS
   INTEGER, PARAMETER :: NUM_CUST = 1000, &
                         NUM_SUPP = 100, &
                         NUM_EMP  = 10
CONTAINS
   SUBROUTINE ACCTS_RECEIVABLE (CUST_ID, AMOUNT)
      . . .
   END SUBROUTINE ACCTS_RECEIVABLE
   SUBROUTINE ACCTS_PAYABLE (CUST_ID, AMOUNT)
      . . .
   END SUBROUTINE ACCTS_PAYABLE
   SUBROUTINE PAYROLL (EMP_ID, AMOUNT)
      . . .
   END SUBROUTINE PAYROLL
   FUNCTION BOTTOM_LINE (AMOUNT)
      . . .
   END FUNCTION BOTTOM_LINE
END MODULE
```

11.6.6 Independent Compilation

Independent compilation is the practice of compiling or processing sub-programs in a separate run on the computer and then using the compiled program unit in a number of applications without the inconvenience or cost of recompiling that unit. In Fortran 66 and 77, each program unit was entirely independent of other units. Thus, each unit could be compiled independently and used in any other program regardless of its source. This was a convenient way of giving routines to others without providing the Fortran source statements. It also saved compilation costs.

The INCLUDE facility in Fortran 90 was added to the language because the INCLUDE line is a popular extension in most implementations of Fortran 77. The INCLUDE facility behaves as if the source text from another file were inserted in place of the INCLUDE line prior to compilation. This departs from pure independent compilation, because the program unit using the INCLUDE line is now dependent on material from other places. The use of modules is a departure from pure independent compilation in this same sense, in that a program unit being compiled is dependent upon information from other sources.

If the program unit contains a reference to a module, the module must be available (in some form) when that program unit is compiled. However, if no modules or INCLUDE lines are used, compilation of a program unit is completely independent of other sources of information. With regard to independent compilation, while there are similarities between the use of INCLUDE and modules, there also could be noticeable differences in any given implementation.

There are a number of ways modules can be implemented, and different implementations may choose different approaches. Because a module is a complete program unit, it may itself be compiled, independent of any using program units. An advantage is that the module contents may be put into a form that can be incorporated much more efficiently during compilation of using program units. Some implementations may require compilation of modules prior to compilation of any program units that use the modules.

Although there are frequently some dependencies using modules, it is often possible to put together a self-contained "package" consisting of certain modules and the program units that use them. This package is independent of other packages that might be part of the Fortran program; packages may be used in the same way as independent compilation has been used in the past. For example, such a module package may be compiled independently of the main program and external procedures, both of which may be compiled independently of the module package as long as these external procedures do not use the module package. In cases where program units use the module package, such program units are probably required to be compiled after compilation of the module package.

11.7 Block Data Program Units

A block data program unit initializes data values in a named common block. The block data program unit contains data specifications and initial data values. There are no executable statements in a block data program unit and the block data program unit is referenced only in EXTERNAL statements in other program units; its only purpose is to initialize data. The module facility is a natural extension to the very limited Fortran 77 block data facility, making block data program units superfluous.

The form of the block data program unit (R1110) is:

```
BLOCK DATA [ block-data-name ]
    [ specification-part ]
END [ BLOCK DATA [ block-data-name ] ]
```

An example of a block data program unit is:

```
BLOCK DATA SUMMER
    COMMON / BLOCK_2 / X, Y
    DATA X / 1.0 /,  Y / 0.0 /
END BLOCK DATA SUMMER
```

The name SUMMER appears on the BLOCK DATA statement and the END statement. X and Y are initialized in a DATA statement; both variables are in named common block BLOCK_2.

Rules and restrictions:

1. There may be only one block data program unit without a name.

2. The block data name on the END statement, if present, must be the same as on the BLOCK DATA statement.

3. The specification part may contain any of the following statements or attributes. Other statements are prohibited.

COMMON	POINTER
DATA	SAVE
DIMENSION	TARGET
EQUIVALENCE	USE
IMPLICIT	derived-type definition
INTRINSIC	type declaration
PARAMETER	

A USE statement in a block data program unit may give access, in essence, to only named constants, because use of any other accessible entity in specification statements is disallowed.

4. The block data program unit may initialize more than one named common block.

5. It is not necessary to initialize an entire common block.

6. A common block must be completely specified, if any object in it is initialized.

7. A given named common block may appear in only one block data program unit.

11.8 Summary

A Fortran Program

A Fortran program contains one or more program units. The program must contain one and only one main program unit. Other units may be subroutines, functions, modules, and block data units in any combination. The following example of a program consists of a main program and an external function ALLIGATOR.

```
PROGRAM MAINSAIL
   . . .
END


FUNCTION ALLIGATOR (X)
   . . .
END
```

A Main Program

A main program of a Fortran program contains the first statement that is executed. The main program may be used as the overall driver program for a collection of procedures. A Fortran program must contain a main program; other procedures are optional.

```
PROGRAM SHUTTLE_SIMULATION
   . . .               ! Specification statements
   TEST_NUMBER = 1  ! Executable statement or construct
   IF (A_OK) CALL BLAST_OFF (TEST_NUMBER)
   . . .
END PROGRAM SHUTTLE_SIMULATION
```

Procedures

A procedure is either a function or subroutine. It may be external (a stand-alone program unit) or internal to another program unit. A procedure may be an external procedure that is defined by a separate program unit or by means other than Fortran, an internal procedure that is defined within another executable program unit, a module procedure that is defined in a module program unit, a procedure that is intrinsic or supplied by the processor, or a statement function.

External Procedures

An external procedure is a function or subroutine that is defined in a separate program unit. External procedures are global and may be used by any other program unit in the executing program. An external procedure must not be used as a "main program"; that is, it must not contain the first executable statement of a Fortran program. External procedures may contain internal procedures. External procedures that are not written in Fortran are permitted. External procedures may be compiled independently. The following program consists of a main program BLUE_SKY and an external function POLLUTION.

```
PROGRAM BLUE_SKY
   . . .
   OZONE_LEVEL = POLLUTION (TODAY)
   . . .
END PROGRAM BLUE_SKY

FUNCTION POLLUTION (DAY)
   . . .
END FUNCTION POLLUTION
```

Internal Procedures

An internal procedure is local to the host program unit and is contained within it. Internal procedures may be functions or subroutines.

Restrictions are that there must be no ENTRY statements in an internal procedure, and an internal procedure must not be used as an actual argument corresponding to a dummy procedure. In a program unit, internal procedures appear after the other source text at the end following a "marker" statement called the CONTAINS statement.

```
PROGRAM BLUE_SKY
    . . .
    OZONE_LEVEL = POLLUTION (TODAY)
    . . .
CONTAINS
    FUNCTION POLLUTION (DAY)
    . . .
    END FUNCTION POLLUTION
END PROGRAM BLUE_SKY
```

Module Procedures

A module procedure is defined within a module. That is, a module procedure is defined by a module subprogram. A module subprogram is similar to an external subprogram and is contained within a module program unit. A module subprogram has access to module entities via host association.

Host Association

A program unit that contains an internal procedure or a module procedure is called a **host**. A contained procedure has access to the host environment. The association between the host entities and internal or module procedure entities is called **host association**. The rules of host association determine whether an object is available only in the host, only in the contained procedures, or both.

Modules

A module is a nonexecutable program unit used to collect related common blocks, specification statements, derived-type definitions, operator definitions, procedure interfaces, and procedure definitions. A module has some similarity to a block data program unit, but has far greater capabilities, for example, for packaging data types along with new operator definitions for that type. Main programs and other program units may access the module with a USE statement. The contents of a module . are not repeated in other program units that use it.

```
PROGRAM HEAVY_METAL
   USE GOLD
   . . .

END PROGRAM HEAVY_METAL

MODULE GOLD
      . . .          ! Specifications
      . . .          ! Module procedures
END MODULE GOLD
```

To capture all the specifications and definitions in a module, a program unit must "use" the module via a USE statement.

```
USE GOLD
```

To capture only some of the public entities in a module, a program unit must restrict the access of entities in the USE statement.

```
USE GOLD, ONLY : A, B
```

To use a different name for a module variable, the new name is declared in the USE statement.

```
USE GOLD : ATEMP => A
```

Use Association

Use association is similar to host association in that it makes objects defined or declared in a scoping unit available in another scoping unit. In the case of use association, public entities in a module program unit are made available to other program units.

Block Data Units

A block data program unit initializes data in named common blocks. Only data specifications and initial values may appear. A block data program unit is not executable.

```
BLOCK DATA
   COMMON / PLACE / X
   DATA X / 42.99 /
        . . .  ! Data initialization in named common
END
```

F9◐

12

Using Procedures

Procedures are very useful in structuring a problem solution into understandable segments, and therefore the effective use of procedures is an important aspect of programming. This chapter describes the details for constructing and using procedures in Fortran 90.

After the overall program design is known, including the relationships of its constituent procedures, each individual procedure may be developed, refined, and tested separately before it is incorporated into the more complicated context of the complete Fortran program. This is especially important when a large program, which may contain hundreds of procedures, is assigned to teams of programmers. Organizing such large numbers of procedures is a formidable task in itself, and Fortran 90 provides mechanisms to help manage this organizational complexity. For example, related procedures can be grouped together in modules to form coherent procedure libraries, or just the interfaces can be collected into procedure interface libraries.

The procedure facilities and concepts of Fortran 77 are all available in Fortran 90. The new procedure features that have been added, such as recursion, optional and keyword arguments, defined operators and assignment, generic procedures, and explicit interfaces, have been integrated consistently, in a natural way, within the Fortran 77 framework. All arguments, including those new in Fortran 90, such as array sections and variables with nondefault kinds, require exact match of type properties across procedure boundaries, in the same manner as required by Fortran 77.

The procedure paradigm of Fortran 90 may be viewed as a straightforward extension of Fortran 77, including the ability to explicitly specify procedure interfaces as needed or desired. A procedure interface is explicit when it is known in detail to the calling program. Both internal and module procedures have explicit interfaces by nature. Explicit procedure interfaces not only provide a tool to eliminate one of the most serious problem areas of Fortran 77 (undetected procedure argument mismatches), but also set the scene for profound improvements in the engineering of Fortran software.

With explicit interfaces, the integrity of information flow among different parts of the program is automatically enforced. Such interfaces relieve the programmer (and maintainer) of the considerable mechanics of ensuring such integrity and allow software development resources to be concentrated instead on the functional design of this information flow. The net effect is that a Fortran program becomes more of an integrated, highly reliable, cohesive whole, rather than simply an aggregation of separate program units. Thus, the advantages of modular design are retained, while the effects of a change in one place on other parts of the program are tracked automatically. The result is more productive application development and maintenance—in short, better engineered software.

12.1 Procedure Terms and Concepts

Often a sophisticated technical area gets surrounded and mystified with "jargon"—short and often esoteric terms or phrases that represent key concepts in the technical area. Understanding that jargon is an important part of assimilating an understanding of the technical area. This section is an attempt, at the outset, to describe some of the basic terms and concepts associated with Fortran procedures.

12.1.1 Procedure Terms

There are two basic forms procedures take in a Fortran program: one is a subroutine; the other is a function. These two forms are very similar except in the way they are invoked.

12.1.1.1 Subroutines. A **subroutine** is a procedure whose purpose is to produce some side effect, such as modifying a set of arguments and/or global variables, or performing input/output. In Fortran 77 a subroutine is invoked with a CALL statement. This continues to be the case in Fortran 90, but Fortran 90 also provides an additional form of subroutine reference—the defined assignment. A subroutine may be used to define a new form of assignment, one that is different from those intrinsic to Fortran. Such subroutines may be invoked with assignment syntax (using the = symbol) rather than with the CALL statement.

12.1.1.2 Functions. The purpose of a **function** is to provide a value needed in an expression; normally functions do not produce side effects (though they are not prohibited from having side effects). A function is invoked as an expression operand, as in Fortran 77, and the result is used as the value of that operand. In addition, in Fortran 90, a function may be used to define a new operator or extend the meaning of an intrinsic operator symbol; such a function is invoked by the appearance of the new or extended operator in the expression along with the appropriate operand(s). For example, an interpretation for the operator + may be defined for logical operands, extending the + operation's intrinsic definition, because the intrinsic definition of + involves only numeric operands.

12.1.1.3 Function Results. The main difference between a subroutine and a function is that there is a **function result** value associated with a function. More precisely, there is a result value associated with any particular execution or call to a function. This result may be of any type, including derived type, and may be array-valued. The RESULT option in the FUNCTION statement may be used to give the result a different name than the function name and is required for a recursive function that calls itself directly.

12.1.1.4 External Procedures. External procedures are stand-alone subroutines and functions that are not part of any other program unit. They may share information, such as data and procedures via argument lists, modules, and common blocks, but otherwise they do not share information with any other program unit. They may be developed, compiled, and used completely independently of other procedures and program units. In fact they need not even be written in Fortran.

12.1.1.5 Intrinsic Procedures. Intrinsic procedures such as sine and cosine are already available in the Fortran processor. Intrinsic procedures are sometimes called **built-in procedures** and are automatically available to any Fortran program unit. There are approximately 100 intrinsic procedures in Fortran 90, all of which are described in Chapter 13 and Appendix A. Many of the intrinsic procedures are generic or elemental, or both. The generic properties (when two or more procedures share the same name) of an intrinsic procedure may be extended (12.6.3) and the automatic availability of an intrinsic procedure may be overridden explicitly by an EXTERNAL statement (12.4.4) or a procedure interface block (12.6.2). Many of the intrinsic procedures may be called **elementally** (12.5.8), in which case an array is supplied instead of a scalar for an actual argument. The computation is applied element-by-element to those arguments and returns a conformable array result. User-defined procedures cannot be called elementally.

12.1.1.6 Internal Procedures. Internal procedures are defined within other program units. The program unit containing an internal procedure is called the **host** of the internal procedure. An internal procedure may be either a subroutine or a function and appears between the CONTAINS and END statements of its host. An internal procedure is local to its host and inherits the host's environment via host association.

12.1.1.7 Module Procedures. Module procedures are defined within module program units. A module procedure may be either a subroutine or a function and appears between the CONTAINS and END statements of its host module. A module procedure inherits the host module's environment via host association. A module procedure may be PRIVATE to the module, and hence available only within the module, or it may be PUBLIC.

12.1.1.8 Statement Functions. Statement functions are one-statement function definitions in the specification part of a program unit other than a module or a block data program unit. Their functionality is extended and essentially superseded by internal functions in Fortran 90.

12.1.1.9 Procedure Entry. Normally one procedure is associated with a procedure subprogram. However, a procedure subprogram, which is a syntactic entity, can define any number of conceptual procedures. The name of the procedure subprogram identifies one procedure associated with that subprogram. An ENTRY statement (12.4.3) may be used to specify and identify an additional procedure associated with that subprogram. These statements are **procedure entries** and each defines an additional procedure. This technique is often used in external procedure subprograms to define different actions involving the data environment of the subprogram. (The classic example is the use of the same subprogram to define both the SIN and COS functions, because $\cos(x) = \text{SIN}(\pi/2 - x)$.) This sort of data sharing is provided by host association for internal and module procedures; therefore, procedure entries are not needed for internal and module procedures. In fact, in order to provide some simplification, procedure entries are not even permitted for internal procedures, although they are permitted in module procedures.

12.1.1.10 Procedure Reference. Procedure reference is the term given to the appearance of a procedure name in a program in such a way that causes the procedure to be executed. This is also termed **calling** or **invoking** the procedure. In most cases "reference" is used in this chapter, although occasionally "call" or "invoke" is used. These terms are used for both functions and subroutines. When a procedure is invoked, execution of the program making the call is suspended while the procedure is executed. When execution of the procedure is completed, execution of the invoking program is resumed.

A **subroutine reference** is a stand-alone action in the form of a CALL statement. In some cases the call can take the form of an assignment statement (12.6.5).

A **function reference** occurs as part of an expression, when the name of the function and its argument list appears as a primary in the expression. In some cases a function reference can take the form of a unary or binary operation involving an operator with the arguments as its operands (12.6.4).

12.1.1.11 Actual Arguments. **Actual arguments** appear in a procedure reference and specify the actual entities to be used by the procedure during its execution. These may be variables, for example, with different values for each reference. Some arguments are used as input values, others are variables that receive results from the procedure execution, and some may be both.

12.1.1.12 Dummy Arguments. **Dummy arguments** are the names by which the actual arguments are known inside a procedure. These names are specified when the procedure is defined and are used to represent arguments in computations in the procedure. When the procedure is referenced during program execution, the actual arguments in the reference become associated with the dummy arguments via argument association (12.5). If the procedure interface is explicit, a call to the procedure may use the dummy argument names as actual argument keywords (12.5.4).

12.1.1.13 Alternate Return. Alternate returns are special arguments allowed only in subroutines. They permit control to branch immediately to some spot other than the statement following the call. The actual argument in an alternate return is the label of the statement to which control should be transferred. This is frequently used in accommodating "error exits" from the subroutine. With modern control structures, such as the block-IF and block-CASE, there are usually superior ways to achieve the desired control.

12.1.1.14 Dummy Procedures. Dummy argument names may be treated within the procedure definition as procedure names. That is, they may be used as procedure names in procedure references. This accommodates procedure passing, and the associated actual argument for a dummy procedure must be the name of an actual procedure. The exceptions are that internal procedures, statement functions, and generic names cannot be used as actual arguments.

12.1.1.15 Non-Fortran Procedures. Procedure definitions may be written in a language other than Fortran (assembly language, for example). As long as all references to such a procedure are consistent in terms of the properties of the interface to this procedure, the calling program remains standard conforming. It may, however, not be portable, because the non-Fortran procedure or its method of argument communication might differ across implementations. Currently, the only way to guarantee consistent interfaces across implementations is to write all procedures in standard Fortran.

12.1.2 Argument Association

One of the most pervasive yet elusive concepts pertaining to procedures is that of **argument association**. This refers to the "matching up" of data across procedure boundaries—that is, matching data sources being passed from the calling side with the appropriate receivers in the called procedure. One helpful image of this matching up is the plug/socket analogy in Section 12.5.1.

The term argument association refers first to the overall concept that such a matching up—or association—must take place in order to use procedures and second to the detailed rules governing the matchups. These rules are described in detail in Section 12.5.

12.1.3 Recursion

Transcending a long-standing Fortran tradition, Fortran 90 procedures may be recursive. A procedure involved in either direct or indirect recursion must have the keyword RECURSIVE added to the FUNCTION or SUBROUTINE statement of the procedure definition. Many implementations of Fortran 90 may be expected to extend the standard by not requiring the RECURSIVE keyword. Indeed, many Fortran 77 implementations already support recursion without the need for such an explicit declaration. These implementations generate for all procedure calls the dynamic interface required for recursive calls, which on some architectures is more expensive (less efficient) than interfaces required for nonrecursive calls. The RECURSIVE keyword may help the implementation with the optimization of procedure calls.

An interesting problem that arises in the course of allowing Fortran procedures to be recursive is the treatment of local variables that have been data initialized—that is, have the DATA attribute. There are two quite different possibilities, both compatible extensions of Fortran 77. One possibility is that each layer of recursion has its own local copy of the variable, each initialized to the specified value. The other possibility is that each layer of recursion shares a single copy of the variable and the initialization takes place only once, at the outset of program execution; this is the approach used by Fortran 90. It is equivalent to also specifying SAVE for the variable and so is referred to as DATA-implies-SAVE.

Although each Fortran 77 implementation uses one of these two approaches to implementing initialized local variables, it does not matter to the programmer writing standard Fortran 77 which one it is because a standard Fortran 77 program cannot take advantage of this implementation detail. A standard Fortran 77 program produces the same results regardless of which of these implementation strategies is taken, and so the Fortran 77 standard does not have to specify "what DATA means" to this level of detail. But that's not the case with Fortran 90, because of recursion. Fortran 90 must specify in greater detail what data initialization means.

Because most Fortran 77 implementations employ the "DATA-implies-SAVE" model and there is not an overwhelming technical reason for favoring the other model, DATA-implies-SAVE was chosen for Fortran 90. So this is the rule now, whether or not the procedure is recursive. As an interesting aside, many Fortran 77 programmers discovered that their Fortran compiler implemented DATA-implies-SAVE and used this fact to retain information between executions of the procedure. The resulting programs were not Fortran 77 standard conforming but, if this is the only nonstandard feature in them, become standard conforming under Fortran 90.

12.1.4 Host and Use Association

A procedure may access information specified outside its own scope of definition in four ways:

1. argument association

2. common blocks

3. host association

4. use association

Argument association is fundamentally the same as in Fortran 77 and is extended naturally for the new features in Fortran 90. Argument association is described in detail later in this chapter (12.5). Common blocks, extended with data structures, are the same as in Fortran 77 and are described in detail in Section 5.10.4. Host and use association are new in Fortran 90 and are described in detail in Sections 11.4 and 11.6.4.

Host association applies to a procedure defined (contained) within another (host) program unit. A host may be a main program, module program unit, external procedure, or module procedure. Data and procedure entities specified in or accessible to the host are accessible to the contained procedure through host association. The rules for host association are very similar to the scoping rules of typical block-structured languages, such as Pascal. The main difference is that the Fortran 90 host association rules must take into account implicit as well as explicit declarations. (See Section 11.4 for a complete description of these rules.)

Use association applies to procedures and program units containing USE statements. All public entities of a module are available to a using procedure through use association, although the USE...ONLY mechanism can limit accessibility as the programmer desires. Use association allows shared data and procedure entities to be gathered together in a central place, with selective access to and hiding of these entities as may be appropriate in the specific situation. See Section 11.6.4.5 for a complete description of use association.

12.1.5 Implicit and Explicit Interfaces

The interface to a procedure is the collection of names and attributes of the procedure and its arguments. When this information is not made available explicitly to the calling program, the interface is said to be **implicit** to the calling program. In this case the interface information is assumed by the calling program from the properties of the procedure name and actual arguments in the procedure call. With implicit interfaces the processor in effect assumes that the programmer has specified a valid procedure call and has correctly matched actual argument and dummy argument data types, etc.—for array arguments, element sequence association is assumed (12.5.2), and for pointer arguments, the target is passed (12.5.3).

A procedure interface is said to be **explicit** if the interface information is known at the point of call and does not have to be assumed. In this case the processor can check and guarantee the validity of the call. In Fortran 77, external procedures and statement functions have implicit interfaces and intrinsic functions have explicit interfaces. The explicit nature of the intrinsic function interfaces, for example, permits generic intrinsic functions and keyword calls (both disallowed for statement functions). The processor can, based on the type of the actual argument, generate a call to the correct specific intrinsic, because the processor has explicit interface information for all of the intrinsic functions. In Fortran 77 there are no provisions for explicitly specifying interface information for external procedures.

Fortran 90 puts greater emphasis on explicit interfaces, and, indeed, explicit interfaces are a central concept in Fortran 90. Much of the facility and safety of intrinsic procedures thereby accrues to user-defined procedures as well. The two new forms of procedures in Fortran 90, internal and module procedures, by definition have explicit interfaces and therefore have these advantages. The interface block is provided to allow optional explicit specification of external procedure interfaces, and is described in detail later in this chapter (12.6).

Several important new features in Fortran 90 require explicit interfaces in order to allow correct and efficient procedure calls. These include array section actual arguments, pointer arguments, optional arguments, keyword calls, user-defined operations, user-defined assignment, and user-defined generic procedures.

12.2 Subroutines

A subroutine defines a complete process and is self contained. It has an initial SUBROUTINE statement, a specification part, an execution part that comprises the algorithm, any internal procedures that perform ancillary processes, and an END statement. When a subroutine is invoked, its execution begins with the first executable construct in the subroutine. Data objects and other entities may be communicated to and from the subroutine through argument association, host association, use association, or common storage association.

12.2.1 Subroutine Definition

The form of an external, module, or internal subroutine (R1219) is:

```
[ RECURSIVE ] SUBROUTINE subroutine-name   &
        [ ( [ dummy-argument-list ] ) ]
    [ specification-part ]
    [ execution-part ]
    [ internal-subprogram-part ]
END [ SUBROUTINE [ subroutine-name ] ]
```

A dummy argument is either a dummy argument name or an asterisk (*), where the asterisk designates an alternate return. When a subroutine is executed, the dummy arguments become associated with the actual arguments specified in the call (see Section 12.5).

Examples of subroutine statements are:

```
SUBROUTINE CAMP (SITE)

SUBROUTINE TASK ()

SUBROUTINE INITIALIZE_DATABASE

SUBROUTINE LIGHT (INTENSITY, M, *)

RECURSIVE SUBROUTINE YKTE (Y, KE)
```

An example of a subroutine subprogram is:

```
SUBROUTINE TROUT (STREAM, FLY)
    CHARACTER *10 STREAM
    OPTIONAL FLY
    STREAM = . . .
      . . .
END SUBROUTINE TROUT
```

Rules and restrictions:

1. If the END statement contains a subroutine name, it must be the same name as that in the SUBROUTINE statement.

2. An internal subroutine must not contain an internal subprogram part.

3. An internal subroutine must not contain ENTRY statements.

4. The END statement of an internal or module subroutine must be

```
END SUBROUTINE [ subroutine-name ]
```

that is, the keyword SUBROUTINE is not optional in this case.

5. The * for alternate returns is an obsolescent feature (see Section 12.5.9).

6. If the subroutine is recursive, that is, it calls itself either directly or indirectly, the keyword RECURSIVE is not optional in the SUBROUTINE statement.

7. Dummy argument attributes may be specified explicitly in the body of the subroutine or may be declared implicitly. Each dummy argument is a local variable of the subroutine; therefore, its name must be different from that of any other local variable in the subroutine (14.2).

8. The INTENT and OPTIONAL attributes may be specified for the dummy arguments of the subroutine, except that an INTENT attribute must not be specified for a dummy pointer or a dummy procedure.

9. The PRIVATE and PUBLIC attributes must not be specified in a subroutine.

12.2.2 Subroutine Reference

To use or invoke a subroutine, a CALL statement or defined assignment is placed at that point in a program where the process the subroutine performs is needed. A subroutine invocation specifies the arguments to be used and, in the case of a CALL statement, the name of the subroutine. The form of the CALL statement (R1210) is:

CALL subroutine-name [([subroutine-actual-argument-list])]

and a subroutine actual argument (R1211) has the form:

[keyword =] subroutine-argument

where a keyword is a dummy argument name in the subroutine interface and each actual argument (R1213) is one of the following:

an expression (including a variable)
a procedure name
* label (an alternate return specifier)

Each actual argument is associated with the corresponding dummy argument, as described in Section 12.5, by its position in the argument list or the name of its keyword. Variables are a special case of expression in the context of an actual argument; variables may be associated with dummy arguments used with any intent (IN, OUT, INOUT), whereas other forms of expressions must be associated only with dummy arguments used with intent IN.

Rules and restrictions:

1. Positional arguments must appear first in the argument list if both positional and keyword arguments are used in the same actual argument list. Once the first keyword is used, the rest of the arguments must be keyword arguments.

2. Exactly one actual argument is associated with each nonoptional dummy argument. For an optional dummy argument, the actual argument may be omitted.

3. The keyword is the name of the dummy argument in the explicit interface for the subroutine. If a keyword is present, the actual argument is associated with the dummy argument with that keyword name.

4. If the keyword is omitted, it must be omitted from all preceding actual arguments in that argument list. If no keyword is used, the arguments all have a positional correspondence.

5. The label in the alternate return specifier must be a branch target in the same scoping unit as the CALL statement.

6. An actual argument must not be the name of an internal procedure or statement function.

7. An actual argument associated with a dummy procedure must be the specific name of a procedure. (There may be an identical generic name, but it is the procedure with that specific name that is passed.) Note that certain specific intrinsic function names must not be used as actual arguments (13.9).

Examples of subroutine references:

```
CALL TYR (2.0*A, *99)        ! SUBROUTINE TYR (R, *)
    . . .
99 . . .  ! error recovery
    . . .
CALL TEST (X = 1.1, Y = 4.4)  ! SUBROUTINE TEST (Y, X)
    . . .
```

In the first example, an alternate return to statement 99 in the calling program unit is the last argument. Keyword arguments are used for X and Y in the second CALL statement; therefore, the order of the actual arguments does not matter.

Another way to invoke or reference a subroutine is with user-defined assignment (12.6.5). A subroutine may define forms of assignment different from intrinsic assignment supplied by the Fortran processor. Defined assignment is particularly useful with data structures. Defined assignment subroutines require an ASSIGNMENT interface as described in Section 12.6.5. They have exactly two arguments, arg_1 and arg_2, both nonoptional and the first with intent OUT or INOUT and the second with intent IN. Defined assignment may be invoked with the following assignment syntax:

$$arg_1 = arg_2$$

The attributes of the arguments select the defined assignment, again as described in Section 12.6.5. This facility, in effect, allows the user to extend the generic properties of assignment.

Example of defined assignment:

```
MODULE POLAR_COORDINATES

    TYPE POLAR
        REAL  ::  RHO, THETA
    END TYPE POLAR

    INTERFACE ASSIGNMENT (=)
        MODULE PROCEDURE ASSIGN_POLAR_TO_COMPLEX
    END INTERFACE

        . . .

    SUBROUTINE ASSIGN_POLAR_TO_COMPLEX (C, P)
        COMPLEX, INTENT(OUT)      ::  C
        TYPE (POLAR), INTENT(IN)  ::  P
        C = CMPLX (P%RHO * COS (P%THETA),  &
                   P%RHO * SIN (P%THETA))
    END SUBROUTINE ASSIGN_POLAR_TO_COMPLEX

END MODULE POLAR_COORDINATES


USE POLAR_COORDINATES
COMPLEX ::  CARTESIAN
    . . .
CARTESIAN  =  POLAR (R, PI/6)
```

This last assignment is equivalent to the subroutine call

```
CALL ASSIGN_POLAR_TO_COMPLEX (CARTESIAN, POLAR (R, PI/6))
```

The structure constructor POLAR constructs a value of type POLAR from R and PI/6 and assigns this value to CARTESIAN according to the computations specified in the subroutine.

12.3 Functions

A function is similar to a subroutine, except that its principal use is as a primary in an expression. Analogous to a subroutine, a function has an initial FUNCTION statement, a specification part, an execution part, possibly internal procedures, and an END statement. An argument list provides data communication with the function, but in this case arguments typically serve as input data for the function. The principal output is delivered as the function result to the expression invoking the function. Data objects also may be available to the function via host association, use association, and common storage association.

12.3.1 Function Definition

The form of an external, module, or internal function subprogram (R1215) is:

```
[ function-prefix ] simplest-function-statement   &
        [ RESULT ( result-name ) ]
    [ specification-part ]
    [ execution-part ]
    [ internal-subprogram-part ]
  END [ FUNCTION [ function-name ] ]
```

and the various forms of the function prefix (R1217) are:

```
[ type-spec ] RECURSIVE
[ RECURSIVE ] type-spec
```

and the simplest function statement is:

```
FUNCTION function-name ( [ dummy-argument-name-list ] )
```

When a function is executed, the dummy arguments become associated with the actual arguments specified in the reference (see Section 12.5).

Example function statements are:

```
FUNCTION HOSPITAL (PILLS)

REAL FUNCTION LASER (BEAM)

FUNCTION HOLD (ME, YOU) RESULT (GOOD)

RECURSIVE CHARACTER*10 FUNCTION POLICE (STATION)   &
        RESULT (ARREST)
```

Rules and restrictions:

1. The type of the function may be specified in the function statement or in a type declaration statement, but not both. If the type is not explicitly specified in this way, the default typing rules apply.

2. If the function is array valued, allocatable, or a pointer, the declarations must state these attributes for the function result name.

3. Dummy argument attributes may be specified explicitly in the body of the function or may be declared implicitly. Each dummy argument is a local variable of the function; therefore, its name must be different from that of any other local variable in the function (14.2).

4. If the END statement contains the function name, it must be the same name used in the FUNCTION statement.

5. An internal function must not contain an internal subprogram part.

6. An internal function must not contain ENTRY statements.

7. The END statement of an internal or module function is:

    END FUNCTION [function-name]

    that is, the keyword FUNCTION is required.

8. If there is no result clause, the function name is used as the result variable, and all references to the function are references to the function result variable.

9. If there is a result clause, the result name is used as the result variable, and the function name must not be used as the result variable; in this case, all references to the function name are function references—that is, recursive calls.

10. The function name must not appear in specification statements if there is a result clause.

11. If the result of a function is not a pointer, its value must be completely defined before the end of execution of the function. If the result is an array, all the elements must be defined; if the result is a structure, all of the components must be defined.

12. If the result of the function is an array or a pointer to an array, its shape must be determined before the end of execution of the function.

13. If the result is a pointer, its allocation status must be determined before the end of execution of the function; that is, a target must be associated with the pointer, or the pointer must have been explicitly disassociated from a target.

14. The INTENT and OPTIONAL attributes may be specified for the dummy arguments of the function, except that an INTENT attribute must not be specified for a dummy pointer or a dummy procedure.

15. The PRIVATE and PUBLIC attributes must not be specified in a function.

Note that, in the case of direct recursion, both the RECURSIVE keyword and the RESULT option must be specified; this is the only case in which the RESULT option is required.

12.3.2 The RESULT Option

As with subroutines, when a function is either directly or indirectly recursive, RECURSIVE must appear in the FUNCTION statement but is optional for nonrecursive functions. The RESULT clause specifies a name different from the function name to hold the function result. The result name may be declared, defined, and referenced as an ordinary data object. The function name has the same attributes as the result name. Upon return from a function with a RESULT clause, the value of the function is the last value given to the result name.

Why is there a RESULT option in Fortran 90? In Fortran 77 there is no RESULT clause and the function name is used as the result data object. This is still the case in Fortran 90 for functions not having the RESULT option. If the function is both array valued and directly recursive, however, a recursive reference to the function may be indistinguishable from a reference to the array-valued result. The RESULT clause resolves this ambiguity by providing one name for the result value (the result name) and another name for recursive calls (the function name). For example, if F is a recursive function that returns a rank-one array of reals and has a single integer argument, in the statement

```
A = F(K)
```

the reference to F(K) could be interpreted as either a reference to the K*th* element of the array-valued result of F or a recursive call to F with actual argument K. In these cases, Fortran 90 specifies that such references are to be interpreted as recursive calls. If references to the array element are intended, then the result name is used in the reference rather than the function name.

A result clause is required when the function is recursive and either the result variable is referenced for its value or a direct recursive call is made.

Another simple example of a recursive function is REVERSE that reverses the words in a given phrase.

```
RECURSIVE FUNCTION REVERSE (PHRASE) RESULT (FLIPPED)
    CHARACTER (*)           PHRASE
    CHARACTER (LEN(PHRASE)) FLIPPED
    L = TRIM_LEN (PHRASE)
    N = INDEX (PHRASE(1:L), " ", BACK=.TRUE.)
    IF (N == 0) THEN; FLIPPED = PHRASE
    ELSE; FLIPPED = PHRASE (N+1:L) // " "  &
            // REVERSE (PHRASE (1:N-1))
    END IF
END FUNCTION REVERSE
```

12.3.3 Function Reference

One way a function may be referenced or invoked is by placing the function name with its actual arguments as an operand in an expression. The actual arguments are evaluated, argument association takes place in accordance with the rules in Section 12.5, and the statements in the body of the function are executed. The reference results in a value which is then used as the value of that primary in the expression. For example, in the expression

```
A + F(B)
```

where F is a function of one argument that delivers a numeric result, this result becomes the value of the right-hand operand of the expression.

The form of a function reference (R1209) is:

function-name ([function-actual-argument-list])

the form of a function actual argument (R1211) is:

[keyword =] function-argument

and a function argument (R1213) is one of the following:

an expression (including a variable)
a procedure name

and where a keyword is a dummy argument name in the function interface. As with subroutines (12.2.2), each actual argument is associated with the corresponding dummy argument by position or keyword. Variables are a special case of expression in the context of an actual argument; variables may be associated with dummy arguments used with any intent (IN, OUT, INOUT), whereas other forms of expressions must be associated only with dummy arguments used with intent IN. Note that (A), where A is a variable, is not a variable, but a more general expression.

The only difference between subroutine and function argument lists is that a function argument list must not contain an alternate return. Otherwise the rules and restrictions for actual and dummy arguments are the same for functions and subroutines and are listed in Section 12.2.2.

Examples of function references are:

```
Y = 2.3 * CAPS (4*12, K)      ! FUNCTION CAPS (SIZE, KK)

PRINT *, TIME (TODAYS_DATE)   ! FUNCTION TIME (DATE)
```

Another way to reference a function is with user-defined operators in an expression (12.6.4). A number of arithmetic, logical, relational, and character operators are predefined in Fortran; these are called **intrinsic operators**. These operators may be given additional meanings, and new operators may be defined. Functions define these operations and interface blocks associate them with the desired operator symbols, as described in Section 12.6.4. A function may be invoked by using its associated defined operator in an expression. The rules associated with operator functions are as follows.

Rules and restrictions:

1. Functions of one argument are used to define unary operations; functions of two arguments are used to define binary operations.

2. The arguments must be not be optional and must have intent IN.

3. New operators must have the dot form, contain only letters (underscores not allowed) between the dots, have no more than 31 letters, and must not be the same as the logical literal constants .TRUE. or

.FALSE.   Possibilities   are   .FOURIER.,   .NEWPLUS.,   and .BLAHANDBLAAH.

4. If a defined operator is the same as an intrinsic operator (for example, +, *, .EQ., .AND.), it extends the generic properties of this operator, as described in Section 12.6.4. In such an extension, the attributes of the arguments must not match exactly those of the operands associated with an intrinsic meaning of the operator (Table 7-3).

Example:

```
INTERFACE  OPERATOR (.BETA.)
    FUNCTION BETA_OP (A, B)
            . . .   ! attributes of BETA_OP, A, and B
                    ! (including intent IN for A and B)
    END FUNCTION
END INTERFACE
    . . .
PRINT *, X .BETA. Y
```

The presence of .BETA. in the expression in the PRINT statement invokes the function BETA_OP, with X as the first actual argument and Y as the second actual argument. The function value is returned as the value of X .BETA. Y in the expression.

12.3.4 Statement Functions

A statement function statement (R1226) is a function definition that consists of only one Fortran statement. Its form is:

function-name (dummy-argument-name-list) = scalar-expression

A statement function statement may be replaced (except within an internal procedure) with the following equivalent three-line internal function definition

```
FUNCTION function-name ( dummy-argument-name-list )
    function-name = scalar-expression
END FUNCTION
```

providing the function and its arguments are typed the same in both cases. Additional rules governing statement functions follow these three examples of statement functions.

```
CHARACTER (5)  ZIP_5            ! Notice these are scalar
CHARACTER (10) ZIP_CODE         ! character strings
ZIP_5 (ZIP_CODE) = ZIP_CODE (1:5)

INTEGER TO_POST, MOVE
TO_POST (MOVE) = MOD(MOVE,10)

REAL FAST_ABS
COMPLEX Z
FAST_ABS (Z) = ABS (REAL (Z)) + ABS (AIMAG (Z))
```

Rules and restrictions:

1. Note that the function and all the dummy arguments are scalar.

2. The expression must contain only intrinsic operations and must be scalar valued. (As stated here, this allows the expression to include references to scalar-valued functions having array arguments, such as SUM (A+B), where SUM is the array reduction intrinsic function and A and B are conformable arrays. This is probably the intent of the standard, because Fortran 77 allows array names as function arguments in a statement function expression, but the standard is somewhat contradictory on this point and the intent may have been to disallow general array-valued expressions in statement functions. Because some implementations may interpret the statement function rules in this way, perhaps the prudent programmer should avoid array expressions completely when using statement functions and instead use the internal function form when referencing such expressions.)

3. Note that statement functions are defined in the specification part of a program unit, internal procedure, or module procedure. Any other statement function referenced in the expression must have been defined earlier in the specification part, and hence a statement function cannot be recursive (either directly or indirectly).

4. Named constants and variables used in the expression must have been declared earlier in the specification part or made available by use or host association.

5. If an array element is used in the expression, the parent array must have been declared earlier in the specification part.

6. The appearance of any entity in the expression that has not previously been typed explicitly constitutes an implicit type declaration

and any subsequent explicit type declaration for that entity must be consistent with the implicit type.

7. Statement function dummy arguments have a scope of the statement function statement.

8. Statement function dummy arguments are assumed to be intent IN (that is, function references in the expression must not change the value of any dummy argument of the statement function).

9. A statement function must not be used as an actual argument.

10. A statement function is referenced in the same manner as any other function, except that statement function interfaces are implicit and therefore the keyword form of actual arguments is not allowed; the argument association rules are the same.

Note that statement function interfaces are implicit, not explicit; see Section 12.6.1 for a detailed discussion of explicit interfaces. Explicit interfaces are associated with those procedures that can have array-valued results, assumed-shape dummy arguments, pointer arguments, and keyword arguments, and can have various generic forms. Because none of these apply to statement functions, statement functions do not have and are not allowed to have an explicit interface.

12.4 Procedure-Related Statements

Several procedure-related statements—RETURN, CONTAINS, ENTRY, EXTERNAL, and INTRINSIC—are general in that they apply to both kinds of procedures (functions and subroutines) or to more than one form of procedures (for example, external, internal, module).

12.4.1 RETURN Statement

A RETURN statement terminates execution of a procedure and returns control to the calling program. Often, however, it is not needed because the procedure END statement performs the same function as well as constituting the physical end of the procedure. It is occasionally convenient to use RETURN statements, however, because they may be placed anywhere in the execution part of the procedure.

The form of the RETURN statement (R1224) is:

RETURN [scalar-integer-expression]

The scalar integer expression option is applicable only to subroutines and is used in conjunction with alternate returns. This expression must be of type integer, and its value must be in the range $1:n$ where n is the number of alternate returns in the argument list; the value selects which alternate return, counting from left to right in the argument list, is to be used for this particular return from the procedure. The effect of an alternate return is the same as

```
CALL SUBR (..., IRET)
GO TO ( label-list ), IRET
```

where inside SUBR, the variable IRET is assigned the integer expression alternate return value prior to returning from SUBR. In Fortran 90 there are better ways to achieve the functionality of alternate return, such as with a CASE construct controlled by a return code with an appropriate mnemonic value; for this reason alternate return is an obsolescent feature.

12.4.2 CONTAINS Statement

The CONTAINS statement (R1225) separates the internal procedures from the specification and executable parts of the host and separates module procedures from the specification part of the module; its form is simply:

```
CONTAINS
```

It is a nonexecutable statement that has the effect of making the execution sequence bypass everything following the CONTAINS statement up to the END statement of the program unit. Therefore, if it were executable, the CONTAINS statement would have the effect of a STOP statement in a main program and a RETURN statement in a procedure subprogram.

The CONTAINS statement serves only to delimit the procedure part of a program unit. It is not needed to resolve ambiguities because there are none, but without it some constructs are not resolvable until the entire program unit has been analyzed.

12.4.3 ENTRY Statement

The concept of procedure entry was described in Section 12.1.1. A procedure entry is defined by the appearance of an ENTRY statement in the specification or execution part of the procedure subprogram. An ENTRY statement (R1223) has the form:

```
ENTRY entry-name [ ( [ dummy-argument-list ] ) ]  &
    [ RESULT ( result-name ) ]
```

The attributes of the dummy arguments and entry result, if this is an entry in a function, are prescribed in the specification part of the subprogram.

The ENTRY statement may be thought of as providing auxiliary FUNCTION statements in function subprograms or SUBROUTINE statements in subroutine subprograms, each defining another procedure. The entry names must be different from one another and from the original function or subroutine name. The example below illustrates the typical way of using the ENTRY statement to define several procedures in a single subprogram. Following each ENTRY statement and before the next one, in this example, is the set of executable statements, the last one being a RETURN statement, that represent the procedure corresponding to this entry. When the procedure represented by this entry is called, the procedure is "entered" and execution proceeds from this point. Execution continues in the procedure in the normal manner, ignoring any ENTRY statements subsequently encountered, until a RETURN statement is executed or the end of the procedure is reached.

The following is a typical example of the structure of a subroutine with ENTRY statements.

```
SUBROUTINE name-1 ( argument-list-1 )
    . . .
RETURN

ENTRY name-2 ( argument-list-2 )
    . . .
! This falls through past the next ENTRY statement

ENTRY name-3 ( argument-list-3 )
    . . .
RETURN

END
```

Often, in practical cases, the computations in these entry bodies are similar, involving the same data and code. Rather than duplicating this code, in Fortran 77 a single copy typically is placed at the bottom of the subprogram and branches are made to it as appropriate. In Fortran 90 such common code can be packaged as an internal procedure.

All of the entries in a subroutine subprogram define subroutine procedures and all of the entries in a function subprogram define function procedures. All of the entries in a function subprogram must be storage association compatible. The RESULT option on an ENTRY statement has the same form and meaning as the RESULT option on a FUNCTION statement (12.3.2).

Examples of the ENTRY statement are:

```
ENTRY FAST (CAR, TIRES)

ENTRY LYING (X, Y) RESULT (DOWN)
```

Rules and restrictions:

1. An ENTRY statement may appear only in an external or module subprogram; an internal subprogram must not contain ENTRY statements.

2. An external or module subprogram may contain any number of ENTRY statements.

3. An ENTRY statement must not appear in an executable construct (IF, DO, CASE, or WHERE constructs) or a nonblock DO loop.

4. An entry name must not be the same as any dummy argument name in the subprogram.

5. An entry name must not appear in an EXTERNAL statement, INTRINSIC statement, or procedure interface block in that subprogram.

6. The RESULT option applies only to function entries and thus may appear only in function subprograms.

7. If a result name is specified, it must not be the same as any entry name, the function name, or any other result name. If a result name is specified, the entry name must not appear in any specification statements in the subprogram; it inherits all of its attributes from the result name.

8. The keyword RECURSIVE is not used in an entry statement. Instead the presence or absence of RECURSIVE on the initial SUBROUTINE or FUNCTION statement of the subprogram applies to each entry in the procedure.

9. If each entry result in a function subprogram has the same type, kind, and shape as the function result, each of the entries identifies (is an alias for) the same result variable. In this case there is no restriction on the nature of the result. For example, the result could be of derived type, either scalar or array, and could have the pointer attribute.

10. If all of the entries in a function subprogram (including the function
     result) are not the same type, kind, and shape, then they must all
     be scalar, without the pointer attribute, and must be "equivalence-
     able". This means they all must be of type default character with
     the same length or any mix of default integer, default real, default
     logical, double precision real, or default complex. The reason for
     these rules is that all subprogram entries are storage associated with
     the function result.

11. A dummy argument must not appear in an executable statement
     before the ENTRY statement specifying that dummy argument. A
     dummy argument of the ENTRY statement must not appear in a
     statement function scalar expression before the ENTRY statement
     specifying that dummy argument, unless it is also a dummy argu-
     ment of the statement function.

12. An executable statement or statement function depending on a
     dummy argument of the procedure that was entered, or upon a
     local data object depending on that dummy argument (such as a
     dynamic local array whose size depends on the dummy argument),
     may be executed only if the dummy argument appears in the
     ENTRY statement of the referenced procedure. In addition, an
     associated actual argument must be present if the dummy argument
     is optional.

For either a function or subroutine subprogram the order, number,
types, kind type parameters, and names of the dummy arguments in an
ENTRY statement may differ from those in the FUNCTION or SUBROU-
TINE statement or any other ENTRY statement in that subprogram.
Note, however, that all of the entry result values of a function subprogram must be equivalenceable to the function result value, as described
in items 9 and 10 above.

The interface to a procedure defined by an ENTRY statement in an
external subprogram may be made explicit in another scoping unit (the
calling scoping unit) by supplying an interface body for it in a procedure
interface block. In this case the ENTRY statement appears as the first
statement of the interface body, but the word ENTRY is replaced by the
word FUNCTION or SUBROUTINE, whichever is the appropriate one.
Such an interface body must include RECURSIVE if the subprogram is
recursive and must correctly specify the dummy argument attributes and
the attributes of the result if it is a function. Entry procedures defined in
module procedures already have explicit interfaces in program units that
use the module.

12.4.4 EXTERNAL Statement

Consider the following program segment in a program unit containing no declarations:

```
    . . .
A = X + Y
CALL B (X, Y)
CALL Q (A, B, C)
    . . .
```

It is clear that A is a variable and B and Q are subroutines, but in this code fragment, C could be either a variable name or a procedure name. Other statements in the program might resolve the mystery, and then again they might not. In the cases where they do not, the processor assumes that the argument is a variable. But when the programmer wants it to be a procedure name, there must be some way to so specify. The means for doing this is the EXTERNAL statement.

The EXTERNAL statement is described completely in Section 5.7.1. Note that the EXTERNAL statement appears in the program unit in which the procedure in question is an actual argument; the procedure must be an external procedure or dummy procedure. Internal procedures, statement functions, and generic names must not appear as actual arguments. Use association takes care of module procedures, and intrinsic procedures are handled separately, as described in the next section. Note that an interface block for the external procedure has the same effect (as well as providing argument checking and other benefits) and, therefore, effectively makes the EXTERNAL statement obsolescent for this purpose. Another minor use of the EXTERNAL statement is to identify the relevant block data program unit.

12.4.5 INTRINSIC Statement

The INTRINSIC statement does for intrinsic procedures what the EXTERNAL statement does for external procedures (see the preceding section). The INTRINSIC statement also is described completely in Section 5.7.2. Note that an interface block cannot be provided for an intrinsic procedure because that would specify a duplicate explicit interface; therefore, the INTRINSIC statement is not effectively obsolescent. For example, in the procedure reference

```
CALL Q(A, B, SIN)
```

if the intrinsic function SIN is intended for the third actual argument, SIN must be declared in an INTRINSIC statement if it is not otherwise known to be a procedure name in that scope. (SIN is both a specific and a generic procedure name—it is the specific name that is involved here.)

12.5 Argument Association

When a procedure is referenced, the actual arguments supply the input data to be used for this execution of the procedure and specify the variables to receive any output data. Within the procedure, the dummy arguments assume the roles of these input and output data objects. Thus, during execution of a procedure reference, the appropriate "linkage" must be established between the actual arguments specified in the call and the dummy arguments defined within the procedure. This linkage is called **argument association**.

As shown in Figure 12-1, the fundamental form that a set of actual arguments take in a reference is that of a sequence of expressions separated by commas. The set of names in a procedure definition after the procedure name is a list of dummy argument names. In each case this is called an "argument list"—an **actual argument list** in the former case and a **dummy argument list** in the latter case. The arguments are counted from left to right.

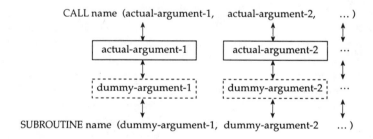

Figure 12-1 Actual and dummy argument lists

In Figure 12-1 the actual arguments are shown as solid boxes because these represent, or identify, actual data values or locations. The dummy arguments are shown as dotted boxes to indicate that they do not represent actual data. The dummy arguments represent "empty names" until they become associated with actual arguments. In effect the procedure call passes unnamed boxes of data to the procedure, and in the course of argument association, the dummy argument names get attached to these boxes. Upon return from the procedure the dummy argument names are stripped from the boxes, and the original names in the calling program are restored.

The principal argument association mechanism is **positional** (but see Section 12.5.4 below); that is, arguments are associated according to their positions in the respective actual and dummy argument lists—the first dummy argument becomes associated with (becomes the name of) the first actual argument, the second dummy argument becomes associated with the second actual argument, and so on. The remainder of this section describes the detailed rules governing this association mechanism and various forms it can take.

This section is also about argument association, in general, and only a portion of it is about pointers. That portion discusses them as actual and dummy arguments. However, there is a very interesting parallel between pointers and argument association—in many respects Fortran 90 pointers are just like dummy arguments, and targets are just like actual arguments. Until a pointer becomes associated with a target (via dynamic allocation or pointer assignment), it is just an "empty box", like a dummy argument. After it becomes associated it can be used as if it were the target. Thus, argument association and pointer association are conceptually identical. The main difference is the form the association takes—procedure references cause argument association, whereas dynamic allocation and pointer assignment cause pointer association.

12.5.1 Type, Kind, and Rank Matching

An actual argument, being an actual data object, has the usual set of data object attributes. These may be determined by the specification part of the calling program (see Chapter 5) or, if the actual argument is an expression, by the rules governing expression results (see Section 7.2.8). The most important of these attributes, for argument association purposes, are the data type, kind type parameter, and rank of an object. This trio of attributes will be referred to as the **TKR pattern** of the object. Thus, each actual argument, except for alternate returns and procedures as arguments, has a TKR pattern. Suppose, for example, that an actual argument ERER has been specified by the statement

```
REAL ERER (100)
```

The TKR pattern of ERER is: real, default kind, rank 1.

Similarly, each dummy argument has a declared TKR pattern. Even though a dummy argument is merely an empty name until it becomes associated with an actual argument, that name is used within the procedure as if it were a regular data object. Therefore it has a set of attributes just like any other data object, and this set includes a TKR pattern. The dummy argument attributes are specified, either explicitly or implicitly, in the procedure definition.

The most fundamental rule of argument association is that the TKR patterns of an actual argument and its associated dummy argument must be the same. Note that statement function references conform to these rules, except that dummy argument attributes are defined in the host.

The set of dummy arguments may be thought of as the procedure "socket"—the means by which the procedure gets connected to the rest of the program; each dummy argument is one of the holes in this socket. One can think of the TKR pattern of a dummy argument as determining the shape of that hole in the socket.

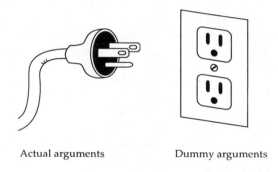

Actual arguments   Dummy arguments

Figure 12-2 The plug and socket analogy for actual and dummy arguments

Similarly, the set of actual arguments in a reference to that procedure may be thought of as a "plug" that connects with the procedure socket (Figure 12-2), with each actual argument representing one prong of the plug. The TKR pattern of an actual argument determines the shape of that prong. For the connection to work properly, the shape of each plug prong must match the shape of the corresponding socket hole.

Because external procedures and their calling programs are usually compiled separately, there is normally no detection of TKR mismatches by the implementation. Therefore, TKR argument matching is extremely error-prone, and such mismatches are among the most common and elusive errors in Fortran applications. Explicit procedure interfaces (see Section 12.6.1) solve this problem by enabling automatic detection of TKR argument mismatches.

Although extremely error-prone with implicit interfaces, this TKR rule is very simple and straightforward: associated actual and dummy arguments must have the same data type, the same kind parameter for that type, and the same rank. This last part means that if one is a scalar, they both must be scalars; otherwise, they must both be arrays with the same number of dimensions. (See 12.5.2 for an exception to this general rule on rank matching.) Alternate returns are a special case (12.5.9), as are procedures used as arguments (12.5.10).

Argument associations involving arrays and pointers also have some special considerations; they are treated in Sections 12.5.2 and 12.5.3, respectively. That leaves scalar data objects without the pointer attribute to discuss here. The rule is almost trivially simple: the associated dummy argument for a scalar actual argument must be scalar and must have the same data type and kind type parameter value as the actual argument. (See the exception to this in Section 12.5.3, in which an array element—which is a scalar—may be passed to a dummy array.) Note that array elements, scalar-valued structure components, and substrings are valid scalar actual arguments. The only slightly complicated case involves arguments of type character because scalar character objects have an additional attribute: the character length.

The cleanest situation is, of course, when the associated actual and dummy argument character lengths are the same. This may be achieved by explicit declaration of the character length in each case, with the length value specified to be the same. In many cases this is an impossibly severe condition, however, because it prevents the development of general-purpose procedures (for example, procedures that can accept character input of any length). **Assumed length** dummy arguments alleviate this problem. In cases involving character arguments, assumed length generally should be used for the dummy argument.

Assumed length may be specified only for dummy argument data objects. This is done by specifying an asterisk (*) for the character length (Section 5.1.6). An assumed-length dummy argument does not have a length until it becomes associated with an actual argument. When it becomes associated, its length becomes the length of the actual argument. In effect, the length of the actual argument is passed as part of the actual argument and is picked up by the dummy argument in the course of argument association.

Therefore, in most cases, that is the way to go—assumed length for dummy arguments of type character. Explicit declared length is permitted for dummy arguments, however, so there must be rules governing those inevitable instances when the lengths of the actual argument and its associated dummy argument are different. Actually, these lengths are not allowed to be different for nondefault type character arguments, so the following discussion applies only to default character arguments. For scalars, the easy case is when the length of the actual argument is greater than that of the dummy argument. In this instance, the procedure has access to only the leftmost characters of the actual argument, up to the length of the dummy argument. Even though the remaining characters of the actual argument are in some sense "passed" by the call, the procedure cannot "see" them or do anything with them.

But what if the actual argument length is less than the dummy argument length? In this case, or so it would seem, the procedure "sees" more than is actually passed. This is, in fact, an untenable situation, so it is disallowed. Thus, in summary, the lengths of associated actual and dummy character arguments may be different only for default type characters and only if the actual argument length is greater than the dummy argument length. Play it safe and simple: for character arguments always use assumed-length dummy arguments for both default and nondefault character types.

For arrays, the rules are somewhat complicated and are described in detail in Section 12.5.2 under the topic of "Array Element Sequence Association".

12.5.2 Array Association

For array arguments the fundamental rule in Fortran 90 is that the shapes of an actual argument and its associated dummy argument must be the same. That is, they must have the same rank and the same extent (number of elements) in each dimension; thus, they also are the same size. To make this simple rule viable and to make passing array sections viable, a new type of dummy argument was introduced in Fortran 90—the **assumed-shape** dummy argument. Assumed-shape dummy arguments for arrays are analogous to assumed-length dummy arguments for character arguments in that assumed-shape dummy arguments assume their shape attributes from the actual argument upon association. The only requirement for the user of assumed-shape dummy arguments is to ensure that the ranks of the actual and dummy arguments agree as well as the type and kind; the rest follows automatically, and association is on an element-by-corresponding-element basis. Thus, again, TKR is the only rule to observe when using assumed-shape dummy arguments. Assumed-shape dummy arguments are declared as described in Section 5.3.1.2.

But, alas, Fortran 77 does not have assumed-shape dummy arrays and therefore does not offer the array argument simplicity they provide. Also, Fortran 77 is conceptually much more "array element sequence" or "storage mapping" oriented than Fortran 90, which is conceptually "array object" oriented. In Fortran 90 an array is considered an object in and of itself, as well as a sequence of related but separate elements. Being array element sequence oriented, the Fortran 77 array argument association mechanisms are geared towards associating array element sequences rather than associating array objects. These mechanisms are considerably more complicated than the simple TKR pattern matches described above, although they do offer somewhat more functionality (described below). Fortran 90, in order to be completely upward compatible with Fortran 77, provides these separate mechanisms, and much of the rest of this section is devoted to the description of array element sequence association.

12.5.2.1 Array Element Sequence Association. If a dummy argument is declared as an explicit-shape array or an assumed-size array (the only kinds provided in Fortran 77), then the ranks of the actual argument and its associated dummy argument do not have to be the same, although the types and kinds still have to match. In this case the actual argument is viewed as defining a sequence of objects, each an element of the actual array. The order of these objects is the array element order (6.4.7) of the actual array. Briefly, array element order is a linear sequence of the array elements obtained by varying the first subscript most rapidly through its range, then the second subscript, and so on. The number of objects in this sequence is the size of the actual array.

Similarly, the dummy array is viewed as defining a linear sequence of dummy array elements, in array element order of the dummy array. The association of the dummy array and actual array is the association of corresponding elements in these sequences. To determine associated elements, the two sequences are superimposed with the initial elements of each corresponding. This is illustrated in Figure 12-3, in which a three-dimensional actual array is associated with a two-dimensional dummy array. In this example, this causes the actual argument element AA(1,2,2) to become associated with dummy argument element DA(4,2), for example. The only additional rule that needs to be observed is that the size of the dummy array cannot exceed the size of the actual array. An assumed-size dummy array extends to and "cuts off" at the end of the actual argument array sequence.

Actual array: REAL AA(2,3,2)

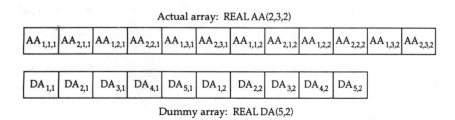

Dummy array: REAL DA(5,2)

Figure 12-3 Example of array element sequence association

For character arrays, the character length issue raises its ugly head again, because the array element length must be specified in this case.

For nondefault type character arrays the rule is (as with scalars) that the actual and dummy array element character lengths must be the same. Thus, in this instance, the situation described above and illustrated in Figure 12-3 applies. But the situation is different with default characters—the lengths of the actual and dummy array elements may be different. Here, the actual and dummy arguments are viewed as sequences of characters. Each array element, in array element order, contributes a subsequence of characters the size of its length to the corresponding sequence of characters representing the argument. The argument association is then on a character-by-corresponding-character basis of these two character sequences. This not-so-pretty picture can result in array element "boundary crossing" between the actual and dummy arguments, as illustrated in Figure 12-4. In this case the size rule is that the number of characters in the dummy array cannot exceed the number of characters in the actual array. Using the example in Figure 12-4, these rules cause the dummy argument element DA(4) to be associated with the last character of the actual argument element AA(2,1) and the first two characters of actual argument element AA(1,2).

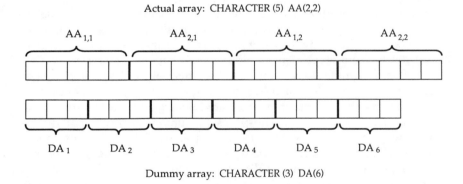

Actual array: CHARACTER (5) AA(2,2)

Dummy array: CHARACTER (3) DA(6)

Figure 12-4 Array element sequence association for default characters

The provision that the ranks of the actual and dummy argument arrays need not match in array element sequence association has an interesting asymmetrical end condition—namely when one is a scalar (effectively a rank of zero). The case of the actual argument having non-zero rank and the dummy argument being scalar occurs for elemental references to intrinsic functions (see Section 12.5.8). The reverse, passing a scalar to a dummy array, is allowed in a limited way in array element sequence association. If the dummy argument meets the conditions for array element sequence association (that is, it is declared as an explicit-shape or assumed-size array), the actual argument may be a single array element but, except for default characters, cannot be any other kind of scalar. This functionality is provided in Fortran 77 to accommodate the passing of certain forms of array sections.

In the array element sequence association paradigm, the appearance of an array element as the actual argument causes the sequence of actual array elements to begin with this element, rather than the first element of the array, and extend to the end of the array in array element order. This sequence is then associated with the full dummy argument sequence. Care must be taken to ensure that the size of the dummy array is not greater than the size of the array element sequence from the specified array element on. An element of an assumed-shape or pointer array cannot be passed to a dummy array.

For default characters, the plot thickens still more—the actual argument can be a substring of an array element. The reason is that for default character arguments the array sequence is character based rather than array-element based. The substring provides a third way (together with an array and an array element) to specify the beginning of the actual argument character sequence. As with the other two, the sequence extends to the end of the actual array in array element order. Also, as with the other two, the number of characters in the associated dummy array must not exceed the number in the specified portion of the actual array. In addition, as in the array element case, the substring must not be from an element of an assumed-shape or pointer array.

Doesn't simple TKR sound good at this point? Use assumed-shape dummy arrays and assumed-length character dummy arguments, make the TKRs match, and never be frustrated by argument association again. Passing array elements and substrings to dummy arrays is not the preferred way to pass array sections in Fortran 90. Allowing the rank of the actual argument array to be different from that of the dummy argument does offer some functionality not available from TKR, but the Fortran 90 array facilities provide superior alternatives for accomplishing the desired effect. TKR is significantly simpler and safer and, in general, should be the preferred array argument association mechanism.

12.5.2.2 Passing Array Sections. The passing of array sections in procedure references represents an important part of the array processing facility and therefore is a significant feature of Fortran 90. This is a conceptual extension over Fortran 77, because most array sections are discontiguous in the array element order sense. Thus, array element sequence association is not a good mechanism for accommodating the passing of array sections. Assumed-shape dummy arguments do constitute a good mechanism for this purpose and provide the normal method of passing array sections.

There are three principal ways of forming an array section (see Sections 6.4.4 and 6.4.5):

1. an array reference containing a subscript triplet

2. an array reference containing a vector subscript

3. a structure component reference in which a part other than the rightmost is array valued

An array section may also be passed to an explicit-shape or assumed-size dummy array. For reasons of compatibility with Fortran 77 compiled code, the array arguments of procedures with implicit interfaces are assumed to be sequence associated with the dummy arguments. In this case the section must be converted (by the compiler) to a form acceptable for array element sequence association, and possibly reconverted upon return (for example, if it returns results from the procedure execution). Such conversion is likely to result in performance inferior to that obtained from the use of assumed-shape dummy arguments, but is the price of passing array sections to explicit-shape or assumed-size arrays. (Note that assumed-shape dummy arguments require explicit interfaces.)

With this understanding, passing array sections poses no particular conceptual problems. In the case of assumed-shape dummy arguments, the TKR association rules apply. Otherwise the array element sequence association rules apply to the "compacted" section. One restriction that applies to the use of array sections as actual arguments, regardless of the nature of the dummy argument, is that array sections generated by vector subscripts are not definable—that is, they must not be assigned new values by the procedure. The associated dummy argument must not have intent OUT or intent INOUT, or be treated as if they did have either of these attributes. The reason is that with vector subscripts the same actual array element could be part of the array section more than once, and thereby this actual array element becomes associated with more than one dummy argument element. If such an object could be defined, conflicting values could be specified for the same actual array element.

12.5.2.3 Miscellaneous Array Association Rules

1. If the dummy argument is assumed shape, the actual argument must not be an assumed-size array. The reason is that assumed-shape dummy arguments require that complete shape information about the actual argument be supplied to the dummy argument.

Because the size of an assumed-size array is "open ended", complete shape information is not available for assumed-size arrays. Note that a section of an assumed-size array may be used as an actual argument, provided such a section is not open ended (that is, the extent of the last dimension is explicitly specified).

2. Related to the above restriction on not defining dummy arguments associated with array sections containing vector subscripts, the same data object coming into a procedure through two or more arguments must not be defined. For example, if A(1:5) is an actual argument and A(3:9) is another actual argument, then the three elements A(3:5) have come in through two arguments. In this case none of the three elements A(3:5) can be defined in the procedure. This restriction need not involve arrays, and applies to any data object associated to two dummy arguments. If A in the above example were a character string, the same associations are possible and the same restrictions apply. Even for a simple scalar this can be the case. If K is a scalar integer variable, it may appear twice in the actual argument list, but if it does, it must not become defined as a result of a reference to the procedure.

3. Related to the immediately preceding rule, a data object may be available to a procedure through argument association and by a different method of association. For example, it might come in as an actual argument and also be available through use or host association. In this case it can be defined and referenced only as a dummy argument. It would be illegal to assign A a value within subroutine S in the following example:

```
CALL S(A)
  . . .
CONTAINS
  SUBROUTINE S(D)
  D = 5

    . . .
```

4. If the dummy argument is an array that has the pointer attribute, it is effectively an assumed-shape dummy. Therefore the TKR rules apply to associated actual arguments. (The argument association rules that apply to pointers is the topic of the next section.)

5. For generic references, defined operators, or defined assignments, the TKR method is required for all arguments and operands. Thus, an array element must not be passed to an array dummy argument under any circumstance. For example, if SQUIRT is a generic

procedure name, then SQUIRT(A(7)) has a scalar actual argument and the associated dummy argument must be scalar. If the generic procedure procedure allows both a scalar dummy argument and an array dummy argument, the specific procedure with the scalar dummy argument is selected.

6. An array is never passed to an intrinsic procedure (12.5.8) if the actual argument is an array element—only the array element is passed.

12.5.3 Pointer Association

In Fortran 90 a data object may have the POINTER attribute, the TARGET attribute, or neither of these attributes, but not both. Of these three, only the last is provided in Fortran 77. A dummy argument may be any of these three, as may be an actual argument, but of the nine possible combinations for associated actual and dummy arguments two are disallowed and of the remaining cases only the five labeled A–E in Figure 12-5 are distinct (the other two are equivalent to the cases below them in the figure). A pointer is depicted by a bold arrow, and a target by a bull's eye; objects with neither the POINTER nor TARGET attribute are shown as rectangular boxes.

Combination E in Figure 12-5 is where neither the actual nor dummy argument has either the POINTER or TARGET attribute. This situation is completely covered by Sections 12.5.1 and 12.5.2. Combinations B, C, and D are similar; they are the cases in which either the actual or dummy argument, or both, have the target attribute. As far as argument association, per se, is concerned, these cases are very much like combination E. That is, either TKR or array element sequence association (AESA) applies, according to the rules given in Sections 12.5.1.and 12.5.2.

Because cases B, C, and D in Figure 12-5 involve arguments with the target attribute, there may be pointers associated with these targets. In the calling program, a target object may be used as an actual argument (cases B and C), and at the time of the call there may be pointers associated with this target. In the procedure, a dummy argument may have the target attribute (combinations B and D), which means that during execution of the procedure a pointer, including another dummy argument with the pointer attribute, may become associated with this target argument.

The rules governing the associated pointers of target arguments are:

1. During argument association, any pointers associated with a target actual argument remain pointer associated with that object, but do not become pointer associated with the dummy argument. This

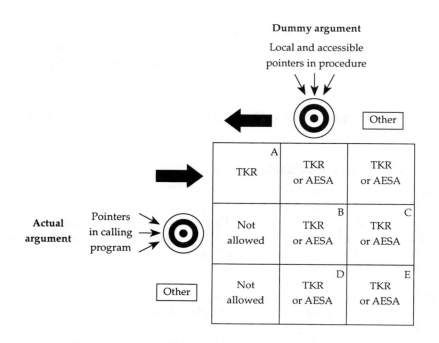

Figure 12-5 Association of objects with POINTER and TARGET attributes

means that even if the actual argument has pointers pointing to it, the procedure does not know what they are, and therefore cannot use this information in any way and cannot affect any such pointer associations in any way.

2. Upon completion of procedure execution and disassociation of the actual and dummy arguments, any pointers associated with the actual argument before the call remain pointing to it.

3. For a dummy argument having the TARGET attribute, its pointer association status with local pointers before argument association is undefined. Upon completion of procedure execution and disassociation of the actual and dummy arguments, the pointer association status of all previously pointer-associated pointers with a dummy argument having the TARGET attribute becomes undefined.

In cases B and D in Figure 12-5, pointer association between the dummy target and pointers has no effect in the calling program. Rule 3 above says that even if the calling program passes a pointer and a target as two different actual arguments, pointer association between these two within the scope of the calling program cannot be established (or removed) by the called procedure.

Case A in Figure 12-5 illustrates that both the actual argument and the dummy argument may have the pointer attribute. When the dummy argument is a pointer, the procedure interface must be explicit in the calling program (see Section 12.6.1), and the associated actual argument must also be a pointer. In this case the following rules apply:

1. The TKR association rules apply.

2. Upon argument association, the dummy argument acquires the same pointer association status as the actual argument and becomes pointer associated with the same target as is the actual argument, if the actual argument is associated with a target.

3. During procedure execution, the pointer association status of the dummy argument may change, and any such changes are reflected in the actual argument.

The two unlabeled allowed cases in Figure 12-5 are those in which the actual argument is a pointer but the dummy argument is not. In this case the actual argument must be associated with a target, and it is this target that becomes argument associated with the dummy argument. Thus, these two cases are equivalent to cases B and C. In effect, the appearance of a pointer as an actual argument, without the dummy argument known to be a pointer, is treated as a pointer reference. In Fortran 90 a pointer reference is treated as a reference to the target. The two cases in Figure 12-5 described as "not allowed" are illegal because the actual arguments would be incompatible with (pointer) operations allowable on the dummy argument.

In case C the procedure interface may or may not be explicit in the calling program. In cases A, B, and D the Fortran 90 rules require explicit interfaces (but in cases B and D there is no real technical need for this requirement). Thus, for example, calling programs may pass target-associated pointers to Fortran 77 procedures, because in reality the underlying (pointed to) object is passed.

12.5.4 Argument Keywords

The fundamental "pairing" of arguments in the actual argument list with those in the dummy argument list is positional, as shown in Figure 12-1. But Fortran 90 also provides an order-independent way of constructing actual argument lists. With this option the programmer can explicitly specify in the call which actual argument is to be associated with an dummy argument rather than using its position in the actual argument list to determine the pairing. To do this the name of the dummy argument, which in this context is referred to as a "keyword", is specified in the actual argument list along with the actual argument. The form that this takes is:

dummy-argument-name = actual-argument

This form may be used for all of the actual arguments in an actual argument list, and the arguments may be in any order. A reference may use keywords for only some of the actual arguments. For those actual arguments not having keywords, the positional mechanism is used to determine the associated dummy arguments. Positionally associated actual arguments must appear in the actual argument list before the keyword actual arguments. After the appearance of the first keyword actual argument (if any) in the actual argument list, all subsequent actual arguments must use keywords. Examples are:

```
CALL GO (X, HT=40)

CALL TELL (XYLOPHONE, NET=10, QP=PI/6)
```

Thus, when only some arguments in the actual argument list use keywords, the first part is positional, with no argument keywords, and the last part uses keywords. In the keyword portion of the list the order of the arguments is completely immaterial, and the keyword alone is used to determine which dummy argument is associated with a given actual argument. Care must be taken with keyword arguments in each call to make sure that one and only one actual argument is specified for each nonoptional dummy argument and that at most one actual argument is specified for each dummy argument.

Keyword actual argument lists can aid readability by decreasing the need to remember the precise sequence of dummy arguments in dummy argument lists. This functionality, and the form that it takes, is modeled after keyword specifiers in input/output statements. The one situation that requires keyword arguments is when an optional argument *not* at the end of the argument list is omitted; keyword arguments constitute the only way to "skip" such arguments in an actual argument list.

To use keyword actual arguments the procedure interface must be explicit in the scope of the program containing the reference. In this case, the defined sequence of dummy argument names (keywords) is known to the calling program, and hence the compiler can generate the proper reference. Intrinsic, internal, and module procedure interfaces are always explicit, and hence keyword references can be used with these. An interface block (12.6.2) must be provided in the calling program for an external procedure before keyword references can be made to it. This "price" of an interface block comes with an interesting benefit not available from the automatic explicitness of intrinsic, internal, and module procedure interfaces—the keywords do not have to be the same as the dummy argument names in the procedure definition. This ability to "tailor" the argument keywords to the application is available only with external procedures.

12.5.5 Optional Arguments

Fortran 90 includes the ability to specify that an argument be optional. This means that an actual argument need not be supplied for it in a particular reference, even though it is in the list of dummy arguments. An optional argument is so specified by giving the dummy argument the optional attribute (see 5.6.3) either in an entity-oriented declaration that includes the OPTIONAL attribute or by its inclusion in an OPTIONAL statement in the procedure definition. The optional attribute can be specified only for a dummy argument. Any dummy argument in any procedure can be specified to be optional.

In a positional argument list, an optional argument at the right-hand end of the list may be simply omitted from the reference. To omit an argument from the keyword part of an actual argument list (12.5.4), that dummy argument name is not used as one of the keywords. Note that the keyword technique must be used to omit an optional argument that is not at the end of the list, unless all of the remaining arguments are also being omitted in this reference. An example of this is:

```
CALL TELL (1.3, T=F(K))
   . . .
SUBROUTINE TELL (X, N, T)
   OPTIONAL N, T
      . . .
END
```

For this reason, optional arguments require explicit procedure interfaces. Note also that a number of the new intrinsic procedures in Fortran 90 have optional arguments. Some of the intrinsic functions from Fortran 77 have been extended with optional arguments as well.

During execution of a procedure with an optional dummy argument, it is usually necessary to know in that particular reference if an actual argument has been supplied for that dummy argument. The PRESENT intrinsic function is available for that purpose (see Sections 13.3.6 and A.80). It is an inquiry function and has one argument, the name of an optional argument in the procedure. Upon execution it returns a value of default logical type, depending on whether or not the dummy argument is associated with an actual argument (see rule 4 below). For example,

```
IF (PRESENT (NUM_CHAR)) THEN
   ! Processing if an actual argument has been
   ! supplied for optional dummy argument NUM_CHAR
   USABLE_NUM_CHAR = NUM_CHAR
ELSE
   ! Processing if nothing is supplied for NUM_CHAR
   USABLE_NUM_CHAR = DEFAULT_NUM_CHAR
END IF
```

illustrates how the PRESENT function can be used to control the processing in the procedure as is appropriate depending on the presence or absence of an optional argument. For an optional dummy argument not present (corresponding actual argument not supplied), the following rules apply.

Rules and restrictions:

1. A dummy argument not present must not be referenced or defined.

2. A dummy procedure not present must not be invoked.

3. A dummy argument not present must not be supplied as an actual argument corresponding to a nonoptional dummy argument, except in a reference to the PRESENT intrinsic function.

4. A dummy argument not present may be supplied as an actual argument corresponding to an optional dummy argument. In this case, the latter dummy argument is also considered to be not present.

Because Fortran 77 does not allow arguments to be optional, a common use of the ENTRY statement (12.4.3) is to define an alternate entry to a procedure whose only difference was an extra argument. With optional arguments in Fortran 90, those uses of the ENTRY statement are now obsolescent, especially when the same procedure name is preferable to separate entry names.

12.5.6 Argument Intent

Any dummy argument, except a procedure or pointer, may be given an INTENT attribute (see Section 5.6.2). There are three possible forms for this attribute:

```
INTENT (IN)
INTENT (OUT)
INTENT (INOUT)
```

The INTENT attribute may be specified only for dummy arguments and indicates something about the intended use of the argument in the procedure. The use of this attribute enables the compiler to detect uses of the argument within the procedure that are inconsistent with the intent.

INTENT(IN) specifies that an argument is to be used to input data to the procedure, is therefore defined upon entry to the procedure, is not to be used to return results to the calling program, and must not be redefined by the procedure. Attempts to change this argument in the procedure cause errors that could be detected.

INTENT(OUT) specifies that an argument is to be used to return results to the calling program and cannot be used to supply input data. A dummy argument with INTENT(OUT) must not be referenced within the procedure before it is defined. The actual argument associated with an INTENT(OUT) dummy must be a definable data object, that is, a variable.

INTENT(INOUT) specifies that an argument has a defined value upon entry to the procedure and that this value may be redefined during execution of the procedure; it may be referenced before being changed. This would be the intent, for example, of a data object whose value is to be updated by the procedure. The actual argument associated with an INTENT(INOUT) dummy must be a definable data object.

Note that actual arguments that are array sections with vector-valued subscripts are not allowed to be associated with dummy arguments having INTENT(OUT) or INTENT(INOUT); that is, the associated dummy argument must not be defined (12.5.2).

The use of the INTENT attribute for a dummy argument does not require an explicit interface, because it governs use within the procedure. Making the interface of a procedure containing an INTENT(OUT) or INTENT(INOUT) dummy argument explicit in the calling program, although not required, can nevertheless be useful in detecting possible attempts to use nondefinable data objects for the associated actual argument.

12.5.7 Resolving References to Generic Procedures

User-defined generic procedures (12.6.3) represent significant functionality in Fortran 90 that is not provided in Fortran 77. Interestingly, generic *intrinsic* procedures are provided in Fortran 77, but not generic *user-defined* procedures. Thus, Fortran 77 programmers are familiar with the concept and use of generic procedures, and generic intrinsics have been very popular with Fortran 77 programmers.

Two or more procedures are generic if they can be referenced with the same name. With such a reference it must be possible to determine which of the procedures is being called. That is, a generic reference must be resolved to that specific procedure in the set of procedures sharing the generic name to which the call applies. The distinguishing property of the reference that is used for this resolution is the nature of the actual argument list. The sequence of TKR patterns in the actual argument in effect selects the appropriate specific procedure to be called. Examples of generic references are:

```
SQRT (32.6)

SQRT (3D+10)

SQRT ((1.1, 2.2))
```

The set of specific procedures making up the generic set are restricted such that any given sequence of actual argument TKR patterns will match only one of the dummy argument lists of this set. Thus, the requirement of TKR matches in the argument lists can be used to resolve generic references. The operational rules follow; for further details see Section 14.2.7. Considering the dummy argument lists of any two procedures in the generic set, one of them must have a nonoptional dummy argument that satisfies both of the following conditions:

1. It must be in a position in the list at which the other list has no dummy argument or it has a TKR pattern different from that of the dummy argument in the same position in the other list.

2. It must have a name different from all the dummy argument names in the other list or it must have a TKR pattern different from that of the dummy argument with the same name in the other list.

The reason for the second of these rules is the need for unique resolution with respect to references with keyword arguments, as well as strictly positional actual argument lists. Section 12.6.3 contains an example that illustrates why just the first rule is not enough.

Because resolution of a generic reference requires matching the actual argument list with the candidate dummy argument lists from the generic set, clearly the interfaces of the procedures in the generic set must be explicit in the scoping unit containing the reference. How this is done and how a procedure is added to a generic set is described in Section 12.6.3.

12.5.8 Elemental References to Intrinsic Procedures

As mentioned briefly in Section 12.5.2, in certain special cases involving references to intrinsic procedures, the rule that disallows passing an actual array to a scalar dummy is relaxed. Many intrinsic procedures have scalar dummy arguments, and many of these may be called with array actual arguments. These are called **elemental** intrinsic procedures. In Fortran 90 there are 64 elemental intrinsic functions and one elemental intrinsic subroutine.

Elemental functions are defined to have scalar results as well as scalar dummy arguments. For an elemental intrinsic function with one argument, calling that function with an array argument causes the function to be applied to each element of that array, with each application yielding a corresponding scalar result value. This collection of result values, one for each element of the actual argument, is returned to the calling program as the result of the function call in the form of an array of the same shape as the actual argument. Thus, the function is applied element-by-element (hence the term elemental reference) to the actual argument, resulting in an array of the same shape as the argument and whose element values are the same as if the function had been individually applied to the corresponding elements of the argument.

The square root function SQRT is an example of an elemental intrinsic function. Its dummy argument is a scalar, and it returns a scalar result. A typical reference to SQRT might be

```
Y = SQRT(X)
```

If both X and Y are scalar variables, this would be a normal call to SQRT, familiar in Fortran 77. In Fortran 90, X and Y can be arrays. Suppose that both are one-dimensional arrays with bounds X(1:100) and Y(1:100). Then the above assignment statement is still valid and has a result equivalent to:

```
DO J = 1, 100
   Y (J) = SQRT (X (J))
END DO
```

except that the elemental call to SQRT does not imply the ordering of the individual computations that is specified by the DO construct. In this case, X and Y have the same shape. What would happen in this example if they did not? Answer: the assignment statement would be invalid, because the result returned by SQRT(X) has the same shape as X, and the assignment statement requires conformable objects on both sides of the equal sign.

If the procedure has more than one dummy argument, can it be called elementally? Yes, if all of the dummy arguments and the result are scalar and the actual arguments are conformable. Of course, there is always an exception: if the name of the dummy argument is KIND (which means its value is a kind type value), its associated actual argument must be scalar; the other actual arguments may be scalars or arrays, as long as they are conformable, and the result has the shape of these arrays or a scalar. The KIND actual argument specifies the kind value for the resulting array.

All of the elemental intrinsic procedures are identified as such in the Appendix A intrinsic procedure descriptions under the heading **class**. Many of these have multiple arguments (including the single intrinsic subroutine MVBITS) and many have a KIND dummy argument. In the case of MVBITS there is no function result, of course (one of the arguments returns the result), but the rule for conformable actual arguments is the same as for the elemental functions.

Prediction: Elemental references will become very popular with Fortran programmers, generating pressure to extend this functionality to user-defined procedures in the next version of the Fortran standard. In some respects elemental references are to Fortran 90 what generic references are to Fortran 77—allowed for intrinsic procedures, but not yet allowed for user-defined procedures. Fortran 90 allows generic references for user-defined procedures as well as intrinsic procedures, and only time will tell if a similar evolution will take place for elemental references.

12.5.9 Alternate Returns

An alternate return is one of the two kinds of procedure arguments that are not data objects (the other is a dummy procedure—see Section 12.5.10). Alternate returns can appear only in subroutine argument lists. They are used to specify a return different than the normal execution upon completion of the subroutine. As mentioned in Section 12.1.1, there are usually superior ways of achieving the desired control, and therefore alternate return is an obsolescent feature. It could be removed from the next revision of the Fortran standard.

There may be any number of alternate returns in a subroutine argument list, and they may appear at any position in the list. In the dummy argument list each alternate return is simply an asterisk. For example, the following dummy argument list for subroutine CALC_2 has two alternate return indicators, in the second and fifth argument positions.

```
SUBROUTINE CALC_2 (A, *, P, Q, *)
```

Alternate returns cannot be optional, and the associated actual arguments cannot have keywords.

Actual arguments associated with alternate return dummy arguments must be asterisks followed by labels of branch targets in the scope of the calling program. They specify the return points for the corresponding alternate returns. For example, the following is a valid reference to CALC_2:

```
CALL CALC_2 (X, *330, Y, Z, *200)
```

provided the statements labeled 200 and 330 are branch targets. The statement having the label 330 is the return point for the first alternate return, and the statement having the label 200 is the return point for the second alternate return.

Use of an alternate return is accomplished with the extended form of the RETURN statement (R1224) described in Section 12.4.1. That form is:

RETURN scalar-integer-expression

The scalar integer expression must have an integer value between 1 and the number of asterisks in the dummy argument list, inclusive. The integer scalar expression value selects which of the alternate returns, counting from left to right, is to be utilized. Using the above example call:

```
RETURN  2   ! returns to statement 200 in the calling program
RETURN (1)  ! returns to statement 330
RETURN      ! normal return from the call
```

12.5.10 Dummy Procedures

A dummy argument may be a name that is subsequently used in the procedure as a procedure name. That is, it may appear in an interface block, in an EXTERNAL or INTRINSIC statement, or as the name of the procedure referenced in a function or subroutine reference. The associated actual argument must be the name (without an argument list) of an external, module, intrinsic, or dummy procedure.

Rules and restrictions:

1. The actual argument must not be the name of an internal procedure or a statement function.

2. The actual argument must not be a generic procedure name, unless there is a specific procedure with the same name; only specific procedures may be passed in argument lists.

3. If the interface of the dummy procedure is explicit, the associated actual procedure must be consistent with this interface as described in Section 12.6.2.2.

4. If the dummy procedure is typed, referenced as a function, or has an explicit function interface, the actual argument must be a function.

5. If the dummy procedure is referenced as a subroutine or has an explicit subroutine interface, the actual argument must be a subroutine.

Dummy procedures may be optional, but must not have the INTENT attribute. They may occur in either function or subroutine subprograms. The associated actual argument may be specified using a keyword.

12.6 Procedure Interfaces

The term **procedure interface** refers to those properties of a procedure that interact with or are of direct concern to a calling program in referencing the procedure. These properties are the names of the procedure and its dummy arguments, the attributes of the procedure (if it is a function), and the attributes and order of the dummy arguments. If these properties are all known to the calling program—that is, known within the scope of the calling program—then the procedure interface is said to be **explicit** in that scope; otherwise, the interface is **implicit** in that scope. Examples of explicit interfaces are Fortran 77 intrinsic procedures; examples of implicit interfaces are Fortran 77 external procedures and statement functions.

Interface blocks may be used in the specification part of a scoping unit to make explicit a procedure interface (other than a statement function) that otherwise would be implicit in that scoping unit. In addition, interface blocks serve four other purposes in Fortran 90:

1. to allow the user to give generic properties to procedures

2. to define new user-defined operators and to extend the generic properties of intrinsic operators

3. to extend the assignment operation to new data combinations (user-defined coercions)

4. to specify that a procedure is external

The following sections describe the roles of explicit interfaces, situations in which explicit interfaces are needed, when a procedure definition provides an explicit interface, and all of the uses of interface blocks.

12.6.1 Explicit Interfaces

The explicit procedure interface is one of the most important features of Fortran 90, for two principal reasons. First, its use can significantly diminish what may be the biggest source of errors in Fortran 77: mismatched data types in procedure references. Second, explicit interfaces enable significant functionality; the following ten situations require explicit interfaces:

1. optional arguments

2. array-valued functions

3. pointer-valued functions

4. character-valued functions whose lengths are determined dynamically

5. assumed-shape dummy arguments (needed for efficient passing of array sections)

6. dummy arguments with the pointer or target attribute

7. keyword actual arguments (which allow for better argument identification and order independence of the argument list)

8. generic procedures (calling different procedures with the same name)

9. user-defined operators (which is just an alternate form for calling certain functions)

10. user-defined assignment (which is just an alternate form for calling certain subroutines)

Explicit interfaces are required for items 1 and 7 in this list so that the proper association between actual and dummy arguments can be established. In Fortran 90 any of the arguments in the dummy argument list may be declared to be optional and any such argument may be omitted in a reference to the procedure. Keyword arguments allow actual arguments to occur in any order and are needed when omitting an optional argument that is not the last in the dummy argument list. Consider, for example, the procedure:

```
SUBROUTINE EX (P, Q, R, S, T); OPTIONAL Q, R, T
```

The following are all valid calls:

```
CALL EX (V, W, X, Y, Z)
CALL EX (V, W, X, Y)                    ! last argument omitted
CALL EX (P=V, Q=W, R=X, S=Y, T=Z) ! same as first call
CALL EX (P=V, Q=W, R=X, S=Y)        ! same as second call
CALL EX (P=V, S=Y)            ! all optional arguments omitted
CALL EX (S=Y, P=V)                ! same as fifth call
CALL EX (R=X, S=Y, P=V, Q=W) ! same as second call
CALL EX (S=Y, T=Z, Q=W, P=V) ! an optional argument omitted
```

The last four of these example CALL statements illustrate why explicit
• interfaces are needed for optional and keyword arguments—namely, so
that the calling routine knows the names of the dummy arguments in
order that the proper subroutine reference can be generated.

Items 2 and 4 in the above list involve function results whose size
(number of "things" returned) is determined by the procedure and may
be different from reference to reference. Explicit interfaces convey the
necessary information to the calling routines to process such references
correctly. Note that other means—for example, additional
declarations—could have been used to convey the necessary information.
As it happens, the design choice made in Fortran 90 was to specify
explicit interfaces, which come "for free" with internal and module procedures.

Item 3 is another case in which the necessary information could
have been conveyed in other ways, but explicit interfaces are again sufficient and, at least for internal and module procedures, place a minimal
burden on the user. In this case the calling procedure needs to know
that there is a layer of indirection (the pointer) buffering the actual data
involved.

Item 5 represents a significant new functionality in Fortran 90, one
that requires additional information in the calling program that is nicely
provided by explicit interfaces. With discontiguous arrays, additional
information must be passed in the call. The Fortran 77 array passing
mechanism requires contiguous arrays and does not require passing the
array shape and size. In contrast, Fortran 90 also allows passing sections
of arrays as arguments, which may comprise array elements discontiguous in storage, and indeed may represent very sparse array sections.
Assumed-shape dummy arrays are provided to accommodate this new
form of array passing. Any array, contiguous or not, may be passed to
either form of dummy argument, assumed-shape or otherwise. For
implicit interfaces an explicit-shape or assumed-size (Fortran 77 style)
dummy argument is the default, and therefore assumed-shaped arguments require explicit interfaces. Discontiguous array sections can be
passed to explicit-shape or assumed-size dummy arguments, but in this

case the processor must pack such sections into contiguous temporaries on entry to the procedure and unpack them on return, possibly incurring performance penalties.

Item 6 is on the list because an actual argument may be a pointer, but what is passed may be either the pointer itself or the target. Which one is passed depends upon what the procedure expects, and hence whether or not the dummy argument has the pointer attribute. The explicit interface provides the required information. The default for implicit interfaces is that the target is passed. This is consistent with both the basic nature of Fortran 77 and the Fortran 90 pointer mechanism—except in extenuating circumstances a pointer reference is a reference to the target. This means that a pointer object can be passed to a Fortran 77 procedure with the effect of passing the target object.

For generic procedures (item 8) the calling routine must be able to disambiguate a generic procedure name; that is, because generic means two or more procedures with the same name, the calling routine must have enough information to determine which specific procedure to invoke for a given reference. Explicit interfaces provide this information by making dummy argument attribute information available to the calling routine. The specific procedure called is the one for which the dummy argument attribute pattern matches that for the actual arguments. Generic procedures, including the use of interface blocks for configuring generic names, are discussed in detail in Section 12.6.3.

User-defined operators (item 9) merely represent an alternative way to reference certain functions. They allow the use of infix operator notation, rather than traditional function notation for two-argument functions. Thus, for example, $A + B$ can be used in place of RATIONAL_ADD (A, B) if A and B are of the derived type representing rational numbers, and the operator " $+$ " has been extended as the operator form of RATIONAL_ADD. An example of using a new operator, rather than extending an intrinsic operator, is P .SMOOTH. 3, where P represents a matrix of picture elements to be "smoothed" and 3 is the size of the smoothing neighborhood. This is alternative syntax for the function reference PICTURE_SMOOTH $(P,3)$. Such alternative syntax provisions are similar to generic procedures, and the same sort of interface information is needed to resolve such references. This topic is treated in detail in Section 12.6.4.

A third form of generic interface provided by Fortran 90 for which explicit interface information is used to resolve references is that of assignment coercion (item 10). This allows a value of one data type to be converted to a corresponding value of another data type and assigned to an object of the latter type. A simple example of coercion, intrinsic to Fortran 77, is $K = X + 2.2$, where X is of type real and K is integer.

Examples of desirable new coercions might be R = K where R is of the derived type representing rational numbers, and K is an integer, and P = M2D where P is of the derived type representing a two-dimensional picture and M2D is a two-dimensional integer array. In Fortran 77 these last two effects would be achieved by subroutine calls:

```
CALL RATINT (R, K)
CALL PXINIT (P, M2D)
```

In Fortran 90 these coercion operations are performed by the same subroutines, but these subroutines may be invoked by the assignment syntax rather than the traditional subroutine call syntax. This topic is treated in more detail in Section 12.6.5.

12.6.2 Interface Blocks

A procedure interface block is used to

1. make explicit interfaces for external and dummy procedures

2. define a generic procedure name, specify the set of procedures to which that name applies, and make explicit the interfaces of any external procedures included in the set

3. define a new operator symbol or specify extension of an intrinsic or already defined operator, identify the function or functions to which it applies, and make explicit the interfaces of any of those functions that are external

4. define one or more new assignment coercions, identify the subroutine or subroutines involved, and make explicit the interfaces of any of those subroutines that are external

In all of these cases, the purpose of the interface block is to make the necessary information available to the calling routine so that a procedure reference can be processed correctly. Therefore, the interface block must either appear in the specification part of the calling routine or be in a module used by the calling routine.

Of the four items listed above, the first is further described below in this section, the second in Section 12.6.3, the third in Section 12.6.4, and the fourth in Section 12.6.5. In the remainder of this section, the general form of interface blocks, covering all four of these cases, is described, followed by a discussion of the simplified form that applies to just the first case. Sections 12.6.3, 12.6.4, and 12.6.5 each deal with specific forms of the interface block that apply to these cases.

12.6.2.1 General Form of Procedure Interface Blocks. Interface blocks (R1201) have the form:

```
INTERFACE [ generic-spec ]
    [ interface-body ] ...
    [ MODULE PROCEDURE procedure-name-list ] ...
END INTERFACE
```

where a generic specification (R1206) is one of the following three things:

```
generic-name
OPERATOR ( defined-operator )
ASSIGNMENT (=)
```

and an interface body (R1204) specifies the interface for either a function or a subroutine:

```
function-statement
    [ specification-part ]
END FUNCTION [ function-name ]
```

```
subroutine-statement
    [ specification-part ]
END SUBROUTINE [ subroutine-name ]
```

Rules and restrictions:

1. If the generic specification is omitted, the MODULE PROCEDURE option must also be omitted; the form without the generic specification applies to case 1 in the list of four above.

2. The choice of a generic name for a generic specification is case 2; the OPERATOR choice for a generic specification is case 3; and the ASSIGNMENT choice for a generic specification is case 4.

3. In all cases an interface body must be for an external or dummy procedure.

4. The specification part of an interface body contains specifications pertaining only to the dummy arguments and, in the case of functions, the function result. This means, for example, that an interface body cannot contain an ENTRY statement, DATA statement, FORMAT statement, or statement function statement.

5. The attributes of the dummy arguments and function result must be completely specified in the specification part, and these specifications must be consistent with those specified in the procedure definition. Note that dummy argument names may be different, but the attributes must be the same.

6. Because an interface block describes properties defined in an external scope rather than in its host's scope, an interface block comprises its own scoping unit, separate from any other scoping unit; an interface block does not inherit anything from its host via host association, such as named constants or implicit type rules.

7. An interface body may contain a USE statement and access entities, such as derived-type definitions, via use association.

8. A procedure name in a MODULE PROCEDURE statement must be the name of a module procedure either in that module (if the host of the interface block is a module) or accessible to the host through use association.

9. An interface block must not contain an ENTRY statement, but an entry interface may be specified by using the entry name as the function or subroutine name in an interface body.

10. A procedure must not have more than one explicit interface in a given scoping unit.

11. An interface block must not appear in a block data program unit.

12. Note that the keywords FUNCTION and SUBROUTINE are not optional in the END statements of interface bodies.

12.6.2.2 Explicit Interfaces for External Procedures. The simplest use of interface blocks is to make the interfaces for external (and dummy) procedures explicit. The form of the interface block for this purpose is:

```
INTERFACE
    [ interface-body ] ...
END INTERFACE
```

Rules and restrictions 3–7 and 9–12 apply in this case. Rule 6 means that IMPLICIT statements, type declarations, and derived-type definitions in the host do not carry down into an interface block. Rule 10 means that an interface body for a given external procedure may be specified at most once in a host program unit. An interface body cannot be specified for intrinsic, internal, and module procedures, because these procedures already have explicit interfaces.

12.6.3 Generic Procedures

Fortran 77 programmers are familiar with generic procedures, because many of the intrinsic procedures in Fortran 77 are generic. An example is:

```
INT (R)
INT (D)
```

where R and D are respectively REAL and DOUBLE PRECISION objects. It looks like there is only one procedure involved here (INT), but there are really two. There is a specific procedure lurking around that accepts a real argument and another one that accepts a double precision argument. Because the purpose of these two procedures is virtually identical, it is desirable to refer to each of them with the same generic name. The type of the argument is sufficient to identify which of the specific procedures is involved in a given reference.

Thus, generic refers to a set of different procedures with different specific names that all have the same (generic) name. Fortran 77 limits this functionality to intrinsic procedures with the generic aspects predefined in the language. This extremely popular feature of Fortran 77 has been extended in Fortran 90 to allow users to define additional generic properties involving intrinsic and user-defined procedures. The mechanism for this is the interface block, which in this case has the form:

```
INTERFACE generic-name
    [ interface-body ] ...
    [ MODULE PROCEDURE procedure-name-list ] ...
END INTERFACE
```

Rules and restrictions 3–12 in Section 12.6.2.1 apply in this case. The generic name in the INTERFACE statement, of course, specifies the generic name to be used in this host. All the procedures being assigned this generic name are specified in the interface block. This potentially includes both external procedures and module procedures. In the case of an external procedure, the procedure is identified by its specific name and its interface, thereby making its interface explicit as well as defining a generic name for it. In the case of a module procedure, only the specific name of the procedure is given (in order to identify the procedure) because its interface is already explicit. Note that because of rule 10 (Section 12.6.2.1) an external procedure can be included in only one generic set in a given host. Because the MODULE PROCEDURE statement does not specify an explicit interface, however, a module procedure may be included in any number of generic sets.

Note also that internal procedures cannot be given generic names, nor can statement functions. Similarly, intrinsic procedures cannot be included in an interface block, but a generic name may be the same as an intrinsic procedure name, including a generic intrinsic procedure name. For example:

```
INTERFACE INT
    MODULE PROCEDURE RATIONAL_TO_INTEGER
END INTERFACE
```

is allowed, which extends the generic properties of INT to include a user-defined procedure. The generic name may also be the same as one of the specific names of the procedures included in the generic set, or the same as any other generic name, or completely different. The only real requirement is that any procedure reference involving a generic procedure name be resolvable to one specific procedure. Thus, for example, the generic name INT cannot be applied to a user-defined function that has a single real argument, because then a reference to INT with a real actual argument would be ambiguous as to whether the reference was to the corresponding intrinsic function or to the user-defined function.

Moreover, there may be any number of generic names active in any given scoping unit. A common situation will be that a number of generic names will be imported by USE statements. Any of these generic sets may be increased arbitrarily, as long as any procedure reference can be uniquely resolved to a specific procedure.

The rules for resolving a generic reference involve the number of arguments and the type, kind type parameter, and rank of each argument. Based upon these rules, and only these rules, a given procedure reference must be consistent with precisely one of the specific procedures in the generic set. This concept is fairly simple, but there is a subtle aspect to it. Consider, for example, a simple two-argument subroutine G (P, Q) with generic name G, dummy argument names P and Q, and neither argument optional. A reference to G, with actual arguments X and Y could take any of the following four forms:

```
CALL G (X, Y)
CALL G (X, Q=Y)
CALL G (P=X, Q=Y)
CALL G (Q=Y, P=X)
```

The last three are allowed because the interface to G is explicit and keyword references may be used when the interface is explicit. What subroutine H could be added to the generic set with G? The first of the above four calls rules out any two-argument H whose first argument has the same type, kind type parameter, and rank (TKR) as the P argument of G and whose second argument has the same TKR as the Q argument of G. The third and fourth of these four calls rules out any subroutine H of the form H (Q, P), whose first argument is named Q and has the same TKR as the Q (second) argument of G and whose second argument is named P and has the same TKR as the P (first) argument of G. The reason for this last case is that a reference to H in which all the actual arguments had keywords would look exactly like a call to G, in terms of TKR patterns; such a reference would not be uniquely resolvable to either a call to G only or to H only. Any other H could be included in the generic set with G.

Thus, the essence of the generic reference resolution rules is uniqueness with respect to TKR patterns under both positional or keyword references. The complete formal rules for this are given in Section 14.2.7.

A procedure may always be referenced by its specific name. It may also be referenced by any generic name it might also have been given.

12.6.4 Defind Operators

Just as generic names allow the user to give procedures alternative and presumably "better" forms of reference, so do defined operators. In this case functions of one or two nonoptional arguments are involved.

Often the purpose of a function is to perform some computation (operation) on the values represented by its arguments and to return the result for computational use in the calling program. In mathematical tradition, such operations of one or two arguments are usually expressed as operators in an expression, with the arguments as the operands. A good example is the INVERSE function given in Section 11.6.5.4. The defined operator provisions of the interface block give users the option of specifying a function reference with operator syntax. Conceptually, it is very similar to that of generic procedures, although syntactically quite different, and may be considered a special form of generic functions.

The form of the interface block for defining a new operator or extending the generic properties of an existing operator is:

```
INTERFACE OPERATOR ( defined-operator )
     [ interface-body ] ...
     [ MODULE PROCEDURE procedure-name-list ] ...
END INTERFACE
```

Pretty much the same rules apply here as in the generic name case. In addition, each interface body must be for a one- or two-argument function, and each procedure name in the MODULE PROCEDURE statement must be that of a one- or two-argument function. The arguments must all be nonoptional and all must be specified with INTENT(IN).

The defined operator in the INTERFACE statement specifies the operator that can be used in the operation form of reference for each of the functions identified in the interface block. The operation takes the infix (operator between the arguments) form for two-argument functions and takes the prefix form for one-argument functions. For example:

```
INTERFACE OPERATOR (+)
   FUNCTION INTEGER_PLUS_INTERVAL (X, Y)
      USE INTERVAL_ARITHMETIC
      TYPE (INTERVAL)              :: INTEGER_PLUS_INTERVAL
      INTEGER                      :: X
      TYPE (INTERVAL), INTENT (IN) :: Y
   END FUNCTION INTEGER_PLUS_INTERVAL
   MODULE PROCEDURE RATIONAL_ADD
END INTERFACE
```

extends the "+" operator to two user-defined functions, an external function INTEGER_PLUS_INTERVAL that presumably computes an appropriate value for the sum of an integer value and something called an "interval", and a module function RATIONAL_ADD that probably computes the sum of two "rational numbers". Both functions now can be called in the form A+B, where A and B are the two actual arguments. An example of new operator definition, rather than extending existing operators, is:

```
INTERFACE OPERATOR (.INVERSETIMES.)
   MODULE PROCEDURE MATRIX_INVERSE_TIMES
END INTERFACE
```

Now the inverse of matrix A can be multiplied by B using the expression A .INVERSETIMES. B, which produces $A^{-1} \times B$, and in effect solves the system of linear equations, $Ax = B$, for x.

Functions with operator interfaces may be referenced with the operator form, but they also may be referenced via the traditional functional form using the specific function name.

Note that the two forms for a defined operator given by (R311, R704, R724):

intrinsic-operator
   . letter [letter] ... .

are the same as some of the intrinsic operators and that neither .TRUE. nor .FALSE. may be chosen as a defined operator. Note also that if an operator has the same name as an intrinsic operator, it must have the same number of operands as the intrinsic operator; for example, .NOT. must not be defined as a binary operator.

Operator interfaces define a set of generic procedures, with the operator being the "generic name". This is particularly obvious with intrinsic operators, as each intrinsic operation may be thought of as being performed by a "hidden intrinsic function" and the operator interface merely extends the set of functions that share that operator form. As with the use of generic procedure names, a function reference via a generic operator must resolve to a unique specific function. The resolution rules in this case are exactly the same TKR rules used for the generic name case when the functional form is used (see the previous section), but are somewhat simpler when the operator syntax is used, because this syntax does not allow the use of argument keywords. Thus, the argument TKR pattern must be unique solely on the basis of argument position.

This means, for example, that "+" cannot be specified in an operator interface for a function with a scalar integer argument and a scalar real argument, because "+" already has a meaning for any such TKR pattern. Specifying such an operator extension would mean that $I+R$, where I is a scalar integer and R is a scalar real, would be ambiguous between the intrinsic meaning and the extended meaning. Therefore, the Fortran 90 TKR rules disallow such extensions. Of course, because the interfaces of all generic procedures, including defined operators, are explicit, the compiler can detect when a violation of these TKR rules is attempted.

12.6.5 Defined Assignment

The last form of generic procedures in Fortran 90 is assignment (or conversion) subroutines. These specify the conversion of data values (see Section 12.6.3) with one set of TKR attributes into another set with a different pattern of TKR attributes. Although such conversions can be performed by ordinary subroutines, it is convenient and "natural" to express their use with assignment syntax, and hence defined assignment extensions. If one wishes to think of assignment as an "operation", then defined assignment is precisely the same as defined operators, except that there is only one defined assignment operator symbol (=), and all defined assignment procedures are two-argument subroutines rather than functions. As with the other forms of generic procedures, the interface block is used to specify defined assignments.

The form of the interface block for defining new assignment operations is:

```
INTERFACE ASSIGNMENT (=)
    [ interface-body ] ...
    [ MODULE PROCEDURE procedure-name-list ] ...
END INTERFACE
```

Again, most of the same rules apply here as in the generic name case, except that each interface body must be for a two-argument external subroutine and each procedure name in the MODULE PROCEDURE

statement must be that of an accessible two-argument module subroutine.
Neither argument may be optional. The first argument must have the
attribute INTENT(OUT) or INTENT(INOUT); this is the location for the
converted value. The second argument must have the attribute
INTENT(IN); this is the value to be converted.

The assignment interface specifies that an assignment statement can
be used in place of a traditional subroutine call for the subroutines identified in the interface block. The form of this assignment is:

variable = expression

where the variable would be the first actual argument in a traditional call
to the subroutine and the expression would be the second argument. The
variable must be a variable designator legitimate for the left-hand side of
an assignment. The traditional subroutine call may continue to be used
as well as the assignment syntax.

An example of an assignment interface block is:

```
INTERFACE ASSIGNMENT (=)
   SUBROUTINE ASSIGN_STRING_TO_CHARACTER (C, S)
      USE STRING_DATA
      CHARACTER (*), INTENT (OUT) :: C
      TYPE (STRING), INTENT (IN)  :: S
   END SUBROUTINE ASSIGN_STRING_TO_CHARACTER
   MODULE PROCEDURE  RATIONAL_TO_INTEGER
END INTERFACE
```

This interface block allows ASSIGN_STRING_TO_CHARACTER (which
extracts the character value) to be called in the form:

C = S

In addition, RATIONAL_TO_INTEGER may be called in the form

R = K

where R is of derived type RATIONAL and K is an integer. The purpose of RATIONAL_TO_INTEGER presumably is to convert an integer
value into the appropriate RATIONAL form.

In analogy with the discussion of generic operators in the preceding
section, each intrinsically defined assignment operation may be thought
of as being performed by a hidden intrinsic subroutine. Thus, the assignment symbol is the generic name of a set of generic subroutines. The
assignment interface block allows the user to add user-defined external
and module subroutines to that generic set. In analogy with generic
operators, any given assignment must be resolvable to the specific

subroutine. Not surprisingly, when assignment syntax is used, it is the TKR pattern rules (see Section 12.6.3) without the keyword argument complication that are applied to perform this resolution, exactly as with defined operators.

This means, for example, that an assignment interface cannot be specified for a subroutine whose first argument is a scalar of type integer and whose second argument is a scalar of type real. All such coercions have intrinsic meanings, and thus an assignment interface block of this form would introduce an unresolvable ambiguity. The TKR rules prevent this from happening, and the compiler can detect when a violation of these rules is attempted.

12.7 Summary

Procedure Properties

Table 12-1 summarizes the properties of Fortran procedures.

Table 12-1 Summary of Fortran procedure properties

Property of procedure	External	Intrinsic	Module	Internal	Statement function
Dummy arguments may be optional	Yes	Yes	Yes	Yes	No
Call may use keywords	Yes	Yes	Yes	Yes	No
Call may be recursive	Yes	N/A	Yes	Yes	No
Definition may have CONTAINS	Yes	N/A	Yes	No	No
May be passed	Yes	Yes	Yes	No	No
May appear in an interface body	Yes	No	No	No	No
Interface automatically explicit	No	Yes	Yes	Yes	No
May be called elementally	No	Yes	No	No	No
May be used to define operators	Yes	No	Yes	No	No
May be generic	Yes	Yes	Yes	No	No
May contain ENTRY statements	Yes	N/A	Yes	No	N/A

Subroutine

A user-defined subroutine is either an external, a module, or an internal procedure. Five intrinsic procedures are subroutines. A subroutine consists of a self-contained body of statements describing a particular task that may be called upon in a Fortran program. Subroutines are invoked with a CALL statement. The subroutine argument list contains both input and output data objects. (See Section 12.2.)

```
SUBROUTINE MARY (X, ROBERT, DUST)
   REAL, OPTIONAL :: X, ROBERT, DUST
   . . .
END SUBROUTINE MARY
   . . .
CALL MARY (DUST = 21, X = 4.3)
```

Function

A user-defined function is either an external, a module, or an internal procedure. There are over 100 intrinsic functions. Functions and subroutines are similar in definition. A function is referenced as an operand in an expression by using its name followed by actual arguments, if any. The arguments to a function serve primarily as input to the function; the function result is the principal output. (See Section 12.3.)

```
FUNCTION PRESSURE (TE)
   . . .
END
   . . .
X = PRESSURE (Y*2.3) + XSET
```

ENTRY Statement

The ENTRY statement defines an additional procedure associated with a subprogram. The number of procedures defined by a procedure subprogram is $n+1$, where n is the number of ENTRY statements in the subprogram. (See Section 12.4.3.)

```
ENTRY GG (X)
```

Statement Function

The statement function is a facility that allows the programmer to encapsulate a computation that can be defined with a single scalar expression. (See Section 12.3.4.)

```
FCOS (Y) = Y * Q
   . . .
TEMP = FCOS (T) ** 5
```

Assignment Subroutines

A subroutine may be configured as a defined assignment, which extends the use of the assignment statement for making coercions and assigning values. (See Section 12.6.5.)

```
INTERFACE ASSIGNMENT (=)
   SUBROUTINE ASSIGN_ARRAY_MATRIX (MATRIX, ARRAY)
      TYPE (MATRIX_TYPE)  MATRIX
      REAL                ARRAY(:,:)
      . . .
   END SUBROUTINE
END INTERFACE
. . .
TYPE (MATRIX_TYPE)  MATRIX_A
REAL                A(10,10)
. . .
MATRIX_A = A
```

Operator Functions

A function may be configured as a defined operation. New operators may be defined, and intrinsic operators extended. (See Section 12.6.4.)

```
INTERFACE OPERATOR (.SQUARE.)
   FUNCTION OP (X)
      OP = X * X
   END FUNCTION OP
END INTERFACE
. . .
PRINT *, A + .SQUARE. B
```

Generic Procedures

A set of procedures may be given a generic name, and generic intrinsic names may be applied to user-defined procedures. (See Section 12.6.3.)

Explicit Interfaces

The interfaces of intrinsic, module, and internal procedures are always explicit. The interface of an external procedure is normally implicit, but may be made explicit with an interface block. The interfaces of statement functions are always implicit. (See Section 12.6.1.)

Optional Arguments

Arguments may be specified as optional in external, module, and internal procedures. Some of the intrinsic procedures have optional arguments. The PRESENT intrinsic function allows user-defined procedures to determine the presence or absence of an actual argument associated with an optional dummy argument. (See Section 12.5.5.)

Keyword Arguments

Actual arguments may be specified with keywords, which provide order independence and accommodate the omission of optional arguments. Keywords are dummy argument names, and their use requires explicit interfaces. (See Section 12.5.4.)

Recursion

External, module, and internal procedures may be directly and indirectly recursive. Recursive procedures require use of the RECURSIVE keyword in the procedure definition, and recursive functions often require use of the RESULT clause. (See Sections 12.1.2, 12.2.1, 12.3.1, and 12.3.2.)

```
RECURSIVE FUNCTION F(I)  RESULT (R)
   IF (I<0) THEN;   R = 1
   ELSE;   R = I*G(I-1)
   END IF
END FUNCTION   F

RECURSIVE FUNCTION G(I)  RESULT (R)
   IF (I<0) THEN;   R = 1
   ELSE;   R = I+F(I-1)
   END IF
END FUNCTION   G
```

F9◐

13

Intrinsic Procedures

Intrinsic procedures are functions and subroutines that are part of any standard-conforming implementation of Fortran 90; they are specified in the standard and thus are called **intrinsic**. Examples of intrinsic procedures are SIN, COS, SUM, RANDOM_NUMBER, and SHAPE. There are 113 intrinsic procedures available in Fortran 90—five intrinsic subroutines and 108 intrinsic functions.

Intrinsic procedures are always "there", and may be called from any program unit or subprogram. However, a user-written function or subroutine with the same name as an intrinsic function or subroutine takes precedence over the intrinsic procedure in a given scoping unit if its interface is explicit, it is listed in an EXTERNAL statement in that scoping unit, or it is a statement function. The intrinsic procedure takes precedence if and only if there is no statement function with this name, and it is either listed in an INTRINSIC statement or the user-defined procedure's interface is implicit in that scoping unit. For example, a module or internal procedure always overrides an intrinsic procedure with the same name (in the absence of an applicable INTRINSIC statement) because its interface is explicit.

All of the Fortran 90 intrinsic procedures are listed in Table 13-1, and each of these procedures is described in detail in Appendix A.

13.1 Intrinsic Procedure Terms and Concepts

Intrinsic procedures are "pre-defined" by the language, but otherwise conform to the principles and rules for procedures as described in Chapter 12. In particular, intrinsic procedures are invoked in the same way as other procedures (12.2.2 and 12.3.3) and employ the same argument association mechanisms (12.5). An intrinsic procedure's interface is explicit in all scoping units, but may be superseded by a user-defined procedure. The intrinsic procedure interfaces, including the argument keywords (dummy argument names) and argument optionality, are all described partially in Section 13.8 and completely in Appendix A.

Generic Procedures. All the intrinsic procedures except four functions (LGE, LGT, LLE, LLT) are generic and each corresponds to two or more underlying specific intrinsic procedures. Each specific intrinsic procedure has a specific type/kind pattern and sometimes rank requirements for its argument list, and resolution of a reference to a generic intrinsic procedure is based upon this pattern as described in Section 12.5.7.

Some of the specific intrinsic functions have names, which are listed in Table 13-2. The specific names may be used in procedure references, although this is not recommended. When passing intrinsic functions as actual arguments, the specific names must be used; thus, only the specific intrinsic functions listed in Table 13-2 can be passed. Note that several of these (marked with an asterisk) are explicitly disallowed from being used as actual arguments. Note also from Table 13-2 that some of the specific intrinsic names are the same as the generic names.

Elemental Procedures. As mentioned in Section 12.5.8, many of the intrinsic functions and one intrinsic subroutine may be referenced elementally. This extends those intrinsic procedures to array arguments and results in a natural way. The intrinsic procedures that can be called elementally are the conversion functions (13.4), the computation functions (13.5, except for REPEAT, TRIM, and the vector and matrix multiplication functions DOT_PRODUCT and MATMUL), and the MVBITS subroutine. The inquiry and numeric manipulation functions (13.3) and array functions (13.6) are not elemental.

Transformational Procedures. A transformational intrinsic procedure is one that is not elemental. A transformational procedure has either a dummy argument that is array valued (for example, the SUM function) or an actual argument that is array valued without causing an elemental interpretation (for example, the SHAPE function). The inquiry and numeric manipulation functions (13.3), the array functions (13.6), and the vector and matrix multiplication functions DOT_PRODUCT and MATMUL (13.5) are all transformational. In essence, a transformational function "transforms" an array actual argument into a scalar result or another array, rather than applying the argument element-by-element.

Argument Keywords. Intrinsic procedure references may use keyword arguments, as described in Section 12.5.4. A number of Fortran 90 intrinsic procedure arguments are optional (12.5.5), and the use of keywords helps in omitting corresponding actual arguments. For example, in

```
CALL RANDOM_SEED (PUT=SEED_VALUE)
```

the keyword form shown must be used because the optional first argument SIZE is omitted.

Intrinsic procedure keywords (dummy argument names) have been made as consistent as possible, including using the same name in different intrinsic procedures for dummy arguments that play a corresponding or identical role. These include DIM, MASK, KIND, and BACK.

DIM is used, mostly in the array reduction functions and in some of the other array functions (13.6), to specify which dimension of the array is involved, if not the whole array. DIM is a scalar integer and usually is optional.

MASK is used, mostly in the array functions, to "mask out" elements of an array that are not to be involved in the operation. For example, in the function SUM, any element of the array that is not to be included in the sum of the elements can be excluded by use of an appropriate mask. The MASK is a logical array with the same shape as the array it is masking; it usually is an optional argument.

KIND is an argument that is used mainly in the transfer and conversion functions (13.4) to specify the kind type parameter of the function result. The KIND actual argument must be a scalar integer initialization expression, even in elemental references; it is usually optional.

BACK is an optional logical argument used in several of the intrinsic functions to specify reverse order (backward) processing. For example, if BACK=.TRUE. in the INDEX function, then the search is performed beginning from the right end of the string rather than the left end.

13.2 Representation Models

Some of the Fortran 90 intrinsic functions compute values related to how data is represented. These values are based upon and determined by the underlying **representation model**. There are three such models in Fortran 90: the **bit model**, the **integer number system model**, and the **real number system model**.

These models, and the corresponding functions returning values related to the models, allow development of robust and portable code. For example, by obtaining information about the spacing of real numbers, the convergence of a numerical algorithm can be controlled so that maximum accuracy may be achieved while attaining convergence.

In a given implementation the model parameters are chosen to match the implementation as closely as possible, but an exact match is not required and the model does not impose any particular arithmetic on the implementation.

13.2.1 The Bit Model

The bit model interprets a nonnegative scalar data object of type integer as a sequence of binary digits (bits), based upon the model

$$\sum_{k=0}^{n-1} b_k 2^k$$

where n is the number of bits and each b_k has a bit value of 0 or 1. The bits are numbered from right to left beginning with 0.

The bit computation functions in Section 13.5 are based upon the bit model. The model deals only with nonnegative integers interpreted through these functions and the MVBITS subroutine, and it is not necessarily related to the implementation of the integer data type. It also is independent of the BOZ constants (4.3.1.4).

13.2.2 The Integer Number System Model

The integer number system is modeled by

$$i = s \sum_{k=0}^{q-1} d_k r^k$$

where

i is the integer value
s is the sign (+1 or –1)
r is the radix (integer greater than 1)
q is the number of digits (integer greater than 0)
d_k is the kth digit and is an integer $0 \le d_k < r$

The integer number system model may model the implementation's integer data type exactly, but it need not. It does, however, provide accurate information about the implementation, such as its largest integer value.

13.2.3 The Real Number System Model

The real number system is modeled by

$$x = s\, b^e \sum_{k=1}^{p} f_k b^{-k}$$

where

x is the real value
s is the sign (+1 or –1)
b is the base (real radix) and is an integer greater than 1
e is an integer between some minimum and maximum value
p is the number of mantissa digits and is an integer greater than 1
f_k is the kth digit and is an integer $0 \le f_k < b$,
       but f_1 may be zero only if all the f_k are zero

The real number system model may model the implementation's real data type exactly, but it need not. One common implementation is the IEEE floating point standard, which has single precision model numbers:

$b = 2$
$p = 24$
$-126 \le e \le 127$

This IEEE standard does not represent f_1, which is presumed to be 1. Thus, the mantissa, including its sign, can be represented in 24 bits. The exponent, including sign, takes 8 bits, for a total of 32 bits in the single precision representation. What normally would be an exponent value of –127 is not included in the exponent range; rather, IEEE uses this case to identify, for example, the real value zero (the one case in which f_1 is 0) and NaNs (illegal or out-of-range values).

The numeric inquiry and manipulation functions return much useful information about the real number system model pertaining to an implementation.

13.3 Inquiry and Numeric Manipulation Functions

Fortran 90 has a number of intrinsic functions known as **inquiry functions** and **numeric manipulation functions**. These are sometimes called the "environmental intrinsics". These functions, rather than performing some computation with their arguments, return information concerning the status or nature of the argument. An inquiry function returns information about the data type of its argument, and the returned value is independent of the value of the argument; the actual argument of a reference to such a function need not be defined. A numeric manipulation function, on the other hand, returns numeric environmental information dependent on the value of the actual argument; the actual argument of a reference to such a function must be defined. Fortran 77 has one inquiry function, LEN, that returned the declared length (number of characters) of the argument character string, and no numeric manipulation functions. Fortran 90 has a large set of inquiry and numeric manipulation functions.

Character Inquiry Function (LEN). The LEN intrinsic function, as in Fortran 77, returns the declared length (number of characters) of the argument character string. The argument need not be defined, as its value is not required in order to determine its length. For assumed-length dummy arguments, LEN returns the length of the actual argument.

Bit Inquiry Function (BIT_SIZE). The BIT_SIZE function returns the number of bits n provided by the bit model (13.2.1) in a scalar data object of type integer. The argument for BIT_SIZE is an integer, which need not be defined.

Kind Functions. The KIND inquiry function returns the kind type parameter of its argument, which may be of any intrinsic type. The value of the argument need not be defined. Somewhat related to the KIND function, but providing a complementary functionality, are two transformational functions, SELECTED_REAL_KIND and SELECTED_INT_KIND.

SELECTED_REAL_KIND returns the real kind type parameter corresponding to the decimal precision and exponent range specified by its arguments. SELECTED_INT_KIND returns the integer kind type parameter corresponding to the decimal exponent range specified by its argument. Figure 13-1 illustrates these three functions. KIND maps "variable space" into kind values. SELECTED_INTEGER_KIND maps "decimal integer model space" into kind values. The SELECTED_REAL_KIND function maps "decimal real model space" into kind values.

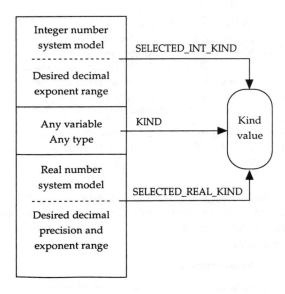

Figure 13-1 The three intrinsic functions returning KIND values

Numeric Inquiry Functions. There are nine environmental intrinsic inquiry functions that together describe the numerical environment in terms of the integer model (13.2.2) and real model (13.2.3).

Function	Value returned
DIGITS	q for an integer argument and p for a real argument
EPSILON	b^{1-p} for a real argument (small compared to 1)
HUGE	Largest number in the model (real or integer)
MINEXPONENT	The minimum value of e for a real argument
MAXEXPONENT	The maximum value of e for a real argument
PRECISION	Decimal precision (real or complex)
RADIX	The base b of the model (real or integer)
RANGE	Decimal exponent range (real, complex, or integer)
TINY	Smallest positive value for a real argument

The arguments for these nine functions need not be defined. Note that all are generic in that each can be used with any kind of real argument, and all but MINEXPONENT, MAXEXPONENT, and EPSILON can be used with any kind of integer argument as well.

There are seven numeric manipulation functions that deal with values, based upon the real number model associated with a single numeric object, rather than the model properties that apply to the entire type kind. Therefore, the actual arguments of these seven must be defined before the function is referenced.

Function	Value returned
EXPONENT	Value of e for the real value
FRACTION	Fractional part of a real value
NEAREST	Nearest processor number in a given direction
RRSPACING	Reciprocal of the relative spacing near the argument
SCALE	Change the value of e by a specified value
SET_EXPONENT	Set the value of e to a specified value
SPACING	Model absolute spacing near the argument

These seven functions apply only to the real environment but are generic over all of the kinds of real supported by the implementation and may be called elementally.

Array Inquiry Functions. Many of the intrinsic functions added in Fortran 90 are related to arrays and constitute a rich set of array operations. The array inquiry functions allow certain properties of an array to be determined dynamically.

Function	Value returned
ALLOCATED	Allocation status of the argument array
LBOUND	Lower bound(s) of an array or a dimension of an array
SHAPE	Number of elements in each dimension of an array
SIZE	The size (total number of elements) of an array
UBOUND	Upper bound(s) of an array or a dimension of an array

The array argument for these five functions need not be defined, but the optional DIM argument must be defined if it is used (in SIZE, LBOUND, or UBOUND).

Pointer Association Status Inquiry Function (ASSOCIATED). The inquiry function ASSOCIATED returns true if the argument, which must have the pointer attribute, is currently associated with a target. If the optional second argument is supplied, ASSOCIATED returns true if the pointer is currently associated with this second argument; if the second argument is a pointer, ASSOCIATED returns true if both arguments are associated with the same target.

Argument Presence Inquiry Function (PRESENT). The inquiry function PRESENT permits the programmer to determine if an actual argument has been supplied for a dummy argument specified as optional. The argument to the PRESENT function must be the name of an optional dummy argument. In general, PRESENT returns true if an actual argument has been supplied and returns false otherwise (but see 12.5.5 for the details).

13.4 Transfer and Conversion Functions

Fortran 90 contains a number of intrinsic functions to transfer or convert data values from one type and kind (TK) combination to another TK combination. Most of these are also intrinsic functions in Fortran 77, though the optional KIND argument has been added to many in Fortran 90. Most are also generic, as they are in Fortran 77, providing the appropriate conversion for a number of different argument TK patterns.

Function	Value returned
ACHAR	Character in the specified position of the ASCII character set
AIMAG	The imaginary part of a complex argument value
AINT	A real value truncated to an integer (result is still real)
ANINT	A real value rounded to the nearest integer (result is still real)
CHAR	Character in the specified position of the processor character set
CMPLX	The corresponding complex value of the argument
CONJG	The complex conjugate of a complex argument
DBLE	The corresponding double precision value of the argument
IACHAR	Position of the specified character in the ASCII character set
IBITS	A specified substring of bits of an integer argument
ICHAR	Position of the specified character in the processor character set
INT	The corresponding (truncated) integer value of the argument
LOGICAL	The corresponding logical value of the argument
NINT	A real value rounded to the nearest integer
REAL	The corresponding real value of the argument

All of the functions in this list may be called elementally.

The TRANSFER Intrinsic Function. The TRANSFER function allows "binary transfer" of data between different TK patterns without conversion of any sort. The physical representation (for example, bit pattern) of the source data is transferred to the function result unchanged; the TK pattern of the function result is that of the MOLD argument. The TRANSFER function is transformational, not elemental. Note that the TRANSFER function cannot produce portable results.

13.5 Computation Functions

The computation intrinsic functions perform certain computational operations, delivering the results of these computations as the function results. These 47 computation functions are organized into three groups: numeric computation functions (26), character computation functions (12), and bit computation functions (9).

Because of the dependence on the number of bits in the bit model, the bit manipulation procedures may yield nonportable results.

Numeric Computation Functions

Function	Value returned
ABS	The absolute value of the argument
ACOS	The arc cosine of the argument
ASIN	The arc sine of the argument
ATAN	The arc tangent of the argument
ATAN2	The angle in radians of a complex argument (X,Y)
CEILING	The smallest integer greater than or equal to the argument value
COS	The cosine of the argument
COSH	The hyperbolic cosine of the argument
DIM	The difference of two values, if positive, or zero otherwise
DOT_PRODUCT	The dot product of two vectors
DPROD	The double precision product of two single precision values
EXP	The natural exponential function
FLOOR	The greatest integer less than or equal to the argument value
LOG	The natural logarithm function
LOG10	The logarithm to the base 10
MATMUL	Matrix multiplication
MAX	The maximum of a set of values
MIN	The minimum of a set of values
MOD	The remainder function, having the sign of the first argument
MODULO	The remainder function, having the sign of the second argument
SIGN	Apply a given sign to a given value
SIN	The sine of the argument
SINH	The hyperbolic sine of the argument
SQRT	The square root of the argument
TAN	The tangent of the argument
TANH	The hyperbolic tangent of the argument

Character Computation Functions

Function	Value returned
ADJUSTL	Remove leading blanks (and place them on the right)
ADJUSTR	Remove trailing blanks (and place them on the left)
INDEX	Find the location of a given substring in a character string
LEN_TRIM	Length of a string after trailing blanks have been removed
LGE	Greater than or equal to comparison based on ASCII
LGT	Greater than comparison based on ASCII
LLE	Less than or equal to comparison based on ASCII
LLT	Less than comparison based on ASCII
REPEAT	Concatenate several copies of a character string
SCAN	Scan a string for any one of a given set of characters
TRIM	The argument with trailing blank characters removed
VERIFY	Location of a character in a string that is not one of a given set

Bit Computation Functions

Function	Value returned
BTEST	The bit value of a specified position in an integer argument
IAND	Logical AND of two integer arguments
IBCLR	Clear a specified bit to zero in the integer argument
IBSET	Set a specified bit to one in the integer argument
IEOR	Logical exclusive-OR of two integer arguments
IOR	Logical inclusive-OR of two integer arguments
ISHFT	Logical end-off shift of the bits in the argument
ISHFTC	Logical circular shift of the bits in the argument
NOT	Logical complement of an integer argument

All of these functions, in all three groups, are generic except for LGE, LGT, LLE, and LLT, and all are elemental except DOT_PRODUCT, MATMUL, REPEAT, and TRIM. Note that the bit computation function cannot produce portable results.

13.6 Array Functions

The 17 array functions provide various generic array operations and may be classified as reduction (7), construction (4), reshape (1), manipulation (3), and location functions (2). All are transformational except MERGE, which is elemental.

Array Reduction Functions. The reduction functions "reduce" an argument array in the sense that all of the array elements are reflected in (reduced to) a scalar result, or the reduction takes place not over the whole array but rather along a specified dimension. In the latter case the function result is an array whose rank is one less than that of the argument array.

Function	Value returned
ALL	True if all of the argument array elements are true
ANY	True if any of the argument array elements are true
COUNT	The number of true elements in the argument array
MAXVAL	Maximum value of the argument array elements
MINVAL	Minimum value of the argument array elements
PRODUCT	The product of the argument array elements
SUM	The sum of the argument array elements

Array Construction Functions. The construction functions construct new array values from the elements of existing arrays.

Function	Value returned
MERGE	Combines two (conformable) arrays under control of a mask
PACK	Packs a masked array into a vector
SPREAD	Replicates an array by adding a dimension
UNPACK	Unpacks a masked array from a vector

The Array Reshape Function (RESHAPE). The RESHAPE function allows the reshaping of the elements of a rank-one array into an array with any specified shape.

Array Manipulation Functions. The manipulation functions rearrange the elements of an array.

Function	Value returned
CSHIFT	Circular shift of the elements of the argument array
EOSHIFT	End-off shift of the elements of the argument array
TRANSPOSE	The matrix transpose of the argument array

Array Location Functions. The location functions locate the maximum and minimum values in the array or along a specified dimension.

Function	Value returned
MAXLOC	The rank-one array which is the location of the maximum element
MINLOC	The rank-one array which is the location of the minimum element

13.7 Intrinsic Subroutines

Intrinsic subroutines are new in Fortran 90; Fortran 77 has only intrinsic functions. There are five intrinsic subroutines: DATE_AND_TIME, MVBITS, RANDOM_NUMBER, RANDOM_SEED, and SYSTEM_CLOCK. These are referenced in the same way as any other subroutine, as described in Section 12.2.2. None of these intrinsic subroutines may be used as actual arguments (that is, intrinsic subroutines must not be passed).

DATE_AND_TIME. This subroutine returns date and time information in several INTENT (OUT) arguments.

MVBITS. This subroutine copies a sequence of bits from one integer data object to another. It is the only elemental intrinsic subroutine.

RANDOM_NUMBER. This subroutine returns a pseudorandom number or an array of pseudorandom numbers as the value of its argument. It is a subroutine rather than a function because its execution has the side effect of changing the value of the underlying random number generator seed; intrinsic functions have no side effects.

RANDOM_SEED. This subroutine allows the value of the random number generator seed value to be initialized or retrieved.

SYSTEM_CLOCK. This subroutine returns data from the processor's real-time system clock in various formats in several INTENT (OUT) arguments.

13.8 Alphabetical List of All Intrinsic Procedures

The following table lists all of the intrinsic procedures in Fortran 90. The argument names shown are the keywords for keyword argument calls. All of the optional arguments are noted as such. These procedures are described in detail, in alphabetical order, in Appendix A.

Table 13-1 List of intrinsic procedures and arguments

Function	Optional arguments
ABS (A)	
ACHAR (I)	
ACOS (X)	
ADJUSTL (STRING)	
ADJUSTR (STRING)	
AIMAG (Z)	
AINT (A, KIND)	KIND
ALL (MASK, DIM)	DIM
ALLOCATED (ARRAY)	
ANINT (A, KIND)	KIND
ANY (MASK, DIM)	DIM
ASIN (X)	
ASSOCIATED (POINTER, TARGET)	TARGET
ATAN (X)	
ATAN2 (Y, X)	
BIT_SIZE (I)	
BTEST (I, POS)	
CEILING (A)	
CHAR (I, KIND)	KIND

Table 13-1 (*continued*)

Function	Optional arguments
CMPLX (X, Y, KIND)	Y, KIND
CONJG (Z)	
COS (X)	
COSH (X)	
COUNT (MASK, DIM)	DIM
CSHIFT (ARRAY, SHIFT, DIM)	DIM
DATE_AND_TIME (DATE, TIME, ZONE, VALUES)	DATE, TIME, ZONE, VALUES
DBLE (A)	
DIGITS (X)	
DIM (X, Y)	
DOT_PRODUCT (VECTOR_A, VECTOR_B)	
DPROD (X, Y)	
EOSHIFT (ARRAY, SHIFT, BOUNDARY, DIM)	BOUNDARY, DIM
EPSILON (X)	
EXP (X)	
EXPONENT (X)	
FLOOR (A)	
FRACTION (X)	
HUGE (X)	
IACHAR (C)	
IAND (I, J)	
IBCLR (I, POS)	
IBITS (I, POS, LEN)	
IBSET (I, POS)	
ICHAR (C)	
IEOR (I, J)	
INDEX (STRING, SUBSTRING, BACK)	BACK
INT (A, KIND)	KIND
IOR (I, J)	
ISHFT (I, SHIFT)	
ISHFTC (I, SHIFT, SIZE)	SIZE
KIND (X)	
LBOUND (ARRAY, DIM)	DIM
LEN (STRING)	
LEN_TRIM (STRING)	
LGE (STRING_A, STRING_B)	
LGT (STRING_A, STRING_B)	
LLE (STRING_A, STRING_B)	
LLT (STRING_A, STRING_B)	

Table 13-1 (*continued*)

Function	Optional arguments
LOG (X)	
LOG10 (X)	
LOGICAL (L, KIND)	KIND
MATMUL (MATRIX_A, MATRIX_B)	
MAX (A1, A2, A3, ...)	A3, ...
MAXEXPONENT (X)	
MAXLOC (ARRAY, MASK)	MASK
MAXVAL (ARRAY, DIM, MASK)	DIM, MASK
MERGE (TSOURCE, ISOURCE, MASK)	
MIN (A1, A2, A3, ...)	A3, ...
MINEXPONENT (X)	
MINLOC (ARRAY, MASK)	MASK
MINVAL (ARRAY, DIM, MASK)	DIM, MASK
MOD (A, P)	
MODULO (A, P)	
MVBITS (FROM, FROMPOS, LEN, TO, TOPOS)	
NEAREST (X, S)	
NINT (A, KIND)	KIND
NOT (I)	
PACK (ARRAY, MASK, VECTOR)	VECTOR
PRECISION (X)	
PRESENT (A)	
PRODUCT (ARRAY, DIM, MASK)	DIM, MASK
RADIX (X)	
RANDOM_NUMBER (HARVEST)	
RANDOM_SEED (SIZE, PUT, GET)	SIZE, PUT, GET
RANGE (X)	
REAL (X, KIND)	KIND
REPEAT (STRING, NCOPIES)	
RESHAPE (SOURCE, SHAPE, PAD, ORDER)	PAD, ORDER
RRSPACING (X)	
SCALE (X, I)	
SCAN (STRING, SET, BACK)	BACK
SELECTED_INT_KIND (R)	
SELECTED_REAL_KIND (P, R)	P, R
SET_EXPONENT (X, I)	
SHAPE (SOURCE)	
SIGN (A, B)	
SIN (X)	
SINH (X)	
SIZE (ARRAY, DIM)	DIM
SPACING (X)	

Table 13-1 (*continued*)

Function	Optional arguments
SPREAD (SOURCE, DIM, NCOPIES)	
SQRT (X)	
SUM (ARRAY, DIM, MASK)	DIM, MASK
SYSTEM_CLOCK (COUNT, COUNT_RATE, COUNT_MAX)	COUNT, COUNT_RATE, COUNT_MAX
TAN (X)	
TANH (X)	
TINY (X)	
TRANSFER (SOURCE, MOLD, SIZE)	SIZE
TRANSPOSE (MATRIX)	
TRIM (STRING)	
UBOUND (ARRAY, DIM)	DIM
UNPACK (VECTOR, MASK, FIELD)	
VERIFY (STRING, SET, BACK)	BACK

13.9 Specific Names for Generic Intrinsic Procedures

The intrinsic functions having specific names may be called with those names as well as with the generic names. To pass an intrinsic procedure as an actual argument, however, the specific name must be used. The following table gives the specific intrinsic procedure names available in Fortran 90, but the ones marked with an asterisk (for example, CHAR) must not be used as actual arguments.

Table 13-2 List of intrinsic procedures and arguments

Generic name	Specific name and arguments	Specific argument types
ABS	ABS (A)	Default real
	CABS (A)	Default complex
	DABS (A)	Double precision real
	IABS (A)	Default integer
ACOS	ACOS (X)	Default real
	DACOS (X)	Double precision real
AIMAG	AIMAG (Z)	Default complex
AINT	AINT (A)	Default real
	DINT (A)	Double precision real
ANINT	ANINT (A)	Default real
	DNINT (A)	Double precision real
ASIN	ASIN (X)	Default real

Table 13-2 (*continued*)

Generic name	Specific name and arguments	Specific argument types
	DSIN (X)	Double precision real
ATAN	ATAN (A)	Default real
	DTAN (A)	Double precision real
ATAN2	ATAN2 (A)	Default real
	DTAN2 (A)	Double precision real
CHAR	* CHAR (I)	Default integer
COS	COS (X)	Default real
	CCOS (X)	Default complex
	DCOS (X)	Double precision real
CONJG	CONJG (X)	Default complex
COSH	COSH (X)	Default real
	DCOSH (X)	Double precision real
DIM	DIM (X,Y)	Default real
	IDIM (X,Y)	Default integer
DPROD	DPROD (X,Y)	Default real
EXP	EXP (X)	Default real
	CEXP (X)	Default complex
	DEXP (X)	Double precision real
ICHAR	* ICHAR (C)	Default character
INDEX	INDEX (STRING, SUBSTRING)	Default character
INT	* INT (A)	Default real
	* IFIX (A)	Default real
	* IDINT (A)	Double precision real
LEN	LEN (STRING)	Default character
LGE	* LGE (STRING_A, STRING_B)	Default character
LGT	* LGT (STRING_A, STRING_B)	Default character
LLE	* LLE (STRING_A, STRING_B)	Default character
LLT	* LLT (STRING_A, STRING_B)	Default character
LOG	ALOG (X)	Default real
	CLOG (X)	Default complex
	DLOG (X)	Double precision real
LOG10	ALOG10 (X)	Default real
	DLOG10 (X)	Double precision real
MAX	* MAX0 (A1, A2, A3 ...)	Default integer

Table 13-2 (*continued*)

Generic name	Specific name and arguments	Specific argument types
	* AMAX1 (A1, A2, A3 ...)	Default real
	* DMAX1 (A1, A2, A3 ...)	Double precision real
Note 1	* MAX1 (A1, A2, A3 ...)	Default real
Note 2	* AMAX0 (A1, A2, A3 ...)	Default integer
MIN	* MIN0 (A1, A2, A3 ...)	Default integer
	* AMIN1 (A1, A2, A3 ...)	Default real
	* DMIN1 (A1, A2, A3 ...)	Double precision real
Note 1	* MIN1 (A1, A2, A3 ...)	Default real
Note 2	* AMIN0 (A1, A2, A3 ...)	Default integer
MOD	MOD (A, P)	Default integer
	AMOD (A, P)	Default real
	DMOD (A, P)	Double precision real
NINT	NINT (A)	Default real
	IDNINT (A)	Double precision real
REAL	* REAL (A)	Default integer
	* FLOAT (A)	Default integer
	* SNGL (A)	Double precision real
SIGN	SIGN (A, B)	Default real
	DSIGN (A, B)	Double precision real
	ISIGN (A, B)	Default integer
SIN	SIN (X)	Default real
	CSIN (X)	Default complex
	DSIN (X)	Double precision real
SINH	SINH (X)	Default real
	DSINH (X)	Double precision real
SQRT	SQRT (X)	Default real
	CSQRT (X)	Default complex
	DSQRT (X)	Double precision real
TAN	TAN (X)	Default real
	DTANH (X)	Double precision real
TANH	TANH (X)	Default real
	DTANH (X)	Double precision real

Note 1: The result of this function is of type default integer and has no generic name.

Note 2: The result of this function is of type default real and has no generic name.

13.10 Summary

There are 113 intrinsic procedures in Fortran 90—108 intrinsic functions and 5 intrinsic subroutines. All 113 intrinsic procedures are described in detail in Appendix A.

Generic Procedures

Two or more procedures may be referenced with the same name if they each have a unique set of argument attributes. Such procedures are called generic procedures. SQRT is an example of a generic procedure.

Specific Procedures

A specific procedure is one that has a name that is not shared by any other procedures. Many of the procedures sharing a generic name also have specific names. The specific name must be used if the procedure is passed as an actual argument. CSQRT is an example of a specific procedure.

Elemental Procedures

Many of the intrinsic procedures have a scalar dummy argument and deliver a corresponding scalar result. Except for TRIM, these intrinsic procedures may be called elementally—that is, they may be called with an array actual argument. In this case the result is an array conformable with the argument, with each result element having the value that would be returned if the procedure were called with the corresponding actual argument element. SQRT is an example of an elemental procedure.

Transformational Procedures

Transformational procedures are those that have array dummy arguments. The result of a transformational procedure may be an array, but the result value is not related to the arguments in the same way as with elemental procedures. MATMUL is an example of a transformational procedure.

Inquiry and Numeric Manipulation Functions

There are 28 inquiry and numeric manipulation functions. These functions return information about data objects and their representation. LEN is an example of an inquiry function; NEAREST is an example of a numeric manipulation function.

Transfer and Conversion Functions

There are 16 transfer and conversion functions. These functions convert values from one type and kind combination to another type and kind combination. INT is an example of a conversion function.

Computation Functions

There are 47 computation functions: 26 numeric, 12 character, and 9 bit. These functions perform various computations on the supplied argument values. SQRT is an example of a computation function.

Array Functions

There are 17 array functions. These functions perform various reduction, construction, reshape, manipulation, and location operations on their arguments. SUM is an example of an array reduction function.

Intrinsic Subroutines

There are five intrinsic subroutines: DATE_AND_TIME, MVBITS, RANDOM_NUMBER, RANDOM_SEED, and SYSTEM_CLOCK. Fortran 90 marks the first time that Fortran has included standard intrinsic subroutines.

F90

14

Scope, Association, and Definition

This handbook began with a sneak preview of the new features in Fortran 90 and ends with a discussion of three of the oldest concepts in Fortran. Scope, association, and definition have always been the glue binding Fortran into a powerful greater-than-the-sum-of-its-parts whole. Yet, until fully understood and assimilated, these concepts may seem daunting and leave one feeling like their first-letter acronym rather than with the comfortable sense of a firm grip on the language.

The reason for the importance of scope, association, and definition is communication; they provide the communication pathways among the different parts of the program. As with any other organism whose function is made up of interacting parts (say a business), without effective communication among its parts a Fortran program would have limited capabilities. Scope, association, and definition provide Fortran with a very good communications framework.

With the new data types, program units, and procedure provisions, Fortran 90 builds significantly on the concepts of scope, association, and definition, making these concepts even more comprehensive and central to the working of Fortran. Fully understanding them is the key to understanding Fortran 90. Although perhaps initially daunting, assimilating these concepts is a bit like learning to ride a bicycle—seemingly impossible at first, but once you get the hang of it nothing could be simpler and it becomes natural and thrilling. The purpose of this chapter is to facilitate a similar mastery of scope, association, and definition.

Various aspects of scope, association, and definition have already been discussed throughout the earlier chapters of this handbook. The only reason this material is not presented completely in these chapters is that a comprehensive and thorough understanding of the entire language is needed to fully assimilate these topics. Fortunately, all of the detailed rules and conditions presented in this chapter usually are not necessary in order to construct pieces of Fortran programs. If simple programming disciplines are followed, many of the subtle issues and concerns related to scope, association, and definition can be avoided in writing correct programs. However, there are some situations in which it is necessary to know all the details, particularly when modifying or maintaining programs, looking for subtle bugs, or, of course, when implementing a compiler.

Scope is introduced in Chapter 2. Recall that it specifies that part of a program in which a particular entity is known and accessible. The spectrum of scope varies from an entire program (global) to individual program units (local) to statements or parts of statements. But, to both communicate data between program units and limit and control accessibility of data, the language defines the concept of association which relates local objects within and between program units. The association methods have all been introduced in the early chapters and include association via arguments (argument association), association via storage (storage association), association via modules (use association), association via hosts (host association), and association via name aliases (pointer association).

Once objects can be associated, there may be multiple ways to define values for them. For example, assignment statements and input statements define objects directly by name, which may also cause associated items to become defined. In some cases, such associated object values may be unpredictable or unreliable. For example, if a real object is equivalenced (storage associated) with an integer object, defining the real object with a valid real value causes the integer object to acquire a "meaningless" value. Referencing such unpredictable values causes the program to be nonportable, and therefore such references must be avoided. The mechanism for addressing this problem is the concept of **undefined value**, introduced in Fortran 66 and continued in both Fortran 77 and Fortran 90. In certain cases, such as for the integer object in the preceding example, certain values are considered to be undefined; references to undefined values are nonstandard conforming.

Thus, the three topics, scope, association, and definition, are related. Scope specifies the part of a program where an entity is known and accessible. Association is the pathway along which entities in the same or different scopes communicate. Definition, and its opposite, undefinition, characterize the ways in which variables are defined and become undefined indirectly as a consequence of being associated with other objects.

14.1 The Use of Names

Picking names for variables, functions, and other entities is a more important and more complicated matter than it may at first seem. On the one hand, wise choice of names makes the program "readable"—the names correctly communicate the algorithm to the reader of the program. This can lead, on the other hand, to conflicting use of names, which, of course, must be avoided.

One philosophy might be to pick a unique name for everything in the program that has a name so that there is no possibility of conflicting uses of a name. This approach, taken to its extreme, would require avoiding all intrinsic procedure (and keyword) names for programmer-chosen names. For example, the names CASE, CHAR, SIZE, and SUM could not be used as variable names. Actually, the use of such a name for a variable causes no real problem, unless later an intrinsic function with that name is needed.

There are more serious problems with this approach, however. First, such a system generates too many different names, particularly for large programs. It inhibits the choice of mnemonic and common names, appropriate for the programming task at hand. Finally, it makes it difficult to modularize the development of programs and to write parts of the program independently. In fact, for most software programming projects, this approach is unworkable.

Despite this, the good programmer will apply this philosophy to small programs or within the confines of a program unit. A good programmer knows as many keywords, statement names, intrinsic names, etc., as possible and avoids them simply for the reason that confusion can result otherwise.

With the possibility that different parts of a program are developed by different programmers, it is reasonable to allow and expect that something named X in one subprogram, for example, has nothing (necessarily) to do with something named X in another subprogram. This permits different programmers to work independently. The concepts of scope and classes of names are the mechanisms that provide this capability and eliminate the need to strictly adhere to the scheme of picking a different name for everything. These concepts are not new in Fortran 90, but are more pervasive than in earlier versions of Fortran due to the introduction of internal procedures, modules, derived data types, interface blocks, and array constructors. Fortran has always allowed the programmer great latitude to use the same name for as many different things as possible, and this becomes even more important as programming tools and applications become more complex and sophisticated.

Because it is possible to use X to mean two different things, the natural question is: Where does X mean what? This is what scope is all about.

14.2 Scope

Named things such as variables, constants, procedures, block data subprograms, modules, and namelist groups, have scope. Other (unnamed) entities that have scope are operator symbols, the assignment symbol, labels, and input/output unit numbers.

The **scope** of an entity is that part of a Fortran program in which that entity has a given meaning and can be used, defined, or referenced by its designator. The scope of an entity might be as large as the whole executable program or as small as part of a Fortran statement. Entities that can be used with the same meaning throughout the executable program are said to be **global entities** and have a global scope. An example of a global entity is an external procedure name. Entities that can be used only within the smaller context of a subprogram are said to be **local entities** and have a local scope. An example of a local entity is a statement label. An even smaller context for scope might be a Fortran statement (or part of one); entities valid for only this context are said to be **statement entities**, such as the dummy arguments in a statement function.

The terms scope and scoping unit are not defined in Fortran 77, but the concept of scope and the global, local, and statement varieties of scope are all implicitly part of Fortran 77. Scoping units in Fortran 77 are program units, with each program unit being a separate scoping unit. To this Fortran 90 adds internal procedures, interface blocks, and derived-type definitions as separate scoping units. (Certain entities in statement functions and implied-dos have their scopes limited to these constructs, but statement functions and implied-dos are not considered to be scoping units.)

Some scoping units can contain other scoping units. For example, an external function can contain interface blocks and internal procedures. In such cases, different scoping units are properly thought of as "nonoverlapping" rather than "nested". Putting an interface block, say, into a subprogram causes a "hole" in the subprogram scoping unit that is filled with the scoping unit of the interface block. Scoping units surrounded by another scoping unit may or may not inherit properties from the surrounding scope. For example, internal procedures, module procedures, and derived-type definitions inherit implicit rules from the surrounding scope; interface blocks, on the other hand, do not inherit implicit rules from the surrounding scope.

A scoping unit in Fortran 90 is one of the following:

1. a derived-type definition

2. a procedure interface body, excluding any derived-type definitions and procedure interface bodies contained within it

3. a program unit or subprogram, excluding derived-type definitions, procedure interface bodies, and subprograms contained within it

To visualize the concept of scope and scoping units, consider Figure 14-1. The outer rectangle bounds the pieces of an executable Fortran program; it is not a scoping unit but could be said to represent global scope. Within the executable program four other rectangles depict program units. One is the main program, two others are external subprogram units, and the fourth one is a module program unit.

All four of these program unit rectangles represent scoping units, excluding any rectangles within them. The main program in this example encloses no rectangle and so is an integral scoping unit without holes. External subprogram A has two internal procedures within it, and therefore procedure A's scoping unit is this rectangle, excluding internal procedures B and C. External subprogram D has an interface block in it and no internal procedures. Its scoping unit is procedure D, excluding the interface block. Module E has a derived-type definition and two module procedures within it. Its scoping unit is similarly the module program unit, excluding the derived-type definition and the module procedures.

In addition, the interface block, the derived-type definition, and each of the internal and module procedures are scoping units. In this example, these latter scoping units have no holes, as they do not themselves contain internal procedures, module procedures, interface blocks, or derived-type definitions, although they could in general.

14.2.1 Scope of Names

A name has one of the following scopes:

1. global—scope of an executable program (for example, an external function name)

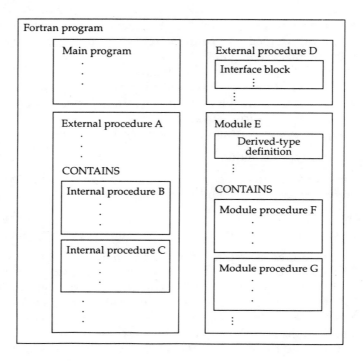

Figure 14-1 Scoping units

2.   local—scope of a scoping unit (for example, an array name in a subroutine subprogram)

3.   statement—scope of a Fortran statement (for example, a statement function argument) or a part of a Fortran statement (for example, an implied-do variable)

14.2.1.1 Names as Global Entities. The name of a main program, an external procedure, a module, a block data program unit, or a common block has global scope. No two global entities may have the same name. For example, the main program name may not also be used as the name of an external procedure or a common block.

14.2.1.2 Names as Local Entities. There are three classes of names having local scope:

1.   names of variables, constants, control constructs, statement functions, internal procedures, module procedures, dummy procedures,

intrinsic procedures, user-defined generic procedures, derived types, and namelist groups

2. names of the components of a derived type—there is a separate class of names for each derived type, which means that two different derived types can have the same component names

3. names of argument keywords—there is a separate class of names for each procedure with an explicit interface, which means that two different procedures can have the same argument keyword names

Rules and restrictions:

1. A global entity name may not be used to identify a local entity, except that a local entity may have the same name as a common block.

2. A nongeneric local name is unique within the same scoping unit and within the same class; that is, it identifies exactly one entity. That name may also be used to identify a different object in a different scoping unit or a different object in a different class in the same scoping unit. When that name or a different name is used in other scoping units, it usually represents a different entity but may represent the same entity because of association.

3. A generic local name may be used for two or more different procedures in that scoping unit. The rules for generic names are described in Sections 14.2.6 and 14.2.7.

4. A local name may be used for another local entity in a different class in that scoping unit. For example, a structure component of type logical may have the same name as a local integer variable.

5. Components of a derived type have the scope of the derived-type definition, and when used in a qualified structure reference have the scope of the structure reference itself.

6. Argument keywords are local entities, and are in a separate class for each procedure with an explicit interface. This means that an argument keyword used for one procedure can be used as an argument keyword for another procedure, as a local variable or procedure name, and as a component name of a derived type.

7. If a common block name is the same as the name of a local entity, the name is the local entity except where it appears to identify the common block. Uniqueness of the reference is determined by the context of the name. For example, a name enclosed in slashes in a SAVE statement must be a common block name rather than the name of a local variable of the same name.

8. The name of an intrinsic function (and there are many of them) may be used as a local entity provided the intrinsic function itself is not used in that scoping unit. For example, if the scoping unit uses the name SIN as a local variable name, the intrinsic function SIN may not be used in the same program unit.

9. For each function and function entry that does not have a result variable, there is a local variable within the function subprogram scoping unit whose name is the same as the function or entry name. This local variable is used to define the value of the function or entry name within the function subprogram.

10. For each internal or module procedure, the name of the procedure is also a name local to the host scoping unit. Similarly, for any entry name used in a module procedure, the name of the entry is also a name local to the host scoping unit.

14.2.1.3 Names as Statement Entities. The name of a dummy argument in a statement function statement, or a DO variable in an implied-do list of a DATA statement or array constructor, has a scope that is the statement or part of the statement. Such a name may be used elsewhere as a local or global name without a name conflict and refers to a different entity when so used.

Rules and restrictions:

1. The name of a dummy argument used in a statement function statement has the scope of the statement. The type and type parameters of the name are determined by the declarations in the containing scoping unit.

2. The DO variable in an array constructor or an implied-do loop in a DATA statement has the scope of that part of the statement in which it appears. The type, which must be integer, and type parameters of the name are determined by the declarations in the containing scoping unit. (Note that the scope of the DO variable in these implied-do lists is part of a statement, whereas the scope of the DO variable in a DO construct is local to the scoping unit containing the DO construct.)

Note that the DO variable of an implied-do in an input/output item list has the scope of the program unit containing the input/output statement.

14.2.2 Scope of Labels

A label is a local entity. No two statements in the same scoping unit may have the same label, but the same label may be used in different scoping units.

14.2.3 Scope of Input/Output Units

External input/output unit numbers are global entities and have global scope. Within an executable program, a unit number refers to the same input/output unit wherever it appears in a unit number context in an input/output statement.

14.2.4 Scope of Operators

Operator symbols are either intrinsic or defined. Intrinsic operators have global scope; the scope of a defined operator is a scoping unit. An operator symbol may refer to both an intrinsic operator and a defined operator. For example, the operator symbol + can be both global (its intrinsic meaning) and local (its defined meaning). Operators may be generic; that is, two or more operators may be designated by the same operator symbol. The types, kind parameter values, and the ranks of the operands distinguish which operator is used (see Section 7.3.2).

14.2.5 Scope of Assignment

Like operators (14.2.4), intrinsic assignment has global scope; defined assignment has the scope of a scoping unit. The assignment symbol (=) always has global meanings and may, like operator symbols, also have local meanings. Assignment is generic; many assignment operations are designated by the same operator symbol. The types, kind parameter values, and the ranks of the entities on the left and right sides of the equal sign distinguish which assignment is used (see Section 7.5.2).

14.2.6 Scope of Unambiguous Procedure References

A procedure reference is unambiguous if the procedure name in the reference is a specific procedure name that is not the same as any generic procedure name in that scoping unit. This is the case in references to

1. internal procedures

2.   module and external procedures not appearing in an interface block with a generic specification in that scoping unit or available via use or host association

3.   nongeneric specific names of intrinsic functions

4.   statement functions

5.   dummy procedures

Specific names of external and intrinsic procedures are global; all other specific procedure names are local.

Procedure references involving generic procedure names are also unambiguous if the two rules of Section 12.5.7 apply. These rules are repeated here. Considering the dummy argument lists of any two procedures sharing the same generic name, one of these lists must have a non-optional dummy argument that satisfies both of the following conditions:

1.   It is either in a position in the list at which the other list it has no dummy argument or it has a type, kind type parameter, and rank (TKR) pattern different from that of the dummy argument in the same position in the other list.

2.   It has either a name different from all the dummy argument names in the other list or has a TKR pattern different from that of the dummy argument with the same name in the other list.

These rules apply regardless of whether the generic names are intrinsic, defined by interface blocks with generic specifications, or both. They also apply to generic operator and assignment symbols. Generic names of intrinsic functions are global and defined generic names are local.

14.2.7 Resolving Procedure References

A procedure reference is involved in

1.   executing a CALL statement

2.   executing a defined assignment statement

3.   evaluating a defined operation

4.   evaluating an expression containing a function reference

In this last case, an expression contains a function reference if the form of one of the operands is a name followed by a parenthesized list of expressions and that name is not declared in the scoping unit to be an array name.

In case 2, a generic "name" (the assignment symbol, =) is involved, and there must be an interface block with an ASSIGNMENT generic specification in the scoping unit or available through use or host association that identifies a specific external or module subroutine that defines this assignment. The rules of Sections 12.5.7, 12.6.5, and 14.2.6 determine which specific subroutine is involved in the reference.

In case 3, a generic "name" (the operator symbol) is involved, and there must be an interface block with an OPERATOR generic specification in the scoping unit or available through use or host association that identifies a specific external or module function that defines this operation. The rules of Sections 12.5.7, 12.6.4, and 14.2.6 determine which specific function is involved in the reference.

In cases 1 and 4, the following sequence of rules may be used to resolve the reference (that is, determine which specific procedure is involved in the reference). The first of these rules that applies, taken in order, resolves the reference.

1. If the procedure name in the reference is a dummy argument in that scoping unit, then the dummy argument is a dummy procedure and the reference is to that dummy procedure. Thus, the procedure invoked by the reference is the procedure supplied as the associated actual argument.

2. If the procedure name appears in an EXTERNAL statement in that scoping unit, the reference is to an external procedure with that name.

3. If the procedure name is that of an accessible internal procedure or statement function, the reference is to that internal procedure or statement function.

4. If the procedure name is specified as a generic name in an interface in that scoping unit or in an interface block made accessible by use or host association, and the reference is consistent with one of the specific interfaces for that generic name, the reference is to that specific procedure. The rules of Section 12.5 determine which specific procedure is invoked (the rules of Sections 12.5.7 and 14.2.6 guarantee that there will be at most one such procedure).

5. If the procedure name appears in an INTRINSIC statement in that scoping unit, the reference is to the corresponding specific intrinsic procedure.

6. If the procedure name is accessible via use association, the reference is to that specific procedure. Note that it is possible, because of the renaming facility, for the procedure name in the reference to be different from that in the module.

7. If the scoping unit of the reference has a host scoping unit, and if application in the host of the preceding six rules resolves the reference, then the reference is so resolved.

8. If the procedure name is either the specific or generic name of an intrinsic procedure, the reference is to the corresponding specific intrinsic procedure.

9. If the procedure name is not a generic name, the reference is to an external procedure with that name.

10. Otherwise the reference cannot be resolved and is not standard conforming.

14.3 Association

Fortran uses the concept of scoping so that the same name can be used for different things in different parts of a program. This is desirable so that programmers do not have to worry about conflicting uses of a name.

However, there are times when just the opposite is desired: the programmer wants different names in the same or different parts of a program to refer to the same entity. For example, there may be a need to have one data value that may be examined and modified by all of the procedures of a program. In general, particularly with external program units, the names used will be different in the different parts of the program, but they can be the same.

Association is the mechanism used to indicate that local names in different scoping units or different local names in the same scoping unit refer to the same entity. There are four forms of association:

1. Name association involves the use of names, always in different scoping units, to establish an association.

2. Pointer association allows dynamic association of names within a scoping unit and is essentially an aliasing mechanism.

3. Storage association involves the use of storage sequences to establish an association between data objects. The association may be between two objects in the same scoping unit (EQUIVALENCE) or in different scoping units (COMMON).

4. Sequence association is a combination of name association and storage association. It applies to the association of actual and array dummy arguments using storage sequence association. It associates names in different scoping units.

Figures 14-2 and 14-3 illustrate the various kinds of association in an executable program.

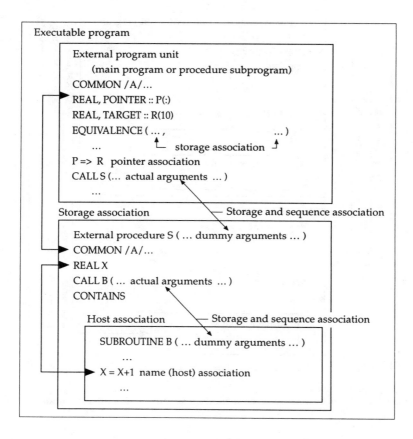

Figure 14-2 Associations between two nonmodule scoping units

14.3.1 Name Association

Name association permits access to the same entity (either data or a procedure) from different scoping units by the same or a different name. There are three forms of name association: argument, use, and host.

14.3.1.1 Argument Association. Argument association is explained in detail in Section 12.5. It establishes a correspondence between the actual argument in the scoping unit containing the procedure reference and the dummy argument in the scoping unit defining the procedure. An actual argument may be the name of a variable or procedure, or it may be

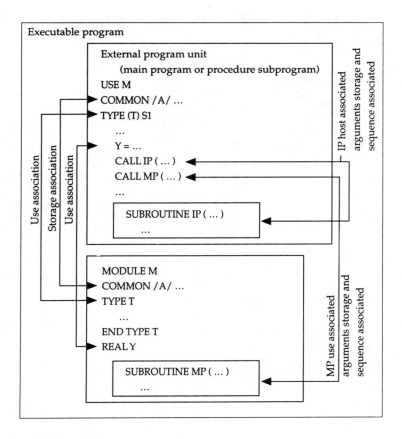

Figure 14-3 Associations between a module scoping unit and a nonmodule scoping unit

an expression. The dummy argument name is used in the procedure definition to refer to the actual argument, whether it is a name or an expression. When the program returns from the procedure, the actual and dummy arguments become disassociated.

14.3.1.2 Use Association. Use association causes an association between entities in the scoping unit of a module and the scoping unit containing a USE statement referring to the module. It provides access to entities specified in the module. The default situation is that all public entities in the module are accessed by the name used in the module, but entities can be renamed selectively in the USE statement and excluded with the ONLY option. Use association is explained in Section 11.6.4.5.

14.3.1.3 Host Association. Host association causes an association between entities in a host scoping unit and the scoping unit of either an internal procedure, module procedure, or derived-type definition. The basic idea of host association is that entities in the host (for example, host variables) are also available in any procedures or derived-type definitions within the host. As with default use association, such entities are known by the same name in the internal or module procedure or derived-type definition as they are known in the host. There is no mechanism for renaming entities, but the association of names between the host and the contained scoping unit can be replaced by the local declaration of an entity with that name; such a declaration blocks access to the entity of the same name in the host scoping unit. Host association is described in Section 11.4.

Rules and restrictions:

1. If renaming occurs by a USE statement, the type, type parameters, and other attributes of the local name are those of the module entity. No respecification can occur in the scoping unit containing the USE statement.

2. When an entity is renamed by a USE statement, the original name in the module can be used as a local name for a different entity in the scoping unit containing the USE statement. There would be no name conflict.

3. The PUBLIC and PRIVATE access specifications are determined in the module scoping unit referenced in the USE statement, and cannot be changed or overridden by the referencing scoping unit (but see the example in 11.6.4.5).

14.3.2 Pointer Association

A pointer is a variable with the pointer attribute. During program execution, the pointer variable is undefined, disassociated, or associated with a scalar or an array data object or function result. The association of pointers is dynamic throughout a program; that is, it can be changed as needed during execution.

Rules and restrictions:

1. Pointers are initially undefined.

2. There are two ways that pointers may be associated:

    a. by pointer assignment, pointers are associated with other pointers or with scalar or array data objects that have the TARGET attribute

b.   by execution of an ALLOCATE statement, pointers are associated with previously unnamed space

3.   Associated pointers may become disassociated or undefined. Disassociated pointers may become associated or undefined. Undefined pointers may become associated.

4.   Associated pointers become disassociated when the association is nullified (NULLIFY statement) or when the pointer is deallocated (DEALLOCATE statement).

14.3.3 Storage Association

Storage association is the provision that two or more variables may share the same memory space. This allows the same value to be referenced by more than one name, achieving an effect similar to that of name association and pointer association. Consider the following simple example:

```
EQUIVALENCE (X, Y)
```

Variables X and Y share the same computer memory; changing the value of either one affects the value of the other.

The effects of EQUIVALENCE and COMMON statements can be complicated because of partially overlapping variables and storage association between different data types. The concept of storage association is used to describe these effects. Note that, although terms like "computer memory" are used in this discussion, implementation of Fortran does not require any particular method of storing values. However, implementations commonly use memory to store values in a way that closely reflects this description.

14.3.3.1 Storage Units and Storage Sequence. A storage unit corresponds to a particular part of memory that usually holds a single Fortran value. Thus, memory may be thought of as a sequence of storage units, each possibly holding a Fortran value. A storage unit may be a **numeric storage unit**, **character storage unit**, or an **unspecified storage unit**.

A sequence of any number of consecutive storage units is a **storage sequence**. A storage sequence has a size, which is the number of storage units in the sequence.

14.3.3.2 Fortran Data and Storage Units. Some of the relationships between Fortran data and storage units are as follows. All of the following data objects are nonpointer values unless explicitly specified otherwise.

- A scalar data object of type default integer, default real, or default logical occupies one numeric storage unit. Default complex and double precision real values occupy two consecutive numeric storage units.

- A single default character occupies one character storage unit.

- All other values, that is, pointers and all values with nondefault kinds, occupy unspecified storage units. An unspecified storage unit is treated as a different object for each of these types of values. For example, a storage unit for a pointer to a default integer occupies an unspecified storage unit that is different than the unspecified storage unit for an integer of nondefault type.

Composite objects occupy storage sequences, depending on their form.

- A default scalar character object of length *len* has *len* consecutive character storage units.

- An array occupies a storage sequence consisting of one storage unit of the appropriate sort for each element of the array in array element order.

- A scalar of a sequence derived type occupies a storage sequence consisting of storage units corresponding to the components of the structure, in the order they occur in the derived-type definition. Recall that to be a sequence type, the derived type must have the SEQUENCE attribute.

- Each common block has a storage sequence as described in Section 5.10.4.

- Each ENTRY statement in a function subprogram has a storage sequence as described in Section 12.4.3.

- EQUIVALENCE statements create storage sequences from the storage units of the objects making up the equivalence lists.

Two objects that occupy the same storage sequence are **storage associated**. Two objects that occupy parts of the same storage sequence are **partially storage associated**.

14.3.3.3 Partial Association. Partial association applies to character data and other composite objects in COMMON, EQUIVALENCE, or ENTRY statements. When such objects only partially overlap in storage, they are then said to be **partially associated**. For example, two character strings are partially associated if substrings of each share the same storage but the entire strings do not.

14.3.3.4 Examples. In this section are examples of storage sequences of various sorts and illustrations of how equivalencing causes association of storage sequences and the data objects in them. First, a simple example involving numeric storage units is:

```
COMPLEX :: C
REAL    :: X (0:5)
EQUIVALENCE (C, X(3))
```

The storage sequence occupied by C consists of two numeric storage units, one for the real part and one for the imaginary part.

The storage sequence occupied by X consists of six numeric storage units, one for each element of the array.

X(0)	X(1)	X(2)	X(3)	X(4)	X(5)

The EQUIVALENCE statement indicates that X(3) and the real part of C occupy the same storage unit, creating the following association; items above and below each other are storage associated.

X(0)	X(1)	X(2)	X(3)	X(4)	X(5)
			C_r	C_i	

Next, consider an example with character data. If two character objects are to become associated, they must have the same kind type parameter.

```
CHARACTER (KIND = GREEK) A(2:2)*2, B(2)*3, C*5
EQUIVALENCE (A (2,1) (1:1), B (1) (2:3), C (3:5))
```

A, B, and C occupy character storage sequences of size 8, 6, and 5 respectively, and the EQUIVALENCE statement sets up the following associations.

A(1,1)(1:1)	A(1,1)(2:2)	A(2,1)(1:1)	A(2,1)(2:2)	A(1,2)(1:1)	A(1,2)(2:2)	A(2,2)(1:1)	A(2,2)(2:2)
	B(1)(1:1)	B(1)(2:2)	B(1)(3:3)	B(2)(1:1)	B(2)(2:2)	B(2)(3:3)	
C(1:1)	C(2:2)	C(3:3)	C(4:4)	C(5:5)			

14.3.4 Sequence Association

Sequence association is a special form of argument association that applies to character, array, and sequence structure arguments. The rules for such association are found in Section 12.5.2.

14.4 Definition Status

When can the value of a variable be used safely? Answer: when that value is well-defined and predictable. There are a number of things, exhaustively listed below, that can cause a variable's value to become ill-defined or unpredictable during the course of program execution. For example, an I/O error can corrupt a variable's value; another example is assigning a value to an integer variable, which makes the value of any storage-associated real variable unpredictable (in any portable sense). Informally, "defined" is the Fortran term given to a variable whose value is well-defined and predictable; the "undefined" is given to a variable whose value is ill-defined or unpredictable.

The use of undefined values is not portable, and hence is not standard conforming. Unfortunately, because either the compiler cannot always check for undefined conditions, or it might be too costly to do so, the responsibility for avoiding the use of undefined values rests mainly with the programmer.

During execution of a program, variables are said to be **defined** or **undefined**. If a variable is defined, it has a value established during some statement execution (or event) in the program. If a variable is undefined, it is considered to not have a value. Variables are initially undefined except for initial values specified in DATA statements and type statements. As execution proceeds, other events may cause a variable to become defined or undefined. There is no specific representation for an undefined variable. Undefined variables must not be referenced in a context in which the value of the variable is used.

14.4.1 Definition Status of Subobjects

An array element or array section is part of an array. A substring is part of a character variable. A component is part of a structure. An object of type complex consists of two parts, its real and imaginary parts. All parts of an object must be defined for the object to be defined. If any part of an object is undefined, that object is undefined. Zero-sized arrays and zero-length strings are always defined.

14.4.2 Events that Affect Definition Status of Variables

Assignment defines the value of the variable on the left of the equal sign. Similarly, reading input establishes values for variables in the input list. Certain specifier variables are defined when a statement such as the INQUIRE statement is executed.

Returning from a procedure causes all unsaved local variables to become undefined. Deallocation and disassociation during program execution causes variables to become undefined. In addition, the process of defining an entity may cause certain associated or partially associated entities to become undefined. Lists of events that cause variables to be defined and undefined follow.

14.4.3 Events that Cause Variables to Become Defined

Variables become defined as follows:

1. Execution of an intrinsic assignment statement other than a masked array assignment statement causes the variable that precedes the equal sign to become defined. Execution of a defined assignment statement may cause all or part of the variable that precedes the equal sign to become defined.

2. Execution of a masked array assignment statement may cause some or all of the array elements in the assignment statement to become defined.

3. As execution of an input statement proceeds, each variable that is assigned a value from the input file becomes defined at the time that data is transferred to it. Execution of a WRITE statement

whose unit specifier identifies an internal file causes each record that is written to become defined.

4. Execution of a DO statement causes the DO variable, if any, to become defined.

5. Beginning execution of the action specified by an implied-do list in an input/output statement causes the implied-do variable to become defined.

6. Execution of an ASSIGN statement causes the variable in the statement to become defined with a statement label value.

7. A reference to a procedure causes a dummy argument data object to become defined if the associated actual argument is defined with a value that is not a statement label. If only a subobject of an actual argument is defined, only the corresponding subobject of the associated dummy argument is defined.

8. Execution of an input/output statement containing an input/output IOSTAT= specifier causes the specified integer variable to become defined.

9. Execution of a READ statement containing a SIZE= specifier causes the specified integer variable to become defined.

10. Execution of an INQUIRE statement causes any variable that is assigned a value during the execution of the statement to become defined if no error condition exists.

11. When a character storage unit becomes defined, all associated character data objects become defined.

12. When a numeric storage unit becomes defined, all associated numeric data objects of the same type become defined, except that variables associated with the variable in an ASSIGN statement become undefined when the ASSIGN statement is executed. When an entity of double precision real type becomes defined, all totally associated entities of double precision real type become defined.

13. When an unspecified storage unit becomes defined, all associated data objects become defined.

14. When a default complex entity becomes defined, all partially associated default real entities become defined.

15. When both parts of a default complex entity become defined as a result of partially associated default real or default complex entities becoming defined, the default complex entity becomes defined.

16. When all components of a numeric sequence structure or character sequence structure become defined as a result of partially associated objects becoming defined, the structure becomes defined.

17. Execution of an ALLOCATE or DEALLOCATE statement with a STAT= specifier causes the variable specified by the STAT= specifier to become defined.

18. Execution of a pointer assignment statement that associates a pointer with a target that is defined causes the pointer to become defined.

14.4.4 Events that Cause Variables to Become Undefined

Variables become undefined as follows:

1. When a variable of a given type becomes defined, all associated variables of different type become undefined. However, when a variable of type default real is partially associated with a variable of type default complex, the complex variable does not become undefined when the real variable becomes defined and the real variable does not become undefined when the complex variable becomes defined. When a variable of type default complex is partially associated with another variable of type default complex, definition of one does not cause the other to become undefined.

2. Execution of an ASSIGN statement causes the variable in the statement to become undefined as an integer. Variables that are associated with the variable also become undefined.

3. If the evaluation of a function may cause an argument of the function or a variable in a module or in a common block to become defined, and if a reference to the function appears in an expression in which the value of the function is not needed to determine the value of the expression, the argument or variable becomes undefined when the expression is evaluated.

4. The execution of a RETURN statement or an END statement within a subprogram causes all variables local to its scoping unit or local to the current instance of its scoping unit for a recursive invocation to become undefined, except for the following:

    a. variables with the SAVE attribute

    b. variables in blank common

    c.   variables in a named common block that appears in the subprogram and appears in at least one other scoping unit that is making either a direct or indirect reference to the subprogram

    d.   variables accessed from the host scoping unit

    e.   variables accessed from a module that also is accessed in at least one other scoping unit that is making either a direct or indirect reference to the module

    f.   variables in a named common block that are initially defined and that have not been subsequently defined or redefined

5. When an error condition or end-of-file condition occurs during execution of an input statement, all of the variables specified by the input list or namelist group of the statement become undefined.

6. When an error or end-of-file condition occurs during execution of an input/output statement, some or all of the implied-do variables may become undefined.

7. Execution of a defined assignment statement may leave all or part of the variable that precedes the equal sign undefined.

8. Execution of a direct access input statement that specifies a record that has not been written previously causes all of the variables specified by the input list of the statement to become undefined.

9. Execution of an INQUIRE statement may cause the NAME=, RECL=, and NEXTREC= variables to become undefined.

10. When a character storage unit becomes undefined, all associated character data objects units become undefined.

11. When a numeric storage unit becomes undefined, all associated numeric data objects units become undefined unless the undefinition is a result of defining an associated numeric data object of different type (see 1 above).

12. When an entity of double precision real type becomes undefined, all totally associated entities of double precision real type become undefined.

13. When an unspecified storage unit becomes undefined, all associated data objects become undefined.

14. A reference to a procedure causes part of a dummy argument to become undefined if the corresponding part of the actual argument is defined with a value that is a statement label.

15. When an allocatable array is deallocated, it becomes undefined. Successful execution of an ALLOCATE statement creates an array that is undefined.

16. Execution of an INQUIRE statement causes all inquire specifier variables to become undefined if an error condition exists, except for the variable in the IOSTAT= specifier, if any.

17. When a procedure is invoked:

    a. An optional dummy argument that is not associated with an actual argument is undefined.

    b. A dummy argument with INTENT (OUT) is undefined.

    c. An actual argument associated with a dummy argument with INTENT (OUT) becomes undefined.

    d. A subobject of a dummy argument is undefined if the corresponding subobject of the actual argument is undefined.

    e. The result variable of a function is undefined.

18. When the association status of a pointer becomes undefined or disassociated, the pointer becomes undefined.

A

Intrinsic Procedures

This appendix contains detailed specifications of the generic intrinsic procedures in alphabetical order.

For each procedure there are examples. The examples use type kind parameters for which the following assumptions are made:

1. The default real type has eight decimal digits of precision.

2. The value of the integer named constant HIGH is a kind parameter value for a real data type with 14 decimal digits of precision and an exponent range of at least 100.

3. The value of the integer named constant GREEK is a kind parameter value for a character data type that contains Greek letters.

4. The value of the integer named constant BIT is a kind parameter value for a logical data type that is an alternative to the default logical data type.

5. The value of the integer named constant SHORT is a kind parameter value for an integer data type with eight bits to represent integer values, that is, s in the bit model (13.2.1) for this integer type is 8.

All real values cannot be represented exactly in any processor; therefore, when the following text says something like "ACOS (.1_HIGH) has the value 1.4706289056333", it means that the value is a processor approximation to 1.4706289056333. The Fortran 90 standard does not specify how accurate the approximation must be.

A.1 ABS (A)

Description. Absolute value.

Class. Elemental function.

Argument. A must be of type integer, real, or complex.

Result Type and Type Parameter. The same as A except that if A is complex, the result is real.

Result Value. If A is of type integer or real, the value of the result is $|A|$; if A is complex with value (x, y), the result is equal to a processor-dependent approximation to $\sqrt{x^2 + y^2}$.

Examples. ABS (−1) has the value 1. ABS (−1.5) has the value 1.5. ABS ((3.0, 4.0)) has the value 5.0.

A.2 ACHAR (I)

Description. Returns the character in a specified position of the ASCII collating sequence. It is the inverse of the IACHAR function.

Class. Elemental function.

Argument. I must be of type integer.

Result Type and Type Parameter. Character of length one with kind type parameter value KIND ('A').

Result Value. If I has a value in the range $0 \leq I \leq 127$, the result is the character in position I of the ASCII collating sequence, provided the processor is capable of representing that character; otherwise, the result is processor dependent. If the processor is not capable of representing both uppercase and lowercase letters and I corresponds to a letter in a case that the processor is not capable of representing, the result is the letter in the case that the processor is capable of representing. ACHAR (IACHAR (C)) must have the value C for any character C capable of representation in the processor.

Examples. ACHAR (88) is 'X'. ACHAR (42) is '*'.

A.3 ACOS (X)

Description. Arccosine (inverse cosine) function.

Class. Elemental function.

Argument. X must be of type real with a value that satisfies the inequality $|X| \leq 1$.

Result Type and Type Parameter. Same as X.

Result Value. The result has a value equal to a processor-dependent approximation to arccos(X), expressed in radians. It lies in the range $0 \leq ACOS (X) \leq \pi$.

Examples. ACOS (0.54030231) has the value 1.0. ACOS (.1_HIGH) has the value 1.4706289056333 with kind HIGH.

A.4 ADJUSTL (STRING)

Description. Adjust to the left, removing leading blanks and inserting trailing blanks.

Class. Elemental function.

Argument. STRING must be of type character.

Result Type. Character of the same length and kind type parameter as STRING.

Result Value. The value of the result is the same as STRING except that any leading blanks have been deleted and the same number of trailing blanks have been inserted.

Examples. ADJUSTL (' WORD') is 'WORD '. ADJUSTL (GREEK_' $\tau\rho\iota\alpha$') is GREEK_'$\tau\rho\iota\alpha$ '.

A.5 ADJUSTR (STRING)

Description. Adjust to the right, removing trailing blanks and inserting leading blanks.

Class. Elemental function.

Argument. STRING must be of type character.

Result Type. Character of the same length and kind type parameter as STRING.

Result Value. The value of the result is the same as STRING except that any trailing blanks have been deleted and the same number of leading blanks have been inserted.

Examples. ADJUSTR ('WORD ') has the value ' WORD'. ADJUSTR (GREEK_'$\tau\rho\iota\alpha$ ') has the value GREEK_' $\tau\rho\iota\alpha$'.

A.6 AIMAG (Z)

Description. Imaginary part of a complex number.

Class. Elemental function.

Argument. Z must be of type complex.

Result Type and Type Parameter. Real with the same kind type parameter as Z.

Result Value. If Z has the value (x, y), the result has value y.

Examples. AIMAG ((2.0, 3.0)) has the value 3.0. AIMAG ((2.0_HIGH, 3.0)) has the value 3.0 with kind HIGH; the parts of a complex literal constant have the same precision, which is that of the part with the greatest precision.

A.7 AINT (A, KIND)

Optional Argument. KIND

Description. Truncation to a whole number.

Class. Elemental function.

Arguments.

A   must be of type real.

KIND (optional)   must be a scalar integer initialization expression.

Result Type and Type Parameter. The result is of type real. If KIND is present, the kind type parameter is that specified by KIND; otherwise, the kind type parameter is that of A.

Result Value. If $|A| < 1$, AINT (A) has the value 0; if $|A| \geq 1$, AINT (A) has a value equal to the integer whose magnitude is the largest integer that does not exceed the magnitude of A and whose sign is the same as the sign of A.

Examples. AINT (2.783) has the value 2.0. AINT (–2.783) has the value –2.0. AINT (2.1111111111111_HIGH) and AINT (2.1111111111111, HIGH) have the value 2.0 with kind HIGH.

A.8 ALL (MASK, DIM)

Optional Argument. DIM

Description. Determine whether all values are true in MASK along dimension DIM.

Class. Transformational function.

Arguments.

MASK   must be of type logical. It must not be scalar.

DIM (optional)   must be scalar and of type integer with value in the
                        range $1 \le \text{DIM} \le n$, where n is the rank of MASK.
                        The corresponding actual argument must not be an
                        optional dummy argument.

Result Type, Type Parameter, and Shape. The result is of type logical
with the same kind type parameter as MASK. It is scalar if DIM is
absent or MASK has rank one; otherwise, the result is an array of rank
$n-1$ and of shape $(d_1, d_2, ..., d_{\text{DIM}-1}, d_{\text{DIM}+1}, ..., d_n)$ where $(d_1, d_2,$
$..., d_n)$ is the shape of MASK.

Result Value.

Case (i):   The result of ALL (MASK) has the value true if all elements
                of MASK are true or if MASK has size zero, and the result
                has value false if any element of MASK is false.

Case (ii):   If MASK has rank one, ALL (MASK, DIM) has a value
                equal to that of ALL (MASK). Otherwise, the value of ele-
                ment $(s_1, s_2, ..., s_{\text{DIM}-1}, s_{\text{DIM}+1}, ..., s_n)$ of ALL (MASK,
                DIM) is equal to ALL (MASK $(s_1, s_2, ..., s_{\text{DIM}-1}, :, s_{\text{DIM}+1},$
                $..., s_n))$.

Examples.

Case (i):   The value of ALL ((/ .TRUE., .FALSE., .TRUE. /)) is false.
                ALL ((/ .TRUE._BIT, .TRUE._BIT, .TRUE._BIT /)) is the
                value true with kind parameter BIT. Note that all values in
                an array constructor must have the same type and type
                parameter (4.6).

Case (ii):   If B is the array $\begin{bmatrix} 1 & 3 & 5 \\ 2 & 4 & 6 \end{bmatrix}$ and C is the array $\begin{bmatrix} 0 & 3 & 5 \\ 7 & 4 & 8 \end{bmatrix}$
                then ALL (B .NE. C, DIM = 1) is (true, false, false) and
                ALL (B .NE. C, DIM = 2) is (false, false).

A.9 ALLOCATED (ARRAY)

Description. Indicate whether or not an allocatable array is currently
allocated.

Class. Inquiry function.

Argument. ARRAY must be an allocatable array.

Result Type, Type Parameter, and Shape. Default logical scalar.

Result Value. The result has the value true if ARRAY is currently allocated and has the value false if ARRAY is not currently allocated. The result is undefined if the allocation status (6.5.1.1) of the array is undefined.

Example. If the followed statements are processed

```
REAL, ALLOCATABLE :: A(:,:)
ALLOCATE (A(10,10))
PRINT *, ALLOCATED (A)
```

then .TRUE. is printed.

A.10 ANINT (A, KIND)

Optional Argument. KIND

Description. Nearest whole number.

Class. Elemental function.

Arguments.

A   must be of type real.

KIND (optional)   must be a scalar integer initialization expression.

Result Type and Type Parameter. The result is of type real. If KIND is present, the kind type parameter is that specified by KIND; otherwise, the kind type parameter is that of A.

Result Value. If $A > 0$, ANINT (A) has the value AINT $(A + 0.5)$; if $A \leq 0$, ANINT (A) has the value AINT $(A - 0.5)$.

Examples. ANINT (2.783) has the value 3.0. ANINT (−2.783) has the value −3.0. ANINT (2.7837837837837_HIGH) and ANINT (2.7837837837837, HIGH) have the value 3.0 with kind HIGH.

A.11 ANY (MASK, DIM)

Optional Argument. DIM

Description. Determine whether any value is true in MASK along dimension DIM.

Class. Transformational function.

Arguments.

MASK   must be of type logical. It must not be scalar.

DIM (optional)　　　　must be scalar and of type integer with a value in the range $1 \le \text{DIM} \le n$, where n is the rank of MASK. The corresponding actual argument must not be an optional dummy argument.

Result Type, Type Parameter, and Shape. The result is of type logical with the same kind type parameter as MASK. It is scalar if DIM is absent or MASK has rank one; otherwise, the result is an array of rank $n-1$ and of shape $(d_1, d_2, ..., d_{\text{DIM}-1}, d_{\text{DIM}+1}, ..., d_n)$ where $(d_1, d_2, ..., d_n)$ is the shape of MASK.

Result Value.

Case (i):　　The result of ANY (MASK) has the value true if any element of MASK is true and has the value false if no elements are true or if MASK has size zero.

Case (ii):　　If MASK has rank one, ANY (MASK, DIM) has a value equal to that of ANY (MASK). Otherwise, the value of element $(s_1, s_2, ..., s_{\text{DIM}-1}, s_{\text{DIM}+1}, ..., s_n)$ of ANY (MASK, DIM) is equal to ANY (MASK $(s_1, s_2, ..., s_{\text{DIM}-1}, :, s_{\text{DIM}+1}, ..., s_n))$.

Examples.

Case (i):　　The value of ANY ((/ .TRUE., .FALSE., .TRUE. /)) is true. ANY ((/ .FALSE._BIT, .FALSE._BIT, .FALSE._BIT /)) is false with kind parameter BIT.

Case (ii):　　If B is the array $\begin{bmatrix} 1 & 3 & 5 \\ 2 & 4 & 6 \end{bmatrix}$ and C is the array $\begin{bmatrix} 0 & 3 & 5 \\ 7 & 4 & 8 \end{bmatrix}$ ANY (B .NE. C, DIM = 1) is (true, false, true) and ANY (B .NE. C, DIM = 2) is (true, true).

A.12 ASIN (X)

Description. Arcsine (inverse sine) function.

Class. Elemental function.

Argument. X must be of type real. Its value must satisfy the inequality $|X| \le 1$.

Result Type and Type Parameter. Same as X.

Result Value. The result has a value equal to a processor-dependent approximation to arcsin(X), expressed in radians. It lies in the range $-\pi/2 \le \text{ASIN}(X) \le \pi/2$.

Examples. ASIN (0.84147098) has the value 1.0. ASIN (1.0_HIGH) has the value 1.5707963267949 with kind HIGH.

A.13 ASSOCIATED (POINTER, TARGET)

Optional Argument. TARGET

Description. Returns the association status of its pointer argument or indicates the pointer is associated with the target.

Class. Inquiry function.

Arguments.

POINTER   must be a pointer and may be of any type. Its pointer association status must not be undefined.

TARGET (optional) must be a pointer or target. If it is a pointer, its pointer association status must not be undefined.

Result Type. The result is of type default logical.

Result Value.

Case (i):   If TARGET is absent, the result is true if POINTER is currently associated with a target and false if it is not.

Case (ii):   If TARGET is present and is a target, the result is true if POINTER is currently associated with TARGET and false if it is not.

Case (iii):   If TARGET is present and is a pointer, the result is true if both POINTER and TARGET are currently associated with the same target, and is false otherwise. If either POINTER or TARGET is disassociated, the result is false.

Examples.

Case (i):   ASSOCIATED (PTR) is true if PTR is currently associated with a target.

Case (ii):   ASSOCIATED (PTR, TAR) is true if the following statements have been processed:

```
REAL, TARGET  :: TAR (0:100)
REAL, POINTER :: PTR(:)
PTR => TAR
```

The subscript range for PTR is 0:100. If the pointer assignment statement is either of

```
PTR => TAR (:)
```

```
PTR => TAR (0:100)
```

ASSOCIATED (PTR, TAR) is still true, but in both cases the subscript range for PTR is 1:101 (5.3.1.3). However, if the pointer assignment statement is

```
PTR => TAR (0:99)
```

ASSOCIATED (PTR, TAR) is false, because TAR (0:99) is not the same as TAR.

Case (iii):   ASSOCIATED (PTR1, PTR2) is true if the following statements have been processed:

```
REAL, POINTER :: PTR1(:), PTR2(:)
ALLOCATE (PTR1(0:10))
PTR2 => PTR1
```

After the execution of either of the statements:

```
NULLIFY (PTR1)
NULLIFY (PTR2)
```

ASSOCIATED (PTR1, PTR2) is false.

A.14 ATAN (X)

Description. Arctangent (inverse tangent) function.

Class. Elemental function.

Argument. X must be of type real.

Result Type and Type Parameter. Same as X.

Result Value. The result has a value equal to a processor-dependent approximation to arctan(X), expressed in radians, that lies in the range $-\pi/2 \le$ ATAN (X) $\le \pi/2$.

Examples. ATAN (1.5574077) has the value 1.0. ATAN (2.0_HIGH/3.0) has the value 0.58800260354757 with kind HIGH.

A.15 ATAN2 (Y, X)

Description. Arctangent (inverse tangent) function. The result is the principal value of the argument of the nonzero complex number (X, Y).

Class. Elemental function.

Arguments.

Y   must be of type real.

X   must be of the same type and kind type parameter
                              as Y. If Y has the value zero, X must not have the
                              value zero.

Result Type and Type Parameter. Same as X.

Result Value. The result has a value equal to a processor-dependent
approximation to the principal value of the argument of the complex
number (X, Y), expressed in radians. It lies in the range $-\pi < $ ATAN2
(Y, X) $\leq \pi$ and is equal to a processor-dependent approximation to a
value of arctan(Y/X) if X $\neq$ 0. If Y > 0, the result is positive. If Y = 0,
the result is zero if X > 0 and the result is π if X < 0. If Y < 0, the result
is negative. If X = 0, the absolute value of the result is $\pi/2$.

Examples. ATAN2 (1.5574077, 1.0) has the value 1.0. If Y has the

value $\begin{bmatrix} 1 & 1 \\ -1 & -1 \end{bmatrix}$ and X has the value $\begin{bmatrix} -1 & 1 \\ -1 & 1 \end{bmatrix}$, the value of

ATAN2 (Y, X) is $\begin{bmatrix} \dfrac{3\pi}{4} & \dfrac{\pi}{4} \\ \dfrac{-3\pi}{4} & -\dfrac{\pi}{4} \end{bmatrix}$.

A.16 BIT—SIZE (I)

Description. Returns the number of bits s defined by the model of 13.2.1
for integers with the kind parameter of the argument.

Class. Inquiry function.

Argument. I must be of type integer.

Result Type, Type Parameter, and Shape. Scalar integer with the same
kind type parameter as I.

Result Value. The result has the value of the number of bits s in the
model integer defined for bit manipulation contexts in 13.2.1 for integers
with the kind parameter of the argument.

Examples. BIT_SIZE (1) has the value 32 if s in the model is 32.
BIT_SIZE (1_SHORT) is 8 with kind SHORT.

A.17 BTEST (I, POS)

Description. Tests a bit of an integer value.

Class. Elemental function.

Arguments.

I   must be of type integer.

POS   must be of type integer. It must be nonnegative and be less than BIT_SIZE (I).

Result Type. The result is of type default logical.

Result Value. The result has the value true if bit POS of I has the value 1 and has the value false if bit POS of I has the value 0. The model for the interpretation of an integer value as a sequence of bits is in 13.2.1.

Examples. BTEST (8, 3) has the value true. BTEST (8_SHORT, 3) has the value true. If A has the value $\begin{bmatrix} 1 & 2 \\ 3 & 4 \end{bmatrix}$, the value of BTEST (A, 2) is $\begin{bmatrix} \text{false} & \text{false} \\ \text{false} & \text{true} \end{bmatrix}$, and the value of BTEST (2, A) is $\begin{bmatrix} \text{true} & \text{false} \\ \text{false} & \text{false} \end{bmatrix}$.

A.18 CEILING (A)

Description. Returns the least integer greater than or equal to its argument.

Class. Elemental function.

Argument. A must be of type real.

Result Type and Type Parameter. Default integer.

Result Value. The result has a value equal to the least integer greater than or equal to A. The result is undefined if the processor cannot represent this value in the default integer type.

Examples. CEILING (3.7) has the value 4. CEILING (–3.7) has the value –3. CEILING (20.0_HIGH/3) has the value 7.

A.19 CHAR (I, KIND)

Optional Argument. KIND

Description. Returns the character in a given position of the processor collating sequence associated with the specified kind type parameter. It is the inverse of the function ICHAR.

Class. Elemental function.

Arguments.

I   must be of type integer with a value in the range
                          $0 \le I \le n - 1$, where n is the number of characters
                          in the collating sequence associated with the speci-
                          fied kind type parameter.

KIND (optional)   must be a scalar integer initialization expression.

Result Type and Type Parameters. Character of length one. If KIND is
present, the kind type parameter is that specified by KIND; otherwise,
the kind type parameter is that of default character type.

Result Value. The result is the character in position I of the collating
sequence associated with the specified kind type parameter. ICHAR
(CHAR (I, KIND (C))) must have the value I for $0 \le I \le n - 1$ and
CHAR (ICHAR (C), KIND (C)) must have the value C for any character
C capable of representation in the processor.

Examples. CHAR (88) is 'X' on a processor using the ASCII collating
sequence. CHAR (97, GREEK) might be 'α' on a processor that supports
a character type containing Greek letters.

A.20 CMPLX (X, Y, KIND)

Optional Arguments. Y, KIND

Description. Convert to complex type.

Class. Elemental function.

Arguments.

X   must be of type integer, real, or complex.

Y (optional)   must be of type integer or real. It must not be pre-
                          sent if X is of type complex.

KIND (optional)   must be a scalar integer initialization expression.

Result Type and Type Parameter. The result is of type complex. If
KIND is present, the kind type parameter is that specified by KIND; otherwise, the kind type parameter is that of default real type.

Result Value. If Y is absent and X is not complex, it is as if Y were present with the value zero. If Y is absent and X is complex, it is as if Y
were present with the value AIMAG (X). CMPLX (X, Y, KIND) has the
complex value whose real part is REAL (X, KIND) and whose imaginary
part is REAL (Y, KIND).

Examples. CMPLX (–3) is –3.0 + 0ι. CMPLX ((4.1, 0.0), KIND=HIGH), CMPLX ((4.1, 0), KIND=HIGH), and CMPLX (4.1, KIND=HIGH) are each 4.1 + 0 with kind HIGH.

A.21 CONJG (Z)

Description. Conjugate of a complex number.

Class. Elemental function.

Argument. Z must be of type complex.

Result Type and Type Parameter. Same as Z.

Result Value. If Z has the value (x, y), the result has the value $(x, -y)$.

Examples. CONJG ((2.0, 3.0)) is 2.0 – 3.0ι. CONJG ((0, –4.1_HIGH)) is 0 + 4.1ι with kind HIGH.

A.22 COS (X)

Description. Cosine function.

Class. Elemental function.

Argument. X must be of type real or complex.

Result Type and Type Parameter. Same as X.

Result Value. The result has a value equal to a processor-dependent approximation to cos(X). If X is of type real, it is regarded as a value in radians. If X is of type complex, its real part is regarded as a value in radians.

Examples. COS (1.0) has the value 0.54030231. COS (1.0_HIGH, 1.0) has the value 0.83373002513115 – 0.98889770576287ι with kind HIGH.

A.23 COSH (X)

Description. Hyperbolic cosine function.

Class. Elemental function.

Argument. X must be of type real.

Result Type and Type Parameter. Same as X.

Result Value. The result has a value equal to a processor-dependent approximation to cosh(X).

Examples. COSH (1.0) has the value 1.5430806. COSH (0.1_HIGH) has the value 1.0050041680558 with kind HIGH.

A.24 COUNT (MASK, DIM)

Optional Argument. DIM

Description. Count the number of true elements of MASK along dimension DIM.

Class. Transformational function.

Arguments.

MASK   must be of type logical. It must not be scalar.

DIM (optional)   must be scalar and of type integer with a value in the range $1 \leq \text{DIM} \leq n$, where n is the rank of MASK. The corresponding actual argument must not be an optional dummy argument.

Result Type, Type Parameter, and Shape. The result is of type default integer. It is scalar if DIM is absent or MASK has rank one; otherwise, the result is an array of rank $n-1$ and of shape $(d_1, d_2, ..., d_{\text{DIM}-1}, d_{\text{DIM}+1}, ..., d_n)$ where $(d_1, d_2, ..., d_n)$ is the shape of MASK.

Result Value.

Case (i):   The result of COUNT (MASK) has a value equal to the number of true elements of MASK or has the value zero if MASK has size zero.

Case (ii):   If MASK has rank one, COUNT (MASK, DIM) has a value equal to that of COUNT (MASK). Otherwise, the value of element $(s_1, s_2, ..., s_{\text{DIM}-1}, s_{\text{DIM}+1}, ..., s_n)$ of COUNT (MASK, DIM) is equal to COUNT (MASK $(s_1, s_2, ..., s_{\text{DIM}-1}, :, s_{\text{DIM}+1}, ..., s_n)$).

Examples.

Case (i):   The value of COUNT ((/ .TRUE., .FALSE., .TRUE. /)) is 2.

Case (ii):   If B is the array $\begin{bmatrix} 1 & 3 & 5 \\ 2 & 4 & 6 \end{bmatrix}$ and C is the array $\begin{bmatrix} 0 & 3 & 5 \\ 7 & 4 & 8 \end{bmatrix}$, COUNT (B .NE. C, DIM = 1) is (2, 0, 1) and COUNT (B .NE. C, DIM = 2) is (1, 2).

A.25 CSHIFT (ARRAY, SHIFT, DIM)

Optional Argument. DIM

Description. Perform a circular shift on an array expression of rank one or perform circular shifts on all the complete rank one sections along a given dimension of an array expression of rank two or greater. Elements shifted out at one end of a section are shifted in at the other end.

Different sections may be shifted by different amounts and in different directions.

Class. Transformational function.

Arguments.

ARRAY   may be of any type. It must not be scalar.

SHIFT   must be of type integer and must be scalar if ARRAY has rank one; otherwise, it must be scalar or of rank $n-1$ and of shape $(d_1, d_2, ..., d_{DIM-1}, d_{DIM+1}, ..., d_n)$ where $(d_1, d_2, ..., d_n)$ is the shape of ARRAY.

DIM (optional)   must be a scalar and of type integer with a value in the range $1 \le DIM \le n$, where n is the rank of ARRAY. If DIM is omitted, it is as if it were present with the value 1.

Result Type, Type Parameter, and Shape. The result is of the type and type parameters of ARRAY, and has the shape of ARRAY.

Result Value.

Case (i):   If ARRAY has rank one, element i of the result is ARRAY $(1 + MODULO (i + SHIFT - 1, SIZE (ARRAY)))$.

Case (ii):   If ARRAY has rank greater than one, section $(s_1, s_2, ..., s_{DIM-1}, :, s_{DIM+1}, ..., s_n)$ of the result has a value equal to CSHIFT (ARRAY $(s_1, s_2, ..., s_{DIM-1}, :, s_{DIM+1}, ..., s_n)$, 1, sh), where sh is SHIFT or SHIFT $(s_1, s_2, ..., s_{DIM-1}, s_{DIM+1}, ..., s_n)$.

Examples.

Case (i):   If V is the array (1, 2, 3, 4, 5, 6), the effect of shifting V circularly to the left by two positions is achieved by CSHIFT (V, SHIFT = 2) which has the value (3, 4, 5, 6, 1, 2); CSHIFT (V, SHIFT = –2) achieves a circular shift to the right by two positions and has the value (5, 6, 1, 2, 3, 4).

Case (ii):   The rows of an array of rank two may all be shifted by the same amount or by different amounts. If M is the array $\begin{bmatrix} 1 & 2 & 3 \\ 4 & 5 & 6 \\ 7 & 8 & 9 \end{bmatrix}$, the value of CSHIFT (M, SHIFT = –1, DIM = 2) is $\begin{bmatrix} 3 & 1 & 2 \\ 6 & 4 & 5 \\ 9 & 7 & 8 \end{bmatrix}$, and the value of CSHIFT (M,

$$\text{SHIFT} = (/ -1, 1, 0 \, /), \text{DIM} = 2) \text{ is } \begin{bmatrix} 3 & 1 & 2 \\ 5 & 6 & 4 \\ 7 & 8 & 9 \end{bmatrix}.$$

A.26 DATE_AND_TIME (DATE, TIME, ZONE, VALUES)

Optional Arguments. DATE, TIME, ZONE, VALUES

Description. Returns data on the real-time clock and date in a form compatible with the representations defined in ISO 8601:1988.

Class. Subroutine.

Arguments.

DATE (optional)   must be scalar and of type default character, and must be of length at least 8 in order to contain the complete value. It is an INTENT (OUT) argument. Its leftmost 8 characters are set to a value of the form *CCYYMMDD*, where *CC* is the century, *YY* the year within the century, *MM* the month within the year, and *DD* the day within the month. If there is no date available, they are set to blank.

TIME (optional)   must be scalar and of type default character, and must be of length at least 10 in order to contain the complete value. It is an INTENT (OUT) argument. Its leftmost 10 characters are set to a value of the form *hhmmss.sss*, where *hh* is the hour of the day, *mm* is the minutes of the hour, and *ss.sss* is the seconds and milliseconds of the minute. If there is no clock available, they are set to blank.

ZONE (optional)   must be scalar and of type default character, and must be of length at least 5 in order to contain the complete value. It is an INTENT (OUT) argument. Its leftmost 5 characters are set to a value of the form $\pm hhmm$, where *hh* and *mm* are the time difference with respect to Coordinated Universal Time (UTC) in hours and parts of an hour expressed in minutes, respectively. If there is no clock available, they are set to blank.

VALUES (optional)   must be of type default integer and of rank one. It is an INTENT (OUT) argument. Its size must be at least 8. The values returned in VALUES are as follows:

VALUES (1)	the year (for example, 1990), or −HUGE (0) if there is no date available;
VALUES (2)	the month of the year, or −HUGE (0) if there is no date available;
VALUES (3)	the day of the month, or −HUGE (0) if there is no date available;
VALUES (4)	the time difference with respect to Coordinated Universal Time (UTC) in minutes, or −HUGE (0) if this information is not available;
VALUES (5)	the hour of the day, in the range of 0 to 23, or −HUGE (0) if there is no clock;
VALUES (6)	the minutes of the hour, in the range 0 to 59, or −HUGE (0) if there is no clock;
VALUES (7)	the seconds of the minute, in the range 0 to 60, or −HUGE (0) if there is no clock;
VALUES (8)	the milliseconds of the second, in the range 0 to 999, or −HUGE (0) if there is no clock.

HUGE is described in A.38.

Example.

```
INTEGER DATE_TIME (8)
CHARACTER (LEN = 10) BIG_BEN (3)
CALL DATE_AND_TIME (BIG_BEN (1), BIG_BEN (2),  &
                    BIG_BEN (3), DATE_TIME)
```

if called in Geneva, Switzerland on 1985 April 12 at 15:27:35.5 would have assigned the value "19850412 " to BIG_BEN (1), the value "152735.500" to BIG_BEN (2), and the value "+0100   " to BIG_BEN (3), and the following values to DATE_TIME: 1985, 4, 12, 60, 15, 27, 35, 500.

Note that UTC is defined by CCIR Recommendation 460-2 (and is also known as Greenwich Mean Time).

A.27 DBLE (A)

Description. Convert to double precision real type.
Class. Elemental function.

Argument. A must be of type integer, real, or complex.

Result Type and Type Parameter. Double precision real.

Result Value.

Case (i):   If A is of type double precision real, DBLE (A) = A.

Case (ii):   If A is of type integer or real, the result is as much precision of the significant part of A as a double precision real datum can contain.

Case (iii): If A is of type complex, the result is as much precision of the significant part of the real part of A as a double precision real datum can contain.

Examples. DBLE (–.3) is –0.3 of type double precision real. DBLE (1.0_HIGH/3) is 0.33333333333333 of type double precision real.

A.28 DIGITS (X)

Description. Returns the number of significant digits in the model representing numbers of the same type and kind type parameter as the argument.

Class. Inquiry function.

Argument. X must be of type integer or real. It may be scalar or array valued.

Result Type, Type Parameter, and Shape. Default integer scalar.

Result Value. The result has the value q if X is of type integer and p if X is of type real, where q and p are as defined in 13.2 for the model representing numbers of the same type and kind type parameter as X.

Examples. DIGITS (X) has the value 24 for real X whose model described in 13.2.3. DIGITS (ARRAY_A), where ARRAY_A is declared as

```
    REAL (KIND=HIGH) ARRAY_A (100)
```

might have the value 48 for a model somewhat different from the one described in 13.2.3.

A.29 DIM (X, Y)

Description. The difference X–Y if it is positive; otherwise zero.

Class. Elemental function.

Arguments.

X   must be of type integer or real.

Y   must be of the same type and kind type parameter as X.

Result Type and Type Parameter. Same as X.

Result Value. The value of the result is X–Y if $X > Y$ and zero otherwise.

Examples. DIM (5, 3) has the value 2. DIM (–3.0, 2.0) has the value 0.0.

A.30 DOT_PRODUCT (VECTOR_A, VECTOR_B)

Description. Performs dot-product multiplication of numeric or logical vectors.

Class. Transformational function.

Arguments.

VECTOR_A   must be of numeric type (integer, real, or complex) or of logical type. It must be array valued and of rank one.

VECTOR_B   must be of numeric type if VECTOR_A is of numeric type or of type logical if VECTOR_A is of type logical. It must be array valued and of rank one. It must be of the same size as VECTOR_A.

Result Type, Type Parameter, and Shape. If the arguments are of numeric type, the type and kind type parameter of the result are those of the expression VECTOR_A * VECTOR_B determined by the types of the arguments according to 7.2.8. If the arguments are of type logical, the result is of type logical with the kind type parameter of the expression VECTOR_A .AND. VECTOR_B according to 7.2.8. The result is scalar.

Result Value.

Case (i):   If VECTOR_A is of type integer or real, the result has the value SUM (VECTOR_A*VECTOR_B). If the vectors have size zero, the result has the value zero.

Case (ii):   If VECTOR_A is of type complex, the result has the value SUM (CONJG (VECTOR_A)*VECTOR_B). If the vectors have size zero, the result has the value zero.

Case (iii):   If VECTOR_A is of type logical, the result has the value ANY (VECTOR_A .AND. VECTOR_B). If the vectors have size zero, the result has the value false.

Examples.

Case (i):   DOT_PRODUCT ((/ 1, 2, 3 /), (/ 2, 3, 4 /)) has the value 20.

Case (ii):   DOT_PRODUCT ((/ (1.0, 2.0), (2.0, 3.0) /), (/ (1.0, 1.0), (1.0, 4.0) /)) has the value $17 + 4\iota$.

Case (iii):   DOT_PRODUCT ((/ .TRUE., .FALSE. /), (/ .TRUE., .TRUE. /)) has the value true.

A.31 DPROD (X, Y)

Description. Double precision real product.
Class. Elemental function.
Arguments.

X   must be of type default real.

Y   must be of type default real.

Result Type and Type Parameters. Double precision real.
Result Value. The result has a value equal to a processor-dependent approximation to the product of X and Y.
Example. DPROD (–3.0, 2.0) has the value –6.0 of type double precision real.

A.32 EOSHIFT (ARRAY, SHIFT, BOUNDARY, DIM)

Optional Arguments. BOUNDARY, DIM
Description. Perform an end-off shift on an array expression of rank one or perform end-off shifts on all the complete rank-one sections along a given dimension of an array expression of rank two or greater. Elements are shifted off at one end of a section and copies of a boundary value are shifted in at the other end. Different sections may have different boundary values and may be shifted by different amounts and in different directions.
Class. Transformational function.
Arguments.

ARRAY   may be of any type. It must not be scalar.

SHIFT   must be of type integer and must be scalar if ARRAY has rank one; otherwise, it must be scalar or of rank $n-1$ and of shape $(d_1, d_2, ..., d_{DIM-1},$

$d_{\text{DIM}+1}$, ..., d_n) where $(d_1, d_2, ..., d_n)$ is the shape of ARRAY.

BOUNDARY (optional)

must be of the same type and type parameters as ARRAY and must be scalar if ARRAY has rank one; otherwise, it must be either scalar or of rank $n - 1$ and of shape $(d_1, d_2, ..., d_{\text{DIM}-1}, d_{\text{DIM}+1}, ..., d_n)$. BOUNDARY may be omitted for the data types in the following table and, in this case, it is as if it were present with the scalar value shown.

Type of ARRAY	Value of BOUNDARY
Integer	0
Real	0.0
Complex	(0.0, 0.0)
Logical	false
Character (*len*)	*len* blanks

DIM (optional)

must be scalar and of type integer with a value in the range $1 \leq \text{DIM} \leq n$, where n is the rank of ARRAY. If DIM is omitted, it is as if it were present with the value 1.

Result Type, Type Parameter, and Shape. The result has the type, type parameters, and shape of ARRAY.

Result Value. Element $(s_1, s_2, ..., s_n)$ of the result has the value ARRAY $(s_1, s_2, ..., s_{\text{DIM}-1}, s_{\text{DIM}}+sh, s_{\text{DIM}+1}, ..., s_n)$ where sh is SHIFT or SHIFT $(s_1, s_2, ..., s_{\text{DIM}-1}, s_{\text{DIM}+1}, ..., s_n)$ provided the inequality LBOUND (ARRAY, DIM) $\leq s_{\text{DIM}} + sh \leq$ UBOUND (ARRAY, DIM) holds and is otherwise BOUNDARY or BOUNDARY $(s_1, s_2, ..., s_{\text{DIM}-1}, s_{\text{DIM}+1}, ..., s_n)$.

Examples.

Case (i): If V is the array (1, 2, 3, 4, 5, 6), the effect of shifting V end-off to the left by 3 positions is achieved by EOSHIFT (V, SHIFT = 3) which has the value (4, 5, 6, 0, 0, 0); EOSHIFT (V, SHIFT = –2, BOUNDARY = 99) achieves an end-off shift to the right by 2 positions with the boundary value of 99 and has the value (99, 99, 1, 2, 3, 4).

Case (ii): The rows of an array of rank two may all be shifted by the same amount or by different amounts and the boundary elements can be the same or different. If M is the array

$$\begin{bmatrix} A & B & C \\ D & E & F \\ G & H & I \end{bmatrix}, \text{ then the value of EOSHIFT (M, SHIFT} = -1,$$

BOUNDARY = '*', DIM = 2) is $\begin{bmatrix} * & A & B \\ * & D & E \\ * & G & H \end{bmatrix}$, and the

value of EOSHIFT (M, SHIFT = (/ -1, 1, 0 /),

BOUNDARY = (/ '*', '/', '?' /), DIM = 2) is $\begin{bmatrix} * & A & B \\ E & F & / \\ G & H & I \end{bmatrix}$.

A.33 EPSILON (X)

Description. Returns a positive model number that is almost negligible compared to unity in the model representing numbers of the same type and kind type parameter as the argument.

Class. Inquiry function.

Argument. X must be of type real. It may be scalar or array valued.

Result Type, Type Parameter, and Shape. Scalar of the same type and kind type parameter as X.

Result Value. The result has the value b^{1-p} where b and p are as defined in 13.2.3 for the model representing numbers of the same type and kind type parameter as X.

Examples. EPSILON (X) has the value 2^{-23} for real X whose model is described in 13.2.3. EPSILON (Y), where Y has kind parameter HIGH, would be 2^{-47} if p is 48 for the model of kind HIGH.

A.34 EXP (X)

Description. Exponential.

Class. Elemental function.

Argument. X must be of type real or complex.

Result Type and Type Parameter. Same as X.

Result Value. The result has a value equal to a processor-dependent approximation to e^X. If X is of type complex, its imaginary part is regarded as a value in radians.

Examples. EXP (1.0) has the value 2.7182818. EXP (2.0_HIGH/3.0) has the value 1.9477340410547 with kind HIGH.

A.35 EXPONENT (X)

Description. Returns the exponent part of the argument when represented as a model number.

Class. Elemental function.

Argument. X must be of type real.

Result Type. Default integer.

Result Value. The result has a value equal to the exponent e of the model representation (13.2.3) for the value of X, provided X is nonzero and e is within the range for default integers. The result is undefined if the processor cannot represent e in the default integer type. EXPONENT (X) has the value zero if X is zero.

Examples. EXPONENT (1.0) has the value 1 and EXPONENT (4.1) has the value 3 for reals whose model is described in 13.2.3.

A.36 FLOOR (A)

Description. Returns the greatest integer less than or equal to its argument.

Class. Elemental function.

Argument. A must be of type real.

Result Type and Type Parameter. Default integer.

Result Value. The result has value equal to the greatest integer less than or equal to A. The result is undefined if the processor cannot represent this value in the default integer type.

Examples. FLOOR (3.7) has the value 3. FLOOR (–3.7) has the value –4. FLOOR (10.0_HIGH/3) has the value 3.

A.37 FRACTION (X)

Description. Returns the fractional part of the model representation of the argument value.

Class. Elemental function.

Argument. X must be of type real.

Result Type and Type Parameter. Same as X.

Result Value. The result has the value $X \times b^{-e}$, where b and e are as defined in 13.2.3 for the model representation of X. If X has the value zero, the result has the value zero.

Example. FRACTION (3.0) has the value 0.75 for reals whose model is described in 13.2.3.

A.38 HUGE (X)

Description. Returns the largest number in the model representing numbers of the same type and kind type parameter as the argument.

Class. Inquiry function.

Argument. X must be of type integer or real. It may be scalar or array valued.

Result Type, Type Parameter, and Shape. Scalar of the same type and kind type parameter as X.

Result Value. The result has the value $r^q - 1$ if X is of type integer and $(1 - b^{-p})b^{e_{max}}$ if X is of type real, where r, q, b, p, and e_{max} are as defined in 13.2.3 for the model representing numbers of the same type and kind type parameter as X.

Example. HUGE (X) has the value $(1 - 2^{-24}) \times 2^{127}$ for real X whose model is described in 13.2.3.

A.39 IACHAR (C)

Description. Returns the position of a character in the ASCII collating sequence.

Class. Elemental function.

Argument. C must be of type default character and of length one.

Result Type and Type Parameter. Default integer.

Result Value. If C is in the collating sequence defined by the codes specified in ISO 646:1983 (International Reference Version), the result is the position of C in that sequence and satisfies the inequality ($0 \le$ IACHAR (C) ≤ 127). A processor-dependent value is returned if C is not in the ASCII collating sequence. The results are consistent with the LGE, LGT, LLE, and LLT lexical comparison functions. For example, if LLE (C, D) is true, IACHAR (C) .LE. IACHAR (D) is true where C and D are any two characters representable by the processor.

Examples. IACHAR ('X') has the value 88. IACHAR ('*') has the value 42.

A.40 IAND (I, J)

Description. Performs a logical AND.

Class. Elemental function.

Arguments.

I   must be of type integer.

J   must be of type integer with the same kind type
                          parameter as I.

Result Type and Type Parameter. Same as I.

Result Value. The result has the value obtained by combining I and J
bit-by-bit according to the following truth table:

I	J	IAND (I, J)
1	1	1
1	0	0
0	1	0
0	0	0

The model for the interpretation of an integer value as a sequence of bits
is in 13.2.1.

Examples. IAND (1, 3) has the value 1. IAND (2_SHORT, 10_SHORT)
is 2 with kind SHORT.

A.41 IBCLR (I, POS)

Description. Clears one bit to zero.

Class. Elemental function.

Arguments.

I   must be of type integer.

POS   must be of type integer. It must be nonnegative
                          and less than BIT_SIZE (I).

Result Type and Type Parameter. Same as I.

Result Value. The result has the value of the sequence of bits of I,
except that bit POS of I is set to zero. The model for the interpretation
of an integer value as a sequence of bits is in 13.2.1.

Examples. IBCLR (14, 1) has the result 12. If V has the value
(1, 2, 3, 4), the value of IBCLR (POS = V, I = 31) is (29, 27, 23, 15).
The value of IBCLR ((/ 15_SHORT, 31_SHORT, 7_SHORT /), 3) is
(7, 23, 7) with kind SHORT.

A.42 IBITS (I, POS, LEN)

Description. Extracts a sequence of bits.

Class. Elemental function.

Arguments.

I   must be of type integer.

POS   must be of type integer. It must be nonnegative
                         and POS + LEN must be less than or equal to
                         BIT_SIZE (I).

LEN   must be of type integer and nonnegative.

Result Type and Type Parameter. Same as I.

Result Value. The result has the value of the sequence of LEN bits in I
beginning at bit POS right-adjusted and with all other bits zero. The
model for the interpretation of an integer value as a sequence of bits is in
13.2.1.

Examples. IBITS (14, 1, 3) has the value 7. The value of
IBITS ((/ 15_SHORT, 31_SHORT, 7_SHORT /), 2_SHORT, 3_SHORT)
is (3, 7, 1) with kind SHORT.

A.43   IBSET (I, POS)

Description. Sets one bit to one.

Class. Elemental function.

Arguments.

I   must be of type integer.

POS   must be of type integer. It must be nonnegative
                         and less than BIT_SIZE (I).

Result Type and Type Parameter. Same as I.

Result Value. The result has the value of the sequence of bits of I,
except that bit POS of I is set to one. The model for the interpretation
of an integer value as a sequence of bits is in 13.2.1.

Examples. IBSET (12, 1) has the value 14. If V has the value
(1, 2, 3, 4), the value of IBSET (POS = V, I = 0) is (2, 4, 8, 16). The
value of IBSET ((/ 15_SHORT, 31_SHORT, 7_SHORT /), 3) is
(15, 31, 15) with kind SHORT.

A.44   ICHAR (C)

Description. Returns the position of a character in the processor collating sequence associated with the kind type parameter of the character.

Class. Elemental function.

Argument. C must be of type character and of length one. Its value must be that of a character capable of representation in the processor.

Result Type and Type Parameter. Default integer.

Result Value. The result is the position of C in the processor collating sequence associated with the kind type parameter of C and is in the range $0 \le$ ICHAR (C) $\le n - 1$, where n is the number of characters in the collating sequence. For any characters C and D capable of representation in the processor, C .LE. D is true if and only if ICHAR (C) .LE. ICHAR (D) is true and C .EQ. D is true if and only if ICHAR (C). EQ. ICHAR (D) is true.

Examples. ICHAR ('X') has the value 88 on a processor using the ASCII collating sequence for the default character type. ICHAR ('*') has the value 42 on such a processor.

A.45 IEOR (I, J)

Description. Performs an exclusive OR.

Class. Elemental function.

Arguments.

I   must be of type integer.

J   must be of type integer with the same kind type parameter as I.

Result Type and Type Parameter. Same as I.

Result Value. The result has the value obtained by combining I and J bit-by-bit according to the following truth table:

I	J	IEOR (I, J)
1	1	0
1	0	1
0	1	1
0	0	0

The model for the interpretation of an integer value as a sequence of bits is in 13.2.1.

Examples. IEOR (1, 3) has the value 2. IEOR ((/ 3_SHORT, 10_SHORT /), 2_SHORT) is (1, 8) with kind SHORT.

A.46 INDEX (STRING, SUBSTRING, BACK)

Optional Argument. BACK

Description. Returns the starting position of a substring within a string.

Class. Elemental function.

Arguments.

STRING   must be of type character.

SUBSTRING   must be of type character with the same kind type parameter as STRING.

BACK (optional)   must be of type logical.

Result Type and Type Parameter. Default integer.

Result Value.

Case (i):   If BACK is absent or present with the value false, the result is the minimum positive value of I such that STRING (I : I + LEN (SUBSTRING) – 1) = SUBSTRING or zero if there is no such value. Zero is returned if LEN (STRING) < LEN (SUBSTRING) and one is returned if LEN (SUBSTRING) = 0.

Case (ii):   If BACK is present with the value true, the result is the maximum value of I less than or equal to LEN (STRING) – LEN (SUBSTRING) + 1 such that STRING (I : I + LEN (SUBSTRING) – 1) = SUBSTRING or zero if there is no such value. Zero is returned if LEN (STRING) < LEN (SUBSTRING) and LEN (STRING) + 1 is returned if LEN (SUBSTRING) = 0.

Examples. INDEX ('FORTRAN', 'R') has the value 3. INDEX ('FOR-TRAN', 'R', BACK = .TRUE.) has the value 5. INDEX (GREEK_"$\tau\rho\iota\alpha$", GREEK_"ι") has the value 3. INDEX ("XXX", " ") has the value 1. INDEX ("XXX", " ", BACK=.TRUE.) has the value 4.

A.47 INT (A, KIND)

Optional Argument. KIND

Description. Convert to integer type.

Class. Elemental function.

Arguments.

A   must be of type integer, real, or complex.

KIND (optional)   must be a scalar integer initialization expression.

Result Type and Type Parameter. Integer. If KIND is present, the kind type parameter is that specified by KIND; otherwise, the kind type parameter is that of default integer type.

Result Value.

Case (i):   If A is of type integer, INT (A) = A.

Case (ii):   If A is of type real, there are two cases: if $|A| < 1$, INT (A) has the value 0; if $|A| \geq 1$, INT (A) is the integer whose magnitude is the largest integer that does not exceed the magnitude of A and whose sign is the same as the sign of A.

Case (iii):   If A is of type complex, INT (A) is the value obtained by applying the case (ii) rule to the real part of A.

The result is undefined if the processor cannot represent the result in the specified integer type.

Examples. INT (–3.7) has the value –3. INT (9.1_HIGH/4.0_HIGH, SHORT) is 2 with kind SHORT.

A.48 IOR (I, J)

Description. Performs an inclusive OR.

Class. Elemental function.

Arguments.

I   must be of type integer.

J   must be of type integer with the same kind type parameter as I.

Result Type and Type Parameter. Same as I.

Result Value. The result has the value obtained by combining I and J bit-by-bit according to the following truth table:

I	J	IOR (I, J)
1	1	1
1	0	1
0	1	1
0	0	0

The model for the interpretation of an integer value as a sequence of bits is in 13.2.1.

Examples. IOR (1, 3) has the value 3. IOR ((/ 3_SHORT, 2_SHORT /), (/ 1_SHORT, 10_SHORT /))) is (3, 10) with kind SHORT.

A.49 ISHFT (I, SHIFT)

Description. Performs a logical shift.

Class. Elemental function.

Arguments.

I   must be of type integer.

SHIFT   must be of type integer. The absolute value of SHIFT must be less than or equal to BIT_SIZE (I).

Result Type and Type Parameter. Same as I.

Result Value. The result has the value obtained by shifting the bits of I by SHIFT positions. If SHIFT is positive, the shift is to the left; if SHIFT is negative, the shift is to the right; and if SHIFT is zero, no shift is performed. Bits shifted out from the left or from the right, as appropriate, are lost. Zeros are shifted in from the opposite end. The model for the interpretation of an integer value as a sequence of bits is in 13.2.1.

Examples. ISHFT (3, 1) has the value 6. ISHFT (3, –1) has the value 1.

A.50 ISHFTC (I, SHIFT, SIZE)

Optional Argument. SIZE

Description. Performs a circular shift of the rightmost bits.

Class. Elemental function.

Arguments.

I   must be of type integer.

SHIFT   must be of type integer. The absolute value of SHIFT must be less than or equal to SIZE.

SIZE (optional)   must be of type integer. The value of SIZE must be positive and must not exceed BIT_SIZE (I). If SIZE is absent, it is as if it were present with the value of BIT_SIZE (I).

Result Type and Type Parameter. Same as I.

Result Value. The result has the value obtained by shifting the SIZE rightmost bits of I circularly by SHIFT positions. If SHIFT is positive, the shift is to the left; if SHIFT is negative, the shift is to the right; and if

SHIFT is zero, no shift is performed. No bits are lost. The unshifted bits are unaltered. The model for the interpretation of an integer value as a sequence of bits is in 13.2.1.

Examples. ISHFTC (3, 2, 3) has the value 5. ISHFTC (3_SHORT, –2_SHORT) is 192 with kind SHORT.

A.51 KIND (X)

Description. Returns the value of the kind type parameter of X.

Class. Inquiry function.

Argument. X may be of any intrinsic type.

Result Type, Type Parameter, and Shape. Default integer scalar.

Result Value. The result has a value equal to the kind type parameter value of X.

Examples. KIND (0.0) has the kind type parameter value of default real. KIND (1.0_HIGH) has the value of the named constant HIGH.

A.52 LBOUND (ARRAY, DIM)

Optional Argument. DIM

Description. Returns all the lower bounds or a specified lower bound of an array.

Class. Inquiry function.

Arguments.

ARRAY   may be of any type. It must not be scalar. It must not be a pointer that is disassociated or an allocatable array that is not allocated.

DIM (optional)   must be scalar and of type integer with a value in the range $1 \leq DIM \leq n$, where n is the rank of ARRAY. The corresponding actual argument must not be an optional dummy argument.

Result Type, Type Parameter, and Shape. The result is of type default integer. It is scalar if DIM is present; otherwise, the result is an array of rank one and size n, where n is the rank of ARRAY.

Result Value.

Case (i):   For an array section or for an array expression, other than a whole array or array structure component, LBOUND (ARRAY, DIM) has the value 1; otherwise, it has a value equal to the lower bound for subscript DIM of ARRAY if dimension DIM of ARRAY does not have size zero and has the value 1 if dimension DIM has size zero.

Case (ii):   LBOUND (ARRAY) has a value whose ith component is equal to LBOUND (ARRAY, i), for $i = 1, 2, ..., n$, where n is the rank of ARRAY.

Examples. If the following statements are processed

```
REAL, TARGET :: A (2:3, 7:10)
REAL, POINTER, DIMENSION (:,:) :: B, C, D
B => A
C => A(:,:)
ALLOCATE ( D(-3:3,-7:7) )
```

LBOUND (A) is (2, 7), LBOUND (A, DIM=2) is 7, LBOUND (B) is (2,7), LBOUND (C) is (1,1), LBOUND (D) is (-3,-7),

A.53 LEN (STRING)

Description. Returns the length of a character entity.

Class. Inquiry function.

Argument. STRING must be of type character. It may be scalar or array valued.

Result Type, Type Parameter, and Shape. Default integer scalar.

Result Value. The result has a value equal to the number of characters in STRING if it is scalar or in an element of STRING if it is array valued.

Example. If C and D are declared by the statements

```
CHARACTER (11) C (100)
CHARACTER (KIND=GREEK, LEN=31) D
```

LEN (C) has the value 11 and LEN (D) has the value 31.

A.54 LEN_TRIM (STRING)

Description. Returns the length of the character argument without counting trailing blank characters.

Class. Elemental function.

Argument. STRING must be of type character.

Result Type and Type Parameter. Default integer.

Result Value. The result has a value equal to the number of characters remaining after any trailing blanks in STRING are removed. If the argument contains no nonblank characters, the result is zero.

Examples. LEN_TRIM (' A B ') has the value 4 and LEN_TRIM (' ') has the value 0.

A.55 LGE (STRING_A, STRING_B)

Description. Test whether a string is lexically greater than or equal to another string, based on the ASCII collating sequence.

Class. Elemental function.

Arguments.

STRING_A   must be of type default character.

STRING_B   must be of type default character.

Result Type and Type Parameters. Default logical.

Result Value. If the strings are of unequal length, the comparison is made as if the shorter string were extended on the right with blanks to the length of the longer string. If either string contains a character not in the ASCII character set, the result is processor dependent. The result is true if the strings are equal or if STRING_A follows STRING_B in the ASCII collating sequence; otherwise, the result is false. Note that the result is true if both STRING_A and STRING_B are of zero length.

Example. LGE ('ONE', 'TWO') has the value false.

A.56 LGT (STRING_A, STRING_B)

Description. Test whether a string is lexically greater than another string, based on the ASCII collating sequence.

Class. Elemental function.

Arguments.

STRING_A   must be of type default character.

STRING_B   must be of type default character.

Result Type and Type Parameters. Default logical.

Result Value. If the strings are of unequal length, the comparison is made as if the shorter string were extended on the right with blanks to the length of the longer string. If either string contains a character not in the ASCII character set, the result is processor dependent. The result is true if STRING_A follows STRING_B in the ASCII collating sequence; otherwise, the result is false. Note that the result is false if both STRING_A and STRING_B are of zero length.

Example. LGT ('ONE', 'TWO') has the value false.

A.57 LLE (STRING_A, STRING_B)

Description. Test whether a string is lexically less than or equal to another string, based on the ASCII collating sequence.

Class. Elemental function.

Arguments.

STRING_A   must be of type default character.

STRING_B   must be of type default character.

Result Type and Type Parameters. Default logical.

Result Value. If the strings are of unequal length, the comparison is made as if the shorter string were extended on the right with blanks to the length of the longer string. If either string contains a character not in the ASCII character set, the result is processor dependent. The result is true if the strings are equal or if STRING_A precedes STRING_B in the ASCII collating sequence; otherwise, the result is false. Note that the result is true if both STRING_A and STRING_B are of zero length.

Example. LLE ('ONE', 'TWO') has the value true.

A.58 LLT (STRING_A, STRING_B)

Description. Test whether a string is lexically less than another string, based on the ASCII collating sequence.

Class. Elemental function.

Arguments.

STRING_A   must be of type default character.

STRING_B   must be of type default character.

Result Type and Type Parameters. Default logical.

Result Value. If the strings are of unequal length, the comparison is made as if the shorter string were extended on the right with blanks to the length of the longer string. If either string contains a character not in the ASCII character set, the result is processor dependent. The result is true if STRING_A precedes STRING_B in the ASCII collating sequence; otherwise, the result is false. Note that the result is false if both STRING_A and STRING_B are of zero length.

Example. LLT ('ONE', 'TWO') has the value true.

A.59 LOG (X)

Description. Natural logarithm.

Class. Elemental function.

Argument. X must be of type real or complex. If X is real, its value must be greater than zero. If X is complex, its value must not be zero.

Result Type and Type Parameter. Same as X.

Result Value. The result has a value equal to a processor-dependent approximation to $\log_e X$. A result of type complex is the principal value with imaginary part ω in the range $-\pi < \omega \leq \pi$. The imaginary part of the result is π only when the real part of the argument is less than zero and the imaginary part of the argument is zero.

Examples. LOG (10.0) has the value 2.3025851. LOG ((−0.5_HIGH,0)) has the value −0.69314718055994 + 3.1415926535898ι with kind HIGH.

A.60 LOG10 (X)

Description. Common logarithm.

Class. Elemental function.

Argument. X must be of type real. The value of X must be greater than zero.

Result Type and Type Parameter. Same as X.

Result Value. The result has a value equal to a processor-dependent approximation to $\log_{10} X$.

Examples. LOG10 (10.0) has the value 1.0. LOG10 (10.0E1000_HIGH) has the value 1001.0 with kind HIGH.

A.61 LOGICAL (L, KIND)

Optional Argument. KIND

Description. Converts between kinds of logical.

Class. Elemental function.

Arguments.

L   must be of type logical.

KIND (optional)   must be a scalar integer initialization expression.

Result Type and Type Parameter. Logical. If KIND is present, the kind type parameter is that specified by KIND; otherwise, the kind type parameter is that of default logical.

Result Value. The value is that of L.

Examples. LOGICAL (L .OR. .NOT. L) has the value true and is of type default logical, regardless of the kind type parameter of the logical variable L. LOGICAL (L, BIT) has kind parameter BIT and has the same value as L.

A.62 MATMUL (MATRIX_A, MATRIX_B)

Description. Performs matrix multiplication of numeric or logical matrices.

Class. Transformational function.

Arguments.

MATRIX_A   must be of numeric type (integer, real, or complex) or of logical type. It must be array valued and of rank one or two.

MATRIX_B   must be of numeric type if MATRIX_A is of numeric type and of logical type if MATRIX_A is of logical type. It must be array valued and of rank one or two. If MATRIX_A has rank one, MATRIX_B must have rank two. If MATRIX_B has rank one, MATRIX_A must have rank two. The size of the first (or only) dimension of MATRIX_B must equal the size of the last (or only) dimension of MATRIX_A.

Result Type, Type Parameter, and Shape. If the arguments are of numeric type, the type and kind type parameter of the result are determined by the types of the arguments according to 7.2.8.2. If the arguments are of type logical, the result is of type logical with the kind type parameter of the arguments according to 7.2.8.2. The shape of the result depends on the shapes of the arguments as follows:

Case (i):   If MATRIX_A has shape (n, m) and MATRIX_B has shape (m, k), the result has shape (n, k).

Case (ii):   If MATRIX_A has shape (m) and MATRIX_B has shape (m, k), the result has shape (k).

Case (iii):   If MATRIX_A has shape (n, m) and MATRIX_B has shape (m), the result has shape (n).

Result Value.

Case (i):   Element (i, j) of the result has the value SUM (MATRIX_A $(i, :)$ * MATRIX_B $(:, j)$) if the arguments are of numeric type and has the value ANY (MATRIX_A $(i, :)$ .AND. MATRIX_B $(:, j)$) if the arguments are of logical type.

Case (ii):   Element (j) of the result has the value SUM (MATRIX_A $(:)$ * MATRIX_B $(:, j)$) if the arguments are of numeric type and has the value ANY (MATRIX_A $(:)$ .AND. MATRIX_B $(:, j)$) if the arguments are of logical type.

Case (iii): Element (i) of the result has the value SUM (MATRIX_A $(i, :)$ * MATRIX_B $(:)$) if the arguments are of numeric type and has the value ANY (MATRIX_A $(i, :)$ .AND. MATRIX_B $(:)$) if the arguments are of logical type.

Examples. Let A and B be the matrices $\begin{bmatrix} 1 & 2 & 3 \\ 2 & 3 & 4 \end{bmatrix}$ and $\begin{bmatrix} 1 & 2 \\ 2 & 3 \\ 3 & 4 \end{bmatrix}$; let X and Y be the vectors (1, 2) and (1, 2, 3).

Case (i):   The result of MATMUL (A, B) is the matrix-matrix product AB with the value $\begin{bmatrix} 14 & 20 \\ 20 & 29 \end{bmatrix}$.

Case (ii):   The result of MATMUL (X, A) is the vector-matrix product XA with the value (5, 8, 11).

Case (iii): The result of MATMUL (A, Y) is the matrix-vector product AY with the value (14, 20).

A.63 MAX (A1, A2, A3, ...)

Optional Arguments. A3, ...

Description. Maximum value.

Class. Elemental function.

Arguments. The arguments must all have the same type which must be integer or real and they must all have the same kind type parameter.

Result Type and Type Parameter. Same as the arguments.

Result Value. The value of the result is that of the largest argument.

Examples. MAX (–9.0, 7.0, 2.0) has the value 7.0. MAX (–1.0_HIGH/3, –0.1_HIGH) is –0.1 with kind HIGH.

A.64 MAXEXPONENT (X)

Description. Returns the maximum exponent in the model representing numbers of the same type and kind type parameter as the argument.

Class. Inquiry function.

Argument. X must be of type real. It may be scalar or array valued.

Result Type, Type Parameter, and Shape. Default integer scalar.

Result Value. The result has the value e_{max}, as defined in 13.2.3 for the model representing numbers of the same type and kind type parameter as X.

Example. MAXEXPONENT (X) has the value 127 for real X whose model is described in 13.2.3.

A.65 MAXLOC (ARRAY, MASK)

Optional Argument. MASK

Description. Determine the location of the first element of ARRAY having the maximum value of the elements identified by MASK.

Class. Transformational function.

Arguments.

ARRAY   must be of type integer or real. It must not be scalar.

MASK (optional)   must be of type logical and must be conformable with ARRAY.

Result Type, Type Parameter, and Shape. The result is of type default integer; it is an array of rank one and of size equal to the rank of ARRAY.

Result Value.

Case (i):   If MASK is absent, the result is a rank-one array whose element values are the values of the subscripts of an element of ARRAY whose value equals the maximum value of all of the elements of ARRAY. The ith subscript returned lies in the range 1 to e_i, where e_i is the extent of the ith dimension of ARRAY. If more than one element has the maximum value, the element whose subscripts are returned is the first such element, taken in array element order. If ARRAY has size zero, the value of the result is processor dependent.

Case (ii):   If MASK is present, the result is a rank-one array whose element values are the values of the subscripts of an element of ARRAY, corresponding to a true element of MASK, whose value equals the maximum value of all such elements of ARRAY. The ith subscript returned lies in the range 1 to e_i, where e_i is the extent of the ith dimension of ARRAY. If more than one such element has the maximum value, the element whose subscripts are returned is the first such element taken in array element order. If there are no such elements (that is, if ARRAY has size zero or every element of MASK has the value false), the value of the result is processor dependent.

An element of the result is undefined if the processor cannot represent the value as a default integer.

Examples.

Case (i):   The value of MAXLOC ((/ 2, 6, 4, 6 /)) is (2).

Case (ii):   If A has the value $\begin{bmatrix} 0 & -5 & 8 & -3 \\ 3 & 4 & -1 & 2 \\ 1 & 5 & 6 & -4 \end{bmatrix}$, MAXLOC (A,

MASK = A .LT. 6) has the value (3, 2). Note that this is true even if A has a declared lower bound other than 1.

A.66 MAXVAL (ARRAY, DIM, MASK)

Optional Arguments. DIM, MASK

Description. Maximum value of the elements of ARRAY along dimension DIM corresponding to the true elements of MASK.

Class. Transformational function.

Arguments.

ARRAY   must be of type integer or real. It must not be scalar.

DIM (optional)   must be scalar and of type integer with a value in the range $1 \le DIM \le n$, where n is the rank of ARRAY. The corresponding actual argument must not be an optional dummy argument.

MASK (optional)   must be of type logical and must be conformable with ARRAY.

Result Type, Type Parameter, and Shape. The result is of the same type and kind type parameter as ARRAY. It is scalar if DIM is absent or ARRAY has rank one; otherwise, the result is an array of rank $n-1$ and of shape $(d_1, d_2, ..., d_{DIM-1}, d_{DIM+1}, ..., d_n)$ where $(d_1, d_2, ..., d_n)$ is the shape of ARRAY.

Result Value.

Case (i):   The result of MAXVAL (ARRAY) has a value equal to the maximum value of all the elements of ARRAY or has the value of the negative number of the largest magnitude supported by the processor for numbers of the type and kind type parameter of ARRAY if ARRAY has size zero.

Case (ii):   The result of MAXVAL (ARRAY, MASK = MASK) has a value equal to the maximum value of the elements of ARRAY corresponding to true elements of MASK or has the value of the negative number of the largest magnitude supported by the processor for numbers of the type and kind type parameter of ARRAY if there are no true elements.

Case (iii): If ARRAY has rank one, MAXVAL (ARRAY, DIM [,MASK]) has a value equal to that of MAXVAL (ARRAY [,MASK = MASK]). Otherwise, the value of element $(s_1, s_2, ..., s_{DIM-1}, s_{DIM+1}, ..., s_n)$ of MAXVAL (ARRAY, DIM [,MASK]) is equal to MAXVAL (ARRAY $(s_1, s_2, ..., s_{DIM-1}, :, s_{DIM+1}, ..., s_n)$, [, MASK = MASK $(s_1, s_2, ..., s_{DIM-1}, :, s_{DIM+1}, ..., s_n)$]).

Examples.

Case (i):   The value of MAXVAL ((/ 1, 2, 3 /)) is 3.

Case (ii):   MAXVAL (C, MASK = C .LT. 0.0) finds the maximum of the negative elements of C.

Case (iii): If B is the array $\begin{bmatrix} 1 & 3 & 5 \\ 2 & 4 & 6 \end{bmatrix}$, MAXVAL (B, DIM = 1) is (2, 4, 6) and MAXVAL (B, DIM = 2) is (5, 6).

A.67 MERGE (TSOURCE, FSOURCE, MASK)

Description. Choose alternative value according to the value of a mask.

Class. Elemental function.

Arguments.

TSOURCE   may be of any type.

FSOURCE   must be of the same type and type parameters as TSOURCE.

MASK   must be of type logical.

Result Type and Type Parameters. Same as TSOURCE.

Result Value. The result is TSOURCE if MASK is true and FSOURCE otherwise.

Examples. If TSOURCE is the array $\begin{bmatrix} 1 & 6 & 5 \\ 2 & 4 & 6 \end{bmatrix}$, FSOURCE is the array $\begin{bmatrix} 0 & 3 & 2 \\ 7 & 4 & 8 \end{bmatrix}$ and MASK is the array $\begin{bmatrix} T & . & T \\ . & . & T \end{bmatrix}$, where "T" represents true and "." represents false, then MERGE (TSOURCE, FSOURCE, MASK) is $\begin{bmatrix} 1 & 3 & 5 \\ 7 & 4 & 6 \end{bmatrix}$. The value of MERGE (1.0, 0.0, K > 0) is 1.0 for K = 5 and 0.0 for K = -2.

A.68 MIN (A1, A2, A3, ...)

Optional Arguments. A3, ...

Description. Minimum value.

Class. Elemental function.

Arguments. The arguments must all be of the same type which must be integer or real and they must all have the same kind type parameter.

Result Type and Type Parameter. Same as the arguments.

Result Value. The value of the result is that of the smallest argument.

Examples. MIN (-9.0, 7.0, 2.0) has the value -9.0. MIN (-0.4_HIGH, -1.0_HIGH/3) is -0.4 with kind HIGH.

A.69 MINEXPONENT (X)

Description. Returns the minimum (most negative) exponent in the model representing numbers of the same type and kind type parameter as the argument.

Class. Inquiry function.

Argument. X must be of type real. It may be scalar or array valued.

Result Type, Type Parameter, and Shape. Default integer scalar.

Result Value. The result has the value e_{min}, as defined in 13.2.3 for the model representing numbers of the same type and kind type parameter as X.

Example. MINEXPONENT (X) has the value -126 for real X whose model is described in 13.2.3.

A.70 MINLOC (ARRAY, MASK)

Optional Argument. MASK

Description. Determine the location of the first element of ARRAY having the minimum value of the elements identified by MASK.

Class. Transformational function.

Arguments.

ARRAY   must be of type integer or real. It must not be scalar.

MASK (optional)   must be of type logical and must be conformable with ARRAY.

Result Type, Type Parameter, and Shape. The result is of type default integer; it is an array of rank one and of size equal to the rank of ARRAY.

Result Value.

Case (i):   If MASK is absent, the result is a rank-one array whose element values are the values of the subscripts of an element of ARRAY whose value equals the minimum value of all the elements of ARRAY. The ith subscript returned lies in the range 1 to e_i, where e_i is the extent of the ith dimension of ARRAY. If more than one element has the minimum value, the element whose subscripts are returned is the first such element, taken in array element order. If ARRAY has size zero, the value of the result is processor dependent.

Case (ii):   If MASK is present, the result is a rank-one array whose element values are the values of the subscripts of an element of ARRAY, corresponding to a true element of MASK, whose value equals the minimum value of all such elements of ARRAY. The ith subscript returned lies in the range 1 to e_i, where e_i is the extent of the ith dimension of ARRAY. If more than one such element has the minimum value, the element whose subscripts are returned is the first such element taken in array element order. If ARRAY has size zero or every element of MASK has the value false, the value of the result is processor dependent.

An element of the result is undefined if the processor cannot represent the value as a default integer.

Examples.

Case (i):   The value of MINLOC ((/ 4, 3, 6, 3 /)) is (2).

Case (ii):   If A has the value $\begin{bmatrix} 0 & -5 & 8 & -3 \\ 3 & 4 & -1 & 2 \\ 1 & 5 & 6 & -4 \end{bmatrix}$, MINLOC (A,

MASK = A .GT. -4) has the value (1, 4). Note that this is true even if A has a declared lower bound other than 1.

A.71 MINVAL (ARRAY, DIM, MASK)

Optional Arguments. DIM, MASK

Description. Minimum value of all the elements of ARRAY along dimension DIM corresponding to true elements of MASK.

Class. Transformational function.

Arguments.

ARRAY   must be of type integer or real. It must not be scalar.

DIM (optional)   must be scalar and of type integer with a value in the range $1 \le \text{DIM} \le n$, where n is the rank of ARRAY. The corresponding actual argument must not be an optional dummy argument.

MASK (optional)   must be of type logical and must be conformable with ARRAY.

Result Type, Type Parameter, and Shape. The result is of the same type and kind type parameter as ARRAY. It is scalar if DIM is absent or ARRAY has rank one; otherwise, the result is an array of rank $n-1$ and of shape $(d_1, d_2, ..., d_{\text{DIM}-1}, d_{\text{DIM}+1}, ..., d_n)$ where $(d_1, d_2, ..., d_n)$ is the shape of ARRAY.

Result Value.

Case (i):   The result of MINVAL (ARRAY) has a value equal to the minimum value of all the elements of ARRAY or has the value of the positive number of the largest magnitude supported by the processor for numbers of the type and kind type parameter of ARRAY if ARRAY has size zero.

Case (ii):   The result of MINVAL (ARRAY, MASK = MASK) has a value equal to the minimum value of the elements of ARRAY corresponding to true elements of MASK or has the value of the positive number of the largest magnitude supported by the processor for numbers of the type and kind type parameter of ARRAY if there are no true elements.

Case (iii):   If ARRAY has rank one, MINVAL (ARRAY, DIM [,MASK]) has a value equal to that of MINVAL (ARRAY [,MASK = MASK]). Otherwise, the value of element $(s_1, s_2, ..., s_{DIM-1}, s_{DIM+1}, ..., s_n)$ of MINVAL (ARRAY, DIM [,MASK]) is equal to MINVAL (ARRAY $(s_1, s_2, ..., s_{DIM-1}, :, s_{DIM+1}, ..., s_n)$ [, MASK= MASK $(s_1, s_2, ..., s_{DIM-1}, :, s_{DIM+1}, ..., s_n)$]).

Examples.

Case (i):   The value of MINVAL ((/ 1, 2, 3 /)) is 1.

Case (ii):   MINVAL (C, MASK = C .GT. 0.0) forms the minimum of the positive elements of C.

Case (iii):   If B is the array $\begin{bmatrix} 1 & 3 & 5 \\ 2 & 4 & 6 \end{bmatrix}$, MINVAL (B, DIM = 1) is (1, 3, 5) and MINVAL (B, DIM = 2) is (1, 2).

A.72 MOD (A, P)

Description. Remainder function.

Class. Elemental function.

Arguments.

A   must be of type integer or real.

P   must be of the same type and kind type parameter as A.

Result Type and Type Parameter. Same as A.

Result Value. If $P \neq 0$, the value of the result is A – INT (A / P) * P. If $P = 0$, the result is processor dependent.

Examples. MOD (3.0, 2.0) has the value 1.0. MOD (8, 5) has the value 3. MOD (–8, 5) has the value –3. MOD (8, –5) has the value 3. MOD (–8, –5) has the value –3. MOD (2.0_HIGH, 3.0_HIGH) has the value 2.0 with kind HIGH.

A.73 MODULO (A, P)

Description. Modulo function.

Class. Elemental function.

Arguments.

A   must be of type integer or real.

P   must be of the same type and kind type parameter as A.

Result Type and Type Parameter. Same as A.

Result Value.

Case (i):   A is of type integer. If $P \neq 0$, MODULO (A, P) has the value R such that $A = Q \times P + R$, where Q is an integer, the inequalities $0 \leq R < P$ hold if $P > 0$, and $P < R \leq 0$ hold if $P < 0$. If $P = 0$, the result is processor dependent.

Case (ii):   A is of type real. If $P \neq 0$, the value of the result is A – FLOOR (A / P) * P. If $P = 0$, the result is processor dependent.

Examples. MODULO (8, 5) has the value 3. MODULO (–8, 5) has the value 2. MODULO (8, –5) has the value –2. MODULO (–8, –5) has the value –3. MODULO (3.0, 2.0) has the value 1.0. MODULO (2.0_HIGH, 3.0_HIGH) has the value 2.0 with kind HIGH.

A.74 MVBITS (FROM, FROMPOS, LEN, TO, TOPOS)

Description. Copies a sequence of bits from one data object to another.

Class. Elemental subroutine.

Arguments.

FROM   must be of type integer. It is an INTENT (IN) argument.

FROMPOS   must be of type integer and nonnegative. It is an INTENT (IN) argument. FROMPOS + LEN must be less than or equal to BIT_SIZE (FROM). The model for the interpretation of an integer value as a sequence of bits is in 13.2.1.

LEN   must be of type integer and nonnegative. It is an INTENT (IN) argument.

TO   must be a variable of type integer with the same kind type parameter value as FROM and may be the same variable as FROM. It is an INTENT (INOUT) argument. TO is set by copying the sequence of bits of length LEN, starting at position FROMPOS of FROM to position TOPOS of TO.

No other bits of TO are altered. On return, the LEN bits of TO starting at TOPOS are equal to the value that the LEN bits of FROM starting at FROMPOS had on entry. The model for the interpretation of an integer value as a sequence of bits is in 13.2.1.

TOPOS   must be of type integer and nonnegative. It is an INTENT (IN) argument. TOPOS + LEN must be less than or equal to BIT_SIZE (TO).

Examples. If TO has the initial value 6, the value of TO after the statement CALL MVBITS (7, 2, 2, TO, 0) is 5. After the statement

```
CALL MVBITS (PATTERN, 0_SHORT, 1_SHORT, PATTERN, 7_SHORT)
```

is executed, the integer variable PATTERN of kind SHORT has a leading bit that is identical to its terminal bit.

A.75 NEAREST (X, S)

Description. Returns the nearest different machine representable number in a given direction.

Class. Elemental function.

Arguments.

X   must be of type real.

S   must be of type real and not equal to zero.

Result Type and Type Parameter. Same as X.

Result Value. The result has a value equal to the machine representable number distinct from X and nearest to it in the direction of the infinity with the same sign as S.

Example. NEAREST (3.0, 2.0) has the value $3 + 2^{-22}$ on a machine whose representation is that of the model described in 13.2.3.

A.76 NINT (A, KIND)

Optional Argument. KIND
Description. Nearest integer.
Class. Elemental function.

Arguments.

A   must be of type real.

KIND (optional)   must be a scalar integer initialization expression.
Result Type and Type Parameter. Integer. If KIND is present, the kind type parameter is that specified by KIND; otherwise, the kind type parameter is that of default integer type.
Result Value. If A > 0, NINT (A) has the value INT (A+0.5); if A ≤ 0, NINT (A) has the value INT (A–0.5). The result is undefined if the processor cannot represent the result in the specified integer type.
Examples. NINT (2.783) has the value 3. NINT (1.99999999999_HIGH) has the value 2.

A.77 NOT (I)

Description. Performs a logical complement.
Class. Elemental function.
Argument. I must be of type integer.
Result Type and Type Parameter. Same as I.
Result Value. The result has the value obtained by complementing I bit-by-bit according to the following truth table:

I	NOT (I)
1	0
0	1

The model for the interpretation of an integer value as a sequence of bits is in 13.2.1.
Example. If I is an integer of kind SHORT and has a value that is equal to 01010101 (base 2), NOT (I) has the value which is equal to 10101010 (base 2).

A.78 PACK (ARRAY, MASK, VECTOR)

Optional Argument. VECTOR
Description. Pack an array into an array of rank one under the control of a mask.
Class. Transformational function.

Arguments.

ARRAY	may be of any type. It must not be scalar.
MASK	must be of type logical and must be conformable with ARRAY.
VECTOR (optional)	must be of the same type and type parameters as ARRAY and must have rank one. VECTOR must have at least as many elements as there are true elements in MASK. If MASK is scalar with the value true, VECTOR must have at least as many elements as there are in ARRAY.

Result Type, Type Parameter, and Shape. The result is an array of rank one with the same type and type parameters as ARRAY. If VECTOR is present, the result size is that of VECTOR; otherwise, the result size is the number t of true elements in MASK unless MASK is scalar with the value true, in which case the result size is the size of ARRAY.

Result Value. Element i of the result is the element of ARRAY that corresponds to the ith true element of MASK, taking elements in array element order, for $i = 1, 2, ..., t$. If VECTOR is present and has size $n > t$, element i of the result has the value VECTOR (i), for $i = t + 1, ..., n$.

Examples. The nonzero elements of an array M with the value
$$\begin{bmatrix} 0 & 0 & 0 \\ 9 & 0 & 0 \\ 0 & 0 & 7 \end{bmatrix}$$
may be "gathered" by the function PACK. The result of PACK (M, MASK = M .NE. 0) is (9, 7) and the result of PACK (M, M .NE. 0, VECTOR = (/ 2, 4, 6, 8, 10, 12 /)) is (9, 7, 6, 8, 10, 12).

A.79 PRECISION (X)

Description. Returns the decimal precision in the model representing real numbers with the same kind type parameter as the argument.

Class. Inquiry function.

Argument. X must be of type real or complex. It may be scalar or array valued.

Result Type, Type Parameter, and Shape. Default integer scalar.

Result Value. The result has the value INT $((p - 1) * \text{LOG10} (b)) + k$, where b and p are as defined in 13.2.3 for the model representing real numbers with the same value for the kind type parameter as X, and where k is 1 if b is an integral power of 10 and 0 otherwise.

Example. PRECISION (X) has the value INT (23 * LOG10 (2.)) = INT (6.92...) = 6 for real X whose model is described in 13.2.3.

A.80 PRESENT (A)

Description. Determine whether an optional argument is present.

Class. Inquiry function.

Argument. A must be an optional argument of the procedure in which the PRESENT function reference appears.

Result Type and Type Parameters. Default logical scalar.

Result Value. The result has the value true if A is present (12.5.5) and otherwise has the value false.

Example.

```
SUBROUTINE SUB (A, B, EXTRA)
   REAL A, B, C
   REAL, OPTIONAL :: EXTRA
   . . .
   IF (PRESENT (EXTRA)) THEN
      C = EXTRA
   ELSE
      C = (A+B)/2
   END IF
   . . .
END
```

If SUB is called with the statement

```
CALL SUB (10.0, 20.0, 30.0)
```

C is set to 30.0. If SUB is called with the statement

```
CALL SUB (10.0, 20.0)
```

C is set to 15.0. An optional argument that is not present must not be referenced or defined or supplied as a nonoptional actual argument, except as the argument of the PRESENT intrinsic function.

A.81 PRODUCT (ARRAY, DIM, MASK)

Optional Arguments. DIM, MASK

Description. Product of all the elements of ARRAY along dimension DIM corresponding to the true elements of MASK.

Class. Transformational function.

Arguments.

ARRAY   must be of type integer, real, or complex. It must
                         not be scalar.

DIM (optional)   must be scalar and of type integer with a value in
                         the range $1 \le \text{DIM} \le n$, where n is the rank of
                         ARRAY. The corresponding actual argument must
                         not be an optional dummy argument.

MASK (optional)   must be of type logical and must be conformable
                         with ARRAY.

Result Type, Type Parameter, and Shape. The result is of the same type
and kind type parameter as ARRAY. It is scalar if DIM is absent or
ARRAY has rank one; otherwise, the result is an array of rank $n-1$ and
of shape $(d_1, d_2, ..., d_{\text{DIM}-1}, d_{\text{DIM}+1}, ..., d_n)$ where $(d_1, d_2, ..., d_n)$ is
the shape of ARRAY.

Result Value.

Case (i):   The result of PRODUCT (ARRAY) has a value equal to a
                 processor-dependent approximation to the product of all the
                 elements of ARRAY or has the value one if ARRAY has size
                 zero.

Case (ii):   The result of PRODUCT (ARRAY, MASK = MASK) has a
                 value equal to a processor-dependent approximation to the
                 product of the elements of ARRAY corresponding to the
                 true elements of MASK or has the value one if there are no
                 true elements.

Case (iii):   If ARRAY has rank one, PRODUCT (ARRAY, DIM
                 [,MASK]) has a value equal to that of PRODUCT (ARRAY
                 [,MASK = MASK]). Otherwise, the value of element $(s_1,$
                 $s_2, ..., s_{\text{DIM}-1}, s_{\text{DIM}+1}, ..., s_n)$ of PRODUCT (ARRAY,
                 DIM [,MASK]) is equal to PRODUCT (ARRAY $(s_1, s_2, ...,$
                 $s_{\text{DIM}-1}, :, s_{\text{DIM}+1}, ..., s_n)$ [, MASK = MASK $(s_1, s_2, ...,$
                 $s_{\text{DIM}-1}, :, s_{\text{DIM}+1}, ..., s_n)$]).

Examples.

Case (i):   The value of PRODUCT ((/ 1, 2, 3 /)) and PRODUCT
                 ((/ 1, 2, 3 /), DIM=1) is 6.

Case (ii):   PRODUCT (C, MASK = C .GT. 0.0) forms the product of
                 the positive elements of C.

Case (iii):   If B is the array $\begin{bmatrix} 1 & 3 & 5 \\ 2 & 4 & 6 \end{bmatrix}$, PRODUCT (B, DIM = 1) is
                 (2, 12, 30) and PRODUCT (B, DIM = 2) is (15, 48).

A.82 RADIX (X)

Description. Returns the base of the model representing numbers of the same type and kind type parameter as the argument.

Class. Inquiry function.

Argument. X must be of type integer or real. It may be scalar or array valued.

Result Type, Type Parameter, and Shape. Default integer scalar.

Result Value. The result has the value r if X is of type integer and the value b if X is of type real, where r and b are as defined in 13.2.3 for the model representing numbers of the same type and kind type parameter as X.

Example. RADIX (X) has the value 2 for real X whose model is described in 13.2.3.

A.83 RANDOM_NUMBER (HARVEST)

Description. Returns one pseudorandom number or an array of pseudo-random numbers from the uniform distribution over the range $0 \le x < 1$.

Class. Subroutine.

Argument. HARVEST must be of type real. It is an INTENT (OUT) argument. It may be a scalar or an array variable. It is set to contain pseudorandom numbers from the uniform distribution in the interval $0 \le x < 1$.

Examples.

```
REAL X, Y (10, 10)
! Initialize X with a pseudorandom number
CALL RANDOM_NUMBER (HARVEST = X)
CALL RANDOM_NUMBER (Y)
! X and Y contain uniformly distributed random numbers
```

A.84 RANDOM_SEED (SIZE, PUT, GET)

Optional Arguments. SIZE, PUT, GET

Description. Restarts or queries the pseudorandom number generator used by RANDOM_NUMBER.

Class. Subroutine.

Arguments. There must either be exactly one or no arguments present.

SIZE (optional)	must be scalar and of type default integer. It is an INTENT (OUT) argument. It is set to the number N of integers that the processor uses to hold the value of the seed.
PUT (optional)	must be a default integer array of rank one and size $\geq N$. It is an INTENT (IN) argument. It is used by the processor to set the seed value.
GET (optional)	must be a default integer array of rank one and size $\geq N$. It is an INTENT (OUT) argument. It is set by the processor to the current value of the seed.

If no argument is present, the processor sets the seed to a processor-dependent value.

Examples.

```
CALL RANDOM_SEED                   ! Processor initialization
CALL RANDOM_SEED (SIZE = K)        ! Sets K = N
CALL RANDOM_SEED (PUT = SEED (1 : K)) ! Set user seed
CALL RANDOM_SEED (GET = OLD (1 : K))  ! Read current seed
```

A.85 RANGE (X)

Description. Returns the decimal exponent range in the model representing integer or real numbers with the same kind type parameter as the argument.

Class. Inquiry function.

Argument. X must be of type integer, real, or complex. It may be scalar or array valued.

Result Type, Type Parameter, and Shape. Default integer scalar.

Result Value.

Case (i):	For an integer argument, the result has the value INT (LOG10 (*huge*)), where *huge* is the largest positive integer in the model representing integer numbers with same kind type parameter as X (13.2.2).
Case (ii):	For a real or complex argument, the result has the value INT (MIN (LOG10 (*huge*), –LOG10 (*tiny*))), where *huge* and *tiny* are the largest and smallest positive numbers in the model representing real numbers with the same value for the kind type parameter as X (13.2.3).

Example. RANGE (X) has the value 38 for real X whose model is described in 13.2.3, because in this case $huge = (1 - 2^{-24}) \times 2^{127}$ and $tiny = 2^{-127}$.

A.86 REAL (A, KIND)

Optional Argument. KIND

Description. Convert to real type.

Class. Elemental function.

Arguments.

A   must be of type integer, real, or complex.

KIND (optional)   must be a scalar integer initialization expression.

Result Type and Type Parameter. Real.

Case (i):   If A is of type integer or real and KIND is present, the kind type parameter is that specified by KIND. If A is of type integer or real and KIND is not present, the kind type parameter is the processor-dependent kind type parameter for the default real type.

Case (ii):   If A is of type complex and KIND is present, the kind type parameter is that specified by KIND. If A is of type complex and KIND is not present, the kind type parameter is the kind type parameter of A.

Result Value.

Case (i):   If A is of type integer or real, the result is equal to a processor-dependent approximation to A.

Case (ii):   If A is of type complex, the result is equal to a processor-dependent approximation to the real part of A.

Examples. REAL (–3) has the value –3.0. REAL (Z) has the same kind type parameter and the same value as the real part of the complex variable Z. REAL (2.0_HIGH/3.0) is 0.66666666666666 with kind HIGH.

A.87 REPEAT (STRING, NCOPIES)

Description. Concatenate several copies of a string.

Class. Transformational function.

Arguments.

STRING   must be scalar and of type character.

NCOPIES   must be scalar and of type integer. Its value must
                    not be negative.

Result Type, Type Parameter, and Shape. Character scalar of length
NCOPIES times that of STRING, with the same kind type parameter as
STRING.

Result Value. The value of the result is the concatenation of NCOPIES
copies of STRING.

Examples. REPEAT ('H', 2) has the value HH. REPEAT ('XYZ', 0) has
the value of a zero-length string.

A.88 RESHAPE (SOURCE, SHAPE, PAD, ORDER)

Optional Arguments. PAD, ORDER

Description. Constructs an array of a specified shape from the elements
of a given array.

Class. Transformational function.

Arguments.

SOURCE   may be of any type. It must be array valued. If
                    PAD is absent or of size zero, the size of SOURCE
                    must   be   greater   than   or   equal   to
                    PRODUCT (SHAPE). The size of the result is the
                    product of the values of the elements of SHAPE.

SHAPE   must be of type integer, rank one, and constant
                    size. Its size must be positive and less than 8. It
                    must not have an element whose value is negative.

PAD (optional)   must be of the same type and type parameters as
                    SOURCE. PAD must be array valued.

ORDER (optional)   must be of type integer, must have the same shape
                    as SHAPE, and its value must be a permutation of
                    $(1, 2, ..., n)$, where n is the size of SHAPE. If
                    absent, it is as if it were present with value $(1, 2,
                    ..., n)$.

Result Type, Type Parameter, and Shape. The result is an array of
shape SHAPE (that is, SHAPE (RESHAPE (SOURCE, SHAPE, PAD,
ORDER)) is equal to SHAPE) with the same type and type parameters as
SOURCE.

Result Value. The elements of the result, taken in permuted subscript order ORDER (1), ..., ORDER (n), are those of SOURCE in normal array element order followed if necessary by those of PAD in array element order, followed if necessary by additional copies of PAD in array element order.

Examples. RESHAPE ((/ 1, 2, 3, 4, 5, 6 /), (/ 2, 3 /)) has the value

$$\begin{bmatrix} 1 & 3 & 5 \\ 2 & 4 & 6 \end{bmatrix}.$$ RESHAPE ((/ 1, 2, 3, 4, 5, 6 /),   (/ 2, 4 /),   (/ 0, 0 /),

(/ 2, 1 /)) has the value $\begin{bmatrix} 1 & 2 & 3 & 4 \\ 5 & 6 & 0 & 0 \end{bmatrix}.$

A.89 RRSPACING (X)

Description. Returns the reciprocal of the relative spacing of model numbers near the argument value.

Class. Elemental function.

Argument. X must be of type real.

Result Type and Type Parameter. Same as X.

Result Value. The result has the value $|X \times b^{-e}| \times b^p$, where b, e, and p are as defined in 13.2.3 for the model representation of X.

Example. RRSPACING (–3.0) has the value 0.75×2^{24} for reals whose model is described in 13.2.3.

A.90 SCALE (X, I)

Description. Returns $X \times b^I$ where b is the base in the model representation of X.

Class. Elemental function.

Arguments.

X   must be of type real.

I   must be of type integer.

Result Type and Type Parameter. Same as X.

Result Value. The result has the value $X \times b^I$, where b is defined in 13.2.3 for model numbers representing values of X, provided this result is within range; if not, the result is processor dependent.

Example. SCALE (3.0, 2) has the value 12.0 for reals whose model is described in 13.2.3.

A.91 SCAN (STRING, SET, BACK)

Optional Argument. BACK

Description. Scan a string for any one of the characters in a set of characters.

Class. Elemental function.

Arguments.

STRING   must be of type character.

SET   must be of type character with the same kind type
                    parameter as STRING.

BACK (optional)   must be of type logical.

Result Type and Type Parameter. Default integer.

Result Value.

Case (i):   If BACK is absent or is present with the value false and if
                STRING contains at least one character that is in SET, the
                value of the result is the position of the leftmost character
                of STRING that is in SET.

Case (ii):   If BACK is present with the value true and if STRING contains at least one character that is in SET, the value of the
                result is the position of the rightmost character of STRING
                that is in SET.

Case (iii):   The value of the result is zero if no character of STRING is
                in SET or if the length of STRING or SET is zero.

Examples.

Case (i):   SCAN ('FORTRAN', 'TR') has the value 3.

Case (ii):   SCAN ('FORTRAN', 'TR', BACK = .TRUE.) has the value
                5.

Case (iii):   SCAN ('FORTRAN', 'BCD') has the value 0.

A.92 SELECTED_INT_KIND (R)

Description. Returns a value of the kind type parameter of an integer
data type that represents all integer values n with $-10^R < n < 10^R$.

Class. Transformational function.

Argument. R must be scalar and of type integer.

Result Type, Type Parameter, and Shape. Default integer scalar.

Result Value. The result has a value equal to the value of the kind type parameter of an integer data type that represents all values n in the range of values n with $-10^R < n < 10^R$, or if no such kind type parameter is available on the processor, the result is –1. If more than one kind type parameter meets the criteria, the value returned is the one with the smallest decimal exponent range, unless there are several such values, in which case the smallest of these kind values is returned.

Examples. SELECTED_INT_KIND (6) has the value KIND (0) on a machine that supports a default integer representation method with $r = 2$ and $q = 31$ as defined in the model for the integer number systems in 13.2.2. SELECTED_INT_KIND (2) has the value of SHORT on a machine that supports this integer kind.

A.93 SELECTED_REAL_KIND (P, R)

Optional Arguments. P, R

Description. Returns a value of the kind type parameter of a real data type with decimal precision of at least P digits and a decimal exponent range of at least R.

Class. Transformational function.

Arguments. At least one argument must be present.

P (optional)   must be scalar and of type integer.

R (optional)   must be scalar and of type integer.

Result Type, Type Parameter, and Shape. Default integer scalar.

Result Value. The result has a value equal to a value of the kind type parameter of a real data type with decimal precision, as returned by the function PRECISION, of at least P digits and a decimal exponent range, as returned by the function RANGE, of at least R, or if no such kind type parameter is available on the processor, the result is –1 if the precision is not available, –2 if the exponent range is not available, and –3 if neither is available. If more than one kind type parameter value meets the criteria, the value returned is the one with the smallest decimal precision, unless there are several such values, in which case the smallest of these kind values is returned.

Examples. SELECTED_REAL_KIND (6, 70) has the value KIND (0.0) on a machine that supports a default real approximation method with $b = 16$, $p = 6$, $e_{min} = -64$, and $e_{max} = 63$ as defined in the model for the real number system in 13.2.3. SELECTED_REAL_KIND (P=14) returns the value of HIGH on a machine that supports this real kind.

A.94 SET_EXPONENT (X, I)

Description. Returns the model number whose fractional part is the fractional part of the model representation of X and whose exponent part is I.

Class. Elemental function.

Arguments.

X   must be of type real.

I   must be of type integer.

Result Type and Type Parameter. Same as X.

Result Value. The result has the value $X \times b^{1-e}$, where b and e are as defined in 13.2.3 for the model representation of X, provided this result is within range; if not, the result is processor dependent. If X has value zero, the result has value zero.

Example. SET_EXPONENT (3.0, 1) has the value 1.5 for reals whose model is as described in 13.2.3.

A.95 SHAPE (SOURCE)

Description. Returns the shape of an array or a scalar.

Class. Inquiry function.

Argument. SOURCE may be of any type. It may be array valued or scalar. It must not be a pointer that is disassociated or an allocatable array that is not allocated. It must not be an assumed-size array.

Result Type, Type Parameter, and Shape. The result is a default integer array of rank one whose size is equal to the rank of SOURCE.

Result Value. The value of the result is the shape of SOURCE.

Examples. The value of SHAPE (A (2:5, –1:1)) is (4, 3). The value of SHAPE (3) is the rank-one array of size zero.

A.96 SIGN (A, B)

Description. Absolute value of A times the sign of B.

Class. Elemental function.

Arguments.

A   must be of type integer or real.

B   must be of the same type and kind type parameter as A.

Result Type and Type Parameter. Same as A.

Result Value. The value of the result is $|A|$ if $B \geq 0$ and $-|A|$ if $B < 0$.

Example. SIGN (–3.0, 2.0) has the value 3.0.

A.97 SIN (X)

Description. Sine function.

Class. Elemental function.

Argument. X must be of type real or complex.

Result Type and Type Parameter. Same as X.

Result Value. The result has a value equal to a processor-dependent approximation to sin(X). If X is of type real, it is regarded as a value in radians. If X is of type complex, its real part is regarded as a value in radians.

Examples. SIN (1.0) has the value 0.84147098. SIN ((0.5_HIGH, 0.5)) has the value $0.54061268571316 + 0.45730415318425\iota$ with kind HIGH.

A.98 SINH (X)

Description. Hyperbolic sine function.

Class. Elemental function.

Argument. X must be of type real.

Result Type and Type Parameter. Same as X.

Result Value. The result has a value equal to a processor-dependent approximation to sinh(X).

Examples. SINH (1.0) has the value 1.1752012. SINH (0.5_HIGH) has the value 0.52109530549375 with kind HIGH.

A.99 SIZE (ARRAY, DIM)

Optional Argument. DIM

Description. Returns the extent of an array along a specified dimension or the total number of elements in the array.

Class. Inquiry function.

Arguments.

ARRAY   may be of any type. It must not be scalar. It must not be a pointer that is disassociated or an allocatable array that is not allocated. If ARRAY is an assumed-size array, DIM must be present with a value less than the rank of ARRAY.

DIM (optional)   must be scalar and of type integer with a value in the range $1 \le \text{DIM} \le n$, where n is the rank of ARRAY.

Result Type, Type Parameter, and Shape. Default integer scalar.

Result Value. The result has a value equal to the extent of dimension DIM of ARRAY or, if DIM is absent, the total number of elements of ARRAY.

Examples. The value of SIZE (A (2:5, –1:1), DIM=2) is 3. The value of SIZE (A (2:5, –1:1)) is 12.

A.100 SPACING (X)

Description. Returns the absolute spacing of model numbers near the argument value.

Class. Elemental function.

Argument. X must be of type real.

Result Type and Type Parameter. Same as X.

Result Value. The result has the value b^{e-p}, where b, e, and p are as defined in 13.2.3 for the model representation of X, provided this result is within range; otherwise, the result is the same as that of TINY (X).

Example. SPACING (3.0) has the value 2^{-22} for reals whose model is described in 13.2.3.

A.101 SPREAD (SOURCE, DIM, NCOPIES)

Description. Replicates an array by adding a dimension. Broadcasts several copies of SOURCE along a specified dimension (as in forming a book from copies of a single page) and thus forms an array of rank one greater.

Class. Transformational function.

Arguments.

SOURCE   may be of any type. It may be scalar or array valued. The rank of SOURCE must be less than 7.

DIM   must be scalar and of type integer with value in the range $1 \le \text{DIM} \le n+1$, where n is the rank of SOURCE.

NCOPIES   must be scalar and of type integer.

Result Type, Type Parameter, and Shape. The result is an array of the same type and type parameters as SOURCE and of rank $n+1$, where n is the rank of SOURCE.

Case (i):   If SOURCE is scalar, the shape of the result is (MAX (NCOPIES, 0)).

Case (ii): If SOURCE is array valued with shape $(d_1, d_2, ..., d_n)$, the shape of the result is $(d_1, d_2, ..., d_{DIM-1}, $ MAX (NCOPIES, 0), $d_{DIM}, ..., d_n)$.

Result Value.

Case (i):   If SOURCE is scalar, each element of the result has a value equal to SOURCE.

Case (ii): If SOURCE is array valued, the element of the result with subscripts $(r_1, r_2, ..., r_{n+1})$ has the value SOURCE $(r_1, r_2, ..., r_{DIM-1}, r_{DIM+1}, ..., r_{n+1})$.

Examples.

Case (i):   SPREAD ("A", 1, 3) is the character array (/ "A", "A", "A" /).

Case (ii): If A is the array (2, 3, 4), SPREAD (A, DIM=1,

NCOPIES=NC) is the array $\begin{bmatrix} 2 & 3 & 4 \\ 2 & 3 & 4 \\ 2 & 3 & 4 \end{bmatrix}$ if NC has the value

3 and is a zero-sized array if NC has the value 0.

A.102 SQRT (X)

Description. Square root.

Class. Elemental function.

Argument. X must be of type real or complex. Unless X is complex, its value must be greater than or equal to zero.

Result Type and Type Parameter. Same as X.

Result Value. The result has a value equal to a processor-dependent approximation to the square root of X. A result of type complex is the principal value with the real part greater than or equal to zero. When the real part of the result is zero, the imaginary part is greater than or equal to zero.

Examples. SQRT (4.0) has the value 2.0. SQRT (5.0_HIGH) has the value 2.23606774998 with kind HIGH.

A.103 SUM (ARRAY, DIM, MASK)

Optional Arguments. DIM, MASK

Description. Sum all the elements of ARRAY along dimension DIM corresponding to the true elements of MASK.

Class. Transformational function.

Arguments.

ARRAY   must be of type integer, real, or complex. It must not be scalar.

DIM (optional)   must be scalar and of type integer with a value in the range $1 \leq \text{DIM} \leq n$, where n is the rank of ARRAY. The corresponding actual argument must not be an optional dummy argument.

MASK (optional)   must be of type logical and must be conformable with ARRAY.

Result Type, Type Parameter, and Shape. The result is of the same type and kind type parameter as ARRAY. It is scalar if DIM is absent or ARRAY has rank one; otherwise, the result is an array of rank $n-1$ and of shape $(d_1, d_2, ..., d_{\text{DIM}-1}, d_{\text{DIM}+1}, ..., d_n)$ where $(d_1, d_2, ..., d_n)$ is the shape of ARRAY.

Result Value.

Case (i):   The result of SUM (ARRAY) has a value equal to a processor-dependent approximation to the sum of all the elements of ARRAY or has the value zero if ARRAY has size zero.

Case (ii):   The result of SUM (ARRAY, MASK = MASK) has a value equal to a processor-dependent approximation to the sum of the elements of ARRAY corresponding to the true elements of MASK or has the value zero if there are no true elements.

Case (iii): If ARRAY has rank one, SUM (ARRAY, DIM [,MASK]) has a value equal to that of SUM (ARRAY [,MASK = MASK]). Otherwise, the value of element $(s_1, s_2, ..., s_{\text{DIM}-1}, s_{\text{DIM}+1}, ..., s_n)$ of SUM (ARRAY, DIM [,MASK]) is equal to SUM (ARRAY $(s_1, s_2, ..., s_{\text{DIM}-1}, :, s_{\text{DIM}+1}, ..., s_n)$ [, MASK= MASK $(s_1, s_2, ..., s_{\text{DIM}-1}, :, s_{\text{DIM}+1}, ..., s_n)$]).

Examples.

Case (i):   The value of SUM ((/ 1, 2, 3 /)) and SUM ((/ 1, 2, 3 /), DIM=1) is 6.

Case (ii):   SUM (C, MASK= C .GT. 0.0) forms the arithmetic sum of the positive elements of C.

Case (iii):   If B is the array $\begin{bmatrix} 1 & 3 & 5 \\ 2 & 4 & 6 \end{bmatrix}$, SUM (B, DIM = 1) is (3, 7, 11) and SUM (B, DIM = 2) is (9, 12).

A.104 SYSTEM_CLOCK (COUNT, COUNT_RATE, COUNT_MAX)

Optional Arguments. COUNT, COUNT_RATE, COUNT_MAX
Description. Returns integer data from a real-time clock.
Class. Subroutine.
Arguments.

COUNT (optional)   must be scalar and of type default integer. It is an INTENT (OUT) argument. It is set to a processor-dependent value based on the current value of the processor clock or to –HUGE (0) if there is no clock. The processor-dependent value is incremented by one for each clock count until the value COUNT_MAX is reached and is reset to zero at the next count. It lies in the range 0 to COUNT_MAX if there is a clock.

COUNT_RATE (optional)
   must be scalar and of type default integer. It is an INTENT (OUT) argument. It is set to the number of processor clock counts per second, or to zero if there is no clock.

COUNT_MAX (optional)
   must be scalar and of type default integer. It is an INTENT (OUT) argument. It is set to the maximum value that COUNT can have, or to zero if there is no clock.

Example. If the processor clock is a 24-hour clock that registers time in 1-second intervals, at 11:30 A.M. the reference

```
CALL SYSTEM_CLOCK (COUNT = C, COUNT_RATE = R, COUNT_MAX = M)
```

sets $C = 11 \times 3600 + 30 \times 60 = 41400$, $R = 1$, and $M = 24 \times 3600 - 1 = 86399$.

A.105 TAN (X)

Description. Tangent function.

Class. Elemental function.

Argument. X must be of type real.

Result Type and Type Parameter. Same as X.

Result Value. The result has a value equal to a processor-dependent approximation to tan(X), with X regarded as a value in radians.

Examples. TAN (1.0) has the value 1.5574077. TAN (2.0_HIGH) has the value –2.1850398632615 with kind HIGH.

A.106 TANH (X)

Description. Hyperbolic tangent function.

Class. Elemental function.

Argument. X must be of type real.

Result Type and Type Parameter. Same as X.

Result Value. The result has a value equal to a processor-dependent approximation to tanh(X).

Examples. TANH (1.0) has the value 0.76159416. TANH (2.0_HIGH) has the value 0.96402758007582 with kind HIGH.

A.107 TINY (X)

Description. Returns the smallest positive number in the model representing numbers of the same type and kind type parameter as the argument.

Class. Inquiry function.

Argument. X must be of type real. It may be scalar or array valued.

Result Type, Type Parameter, and Shape. Scalar with the same type and kind type parameter as X.

Result Value. The result has the value $b^{e_{min}-1}$ where b and e_{min} are as defined in 13.2.3 for the model representing numbers of the same type and kind type parameter as X.

Example. TINY (X) has the value 2^{-127} for real X whose model is described in 13.2.3.

A.108 TRANSFER (SOURCE, MOLD, SIZE)

Optional Argument. SIZE

Description. Returns a result with a physical representation identical to that of SOURCE but interpreted with the type and type parameters of MOLD.

Class. Transformational function.

Arguments.

SOURCE   may be of any type and may be scalar or array val-
                      ued.

MOLD   may be of any type and may be scalar or array val-
                      ued.

SIZE (optional)   must be scalar and of type integer. The corre-
                      sponding actual argument must not be an optional
                      dummy argument.

Result Type, Type Parameter, and Shape. The result is of the same type and type parameters as MOLD.

Case (i):   If MOLD is a scalar and SIZE is absent, the result is a sca-
                lar.

Case (ii):   If MOLD is array valued and SIZE is absent, the result is
                array valued and of rank one. Its size is as small as possi-
                ble such that its physical representation is not shorter than
                that of SOURCE.

Case (iii):   If SIZE is present, the result is array valued of rank one and
                size SIZE.

Result Value. If the physical representation of the result has the same length as that of SOURCE, the physical representation of the result is that of SOURCE. If the physical representation of the result is longer than that of SOURCE, the physical representation of the leading part is that of SOURCE and the remainder is undefined. If the physical representation of the result is shorter than that of SOURCE, the physical representation of the result is the leading part of SOURCE. If D and E are scalar variables such that the physical representation of D is as long as or longer than that of E, the value of TRANSFER (TRANSFER (E, D), E) must be the value of E. IF D is an array and E is an array of rank one, the value of TRANSFER (TRANSFER (E, D), E, SIZE (E)) must be the value of E.

Examples.

Case (i):   TRANSFER (1082130432, 0.0) has the value 4.0 on a processor that represents the values 4.0 and 1082130432 as the string of binary digits 0100 0000 1000 0000 0000 0000 0000 0000.

Case (ii):   TRANSFER ((/ 1.1, 2.2, 3.3 /), (/ (0.0, 0.0) /)) is a complex rank-one array of length two whose first element is (1.1, 2.2) and whose second element has a real part with the value 3.3. The imaginary part of the second element is undefined.

Case (iii):   TRANSFER ((/ 1.1, 2.2, 3.3 /), (/ (0.0, 0.0) /), 1) has the value $1.1 + 2.2\iota$, which is a rank-one array with one complex element.

A.109 TRANSPOSE (MATRIX)

Description. Transpose an array of rank two.

Class. Transformational function.

Argument. MATRIX may be of any type and must have rank two.

Result Type, Type Parameters, and Shape. The result is an array of the same type and type parameters as MATRIX and with rank two and shape (n, m) where (m, n) is the shape of MATRIX.

Result Value. Element (i, j) of the result has the value MATRIX (j, i), $i = 1, 2, ..., n; j = 1, 2, ..., m$.

Example. If A is the array $\begin{bmatrix} 1 & 2 & 3 \\ 4 & 5 & 6 \\ 7 & 8 & 9 \end{bmatrix}$, then TRANSPOSE (A) has the value $\begin{bmatrix} 1 & 4 & 7 \\ 2 & 5 & 8 \\ 3 & 6 & 9 \end{bmatrix}$.

A.110 TRIM (STRING)

Description. Returns the argument with trailing blank characters removed.

Class. Transformational function.

Argument. STRING must be of type character and must be a scalar.

Result Type and Type Parameters. Character with the same kind type parameter value as STRING and with a length that is the length of STRING less the number of trailing blanks in STRING.

Result Value. The value of the result is the same as STRING except any trailing blanks are removed. If STRING contains no nonblank characters, the result has zero length.

Examples. TRIM (' A B ') is ' A B'. TRIM (GREEK_' Π ') is GREEK_' Π'.

A.111 UBOUND (ARRAY, DIM)

Optional Argument. DIM

Description. Returns all the upper bounds of an array or a specified upper bound.

Class. Inquiry function.

Arguments.

ARRAY	may be of any type. It must not be scalar. It must not be a pointer that is disassociated or an allocatable array that is not allocated. If ARRAY is an assumed-size array, DIM must be present with a value less than the rank of ARRAY.
DIM (optional)	must be scalar and of type integer with a value in the range $1 \leq DIM \leq n$, where n is the rank of ARRAY. The corresponding actual argument must not be an optional dummy argument.

Result Type, Type Parameter, and Shape. The result is of type default integer. It is scalar if DIM is present; otherwise, the result is an array of rank one and size n, where n is the rank of ARRAY.

Result Value.

Case (i):	For an array section or for an array expression, other than a whole array or array structure component, UBOUND (ARRAY, DIM) has a value equal to the number of elements in the given dimension; otherwise, it has a value equal to the upper bound for subscript DIM of ARRAY if dimension DIM of ARRAY does not have size zero and has the value zero if dimension DIM has size zero.

Case (ii): UBOUND (ARRAY) has a value whose ith component is equal to UBOUND (ARRAY, i), for $i = 1, 2, ..., n$, where n is the rank of ARRAY.

Examples. If the following statements are processed

```
REAL, TARGET :: A (2:3, 7:10)
REAL, POINTER, DIMENSION (:,:) :: B, C, D
B => A;  C => A(:,:)
ALLOCATE (D(-3:3,-7:7))
```

UBOUND (A) is (3, 10), UBOUND (A, DIM = 2) is 10, UBOUND (B) is (3, 10), UBOUND (C) is (2, 4), and UBOUND (D) is (3, 7); see Section 7.5.3, rules and restrictions, item 9.

A.112 UNPACK (VECTOR, MASK, FIELD)

Description. Unpack an array of rank one into an array under the control of a mask.

Class. Transformational function.

Arguments.

VECTOR   may be of any type. It must have rank one. Its size must be at least t where t is the number of true elements in MASK.

MASK   must be array valued and of type logical.

FIELD   must be of the same type and type parameters as VECTOR and must be conformable with MASK.

Result Type, Type Parameter, and Shape. The result is an array of the same type and type parameters as VECTOR and the same shape as MASK.

Result Value. The element of the result that corresponds to the ith true element of MASK, in array element order, has the value VECTOR (i) for $i = 1, 2, ..., t$, where t is the number of true values in MASK. Each other element has a value equal to FIELD if FIELD is scalar or to the corresponding element of FIELD if it is an array.

Examples. Specific values may be "scattered" to specific positions in an array by using UNPACK. If M is the array $\begin{bmatrix} 1 & 0 & 0 \\ 0 & 1 & 0 \\ 0 & 0 & 1 \end{bmatrix}$, V is the array

(1, 2, 3), and Q is the logical mask $\begin{bmatrix} . & T & . \\ T & . & . \\ . & . & T \end{bmatrix}$, where "T" represents

true and "." represents false, then the result of UNPACK (V,

MASK = Q, FIELD = M) has the value $\begin{bmatrix} 1 & 2 & 0 \\ 1 & 1 & 0 \\ 0 & 0 & 3 \end{bmatrix}$ and the result of

UNPACK (V, MASK = Q, FIELD = 0) has the value $\begin{bmatrix} 0 & 2 & 0 \\ 1 & 0 & 0 \\ 0 & 0 & 3 \end{bmatrix}$.

A.113 VERIFY (STRING, SET, BACK)

Optional Argument. BACK

Description. Verify that a set of characters contains all the characters in a string by identifying the position of the first character in a string of characters that does not appear in a given set of characters.

Class. Elemental function.

Arguments.

STRING   must be of type character.

SET   must be of type character with the same kind type parameter as STRING.

BACK (optional)   must be of type logical.

Result Type and Type Parameter. Default integer.

Result Value.

Case (i):   If BACK is absent or present with the value false and if STRING contains at least one character that is not in SET, the value of the result is the position of the leftmost character of STRING that is not in SET.

Case (ii):   If BACK is present with the value true and if STRING contains at least one character that is not in SET, the value of the result is the position of the rightmost character of STRING that is not in SET.

Case (iii):   The value of the result is zero if each character in STRING is in SET or if STRING has zero length.

Examples.

Case (i):   VERIFY ('ABBA', 'A') has the value 2.

Case (ii):   VERIFY ('ABBA', 'A', BACK = .TRUE.) has the value 3.

Case (iii):   VERIFY ('ABBA', 'AB') has the value 0.

F 9 ⊚

B

Fortran 90 Syntax

This appendix contains a complete description of the Fortran 90 syntax. Section B.1 describes the form of the syntax. Section B.2 contains the complete syntax and constraints as they appear in the standard. Section B.3 is a cross reference of each syntax term, the rule in which it is defined, and the rules in which it is referenced. A high-level summary of the syntax appears in Chapter 2.

B.1 The Form of the Syntax

The syntax of Fortran programs is described using a variant of the Backus-Naur Form (BNF).

B.1.1 Syntax Rules Expressed in BNF

The BNF syntax rules are expressed as a definition; the metalanguage class being defined is first, followed by the symbol is, and finally the syntax definition, as in the following example:

goto-stmt	**is**	GO TO *label*

The term *goto-stmt* represents the GO TO statement; such terms are called **nonterminal symbols** or simply **nonterminals**. The syntax rule defines *goto-stmt* to be GO TO *label*, which describes the form of the GO TO statement. The description of the GO TO statement is not complete until the definition of *label* is given; *label* is also a nonterminal symbol. A further search for *label* in the BNF will result in a specification of *label* and thereby provide the complete statement definition. A **terminal** part of a syntax rule does not need further definition. For example, GO TO is a terminal and is a required part of the statement form.

In many cases, information about the metalanguage class can be derived from part of the descriptive term. The part may be a complete word, like *-list*, or a common abbreviation. Some of the abbreviations used consistently in metalanguage classes are given in Table B-1. For example, all class definitions that end with *-stmt* might be used to generate a complete list of the statements in Fortran 90.

Table B-1 Syntax metalanguage abbreviations

Abbreviation	Term
stmt	statement
expr	expression
op	operator
int	integer
char	character
spec	specifier or specification
arg	argument
attr	attribute
decl	declaration
def	definition
desc	descriptor

B.1.2 Definition Syntax Symbol "is"

The term **is** separates the syntax class name from its definition. Examples:

goto-stmt	**is**	GO TO *label*
power-op	**is**	★★

B.1.3 Alternative Syntax Symbol "or"

The symbol **or** indicates an alternative definition for the syntactic class being defined.

> *add-op*   **is**   +
>   **or**   –

This indicates that the add operator may be either plus or minus.

B.1.4 Optional Symbol "( )"

In some syntactic definitions, there may be items that are optional. These are enclosed in square brackets. The term *sign* is optional in the following example.

> *signed-int-literal-constant* **is**   [*sign*] *int-literal-constant*

The fact that the sign is optional indicates that both 75 and +75 are signed integer literal constants.

B.1.5 Symbol for Repeated Items "( ) . . ."

Enclosing an item in square brackets followed by an ellipsis indicates that the item may occur zero or more times. In the following example, the term *digit* is repeated as many times as required to define the integer literal constant.

> *int-literal-constant*   **is**   *digit* [*digit*] . . .

For example, there are five digits in the integer literal constant 94024.

B.1.6 Syntax Rule Continuation Symbol "■"

If a rule does not fit on one line, the convention is to use the symbol ■ at the end of the line being continued as well as at the beginning of the line that continues or completes the statement.

> *allocatable-stmt*   **is**   ALLOCATABLE [::] *array-name* ■
>   ■ [(*deferred-shape-spec-list*)] ■
>   ■ [, *array-name* [(*deferred-shape-spec-list*)]] ...

The following statement, written all on one line, is an example of an ALLOCATABLE statement satisfying this syntax rule.

```
ALLOCATABLE :: A1, A2
```

B.1.7 Assumed Syntax Rules

Certain assumptions have been made in the use of the nonterminal *xyz* in the syntax rules. For example,

xyz-list	means	*xyz* [, *xyz*] ...
xyz-name	is	a name
scalar-xyz	is	an *xyz* that is a scalar

B.1.8 Example BNF Syntax

read-stmt	**is**	READ (*io-control-spec-list*) [*input-item-list*]
	or	READ *format* [, *input-item-list*]
format	**is**	*char-expr*
	or	*label*
	or	*
	or	*scalar-int-variable*

In this example, there are two alternatives to the READ statement. The first uses an input/output control specification list; the second is a formatted READ statement to a processor-dependent unit. Both alternatives have an optional input item list, indicated by [ ]. The syntax class *format* (a nonterminal) is further defined as either a character expression containing the format specifications, or a statement label referring to a separate FORMAT statement that contains the format specifications, or an asterisk (*) indicating that the READ statement is list-directed, or a scalar integer variable whose value specifies the label of a FORMAT statement. In the standard, the last alternative is printed in a smaller font because it is a feature that may be removed in the next revision; this convention is not used in the handbook, except in Appendix B.

There are other nonterminal symbols in the description of the READ statement and further BNF rules need to be examined to determine the complete description of the READ statement.

B.1.9 Constraints

The BNF forms do not, by themselves, provide a complete description of the syntax; additional constraints are described with text. The BNF rules and the constraints together describe the syntax of Fortran. Constraints are restrictions to the syntax rules that limit the form of the statement described. Constraints, if present, appear following a syntax rule.

B.1.10 Identifying Numbers

In the text of the standard, each BNF rule is given an identifying number, for example, R201. These rules appear throughout the text of the standard, and again in a BNF listing in an Annex to the standard. The numbering of the rules in the following section matches the numbering of the rules in the standard. These numbers also are used in the chapters of this book.

B.2 Syntax Rules and Constraints

Each of the following sections contains the syntax rules and constraints from one section of the Fortran standard.

B.2.1 Introduction

B.2.2 Fortran Terms and Concepts

R201	*executable-program*	**is**	*program-unit*
			[*program-unit*] ...
R202	*program-unit*	**is**	*main-program*
		or	*external-subprogram*
		or	*module*
		or	*block-data*
R1101	*main-program*	**is**	[*program-stmt*]
			[*specification-part*]
			[*execution-part*]
			[*internal-subprogram-part*]
			end-program-stmt
R203	*external-subprogram*	**is**	*function-subprogram*
		or	*subroutine-subprogram*
R1215	*function-subprogram*	**is**	*function-stmt*
			[*specification-part*]
			[*execution-part*]
			[*internal-subprogram-part*]
			end-function-stmt
R1219	*subroutine-subprogram*	**is**	*subroutine-stmt*
			[*specification-part*]
			[*execution-part*]
			[*internal-subprogram-part*]
			end-subroutine-stmt
R1104	*module*	**is**	*module-stmt*
			[*specification-part*]
			[*module-subprogram-part*]
			end-module-stmt
R1110	*block-data*	**is**	*block-data-stmt*
			[*specification-part*]
			end-block-data-stmt
R204	*specification-part*	**is**	[*use-stmt*] ...
			[*implicit-part*]
			[*declaration-construct*] ...
R205	*implicit-part*	**is**	[*implicit-part-stmt*] ...
			implicit-stmt
R206	*implicit-part-stmt*	**is**	*implicit-stmt*
		or	*parameter-stmt*

		or	*format-stmt*
		or	*entry-stmt*
R207	*declaration-construct*	is	*derived-type-def*
		or	*interface-block*
		or	*type-declaration-stmt*
		or	*specification-stmt*
		or	*parameter-stmt*
		or	*format-stmt*
		or	*entry-stmt*
		or	*stmt-function-stmt*
R208	*execution-part*	is	*executable-construct*
			[*execution-part-construct*] ...
R209	*execution-part-construct*	is	*executable-construct*
		or	*format-stmt*
		or	*data-stmt*
		or	*entry-stmt*
R210	*internal-subprogram-part*	is	*contains-stmt*
			internal-subprogram
			[*internal-subprogram*] ...
R211	*internal-subprogram*	is	*function-subprogram*
		or	*subroutine-subprogram*
R212	*module-subprogram-part*	is	*contains-stmt*
			module-subprogram
			[*module-subprogram*] ...
R213	*module-subprogram*	is	*function-subprogram*
		or	*subroutine-subprogram*
R214	*specification-stmt*	is	*access-stmt*
		or	*allocatable-stmt*
		or	*common-stmt*
		or	*data-stmt*
		or	*dimension-stmt*
		or	*equivalence-stmt*
		or	*external-stmt*
		or	*intent-stmt*
		or	*intrinsic-stmt*
		or	*namelist-stmt*
		or	*optional-stmt*
		or	*pointer-stmt*
		or	*save-stmt*
		or	*target-stmt*
R215	*executable-construct*	is	*action-stmt*
		or	*case-construct*
		or	*do-construct*
		or	*if-construct*
		or	*where-construct*
R216	*action-stmt*	is	*allocate-stmt*
		or	*assignment-stmt*
		or	*backspace-stmt*
		or	*call-stmt*
		or	*close-stmt*
		or	*computed-goto-stmt*
		or	*continue-stmt*
		or	*cycle-stmt*
		or	*deallocate-stmt*
		or	*endfile-stmt*
		or	*end-function-stmt*
		or	*end-program-stmt*

	or	*end-subroutine-stmt*
	or	*exit-stmt*
	or	*goto-stmt*
	or	*if-stmt*
	or	*inquire-stmt*
	or	*nullify-stmt*
	or	*open-stmt*
	or	*pointer-assignment-stmt*
	or	*print-stmt*
	or	*read-stmt*
	or	*return-stmt*
	or	*rewind-stmt*
	or	*stop-stmt*
	or	*where-stmt*
	or	*write-stmt*
	or	*arithmetic-if-stmt*
	or	*assign-stmt*
	or	*assigned-goto-stmt*
	or	*pause-stmt*

Constraint: An *execution-part* must not contain an *end-function-stmt*, *end-program-stmt*, or *end-subroutine-stmt*.

B.2.3 Characters, Lexical Tokens, and Source Form

R301	*character*	**is**	*alphanumeric-character*
		or	*special-character*
R302	*alphanumeric-character*	**is**	*letter*
		or	*digit*
		or	*underscore*
R303	*underscore*	**is**	__
R304	*name*	**is**	*letter* [*alphanumeric-character*] ...

Constraint: The maximum length of a *name* is 31 characters.

R305	*constant*	**is**	*literal-constant*
		or	*named-constant*
R306	*literal-constant*	**is**	*int-literal-constant*
		or	*real-literal-constant*
		or	*complex-literal-constant*
		or	*logical-literal-constant*
		or	*char-literal-constant*
		or	*boz-literal-constant*
R307	*named-constant*	**is**	*name*
R308	*int-constant*	**is**	*constant*

Constraint: *int-constant* must be of type integer.

R309	*char-constant*	**is**	*constant*

Constraint: *char-constant* must be of type character.

R310	*intrinsic-operator*	**is**	*power-op*
		or	*mult-op*
		or	*add-op*
		or	*concat-op*
		or	*rel-op*
		or	*not-op*
		or	*and-op*
		or	*or-op*
		or	*equiv-op*

R708	*power-op*	**is**	**
R709	*mult-op*	**is**	*
		or	/
R710	*add-op*	**is**	+
		or	–
R712	*concat-op*	**is**	//
R714	*rel-op*	**is**	.EQ.
		or	.NE.
		or	.LT.
		or	.LE.
		or	.GT.
		or	.GE.
		or	==
		or	/=
		or	<
		or	<=
		or	>
		or	>=
R719	*not-op*	**is**	.NOT.
R720	*and-op*	**is**	.AND.
R721	*or-op*	**is**	.OR.
R722	*equiv-op*	**is**	.EQV.
		or	.NEQV.
R311	*defined-operator*	**is**	*defined-unary-op*
		or	*defined-binary-op*
		or	*extended-intrinsic-op*
R704	*defined-unary-op*	**is**	. *letter* [*letter*] ... .
R724	*defined-binary-op*	**is**	. *letter* [*letter*] ... .
R312	*extended-intrinsic-op*	**is**	*intrinsic-operator*

Constraint: A *defined-unary-op* and a *defined-binary-op* must not contain more than 31 letters and must not be the same as any *intrinsic-operator* or *logical-literal-constant*.

R313	*label*	**is**	*digit* [*digit* [*digit* [*digit* [*digit*]]]]

Constraint: At least one digit in a *label* must be nonzero.

B.2.4 Intrinsic and Derived Data Types

R401	*signed-digit-string*	**is**	[*sign*] *digit-string*
R402	*digit-string*	**is**	*digit* [*digit*] ...
R403	*signed-int-literal-constant*	**is**	[*sign*] *int-literal-constant*
R404	*int-literal-constant*	**is**	*digit-string* [_*kind-param*]
R405	*kind-param*	**is**	*digit-string*
		or	*scalar-int-constant-name*
R406	*sign*	**is**	+
		or	–

Constraint: The value of *kind-param* must be nonnegative.
Constraint: The value of *kind-param* must specify a representation method that exists on the processor.

R407	*boz-literal-constant*	**is**	*binary-constant*
		or	*octal-constant*
		or	*hex-constant*

Constraint: A *boz-literal-constant* may appear only in a DATA statement.

R408   *binary-constant*   **is** B ' *digit* [*digit*] ... '
                                             or B " *digit* [*digit*] ... "
Constraint: *digit* must have one of the values 0 or 1.

R409   *octal-constant*   **is** O ' *digit* [*digit*] ... '
                                             or O " *digit* [*digit*] ... "
Constraint: *digit* must have one of the values 0 through 7.

R410   *hex-constant*   **is** Z ' *hex-digit* [*hex-digit*] ... '
                                             or Z " *hex-digit* [*hex-digit*] ... "

R411   *hex-digit*   **is** *digit*
                                             or A
                                             or B
                                             or C
                                             or D
                                             or E
                                             or F

R412   *signed-real-literal-constant* **is** [*sign*] *real-literal-constant*

R413   *real-literal-constant*   **is** *significand* [*exponent-letter exponent*] [_*kind-param*]
                                          or *digit-string exponent-letter exponent* [_*kind-param*]

R414   *significand*   **is** *digit-string* **.** [*digit-string*]
                                          or **.** *digit-string*

R415   *exponent-letter*   **is** E
                                          or D

R416   *exponent*   **is** *signed-digit-string*
Constraint: If both *kind-param* and *exponent-letter* are present, *exponent-letter* must be E.
Constraint: The value of *kind-param* must specify an approximation method that exists on the processor.

R417   *complex-literal-constant* **is** (*real-part* , *imag-part*)

R418   *real-part*   **is** *signed-int-literal-constant*
                                          or *signed-real-literal-constant*

R419   *imag-part*   **is** *signed-int-literal-constant*
                                          or *signed-real-literal-constant*

R420   *char-literal-constant*   **is** [*kind-param* _] ' [*rep-char*] ... '
                                          or [*kind-param* _] " [*rep-char*] ... "
Constraint: The value of *kind-param* must specify a representation method that exists on the processor.

R421   *logical-literal-constant*   **is** .TRUE. [_*kind-param*]
                                          or .FALSE. [_*kind-param*]
Constraint: The value of *kind-param* must specify a representation method that exists on the processor.

R422   *derived-type-def*   **is** *derived-type-stmt*
                                               [*private-sequence-stmt*] ...
                                             component-def-stmt
                                               [*component-def-stmt*] ...
                                               end-type-stmt

R423   *private-sequence-stmt* **is** PRIVATE
                                          or SEQUENCE

R424   *derived-type-stmt*   **is** TYPE [[, *access-spec*] ::] *type-name*
Constraint: The same *private-sequence-stmt* must not appear more than once in a given *derived-type-def*.
Constraint: If SEQUENCE is present, all derived types specified in component definitions must be sequence types.
Constraint: An *access-spec* (5.1.2.2) or a PRIVATE statement within the definition is permitted only if the type definition is within the specification part of a module.

Constraint: If a component of a derived type is of a type declared to be private, either the derived type definition must contain the PRIVATE statement or the derived type must be private.

Constraint: A derived type *type-name* must not be the same as the name of any intrinsic type nor the same as any other accessible derived type *type-name*.

R425   *end-type-stmt*   **is**   END TYPE [*type-name*]

Constraint: If END TYPE is followed by a *type-name*, the *type-name* must be the same as that in the corresponding *derived-type-stmt*.

R426   *component-def-stmt*   **is**   *type-spec* [[, *component-attr-spec-list*] ::] ■
                                   ■ *component-decl-list*

R427   *component-attr-spec*   **is**   POINTER
                                   or   DIMENSION (*component-array-spec*)

Constraint: No *component-attr-spec* may appear more than once in a given *component-def-stmt*.

Constraint: If the POINTER attribute is not specified for a component, a *type-spec* in the *component-def-stmt* must specify an intrinsic type or a previously defined derived type.

Constraint: If the POINTER attribute is specified for a component, a *type-spec* in the *component-def-stmt* must specify an intrinsic type or any accessible derived type including the type being defined.

R428   *component-array-spec*   **is**   *explicit-shape-spec-list*
                                   or   *deferred-shape-spec-list*

R429   *component-decl*   **is**   *component-name* [(*component-array-spec*)] ■
                                   ■ [* *char-length*]

Constraint: If the POINTER attribute is not specified, each *component-array-spec* must be an *explicit-shape-spec-list*.

Constraint: If the POINTER attribute is specified, each *component-array-spec* must be a *deferred-shape-spec-list*.

Constraint: The * *char-length* option is permitted only if the type specified is character.

Constraint: A *char-length* in a *component-decl* must be a constant specification expression (7.1.6.2).

Constraint: Each bound in the *explicit-shape-spec* (R428) must be a constant specification expression (7.1.6.2).

R430   *structure-constructor*   **is**   *type-name* (*expr-list*)

R431   *array-constructor*   **is**   (/ *ac-value-list* /)

R432   *ac-value*   **is**   *expr*
                                   or   *ac-implied-do*

R433   *ac-implied-do*   **is**   (*ac-value-list* , *ac-implied-do-control*)

R434   *ac-implied-do-control*   **is**   *ac-do-variable* = *scalar-int-expr* , ■
                                   ■ *scalar-int-expr* [, *scalar-int-expr*]

R435   *ac-do-variable*   **is**   *scalar-int-variable*

Constraint: *ac-do-variable* must be a named variable.

Constraint: Each *ac-value* expression in the *array-constructor* must have the same type and type parameters.

B.2.5   Data Object Declarations and Specifications

R501   *type-declaration-stmt*   **is**   *type-spec* [[, *attr-spec*] ... ::] *entity-decl-list*

R502   *type-spec*   **is**   INTEGER [*kind-selector*]
                                   or   REAL [*kind-selector*]
                                   or   DOUBLE PRECISION
                                   or   COMPLEX [*kind-selector*]
                                   or   CHARACTER [*char-selector*]

		or	LOGICAL [*kind-selector*]
		or	TYPE (*type-name*)
R503	*attr-spec*	is	PARAMETER
		or	*access-spec*
		or	ALLOCATABLE
		or	DIMENSION (*array-spec*)
		or	EXTERNAL
		or	INTENT (*intent-spec*)
		or	INTRINSIC
		or	OPTIONAL
		or	POINTER
		or	SAVE
		or	TARGET
R504	*entity-decl*	is	*object-name* [(*array-spec*)] ■
			■ [* *char-length*] [= *initialization-expr*]
		or	*function-name* [(*array-spec*)] [* *char-length*]
R505	*kind-selector*	is	([KIND =] *scalar-int-initialization-expr*)

Constraint: The same *attr-spec* must not appear more than once in a given *type-declaration-stmt*.

Constraint: The *function-name* must be the name of an external function, an intrinsic function, a function dummy procedure, or a statement function.

Constraint: The = *initialization-expr* must appear if the statement contains a PARAMETER attribute (5.1.2.1).

Constraint: If = *initialization-expr* appears, a double colon separator must appear before the *entity-decl-list*.

Constraint: The = *initialization-expr* must not appear if *object-name* is a dummy argument, a function result, an object in a named common block unless the type declaration is in a block data program unit, an object in blank common, an allocatable array, a pointer, an external name, an intrinsic name, or an automatic object.

Constraint: The * *char-length* option is permitted only if the type specified is character.

Constraint: The ALLOCATABLE attribute may be used only when declaring an array that is not a dummy argument or a function result.

Constraint: An array declared with a POINTER or an ALLOCATABLE attribute must be specified with an *array-spec* that is a *deferred-shape-spec-list* (5.1.2.4.3).

Constraint: An *array-spec* for a *function-name* that does not have the POINTER attribute must be an *explicit-shape-spec-list*.

Constraint: An *array-spec* for a *function-name* that does have the POINTER attribute must be a *deferred-shape-spec-list*.

Constraint: If the POINTER attribute is specified, the TARGET, INTENT, EXTERNAL, or INTRINSIC attribute must not be specified.

Constraint: If the TARGET attribute is specified, the POINTER, EXTERNAL, INTRINSIC, or PARAMETER attribute must not be specified.

Constraint: The PARAMETER attribute must not be specified for dummy arguments, pointers, allocatable arrays, functions, or objects in a common block.

Constraint: The INTENT and OPTIONAL attributes may be specified only for dummy arguments.

Constraint: An entity must not have the PUBLIC attribute if its type has the PRIVATE attribute.

Constraint: The SAVE attribute must not be specified for an object that is in a common block, a dummy argument, a procedure, a function result, or an automatic data object.

Constraint: An entity must not have the EXTERNAL attribute if it has the INTRINSIC attribute.

Constraint: An entity in a *type-declaration-stmt* must not have the EXTERNAL or
              INTRINSIC attribute specified unless it is a function.
Constraint: An array must not have both the ALLOCATABLE attribute and the
              POINTER attribute.
Constraint: An entity must not be given explicitly any attribute more than once in a scop-
              ing unit.
Constraint: The value of *scalar-int-initialization-expr* must be nonnegative and must spec-
              ify a representation method that exists on the processor.

R506   *char-selector*   is   *length-selector*
                              or   (LEN = *type-param-value* , ■
                                   ■ KIND = *scalar-int-initialization-expr*)
                              or   (*type-param-value* , ■
                                   ■ [KIND =] *scalar-int-initialization-expr*)
                              or   (KIND = *scalar-int-initialization-expr* ■
                                   ■ [, LEN = *type-param-value*])
R507   *length-selector*   is   ([LEN =] *type-param-value*)
                              or   * *char-length* [,]
R508   *char-length*   is   (*type-param-value*)
                              or   *scalar-int-literal-constant*
Constraint: The optional comma in a *length-selector* is permitted only in a *type-spec* in a
              type-declaration-stmt.
Constraint: The optional comma in a *length-selector* is permitted only if no double colon
              separator appears in the *type-declaration-stmt*.
Constraint: The value of *scalar-int-initialization-expr* must be nonnegative and must spec-
              ify a representation method that exists on the processor.
Constraint: The *scalar-int-literal-constant* must not include a *kind-param*.
R509   *type-param-value*   is   *specification-expr*
                              or   *
Constraint: A function name must not be declared with an asterisk *type-param-value* if
              the function is an internal or module function, array-valued, pointer-valued,
              or recursive.
R510   *access-spec*   is   PUBLIC
                              or   PRIVATE
Constraint: An *access-spec* attribute may appear only in the scoping unit of a module.
R511   *intent-spec*   is   IN
                              or   OUT
                              or   INOUT
Constraint: The INTENT attribute must not be specified for a dummy argument that is a
              dummy procedure or a dummy pointer.
R512   *array-spec*   is   *explicit-shape-spec-list*
                              or   *assumed-shape-spec-list*
                              or   *deferred-shape-spec-list*
                              or   *assumed-size-spec*
Constraint: The maximum rank is seven.
R513   *explicit-shape-spec* is   [*lower-bound* :] *upper-bound*
R514   *lower-bound*   is   *specification-expr*
R515   *upper-bound*   is   *specification-expr*
Constraint: An explicit-shape array whose bounds depend on the values of nonconstant
              expressions must be a dummy argument, a function result, or an automatic
              array of a procedure.
R516   *assumed-shape-spec*   is   [*lower-bound*] :
R517   *deferred-shape-spec* is   :
R518   *assumed-size-spec*   is   [*explicit-shape-spec-list* ,] [*lower-bound* :] *
Constraint: The function name of an array-valued function must not be declared as an
              assumed-size array.

R519   *intent-stmt*   **is**   INTENT (*intent-spec*) [::] *dummy-arg-name-list*

Constraint: An *intent-stmt* may appear only in the *specification-part* of a subprogram or an interface body (12.3.2.1).

Constraint: *dummy-arg-name* must not be the name of a dummy procedure or a dummy pointer.

R520   *optional-stmt*   **is**   OPTIONAL [::] *dummy-arg-name-list*

Constraint: An *optional-stmt* may occur only in the scoping unit of a subprogram or an interface body.

R521   *access-stmt*   **is**   *access-spec* [[::] *access-id-list*]

R522   *access-id*   **is**   *use-name*
                                   or   *generic-spec*

Constraint: An *access-stmt* may appear only in the scoping unit of a module. Only one accessibility statement with an omitted *access-id-list* is permitted in the scoping unit of a module.

Constraint: Each *use-name* must be the name of a named variable, procedure, derived type, named constant, or namelist group.

Constraint: A module procedure that has a dummy argument or function result of a type that has PRIVATE accessibility must have PRIVATE accessibility and must not have a generic identifier that has PUBLIC accessibility.

R523   *save-stmt*   **is**   SAVE [[::] *saved-entity-list*]

R524   *saved-entity*   **is**   *object-name*
                                   or   / *common-block-name* /

Constraint: An *object-name* must not be a dummy argument name, a procedure name, a function result name, an automatic data object name, or the name of an entity in a common block.

Constraint: If a SAVE statement with an omitted saved entity list occurs in a scoping unit, no other explicit occurrence of the SAVE attribute or SAVE statement is permitted in the same scoping unit.

R525   *dimension-stmt*   **is**   DIMENSION [::] *array-name* (*array-spec*) ■
                                        ■   [, *array-name* (*array-spec*)] ...

R526   *allocatable-stmt*   **is**   ALLOCATABLE [::] *array-name* ■
                                        ■   [(*deferred-shape-spec-list*)] ■
                                        ■   [, *array-name* [(*deferred-shape-spec-list*)]] ...

Constraint: The *array-name* must not be a dummy argument or function result.

Constraint: If the DIMENSION attribute for an *array-name* is specified elsewhere in the scoping unit, the *array-spec* must be a *deferred-shape-spec-list*.

R527   *pointer-stmt*   **is**   POINTER [::] *object-name* ■
                                        ■   [(*deferred-shape-spec-list*)] ■
                                        ■   [, *object-name* [(*deferred-shape-spec-list*)]] ...

Constraint: The INTENT attribute must not be specified for an *object-name*.

Constraint: If the DIMENSION attribute for an *object-name* is specified elsewhere in the scoping unit, the *array-spec* must be a *deferred-shape-spec-list*.

Constraint: The PARAMETER attribute must not be specified for an *object-name*.

R528   *target-stmt*   **is**   TARGET [::] *object-name* [(*array-spec*)] ■
                                        ■   [, *object-name* [(*array-spec*)]] ...

Constraint: The PARAMETER attribute must not be specified for an *object-name*.

R529   *data-stmt*   **is**   DATA *data-stmt-set* [[,] *data-stmt-set*] ...

R530   *data-stmt-set*   **is**   *data-stmt-object-list* / *data-stmt-value-list* /

R531   *data-stmt-object*   **is**   *variable*
                                   or   *data-implied-do*

R532   *data-stmt-value*   **is**   [*data-stmt-repeat* *] *data-stmt-constant*

R533   *data-stmt-constant*   **is**   *scalar-constant*
                                   or   *signed-int-literal-constant*
                                   or   *signed-real-literal-constant*

		or	*structure-constructor*
		or	*boz-literal-constant*
R534	*data-stmt-repeat*	is	*scalar-int-constant*
R535	*data-implied-do*	is	(*data-i-do-object-list* , *data-i-do-variable* = ■
			■ *scalar-int-expr* , *scalar-int-expr* [, *scalar-int-expr*])
R536	*data-i-do-object*	is	*array-element*
		or	*scalar-structure-component*
		or	*data-implied-do*

Constraint: The *array-element* must not have a constant parent.

Constraint: The *scalar-structure-component* must not have a constant parent.

R537	*data-i-do-variable*	is	*scalar-int-variable*

Constraint: *data-i-do-variable* must be a named variable.

Constraint: The DATA statement repeat factor must be positive or zero. If the DATA statement repeat factor is a named constant, it must have been declared previously in the scoping unit or made accessible by use association or host association.

Constraint: If a *data-stmt-constant* is a *structure-constructor*, each component must be an initialization expression.

Constraint: In a *variable* that is a *data-stmt-object*, any subscript, section subscript, substring starting point, and substring ending point must be an initialization expression.

Constraint: A variable whose name or designator is included in a *data-stmt-object-list* or a *data-i-do-object-list* must not be: a dummy argument, made accessible by use association or host association, in a named common block unless the DATA statement is in a block data program unit, in a blank common block, a function name, a function result name, an automatic object, a pointer, or an allocatable array.

Constraint: In an *array-element* or a *scalar-structure-component* that is a *data-i-do-object*, any subscript must be an expression whose primaries are either constants or DO variables of the containing *data-implied-do*s, and each operation must be intrinsic.

Constraint: A *scalar-int-expr* of a *data-implied-do* must involve as primaries only constants or DO variables of the containing *data-implied-do*s, and each operation must be intrinsic.

R538	*parameter-stmt*	is	PARAMETER (*named-constant-def-list*)
R539	*named-constant-def*	is	*named-constant* = *initialization-expr*
R540	*implicit-stmt*	is	IMPLICIT *implicit-spec-list*
		or	IMPLICIT NONE
R541	*implicit-spec*	is	*type-spec* (*letter-spec-list*)
R542	*letter-spec*	is	*letter* [– *letter*]

Constraint: If IMPLICIT NONE is specified in a scoping unit, it must precede any PARAMETER statements that appear in the scoping unit and there must be no other IMPLICIT statements in the scoping unit.

Constraint: If the minus and second letter appear, the second letter must follow the first letter alphabetically.

R543	*namelist-stmt*	is	NAMELIST / *namelist-group-name* / ■
			■ *namelist-group-object-list* ■
			■ [[,] / *namelist-group-name* / ■
			■ *namelist-group-object-list*] ...
R544	*namelist-group-object*	is	*variable-name*

Constraint: A *namelist-group-object* must not be an array dummy argument with a nonconstant bound, a variable with nonconstant character length, an automatic object, a pointer, a variable of a type that has an ultimate component that is a pointer, or an allocatable array.

Constraint: If a *namelist-group-name* has the PUBLIC attribute, no item in the *namelist-group-object-list* may have the PRIVATE attribute.

R545   *equivalence-stmt*   **is**   EQUIVALENCE *equivalence-set-list*

R546   *equivalence-set*   **is**   (*equivalence-object* , *equivalence-object-list*)

R547   *equivalence-object*   **is**   *variable-name*
                               or   *array-element*
                               or   *substring*

Constraint: An *equivalence-object* must not be a dummy argument, a pointer, an allocatable array, an object of a nonsequence derived type or of a sequence derived type containing a pointer at any level of component selection, an automatic object, a function name, an entry name, a result name, a named constant, a structure component, or a subobject of any of the preceding objects.

Constraint: Each subscript or substring range expression in an *equivalence-object* must be an integer initialization expression (7.1.6.1).

Constraint: If an *equivalence-object* is of type default integer, default real, double precision real, default complex, default logical, or numeric sequence type, all of the objects in the equivalence set must be of these types.

Constraint: If an *equivalence-object* is of type default character or character sequence type, all of the objects in the equivalence set must be of these types.

Constraint: If an *equivalence-object* is of a derived type that is not a numeric sequence or character sequence type, all of the objects in the equivalence set must be of the same type.

Constraint: If an *equivalence-object* is of an intrinsic type other than default integer, default real, double precision real, default complex, default logical, or default character, all of the objects in the equivalence set must be of the same type with the same kind type parameter value.

R548   *common-stmt*   **is**   COMMON [/ [*common-block-name*] /] ■
                            ■ *common-block-object-list* ■
                            ■ [[,] / [*common-block-name*] / ■
                            ■ *common-block-object-list*] ...

R549   *common-block-object*   **is**   *variable-name* [(*explicit-shape-spec-list*)]

Constraint: Only one appearance of a given *variable-name* is permitted in all *common-block-object-list*s within a scoping unit.

Constraint: A *common-block-object* must not be a dummy argument, an allocatable array, an automatic object, a function name, an entry name, or a result name.

Constraint: Each bound in the *explicit-shape-spec* must be a constant specification expression (7.1.6.2).

Constraint: If a *common-block-object* is of a derived type, it must be a sequence type (4.4.1).

Constraint: If a *variable-name* appears with an *explicit-shape-spec-list*, it must not have the POINTER attribute.

B.2.6 Use of Data Objects

R601   *variable*   **is**   *scalar-variable-name*
                              or   *array-variable-name*
                              or   *subobject*

Constraint: *array-variable-name* must be the name of a data object that is an array.

Constraint: *array-variable-name* must not have the PARAMETER attribute.

Constraint: *scalar-variable-name* must not have the PARAMETER attribute.

Constraint: *subobject* must not be a subobject designator (for example, a substring) whose parent is a constant.

R602	*subobject*	**is**	*array-element*
		or	*array-section*
		or	*structure-component*
		or	*substring*
R603	*logical-variable*	**is**	*variable*

Constraint: *logical-variable* must be of type logical.

| R604 | *default-logical-variable* | **is** | *variable* |

Constraint: *default-logical-variable* must be of type default logical.

| R605 | *char-variable* | **is** | *variable* |

Constraint: *char-variable* must be of type character.

| R606 | *default-char-variable* | **is** | *variable* |

Constraint: *default-char-variable* must be of type default character.

| R607 | *int-variable* | **is** | *variable* |

Constraint: *int-variable* must be of type integer.

| R608 | *default-int-variable* | **is** | *variable* |

Constraint: *default-int-variable* must be of type default integer.

R609	*substring*	**is**	*parent-string* (*substring-range*)
R610	*parent-string*	**is**	*scalar-variable-name*
		or	*array-element*
		or	*scalar-structure-component*
		or	*scalar-constant*
R611	*substring-range*	**is**	[*scalar-int-expr*] : [*scalar-int-expr*]

Constraint: *parent-string* must be of type character.

| R612 | *data-ref* | **is** | *part-ref* [% *part-ref*] ... |
| R613 | *part-ref* | **is** | *part-name* [(*section-subscript-list*)] |

Constraint: In a *data-ref*, each *part-name* except the rightmost must be of derived type.

Constraint: In a *data-ref*, each *part-name* except the leftmost must be the name of a component of the derived type definition of the type of the preceding *part-name*.

Constraint: In a *part-ref* containing a *section-subscript-list*, the number of *section-subscript*s must equal the rank of *part-name*.

Constraint: In a *data-ref*, there must not be more than one *part-ref* with nonzero rank. A *part-name* to the right of a *part-ref* with nonzero rank must not have the POINTER attribute.

| R614 | *structure-component* | **is** | *data-ref* |

Constraint: In a *structure-component*, there must be more than one *part-ref* and the rightmost *part-ref* must be of the form *part-name*.

| R615 | *array-element* | **is** | *data-ref* |

Constraint: In an *array-element*, every *part-ref* must have rank zero and the last *part-ref* must contain a *subscript-list*.

| R616 | *array-section* | **is** | *data-ref* [(*substring-range*)] |

Constraint: In an *array-section*, exactly one *part-ref* must have nonzero rank, and either the final *part-ref* has a *section-subscript-list* with nonzero rank or another *part-ref* has nonzero rank.

Constraint: In an *array-section* with a *substring-range*, the rightmost *part-name* must be of type character.

R617	*subscript*	**is**	*scalar-int-expr*
R618	*section-subscript*	**is**	*subscript*
		or	*subscript-triplet*
		or	*vector-subscript*
R619	*subscript-triplet*	**is**	[*subscript*] : [*subscript*] [: *stride*]
R620	*stride*	**is**	*scalar-int-expr*
R621	*vector-subscript*	**is**	*int-expr*

Constraint: A *vector-subscript* must be an integer array expression of rank one.

Constraint: The second *subscript* must not be omitted from a *subscript-triplet* in the last
dimension of an assumed-size array.

R622	*allocate-stmt*	**is**	ALLOCATE (*allocation-list* ■
			■ [, STAT = *stat-variable*])
R623	*stat-variable*	**is**	*scalar-int-variable*
R624	*allocation*	**is**	*allocate-object* [(*allocate-shape-spec-list*)]
R625	*allocate-object*	**is**	*variable-name*
		or	*structure-component*
R626	*allocate-shape-spec*	**is**	[*allocate-lower-bound* :] *allocate-upper-bound*
R627	*allocate-lower-bound*	**is**	*scalar-int-expr*
R628	*allocate-upper-bound*	**is**	*scalar-int-expr*

Constraint: Each *allocate-object* must be a pointer or an allocatable array.

Constraint: The number of *allocate-shape-spec*s in an *allocate-shape-spec-list* must be the
same as the rank of the pointer or allocatable array.

R629	*nullify-stmt*	**is**	NULLIFY (*pointer-object-list*)
R630	*pointer-object*	**is**	*variable-name*
		or	*structure-component*

Constraint: Each *pointer-object* must have the POINTER attribute.

| R631 | *deallocate-stmt* | **is** | DEALLOCATE (*allocate-object-list* ■ |
| | | | ■ [, STAT = *stat-variable*]) |

Constraint: Each *allocate-object* must be a pointer or an allocatable array.

B.2.7 Expressions and Assignment

R701	*primary*	**is**	*constant*
		or	*constant-subobject*
		or	*variable*
		or	*array-constructor*
		or	*structure-constructor*
		or	*function-reference*
		or	(*expr*)
R702	*constant-subobject*	**is**	*subobject*

Constraint: *subobject* must be a subobject designator whose parent is a constant.

Constraint: A *variable* that is a *primary* must not be an assumed-size array.

| R703 | *level-1-expr* | **is** | [*defined-unary-op*] *primary* |
| R704 | *defined-unary-op* | **is** | . *letter* [*letter*] ... . |

Constraint: A *defined-unary-op* must not contain more than 31 letters and must not be
the same as any *intrinsic-operator* or *logical-literal-constant*.

R705	*mult-operand*	**is**	*level-1-expr* [*power-op mult-operand*]
R706	*add-operand*	**is**	[*add-operand mult-op*] *mult-operand*
R707	*level-2-expr*	**is**	[[*level-2-expr*] *add-op*] *add-operand*
R708	*power-op*	**is**	**
R709	*mult-op*	**is**	*
		or	/
R710	*add-op*	**is**	+
		or	−
R711	*level-3-expr*	**is**	[*level-3-expr concat-op*] *level-2-expr*
R712	*concat-op*	**is**	//
R713	*level-4-expr*	**is**	[*level-3-expr rel-op*] *level-3-expr*
R714	*rel-op*	**is**	.EQ.
		or	.NE.
		or	.LT.
		or	.LE.

		or	.GT.
		or	.GE.
		or	==
		or	/=
		or	<
		or	<=
		or	>
		or	>=
R715	*and-operand*	is	[*not-op*] *level-4-expr*
R716	*or-operand*	is	[*or-operand and-op*] *and-operand*
R717	*equiv-operand*	is	[*equiv-operand or-op*] *or-operand*
R718	*level-5-expr*	is	[*level-5-expr equiv-op*] *equiv-operand*
R719	*not-op*	is	.NOT.
R720	*and-op*	is	.AND.
R721	*or-op*	is	.OR.
R722	*equiv-op*	is	.EQV.
		or	.NEQV.
R723	*expr*	is	[*expr defined-binary-op*] *level-5-expr*
R724	*defined-binary-op*	is	. *letter* [*letter*] ... .

Constraint: A *defined-binary-op* must not contain more than 31 letters and must not be the same as any *intrinsic-operator* or *logical-literal-constant*.

R725	*logical-expr*	is	*expr*

Constraint: *logical-expr* must be type logical.

R726	*char-expr*	is	*expr*

Constraint: *char-expr* must be type character.

R727	*default-char-expr*	is	*expr*

Constraint: *default-char-expr* must be of type default character.

R728	*int-expr*	is	*expr*

Constraint: *int-expr* must be type integer.

R729	*numeric-expr*	is	*expr*

Constraint: *numeric-expr* must be of type integer, real or complex.

R730	*initialization-expr*	is	*expr*

Constraint: An *initialization-expr* must be an initialization expression.

R731	*char-initialization-expr*	is	*char-expr*

Constraint: A *char-initialization-expr* must be an initialization expression.

R732	*int-initialization-expr*	is	*int-expr*

Constraint: An *int-initialization-expr* must be an initialization expression.

R733	*logical-initialization-expr*	is	*logical-expr*

Constraint: A *logical-initialization-expr* must be an initialization expression.

R734	*specification-expr*	is	*scalar-int-expr*

Constraint: The *scalar-int-expr* must be a restricted expression.

R735	*assignment-stmt*	is	*variable = expr*

Constraint: A *variable* in an *assignment-stmt* must not be an assumed-size array.

R736	*pointer-assignment-stmt*	is	*pointer-object* => *target*
R737	*target*	is	*variable*
		or	*expr*

Constraint: The *pointer-object* must have the POINTER attribute.

Constraint: The *variable* must have the TARGET attribute or be a subobject of an object with the TARGET attribute, or it must have the POINTER attribute.

Constraint: The *target* must be of the same type, type parameters, and rank as the pointer.

Constraint: The *target* must not be an array section with a vector subscript.

Constraint: The *expr* must deliver a pointer result.

R738   *where-stmt*   is   WHERE (*mask-expr*) *assignment-stmt*

R739   *where-construct*   is   *where-construct-stmt*
                                          [*assignment-stmt*] ...
                                          [*elsewhere-stmt*
                                          [*assignment-stmt*] ...]
                                          end-where-stmt

R740   *where-construct-stmt*   is   WHERE (*mask-expr*)

R741   *mask-expr*   is   *logical-expr*

R742   *elsewhere-stmt*   is   ELSEWHERE

R743   *end-where-stmt*   is   END WHERE

Constraint: In each *assignment-stmt*, the *mask-expr* and the variable being defined must be arrays of the same shape.

Constraint: The *assignment-stmt* must not be a defined assignment.

B.2.8   Execution Control

R801   *block*   is   [*execution-part-construct*] ...

R802   *if-construct*   is   *if-then-stmt*
                                          block
                                          [*else-if-stmt*
                                          block] ...
                                          [*else-stmt*
                                          block]
                                          end-if-stmt

R803   *if-then-stmt*   is   [*if-construct-name* :] IF (*scalar-logical-expr*) THEN

R804   *else-if-stmt*   is   ELSE IF (*scalar-logical-expr*) THEN [*if-construct-name*]

R805   *else-stmt*   is   ELSE [*if-construct-name*]

R806   *end-if-stmt*   is   END IF [*if-construct-name*]

Constraint: If the *if-then-stmt* of an *if-construct* is identified by an *if-construct-name*, the corresponding *end-if-stmt* must specify the same *if-construct-name*. If the *if-then-stmt* of an *if-construct* is not identified by an *if-construct-name*, the corresponding *end-if-stmt* must not specify an *if-construct-name*. If an *else-if-stmt* or *else-stmt* is identified by an *if-construct-name*, the corresponding *if-then-stmt* must specify the same *if-construct-name*.

R807   *if-stmt*   is   IF (*scalar-logical-expr*) *action-stmt*

Constraint: The *action-stmt* in the *if-stmt* must not be an *if-stmt*, *end-program-stmt*, *end-function-stmt*, or *end-subroutine-stmt*.

R808   *case-construct*   is   *select-case-stmt*
                                          [*case-stmt*
                                          block] ...
                                          end-select-stmt

R809   *select-case-stmt*   is   [*case-construct-name* :] SELECT CASE (*case-expr*)

R810   *case-stmt*   is   CASE *case-selector* [*case-construct-name*]

R811   *end-select-stmt*   is   END SELECT [*case-construct-name*]

Constraint: If the *select-case-stmt* of a *case-construct* is identified by a *case-construct-name*, the corresponding *end-select-stmt* must specify the same *case-construct-name*. If the *select-case-stmt* of a *case-construct* is not identified by a *case-construct-name*, the corresponding *end-select-stmt* must not specify a *case-construct-name*. If a *case-stmt* is identified by a *case-construct-name*, the corresponding *select-case-stmt* must specify the same *case-construct-name*.

R812   *case-expr*   is   *scalar-int-expr*
                                  or   *scalar-char-expr*
                                  or   *scalar-logical-expr*

R813   *case-selector*   **is**   (*case-value-range-list*)
                                        or   DEFAULT
Constraint: No more than one of the selectors of one of the CASE statements may be DEFAULT.

R814   *case-value-range*   **is**   *case-value*
                                        or   *case-value* :
                                        or   : *case-value*
                                        or   *case-value* : *case-value*

R815   *case-value*   **is**   *scalar-int-initialization-expr*
                                        or   *scalar-char-initialization-expr*
                                        or   *scalar-logical-initialization-expr*

Constraint: For a given *case-construct*, each *case-value* must be of the same type as *case-expr*. For character type, length differences are allowed, but the kind type parameters must be the same.

Constraint: A *case-value-range* using a colon must not be used if *case-expr* is of type logical.

Constraint: For a given *case-construct*, the *case-value-ranges* must not overlap; that is, there must be no possible value of the *case-expr* that matches more than one *case-value-range*.

R816   *do-construct*   **is**   *block-do-construct*
                                        or   *nonblock-do-construct*

R817   *block-do-construct*   **is**   *do-stmt*
                                               do-block
                                               end-do

R818   *do-stmt*   **is**   *label-do-stmt*
                                        or   *nonlabel-do-stmt*

R819   *label-do-stmt*   **is**   [*do-construct-name* :] DO *label* [*loop-control*]

R820   *nonlabel-do-stmt*   **is**   [*do-construct-name* :] DO [*loop-control*]

R821   *loop-control*   **is**   [,] *do-variable* = *scalar-numeric-expr* , ■
                                          ■ *scalar-numeric-expr* [, *scalar-numeric-expr*]
                                        or   [,] WHILE (*scalar-logical-expr*)

R822   *do-variable*   **is**   *scalar-variable*
Constraint: The *do-variable* must be a named scalar variable of type integer, default real, or double precision real

Constraint: Each *scalar-numeric-expr* in *loop-control* must be of type integer, default real, or double precision real

R823   *do-block*   **is**   *block*

R824   *end-do*   **is**   *end-do-stmt*
                                        or   *continue-stmt*

R825   *end-do-stmt*   **is**   END DO [*do-construct-name*]
Constraint: If the *do-stmt* of a *block-do-construct* is identified by a *do-construct-name*, the corresponding *end-do* must be an *end-do-stmt* specifying the same *do-construct-name*. If the *do-stmt* of a *block-do-construct* is not identified by a *do-construct-name*, the corresponding *end-do* must not specify a *do-construct-name*.

Constraint: If the *do-stmt* is a *nonlabel-do-stmt*, the corresponding *end-do* must be an *end-do-stmt*.

Constraint: If the *do-stmt* is a *label-do-stmt*, the corresponding *end-do* must be identified with the same *label*.

R826   *nonblock-do-construct*   **is**   *action-term-do-construct*
                                        or   *outer-shared-do-construct*

R827   *action-term-do-construct*   **is**   *label-do-stmt*
                                               do-body
                                             do-term-action-stmt

R828 *do-body*   is [*execution-part-construct*] ...

R829 *do-term-action-stmt*   is *action-stmt*

Constraint: A *do-term-action-stmt* must not be a *continue-stmt*, a *goto-stmt*, a *return-stmt*, a *stop-stmt*, an *exit-stmt*, a *cycle-stmt*, an *end-function-stmt*, an *end-subroutine-stmt*, an *end-program-stmt*, an *arithmetic-if-stmt*, or an *assigned-goto-stmt*.

Constraint: The *do-term-action-stmt* must be identified with a label and the corresponding *label-do-stmt* must refer to the same label.

R830 *outer-shared-do-construct* is *label-do-stmt*
                                       do-body
                                       shared-term-do-construct

R831 *shared-term-do-construct*   is *outer-shared-do-construct*
                                   or *inner-shared-do-construct*

R832 *inner-shared-do-construct* is *label-do-stmt*
                                       do-body
                                       do-term-shared-stmt

R833 *do-term-shared-stmt*   is *action-stmt*

Constraint: A *do-term-shared-stmt* must not be a *goto-stmt*, a *return-stmt*, a *stop-stmt*, an *exit-stmt*, a *cycle-stmt*, an *end-function-stmt*, an *end-subroutine-stmt*, an *end-program-stmt*, an *arithmetic-if-stmt*, or an *assigned-goto-stmt*.

Constraint: The *do-term-shared-stmt* must be identified with a label and all of the *label-do-stmts* of the *shared-term-do-construct* must refer to the same label.

R834 *cycle-stmt*   is CYCLE [*do-construct-name*]

Constraint: If a *cycle-stmt* refers to a *do-construct-name*, it must be within the range of that *do-construct*; otherwise, it must be within the range of at least one *do-construct*

R835 *exit-stmt*   is EXIT [*do-construct-name*]

Constraint: If an *exit-stmt* refers to a *do-construct-name*, it must be within the range of that *do-construct*; otherwise, it must be within the range of at least one *do-construct*.

R836 *goto-stmt*   is GO TO *label*

Constraint: The *label* must be the statement label of a branch target statement that appears in the same scoping unit as the *goto-stmt*.

R837 *computed-goto-stmt*   is GO TO (*label-list*) [,] *scalar-int-expr*

Constraint: Each *label* in *label-list* must be the statement label of a branch target statement that appears in the same scoping unit as the *computed-goto-stmt*.

R838 *assign-stmt*   is ASSIGN *label* TO *scalar-int-variable*

Constraint: The *label* must be the statement label of a branch target statement or *format-stmt* that appears in the same scoping unit as the *assign-stmt*.

Constraint: *scalar-int-variable* must be named and of type default integer.

R839 *assigned-goto-stmt*   is GO TO *scalar-int-variable* [[,] (*label-list*)]

Constraint: Each *label* in *label-list* must be the statement label of a branch target statement that appears in the same scoping unit as the *assigned-goto-stmt*.

Constraint: *scalar-int-variable* must be named and of type default integer.

R840 *arithmetic-if-stmt*   is IF (*scalar-numeric-expr*) *label* , *label* , *label*

Constraint: Each *label* must be the label of a branch target statement that appears in the same scoping unit as the *arithmetic-if-stmt*.

Constraint: The *scalar-numeric-expr* must not be of type complex.

R841 *continue-stmt*   is CONTINUE

R842 *stop-stmt*   is STOP [*stop-code*]

R843 *stop-code*   is *scalar-char-constant*
                                   or *digit* [*digit* [*digit* [*digit* [*digit*]]]]

Constraint: *scalar-char-constant* must be of type default character.

R844   *pause-stmt*   **is**   PAUSE [*stop-code*]

B.2.9 Input/Output Statements

R901   *io-unit*   **is**   *external-file-unit*
                                       or   *
                                       or   *internal-file-unit*
R902   *external-file-unit*   **is**   *scalar-int-expr*
R903   *internal-file-unit*   **is**   *default-char-variable*
Constraint: The *default-char-variable* must not be an array section with a vector subscript.
R904   *open-stmt*   **is**   OPEN (*connect-spec-list*)
R905   *connect-spec*   **is**   [UNIT =] *external-file-unit*
                                       or   IOSTAT = *scalar-default-int-variable*
                                       or   ERR = *label*
                                       or   FILE = *file-name-expr*
                                       or   STATUS = *scalar-default-char-expr*
                                       or   ACCESS = *scalar-default-char-expr*
                                       or   FORM = *scalar-default-char-expr*
                                       or   RECL = *scalar-int-expr*
                                       or   BLANK = *scalar-default-char-expr*
                                       or   POSITION = *scalar-default-char-expr*
                                       or   ACTION = *scalar-default-char-expr*
                                       or   DELIM = *scalar-default-char-expr*
                                       or   PAD = *scalar-default-char-expr*
R906   *file-name-expr*   **is**   *scalar-default-char-expr*
Constraint: If the optional characters UNIT= are omitted from the unit specifier, the unit specifier must be the first item in the *connect-spec-list*.
Constraint: Each specifier must not appear more than once in a given *open-stmt*; an *external-file-unit* must be specified.
Constraint: The *label* used in the ERR= specifier must be the statement label of a branch target statement that appears in the same scoping unit as the OPEN statement.
R907   *close-stmt*   **is**   CLOSE (*close-spec-list*)
R908   *close-spec*   **is**   [UNIT =] *external-file-unit*
                                       or   IOSTAT = *scalar-default-int-variable*
                                       or   ERR = *label*
                                       or   STATUS = *scalar-default-char-expr*
Constraint: If the optional characters UNIT= are omitted from the unit specifier, the unit specifier must be the first item in the *close-spec-list*.
Constraint: Each specifier must not appear more than once in a given *close-stmt*; an *external-file-unit* must be specified.
Constraint: The *label* used in the ERR= specifier must be the statement label of a branch target statement that appears in the same scoping unit as the CLOSE statement.
R909   *read-stmt*   **is**   READ (*io-control-spec-list*) [*input-item-list*]
                                       or   READ *format* [, *input-item-list*]
R910   *write-stmt*   **is**   WRITE (*io-control-spec-list*) [*output-item-list*]
R911   *print-stmt*   **is**   PRINT *format* [, *output-item-list*]
R912   *io-control-spec*   **is**   [UNIT =] *io-unit*
                                       or   [FMT =] *format*
                                       or   [NML =] *namelist-group-name*
                                       or   REC = *scalar-int-expr*
                                       or   IOSTAT = *scalar-default-int-variable*

> or ERR = *label*
> or END = *label*
> or ADVANCE = *scalar-default-char-expr*
> or SIZE = *scalar-default-int-variable*
> or EOR = *label*

Constraint: An *io-control-spec-list* must contain exactly one *io-unit* and may contain at most one of each of the other specifiers.

Constraint: An END=, EOR=, or SIZE= specifier must not appear in a *write-stmt*.

Constraint: The *label* in the ERR=, EOR=, or END= specifier must be the statement label of a branch target statement that appears in the same scoping unit as the data transfer statement.

Constraint: A *namelist-group-name* must not be present if an *input-item-list* or an *output-item-list* is present in the data transfer statement.

Constraint: An *io-control-spec-list* must not contain both a *format* and a *namelist-group-name*.

Constraint: If the optional characters UNIT= are omitted from the unit specifier, the unit specifier must be the first item in the control information list.

Constraint: If the optional characters FMT= are omitted from the format specifier, the format specifier must be the second item in the control information list and the first item must be the unit specifier without the optional characters UNIT=.

Constraint: If the optional characters NML= are omitted from the namelist specifier, the namelist specifier must be the second item in the control information list and the first item must be the unit specifier without the optional characters UNIT=.

Constraint: If the unit specifier specifies an internal file, the *io-control-spec-list* must not contain a REC= specifier or a *namelist-group-name*.

Constraint: If the REC= specifier is present, an END= specifier must not appear, a *namelist-group-name* must not appear, and the *format*, if any, must not be an asterisk specifying list-directed input/output.

Constraint: An ADVANCE= specifier may be present only in a formatted sequential input/output statement with explicit format specification (10.1) whose control information list does not contain an internal file unit specifier.

Constraint: If an EOR= specifier is present, an ADVANCE= specifier also must appear.

R913   *format*   is   *default-char-expr*
                            or   *label*
                            or   *
                            or   *scalar-default-int-variable*

Constraint: The *label* must be the label of a FORMAT statement that appears in the same scoping unit as the statement containing the format specifier.

R914   *input-item*   is   *variable*
                            or   *io-implied-do*

R915   *output-item*   is   *expr*
                            or   *io-implied-do*

R916   *io-implied-do*   is   (*io-implied-do-object-list* , *io-implied-do-control*)

R917   *io-implied-do-object*   is   *input-item*
                            or   *output-item*

R918   *io-implied-do-control* is   *do-variable* = *scalar-numeric-expr* , ■
                            ■ *scalar-numeric-expr* [, *scalar-numeric-expr*]

Constraint: A *variable* that is an *input-item* must not be an assumed-size array.

Constraint: The *do-variable* must be a scalar of type integer, default real, or double precision real.

Constraint: Each *scalar-numeric-expr* in an *io-implied-do-control* must be of type integer, default real, or double precision real.

Constraint: In an *input-item-list*, an *io-implied-do-object* must be an *input-item*. In an *output-item-list*, an *io-implied-do-object* must be an *output-item*.

R919 *backspace-stmt* **is** BACKSPACE *external-file-unit*
                                 or BACKSPACE (*position-spec-list*)

R920 *endfile-stmt* **is** ENDFILE *external-file-unit*
                                 or ENDFILE (*position-spec-list*)

R921 *rewind-stmt* **is** REWIND *external-file-unit*
                                 or REWIND (*position-spec-list*)

R922 *position-spec* **is** [UNIT =] *external-file-unit*
                                 or IOSTAT = *scalar-default-int-variable*
                                 or ERR = *label*

Constraint: The *label* in the ERR= specifier must be the statement label of a branch target statement that appears in the same scoping unit as the file positioning statement.

Constraint: If the optional characters UNIT = are omitted from the unit specifier, the unit specifier must be the first item in the *position-spec-list*.

Constraint: A *position-spec-list* must contain exactly one *external-file-unit* and may contain at most one of each of the other specifiers.

R923 *inquire-stmt* **is** INQUIRE (*inquire-spec-list*)
                                 or INQUIRE (IOLENGTH = *scalar-default-int-variable*) ■
                                  ■ *output-item-list*

R924 *inquire-spec* **is** [UNIT =] *external-file-unit*
                                 or FILE = *file-name-expr*
                                 or IOSTAT = *scalar-default-int-variable*
                                 or ERR = *label*
                                 or EXIST = *scalar-default-logical-variable*
                                 or OPENED = *scalar-default-logical-variable*
                                 or NUMBER = *scalar-default-int-variable*
                                 or NAMED = *scalar-default-logical-variable*
                                 or NAME = *scalar-default-char-variable*
                                 or ACCESS = *scalar-default-char-variable*
                                 or SEQUENTIAL = *scalar-default-char-variable*
                                 or DIRECT = *scalar-default-char-variable*
                                 or FORM = *scalar-default-char-variable*
                                 or FORMATTED = *scalar-default-char-variable*
                                 or UNFORMATTED = *scalar-default-char-variable*
                                 or RECL = *scalar-default-int-variable*
                                 or NEXTREC = *scalar-default-int-variable*
                                 or BLANK = *scalar-default-char-variable*
                                 or POSITION = *scalar-default-char-variable*
                                 or ACTION = *scalar-default-char-variable*
                                 or READ = *scalar-default-char-variable*
                                 or WRITE = *scalar-default-char-variable*
                                 or READWRITE = *scalar-default-char-variable*
                                 or DELIM = *scalar-default-char-variable*
                                 or PAD = *scalar-default-char-variable*

Constraint: An *inquire-spec-list* must contain one FILE= specifier or one UNIT= specifier, but not both, and at most one of each of the other specifiers.

Constraint: In the inquire by unit form of the INQUIRE statement, if the optional characters UNIT = are omitted from the unit specifier, the unit specifier must be the first item in the *inquire-spec-list*.

B.2.10 Input/Output Editing

R1001 *format-stmt*   **is** FORMAT *format-specification*
R1002 *format-specification* **is** ([*format-item-list*])
Constraint: The *format-stmt* must be labeled.
Constraint: The comma used to separate *format-item*s in a *format-item-list* may be omit-
     ted as follows:
   Between a P edit descriptor and an immediately following F, E, EN, ES, D, or G edit
   descriptor (10.6.5)
   Before a slash edit descriptor when the optional repeat specification is not present
   (10.6.2)
   After a slash edit descriptor
   Before or after a colon edit descriptor (10.6.3)
R1003 *format-item*   **is** [*r*] *data-edit-desc*
          or *control-edit-desc*
          or *char-string-edit-desc*
          or [*r*] (*format-item-list*)
R1004 *r*   **is** *int-literal-constant*
Constraint: *r* must be positive.
Constraint: *r* must not have a kind parameter specified for it.
R1005 *data-edit-desc*   **is** I *w* [. *m*]
          or B *w* [. *m*]
          or O *w* [. *m*]
          or Z *w* [. *m*]
          or F *w* . *d*
          or E *w* . *d* [E *e*]
          or EN *w* . *d* [E *e*]
          or ES *w* . *d* [E *e*]
          or G *w* . *d* [E *e*]
          or L *w*
          or A [*w*]
          or D *w* . *d*
R1006 *w*   **is** *int-literal-constant*
R1007 *m*   **is** *int-literal-constant*
R1008 *d*   **is** *int-literal-constant*
R1009 *e*   **is** *int-literal-constant*
Constraint: *w* and *e* must be positive.
Constraint: *w*, *m*, *d*, and *e* must not have kind parameters specified for them.
R1010 *control-edit-desc* **is** *position-edit-desc*
          or [*r*] /
          or :
          or *sign-edit-desc*
          or *k* P
          or *blank-interp-edit-desc*
R1011 *k*   **is** *signed-int-literal-constant*
Constraint: *k* must not have a kind parameter specified for it.
R1012 *position-edit-desc* **is** T *n*
          or TL *n*
          or TR *n*
          or *n* X
R1013 *n*   **is** *int-literal-constant*
Constraint: *n* must be positive.
Constraint: *n* must not have a kind parameter specified for it.

R1014	*sign-edit-desc*	**is**	S
		or	SP
		or	SS
R1015	*blank-interp-edit-desc*	**is**	BN
		or	BZ
R1016	*char-string-edit-desc*	**is**	*char-literal-constant*
		or	*c* H *rep-char* [*rep-char*] ...
R1017	*c*	**is**	*int-literal-constant*

Constraint: *c* must be positive.
Constraint: *c* must not have a kind parameter specified for it.
Constraint: The *rep-char* in the *c*H form must be of default character type.
Constraint: The *char-literal-constant* must not have a kind parameter specified for it.

B.2.11 Program Units

R1101	*main-program*	**is**	[*program-stmt*]
			[*specification-part*]
			[*execution-part*]
			[*internal-subprogram-part*]
			end-program-stmt
R1102	*program-stmt*	**is**	PROGRAM *program-name*
R1103	*end-program-stmt*	**is**	END [PROGRAM [*program-name*]]

Constraint: In a *main-program*, the *execution-part* must not contain a RETURN statement or an ENTRY statement.
Constraint: The *program-name* may be included in the *end-program-stmt* only if the optional *program-stmt* is used and, if included, must be identical to the *program-name* specified in the *program-stmt*.
Constraint: An automatic object must not appear in the *specification-part* (R204) of a main program.

R1104	*module*	**is**	*module-stmt*
			[*specification-part*]
			[*module-subprogram-part*]
			end-module-stmt
R1105	*module-stmt*	**is**	MODULE *module-name*
R1106	*end-module-stmt*	**is**	END [MODULE [*module-name*]]

Constraint: If the *module-name* is specified in the *end-module-stmt*, it must be identical to the *module-name* specified in the *module-stmt*.
Constraint: A module *specification-part* must not contain a *stmt-function-stmt*, an *entry-stmt*, or a *format-stmt*.
Constraint: An automatic object must not appear in the *specification-part* (R204) of a module.

R1107	*use-stmt*	**is**	USE *module-name* [, *rename-list*]
		or	USE *module-name* , ONLY : [*only-list*]
R1108	*rename*	**is**	*local-name* = > *use-name*
R1109	*only*	**is**	*access-id*
		or	[*local-name* = >] *use-name*

Constraint: Each *access-id* must be a public entity in the module.
Constraint: Each *use-name* must be the name of a public entity in the module.

R1110	*block-data*	**is**	*block-data-stmt*
			[*specification-part*]
			end-block-data-stmt
R1111	*block-data-stmt*	**is**	BLOCK DATA [*block-data-name*]

R1112 *end-block-data-stmt*   **is** END [BLOCK DATA [*block-data-name*]]

Constraint: The *block-data-name* may be included in the *end-block-data-stmt* only if it was provided in the *block-data-stmt* and, if included, must be identical to the *block-data-name* in the *block-data-stmt*.

Constraint: A *block-data* *specification-part* may contain only USE statements, type declaration statements, IMPLICIT statements, PARAMETER statements, derived-type definitions, and the following specification statements: COMMON, DATA, DIMENSION, EQUIVALENCE, INTRINSIC, POINTER, SAVE, and TARGET.

Constraint: A type declaration statement in a *block-data specification-part* must not contain ALLOCATABLE, EXTERNAL, INTENT, OPTIONAL, PRIVATE, or PUBLIC attribute specifiers.

B.2.12 Procedures

R1201 *interface-block*   **is** *interface-stmt*
                  [*interface-body*] ...
                  [*module-procedure-stmt*] ...
                  end-interface-stmt

R1202 *interface-stmt*   **is** INTERFACE [*generic-spec*]
R1203 *end-interface-stmt*   **is** END INTERFACE
R1204 *interface-body*   **is** *function-stmt*
                  [*specification-part*]
                  end-function-stmt
                or *subroutine-stmt*
                  [*specification-part*]
                  end-subroutine-stmt

R1205 *module-procedure-stmt*   **is** MODULE PROCEDURE *procedure-name-list*
R1206 *generic-spec*   **is** *generic-name*
                or OPERATOR (*defined-operator*)
                or ASSIGNMENT (=)

Constraint: An *interface-body* must not contain an *entry-stmt*, *data-stmt*, *format-stmt*, or *stmt-function-stmt*.

Constraint: The MODULE PROCEDURE specification is allowed only if the *interface-block* has a *generic-spec* and has a host that is a module or accesses a module by use association; each *procedure-name* must be the name of a module procedure that is accessible in the host.

Constraint: An *interface-block* must not appear in a BLOCK DATA program unit.

Constraint: An *interface-block* in a subprogram must not contain an *interface-body* for a procedure defined by that subprogram.

R1207 *external-stmt*   **is** EXTERNAL *external-name-list*
R1208 *intrinsic-stmt*   **is** INTRINSIC *intrinsic-procedure-name-list*

Constraint: Each *intrinsic-procedure-name* must be the name of an intrinsic procedure.

R1209 *function-reference*   **is** *function-name* ([*actual-arg-spec-list*])

Constraint: The *actual-arg-spec-list* for a function reference must not contain an *alt-return-spec*.

R1210 *call-stmt*   **is** CALL *subroutine-name* [([*actual-arg-spec-list*])]
R1211 *actual-arg-spec*   **is** [*keyword* =] *actual-arg*
R1212 *keyword*   **is** *dummy-arg-name*
R1213 *actual-arg*   **is** *expr*
                or *variable*
                or *procedure-name*
                or *alt-return-spec*

R1214   *alt-return-spec*   **is**   * *label*

Constraint: The *keyword* = must not appear if the interface of the procedure is implicit in the scoping unit.

Constraint: The *keyword* = may be omitted from an *actual-arg-spec* only if the *keyword* = has been omitted from each preceding *actual-arg-spec* in the argument list.

Constraint: Each *keyword* must be the name of a dummy argument in the explicit interface of the procedure.

Constraint: A *procedure-name actual-arg* must not be the name of an internal procedure or of a statement function and must not be the generic name of a procedure (12.3.2.1, 13.1).

Constraint: The *label* used in the *alt-return-spec* must be the statement label of a branch target statement that appears in the same scoping unit as the *call-stmt*.

R1215   *function-subprogram*   **is**   *function-stmt*
                                                 [*specification-part*]
                                                 [*execution-part*]
                                                 [*internal-subprogram-part*]
                                                 end-function-stmt

R1216   *function-stmt*   **is**   [*prefix*] FUNCTION *function-name* ■
                                                 ■ ([*dummy-arg-name-list*]) [RESULT (*result-name*)]

Constraint: If RESULT is specified, the *function-name* must not appear in any specification statement in the scoping unit of the function subprogram.

R1217   *prefix*   **is**   *type-spec* [RECURSIVE]
                                         or   RECURSIVE [*type-spec*]

R1218   *end-function-stmt*   **is**   END [FUNCTION [*function-name*]]

Constraint: If RESULT is specified, *result-name* must not be the same as *function-name*.

Constraint: FUNCTION must be present on the *end-function-stmt* of an internal or module function.

Constraint: An internal function must not contain an ENTRY statement.

Constraint: An internal function must not contain an *internal-subprogram-part*.

Constraint: If a *function-name* is present on the *end-function-stmt*, it must be identical to the *function-name* specified in the *function-stmt*.

R1219   *subroutine-subprogram*   **is**   *subroutine-stmt*
                                                 [*specification-part*]
                                                 [*execution-part*]
                                                 [*internal-subprogram-part*]
                                                 end-subroutine-stmt

R1220   *subroutine-stmt*   **is**   [RECURSIVE] SUBROUTINE *subroutine-name* ■
                                                 ■ [([*dummy-arg-list*])]

R1221   *dummy-arg*   **is**   *dummy-arg-name*
                                         or   *

R1222   *end-subroutine-stmt*   **is**   END [SUBROUTINE [*subroutine-name*]]

Constraint: SUBROUTINE must be present on the *end-subroutine-stmt* of an internal or module subroutine.

Constraint: An internal subroutine must not contain an ENTRY statement.

Constraint: An internal subroutine must not contain an *internal-subprogram-part*.

Constraint: If a *subroutine-name* is present on the *end-subroutine-stmt*, it must be identical to the *subroutine-name* specified in the *subroutine-stmt*.

R1223   *entry-stmt*   **is**   ENTRY *entry-name* [([*dummy-arg-list*]) ■
                                                 ■ [RESULT (*result-name*)]]

Constraint: If RESULT is specified, the *entry-name* must not appear in any specification statement in the scoping unit of the function program.

Constraint: An *entry-stmt* may appear only in an *external-subprogram* or *module-subprogram*. An *entry-stmt* must not appear within an *executable-construct*.

Constraint: RESULT may be present only if the *entry-stmt* is contained in a function subprogram.

Constraint: Within the subprogram containing the *entry-stmt*, the *entry-name* must not appear as a dummy argument in the FUNCTION or SUBROUTINE statement or in another ENTRY statement and it must not appear in an EXTERNAL or INTRINSIC statement.

Constraint: A *dummy-arg* may be an alternate return indicator only if the ENTRY statement is contained in a subroutine subprogram.

Constraint: If RESULT is specified, *result-name* must not be the same as *entry-name*.

R1224 *return-stmt*   is   RETURN [*scalar-int-expr*]

Constraint: The *return-stmt* must be contained in the scoping unit of a function or subroutine subprogram.

Constraint: The *scalar-int-expr* is allowed only in the scoping unit of a subroutine subprogram.

R1225 *contains-stmt*   is   CONTAINS

R1226 *stmt-function-stmt*   is   *function-name* ([*dummy-arg-name-list*]) = *scalar-expr*

Constraint: The *scalar-expr* may be composed only of constants (literal and named), references to scalar variables and array elements, references to functions and function dummy procedures, and intrinsic operators. If a reference to a statement function appears in *scalar-expr*, its definition must have been provided earlier in the scoping unit and must not be the name of the statement function being defined.

Constraint: Named constants in *scalar-expr* must have been declared earlier in the scoping unit or made accessible by use or host association. If array elements appear in *scalar-expr*, the parent array must have been declared as an array earlier in the scoping unit or made accessible by use or host association. If a scalar variable, array element, function reference, or dummy function reference is typed by the implicit typing rules, its appearance in any subsequent type declaration statement must confirm this implied type and the values of any implied type parameters.

Constraint: The *function-name* and each *dummy-arg-name* must be specified, explicitly or implicitly, to be scalar data objects.

Constraint: A given *dummy-arg-name* may appear only once in any *dummy-arg-name-list*.

Constraint: Each scalar variable reference in *scalar-expr* may be either a reference to a dummy argument of the statement function or a reference to a variable local to the same scoping unit as the statement function statement.

B.2.13 Intrinsic Procedures

B.2.14 Scope, Association, and Definition

B.3 Cross References

The following is a cross reference of all syntactic symbols used in the BNF, giving the rule in which they are defined and all rules in which they are referenced.

The symbols are sorted alphabetically within three categories: nonterminal symbols that are defined, nonterminal symbols that are not defined, and terminal symbols. Note that except for those ending with

-name, the only undefined nonterminal symbols are *letter, digit, special-character*, and *rep-char*. Symbols ending with *-name* are defined by the rule:

    xyz-name   **is** *name*

    Before processing the cross references, all occurrences of *-list* and *scalar-* in the symbol names were removed.

Symbol	Defined in	Referenced in		
ac-do-variable	R435	R434		
ac-implied-do	R433	R432		
ac-implied-do-control	R434	R433		
ac-value	R432	R431	R433	
access-id	R522	R521	R1109	
access-spec	R510	R424	R503	R521
access-stmt	R521	R214		
action-stmt	R216	R215	R807	R829	R833
action-term-do-construct	R827	R826		
actual-arg	R1213	R1211		
actual-arg-spec	R1211	R1209	R1210	
add-op	R710	R310	R707	
add-operand	R706	R706	R707	
allocatable-stmt	R526	R214		
allocate-lower-bound	R627	R626		
allocate-object	R625	R624	R631	
allocate-shape-spec	R626	R624		
allocate-stmt	R622	R216		
allocate-upper-bound	R628	R626		
allocation	R624	R622		
alphanumeric-character	R302	R301	R304	
alt-return-spec	R1214	R1213		
and-op	R720	R310	R716	
and-operand	R715	R716		
arithmetic-if-stmt	R840	R216		
array-constructor	R431	R701		
array-element	R615	R536	R547	R602	R610
array-section	R616	R602		
array-spec	R512	R503	R504	R525	R528
assign-stmt	R838	R216		
assigned-goto-stmt	R839	R216		
assignment-stmt	R735	R216	R738	R739
assumed-shape-spec	R516	R512		
assumed-size-spec	R518	R512		
attr-spec	R503	R501		
backspace-stmt	R919	R216		
binary-constant	R408	R407		
blank-interp-edit-desc	R1015	R1010		
block	R801	R802	R808	R823
block-data	R1110	R202		
block-data-stmt	R1111	R1110		
block-do-construct	R817	R816		
boz-literal-constant	R407	R306	R533	
c	R1017	R1016		
call-stmt	R1210	R216		
case-construct	R808	R215		

Symbol	Defined in	Referenced in			
case-expr	R812	R809			
case-selector	R813	R810			
case-stmt	R810	R808			
case-value	R815	R814			
case-value-range	R814	R813			
char-constant	R309	R843			
char-expr	R726	R731	R812		
char-initialization-expr	R731	R815			
char-length	R508	R429	R504	R507	
char-literal-constant	R420	R306	R1016		
char-selector	R506	R502			
char-string-edit-desc	R1016	R1003			
char-variable	R605				
character	R301				
close-spec	R908	R907			
close-stmt	R907	R216			
common-block-object	R549	R548			
common-stmt	R548	R214			
complex-literal-constant	R417	R306			
component-array-spec	R428	R427	R429		
component-attr-spec	R427	R426			
component-decl	R429	R426			
component-def-stmt	R426	R422			
computed-goto-stmt	R837	R216			
concat-op	R712	R310	R711		
connect-spec	R905	R904			
constant	R305	R308	R309	R533	R610	R701
constant-subobject	R702	R701			
contains-stmt	R1225	R210	R212		
continue-stmt	R841	R216	R824		
control-edit-desc	R1010	R1003			
cycle-stmt	R834	R216			
d	R1008	R1005			
data-edit-desc	R1005	R1003			
data-i-do-object	R536	R535			
data-i-do-variable	R537	R535			
data-implied-do	R535	R531	R536		
data-ref	R612	R614	R615	R616	
data-stmt	R529	R209	R214		
data-stmt-constant	R533	R532			
data-stmt-object	R531	R530			
data-stmt-repeat	R534	R532			
data-stmt-set	R530	R529			
data-stmt-value	R532	R530			
deallocate-stmt	R631	R216			
declaration-construct	R207	R204			
default-char-expr	R727	R905	R906	R908	R912	R913
default-char-variable	R606	R903	R924		
default-int-variable	R608	R905	R908	R912	R913	R922
		R923	R924		
default-logical-variable	R604	R924			
deferred-shape-spec	R517	R428	R512	R526	R527
defined-binary-op	R724	R311	R723		
defined-operator	R311	R1206			
defined-unary-op	R704	R311	R703		
derived-type-def	R422	R207			

Symbol	Defined in	Referenced in			
derived-type-stmt	R424	R422			
digit-string	R402	R401	R404	R405	R413	R414
dimension-stmt	R525	R214			
do-block	R823	R817			
do-body	R828	R827	R830	R832	
do-construct	R816	R215			
do-stmt	R818	R817			
do-term-action-stmt	R829	R827			
do-term-shared-stmt	R833	R832			
do-variable	R822	R821	R918		
dummy-arg	R1221	R1220	R1223		
e	R1009	R1005			
else-if-stmt	R804	R802			
else-stmt	R805	R802			
elsewhere-stmt	R742	R739			
end-block-data-stmt	R1112	R1110			
end-do	R824	R817			
end-do-stmt	R825	R824			
end-function-stmt	R1218	R216	R1204	R1215	
end-if-stmt	R806	R802			
end-interface-stmt	R1203	R1201			
end-module-stmt	R1106	R1104			
end-program-stmt	R1103	R216	R1101		
end-select-stmt	R811	R808			
end-subroutine-stmt	R1222	R216	R1204	R1219	
end-type-stmt	R425	R422			
end-where-stmt	R743	R739			
endfile-stmt	R920	R216			
entity-decl	R504	R501			
entry-stmt	R1223	R206	R207	R209	
equiv-op	R722	R310	R718		
equiv-operand	R717	R717	R718		
equivalence-object	R547	R546			
equivalence-set	R546	R545			
equivalence-stmt	R545	R214			
executable-construct	R215	R208	R209		
executable-program	R201				
execution-part	R208	R1101	R1215	R1219	
execution-part-construct	R209	R208	R801	R828	
exit-stmt	R835	R216			
explicit-shape-spec	R513	R428	R512	R518	R549
exponent	R416	R413			
exponent-letter	R415	R413			
expr	R723	R430	R432	R701	R723	R725
		R726	R727	R728	R729	R730
		R735	R737	R915	R1213	R1226
extended-intrinsic-op	R312	R311			
external-file-unit	R902	R901	R905	R908	R919	R920
		R921	R922	R924		
external-stmt	R1207	R214			
external-subprogram	R203	R202			
file-name-expr	R906	R905	R924		
format	R913	R909	R911	R912	
format-item	R1003	R1002	R1003		
format-specification	R1002	R1001			
format-stmt	R1001	R206	R207	R209	

Symbol	Defined in	Referenced in			
function-reference	R1209	R701			
function-stmt	R1216	R1204	R1215		
function-subprogram	R1215	R203	R211	R213	
generic-spec	R1206	R522	R1202		
goto-stmt	R836	R216			
hex-constant	R410	R407			
hex-digit	R411	R410			
if-construct	R802	R215			
if-stmt	R807	R216			
if-then-stmt	R803	R802			
imag-part	R419	R417			
implicit-part	R205	R204			
implicit-part-stmt	R206	R205			
implicit-spec	R541	R540			
implicit-stmt	R540	R205	R206		
initialization-expr	R730	R504	R539		
inner-shared-do-construct	R832	R831			
input-item	R914	R909	R917		
inquire-spec	R924	R923			
inquire-stmt	R923	R216			
int-constant	R308	R534			
int-expr	R728	R434	R535	R611	R617	R620
		R621	R627	R628	R732	R734
		R812	R837	R902	R905	R912
		R1224			
int-initialization-expr	R732	R505	R506	R815	
int-literal-constant	R404	R306	R403	R508	R1004	R1006
		R1007	R1008	R1009	R1013	R1017
int-variable	R607	R435	R537	R623	R838	R839
intent-spec	R511	R503	R519		
intent-stmt	R519	R214			
interface-block	R1201	R207			
interface-body	R1204	R1201			
interface-stmt	R1202	R1201			
internal-file-unit	R903	R901			
internal-subprogram	R211	R210			
internal-subprogram-part	R210	R1101	R1215	R1219	
intrinsic-operator	R310	R312			
intrinsic-stmt	R1208	R214			
io-control-spec	R912	R909	R910		
io-implied-do	R916	R914	R915		
io-implied-do-control	R918	R916			
io-implied-do-object	R917	R916			
io-unit	R901	R912			
k	R1011	R1010			
keyword	R1212	R1211			
kind-param	R405	R404	R413	R420	R421
kind-selector	R505	R502			
label	R313	R819	R836	R837	R838	R839
		R840	R905	R908	R912	R913
		R922	R924	R1214		
label-do-stmt	R819	R818	R827	R830	R832
length-selector	R507	R506			
letter-spec	R542	R541			
level-1-expr	R703	R705			
level-2-expr	R707	R707	R711		

Symbol	Defined in	Referenced in			
level-3-expr	R711	R711	R713		
level-4-expr	R713	R715			
level-5-expr	R718	R718	R723		
literal-constant	R306	R305			
logical-expr	R725	R733	R741	R803	R804	R807
		R812	R821		
logical-initialization-expr	R733	R815			
logical-literal-constant	R421	R306			
logical-variable	R603				
loop-control	R821	R819	R820		
lower-bound	R514	R513	R516	R518	
m	R1007	R1005			
main-program	R1101	R202			
mask-expr	R741	R738	R740		
module	R1104	R202			
module-procedure-stmt	R1205	R1201			
module-stmt	R1105	R1104			
module-subprogram	R213	R212			
module-subprogram-part	R212	R1104			
mult-op	R709	R310	R706		
mult-operand	R705	R705	R706		
n	R1013	R1012			
name	R304	R307			
named-constant	R307	R305	R539		
named-constant-def	R539	R538			
namelist-group-object	R544	R543			
namelist-stmt	R543	R214			
nonblock-do-construct	R826	R816			
nonlabel-do-stmt	R820	R818			
not-op	R719	R310	R715		
nullify-stmt	R629	R216			
numeric-expr	R729	R821	R840	R918	
octal-constant	R409	R407			
only	R1109	R1107			
open-stmt	R904	R216			
optional-stmt	R520	R214			
or-op	R721	R310	R717		
or-operand	R716	R716	R717		
outer-shared-do-construct	R830	R826	R831		
output-item	R915	R910	R911	R917	R923
parameter-stmt	R538	R206	R207		
parent-string	R610	R609			
part-ref	R613	R612			
pause-stmt	R844	R216			
pointer-assignment-stmt	R736	R216			
pointer-object	R630	R629	R736		
pointer-stmt	R527	R214			
position-edit-desc	R1012	R1010			
position-spec	R922	R919	R920	R921	
power-op	R708	R310	R705		
prefix	R1217	R1216			
primary	R701	R703			
print-stmt	R911	R216			
private-sequence-stmt	R423	R422			
program-stmt	R1102	R1101			
program-unit	R202	R201			

Symbol	Defined in	Referenced in			
r	R1004	R1003	R1010		
read-stmt	R909	R216			
real-literal-constant	R413	R306	R412		
real-part	R418	R417			
rel-op	R714	R310	R713		
rename	R1108	R1107			
return-stmt	R1224	R216			
rewind-stmt	R921	R216			
save-stmt	R523	R214			
saved-entity	R524	R523			
section-subscript	R618	R613			
select-case-stmt	R809	R808			
shared-term-do-construct	R831	R830			
sign	R406	R401	R403	R412	
sign-edit-desc	R1014	R1010			
signed-digit-string	R401	R416			
signed-int-literal-constant	R403	R418	R419	R533	R1011
signed-real-literal-constant	R412	R418	R419	R533	
significand	R414	R413			
specification-expr	R734	R509	R514	R515	
specification-part	R204	R1101	R1104	R1110	R1204	R1215
		R1219			
specification-stmt	R214	R207			
stat-variable	R623	R622	R631		
stmt-function-stmt	R1226	R207			
stop-code	R843	R842	R844		
stop-stmt	R842	R216			
stride	R620	R619			
structure-component	R614	R536	R602	R610	R625	R630
structure-constructor	R430	R533	R701		
subobject	R602	R601	R702		
subroutine-stmt	R1220	R1204	R1219		
subroutine-subprogram	R1219	R203	R211	R213	
subscript	R617	R618	R619		
subscript-triplet	R619	R618			
substring	R609	R547	R602		
substring-range	R611	R609	R616		
target	R737	R736			
target-stmt	R528	R214			
type-declaration-stmt	R501	R207			
type-param-value	R509	R506	R507	R508	
type-spec	R502	R426	R501	R541	R1217
underscore	R303	R302			
upper-bound	R515	R513			
use-stmt	R1107	R204			
variable	R601	R531	R603	R604	R605	R606
		R607	R608	R701	R735	R737
		R822	R914	R1213		
vector-subscript	R621	R618			
w	R1006	R1005			
where-construct	R739	R215			
where-construct-stmt	R740	R739			
where-stmt	R738	R216			
write-stmt	R910	R216			
array-name		R525	R526		

Symbol	Defined in	Referenced in			
		R809	R813	R821	R837	R839
		R840	R904	R907	R909	R910
		R916	R919	R920	R921	R923
		R1002	R1003	R1206	R1209	R1210
		R1216	R1220	R1223	R1226	
*		R429	R504	R507	R509	R518
		R532	R709	R901	R913	R1214
		R1221				
**		R708				
+		R406	R710			
,		R417	R424	R426	R433	R434
		R501	R506	R507	R518	R525
		R526	R527	R528	R529	R535
		R543	R546	R548	R622	R631
		R821	R837	R839	R840	R909
		R911	R916	R918	R1107	
-		R406	R542	R710		
.		R414	R704	R724	R1005	
.AND.		R720				
.EQ.		R714				
.EQV.		R722				
.FALSE.		R421				
.GE.		R714				
.GT.		R714				
.LE.		R714				
.LT.		R714				
.NE.		R714				
.NEQV.		R722				
.NOT.		R719				
.OR.		R721				
.TRUE.		R421				
/		R524	R530	R543	R548	R709
		R1010				
/)		R431				
//		R712				
/=		R714				
:		R513	R516	R517	R518	R611
		R619	R626	R803	R809	R814
		R819	R820	R1010	R1107	
::		R424	R426	R501	R519	R520
		R521	R523	R525	R526	R527
		R528				
<		R714				
<=		R714				
=		R434	R504	R505	R506	R507
		R535	R539	R622	R631	R735
		R821	R905	R908	R912	R918
		R922	R923	R924	R1206	R1211
		R1226				
==		R714				
=>		R736	R1108	R1109		
>		R714				
>=		R714				
A		R411	R1005			
ACCESS		R905	R924			
ACTION		R905	R924			

Symbol	Defined in	Referenced in			
ADVANCE		R912			
ALLOCATABLE		R503	R526		
ALLOCATE		R622			
ASSIGN		R838			
ASSIGNMENT		R1206			
B		R408	R411	R1005	
BACKSPACE		R919			
BLANK		R905	R924		
BLOCK		R1111	R1112		
BN		R1015			
BZ		R1015			
C		R411			
CALL		R1210			
CASE		R809	R810		
CHARACTER		R502			
CLOSE		R907			
COMMON		R548			
COMPLEX		R502			
CONTAINS		R1225			
CONTINUE		R841			
CYCLE		R834			
D		R411	R415	R1005	
DATA		R529	R1111	R1112	
DEALLOCATE		R631			
DEFAULT		R813			
DELIM		R905	R924		
DIMENSION		R427	R503	R525	
DIRECT		R924			
DO		R819	R820	R825	
DOUBLE		R502			
E		R411	R415	R1005	
ELSE		R804	R805		
ELSEWHERE		R742			
EN		R1005			
END		R425	R743	R806	R811	R825
		R912	R1103	R1106	R1112	R1203
		R1218	R1222			
ENDFILE		R920			
ENTRY		R1223			
EOR		R912			
EQUIVALENCE		R545			
ERR		R905	R908	R912	R922	R924
ES		R1005			
EXIST		R924			
EXIT		R835			
EXTERNAL		R503	R1207		
F		R411	R1005		
FILE		R905	R924		
FMT		R912			
FORM		R905	R924		
FORMAT		R1001			
FORMATTED		R924			
FUNCTION		R1216	R1218		
G		R1005			
GO		R836	R837	R839	
H		R1016			

Symbol	Defined in	Referenced in			
I	R1005				
IF	R803	R804	R806	R807	R840
IMPLICIT	R540				
IN	R511				
INOUT	R511				
INQUIRE	R923				
INTEGER	R502				
INTENT	R503	R519			
INTERFACE	R1202	R1203			
INTRINSIC	R503	R1208			
IOLENGTH	R923				
IOSTAT	R905	R908	R912	R922	R924
KIND	R505	R506			
L	R1005				
LEN	R506	R507			
LOGICAL	R502				
MODULE	R1105	R1106	R1205		
NAME	R924				
NAMED	R924				
NAMELIST	R543				
NEXTREC	R924				
NML	R912				
NONE	R540				
NULLIFY	R629				
NUMBER	R924				
O	R409	R1005			
ONLY	R1107				
OPEN	R904				
OPENED	R924				
OPERATOR	R1206				
OPTIONAL	R503	R520			
OUT	R511				
P	R1010				
PAD	R905	R924			
PARAMETER	R503	R538			
PAUSE	R844				
POINTER	R427	R503	R527		
POSITION	R905	R924			
PRECISION	R502				
PRINT	R911				
PRIVATE	R423	R510			
PROCEDURE	R1205				
PROGRAM	R1102	R1103			
PUBLIC	R510				
READ	R909	R924			
READWRITE	R924				
REAL	R502				
REC	R912				
RECL	R905	R924			
RECURSIVE	R1217	R1220			
RESULT	R1216	R1223			
RETURN	R1224				
REWIND	R921				
S	R1014				
SAVE	R503	R523			
SELECT	R809	R811			

Symbol	Defined in	Referenced in			
SEQUENCE		R423			
SEQUENTIAL		R924			
SIZE		R912			
SP		R1014			
SS		R1014			
STAT		R622	R631		
STATUS		R905	R908		
STOP		R842			
SUBROUTINE		R1220	R1222		
T		R1012			
TARGET		R503	R528		
THEN		R803	R804		
TL		R1012			
TO		R836	R837	R838	R839
TR		R1012			
TYPE		R424	R425	R502	
UNFORMATTED		R924			
UNIT		R905	R908	R912	R922 R924
USE		R1107			
WHERE		R738	R740	R743	
WHILE		R821			
WRITE		R910	R924		
X		R1012			
Z		R410	R1005		
—		R303	R404	R413	R420 R421

F9⬤

C

Decremental Features

C.1 Deleted Features

The deleted features are those features of Fortran 77 that are redundant and considered largely unused. The list of deleted features for Fortran 90 is empty; there are none.

C.2 Obsolescent Features

The obsolescent features are those features of Fortran 77 that are redundant and for which better methods are available in Fortran 77. The obsolescent features are:

1. Arithmetic IF—use the IF statement or IF construct

2. Real and double precision DO control variables and DO loop control expressions — use integer

3. Shared DO termination and termination on a statement other than END DO or CONTINUE — use an END DO or a CONTINUE statement for each DO statement

4. Branching to an END IF statement from outside its IF block — branch to the statement following the END IF

5. Alternate return—see Section C.2.1

6. PAUSE statement—see Section C.2.2

7. ASSIGN and assigned GO TO statements—see Section C.2.3

8. Assigned FORMAT specifiers—see Section C.2.4

9. H edit descriptor—see Section C.2.5

C.2.1 Alternate Return

An alternate return introduces labels into an argument list to allow the called procedure to direct the execution of the caller upon return. The same effect can be achieved with a return code that is used in a computed GO TO statement or CASE construct on return. This avoids an irregularity in the syntax and semantics of argument association. For example,

```
CALL SUBR_NAME (X, Y, Z, *100, *200, *300)
```

may be replaced by

```
CALL SUBR_NAME (X, Y, Z, RETURN_CODE)
SELECT CASE (RETURN_CODE)
   CASE (1)
      ...
   CASE (2)
      ...
   CASE (3)
      ...
   CASE DEFAULT
      ...
END SELECT
```

C.2.2 PAUSE Statement

Execution of a PAUSE statement requires operator or system-specific intervention to resume execution. In most cases, the same functionality can be achieved as effectively and in a more portable way with the use of an appropriate READ statement that awaits some input data.

C.2.3 ASSIGN and Assigned GO TO Statements

The ASSIGN statement allows a label to be dynamically assigned to an integer variable, and the assigned GO TO statement allows "indirect branching" through this variable. This hinders the readability of the program flow, especially if the integer variable also is used in arithmetic operations. The two totally different usages of the integer variable can be an obscure source of error.

These statements have commonly been used to simulate internal procedures, which now can be coded directly.

C.2.4 Assigned FORMAT Specifiers

The ASSIGN statement also allows the label of a FORMAT statement to be dynamically assigned to an integer variable, which can later be used as a format specifier in READ, WRITE, or PRINT statements. This hinders readability, permits inconsistent usage of the integer variable, and can be an obscure source of error.

This functionality is available via character variables, arrays, and constants.

C.2.5 H Editing

This edit descriptor can be a source of error because the number of characters following the descriptor can be miscounted easily. The same functionality is available using the character constant edit descriptor, for which no count is required.

F90

Index of Examples

G

G edit descriptor for reals 418, 419
generic function 9
generic procedure reference 526
global data 10, 471
global data module 464
GO TO statement 309, 317

H

hexadecimal constant 63
host association 31, 458

I

IF construct 4, 287, 290, 315
IF statement 290
implicit typing 134
INCLUDE line 78, 79
initialization expression 250
input/output list item 401
INQUIRE statement 377
integer declaration 93
integer editing 409
integer range 5
INTEGER statement 126
INTENT attribute 155
interface block 9, 242, 473
internal file 356, 389
internal procedure 454, 458, 480
internal procedure scope 30
intrinsic assignment 283
INTRINSIC attribute 162
IOSTAT= specifier 363

K

keyword 66
keyword argument 522, 549

L

L edit descriptor 420
labels 72
linked list 205
list item 405
list-directed formatting 445
list-directed input 429, 432
list-directed output 434
list-directed PRINT statement 353
list-directed READ statement 353, 391
list-directed WRITE statement 353, 391
literal constants 67
logical declaration 99
logical editing 420
logical IF statement 315
LOGICAL statement 128

M

masked array assignment 278, 279, 281, 284
module 10, 32, 464, 481
module name conflict 469
multiplication expression 226

N

name conflict 469
namelist formatting 435, 445
namelist group name declaration 353
namelist input 435, 436, 440
namelist input that is not valid 438
namelist input that is valid 438
namelist input using array values 438
namelist output 435, 442
namelist READ statement 355, 391
NAMELIST statement 164

F90

Index

F

M

N